Emacs Calc Reference Manual

A catalogue record for this book is available from the Hong Kong Public Libraries.

Published in Hong Kong by Samurai Media Limited.

Email: info@samuraimedia.org

ISBN 978-988-8407-05-7

Background Cover Image by https://www.flickr.com/people/webtreatsetc/

Short Contents

Table of Contents

This file documents Calc, the GNU Emacs calculator, included with GNU Emacs 25.1.

Copyright © 1990–1991, 2001–2016 Free Software Foundation, Inc.

1 Getting Started

This chapter provides a general overview of Calc, the GNU Emacs Calculator: What it is, how to start it and how to exit from it, and what are the various ways that it can be used.

1.1 What is Calc?

Calc is an advanced calculator and mathematical tool that runs as part of the GNU Emacs environment. Very roughly based on the HP-28/48 series of calculators, its many features include:

- Choice of algebraic or RPN (stack-based) entry of calculations.
- Arbitrary precision integers and floating-point numbers.
- Arithmetic on rational numbers, complex numbers (rectangular and polar), error forms with standard deviations, open and closed intervals, vectors and matrices, dates and times, infinities, sets, quantities with units, and algebraic formulas.
- Mathematical operations such as logarithms and trigonometric functions.
- Programmer's features (bitwise operations, non-decimal numbers).
- Financial functions such as future value and internal rate of return.
- Number theoretical features such as prime factorization and arithmetic modulo m for any m.
- Algebraic manipulation features, including symbolic calculus.
- Moving data to and from regular editing buffers.
- Embedded mode for manipulating Calc formulas and data directly inside any editing buffer.
- Graphics using GNUPLOT, a versatile (and free) plotting program.
- Easy programming using keyboard macros, algebraic formulas, algebraic rewrite rules, or extended Emacs Lisp.

Calc tries to include a little something for everyone; as a result it is large and might be intimidating to the first-time user. If you plan to use Calc only as a traditional desk calculator, all you really need to read is the "Getting Started" chapter of this manual and possibly the first few sections of the tutorial. As you become more comfortable with the program you can learn its additional features. Calc does not have the scope and depth of a fully-functional symbolic math package, but Calc has the advantages of convenience, portability, and freedom.

1.2 About This Manual

This document serves as a complete description of the GNU Emacs Calculator. It works both as an introduction for novices and as a reference for experienced users. While it helps to have some experience with GNU Emacs in order to get the most out of Calc, this manual ought to be readable even if you don't know or use Emacs regularly.

This manual is divided into three major parts: the "Getting Started" chapter you are reading now, the Calc tutorial, and the Calc reference manual.

If you are in a hurry to use Calc, there is a brief "demonstration" below which illustrates the major features of Calc in just a couple of pages. If you don't have time to go through the full tutorial, this will show you everything you need to know to begin. See Section 1.4 [Demonstration of Calc], page 5.

The tutorial chapter walks you through the various parts of Calc with lots of hands-on examples and explanations. If you are new to Calc and you have some time, try going through at least the beginning of the tutorial. The tutorial includes about 70 exercises with answers. These exercises give you some guided practice with Calc, as well as pointing out some interesting and unusual ways to use its features.

The reference section discusses Calc in complete depth. You can read the reference from start to finish if you want to learn every aspect of Calc. Or, you can look in the table of contents or the Concept Index to find the parts of the manual that discuss the things you need to know.

Every Calc keyboard command is listed in the Calc Summary, and also in the Key Index. Algebraic functions, `M-x` commands, and variables also have their own indices.

You can access this manual on-line at any time within Calc by pressing the `h i` key sequence. Outside of the Calc window, you can press `C-x * i` to read the manual on-line. From within Calc the command `h t` will jump directly to the Tutorial; from outside of Calc the command `C-x * t` will jump to the Tutorial and start Calc if necessary. Pressing `h s` or `C-x * s` will take you directly to the Calc Summary. Within Calc, you can also go to the part of the manual describing any Calc key, function, or variable using `h k`, `h f`, or `h v`, respectively. See Section 3.2 [Help Commands], page 106.

1.3 Notations Used in This Manual

This section describes the various notations that are used throughout the Calc manual.

In keystroke sequences, uppercase letters mean you must hold down the shift key while typing the letter. Keys pressed with Control held down are shown as `C-x`. Keys pressed with Meta held down are shown as `M-x`. Other notations are `RET` for the Return key, `SPC` for the space bar, `TAB` for the Tab key, `DEL` for the Delete key, and `LFD` for the Line-Feed key. The `DEL` key is called Backspace on some keyboards, it is whatever key you would use to correct a simple typing error when regularly using Emacs.

(If you don't have the `LFD` or `TAB` keys on your keyboard, the `C-j` and `C-i` keys are equivalent to them, respectively. If you don't have a Meta key, look for Alt or Extend Char. You can also press `ESC` or `C-[` first to get the same effect, so that `M-x`, `ESC x`, and `C-[ x` are all equivalent.)

Sometimes the `RET` key is not shown when it is "obvious" that you must press `RET` to proceed. For example, the `RET` is usually omitted in key sequences like `M-x calc-keypad RET`.

Commands are generally shown like this: `p` (calc-precision) or `C-x * k` (calc-keypad). This means that the command is normally used by pressing the `p` key or `C-x * k` key sequence, but it also has the full-name equivalent shown, e.g., `M-x calc-precision`.

Commands that correspond to functions in algebraic notation are written: `C` (calc-cos) [cos]. This means the `C` key is equivalent to `M-x calc-cos`, and that the corresponding function in an algebraic-style formula would be 'cos(x)'.

A few commands don't have key equivalents: `calc-sincos` [sincos].

1.4 A Demonstration of Calc

This section will show some typical small problems being solved with Calc. The focus is more on demonstration than explanation, but everything you see here will be covered more thoroughly in the Tutorial.

To begin, start Emacs if necessary (usually the command `emacs` does this), and type `C-x * c` to start the Calculator. (You can also use `M-x calc` if this doesn't work. See Section 1.5.1 [Starting Calc], page 6, for various ways of starting the Calculator.)

Be sure to type all the sample input exactly, especially noting the difference between lower-case and upper-case letters. Remember, `RET`, `TAB`, `DEL`, and `SPC` are the Return, Tab, Delete, and Space keys.

RPN calculation. In RPN, you type the input number(s) first, then the command to operate on the numbers.

Type `2 RET 3 + Q` to compute $\sqrt{2+3} = 2.2360679775$.

Type `P 2 ^` to compute $\pi^2 = 9.86960440109$.

Type `TAB` to exchange the order of these two results.

Type `- I H S` to subtract these results and compute the Inverse Hyperbolic sine of the difference, 2.72996136574.

Type `DEL` to erase this result.

Algebraic calculation. You can also enter calculations using conventional "algebraic" notation. To enter an algebraic formula, use the apostrophe key.

Type `' sqrt(2+3) RET` to compute $\sqrt{2+3}$.

Type `' pi^2 RET` to enter π^2. To evaluate this symbolic formula as a number, type `=`.

Type `' arcsinh($ - $$) RET` to subtract the second-most-recent result from the most-recent and compute the Inverse Hyperbolic sine.

Keypad mode. If you are using the X window system, press `C-x * k` to get Keypad mode. (If you don't use X, skip to the next section.)

Click on the 2, `ENTER`, 3, +, and `SQRT` "buttons" using your left mouse button.

Click on PI, 2, and y^x.

Click on INV, then `ENTER` to swap the two results.

Click on -, `INV`, `HYP`, and `SIN`.

Click on `<-` to erase the result, then click `OFF` to turn the Keypad Calculator off.

Grabbing data. Type `C-x * x` if necessary to exit Calc. Now select the following numbers as an Emacs region: "Mark" the front of the list by typing `C-SPC` or `C-@` there, then move to the other end of the list. (Either get this list from the on-line copy of this manual, accessed by `C-x * i`, or just type these numbers into a scratch file.) Now type `C-x * g` to "grab" these numbers into Calc.

```
1.23   1.97
1.6    2
1.19   1.08
```

The result '[1.23, 1.97, 1.6, 2, 1.19, 1.08]' is a Calc "vector." Type *V R +* to compute the sum of these numbers.

Type *U* to Undo this command, then type *V R ** to compute the product of the numbers.

You can also grab data as a rectangular matrix. Place the cursor on the upper-leftmost '1' and set the mark, then move to just after the lower-right '8' and press *C-x * r*.

Type *v t* to transpose this 3×2 matrix into a 2×3 matrix. Type *v u* to unpack the rows into two separate vectors. Now type *V R + TAB V R +* to compute the sums of the two original columns. (There is also a special grab-and-sum-columns command, *C-x * :*.)

Units conversion. Units are entered algebraically. Type *' 43 mi/hr RET* to enter the quantity 43 miles-per-hour. Type *u c km/hr RET*. Type *u c m/s RET*.

Date arithmetic. Type *t N* to get the current date and time. Type *90 +* to find the date 90 days from now. Type *' <25 dec 87> RET* to enter a date, then *– 7 /* to see how many weeks have passed since then.

Algebra. Algebraic entries can also include formulas or equations involving variables. Type *' [x + y = a, x y = 1] RET* to enter a pair of equations involving three variables. (Note the leading apostrophe in this example; also, note that the space in 'x y' is required.) Type *a S x,y RET* to solve these equations for the variables x and y.

Type *d B* to view the solutions in more readable notation. Type *d C* to view them in C language notation, *d T* to view them in the notation for the TeX typesetting system, and *d L* to view them in the notation for the LaTeX typesetting system. Type *d N* to return to normal notation.

Type *7.5*, then *s l a RET* to let $a = 7.5$ in these formulas. (That's the letter *l*, not the numeral *1*.)

Help functions. You can read about any command in the on-line manual. Type *C-x * c* to return to Calc after each of these commands: *h k t N* to read about the *t N* command, *h f sqrt RET* to read about the sqrt function, and *h s* to read the Calc summary.

Press DEL repeatedly to remove any leftover results from the stack. To exit from Calc, press *q* or *C-x * c* again.

1.5 Using Calc

Calc has several user interfaces that are specialized for different kinds of tasks. As well as Calc's standard interface, there are Quick mode, Keypad mode, and Embedded mode.

1.5.1 Starting Calc

On most systems, you can type *C-x ** to start the Calculator. The key sequence *C-x ** is bound to the command calc-dispatch, which can be rebound if convenient (see Appendix C [Customizing Calc], page 435).

When you press *C-x **, Emacs waits for you to press a second key to complete the command. In this case, you will follow *C-x ** with a letter (upper- or lower-case, it doesn't matter for *C-x **) that says which Calc interface you want to use.

To get Calc's standard interface, type *C-x * c*. To get Keypad mode, type *C-x * k*. Type *C-x * ?* to get a brief list of the available options, and type a second *?* to get a complete list.

To ease typing, *C-x* * * also works to start Calc. It starts the same interface (either *C-x* * c* or *C-x* * k*) that you last used, selecting the *C-x* * c* interface by default.

If *C-x* * doesn't work for you, you can always type explicit commands like *M-x calc* (for the standard user interface) or *M-x calc-keypad* (for Keypad mode). First type *M-x* (that's Meta with the letter *x*), then, at the prompt, type the full command (like *calc-keypad*) and press Return.

The same commands (like *C-x* * c* or *C-x* * **) that start the Calculator also turn it off if it is already on.

1.5.2 The Standard Calc Interface

Calc's standard interface acts like a traditional RPN calculator, operated by the normal Emacs keyboard. When you type *C-x* * c* to start the Calculator, the Emacs screen splits into two windows with the file you were editing on top and Calc on the bottom.

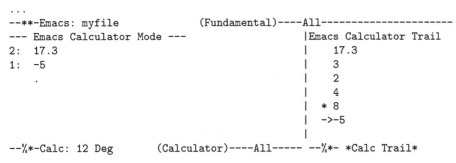

```
     . . .
--**-Emacs: myfile        (Fundamental)----All---------------------
--- Emacs Calculator Mode ---                |Emacs Calculator Trail
2:  17.3                                      |    17.3
1:  -5                                        |    3
      .                                       |    2
                                              |    4
                                              |  * 8
                                              |  ->-5
                                              |
--%*-Calc: 12 Deg      (Calculator)----All----- --%*- *Calc Trail*
```

In this figure, the mode-line for myfile has moved up and the "Calculator" window has appeared below it. As you can see, Calc actually makes two windows side-by-side. The lefthand one is called the *stack window* and the righthand one is called the *trail window*. The stack holds the numbers involved in the calculation you are currently performing. The trail holds a complete record of all calculations you have done. In a desk calculator with a printer, the trail corresponds to the paper tape that records what you do.

In this case, the trail shows that four numbers (17.3, 3, 2, and 4) were first entered into the Calculator, then the 2 and 4 were multiplied to get 8, then the 3 and 8 were subtracted to get −5. (The '>' symbol shows that this was the most recent calculation.) The net result is the two numbers 17.3 and −5 sitting on the stack.

Most Calculator commands deal explicitly with the stack only, but there is a set of commands that allow you to search back through the trail and retrieve any previous result.

Calc commands use the digits, letters, and punctuation keys. Shifted (i.e., upper-case) letters are different from lowercase letters. Some letters are *prefix* keys that begin two-letter commands. For example, *e* means "enter exponent" and shifted *E* means e^x. With the *d* ("display modes") prefix the letter "e" takes on very different meanings: *d e* means "engineering notation" and *d E* means "*eqn* language mode."

There is nothing stopping you from switching out of the Calc window and back into your editing window, say by using the Emacs *C-x o* (other-window) command. When the cursor is inside a regular window, Emacs acts just like normal. When the cursor is in the Calc stack or trail windows, keys are interpreted as Calc commands.

When you quit by pressing C-x * c a second time, the Calculator windows go away but the actual Stack and Trail are not gone, just hidden. When you press C-x * c once again you will get the same stack and trail contents you had when you last used the Calculator.

The Calculator does not remember its state between Emacs sessions. Thus if you quit Emacs and start it again, C-x * c will give you a fresh stack and trail. There is a command (m m) that lets you save your favorite mode settings between sessions, though. One of the things it saves is which user interface (standard or Keypad) you last used; otherwise, a freshly started Emacs will always treat C-x * * the same as C-x * c.

The q key is another equivalent way to turn the Calculator off.

If you type C-x * b first and then C-x * c, you get a full-screen version of Calc (full-calc) in which the stack and trail windows are still side-by-side but are now as tall as the whole Emacs screen. When you press q or C-x * c again to quit, the file you were editing before reappears. The C-x * b key switches back and forth between "big" full-screen mode and the normal partial-screen mode.

Finally, C-x * o (calc-other-window) is like C-x * c except that the Calc window is not selected. The buffer you were editing before remains selected instead. If you are in a Calc window, then C-x * o will switch you out of it, being careful not to switch you to the Calc Trail window. So C-x * o is a handy way to switch out of Calc momentarily to edit your file; you can then type C-x * c to switch back into Calc when you are done.

1.5.3 Quick Mode (Overview)

Quick mode is a quick way to use Calc when you don't need the full complexity of the stack and trail. To use it, type C-x * q (quick-calc) in any regular editing buffer.

Quick mode is very simple: It prompts you to type any formula in standard algebraic notation (like '4 - 2/3') and then displays the result at the bottom of the Emacs screen (3.33333333333 in this case). You are then back in the same editing buffer you were in before, ready to continue editing or to type C-x * q again to do another quick calculation. The result of the calculation will also be in the Emacs "kill ring" so that a C-y command at this point will yank the result into your editing buffer.

Calc mode settings affect Quick mode, too, though you will have to go into regular Calc (with C-x * c) to change the mode settings.

See Section 3.6 [Quick Calculator], page 110, for further information.

1.5.4 Keypad Mode (Overview)

Keypad mode is a mouse-based interface to the Calculator. It is designed for use with terminals that support a mouse. If you don't have a mouse, you will have to operate Keypad mode with your arrow keys (which is probably more trouble than it's worth).

Type C-x * k to turn Keypad mode on or off. Once again you get two new windows, this time on the righthand side of the screen instead of at the bottom. The upper window is the familiar Calc Stack; the lower window is a picture of a typical calculator keypad.

```
|--- Emacs Calculator Mode ---
|2:   17.3
|1:   -5
|             .
|--%*-Calc: 12 Deg        (Calcul
|----+----+--Calc---+----+----1
|FLR |CEIL|RND |TRNC|CLN2|FLT |
|----+----+----+----+----+----|
| LN |EXP |    |ABS |IDIV|MOD |
|----+----+----+----+----+----|
|SIN |COS |TAN |SQRT|y^x |1/x |
|----+----+----+----+----+----|
|  ENTER  |+/- |EEX |UNDO| <- |
|-----+---+-+--+--+-+---++----|
| INV |  7  |  8  |  9  |  /  |
|-----+-----+-----+-----+-----|
| HYP |  4  |  5  |  6  |  *  |
|-----+-----+-----+-----+-----|
|EXEC |  1  |  2  |  3  |  -  |
|-----+-----+-----+-----+-----|
| OFF |  0  |  .  | PI  |  +  |
|-----+-----+-----+-----+-----+
```

Keypad mode is much easier for beginners to learn, because there is no need to memorize lots of obscure key sequences. But not all commands in regular Calc are available on the Keypad. You can always switch the cursor into the Calc stack window to use standard Calc commands if you need. Serious Calc users, though, often find they prefer the standard interface over Keypad mode.

To operate the Calculator, just click on the "buttons" of the keypad using your left mouse button. To enter the two numbers shown here you would click *1 7 . 3 ENTER 5 +/- ENTER*; to add them together you would then click + (to get 12.3 on the stack).

If you click the right mouse button, the top three rows of the keypad change to show other sets of commands, such as advanced math functions, vector operations, and operations on binary numbers.

Because Keypad mode doesn't use the regular keyboard, Calc leaves the cursor in your original editing buffer. You can type in this buffer in the usual way while also clicking on the Calculator keypad. One advantage of Keypad mode is that you don't need an explicit command to switch between editing and calculating.

If you press *C-x * b* first, you get a full-screen Keypad mode (`full-calc-keypad`) with three windows: The keypad in the lower left, the stack in the lower right, and the trail on top.

See Chapter 15 [Keypad Mode], page 345, for further information.

1.5.5 Standalone Operation

If you are not in Emacs at the moment but you wish to use Calc, you must start Emacs first. If all you want is to run Calc, you can give the commands:

```
emacs -f full-calc
```

or

```
emacs -f full-calc-keypad
```

which run a full-screen Calculator (as if by *C-x * b C-x * c*) or a full-screen X-based Calculator (as if by *C-x * b C-x * k*). In standalone operation, quitting the Calculator (by pressing *q* or clicking on the keypad EXIT button) quits Emacs itself.

1.5.6 Embedded Mode (Overview)

Embedded mode is a way to use Calc directly from inside an editing buffer. Suppose you have a formula written as part of a document like this:

```
The derivative of

                          ln(ln(x))

is
```

and you wish to have Calc compute and format the derivative for you and store this derivative in the buffer automatically. To do this with Embedded mode, first copy the formula down to where you want the result to be, leaving a blank line before and after the formula:

```
The derivative of

                          ln(ln(x))

is


                          ln(ln(x))
```

Now, move the cursor onto this new formula and press *C-x * e*. Calc will read the formula (using the surrounding blank lines to tell how much text to read), then push this formula (invisibly) onto the Calc stack. The cursor will stay on the formula in the editing buffer, but the line with the formula will now appear as it would on the Calc stack (in this case, it will be left-aligned) and the buffer's mode line will change to look like the Calc mode line (with mode indicators like '12 Deg' and so on). Even though you are still in your editing buffer, the keyboard now acts like the Calc keyboard, and any new result you get is copied from the stack back into the buffer. To take the derivative, you would type *a d x RET*.

```
    The derivative of

                          ln(ln(x))

    is

    1 / x ln(x)
```

(Note that by default, Calc gives division lower precedence than multiplication, so that '1 / x ln(x)' is equivalent to '1 / (x ln(x))'.)

To make this look nicer, you might want to press *d =* to center the formula, and even *d B* to use Big display mode.

```
The derivative of

                              ln(ln(x))

is
% [calc-mode: justify: center]
% [calc-mode: language: big]


                                 1
                              -------
                              x ln(x)
```

Calc has added annotations to the file to help it remember the modes that were used for this formula. They are formatted like comments in the TEX typesetting language, just in case you are using TEX or LATEX. (In this example TEX is not being used, so you might want to move these comments up to the top of the file or otherwise put them out of the way.)

As an extra flourish, we can add an equation number using a righthand label: Type *d }* *(1) RET*.

```
% [calc-mode: justify: center]
% [calc-mode: language: big]
% [calc-mode: right-label: " (1)"]


                              1
                           -------                          (1)
                           ln(x) x
```

To leave Embedded mode, type *C-x * e* again. The mode line and keyboard will revert to the way they were before.

The related command *C-x * w* operates on a single word, which generally means a single number, inside text. It searches for an expression which "looks" like a number containing the point. Here's an example of its use (before you try this, remove the Calc annotations or use a new buffer so that the extra settings in the annotations don't take effect):

```
A slope of one-third corresponds to an angle of 1 degrees.
```

Place the cursor on the '1', then type *C-x * w* to enable Embedded mode on that number. Now type *3 /* (to get one-third), and *I T* (the Inverse Tangent converts a slope into an angle), then *C-x * w* again to exit Embedded mode.

```
A slope of one-third corresponds to an angle of 18.4349488229 degrees.
```

See Chapter 16 [Embedded Mode], page 351, for full details.

1.5.7 Other *C-x *** Commands

Two more Calc-related commands are *C-x * g* and *C-x * r*, which "grab" data from a selected region of a buffer into the Calculator. The region is defined in the usual Emacs way, by a "mark" placed at one end of the region, and the Emacs cursor or "point" placed at the other.

The *C-x * g* command reads the region in the usual left-to-right, top-to-bottom order. The result is packaged into a Calc vector of numbers and placed on the stack. Calc (in its standard user interface) is then started. Type *v u* if you want to unpack this vector into separate numbers on the stack. Also, *C-u C-x * g* interprets the region as a single number or formula.

The `C-x * r` command reads a rectangle, with the point and mark defining opposite corners of the rectangle. The result is a matrix of numbers on the Calculator stack.

Complementary to these is `C-x * y`, which "yanks" the value at the top of the Calc stack back into an editing buffer. If you type `C-x * y` while in such a buffer, the value is yanked at the current position. If you type `C-x * y` while in the Calc buffer, Calc makes an educated guess as to which editing buffer you want to use. The Calc window does not have to be visible in order to use this command, as long as there is something on the Calc stack.

Here, for reference, is the complete list of `C-x *` commands. The shift, control, and meta keys are ignored for the keystroke following `C-x *`.

Commands for turning Calc on and off:

`*`   Turn Calc on or off, employing the same user interface as last time.

`=, +, -, /, \, &, #`
                 Alternatives for `*`.

`C`   Turn Calc on or off using its standard bottom-of-the-screen interface. If Calc is already turned on but the cursor is not in the Calc window, move the cursor into the window.

`O`   Same as `C`, but don't select the new Calc window. If Calc is already turned on and the cursor is in the Calc window, move it out of that window.

`B`   Control whether `C-x * c` and `C-x * k` use the full screen.

`Q`   Use Quick mode for a single short calculation.

`K`   Turn Calc Keypad mode on or off.

`E`   Turn Calc Embedded mode on or off at the current formula.

`J`   Turn Calc Embedded mode on or off, select the interesting part.

`W`   Turn Calc Embedded mode on or off at the current word (number).

`Z`   Turn Calc on in a user-defined way, as defined by a `Z I` command.

`X`   Quit Calc; turn off standard, Keypad, or Embedded mode if on. (This is like `q` or `OFF` inside of Calc.)

Commands for moving data into and out of the Calculator:

`G`   Grab the region into the Calculator as a vector.

`R`   Grab the rectangular region into the Calculator as a matrix.

`:`   Grab the rectangular region and compute the sums of its columns.

`_`   Grab the rectangular region and compute the sums of its rows.

`Y`   Yank a value from the Calculator into the current editing buffer.

Commands for use with Embedded mode:

A	"Activate" the current buffer. Locate all formulas that contain ':=' or '=>' symbols and record their locations so that they can be updated automatically as variables are changed.
D	Duplicate the current formula immediately below and select the duplicate.
F	Insert a new formula at the current point.
N	Move the cursor to the next active formula in the buffer.
P	Move the cursor to the previous active formula in the buffer.
U	Update (i.e., as if by the = key) the formula at the current point.
`	Edit (as if by `calc-edit`) the formula at the current point.

Miscellaneous commands:

I	Run the Emacs Info system to read the Calc manual. (This is the same as *h i* inside of Calc.)
T	Run the Emacs Info system to read the Calc Tutorial.
S	Run the Emacs Info system to read the Calc Summary.
L	Load Calc entirely into memory. (Normally the various parts are loaded only as they are needed.)
M	Read a region of written keystroke names (like *C-n a b c RET*) and record them as the current keyboard macro.
0	(This is the "zero" digit key.) Reset the Calculator to its initial state: Empty stack, and initial mode settings.

1.6 History and Acknowledgments

Calc was originally started as a two-week project to occupy a lull in the author's schedule. Basically, a friend asked if I remembered the value of 2^{32}. I didn't offhand, but I said, "that's easy, just call up an **xcalc**." Xcalc duly reported that the answer to our question was '4.294967e+09'—with no way to see the full ten digits even though we knew they were there in the program's memory! I was so annoyed, I vowed to write a calculator of my own, once and for all.

I chose Emacs Lisp, a) because I had always been curious about it and b) because, being only a text editor extension language after all, Emacs Lisp would surely reach its limits long before the project got too far out of hand.

To make a long story short, Emacs Lisp turned out to be a distressingly solid implementation of Lisp, and the humble task of calculating turned out to be more open-ended than one might have expected.

Emacs Lisp didn't have built-in floating point math (now it does), so this had to be simulated in software. In fact, Emacs integers would only comfortably fit six decimal digits or so (at the time)—not enough for a decent calculator. So I had to write my own high-precision integer code as well, and once I had this I figured that arbitrary-size integers were just as easy as large integers. Arbitrary floating-point precision was the logical next step. Also, since the large integer arithmetic was there anyway it seemed only fair to give the user direct access to it, which in turn made it practical to support fractions as well as floats. All these features inspired me to look around for other data types that might be worth having.

Around this time, my friend Rick Koshi showed me his nifty new HP-28 calculator. It allowed the user to manipulate formulas as well as numerical quantities, and it could also operate on matrices. I decided that these would be good for Calc to have, too. And once things had gone this far, I figured I might as well take a look at serious algebra systems for further ideas. Since these systems did far more than I could ever hope to implement, I decided to focus on rewrite rules and other programming features so that users could implement what they needed for themselves.

Rick complained that matrices were hard to read, so I put in code to format them in a 2D style. Once these routines were in place, Big mode was obligatory. Gee, what other language modes would be useful?

Scott Hemphill and Allen Knutson, two friends with a strong mathematical bent, contributed ideas and algorithms for a number of Calc features including modulo forms, primality testing, and float-to-fraction conversion.

Units were added at the eager insistence of Mass Sivilotti. Later, Ulrich Mueller at CERN and Przemek Klosowski at NIST provided invaluable expert assistance with the units table. As far as I can remember, the idea of using algebraic formulas and variables to represent units dates back to an ancient article in Byte magazine about muMath, an early algebra system for microcomputers.

Many people have contributed to Calc by reporting bugs and suggesting features, large and small. A few deserve special mention: Tim Peters, who helped develop the ideas that led to the selection commands, rewrite rules, and many other algebra features; François Pinard, who contributed an early prototype of the Calc Summary appendix as well as providing valuable suggestions in many other areas of Calc; Carl Witty, whose eagle eyes discovered many typographical and factual errors in the Calc manual; Tim Kay, who drove the development of Embedded mode; Ove Ewerlid, who made many suggestions relating to the algebra commands and contributed some code for polynomial operations; Randal Schwartz, who suggested the `calc-eval` function; Juha Sarlin, who first worked out how to split Calc into quickly-loading parts; Bob Weiner, who helped immensely with the Lucid Emacs port; and Robert J. Chassell, who suggested the Calc Tutorial and exercises as well as many other things.

Among the books used in the development of Calc were Knuth's *Art of Computer Programming* (especially volume II, *Seminumerical Algorithms*); *Numerical Recipes* by Press, Flannery, Teukolsky, and Vetterling; Bevington's *Data Reduction and Error Analysis for the Physical Sciences*; *Concrete Mathematics* by Graham, Knuth, and Patashnik; Steele's *Common Lisp, the Language*; the *CRC Standard Math Tables* (William H. Beyer, ed.); and Abramowitz and Stegun's venerable *Handbook of Mathematical Functions*. Also, of course, Calc could not have been written without the excellent *GNU Emacs Lisp Reference Manual*, by Bil Lewis and Dan LaLiberte.

Final thanks go to Richard Stallman, without whose fine implementations of the Emacs editor, language, and environment, Calc would have been finished in two weeks.

2 Tutorial

This chapter explains how to use Calc and its many features, in a step-by-step, tutorial way. You are encouraged to run Calc and work along with the examples as you read (see Section 1.5.1 [Starting Calc], page 6). If you are already familiar with advanced calculators, you may wish to skip on to the rest of this manual.

This tutorial describes the standard user interface of Calc only. The Quick mode and Keypad mode interfaces are fairly self-explanatory. See Chapter 16 [Embedded Mode], page 351, for a description of the Embedded mode interface.

The easiest way to read this tutorial on-line is to have two windows on your Emacs screen, one with Calc and one with the Info system. Press `C-x * t` to set this up; the on-line tutorial will be opened in the current window and Calc will be started in another window. From the Info window, the command `C-x * c` can be used to switch to the Calc window and `C-x * o` can be used to switch back to the Info window. (If you have a printed copy of the manual you can use that instead; in that case you only need to press `C-x * c` to start Calc.)

This tutorial is designed to be done in sequence. But the rest of this manual does not assume you have gone through the tutorial. The tutorial does not cover everything in the Calculator, but it touches on most general areas.

The Calc Summary at the end of the reference manual includes some blank space for your own use. You may wish to keep notes there as you learn Calc.

2.1 Basic Tutorial

In this section, we learn how RPN and algebraic-style calculations work, how to undo and redo an operation done by mistake, and how to control various modes of the Calculator.

2.1.1 RPN Calculations and the Stack

Calc normally uses RPN notation. You may be familiar with the RPN system from Hewlett-Packard calculators, FORTH, or PostScript. (Reverse Polish Notation, RPN, is named after the Polish mathematician Jan Łukasiewicz.)

The central component of an RPN calculator is the *stack*. A calculator stack is like a stack of dishes. New dishes (numbers) are added at the top of the stack, and numbers are normally only removed from the top of the stack.

In an operation like $2+3$, the 2 and 3 are called the *operands* and the $+$ is the *operator*. In an RPN calculator you always enter the operands first, then the operator. Each time you type a number, Calc adds or *pushes* it onto the top of the Stack. When you press an operator key like $+$, Calc *pops* the appropriate number of operands from the stack and pushes back the result.

Thus we could add the numbers 2 and 3 in an RPN calculator by typing: *2 RET 3 RET +*. (The RET key, Return, corresponds to the ENTER key on traditional RPN calculators.) Try this now if you wish; type `C-x * c` to switch into the Calc window (you can type `C-x * c` again or `C-x * o` to switch back to the Tutorial window). The first four keystrokes "push" the numbers 2 and 3 onto the stack. The $+$ key "pops" the top two numbers from the stack,

adds them, and pushes the result (5) back onto the stack. Here's how the stack will look
at various points throughout the calculation:

```
              .            1:  2           2:  2          1:  5              .
                                           1:  3                          .
                                               .


              C-x * c           2 RET          3 RET           +            DEL
```

The '.' symbol is a marker that represents the top of the stack. Note that the "top" of
the stack is really shown at the bottom of the Stack window. This may seem backwards,
but it turns out to be less distracting in regular use.

The numbers '1:' and '2:' on the left are *stack level numbers*. Old RPN calculators
always had four stack levels called x, y, z, and t. Calc's stack can grow as large as you like,
so it uses numbers instead of letters. Some stack-manipulation commands accept a numeric
argument that says which stack level to work on. Normal commands like + always work on
the top few levels of the stack.

The Stack buffer is just an Emacs buffer, and you can move around in it using the regular
Emacs motion commands. But no matter where the cursor is, even if you have scrolled the
'.' marker out of view, most Calc commands always move the cursor back down to level
1 before doing anything. It is possible to move the '.' marker upwards through the stack,
temporarily "hiding" some numbers from commands like +. This is called *stack truncation*
and we will not cover it in this tutorial; see Section 6.7.8 [Truncating the Stack], page 157,
if you are interested.

You don't really need the second RET in *2 RET 3 RET* +. That's because if you type any
operator name or other non-numeric key when you are entering a number, the Calculator
automatically enters that number and then does the requested command. Thus *2 RET 3* +
will work just as well.

Examples in this tutorial will often omit RET even when the stack displays shown would
only happen if you did press RET:

```
        1:  2            2:  2          1:  5
            .            1:  3              .
                             .


        2 RET            3              +
```

Here, after pressing *3* the stack would really show '1: 2' with 'Calc: 3' in the minibuffer.
In these situations, you can press the optional RET to see the stack as the figure shows.

(●) **Exercise 1.** (This tutorial will include exercises at various points. Try them if you
wish. Answers to all the exercises are located at the end of the Tutorial chapter. Each
exercise will include a cross-reference to its particular answer. If you are reading with the
Emacs Info system, press *f* and the exercise number to go to the answer, then the letter *l*
to return to where you were.)

Here's the first exercise: What will the keystrokes *1 RET 2 RET 3 RET 4 + * -* compute? ('*'
is the symbol for multiplication.) Figure it out by hand, then try it with Calc to see if
you're right. See Section 2.7.1 [RPN Answer 1], page 71. (●)

(●) **Exercise 2.** Compute $(2 \times 4) + (7 \times 9.5) + \frac{5}{4}$ using the stack. See Section 2.7.2 [RPN
Answer 2], page 71. (●)

The DEL key is called Backspace on some keyboards. It is whatever key you would use
to correct a simple typing error when regularly using Emacs. The DEL key pops and throws

away the top value on the stack. (You can still get that value back from the Trail if you should need it later on.) There are many places in this tutorial where we assume you have used DEL to erase the results of the previous example at the beginning of a new example. In the few places where it is really important to use DEL to clear away old results, the text will remind you to do so.

(It won't hurt to let things accumulate on the stack, except that whenever you give a display-mode-changing command Calc will have to spend a long time reformatting such a large stack.)

Since the – key is also an operator (it subtracts the top two stack elements), how does one enter a negative number? Calc uses the _ (underscore) key to act like the minus sign in a number. So, typing *-5 RET* won't work because the – key will try to do a subtraction, but *_5 RET* works just fine.

You can also press *n*, which means "change sign." It changes the number at the top of the stack (or the number being entered) from positive to negative or vice-versa: *5 n RET*.

If you press RET when you're not entering a number, the effect is to duplicate the top number on the stack. Consider this calculation:

```
1:  3          2:  3          1:  9          2:  9          1:  81
    .          1:  3              .          1:  9              .
                   .                             .


   3 RET           RET              *              RET              *
```

(Of course, an easier way to do this would be *3 RET 4 ^*, to raise 3 to the fourth power.)

The space-bar key (denoted SPC here) performs the same function as RET; you could replace all three occurrences of RET in the above example with SPC and the effect would be the same.

Another stack manipulation key is TAB. This exchanges the top two stack entries. Suppose you have computed *2 RET 3 +* to get 5, and then you realize what you really wanted to compute was $20/(2+3)$.

```
1:  5          2:  5          2:  20         1:  4
    .          1:  20         1:  5              .
                   .              .


  2 RET 3 +         20             TAB              /
```

Planning ahead, the calculation would have gone like this:

```
1:  20         2:  20         3:  20         2:  20         1:  4
    .          1:  2          2:  2          1:  5              .
                   .          1:  3              .
                                  .


  20 RET           2 RET            3              +              /
```

A related stack command is *M-TAB* (hold META and type TAB). It rotates the top three elements of the stack upward, bringing the object in level 3 to the top.

```
1:  10         2:  10         3:  10         3:  20         3:  30
    .          1:  20         2:  20         2:  30         2:  10
                   .          1:  30         1:  10         1:  20
                                  .              .              .


  10 RET           20 RET          30 RET         M-TAB          M-TAB
```

(•) **Exercise 3.** Suppose the numbers 10, 20, and 30 are on the stack. Figure out how to add one to the number in level 2 without affecting the rest of the stack. Also figure out how to add one to the number in level 3. See Section 2.7.3 [RPN Answer 3], page 71. (•)

Operations like +, -, *, /, and ^ pop two arguments from the stack and push a result. Operations like **n** and **Q** (square root) pop a single number and push the result. You can think of them as simply operating on the top element of the stack.

```
    1:  3           1:  9           2:  9           1:  25          1:  5
        .               .           1:  16              .               .
                                        .

    3 RET           RET *           4 RET RET *         +               Q
```

(Note that capital **Q** means to hold down the Shift key while typing q. Remember, plain unshifted q is the Quit command.)

Here we've used the Pythagorean Theorem to determine the hypotenuse of a right triangle. Calc actually has a built-in command for that called **f h**, but let's suppose we can't remember the necessary keystrokes. We can still enter it by its full name using **M-x** notation:

```
    1:  3           2:  3           1:  5
        .           1:  4               .
                        .

    3 RET           4 RET           M-x calc-hypot
```

All Calculator commands begin with the word 'calc-'. Since it gets tiring to type this, Calc provides an **x** key which is just like the regular Emacs **M-x** key except that it types the 'calc-' prefix for you:

```
    1:  3           2:  3           1:  5
        .           1:  4               .
                        .

    3 RET           4 RET           x hypot
```

What happens if you take the square root of a negative number?

```
    1:  4           1:  -4          1:  (0, 2)
        .               .               .

    4 RET           n               Q
```

The notation (a, b) represents a complex number. Complex numbers are more traditionally written $a + bi$; Calc can display in this format, too, but for now we'll stick to the (a, b) notation.

If you don't know how complex numbers work, you can safely ignore this feature. Complex numbers only arise from operations that would be errors in a calculator that didn't have complex numbers. (For example, taking the square root or logarithm of a negative number produces a complex result.)

Complex numbers are entered in the notation shown. The (and , and) keys manipulate "incomplete complex numbers."

```
    1:  ( ...       2:  ( ...       1:  (2, ...     1:  (2, ...     1:  (2, 3)
        .           1:  2               .               3               .
                        .                               .

        (               2               ,               3               )
```

You can perform calculations while entering parts of incomplete objects. However, an incomplete object cannot actually participate in a calculation:

```
1:  ( ...        2:  ( ...        3:  ( ...        1:  ( ...        1:  ( ...
    .            1:  2            2:  2                5                5
                     .           1:  3                .                .
                                     .
                                                                   (error)

    (                2 RET            3                +                +
```

Adding 5 to an incomplete object makes no sense, so the last command produces an error message and leaves the stack the same.

Incomplete objects can't participate in arithmetic, but they can be moved around by the regular stack commands.

```
2:  2            3:  2            3:  3            1:  ( ...        1:  (2, 3)
1:  3            2:  3            2:  ( ...            2                .
    .            1:  ( ...        1:  2                3
                     .                .
                                      .                .

2 RET 3 RET          (                M-TAB            M-TAB            )
```

Note that the , (comma) key did not have to be used here. When you press) all the stack entries between the incomplete entry and the top are collected, so there's never really a reason to use the comma. It's up to you.

(•) **Exercise 4.** To enter the complex number $(2, 3)$, your friend Joe typed (2 , SPC 3). What happened? (Joe thought of a clever way to correct his mistake in only two keystrokes, but it didn't quite work. Try it to find out why.) See Section 2.7.4 [RPN Answer 4], page 72. (•)

Vectors are entered the same way as complex numbers, but with square brackets in place of parentheses. We'll meet vectors again later in the tutorial.

Any Emacs command can be given a *numeric prefix argument* by typing a series of META-digits beforehand. If META is awkward for you, you can instead type *C-u* followed by the necessary digits. Numeric prefix arguments can be negative, as in *M-- M-3 M-5* or *C-u - 3 5*. Calc commands use numeric prefix arguments in a variety of ways. For example, a numeric prefix on the + operator adds any number of stack entries at once:

```
1:  10           2:  10           3:  10           3:  10           1:  60
    .            1:  20           2:  20           2:  20               .
                     .            1:  30           1:  30
                                      .                .

10 RET           20 RET           30 RET           C-u 3            +
```

For stack manipulation commands like RET, a positive numeric prefix argument operates on the top n stack entries at once. A negative argument operates on the entry in level n only. An argument of zero operates on the entire stack. In this example, we copy the second-to-top element of the stack:

```
1:  10           2:  10           3:  10           3:  10           4:  10
    .            1:  20           2:  20           2:  20           3:  20
                     .            1:  30           1:  30           2:  30
                                      .                .           1:  20
                                                                       .

10 RET           20 RET           30 RET           C-u -2           RET
```

Another common idiom is *M-0 DEL*, which clears the stack. (The *M-0* numeric prefix tells DEL to operate on the entire stack.)

2.1.2 Algebraic-Style Calculations

If you are not used to RPN notation, you may prefer to operate the Calculator in Algebraic mode, which is closer to the way non-RPN calculators work. In Algebraic mode, you enter formulas in traditional $2 + 3$ notation.

Notice: Calc gives '/' lower precedence than '*', so that 'a/b*c' is interpreted as 'a/(b*c)'; this is not standard across all computer languages. See below for details.

You don't really need any special "mode" to enter algebraic formulas. You can enter a formula at any time by pressing the apostrophe (') key. Answer the prompt with the desired formula, then press RET. The formula is evaluated and the result is pushed onto the RPN stack. If you don't want to think in RPN at all, you can enter your whole computation as a formula, read the result from the stack, then press DEL to delete it from the stack.

Try pressing the apostrophe key, then *2+3+4*, then RET. The result should be the number 9.

Algebraic formulas use the operators '+', '−', '*', '/', and '^'. You can use parentheses to make the order of evaluation clear. In the absence of parentheses, '^' is evaluated first, then '*', then '/', then finally '+' and '−'. For example, the expression

    2 + 3*4*5 / 6*7^8 - 9

is equivalent to

    2 + ((3*4*5) / (6*(7^8)) - 9

or, in large mathematical notation,

$$2 + \frac{3 \times 4 \times 5}{6 \times 7^8} - 9$$

The result of this expression will be the number -6.99999826533.

Calc's order of evaluation is the same as for most computer languages, except that '*' binds more strongly than '/', as the above example shows. As in normal mathematical notation, the '*' symbol can often be omitted: '2 a' is the same as '2*a'.

Operators at the same level are evaluated from left to right, except that '^' is evaluated from right to left. Thus, '2-3-4' is equivalent to '(2-3)-4' or -5, whereas '2^3^4' is equivalent to '2^(3^4)' (a very large integer; try it!).

If you tire of typing the apostrophe all the time, there is Algebraic mode, where Calc automatically senses when you are about to type an algebraic expression. To enter this mode, press the two letters *m a*. (An 'Alg' indicator should appear in the Calc window's mode line.)

Press *m a*, then *2+3+4* with no apostrophe, then RET.

In Algebraic mode, when you press any key that would normally begin entering a number (such as a digit, a decimal point, or the _ key), or if you press (or [, Calc automatically begins an algebraic entry.

Functions which do not have operator symbols like '+' and '*' must be entered in formulas using function-call notation. For example, the function name corresponding to the square-root key *Q* is sqrt. To compute a square root in a formula, you would use the notation 'sqrt(x)'.

Press the apostrophe, then type *sqrt(5*2) - 3*. The result should be 0.16227766017.

Note that if the formula begins with a function name, you need to use the apostrophe even if you are in Algebraic mode. If you type **arcsin** out of the blue, the **a r** will be taken as an Algebraic Rewrite command, and the **csin** will be taken as the name of the rewrite rule to use!

Some people prefer to enter complex numbers and vectors in algebraic form because they find RPN entry with incomplete objects to be too distracting, even though they otherwise use Calc as an RPN calculator.

Still in Algebraic mode, type:

```
1:  (2, 3)      2:  (2, 3)     1:  (8, -1)    2:  (8, -1)    1:  (9, -1)
    .           1:  (1, -2)        .          1:  1              .
                    .                                .


   (2,3) RET       (1,-2) RET        *              1 RET            +
```

Algebraic mode allows us to enter complex numbers without pressing an apostrophe first, but it also means we need to press RET after every entry, even for a simple number like 1.

(You can type *C-u m a* to enable a special Incomplete Algebraic mode in which the **(** and **[** keys use algebraic entry even though regular numeric keys still use RPN numeric entry. There is also Total Algebraic mode, started by typing *m t*, in which all normal keys begin algebraic entry. You must then use the META key to type Calc commands: *M-m t* to get back out of Total Algebraic mode, *M-q* to quit, etc.)

If you're still in Algebraic mode, press *m a* again to turn it off.

Actual non-RPN calculators use a mixture of algebraic and RPN styles. In general, operators of two numbers (like + and *) use algebraic form, but operators of one number (like *n* and *Q*) use RPN form. Also, a non-RPN calculator allows you to see the intermediate results of a calculation as you go along. You can accomplish this in Calc by performing your calculation as a series of algebraic entries, using the $ sign to tie them together. In an algebraic formula, $ represents the number on the top of the stack. Here, we perform the calculation $\sqrt{2 \times 4 + 1}$, which on a traditional calculator would be done by pressing *2 * 4 + 1 =* and then the square-root key.

```
1:  8          1:  9          1:  3
    .              .              .


 ' 2*4 RET       $+1 RET          Q
```

Notice that we didn't need to press an apostrophe for the *$+1*, because the dollar sign always begins an algebraic entry.

(•) **Exercise 1.** How could you get the same effect as pressing *Q* but using an algebraic entry instead? How about if the *Q* key on your keyboard were broken? See Section 2.7.5 [Algebraic Answer 1], page 72. (•)

The notations *$$*, *$$$*, and so on stand for higher stack entries. For example, *' $$+$ RET* is just like typing +.

Algebraic formulas can include *variables*. To store in a variable, press *s s*, then type the variable name, then press RET. (There are actually two flavors of store command: *s s* stores a number in a variable but also leaves the number on the stack, while *s t* removes

a number from the stack and stores it in the variable.) A variable name should consist of
one or more letters or digits, beginning with a letter.

```
1:  17              .          1:  a + a^2    1:  306
    .                             .               .


    17          s t a RET       ' a+a^2 RET      =
```

The = key *evaluates* a formula by replacing all its variables by the values that were stored
in them.

For RPN calculations, you can recall a variable's value on the stack either by entering
its name as a formula and pressing =, or by using the **s r** command.

```
1:  17       2:  17       3:  17       2:  17       1:  306
    .        1:  17       2:  17       1:  289          .
                 .        1:  2            .
                              .


    s r a RET     ' a RET =      2            ^            +
```

If you press a single digit for a variable name (as in **s t 3**, you get one of ten *quick
variables* q0 through q9. They are "quick" simply because you don't have to type the letter
q or the RET after their names. In fact, you can type simply **s 3** as a shorthand for **s s 3**,
and likewise for **t 3** and **r 3**.

Any variables in an algebraic formula for which you have not stored values are left alone,
even when you evaluate the formula.

```
1:  2 a + 2 b    1:  2 b + 34
    .                .


' 2a+2b RET          =
```

Calls to function names which are undefined in Calc are also left alone, as are calls for
which the value is undefined.

```
1:  log10(0) + log10(x) + log10(5, 6) + foo(3) + 2
    .


' log10(100) + log10(0) + log10(x) + log10(5,6) + foo(3) RET
```

In this example, the first call to `log10` works, but the other calls are not evaluated. In
the second call, the logarithm is undefined for that value of the argument; in the third,
the argument is symbolic, and in the fourth, there are too many arguments. In the fifth
case, there is no function called `foo`. You will see a "Wrong number of arguments" message
referring to 'log10(5,6)'. Press the **w** ("why") key to see any other messages that may
have arisen from the last calculation. In this case you will get "logarithm of zero," then
"number expected: x". Calc automatically displays the first message only if the message
is sufficiently important; for example, Calc considers "wrong number of arguments" and
"logarithm of zero" to be important enough to report automatically, while a message like
"number expected: x" will only show up if you explicitly press the **w** key.

(•) **Exercise 2.** Joe entered the formula '2 x y', stored 5 in x, pressed =, and got the
expected result, '10 y'. He then tried the same for the formula '2 x (1+y)', expecting '10
(1+y)', but it didn't work. Why not? See Section 2.7.6 [Algebraic Answer 2], page 72. (•)

(•) **Exercise 3.** What result would you expect *1 RET 0 /* to give? What if you then type
0 *? See Section 2.7.7 [Algebraic Answer 3], page 72. (•)

One interesting way to work with variables is to use the *evaluates-to* ('=>') operator. It works like this: Enter a formula algebraically in the usual way, but follow the formula with an '=>' symbol. (There is also an *s =* command which builds an '=>' formula using the stack.) On the stack, you will see two copies of the formula with an '=>' between them. The lefthand formula is exactly like you typed it; the righthand formula has been evaluated as if by typing =.

```
2:  2 + 3 => 5                    2:  2 + 3 => 5
1:  2 a + 2 b => 34 + 2 b         1:  2 a + 2 b => 20 + 2 b
        .                                 .


' 2+3 => RET  ' 2a+2b RET s =         10 s t a RET
```

Notice that the instant we stored a new value in **a**, all '=>' operators already on the stack that referred to *a* were updated to use the new value. With '=>', you can push a set of formulas on the stack, then change the variables experimentally to see the effects on the formulas' values.

You can also "unstore" a variable when you are through with it:

```
2:  2 + 5 => 5
1:  2 a + 2 b => 2 a + 2 b
        .


     s u a RET
```

We will encounter formulas involving variables and functions again when we discuss the algebra and calculus features of the Calculator.

2.1.3 Undo and Redo

If you make a mistake, you can usually correct it by pressing shift-*U*, the "undo" command. First, clear the stack (*M-0 DEL*) and exit and restart Calc (*C-x * * C-x * *)* to make sure things start off with a clean slate. Now:

```
1:  2         2:  2        1:  8        2:  2         1:  6
    .         1:  3            .        1:  3             .
                  .                         .


  2 RET          3            ^           U             *
```

You can undo any number of times. Calc keeps a complete record of all you have done since you last opened the Calc window. After the above example, you could type:

```
1:  6         2:  2        1:  2            .              .
    .         1:  3            .
                  .
                                                       (error)
     U             U            U             U
```

You can also type *D* to "redo" a command that you have undone mistakenly.

```
    .         1:  2        2:  2        1:  6         1:  6
              1:  3        1:  3            .             .
                  .            .
                                                      (error)
     D             D            D             D
```

It was not possible to redo past the 6, since that was placed there by something other than an undo command.

You can think of undo and redo as a sort of "time machine." Press *U* to go backward in time, *D* to go forward. If you go backward and do something (like *) then, as any science fiction reader knows, you have changed your future and you cannot go forward again. Thus, the inability to redo past the 6 even though there was an earlier undo command.

You can always recall an earlier result using the Trail. We've ignored the trail so far, but it has been faithfully recording everything we did since we loaded the Calculator. If the Trail is not displayed, press *t d* now to turn it on.

Let's try grabbing an earlier result. The 8 we computed was undone by a *U* command, and was lost even to Redo when we pressed *, but it's still there in the trail. There should be a little '>' arrow (the *trail pointer*) resting on the last trail entry. If there isn't, press *t]* to reset the trail pointer. Now, press *t p* to move the arrow onto the line containing 8, and press *t y* to "yank" that number back onto the stack.

If you press *t]* again, you will see that even our Yank command went into the trail.

Let's go further back in time. Earlier in the tutorial we computed a huge integer using the formula '2^3^4'. We don't remember what it was, but the first digits were "241". Press *t r* (which stands for trail-search-reverse), then type *241*. The trail cursor will jump back to the next previous occurrence of the string "241" in the trail. This is just a regular Emacs incremental search; you can now press *C-s* or *C-r* to continue the search forwards or backwards as you like.

To finish the search, press RET. This halts the incremental search and leaves the trail pointer at the thing we found. Now we can type *t y* to yank that number onto the stack. If we hadn't remembered the "241", we could simply have searched for 2^3^4, then pressed *RET t n* to halt and then move to the next item.

You may have noticed that all the trail-related commands begin with the letter *t*. (The store-and-recall commands, on the other hand, all began with *s*.) Calc has so many commands that there aren't enough keys for all of them, so various commands are grouped into two-letter sequences where the first letter is called the *prefix* key. If you type a prefix key by accident, you can press *C-g* to cancel it. (In fact, you can press *C-g* to cancel almost anything in Emacs.) To get help on a prefix key, press that key followed by *?*. Some prefixes have several lines of help, so you need to press *?* repeatedly to see them all. You can also type *h h* to see all the help at once.

Try pressing *t ?* now. You will see a line of the form,

```
trail/time: Display; Fwd, Back; Next, Prev, Here, [, ]; Yank:  [MORE]  t-
```

The word "trail" indicates that the *t* prefix key contains trail-related commands. Each entry on the line shows one command, with a single capital letter showing which letter you press to get that command. We have used *t n*, *t p*, *t]*, and *t y* so far. The '[MORE]' means you can press *?* again to see more *t*-prefix commands. Notice that the commands are roughly divided (by semicolons) into related groups.

When you are in the help display for a prefix key, the prefix is still active. If you press another key, like *y* for example, it will be interpreted as a *t y* command. If all you wanted was to look at the help messages, press *C-g* afterwards to cancel the prefix.

One more way to correct an error is by editing the stack entries. The actual Stack buffer is marked read-only and must not be edited directly, but you can press ` (grave accent) to edit a stack entry.

Try entering '3.141439' now. If this is supposed to represent π, it's got several errors. Press ` to edit this number. Now use the normal Emacs cursor motion and editing keys to change the second 4 to a 5, and to transpose the 3 and the 9. When you press RET, the number on the stack will be replaced by your new number. This works for formulas, vectors, and all other types of values you can put on the stack. The ` key also works during entry of a number or algebraic formula.

2.1.4 Mode-Setting Commands

Calc has many types of *modes* that affect the way it interprets your commands or the way it displays data. We have already seen one mode, namely Algebraic mode. There are many others, too; we'll try some of the most common ones here.

Perhaps the most fundamental mode in Calc is the current *precision*. Notice the '12' on the Calc window's mode line:

```
--%*-Calc: 12 Deg        (Calculator)----All------
```

Most of the symbols there are Emacs things you don't need to worry about, but the '12' and the 'Deg' are mode indicators. The '12' means that calculations should always be carried to 12 significant figures. That is why, when we type *1 RET 7 /*, we get 0.142857142857 with exactly 12 digits, not counting leading and trailing zeros.

You can set the precision to anything you like by pressing *p*, then entering a suitable number. Try pressing *p 30 RET*, then doing *1 RET 7 /* again:

```
1:  0.142857142857
2:  0.142857142857142857142857142857
    .
```

Although the precision can be set arbitrarily high, Calc always has to have *some* value for the current precision. After all, the true value 1/7 is an infinitely repeating decimal; Calc has to stop somewhere.

Of course, calculations are slower the more digits you request. Press *p 12* now to set the precision back down to the default.

Calculations always use the current precision. For example, even though we have a 30-digit value for 1/7 on the stack, if we use it in a calculation in 12-digit mode it will be rounded down to 12 digits before it is used. Try it; press RET to duplicate the number, then *1 +*. Notice that the RET key didn't round the number, because it doesn't do any calculation. But the instant we pressed +, the number was rounded down.

```
1:  0.142857142857
2:  0.142857142857142857142857142857
3:  1.14285714286
    .
```

In fact, since we added a digit on the left, we had to lose one digit on the right from even the 12-digit value of 1/7.

How did we get more than 12 digits when we computed '2^3^4'? The answer is that Calc makes a distinction between *integers* and *floating-point* numbers, or *floats*. An integer is a number that does not contain a decimal point. There is no such thing as an "infinitely repeating fraction integer," so Calc doesn't have to limit itself. If you asked for '2^10000' (don't try this!), you would have to wait a long time but you would eventually get an exact answer. If you ask for '2.^10000', you will quickly get an answer which is correct only to 12 places. The decimal point tells Calc that it should use floating-point arithmetic to get the answer, not exact integer arithmetic.

You can use the *F* (`calc-floor`) command to convert a floating-point value to an integer, and *c f* (`calc-float`) to convert an integer to floating-point form.

Let's try entering that last calculation:

```
1:  2.          2:  2.          1:  1.99506311689e3010
    .           1:  10000           .


    2.0 RET         10000 RET        ^
```

Notice the letter 'e' in there. It represents "times ten to the power of," and is used by Calc automatically whenever writing the number out fully would introduce more extra zeros than you probably want to see. You can enter numbers in this notation, too.

```
1:  2.          2:  2.          1:  1.99506311678e3010
    .           1:  10000.          .


    2.0 RET         1e4 RET          ^
```

Hey, the answer is different! Look closely at the middle columns of the two examples. In the first, the stack contained the exact integer 10000, but in the second it contained a floating-point value with a decimal point. When you raise a number to an integer power, Calc uses repeated squaring and multiplication to get the answer. When you use a floating-point power, Calc uses logarithms and exponentials. As you can see, a slight error crept in during one of these methods. Which one should we trust? Let's raise the precision a bit and find out:

```
       .        1:  2.          2:  2.          1:  1.995063116880828e3010
                    .           1:  10000.          .


    p 16 RET        2. RET          1e4              ^      p 12 RET
```

Presumably, it doesn't matter whether we do this higher-precision calculation using an integer or floating-point power, since we have added enough "guard digits" to trust the first 12 digits no matter what. And the verdict is. . . Integer powers were more accurate; in fact, the result was only off by one unit in the last place.

Calc does many of its internal calculations to a slightly higher precision, but it doesn't always bump the precision up enough. In each case, Calc added about two digits of precision during its calculation and then rounded back down to 12 digits afterward. In one case, it was enough; in the other, it wasn't. If you really need x digits of precision, it never hurts to do the calculation with a few extra guard digits.

What if we want guard digits but don't want to look at them? We can set the *float format*. Calc supports four major formats for floating-point numbers, called *normal*, *fixed-point*, *scientific notation*, and *engineering notation*. You get them by pressing *d n*, *d f*, *d s*, and *d e*, respectively. In each case, you can supply a numeric prefix argument which says how many digits should be displayed. As an example, let's put a few numbers onto the stack and try some different display modes. First, use *M-0 DEL* to clear the stack, then enter the four numbers shown here:

```
4:  12345      4:  12345      4:  12345      4:  12345      4:  12345
3:  12345.     3:  12300.     3:  1.2345e4   3:  1.23e4     3:  12345.000
2:  123.45     2:  123.       2:  1.2345e2   2:  1.23e2     2:  123.450
1:  12.345     1:  12.3       1:  1.2345e1   1:  1.23e1     1:  12.345
        .              .              .              .              .

    d n            M-3 d n          d s          M-3 d s        M-3 d f
```

Notice that when we typed *M-3 d n*, the numbers were rounded down to three significant digits, but then when we typed *d s* all five significant figures reappeared. The float format does not affect how numbers are stored, it only affects how they are displayed. Only the current precision governs the actual rounding of numbers in the Calculator's memory.

Engineering notation, not shown here, is like scientific notation except the exponent (the power-of-ten part) is always adjusted to be a multiple of three (as in "kilo," "micro," etc.). As a result there will be one, two, or three digits before the decimal point.

Whenever you change a display-related mode, Calc redraws everything in the stack. This may be slow if there are many things on the stack, so Calc allows you to type shift-*H* before any mode command to prevent it from updating the stack. Anything Calc displays after the mode-changing command will appear in the new format.

```
4:  12345      4:  12345      4:  12345      4:  12345      4:  12345
3:  12345.000  3:  12345.000  3:  12345.000  3:  1.2345e4   3:  12345.
2:  123.450    2:  123.450    2:  1.2345e1   2:  1.2345e1   2:  123.45
1:  12.345     1:  1.2345e1   1:  1.2345e2   1:  1.2345e2   1:  12.345
        .              .              .              .              .

    H d s          DEL U            TAB          d SPC            d n
```

Here the *H d s* command changes to scientific notation but without updating the screen. Deleting the top stack entry and undoing it back causes it to show up in the new format; swapping the top two stack entries reformats both entries. The *d SPC* command refreshes the whole stack. The *d n* command changes back to the normal float format; since it doesn't have an *H* prefix, it also updates all the stack entries to be in *d n* format.

Notice that the integer 12345 was not affected by any of the float formats. Integers are integers, and are always displayed exactly.

Large integers have their own problems. Let's look back at the result of *2^3^4*.

    241785163922925834941235

Quick—how many digits does this have? Try typing *d g*:

    2,417,851,639,229,258,349,412,352

Now how many digits does this have? It's much easier to tell! We can actually group digits into clumps of any size. Some people prefer *M-5 d g*:

    24178,51639,22925,83494,12352

Let's see what happens to floating-point numbers when they are grouped. First, type *p 25 RET* to make sure we have enough precision to get ourselves into trouble. Now, type *1e13 /*:

    24,17851,63922.9258349412352

The integer part is grouped but the fractional part isn't. Now try *M-- M-5 d g* (that's meta-minus-sign, meta-five):

    24,17851,63922.92583,49412,352

If you find it hard to tell the decimal point from the commas, try changing the grouping character to a space with *d , SPC*:

    24 17851 63922.92583 49412 352

Type *d , ,* to restore the normal grouping character, then *d g* again to turn grouping off. Also, press *p 12* to restore the default precision.

Press *U* enough times to get the original big integer back. (Notice that *U* does not undo each mode-setting command; if you want to undo a mode-setting command, you have to do it yourself.) Now, type *d r 16 RET*:

    16#20000000000000000000000

The number is now displayed in *hexadecimal*, or "base-16" form. Suddenly it looks pretty simple; this should be no surprise, since we got this number by computing a power of two, and 16 is a power of 2. In fact, we can use *d r 2 RET* to see it in actual binary form:

    2#1000000000000000000000000000000000000000000000000000000000000000 ...

We don't have enough space here to show all the zeros! They won't fit on a typical screen, either, so you will have to use horizontal scrolling to see them all. Press < and > to scroll the stack window left and right by half its width. Another way to view something large is to press ` (grave accent) to edit the top of stack in a separate window. (Press *C-c C-c* when you are done.)

You can enter non-decimal numbers using the # symbol, too. Let's see what the hexadecimal number '5FE' looks like in binary. Type *16#5FE* (the letters can be typed in upper or lower case; they will always appear in upper case). It will also help to turn grouping on with *d g*:

    2#101,1111,1110

Notice that *d g* groups by fours by default if the display radix is binary or hexadecimal, but by threes if it is decimal, octal, or any other radix.

Now let's see that number in decimal; type *d r 10*:

    1,534

Numbers are not *stored* with any particular radix attached. They're just numbers; they can be entered in any radix, and are always displayed in whatever radix you've chosen with *d r*. The current radix applies to integers, fractions, and floats.

(•) **Exercise 1.** Your friend Joe tried to enter one-third as '3#0.1' in *d r 3* mode with a precision of 12. He got '3#0.0222222...' (with 25 2's) in the display. When he multiplied that by three, he got '3#0.222222...' instead of the expected '3#1'. Next, Joe entered '3#0.2' and, to his great relief, saw '3#0.2' on the screen. But when he typed *2 /*, he got '3#0.10000001' (some zeros omitted). What's going on here? See Section 2.7.8 [Modes Answer 1], page 73. (•)

(•) **Exercise 2.** Scientific notation works in non-decimal modes in the natural way (the exponent is a power of the radix instead of a power of ten, although the exponent itself is always written in decimal). Thus '8#1.23e3 = 8#1230.0'. Suppose we have the hexadecimal number 'f.e8f' times 16 to the 15th power: We write '16#f.e8fe15'. What is wrong with this picture? What could we write instead that would work better? See Section 2.7.9 [Modes Answer 2], page 73. (•)

The *m* prefix key has another set of modes, relating to the way Calc interprets your inputs and does computations. Whereas *d*-prefix modes generally affect the way things look, *m*-prefix modes affect the way they are actually computed.

The most popular *m*-prefix mode is the *angular mode*. Notice the 'Deg' indicator in the mode line. This means that if you use a command that interprets a number as an angle, it will assume the angle is measured in degrees. For example,

```
1:  45          1:  0.707106781187   1:  0.500000000001   1:  0.5
    .               .                    .                    .

    45              S                    2 ^                  c 1
```

The shift-*S* command computes the sine of an angle. The sine of 45 degrees is $\sqrt{2}/2$; squaring this yields $2/4 = 0.5$. However, there has been a slight roundoff error because the representation of $\sqrt{2}/2$ wasn't exact. The *c 1* command is a handy way to clean up numbers in this case; it temporarily reduces the precision by one digit while it re-rounds the number on the top of the stack.

(•) **Exercise 3.** Your friend Joe computed the sine of 45 degrees as shown above, then, hoping to avoid an inexact result, he increased the precision to 16 digits before squaring. What happened? See Section 2.7.10 [Modes Answer 3], page 74. (•)

To do this calculation in radians, we would type *m r* first. (The indicator changes to 'Rad'.) 45 degrees corresponds to $\pi/4$ radians. To get π, press the *P* key. (Once again, this is a shifted capital *P*. Remember, unshifted *p* sets the precision.)

```
1:  3.14159265359   1:  0.785398163398   1:  0.707106781187
    .                   .                    .

    P                   4 /       m r        S
```

Likewise, inverse trigonometric functions generate results in either radians or degrees, depending on the current angular mode.

```
1:  0.707106781187   1:  0.785398163398   1:  45.
    .                    .                    .

    .5 Q       m r       I S        m d       U I S
```

Here we compute the Inverse Sine of $\sqrt{0.5}$, first in radians, then in degrees.

Use *c d* and *c r* to convert a number from radians to degrees and vice-versa.

```
1:  45          1:  0.785398163397   1:  45.
    .               .                    .

    45              c r                  c d
```

Another interesting mode is *Fraction mode*. Normally, dividing two integers produces a floating-point result if the quotient can't be expressed as an exact integer. Fraction mode causes integer division to produce a fraction, i.e., a rational number, instead.

```
2:  12          1:  1.33333333333   1:  4:3
1:  9               .                   .
    .

    12 RET 9        /           m f      U /     m f
```

In the first case, we get an approximate floating-point result. In the second case, we get an exact fractional result (four-thirds).

You can enter a fraction at any time using : notation. (Calc uses : instead of / as the fraction separator because / is already used to divide the top two stack elements.) Calculations involving fractions will always produce exact fractional results; Fraction mode only says what to do when dividing two integers.

(•) **Exercise 4.** If fractional arithmetic is exact, why would you ever use floating-point numbers instead? See Section 2.7.11 [Modes Answer 4], page 74. (•)

Typing m f doesn't change any existing values in the stack. In the above example, we had to Undo the division and do it over again when we changed to Fraction mode. But if you use the evaluates-to operator you can get commands like m f to recompute for you.

```
1:  12 / 9 => 1.33333333333    1:  12 / 9 => 1.333    1:  12 / 9 => 4:3
    .                              .                       .


    ' 12/9 => RET                  p 4 RET                 m f
```

In this example, the righthand side of the '=>' operator on the stack is recomputed when we change the precision, then again when we change to Fraction mode. All '=>' expressions on the stack are recomputed every time you change any mode that might affect their values.

2.2 Arithmetic Tutorial

In this section, we explore the arithmetic and scientific functions available in the Calculator.

The standard arithmetic commands are +, -, *, /, and ^. Each normally takes two numbers from the top of the stack and pushes back a result. The n and & keys perform change-sign and reciprocal operations, respectively.

```
1:  5        1:  0.2       1:  5.       1:  -5.      1:  5.
    .            .             .            .            .

    5            &             &            n            n
```

You can apply a "binary operator" like + across any number of stack entries by giving it a numeric prefix. You can also apply it pairwise to several stack elements along with the top one if you use a negative prefix.

```
3:  2        1:  9       3:  2       4:  2       3:  12
2:  3            .        2:  3       3:  3       2:  13
1:  4                     1:  4       2:  4       1:  14
    .                         .        1:  10          .
                                           .

2 RET 3 RET 4    M-3 +       U           10          M-- M-3 +
```

You can apply a "unary operator" like & to the top n stack entries with a numeric prefix, too.

```
3:  2        3:  0.5            3:  0.5
2:  3        2:  0.333333333333  2:  3.
1:  4        1:  0.25            1:  4.
    .            .                   .

2 RET 3 RET 4    M-3 &              M-2 &
```

Notice that the results here are left in floating-point form. We can convert them back to integers by pressing F, the "floor" function. This function rounds down to the next lower integer. There is also R, which rounds to the nearest integer.

```
7:  2.          7:  2           7:  2
6:  2.4         6:  2           6:  2
5:  2.5         5:  2           5:  3
4:  2.6         4:  2           4:  3
3:  -2.         3:  -2          3:  -2
2:  -2.4        2:  -3          2:  -2
1:  -2.6        1:  -3          1:  -3
     .               .               .

             M-7 F         U M-7 R
```

Since dividing-and-flooring (i.e., "integer quotient") is such a common operation, Calc provides a special command for that purpose, the backslash \. Another common arithmetic operator is %, which computes the remainder that would arise from a \ operation, i.e., the "modulo" of two numbers. For example,

```
2:  1234      1:  12        2:  1234      1:  34
1:  100            .         1:  100            .
     .                            .

  1234 RET 100      \           U             %
```

These commands actually work for any real numbers, not just integers.

```
2:  3.1415    1:  3         2:  3.1415    1:  0.1415
1:  1              .         1:  1              .
     .                            .

  3.1415 RET 1      \           U             %
```

(•) **Exercise 1.** The \ command would appear to be a frill, since you could always do the same thing with / F. Think of a situation where this is not true—/ F would be inadequate. Now think of a way you could get around the problem if Calc didn't provide a \ command. See Section 2.7.12 [Arithmetic Answer 1], page 75. (•)

We've already seen the Q (square root) and S (sine) commands. Other commands along those lines are C (cosine), T (tangent), E (e^x) and L (natural logarithm). These can be modified by the I (inverse) and H (hyperbolic) prefix keys.

Let's compute the sine and cosine of an angle, and verify the identity $\sin^2 x + \cos^2 x = 1$. We'll arbitrarily pick -64 degrees as a good value for x. With the angular mode set to degrees (type m d), do:

```
2:  -64       2:  -64       2:  -0.89879  2:  -0.89879  1:  1.
1:  -64       1:  -0.89879  1:  -64       1:  0.43837        .
     .             .             .             .

  64 n RET RET      S             TAB           C             f h
```

(For brevity, we're showing only five digits of the results here. You can of course do these calculations to any precision you like.)

Remember, f h is the calc-hypot, or square-root of sum of squares, command.

Another identity is $\tan x = \dfrac{\sin x}{\cos x}$.

```
2:  -0.89879  1:  -2.0503   1:  -64.
1:  0.43837        .             .
     .

       U             /             I T
```

A physical interpretation of this calculation is that if you move 0.89879 units downward and 0.43837 units to the right, your direction of motion is −64 degrees from horizontal. Suppose we move in the opposite direction, up and to the left:

```
2:  -0.89879    2:  0.89879     1:  -2.0503     1:  -64.
1:  0.43837     1:  -0.43837        .               .
    .               .

    U U             M-2 n           /               I T
```

How can the angle be the same? The answer is that the / operation loses information about the signs of its inputs. Because the quotient is negative, we know exactly one of the inputs was negative, but we can't tell which one. There is an f T [arctan2] function which computes the inverse tangent of the quotient of a pair of numbers. Since you feed it the two original numbers, it has enough information to give you a full 360-degree answer.

```
2:  0.89879    1:  116.      3:  116.       2:  116.     1:  180.
1:  -0.43837       .          2:  -0.89879   1:  -64.         .
    .                         1:  0.43837        .
                                  .

    U U             f T        M-RET M-2 n     f T           -
```

The resulting angles differ by 180 degrees; in other words, they point in opposite directions, just as we would expect.

The META-RET we used in the third step is the "last-arguments" command. It is sort of like Undo, except that it restores the arguments of the last command to the stack without removing the command's result. It is useful in situations like this one, where we need to do several operations on the same inputs. We could have accomplished the same thing by using M-2 RET to duplicate the top two stack elements right after the U U, then a pair of M-TAB commands to cycle the 116 up around the duplicates.

A similar identity is supposed to hold for hyperbolic sines and cosines, except that it is the *difference* $\cosh^2 x - \sinh^2 x$ that always equals one. Let's try to verify this identity.

```
2:  -64      2:  -64          2:  -64         2:  9.7192e54   2:  9.7192e54
1:  -64      1:  -3.1175e27   1:  9.7192e54   1:  -64         1:  9.7192e54
    .            .                .               .               .

64 n RET RET     H C             2 ^             TAB             H S 2 ^
```

Something's obviously wrong, because when we subtract these numbers the answer will clearly be zero! But if you think about it, if these numbers *did* differ by one, it would be in the 55th decimal place. The difference we seek has been lost entirely to roundoff error.

We could verify this hypothesis by doing the actual calculation with, say, 60 decimal places of precision. This will be slow, but not enormously so. Try it if you wish; sure enough, the answer is 0.99999, reasonably close to 1.

Of course, a more reasonable way to verify the identity is to use a more reasonable value for x!

Some Calculator commands use the Hyperbolic prefix for other purposes. The logarithm and exponential functions, for example, work to the base e normally but use base-10 instead if you use the Hyperbolic prefix.

```
1:  1000     1:  6.9077    1:  1000     1:  3
    .            .             .            .

    1000         L             U           H L
```

First, we mistakenly compute a natural logarithm. Then we undo and compute a common logarithm instead.

The *B* key computes a general base-*b* logarithm for any value of *b*.

```
2:  1000      1:  3        1:  1000.     2:  1000.     1:  6.9077
1:  10                                   1:  2.71828
    .             .             .             .             .

1000 RET 10      B           H E           H P           B
```

Here we first use *B* to compute the base-10 logarithm, then use the "hyperbolic" exponential as a cheap hack to recover the number 1000, then use *B* again to compute the natural logarithm. Note that *P* with the hyperbolic prefix pushes the constant *e* onto the stack.

You may have noticed that both times we took the base-10 logarithm of 1000, we got an exact integer result. Calc always tries to give an exact rational result for calculations involving rational numbers where possible. But when we used *H E*, the result was a floating-point number for no apparent reason. In fact, if we had computed *10 RET 3 ^* we *would* have gotten an exact integer 1000. But the *H E* command is rigged to generate a floating-point result all of the time so that *1000 H E* will not waste time computing a thousand-digit integer when all you probably wanted was '1e1000'.

(•) **Exercise 2.** Find a pair of integer inputs to the *B* command for which Calc could find an exact rational result but doesn't. See Section 2.7.13 [Arithmetic Answer 2], page 75. (•)

The Calculator also has a set of functions relating to combinatorics and statistics. You may be familiar with the *factorial* function, which computes the product of all the integers up to a given number.

```
1:  100       1:  93326215443...   1:  100.      1:  9.3326e157
    .             .                     .             .

100           !                     U c f         !
```

Recall, the *c f* command converts the integer or fraction at the top of the stack to floating-point format. If you take the factorial of a floating-point number, you get a floating-point result accurate to the current precision. But if you give *!* an exact integer, you get an exact integer result (158 digits long in this case).

If you take the factorial of a non-integer, Calc uses a generalized factorial function defined in terms of Euler's Gamma function $\Gamma(n)$ (which is itself available as the *f g* command).

```
3:  4.        3:  24.              1:  5.5       1:  52.342777847
2:  4.5       2:  52.3427777847        .             .
1:  5.        1:  120.
    .             .

              M-3 !                M-0 DEL 5.5   f g
```

Here we verify the identity $n! = \Gamma(n+1)$.

The binomial coefficient *n*-choose-*m* or $\binom{n}{m}$ is defined by $\dfrac{n!}{m!\,(n-m)!}$ for all reals *n* and *m*. The intermediate results in this formula can become quite large even if the final result is small; the *k c* command computes a binomial coefficient in a way that avoids large intermediate values.

The *k* prefix key defines several common functions out of combinatorics and number theory. Here we compute the binomial coefficient 30-choose-20, then determine its prime factorization.

```
2:  30          1:  30045015  1:  [3, 3, 5, 7, 11, 13, 23, 29]
1:  20              .             .
    .

    30 RET 20       k c           k f
```

You can verify these prime factors by using *V R ** to multiply together the elements of this vector. The result is the original number, 30045015.

Suppose a program you are writing needs a hash table with at least 10000 entries. It's best to use a prime number as the actual size of a hash table. Calc can compute the next prime number after 10000:

```
1:  10000       1:  10007     1:  9973
    .               .             .

    10000           k n           I k n
```

Just for kicks we've also computed the next prime *less* than 10000.

See Section 7.6 [Financial Functions], page 200, for a description of the Calculator commands that deal with business and financial calculations (functions like `pv`, `rate`, and `sln`).

See Section 7.7 [Binary Functions], page 206, to read about the commands for operating on binary numbers (like `and`, `xor`, and `lsh`).

2.3 Vector/Matrix Tutorial

A *vector* is a list of numbers or other Calc data objects. Calc provides a large set of commands that operate on vectors. Some are familiar operations from vector analysis. Others simply treat a vector as a list of objects.

2.3.1 Vector Analysis

If you add two vectors, the result is a vector of the sums of the elements, taken pairwise.

```
1:  [1, 2, 3]   2:  [1, 2, 3]   1:  [8, 8, 3]
    .           1:  [7, 6, 0]       .

    [1,2,3]  s 1    [7 6 0]  s 2    +
```

Note that we can separate the vector elements with either commas or spaces. This is true whether we are using incomplete vectors or algebraic entry. The *s 1* and *s 2* commands save these vectors so we can easily reuse them later.

If you multiply two vectors, the result is the sum of the products of the elements taken pairwise. This is called the *dot product* of the vectors.

```
2:  [1, 2, 3]   1:  19
1:  [7, 6, 0]       .
    .

    r 1 r 2         *
```

The dot product of two vectors is equal to the product of their lengths times the cosine of the angle between them. (Here the vector is interpreted as a line from the origin $(0,0,0)$

to the specified point in three-dimensional space.) The *A* (absolute value) command can be
used to compute the length of a vector.

```
3:  19              3:  19           1:  0.550782    1:  56.579
2:  [1, 2, 3]       2:  3.741657         .               .
1:  [7, 6, 0]       1:  9.219544
        .                   .

    M-RET               M-2 A            * /              I C
```

First we recall the arguments to the dot product command, then we compute the absolute
values of the top two stack entries to obtain the lengths of the vectors, then we divide the
dot product by the product of the lengths to get the cosine of the angle. The inverse cosine
finds that the angle between the vectors is about 56 degrees.

The *cross product* of two vectors is a vector whose length is the product of the lengths
of the inputs times the sine of the angle between them, and whose direction is perpendicular to both input vectors. Unlike the dot product, the cross product is defined only for
three-dimensional vectors. Let's double-check our computation of the angle using the cross
product.

```
2:  [1, 2, 3]   3:  [-18, 21, -8]   1:  [-0.52, 0.61, -0.23]   1:  56.579
1:  [7, 6, 0]   2:  [1, 2, 3]           .                          .
        .       1:  [7, 6, 0]
                        .

    r 1 r 2         V C  s 3 M-RET   M-2 A * /                      A I S
```

First we recall the original vectors and compute their cross product, which we also store
for later reference. Now we divide the vector by the product of the lengths of the original
vectors. The length of this vector should be the sine of the angle; sure enough, it is!

Vector-related commands generally begin with the *v* prefix key. Some are uppercase
letters and some are lowercase. To make it easier to type these commands, the shift-*V* prefix
key acts the same as the *v* key. (See Section 6.1 [General Mode Commands], page 137, for
a way to make all prefix keys have this property.)

If we take the dot product of two perpendicular vectors we expect to get zero, since the
cosine of 90 degrees is zero. Let's check that the cross product is indeed perpendicular to
both inputs:

```
2:  [1, 2, 3]        1:  0          2:  [7, 6, 0]        1:  0
1:  [-18, 21, -8]        .          1:  [-18, 21, -8]        .
        .                                   .

    r 1 r 3              *           DEL r 2 r 3              *
```

(•) **Exercise 1.** Given a vector on the top of the stack, what keystrokes would you use
to *normalize* the vector, i.e., to reduce its length to one without changing its direction? See
Section 2.7.14 [Vector Answer 1], page 75. (•)

(•) **Exercise 2.** Suppose a certain particle can be at any of several positions along a
ruler. You have a list of those positions in the form of a vector, and another list of the
probabilities for the particle to be at the corresponding positions. Find the average position
of the particle. See Section 2.7.15 [Vector Answer 2], page 75. (•)

2.3.2 Matrices

A *matrix* is just a vector of vectors, all the same length. This means you can enter a matrix using nested brackets. You can also use the semicolon character to enter a matrix. We'll show both methods here:

```
1:  [ [ 1, 2, 3 ]              1:  [ [ 1, 2, 3 ]
      [ 4, 5, 6 ] ]                  [ 4, 5, 6 ] ]
    .                              .


    [[1 2 3] [4 5 6]]          ' [1 2 3; 4 5 6] RET
```

We'll be using this matrix again, so type *s 4* to save it now.

Note that semicolons work with incomplete vectors, but they work better in algebraic entry. That's why we use the apostrophe in the second example.

When two matrices are multiplied, the lefthand matrix must have the same number of columns as the righthand matrix has rows. Row i, column j of the result is effectively the dot product of row i of the left matrix by column j of the right matrix.

If we try to duplicate this matrix and multiply it by itself, the dimensions are wrong and the multiplication cannot take place:

```
1:  [ [ 1, 2, 3 ]   * [ [ 1, 2, 3 ]
      [ 4, 5, 6 ] ]     [ 4, 5, 6 ] ]
    .


    RET *
```

Though rather hard to read, this is a formula which shows the product of two matrices. The '*' function, having invalid arguments, has been left in symbolic form.

We can multiply the matrices if we *transpose* one of them first.

```
2:  [ [ 1, 2, 3 ]     1:  [ [ 14, 32 ]     1:  [ [ 17, 22, 27 ]
      [ 4, 5, 6 ] ]         [ 32, 77 ] ]         [ 22, 29, 36 ]
1:  [ [ 1, 4 ]            .                      [ 27, 36, 45 ] ]
      [ 2, 5 ]
      [ 3, 6 ] ]
    .


    U v t                     *                 U TAB *
```

Matrix multiplication is not commutative; indeed, switching the order of the operands can even change the dimensions of the result matrix, as happened here!

If you multiply a plain vector by a matrix, it is treated as a single row or column depending on which side of the matrix it is on. The result is a plain vector which should also be interpreted as a row or column as appropriate.

```
2:  [ [ 1, 2, 3 ]      1:  [14, 32]
      [ 4, 5, 6 ] ]        .
1:  [1, 2, 3]


    r 4 r 1                     *
```

Multiplying in the other order wouldn't work because the number of rows in the matrix is different from the number of elements in the vector.

(•) **Exercise 1.** Use '*' to sum along the rows of the above 2×3 matrix to get $[6, 15]$. Now use '*' to sum along the columns to get $[5, 7, 9]$. See Section 2.7.16 [Matrix Answer 1], page 75. (•)

An *identity matrix* is a square matrix with ones along the diagonal and zeros elsewhere. It has the property that multiplication by an identity matrix, on the left or on the right, always produces the original matrix.

```
1:  [ [ 1, 2, 3 ]      2:  [ [ 1, 2, 3 ]      1:  [ [ 1, 2, 3 ]
      [ 4, 5, 6 ] ]          [ 4, 5, 6 ] ]          [ 4, 5, 6 ] ]
    .                    1:  [ [ 1, 0, 0 ]      .
                               [ 0, 1, 0 ]
                               [ 0, 0, 1 ] ]
                         .

        r 4                    v i 3 RET              *
```

If a matrix is square, it is often possible to find its *inverse*, that is, a matrix which, when multiplied by the original matrix, yields an identity matrix. The **&** (reciprocal) key also computes the inverse of a matrix.

```
1:  [ [ 1, 2, 3 ]      1:  [ [   -2.4,      1.2,    -0.2 ]
      [ 4, 5, 6 ]            [    2.8,     -1.4,     0.4 ]
      [ 7, 6, 0 ] ]          [ -0.73333, 0.53333, -0.2 ] ]
    .                    .


        r 4 r 2 | s 5          &
```

The vertical bar | *concatenates* numbers, vectors, and matrices together. Here we have used it to add a new row onto our matrix to make it square.

We can multiply these two matrices in either order to get an identity.

```
1:  [ [ 1., 0., 0. ]      1:  [ [ 1., 0., 0. ]
      [ 0., 1., 0. ]            [ 0., 1., 0. ]
      [ 0., 0., 1. ] ]          [ 0., 0., 1. ] ]
    .                        .


        M-RET  *                  U TAB *
```

Matrix inverses are related to systems of linear equations in algebra. Suppose we had the following set of equations:

$$a + 2b + 3c = 6$$
$$4a + 5b + 6c = 2$$
$$7a + 6b \quad\;\; = 3$$

This can be cast into the matrix equation,

$$\begin{pmatrix} 1 & 2 & 3 \\ 4 & 5 & 6 \\ 7 & 6 & 0 \end{pmatrix} \times \begin{pmatrix} a \\ b \\ c \end{pmatrix} = \begin{pmatrix} 6 \\ 2 \\ 3 \end{pmatrix}$$

We can solve this system of equations by multiplying both sides by the inverse of the matrix. Calc can do this all in one step:

```
2:  [6, 2, 3]          1:  [-12.6, 15.2, -3.93333]
1:  [ [ 1, 2, 3 ]          .
      [ 4, 5, 6 ]
      [ 7, 6, 0 ] ]
    .


    [6,2,3] r 5                    /
```

The result is the $[a, b, c]$ vector that solves the equations. (Dividing by a square matrix is equivalent to multiplying by its inverse.)

Let's verify this solution:

```
2:  [ [ 1, 2, 3 ]              1:  [6., 2., 3.]
    [ 4, 5, 6 ]                     .
    [ 7, 6, 0 ] ]
1:  [-12.6, 15.2, -3.93333]
    .


    r 5 TAB                              *
```

Note that we had to be careful about the order in which we multiplied the matrix and
vector. If we multiplied in the other order, Calc would assume the vector was a row vector
in order to make the dimensions come out right, and the answer would be incorrect. If you
don't feel safe letting Calc take either interpretation of your vectors, use explicit $N \times 1$ or
$1 \times N$ matrices instead. In this case, you would enter the original column vector as '[[6],
[2], [3]]' or '[6; 2; 3]'.

(•) **Exercise 2.** Algebraic entry allows you to make vectors and matrices that include
variables. Solve the following system of equations to get expressions for x and y in terms
of a and b.

$$x + ay = 6$$
$$x + by = 10$$

See Section 2.7.17 [Matrix Answer 2], page 75. (•)

(•) **Exercise 3.** A system of equations is "over-determined" if it has more equations than
variables. It is often the case that there are no values for the variables that will satisfy
all the equations at once, but it is still useful to find a set of values which "nearly" satisfy
all the equations. In terms of matrix equations, you can't solve $AX = B$ directly because
the matrix A is not square for an over-determined system. Matrix inversion works only for
square matrices. One common trick is to multiply both sides on the left by the transpose
of A: $A^T A X = A^T B$, where A^T is the transpose 'trn(A)'. Now $A^T A$ is a square matrix
so a solution is possible. It turns out that the X vector you compute in this way will be
a "least-squares" solution, which can be regarded as the "closest" solution to the set of
equations. Use Calc to solve the following over-determined system:

$$a + 2b + 3c = 6$$
$$4a + 5b + 6c = 2$$
$$7a + 6b \qquad = 3$$
$$2a + 4b + 6c = 11$$

See Section 2.7.18 [Matrix Answer 3], page 76. (•)

2.3.3 Vectors as Lists

Although Calc has a number of features for manipulating vectors and matrices as mathematical objects, you can also treat vectors as simple lists of values. For example, we saw
that the **k f** command returns a vector which is a list of the prime factors of a number.

You can pack and unpack stack entries into vectors:

```
3:  10          1:  [10, 20, 30]     3:  10
2:  20              .                2:  20
1:  30                               1:  30
    .                                    .


            M-3 v p                  v u
```

You can also build vectors out of consecutive integers, or out of many copies of a given value:

```
1:  [1, 2, 3, 4]      2:  [1, 2, 3, 4]     2:  [1, 2, 3, 4]
    .                 1:  17               1:  [17, 17, 17, 17]
                          .                    .


    v x 4 RET             17                   v b 4 RET
```

You can apply an operator to every element of a vector using the *map* command.

```
1:  [17, 34, 51, 68]   1:  [289, 1156, 2601, 4624]  1:  [17, 34, 51, 68]
    .                      .                            .


    V M *                  2 V M ^                      V M Q
```

In the first step, we multiply the vector of integers by the vector of 17's elementwise. In the second step, we raise each element to the power two. (The general rule is that both operands must be vectors of the same length, or else one must be a vector and the other a plain number.) In the final step, we take the square root of each element.

(●) **Exercise 1.** Compute a vector of powers of two from 2^{-4} to 2^4. See Section 2.7.19 [List Answer 1], page 77. (●)

You can also *reduce* a binary operator across a vector. For example, reducing '*' computes the product of all the elements in the vector:

```
1:  123123     1:  [3, 7, 11, 13, 41]      1:  123123
    .              .                            .


    123123         k f                          V R *
```

In this example, we decompose 123123 into its prime factors, then multiply those factors together again to yield the original number.

We could compute a dot product "by hand" using mapping and reduction:

```
2:  [1, 2, 3]      1:  [7, 12, 0]      1:  19
1:  [7, 6, 0]          .                   .
    .


    r 1 r 2            V M *               V R +
```

Recalling two vectors from the previous section, we compute the sum of pairwise products of the elements to get the same answer for the dot product as before.

A slight variant of vector reduction is the *accumulate* operation, *V U*. This produces a vector of the intermediate results from a corresponding reduction. Here we compute a table of factorials:

```
1:  [1, 2, 3, 4, 5, 6]     1:  [1, 2, 6, 24, 120, 720]
    .                          .


    v x 6 RET                  V U *
```

Calc allows vectors to grow as large as you like, although it gets rather slow if vectors have more than about a hundred elements. Actually, most of the time is spent formatting these large vectors for display, not calculating on them. Try the following experiment (if your computer is very fast you may need to substitute a larger vector size).

```
1:  [1, 2, 3, 4, ...      1:  [2, 3, 4, 5, ...
    .                         .


    v x 500 RET               1 V M +
```

Now press `v .` (the letter `v`, then a period) and try the experiment again. In `v .` mode, long vectors are displayed "abbreviated" like this:

```
1:  [1, 2, 3, ..., 500]    1:  [2, 3, 4, ..., 501]
     .                          .


    v x 500 RET              1 V M +
```

(where now the '...' is actually part of the Calc display). You will find both operations are now much faster. But notice that even in `v .` mode, the full vectors are still shown in the Trail. Type `t .` to cause the trail to abbreviate as well, and try the experiment one more time. Operations on long vectors are now quite fast! (But of course if you use `t .` you will lose the ability to get old vectors back using the `t y` command.)

An easy way to view a full vector when `v .` mode is active is to press ` (grave accent) to edit the vector; editing always works with the full, unabbreviated value.

As a larger example, let's try to fit a straight line to some data, using the method of least squares. (Calc has a built-in command for least-squares curve fitting, but we'll do it by hand here just to practice working with vectors.) Suppose we have the following list of values in a file we have loaded into Emacs:

x	y
1.34	0.234
1.41	0.298
1.49	0.402
1.56	0.412
1.64	0.466
1.73	0.473
1.82	0.601
1.91	0.519
2.01	0.603
2.11	0.637
2.22	0.645
2.33	0.705
2.45	0.917
2.58	1.009
2.71	0.971
2.85	1.062
3.00	1.148
3.15	1.157
3.32	1.354

If you are reading this tutorial in printed form, you will find it easiest to press `C-x * i` to enter the on-line Info version of the manual and find this table there. (Press `g`, then type *List Tutorial*, to jump straight to this section.)

Position the cursor at the upper-left corner of this table, just to the left of the 1.34. Press `C-@` to set the mark. (On your system this may be `C-2`, `C-SPC`, or *NUL*.) Now position the cursor to the lower-right, just after the 1.354. You have now defined this region as an Emacs "rectangle." Still in the Info buffer, type `C-x * r`. This command (`calc-grab-rectangle`) will pop you back into the Calculator, with the contents of the rectangle you specified in the form of a matrix.

```
1:  [ [ 1.34, 0.234 ]
      [ 1.41, 0.298 ]
      ...
```

(You may wish to use `v .` mode to abbreviate the display of this large matrix.)

We want to treat this as a pair of lists. The first step is to transpose this matrix into a pair of rows. Remember, a matrix is just a vector of vectors. So we can unpack the matrix into a pair of row vectors on the stack.

```
1:  [ [ 1.34,  1.41,  1.49,  ... ]        2:  [1.34, 1.41, 1.49, ... ]
      [ 0.234, 0.298, 0.402, ... ] ]      1:  [0.234, 0.298, 0.402, ... ]
    .                                          .


    v t                                        v u
```

Let's store these in quick variables 1 and 2, respectively.

```
1:  [1.34, 1.41, 1.49, ... ]            .
    .


    t 2                             t 1
```

(Recall that **t** *2* is a variant of **s** *2* that removes the stored value from the stack.)

In a least squares fit, the slope m is given by the formula

$$m = \frac{N \sum xy - \sum x \sum y}{N \sum x^2 - \left(\sum x\right)^2}$$

where $\sum x$ represents the sum of all the values of x. While there is an actual **sum** function in Calc, it's easier to sum a vector using a simple reduction. First, let's compute the four different sums that this formula uses.

```
1:  41.63                       1:  98.0003
    .                               .


  r 1 V R +   t 3               r 1 2 V M ^ V R +   t 4

1:  13.613                      1:  33.36554
    .                               .


  r 2 V R +   t 5               r 1 r 2 V M * V R +   t 6
```

These are $\sum x$, $\sum x^2$, $\sum y$, and $\sum xy$, respectively. (We could have used * to compute $\sum x^2$ and $\sum xy$.)

Finally, we also need N, the number of data points. This is just the length of either of our lists.

```
1:  19
    .


  r 1 v l   t 7
```

(That's **v** followed by a lower-case *l*.)

Now we grind through the formula:

```
1:  633.94526  2:  633.94526  1:  67.23607
    .          1:  566.70919      .


  r 7 r 6 *      r 3 r 5 *        -

2:  67.23607   3:  67.23607   2:  67.23607   1:  0.52141679
1:  1862.0057  2:  1862.0057  1:  128.9488       .
    .          1:  1733.0569      .


  r 7 r 4 *      r 3 2 ^         -               / t 8
```

That gives us the slope m. The y-intercept b can now be found with the simple formula,

$$b = \frac{\sum y - m \sum x}{N}$$

```
1:  13.613     2:  13.613      1:  -8.09358    1:  -0.425978
    .          1:  21.70658        .               .


    r 5            r 8 r 3 *       -              r 7 /    t 9
```

Let's "plot" this straight line approximation, $y \approx mx + b$, and compare it with the original data.

```
1:  [0.699, 0.735, ... ]     1:  [0.273, 0.309, ... ]
    .                            .


    r 1 r 8 *                    r 9 +     s 0
```

Notice that multiplying a vector by a constant, and adding a constant to a vector, can be done without mapping commands since these are common operations from vector algebra. As far as Calc is concerned, we've just been doing geometry in 19-dimensional space!

We can subtract this vector from our original y vector to get a feel for the error of our fit. Let's find the maximum error:

```
1:  [0.0387, 0.0112, ... ]   1:  [0.0387, 0.0112, ... ]   1:  0.0897
    .                            .                            .


    r 2 -                        V M A                        V R X
```

First we compute a vector of differences, then we take the absolute values of these differences, then we reduce the `max` function across the vector. (The `max` function is on the two-key sequence `f x`; because it is so common to use `max` in a vector operation, the letters *X* and *N* are also accepted for `max` and `min` in this context. In general, you answer the *V M* or *V R* prompt with the actual key sequence that invokes the function you want. You could have typed *V R f x* or even *V R x max RET* if you had preferred.)

If your system has the GNUPLOT program, you can see graphs of your data and your straight line to see how well they match. (If you have GNUPLOT 3.0 or higher, the following instructions will work regardless of the kind of display you have. Some GNUPLOT 2.0, non-X-windows systems may require additional steps to view the graphs.)

Let's start by plotting the original data. Recall the "x" and "y" vectors onto the stack and press *g f*. This "fast" graphing command does everything you need to do for simple, straightforward plotting of data.

```
2:  [1.34, 1.41, 1.49, ... ]
1:  [0.234, 0.298, 0.402, ... ]
    .


    r 1 r 2     g f
```

If all goes well, you will shortly get a new window containing a graph of the data. (If not, contact your GNUPLOT or Calc installer to find out what went wrong.) In the X window system, this will be a separate graphics window. For other kinds of displays, the default is to display the graph in Emacs itself using rough character graphics. Press *q* when you are done viewing the character graphics.

Next, let's add the line we got from our least-squares fit.

```
2:  [1.34, 1.41, 1.49, ... ]
1:  [0.273, 0.309, 0.351, ... ]
    .


    DEL r 0    g a  g p
```

It's not very useful to get symbols to mark the data points on this second curve; you can type *g S g p* to remove them. Type *g q* when you are done to remove the X graphics window and terminate GNUPLOT.

(•) **Exercise 2.** An earlier exercise showed how to do least squares fitting to a general system of equations. Our 19 data points are really 19 equations of the form $y_i = mx_i + b$ for different pairs of (x_i, y_i). Use the matrix-transpose method to solve for m and b, duplicating the above result. See Section 2.7.20 [List Answer 2], page 77. (•)

(•) **Exercise 3.** If the input data do not form a rectangle, you can use *C-x * g* (`calc-grab-region`) to grab the data the way Emacs normally works with regions—it reads left-to-right, top-to-bottom, treating line breaks the same as spaces. Use this command to find the geometric mean of the following numbers. (The geometric mean is the *n*th root of the product of *n* numbers.)

```
2.3   6   22   15.1   7
  15   14   7.5
  2.5
```

The *C-x * g* command accepts numbers separated by spaces or commas, with or without surrounding vector brackets. See Section 2.7.21 [List Answer 3], page 78. (•)

As another example, a theorem about binomial coefficients tells us that the alternating sum of binomial coefficients $\binom{n}{0} - \binom{n}{1} + \binom{n}{2} - \cdots \pm \binom{n}{n}$ always comes out to zero. Let's verify this for *n=6*.

```
1:  [1, 2, 3, 4, 5, 6, 7]      1:  [0, 1, 2, 3, 4, 5, 6]
    .                              .


    v x 7 RET                      1 -


1:  [1, -6, 15, -20, 15, -6, 1]        1:  0
    .                                      .


    V M ' (-1)^$ choose(6,$) RET          V R +
```

The *V M '* command prompts you to enter any algebraic expression to define the function to map over the vector. The symbol '$' inside this expression represents the argument to the function. The Calculator applies this formula to each element of the vector, substituting each element's value for the '$' sign(s) in turn.

To define a two-argument function, use '$$' for the first argument and '$' for the second: *V M ' $$-$ RET* is equivalent to *V M -*. This is analogous to regular algebraic entry, where '$$' would refer to the next-to-top stack entry and '$' would refer to the top stack entry, and *' $$-$ RET* would act exactly like *-*.

Notice that the *V M '* command has recorded two things in the trail: The result, as usual, and also a funny-looking thing marked 'oper' that represents the operator function you typed in. The function is enclosed in '< >' brackets, and the argument is denoted by a '#' sign. If there were several arguments, they would be shown as '#1', '#2', and so on. (For example, *V M* ' *$$-$* will put the function '`<#1 - #2>`' on the trail.) This object is a "nameless function"; you can use nameless '`< >`' notation to answer the *V M* ' prompt if you like. Nameless function notation has the interesting, occasionally useful property that a nameless function is not actually evaluated until it is used. For example, *V M* ' *$+random(2.0)* evaluates '`random(2.0)`' once and adds that random number to all elements of the vector, but *V M* ' *<#+random(2.0)>* evaluates the '`random(2.0)`' separately for each vector element.

Another group of operators that are often useful with *V M* are the relational operators: *a =*, for example, compares two numbers and gives the result 1 if they are equal, or 0 if not. Similarly, *a <* checks for one number being less than another.

Other useful vector operations include *v v*, to reverse a vector end-for-end; *V S*, to sort the elements of a vector into increasing order; and *v r* and *v c*, to extract one row or column of a matrix, or (in both cases) to extract one element of a plain vector. With a negative argument, *v r* and *v c* instead delete one row, column, or vector element.

(•) **Exercise 4.** The kth *divisor function* $\sigma_k(n)$ is the sum of the kth powers of all the divisors of an integer n. Figure out a method for computing the divisor function for reasonably small values of n. As a test, the 0th and 1st divisor functions of 30 are 8 and 72, respectively. See Section 2.7.22 [List Answer 4], page 78. (•)

(•) **Exercise 5.** The *k f* command produces a list of prime factors for a number. Sometimes it is important to know that a number is *square-free*, i.e., that no prime occurs more than once in its list of prime factors. Find a sequence of keystrokes to tell if a number is square-free; your method should leave 1 on the stack if it is, or 0 if it isn't. See Section 2.7.23 [List Answer 5], page 78. (•)

(•) **Exercise 6.** Build a list of lists that looks like the following diagram. (You may wish to use the *v /* command to enable multi-line display of vectors.)

```
1:  [ [1],
      [1, 2],
      [1, 2, 3],
      [1, 2, 3, 4],
      [1, 2, 3, 4, 5],
      [1, 2, 3, 4, 5, 6] ]
```

See Section 2.7.24 [List Answer 6], page 79. (•)

(•) **Exercise 7.** Build the following list of lists.

```
1:  [ [0],
      [1, 2],
      [3, 4, 5],
      [6, 7, 8, 9],
      [10, 11, 12, 13, 14],
      [15, 16, 17, 18, 19, 20] ]
```

See Section 2.7.25 [List Answer 7], page 79. (•)

(•) **Exercise 8.** Compute a list of values of Bessel's $J_1(x)$ function '`besJ(1,x)`' for x from 0 to 5 in steps of 0.25. Find the value of x (from among the above set of values) for which '`besJ(1,x)`' is a maximum. Use an "automatic" method, i.e., just reading along the list by hand to find the largest value is not allowed! (There is an *a X* command which does this kind of thing automatically; see Section 10.7 [Numerical Solutions], page 272.) See Section 2.7.26 [List Answer 8], page 80. (•)

(•) **Exercise 9.** You are given an integer in the range $0 \leq N < 10^m$ for $m = 12$ (i.e., an integer of less than twelve digits). Convert this integer into a vector of m digits, each in the range from 0 to 9. In vector-of-digits notation, add one to this integer to produce a vector of $m + 1$ digits (since there could be a carry out of the most significant digit). Convert this vector back into a regular integer. A good integer to try is 25129925999. See Section 2.7.27 [List Answer 9], page 80. (•)

(•) **Exercise 10.** Your friend Joe tried to use V R a = to test if all numbers in a list were equal. What happened? How would you do this test? See Section 2.7.28 [List Answer 10], page 82. (•)

(•) **Exercise 11.** The area of a circle of radius one is π. The area of the 2×2 square that encloses that circle is 4. So if we throw n darts at random points in the square, about $\pi/4$ of them will land inside the circle. This gives us an entertaining way to estimate the value of π. The k r command picks a random number between zero and the value on the stack. We could get a random floating-point number between -1 and 1 by typing 2.0 k r 1 -. Build a vector of 100 random (x, y) points in this square, then use vector mapping and reduction to count how many points lie inside the unit circle. Hint: Use the v b command. See Section 2.7.29 [List Answer 11], page 82. (•)

(•) **Exercise 12.** The *matchstick problem* provides another way to calculate π. Say you have an infinite field of vertical lines with a spacing of one inch. Toss a one-inch matchstick onto the field. The probability that the matchstick will land crossing a line turns out to be $2/\pi$. Toss 100 matchsticks to estimate π. (If you want still more fun, the probability that the GCD (k g) of two large integers is one turns out to be $6/\pi^2$. That provides yet another way to estimate π.) See Section 2.7.30 [List Answer 12], page 83. (•)

(•) **Exercise 13.** An algebraic entry of a string in double-quote marks, '"hello"', creates a vector of the numerical (ASCII) codes of the characters (here, $[104, 101, 108, 108, 111]$). Sometimes it is convenient to compute a *hash code* of a string, which is just an integer that represents the value of that string. Two equal strings have the same hash code; two different strings *probably* have different hash codes. (For example, Calc has over 400 function names, but Emacs can quickly find the definition for any given name because it has sorted the functions into "buckets" by their hash codes. Sometimes a few names will hash into the same bucket, but it is easier to search among a few names than among all the names.) One popular hash function is computed as follows: First set $h = 0$. Then, for each character from the string in turn, set $h = 3h + c_i$ where c_i is the character's ASCII code. If we have 511 buckets, we then take the hash code modulo 511 to get the bucket number. Develop a simple command or commands for converting string vectors into hash codes. The hash code for '"Testing, 1, 2, 3"' is 1960915098, which modulo 511 is 121. See Section 2.7.31 [List Answer 13], page 84. (•)

(•) **Exercise 14.** The H V R and H V U commands do nested function evaluations. H V U takes a starting value and a number of steps n from the stack; it then applies the function you give to the starting value 0, 1, 2, up to n times and returns a vector of the results. Use this command to create a "random walk" of 50 steps. Start with the two-dimensional point $(0, 0)$; then take one step a random distance between -1 and 1 in both x and y; then take another step, and so on. Use the g f command to display this random walk. Now modify your random walk to walk a unit distance, but in a random direction, at each step. (Hint: The sincos function returns a vector of the cosine and sine of an angle.) See Section 2.7.32 [List Answer 14], page 85. (•)

2.4 Types Tutorial

Calc understands a variety of data types as well as simple numbers. In this section, we'll experiment with each of these types in turn.

The numbers we've been using so far have mainly been either *integers* or *floats*. We saw that floats are usually a good approximation to the mathematical concept of real numbers, but they are only approximations and are susceptible to roundoff error. Calc also supports *fractions*, which can exactly represent any rational number.

```
1:  3628800    2:  3628800    1:  518400:7   1:  518414:7   1:  7:518414
               1:  49                     .              .              .
               .

     10 !          49 RET          :              2 +            &
```

The `:` command divides two integers to get a fraction; `/` would normally divide integers to get a floating-point result. Notice we had to type RET between the *49* and the `:` since the `:` would otherwise be interpreted as part of a fraction beginning with 49.

You can convert between floating-point and fractional format using `c f` and `c F`:

```
1:  1.35027217629e-5    1:  7:518414

          .                     .

      c f                   c F
```

The `c F` command replaces a floating-point number with the "simplest" fraction whose floating-point representation is the same, to within the current precision.

```
1:  3.14159265359   1:  1146408:364913   1:  3.1416   1:  355:113

          .                  .                  .              .

      P                   c F      DEL      p 5 RET P      c F
```

(•) **Exercise 1.** A calculation has produced the result 1.26508260337. You suspect it is the square root of the product of π and some rational number. Is it? (Be sure to allow for roundoff error!) See Section 2.7.33 [Types Answer 1], page 86. (•)

Complex numbers can be stored in both rectangular and polar form.

```
1:  -9     1:  (0, 3)    1:  (3; 90.)    1:  (6; 90.)    1:  (2.4495; 45.)

    .          .              .               .               .

    9 n        Q            c p             2 *             Q
```

The square root of -9 is by default rendered in rectangular form $(0 + 3i)$, but we can convert it to polar form (3 with a phase angle of 90 degrees). All the usual arithmetic and scientific operations are defined on both types of complex numbers.

Another generalized kind of number is *infinity*. Infinity isn't really a number, but it can sometimes be treated like one. Calc uses the symbol `inf` to represent positive infinity, i.e., a value greater than any real number. Naturally, you can also write '`-inf`' for minus infinity, a value less than any real number. The word `inf` can only be input using algebraic entry.

```
2:  inf    2:  -inf    2:  -inf    2:  -inf    1:  nan
1:  -17    1:  -inf    1:  -inf    1:  inf         .
    .          .           .           .

' inf RET 17 n    * RET       72 +        A           +
```

Since infinity is infinitely large, multiplying it by any finite number (like -17) has no effect, except that since -17 is negative, it changes a plus infinity to a minus infinity. ("A huge positive number, multiplied by -17, yields a huge negative number.") Adding any finite number to infinity also leaves it unchanged. Taking an absolute value gives us plus infinity again. Finally, we add this plus infinity to the minus infinity we had earlier. If you work it out, you might expect the answer to be -72 for this. But the 72 has been completely lost next to the infinities; by the time we compute 'inf - inf' the finite difference between them, if any, is undetectable. So we say the result is *indeterminate*, which Calc writes with the symbol nan (for Not A Number).

Dividing by zero is normally treated as an error, but you can get Calc to write an answer in terms of infinity by pressing *m i* to turn on Infinite mode.

```
3:  nan        2:  nan        2:  nan        2:  nan        1:  nan
2:  1          1:  1 / 0      1:  uinf       1:  uinf        .
1:  0           .              .              .
     .

    1 RET 0         /          m i    U /        17 n *          +
```

Dividing by zero normally is left unevaluated, but after *m i* it instead gives an infinite result. The answer is actually uinf, "undirected infinity." If you look at a graph of $1/x$ around $x = 0$, you'll see that it goes toward plus infinity as you approach zero from above, but toward minus infinity as you approach from below. Since we said only $1/0$, Calc knows that the answer is infinite but not in which direction. That's what uinf means. Notice that multiplying uinf by a negative number still leaves plain uinf; there's no point in saying '-uinf' because the sign of uinf is unknown anyway. Finally, we add uinf to our nan, yielding nan again. It's easy to see that, because nan means "totally unknown" while uinf means "unknown sign but known to be infinite," the more mysterious nan wins out when it is combined with uinf, or, for that matter, with anything else.

(•) **Exercise 2.** Predict what Calc will answer for each of these formulas: 'inf / inf', 'exp(inf)', 'exp(-inf)', 'sqrt(-inf)', 'sqrt(uinf)', 'abs(uinf)', 'ln(0)'. See Section 2.7.34 [Types Answer 2], page 86. (•)

(•) **Exercise 3.** We saw that 'inf - inf = nan', which stands for an unknown value. Can nan stand for a complex number? Can it stand for infinity? See Section 2.7.35 [Types Answer 3], page 87. (•)

HMS forms represent a value in terms of hours, minutes, and seconds.

```
1:  2@ 30' 0"    1:  3@ 30' 0"    2:  3@ 30' 0"    1:  2.
     .                .           1:  1@ 45' 0."        .
                                       .

   2@ 30' RET          1 +          RET 2 /           /
```

HMS forms can also be used to hold angles in degrees, minutes, and seconds.

```
1:  0.5        1:  26.56505    1:  26@ 33' 54.18"   1:  0.44721
     .              .               .                    .

    0.5            I T            c h                 S
```

First we convert the inverse tangent of 0.5 to degrees-minutes-seconds form, then we take the sine of that angle. Note that the trigonometric functions will accept HMS forms directly as input.

(•) **Exercise 4.** The Beatles' *Abbey Road* is 47 minutes and 26 seconds long, and contains 17 songs. What is the average length of a song on *Abbey Road*? If the Extended Disco

Version of *Abbey Road* added 20 seconds to the length of each song, how long would the album be? See Section 2.7.36 [Types Answer 4], page 87. (•)

A *date form* represents a date, or a date and time. Dates must be entered using algebraic entry. Date forms are surrounded by '< >' symbols; most standard formats for dates are recognized.

```
2:  <Sun Jan 13, 1991>               1:  2.25
1:  <6:00pm Thu Jan 10, 1991>            .
    .


    ' <13 Jan 1991>, <1/10/91, 6pm> RET           -
```

In this example, we enter two dates, then subtract to find the number of days between them. It is also possible to add an HMS form or a number (of days) to a date form to get another date form.

```
1:  <4:45:59pm Mon Jan 14, 1991>     1:  <2:50:59am Thu Jan 17, 1991>
    .                                    .


    t N                                  2 + 10@ 5' +
```

The *t N* ("now") command pushes the current date and time on the stack; then we add two days, ten hours and five minutes to the date and time. Other date-and-time related commands include *t J*, which does Julian day conversions, *t W*, which finds the beginning of the week in which a date form lies, and *t I*, which increments a date by one or several months. See Section 7.5 [Date Arithmetic], page 192, for more.

(•) **Exercise 5.** How many days until the next Friday the 13th? See Section 2.7.37 [Types Answer 5], page 87. (•)

(•) **Exercise 6.** How many leap years will there be between now and the year 10001 AD? See Section 2.7.38 [Types Answer 6], page 88. (•)

An *error form* represents a mean value with an attached standard deviation, or error estimate. Suppose our measurements indicate that a certain telephone pole is about 30 meters away, with an estimated error of 1 meter, and 8 meters tall, with an estimated error of 0.2 meters. What is the slope of a line from here to the top of the pole, and what is the equivalent angle in degrees?

```
1:  8 +/- 0.2     2:  8 +/- 0.2   1:  0.266 +/- 0.011   1:  14.93 +/- 0.594
    .             1:  30 +/- 1        .                     .
                      .


    8 p .2 RET        30 p 1          /                     I T
```

This means that the angle is about 15 degrees, and, assuming our original error estimates were valid standard deviations, there is about a 60% chance that the result is correct within 0.59 degrees.

(•) **Exercise 7.** The volume of a torus (a donut shape) is $2\pi^2 R r^2$ where R is the radius of the circle that defines the center of the tube and r is the radius of the tube itself. Suppose R is 20 cm and r is 4 cm, each known to within 5 percent. What is the volume and the relative uncertainty of the volume? See Section 2.7.39 [Types Answer 7], page 88. (•)

An *interval form* represents a range of values. While an error form is best for making statistical estimates, intervals give you exact bounds on an answer. Suppose we additionally know that our telephone pole is definitely between 28 and 31 meters away, and that it is between 7.7 and 8.1 meters tall.

```
1:  [7.7 .. 8.1]   2:  [7.7 .. 8.1]   1:  [0.24 .. 0.28]   1:  [13.9 .. 16.1]
        .             1:  [28 .. 31]           .                    .


   [ 7.7 .. 8.1 ]     [ 28 .. 31 ]          /                    I T
```

If our bounds were correct, then the angle to the top of the pole is sure to lie in the range shown.

The square brackets around these intervals indicate that the endpoints themselves are allowable values. In other words, the distance to the telephone pole is between 28 and 31, *inclusive*. You can also make an interval that is exclusive of its endpoints by writing parentheses instead of square brackets. You can even make an interval which is inclusive ("closed") on one end and exclusive ("open") on the other.

```
1:  [1 .. 10)     1:  (0.1 .. 1]    2:  (0.1 .. 1]    1:  (0.2 .. 3)
        .                 .          1:  [2 .. 3)              .
                                             .

   [ 1 .. 10 )          &         [ 2 .. 3 )              *
```

The Calculator automatically keeps track of which end values should be open and which should be closed. You can also make infinite or semi-infinite intervals by using '`-inf`' or '`inf`' for one or both endpoints.

(•) **Exercise 8.** What answer would you expect from '1 / (0 .. 10)'? What about '1 / (-10 .. 0)'? What about '1 / [0 .. 10]' (where the interval actually includes zero)? What about '1 / (-10 .. 10)'? See Section 2.7.40 [Types Answer 8], page 89. (•)

(•) **Exercise 9.** Two easy ways of squaring a number are *RET* * and *2* ^. Normally these produce the same answer. Would you expect this still to hold true for interval forms? If not, which of these will result in a larger interval? See Section 2.7.41 [Types Answer 9], page 89. (•)

A *modulo form* is used for performing arithmetic modulo m. For example, arithmetic involving time is generally done modulo 12 or 24 hours.

```
1:  17 mod 24     1:  3 mod 24      1:  21 mod 24     1:  9 mod 24
        .                 .                 .                .


   17 M 24 RET        10 +              n                 5 /
```

In this last step, Calc has divided by 5 modulo 24; i.e., it has found a new number which, when multiplied by 5 modulo 24, produces the original number, 21. If m is prime and the divisor is not a multiple of m, it is always possible to find such a number. For non-prime m like 24, it is only sometimes possible.

```
1:  10 mod 24     1:  16 mod 24     1:  1000000...    1:  16
        .                 .                 .                .


   10 M 24 RET        100 ^           10 RET 100 ^       24 %
```

These two calculations get the same answer, but the first one is much more efficient because it avoids the huge intermediate value that arises in the second one.

(•) **Exercise 10.** A theorem of Pierre de Fermat says that $x^{n-1} \bmod n = 1$ if n is a prime number and x is an integer less than n. If n is *not* a prime number, this will *not* be true for most values of x. Thus we can test informally if a number is prime by trying this formula for several values of x. Use this test to tell whether the following numbers are prime: 811749613, 15485863. See Section 2.7.42 [Types Answer 10], page 89. (•)

It is possible to use HMS forms as parts of error forms, intervals, modulo forms, or as the phase part of a polar complex number. For example, the `calc-time` command pushes the current time of day on the stack as an HMS/modulo form.

```
1:  17@ 34' 45" mod 24@ 0' 0"        1:  6@ 22' 15" mod 24@ 0' 0"
    .                                    .


    x time RET                           n
```

This calculation tells me it is six hours and 22 minutes until midnight.

(•) **Exercise 11.** A rule of thumb is that one year is about $\pi \times 10^7$ seconds. What time will it be that many seconds from right now? See Section 2.7.43 [Types Answer 11], page 90. (•)

(•) **Exercise 12.** You are preparing to order packaging for the CD release of the Extended Disco Version of *Abbey Road*. You are told that the songs will actually be anywhere from 20 to 60 seconds longer than the originals. One CD can hold about 75 minutes of music. Should you order single or double packages? See Section 2.7.44 [Types Answer 12], page 90. (•)

Another kind of data the Calculator can manipulate is numbers with *units*. This isn't strictly a new data type; it's simply an application of algebraic expressions, where we use variables with suggestive names like 'cm' and 'in' to represent units like centimeters and inches.

```
1:  2 in       1:  5.08 cm      1:  0.027778 fath   1:  0.0508 m
    .              .                .                   .


    ' 2in RET      u c cm RET       u c fath RET        u b
```

We enter the quantity "2 inches" (actually an algebraic expression which means two times the variable 'in'), then we convert it first to centimeters, then to fathoms, then finally to "base" units, which in this case means meters.

```
1:  9 acre     1:  3 sqrt(acre)   1:  190.84 m     1:  190.84 m + 30 cm
    .              .                  .                .


    ' 9 acre RET   Q                  u s              ' $+30 cm RET


1:  191.14 m    1:  36536.3046 m^2    1:  365363046 cm^2
    .               .                     .


    u s             2 ^                   u c cgs
```

Since units expressions are really just formulas, taking the square root of 'acre' is undefined. After all, `acre` might be an algebraic variable that you will someday assign a value. We use the "units-simplify" command to simplify the expression with variables being interpreted as unit names.

In the final step, we have converted not to a particular unit, but to a units system. The "cgs" system uses centimeters instead of meters as its standard unit of length.

There is a wide variety of units defined in the Calculator.

```
1:  55 mph     1:  88.5139 kph    1:  88.5139 km / hr   1:  8.201407e-8 c
    .              .                  .                     .


    ' 55 mph RET   u c kph RET        u c km/hr RET         u c c RET
```

We express a speed first in miles per hour, then in kilometers per hour, then again using a slightly more explicit notation, then finally in terms of fractions of the speed of light.

Temperature conversions are a bit more tricky. There are two ways to interpret "20 degrees Fahrenheit"—it could mean an actual temperature, or it could mean a change in temperature. For normal units there is no difference, but temperature units have an offset as well as a scale factor and so there must be two explicit commands for them.

```
1:  20 degF       1:  11.1111 degC      1:  -6.666 degC
    .                 .                     .                 .

    ' 20 degF RET      u c degC RET          U u t degC RET
```

First we convert a change of 20 degrees Fahrenheit into an equivalent change in degrees Celsius (or Centigrade). Then, we convert the absolute temperature 20 degrees Fahrenheit into Celsius.

For simple unit conversions, you can put a plain number on the stack. Then $u\ c$ and $u\ t$ will prompt for both old and new units. When you use this method, you're responsible for remembering which numbers are in which units:

```
1:  55         1:  88.5139          1:  8.201407e-8
    .              .                    .

    55             u c mph RET kph RET   u c km/hr RET c RET
```

To see a complete list of built-in units, type $u\ v$. Press $C\text{-}x\ *\ c$ again to re-enter the Calculator when you're done looking at the units table.

(•) **Exercise 13.** How many seconds are there really in a year? See Section 2.7.45 [Types Answer 13], page 91. (•)

(•) **Exercise 14.** Supercomputer designs are limited by the speed of light (and of electricity, which is nearly as fast). Suppose a computer has a 4.1 ns (nanosecond) clock cycle, and its cabinet is one meter across. Is speed of light going to be a significant factor in its design? See Section 2.7.46 [Types Answer 14], page 91. (•)

(•) **Exercise 15.** Sam the Slug normally travels about five yards in an hour. He has obtained a supply of Power Pills; each Power Pill he eats doubles his speed. How many Power Pills can he swallow and still travel legally on most US highways? See Section 2.7.47 [Types Answer 15], page 91. (•)

2.5 Algebra and Calculus Tutorial

This section shows how to use Calc's algebra facilities to solve equations, do simple calculus problems, and manipulate algebraic formulas.

2.5.1 Basic Algebra

If you enter a formula in Algebraic mode that refers to variables, the formula itself is pushed onto the stack. You can manipulate formulas as regular data objects.

```
1:  2 x^2 - 6      1:  6 - 2 x^2       1:  (3 x^2 + y) (6 - 2 x^2)
    .                  .                   .

    ' 2x^2-6 RET       n                   ' 3x^2+y RET *
```

(•) **Exercise 1.** Do `' x RET Q 2 ^` and `' x RET 2 ^ Q` both wind up with the same result ('x')? Why or why not? See Section 2.7.48 [Algebra Answer 1], page 91. (•)

There are also commands for doing common algebraic operations on formulas. Continuing with the formula from the last example,

```
1:  18 x^2 - 6 x^4 + 6 y - 2 y x^2    1:  (18 - 2 y) x^2 - 6 x^4 + 6 y
    .                                     .


    a x                                   a c x RET
```

First we "expand" using the distributive law, then we "collect" terms involving like powers of x.

Let's find the value of this expression when x is 2 and y is one-half.

```
1:  17 x^2 - 6 x^4 + 3      1:  -25
    .                           .


    1:2 s l y RET               2 s l x RET
```

The **s l** command means "let"; it takes a number from the top of the stack and temporarily assigns it as the value of the variable you specify. It then evaluates (as if by the = key) the next expression on the stack. After this command, the variable goes back to its original value, if any.

(An earlier exercise in this tutorial involved storing a value in the variable **x**; if this value is still there, you will have to unstore it with **s u x RET** before the above example will work properly.)

Let's find the maximum value of our original expression when y is one-half and x ranges over all possible values. We can do this by taking the derivative with respect to x and examining values of x for which the derivative is zero. If the second derivative of the function at that value of x is negative, the function has a local maximum there.

```
1:  17 x^2 - 6 x^4 + 3      1:  34 x - 24 x^3
    .                           .


    U DEL  s 1                  a d x RET  s 2
```

Well, the derivative is clearly zero when x is zero. To find the other root(s), let's divide through by x and then solve:

```
1:  (34 x - 24 x^3) / x     1:  34 - 24 x^2
    .                           .


    ' x RET /                   a x


1:  0.70588 x^2 = 1         1:  x = 1.19023
    .                           .


    0 a =  s 3                  a S x RET
```

Now we compute the second derivative and plug in our values of x:

```
1:  1.19023        2:  1.19023        2:  1.19023
    .              1:  34 x - 24 x^3  1:  34 - 72 x^2
                       .                   .


    a .                r 2                 a d x RET s 4
```

(The **a .** command extracts just the righthand side of an equation. Another method would have been to use **v u** to unpack the equation 'x = 1.19' to 'x' and '1.19', then use *M-- M-2 DEL* to delete the 'x'.)

```
2:  34 - 72 x^2   1:  -68.        2:  34 - 72 x^2     1:  34
1:  1.19023                .      1:  0                      .
            .                                .


    TAB              s 1 x RET       U DEL 0          s 1 x RET
```

The first of these second derivatives is negative, so we know the function has a maximum value at $x = 1.19023$. (The function also has a local *minimum* at $x = 0$.)

When we solved for x, we got only one value even though $0.70588x^2 = 1$ is a quadratic equation that ought to have two solutions. The reason is that **a S** normally returns a single "principal" solution. If it needs to come up with an arbitrary sign (as occurs in the quadratic formula) it picks +. If it needs an arbitrary integer, it picks zero. We can get a full solution by pressing **H** (the Hyperbolic flag) before **a S**.

```
1:  0.70588 x^2 = 1    1:  x = 1.19023 s1     1:  x = -1.19023
            .                      .                      .


    r 3                H a S x RET  s 5        1 n  s 1 s1 RET
```

Calc has invented the variable '**s1**' to represent an unknown sign; it is supposed to be either $+1$ or -1. Here we have used the "let" command to evaluate the expression when the sign is negative. If we plugged this into our second derivative we would get the same, negative, answer, so $x = -1.19023$ is also a maximum.

To find the actual maximum value, we must plug our two values of x into the original formula.

```
2:  17 x^2 - 6 x^4 + 3    1:  24.08333 s1^2 - 12.04166 s1^4 + 3
1:  x = 1.19023 s1                  .
            .


    r 1 r 5                s 1 RET
```

(Here we see another way to use **s 1**; if its input is an equation with a variable on the lefthand side, then **s 1** treats the equation like an assignment to that variable if you don't give a variable name.)

It's clear that this will have the same value for either sign of **s1**, but let's work it out anyway, just for the exercise:

```
2:  [-1, 1]              1:  [15.04166, 15.04166]
1:  24.08333 s1^2 ...              .
            .


    [ 1 n , 1 ] TAB        V M $ RET
```

Here we have used a vector mapping operation to evaluate the function at several values of '**s1**' at once. *V M $* is like *V M '* except that it takes the formula from the top of the stack. The formula is interpreted as a function to apply across the vector at the next-to-top stack level. Since a formula on the stack can't contain '$' signs, Calc assumes the variables in the formula stand for different arguments. It prompts you for an *argument list*, giving the list of all variables in the formula in alphabetical order as the default list. In this case the default is '**(s1)**', which is just what we want so we simply press RET at the prompt.

If there had been several different values, we could have used *V R X* to find the global maximum.

Calc has a built-in **a P** command that solves an equation using *H a S* and returns a vector of all the solutions. It simply automates the job we just did by hand. Applied to our original cubic polynomial, it would produce the vector of solutions $[1.19023, -1.19023, 0]$. (There is also an **a X** command which finds a local maximum of a function. It uses a numerical search method rather than examining the derivatives, and thus requires you to provide some kind of initial guess to show it where to look.)

(•) **Exercise 2.** Given a vector of the roots of a polynomial (such as the output of an **a P** command), what sequence of commands would you use to reconstruct the original polynomial? (The answer will be unique to within a constant multiple; choose the solution where the leading coefficient is one.) See Section 2.7.49 [Algebra Answer 2], page 92. (•)

The **m s** command enables Symbolic mode, in which formulas like 'sqrt(5)' that can't be evaluated exactly are left in symbolic form rather than giving a floating-point approximate answer. Fraction mode (**m f**) is also useful when doing algebra.

```
2:  34 x - 24 x^3       2:  34 x - 24 x^3
1:  34 x - 24 x^3       1:  [sqrt(51) / 6, sqrt(51) / -6, 0]
        .                       .


    r 2 RET     m s   m f     a P x RET
```

One more mode that makes reading formulas easier is Big mode.

```
                  3
2:  34 x - 24 x


        ____    ____
        V 51    V 51
1:  [-----,  -----, 0]
        6       -6



        .


    d B
```

Here things like powers, square roots, and quotients and fractions are displayed in a two-dimensional pictorial form. Calc has other language modes as well, such as C mode, FORTRAN mode, TeX mode and LaTeX mode.

```
2:  34*x - 24*pow(x, 3)         2:  34*x - 24*x**3
1:  {sqrt(51) / 6, sqrt(51) / -6, 0}   1:  /sqrt(51) / 6, sqrt(51) / -6, 0/
        .                                   .


    d C                             d F


3:  34 x - 24 x^3
2:  [{\sqrt{51} \over 6}, {\sqrt{51} \over -6}, 0]
1:  {2 \over 3} \sqrt{5}
        .


    d T    ' 2 \sqrt{5} \over 3 RET
```

As you can see, language modes affect both entry and display of formulas. They affect such things as the names used for built-in functions, the set of arithmetic operators and their precedences, and notations for vectors and matrices.

Notice that 'sqrt(51)' may cause problems with older implementations of C and FOR-TRAN, which would require something more like 'sqrt(51.0)'. It is always wise to check over the formulas produced by the various language modes to make sure they are fully correct.

Type *m s*, *m f*, and *d N* to reset these modes. (You may prefer to remain in Big mode, but all the examples in the tutorial are shown in normal mode.)

What is the area under the portion of this curve from $x = 1$ to 2? This is simply the integral of the function:

```
1:  17 x^2 - 6 x^4 + 3      1:  5.6666 x^3 - 1.2 x^5 + 3 x
    .                           .


    r 1                         a i x
```

We want to evaluate this at our two values for x and subtract. One way to do it is again with vector mapping and reduction:

```
2:  [2, 1]           1:  [12.93333, 7.46666]    1:  5.46666
1:  5.6666 x^3 ...       .                          .


    [ 2 , 1 ] TAB       V M $ RET                  V R -
```

(•) **Exercise 3.** Find the integral from 1 to y of $x \sin \pi x$ (where the sine is calculated in radians). Find the values of the integral for integers y from 1 to 5. See Section 2.7.50 [Algebra Answer 3], page 92. (•)

Calc's integrator can do many simple integrals symbolically, but many others are beyond its capabilities. Suppose we wish to find the area under the curve $\sin x \ln x$ over the same range of x. If you entered this formula and typed *a i x RET* (don't bother to try this), Calc would work for a long time but would be unable to find a solution. In fact, there is no closed-form solution to this integral. Now what do we do?

One approach would be to do the integral numerically. It is not hard to do this by hand using vector mapping and reduction. It is rather slow, though, since the sine and logarithm functions take a long time. We can save some time by reducing the working precision.

```
3:  10                   1:  [1, 1.1, 1.2,  ...  , 1.8, 1.9]
2:  1                        .
1:  0.1
    .


    10 RET 1 RET .1 RET       C-u v x
```

(Note that we have used the extended version of *v x*; we could also have used plain *v x* as follows: *v x 10 RET 9 + .1 *.*)

```
2:  [1, 1.1, ... ]            1:  [0., 0.084941, 0.16993, ... ]
1:  ln(x) sin(x)                  .
    .


    ' sin(x) ln(x) RET  s 1    m r  p 5 RET   V M $ RET


1:  3.4195      0.34195
    .               .


    V R +      0.1 *
```

(If you got wildly different results, did you remember to switch to Radians mode?)

Here we have divided the curve into ten segments of equal width; approximating these segments as rectangular boxes (i.e., assuming the curve is nearly flat at that resolution), we compute the areas of the boxes (height times width), then sum the areas. (It is faster to sum first, then multiply by the width, since the width is the same for every box.)

The true value of this integral turns out to be about 0.374, so we're not doing too well. Let's try another approach.

```
1:  ln(x) sin(x)     1:  0.84147 x + 0.11957 (x - 1)^2 - ...
    .                    .


    r 1                  a t x=1 RET 4 RET
```

Here we have computed the Taylor series expansion of the function about the point $x = 1$. We can now integrate this polynomial approximation, since polynomials are easy to integrate.

```
1:  0.42074 x^2 + ...  1:  [-0.0446, -0.42073]   1:  0.3761
    .                      .                         .


    a i x RET           [ 2 , 1 ] TAB  V M $ RET     V R -
```

Better! By increasing the precision and/or asking for more terms in the Taylor series, we can get a result as accurate as we like. (Taylor series converge better away from singularities in the function such as the one at `ln(0)`, so it would also help to expand the series about the points $x = 2$ or $x = 1.5$ instead of $x = 1$.)

(•) **Exercise 4.** Our first method approximated the curve by stairsteps of width 0.1; the total area was then the sum of the areas of the rectangles under these stairsteps. Our second method approximated the function by a polynomial, which turned out to be a better approximation than stairsteps. A third method is *Simpson's rule*, which is like the stairstep method except that the steps are not required to be flat. Simpson's rule boils down to the formula,

$$\frac{h}{3}(f(a) + 4f(a + h) + 2f(a + 2h) + 4f(a + 3h) + \cdots$$
$$+ 2f(a + (n - 2)h) + 4f(a + (n - 1)h) + f(a + nh))$$

where n (which must be even) is the number of slices and h is the width of each slice. These are 10 and 0.1 in our example. For reference, here is the corresponding formula for the stairstep method:

$$h(f(a) + f(a + h) + f(a + 2h) + f(a + 3h) + \cdots + f(a + (n - 2)h) + f(a + (n - 1)h))$$

Compute the integral from 1 to 2 of $\sin x \ln x$ using Simpson's rule with 10 slices. See Section 2.7.51 [Algebra Answer 4], page 93. (•)

Calc has a built-in `a I` command for doing numerical integration. It uses *Romberg's method*, which is a more sophisticated cousin of Simpson's rule. In particular, it knows how to keep refining the result until the current precision is satisfied.

Aside from the commands we've seen so far, Calc also provides a large set of commands for operating on parts of formulas. You indicate the desired sub-formula by placing the cursor on any part of the formula before giving a *selection* command. Selections won't be covered in the tutorial; see Section 10.1 [Selecting Subformulas], page 243, for details and examples.

2.5.2 Rewrite Rules

No matter how many built-in commands Calc provided for doing algebra, there would always be something you wanted to do that Calc didn't have in its repertoire. So Calc also provides a *rewrite rule* system that you can use to define your own algebraic manipulations.

Suppose we want to simplify this trigonometric formula:

```
1:  2 sec(x)^2 / tan(x)^2 - 2 / tan(x)^2
    .


    ' 2sec(x)^2/tan(x)^2 - 2/tan(x)^2 RET    s 1
```

If we were simplifying this by hand, we'd probably combine over the common denominator. The **a n** algebra command will do this, but we'll do it with a rewrite rule just for practice.

Rewrite rules are written with the ':=' symbol.

```
1:  (2 sec(x)^2 - 2) / tan(x)^2
    .


    a r a/x + b/x := (a+b)/x RET
```

(The "assignment operator" ':=' has several uses in Calc. All by itself the formula 'a/x + b/x := (a+b)/x' doesn't do anything, but when it is given to the **a r** command, that command interprets it as a rewrite rule.)

The lefthand side, 'a/x + b/x', is called the *pattern* of the rewrite rule. Calc searches the formula on the stack for parts that match the pattern. Variables in a rewrite pattern are called *meta-variables*, and when matching the pattern each meta-variable can match any sub-formula. Here, the meta-variable 'a' matched the expression '2 sec(x)^2', the meta-variable 'b' matched the constant '-2' and the meta-variable 'x' matched the expression 'tan(x)^2'.

This rule points out several interesting features of rewrite patterns. First, if a meta-variable appears several times in a pattern, it must match the same thing everywhere. This rule detects common denominators because the same meta-variable 'x' is used in both of the denominators.

Second, meta-variable names are independent from variables in the target formula. Notice that the meta-variable 'x' here matches the subformula 'tan(x)^2'; Calc never confuses the two meanings of 'x'.

And third, rewrite patterns know a little bit about the algebraic properties of formulas. The pattern called for a sum of two quotients; Calc was able to match a difference of two quotients by matching 'a = 2 sec(x)^2', 'b = -2', and 'x = tan(x)^2'.

When the pattern part of a rewrite rule matches a part of the formula, that part is replaced by the righthand side with all the meta-variables substituted with the things they matched. So the result is '(2 sec(x)^2 - 2) / tan(x)^2'.

We could just as easily have written 'a/x - b/x := (a-b)/x' for the rule. It would have worked just the same in all cases. (If we really wanted the rule to apply only to '+' or only to '-', we could have used the **plain** symbol. See Section 10.11.4 [Algebraic Properties of Rewrite Rules], page 294, for some examples of this.)

One more rewrite will complete the job. We want to use the identity 'tan(x)^2 + 1 = sec(x)^2', but of course we must first rearrange the identity in a way that matches our formula. The obvious rule would be '2 sec(x)^2 - 2 := 2 tan(x)^2', but a little thought shows that the rule 'sec(x)^2 := 1 + tan(x)^2' will also work. The latter rule has a more general pattern so it will work in many other situations, too.

```
1:  2

    .


    a r sec(x)^2 := 1 + tan(x)^2 RET
```

You may ask, what's the point of using the most general rule if you have to type it in every time anyway? The answer is that Calc allows you to store a rewrite rule in a variable, then give the variable name in the **a r** command. In fact, this is the preferred way to use rewrites. For one, if you need a rule once you'll most likely need it again later. Also, if the rule doesn't work quite right you can simply Undo, edit the variable, and run the rule again without having to retype it.

```
' a/x + b/x := (a+b)/x RET             s t merge RET
' sec(x)^2 := 1 + tan(x)^2 RET         s t secsqr RET

1:  2 sec(x)^2 / tan(x)^2 - 2 / tan(x)^2    1:  2
    .                                           .


    r 1                    a r merge RET  a r secsqr RET
```

To edit a variable, type **s e** and the variable name, use regular Emacs editing commands as necessary, then type **C-c C-c** to store the edited value back into the variable. You can also use **s e** to create a new variable if you wish.

Notice that the first time you use each rule, Calc puts up a "compiling" message briefly. The pattern matcher converts rules into a special optimized pattern-matching language rather than using them directly. This allows **a r** to apply even rather complicated rules very efficiently. If the rule is stored in a variable, Calc compiles it only once and stores the compiled form along with the variable. That's another good reason to store your rules in variables rather than entering them on the fly.

(•) **Exercise 1.** Type **m s** to get Symbolic mode, then enter the formula '(2 + sqrt(2)) / (1 + sqrt(2))'. Using a rewrite rule, simplify this formula by multiplying the top and bottom by the conjugate '1 - sqrt(2)'. The result will have to be expanded by the distributive law; do this with another rewrite. See Section 2.7.52 [Rewrites Answer 1], page 93. (•)

The **a r** command can also accept a vector of rewrite rules, or a variable containing a vector of rules.

```
1:  [merge, secsqr]        1:  [a/x + b/x := (a + b)/x, ... ]
    .                          .


    ' [merge,sinsqr] RET           =


1:  2 sec(x)^2 / tan(x)^2 - 2 / tan(x)^2    1:  2
    .                                           .


    s t trig RET  r 1              a r trig RET
```

Calc tries all the rules you give against all parts of the formula, repeating until no further change is possible. (The exact order in which things are tried is rather complex, but for simple rules like the ones we've used here the order doesn't really matter. See Section 10.11.7 [Nested Formulas with Rewrite Rules], page 304.)

Calc actually repeats only up to 100 times, just in case your rule set has gotten into an infinite loop. You can give a numeric prefix argument to `a r` to specify any limit. In particular, *M-1* `a r` does only one rewrite at a time.

```
1:  (2 sec(x)^2 - 2) / tan(x)^2         1:  2
    .                                       .


    r 1  M-1 a r trig RET             M-1 a r trig RET
```

You can type *M-0* `a r` if you want no limit at all on the number of rewrites that occur.

Rewrite rules can also be *conditional*. Simply follow the rule with a ':: ' symbol and the desired condition. For example,

```
1:  sin(x + 2 pi) + sin(x + 3 pi) + sin(x + 4 pi)
    .


    ' sin(x+2pi) + sin(x+3pi) + sin(x+4pi) RET


1:  sin(x + 3 pi) + 2 sin(x)
    .


    a r sin(a + k pi) := sin(a) :: k % 2 = 0 RET
```

(Recall, 'k % 2' is the remainder from dividing 'k' by 2, which will be zero only when 'k' is an even integer.)

An interesting point is that the variable 'pi' was matched literally rather than acting as a meta-variable. This is because it is a special-constant variable. The special constants 'e', 'i', 'phi', and so on also match literally. A common error with rewrite rules is to write, say, 'f(a,b,c,d,e) := g(a+b+c+d+e)', expecting to match any 'f' with five arguments but in fact matching only when the fifth argument is literally 'e'!

Rewrite rules provide an interesting way to define your own functions. Suppose we want to define 'fib(n)' to produce the *n*th Fibonacci number. The first two Fibonacci numbers are each 1; later numbers are formed by summing the two preceding numbers in the sequence. This is easy to express in a set of three rules:

```
' [fib(1) := 1, fib(2) := 1, fib(n) := fib(n-1) + fib(n-2)] RET  s t fib

1:  fib(7)             1:  13
    .                      .


    ' fib(7) RET         a r fib RET
```

One thing that is guaranteed about the order that rewrites are tried is that, for any given subformula, earlier rules in the rule set will be tried for that subformula before later ones. So even though the first and third rules both match 'fib(1)', we know the first will be used preferentially.

This rule set has one dangerous bug: Suppose we apply it to the formula 'fib(x)'? (Don't actually try this.) The third rule will match 'fib(x)' and replace it with 'fib(x-1) + fib(x-2)'. Each of these will then be replaced to get 'fib(x-2) + 2 fib(x-3) + fib(x-4)', and so on, expanding forever. What we really want is to apply the third rule only when 'n' is an integer greater than two. Type *s e* `fib` *RET*, then edit the third rule to:

```
fib(n) := fib(n-1) + fib(n-2) :: integer(n) :: n > 2
```

Now:
```
1:  fib(6) + fib(x) + fib(0)      1:  fib(x) + fib(0) + 8
    .                                  .


  ' fib(6)+fib(x)+fib(0) RET        a r fib RET
```
We've created a new function, `fib`, and a new command, `a r fib RET`, which means "evaluate all `fib` calls in this formula." To make things easier still, we can tell Calc to apply these rules automatically by storing them in the special variable `EvalRules`.
```
1:  [fib(1) := ...]      .                     1:  [8, 13]

    .                                              .


  s r fib RET         s t EvalRules RET    ' [fib(6), fib(7)] RET
```
It turns out that this rule set has the problem that it does far more work than it needs to when 'n' is large. Consider the first few steps of the computation of 'fib(6)':
```
fib(6) =
fib(5)                +            fib(4) =
fib(4)     +     fib(3)     +      fib(3)      +      fib(2) =
fib(3) + fib(2) + fib(2) + fib(1) + fib(2) + fib(1) + 1 = ...
```
Note that 'fib(3)' appears three times here. Unless Calc's algebraic simplifier notices the multiple 'fib(3)'s and combines them (and, as it happens, it doesn't), this rule set does lots of needless recomputation. To cure the problem, type `s e EvalRules` to edit the rules (or just `s E`, a shorthand command for editing `EvalRules`) and add another condition:
```
fib(n) := fib(n-1) + fib(n-2) :: integer(n) :: n > 2 :: remember
```
If a ':: remember' condition appears anywhere in a rule, then if that rule succeeds Calc will add another rule that describes that match to the front of the rule set. (Remembering works in any rule set, but for technical reasons it is most effective in `EvalRules`.) For example, if the rule rewrites 'fib(7)' to something that evaluates to 13, then the rule 'fib(7) := 13' will be added to the rule set.

Type `' fib(8) RET` to compute the eighth Fibonacci number, then type `s E` again to see what has happened to the rule set.

With the `remember` feature, our rule set can now compute 'fib(n)' in just n steps. In the process it builds up a table of all Fibonacci numbers up to n. After we have computed the result for a particular n, we can get it back (and the results for all smaller n) later in just one step.

All Calc operations will run somewhat slower whenever `EvalRules` contains any rules. You should type `s u EvalRules RET` now to un-store the variable.

(•) **Exercise 2.** Sometimes it is possible to reformulate a problem to reduce the amount of recursion necessary to solve it. Create a rule that, in about n simple steps and without recourse to the `remember` option, replaces 'fib(n, 1, 1)' with 'fib(1, x, y)' where x and y are the nth and $n+1$st Fibonacci numbers, respectively. This rule is rather clunky to use, so add a couple more rules to make the "user interface" the same as for our first version: enter 'fib(n)', get back a plain number. See Section 2.7.53 [Rewrites Answer 2], page 94. (•)

There are many more things that rewrites can do. For example, there are '&&&' and '|||' pattern operators that create "and" and "or" combinations of rules. As one really simple example, we could combine our first two Fibonacci rules thusly:
```
[fib(1 ||| 2) := 1, fib(n) := ... ]
```

That means "`fib` of something matching either 1 or 2 rewrites to 1."

You can also make meta-variables optional by enclosing them in `opt`. For example, the pattern 'a + b x' matches '2 + 3 x' but not '2 + x' or '3 x' or 'x'. The pattern 'opt(a) + opt(b) x' matches all of these forms, filling in a default of zero for 'a' and one for 'b'.

(•) **Exercise 3.** Your friend Joe had '2 + 3 x' on the stack and tried to use the rule 'opt(a) + opt(b) x := f(a, b, x)'. What happened? See Section 2.7.54 [Rewrites Answer 3], page 94. (•)

(•) **Exercise 4.** Starting with a positive integer a, divide a by two if it is even, otherwise compute $3a + 1$. Now repeat this step over and over. A famous unproved conjecture is that for any starting a, the sequence always eventually reaches 1. Given the formula 'seq(a, 0)', write a set of rules that convert this into 'seq(1, n)' where n is the number of steps it took the sequence to reach the value 1. Now enhance the rules to accept 'seq(a)' as a starting configuration, and to stop with just the number n by itself. Now make the result be a vector of values in the sequence, from a to 1. (The formula '$x\,|\,y$' appends the vectors x and y.) For example, rewriting 'seq(6)' should yield the vector $[6, 3, 10, 5, 16, 8, 4, 2, 1]$. See Section 2.7.55 [Rewrites Answer 4], page 94. (•)

(•) **Exercise 5.** Define, using rewrite rules, a function 'nterms(x)' that returns the number of terms in the sum x, or 1 if x is not a sum. (A *sum* for our purposes is one or more non-sum terms separated by '+' or '−' signs, so that $2 - 3(x + y) + xy$ is a sum of three terms.) See Section 2.7.56 [Rewrites Answer 5], page 95. (•)

(•) **Exercise 6.** A Taylor series for a function is an infinite series that exactly equals the value of that function at values of x near zero.

$$\cos x = 1 - \frac{x^2}{2!} + \frac{x^4}{4!} - \frac{x^6}{6!} + \cdots$$

The **a t** command produces a *truncated Taylor series* which is obtained by dropping all the terms higher than, say, x^2. Calc represents the truncated Taylor series as a polynomial in x. Mathematicians often write a truncated series using a "big-O" notation that records what was the lowest term that was truncated.

$$\cos x = 1 - \frac{x^2}{2!} + O(x^3)$$

The meaning of $O(x^3)$ is "a quantity which is negligibly small if x^3 is considered negligibly small as x goes to zero."

The exercise is to create rewrite rules that simplify sums and products of power series represented as '*polynomial* + O(var^n)'. For example, given '1 - x^2 / 2 + O(x^3)' and 'x - x^3 / 6 + O(x^4)' on the stack, we want to be able to type * and get the result 'x - 2:3 x^3 + O(x^4)'. Don't worry if the terms of the sum are rearranged. (This one is rather tricky; the solution at the end of this chapter uses 6 rewrite rules. Hint: The 'constant(x)' condition tests whether 'x' is a number.) See Section 2.7.57 [Rewrites Answer 6], page 95. (•)

Just for kicks, try adding the rule 2+3 := 6 to **EvalRules**. What happens? (Be sure to remove this rule afterward, or you might get a nasty surprise when you use Calc to balance your checkbook!)

See Section 10.11 [Rewrite Rules], page 291, for the whole story on rewrite rules.

2.6 Programming Tutorial

The Calculator is written entirely in Emacs Lisp, a highly extensible language. If you know Lisp, you can program the Calculator to do anything you like. Rewrite rules also work as a powerful programming system. But Lisp and rewrite rules take a while to master, and often all you want to do is define a new function or repeat a command a few times. Calc has features that allow you to do these things easily.

One very limited form of programming is defining your own functions. Calc's *Z F* command allows you to define a function name and key sequence to correspond to any formula. Programming commands use the shift-*Z* prefix; the user commands they create use the lower case *z* prefix.

```
1:  x + x^2 / 2 + x^3 / 6 + 1        1:  x + x^2 / 2 + x^3 / 6 + 1
    .                                    .


    ' 1 + x + x^2/2! + x^3/3! RET        Z F e myexp RET RET RET y
```

This polynomial is a Taylor series approximation to 'exp(x)'. The *Z F* command asks a number of questions. The above answers say that the key sequence for our function should be *z e*; the *M-x* equivalent should be calc-myexp; the name of the function in algebraic formulas should also be myexp; the default argument list '(x)' is acceptable; and finally *y* answers the question "leave it in symbolic form for non-constant arguments?"

```
1:  1.3495     2:  1.3495     3:  1.3495
    .          1:  1.34986    2:  1.34986
                   .          1:  myexp(a + 1)
                                  .


    .3 z e         .3 E           ' a+1 RET z e
```

First we call our new exp approximation with 0.3 as an argument, and compare it with the true exp function. Then we note that, as requested, if we try to give *z e* an argument that isn't a plain number, it leaves the myexp function call in symbolic form. If we had answered *n* to the final question, 'myexp(a + 1)' would have evaluated by plugging in 'a + 1' for 'x' in the defining formula.

(•) **Exercise 1.** The "sine integral" function $Si(x)$ is defined as the integral of 'sin(t)/t' for $t = 0$ to x in radians. (It was invented because this integral has no solution in terms of basic functions; if you give it to Calc's *a i* command, it will ponder it for a long time and then give up.) We can use the numerical integration command, however, which in algebraic notation is written like 'ninteg(f(t), t, 0, x)' with any integrand 'f(t)'. Define a *z s* command and Si function that implement this. You will need to edit the default argument list a bit. As a test, 'Si(1)' should return 0.946083. (If you don't get this answer, you might want to check that Calc is in Radians mode. Also, ninteg will run a lot faster if you reduce the precision to, say, six digits beforehand.) See Section 2.7.58 [Programming Answer 1], page 96. (•)

The simplest way to do real "programming" of Emacs is to define a *keyboard macro*. A keyboard macro is simply a sequence of keystrokes which Emacs has stored away and can play back on demand. For example, if you find yourself typing *H a S x RET* often, you may wish to program a keyboard macro to type this for you.

```
1:  y = sqrt(x)          1:  x = y^2
    .                        .

    ' y=sqrt(x) RET         C-x ( H a S x RET C-x )

1:  y = cos(x)            1:  x = s1 arccos(y) + 2 n1 pi
    .                        .

    ' y=cos(x) RET          X
```

When you type *C-x* (, Emacs begins recording. But it is also still ready to execute your keystrokes, so you're really "training" Emacs by walking it through the procedure once. When you type *C-x*), the macro is recorded. You can now type *X* to re-execute the same keystrokes.

You can give a name to your macro by typing *Z K*.

```
1:  .              1:  y = x^4          1:  x = s2 sqrt(s1 sqrt(y))
                       .                    .

    Z K x RET          ' y=x^4 RET          z x
```

Notice that we use shift-*Z* to define the command, and lower-case *z* to call it up.

Keyboard macros can call other macros.

```
1:  abs(x)          1:  x = s1 y                1:  2 / x    1:  x = 2 / y
    .                   .                            .            .

    ' abs(x) RET    C-x ( ' y RET a = z x C-x )    ' 2/x RET    X
```

(•) **Exercise 2.** Define a keyboard macro to negate the item in level 3 of the stack, without disturbing the rest of the stack. See Section 2.7.59 [Programming Answer 2], page 96. (•)

(•) **Exercise 3.** Define keyboard macros to compute the following functions:

1. Compute $\dfrac{\sin x}{x}$, where x is the number on the top of the stack.
2. Compute the base-b logarithm, just like the *B* key except the arguments are taken in the opposite order.
3. Produce a vector of integers from 1 to the integer on the top of the stack.

See Section 2.7.60 [Programming Answer 3], page 97. (•)

(•) **Exercise 4.** Define a keyboard macro to compute the average (mean) value of a list of numbers. See Section 2.7.61 [Programming Answer 4], page 97. (•)

In many programs, some of the steps must execute several times. Calc has *looping* commands that allow this. Loops are useful inside keyboard macros, but actually work at any time.

```
1:  x^6          2:  x^6          1: 360 x^2
    .            1:  4                .
                     .

    ' x^6 RET        4            Z < a d x RET Z >
```

Here we have computed the fourth derivative of x^6 by enclosing a derivative command in a "repeat loop" structure. This structure pops a repeat count from the stack, then executes the body of the loop that many times.

If you make a mistake while entering the body of the loop, type *Z C-g* to cancel the loop command.

Here's another example:

```
3:  1              2:  10946
2:  1              1:  17711
1:  20                  .
        .
```

```
1 RET RET 20        Z < TAB C-j + Z >
```

The numbers in levels 2 and 1 should be the 21st and 22nd Fibonacci numbers, respectively. (To see what's going on, try a few repetitions of the loop body by hand; C-j, also on the Line-Feed or LFD key if you have one, makes a copy of the number in level 2.)

A fascinating property of the Fibonacci numbers is that the nth Fibonacci number can be found directly by computing $\phi^n/\sqrt{5}$ and then rounding to the nearest integer, where ϕ ("phi"), the "golden ratio," is $(1+\sqrt{5})/2$. (For convenience, this constant is available from the phi variable, or the $I\,H\,P$ command.)

```
1:  1.61803     1:  24476.0000409   1:  10945.9999817   1:  10946
       .                  .                  .                  .
```

```
    I  H  P           21 ^              5 Q /               R
```

(•) **Exercise 5.** The *continued fraction* representation of ϕ is $1+1/(1+1/(1+1/(\ldots)))$. We can compute an approximate value by carrying this however far and then replacing the innermost $1/(\ldots)$ by 1. Approximate ϕ using a twenty-term continued fraction. See Section 2.7.62 [Programming Answer 5], page 97. (•)

(•) **Exercise 6.** Linear recurrences like the one for Fibonacci numbers can be expressed in terms of matrices. Given a vector $[a, b]$ determine a matrix which, when multiplied by this vector, produces the vector $[b, c]$, where a, b and c are three successive Fibonacci numbers. Now write a program that, given an integer n, computes the nth Fibonacci number using matrix arithmetic. See Section 2.7.63 [Programming Answer 6], page 97. (•)

A more sophisticated kind of loop is the *for* loop. Suppose we wish to compute the 20th "harmonic" number, which is equal to the sum of the reciprocals of the integers from 1 to 20.

```
3:  0              1:  3.597739
2:  1                   .
1:  20
        .
```

```
0 RET 1 RET 20        Z ( & + 1 Z )
```

The "for" loop pops two numbers, the lower and upper limits, then repeats the body of the loop as an internal counter increases from the lower limit to the upper one. Just before executing the loop body, it pushes the current loop counter. When the loop body finishes, it pops the "step," i.e., the amount by which to increment the loop counter. As you can see, our loop always uses a step of one.

This harmonic number function uses the stack to hold the running total as well as for the various loop housekeeping functions. If you find this disorienting, you can sum in a variable instead:

```
1:  0          2:  1                .          1:  3.597739
       .       1:  20                                  .
                      .
```

```
    0 t 7       1 RET 20       Z ( & s + 7 1 Z )       r 7
```

The **s +** command adds the top-of-stack into the value in a variable (and removes that value from the stack).

It's worth noting that many jobs that call for a "for" loop can also be done more easily by Calc's high-level operations. Two other ways to compute harmonic numbers are to use vector mapping and reduction (*v x 20*, then *V M &*, then *V R +*), or to use the summation command **a +**. Both of these are probably easier than using loops. However, there are some situations where loops really are the way to go:

(•) **Exercise 7.** Use a "for" loop to find the first harmonic number which is greater than 4.0. See Section 2.7.64 [Programming Answer 7], page 98. (•)

Of course, if we're going to be using variables in our programs, we have to worry about the programs clobbering values that the caller was keeping in those same variables. This is easy to fix, though:

```
.         1:  0.6667       1:  0.6667      3:  0.6667
          .             .             2:  3.597739
                                      1:  0.6667
                                      .
```

```
    Z `     p 4 RET 2 RET 3 /    s 7 s s a RET    Z ' r 7 s r a RET
```

When we type **Z `** (that's a grave accent), Calc saves its mode settings and the contents of the ten "quick variables" for later reference. When we type **Z '** (that's an apostrophe now), Calc restores those saved values. Thus the **p 4** and **s 7** commands have no effect outside this sequence. Wrapping this around the body of a keyboard macro ensures that it doesn't interfere with what the user of the macro was doing. Notice that the contents of the stack, and the values of named variables, survive past the **Z '** command.

The *Bernoulli numbers* are a sequence with the interesting property that all of the odd Bernoulli numbers are zero, and the even ones, while difficult to compute, can be roughly approximated by the formula $\frac{2n!}{(2\pi)^n}$. Let's write a keyboard macro to compute (approximate) Bernoulli numbers. (Calc has a command, **k b**, to compute exact Bernoulli numbers, but this command is very slow for large n since the higher Bernoulli numbers are very large fractions.)

```
    1:  10                1:  0.0756823
        .                     .
```

```
    10    C-x ( RET 2 % Z [ DEL 0 Z : ' 2 $! / (2 pi)^$ RET = Z ] C-x )
```

You can read **Z [** as "then," **Z :** as "else," and **Z]** as "end-if." There is no need for an explicit "if" command. For the purposes of **Z [**, the condition is "true" if the value it pops from the stack is a nonzero number, or "false" if it pops zero or something that is not a number (like a formula). Here we take our integer argument modulo 2; this will be nonzero if we're asking for an odd Bernoulli number.

The actual tenth Bernoulli number is 5/66.

```
    3:  0.0756823    1:  0      1:  0.25305    1:  0      1:  1.16659
    2:  5:66             .             .             .             .
    1:  0.0757575
        .
```

```
    10 k b RET c f   M-0 DEL 11 X    DEL 12 X       DEL 13 X      DEL 14 X
```

Just to exercise loops a bit more, let's compute a table of even Bernoulli numbers.

```
3:  []                   1:  [0.10132, 0.03079, 0.02340, 0.033197, ...]
2:  2                        .
1:  30

    .


    [ ] 2 RET 30            Z ( X | 2 Z )
```

The vertical-bar | is the vector-concatenation command. When we execute it, the list we are building will be in stack level 2 (initially this is an empty list), and the next Bernoulli number will be in level 1. The effect is to append the Bernoulli number onto the end of the list. (To create a table of exact fractional Bernoulli numbers, just replace X with k b in the above sequence of keystrokes.)

With loops and conditionals, you can program essentially anything in Calc. One other command that makes looping easier is Z /, which takes a condition from the stack and breaks out of the enclosing loop if the condition is true (non-zero). You can use this to make "while" and "until" style loops.

If you make a mistake when entering a keyboard macro, you can edit it using Z E. First, you must attach it to a key with Z K. One technique is to enter a throwaway dummy definition for the macro, then enter the real one in the edit command.

```
1:  3                    1:  3               Calc Macro Edit Mode.
    .                        .               Original keys: 1 <return> 2 +


                                             1                    ;; calc digits
                                             RET                  ;; calc-enter
                                             2                    ;; calc digits
                                             +                    ;; calc-plus


    C-x ( 1 RET 2 + C-x )   Z K h RET     Z E h
```

A keyboard macro is stored as a pure keystroke sequence. The edmacro package (invoked by Z E) scans along the macro and tries to decode it back into human-readable steps. Descriptions of the keystrokes are given as comments, which begin with ';;', and which are ignored when the edited macro is saved. Spaces and line breaks are also ignored when the edited macro is saved. To enter a space into the macro, type SPC. All the special characters RET, LFD, TAB, SPC, DEL, and NUL must be written in all uppercase, as must the prefixes C- and M-.

Let's edit in a new definition, for computing harmonic numbers. First, erase the four lines of the old definition. Then, type in the new definition (or use Emacs M-w and C-y commands to copy it from this page of the Info file; you can of course skip typing the comments, which begin with ';;').

```
Z`                  ;; calc-kbd-push    (Save local values)
0                   ;; calc digits      (Push a zero onto the stack)
st                  ;; calc-store-into  (Store it in the following variable)
1                   ;; calc quick variable  (Quick variable q1)
1                   ;; calc digits      (Initial value for the loop)
TAB                 ;; calc-roll-down   (Swap initial and final)
Z(                  ;; calc-kbd-for     (Begin the "for" loop)
&                   ;; calc-inv         (Take the reciprocal)
s+                  ;; calc-store-plus  (Add to the following variable)
1                   ;; calc quick variable  (Quick variable q1)
1                   ;; calc digits      (The loop step is 1)
```

```
     Z)                     ;; calc-kbd-end-for  (End the "for" loop)
     sr                     ;; calc-recall       (Recall the final accumulated value)
     1                      ;; calc quick variable (Quick variable q1)
     Z'                     ;; calc-kbd-pop       (Restore values)
```

Press *C-c C-c* to finish editing and return to the Calculator.

```
     1:  20          1:  3.597739
         .               .


         20              z h
```

The edmacro package defines a handy read-kbd-macro command which reads the current region of the current buffer as a sequence of keystroke names, and defines that sequence on the *X* (and *C-x e*) key. Because this is so useful, Calc puts this command on the *C-x * m* key. Try reading in this macro in the following form: Press *C-@* (or *C-SPC*) at one end of the text below, then type *C-x * m* at the other.

```
     Z ` 0 t 1
         1 TAB
         Z ( & s + 1  1 Z )
         r 1
     Z '
```

(•) **Exercise 8.** A general algorithm for solving equations numerically is *Newton's Method*. Given the equation $f(x) = 0$ for any function f, and an initial guess x_0 which is reasonably close to the desired solution, apply this formula over and over:

$$x_{\text{new}} = x - \frac{f(x)}{f'(x)}$$

where $f'(x)$ is the derivative of f. The x values will quickly converge to a solution, i.e., eventually x_{new} and x will be equal to within the limits of the current precision. Write a program which takes a formula involving the variable x, and an initial guess x_0, on the stack, and produces a value of x for which the formula is zero. Use it to find a solution of $\sin(\cos x) = 0.5$ near $x = 4.5$. (Use angles measured in radians.) Note that the built-in *a R* (calc-find-root) command uses Newton's method when it is able. See Section 2.7.65 [Programming Answer 8], page 98. (•)

(•) **Exercise 9.** The *digamma* function $\psi(z)$(*"psi"*) is defined as the derivative of $\ln \Gamma(z)$. For large values of z, it can be approximated by the infinite sum

$$\psi(z) \approx \ln z - \frac{1}{2z} - \sum_{n=1}^{\infty} \frac{\text{bern}(2n)}{2n z^{2n}}$$

where $\sum$ represents the sum over n from 1 to infinity (or to some limit high enough to give the desired accuracy), and the bern function produces (exact) Bernoulli numbers. While this sum is not guaranteed to converge, in practice it is safe. An interesting mathematical constant is Euler's gamma, which is equal to about 0.5772. One way to compute it is by the formula, $\gamma = -\psi(1)$. Unfortunately, 1 isn't a large enough argument for the above formula to work (5 is a much safer value for z). Fortunately, we can compute $\psi(1)$ from $\psi(5)$ using the recurrence $\psi(z + 1) = \psi(z) + \frac{1}{z}$. Your task: Develop a program to compute $\psi(z)$; it should "pump up" z if necessary to be greater than 5, then use the above summation formula. Use looping commands to compute the sum. Use your function to compute γ to twelve decimal places. (Calc has a built-in command for Euler's constant, *I P*, which you can use to check your answer.) See Section 2.7.66 [Programming Answer 9], page 99. (•)

(•) **Exercise 10.** Given a polynomial in x and a number m on the stack, where the polynomial is of degree m or less (i.e., does not have any terms higher than x^m), write a program to convert the polynomial into a list-of-coefficients notation. For example, $5x^4 + (x+1)^2$ with $m = 6$ should produce the list $[1, 2, 1, 0, 5, 0, 0]$. Also develop a way to convert from this form back to the standard algebraic form. See Section 2.7.67 [Programming Answer 10], page 101. (•)

(•) **Exercise 11.** The *Stirling numbers of the first kind* are defined by the recurrences,

$$s(n, n) = 1 \quad \text{for } n \geq 0,$$
$$s(n, 0) = 0 \quad \text{for } n > 0,$$
$$s(n + 1, m) = s(n, m - 1) - n\, s(n, m) \quad \text{for } n \geq m \geq 1.$$

(These numbers are also sometimes written $\begin{bmatrix} n \\ m \end{bmatrix}$.)

This can be implemented using a *recursive* program in Calc; the program must invoke itself in order to calculate the two righthand terms in the general formula. Since it always invokes itself with "simpler" arguments, it's easy to see that it must eventually finish the computation. Recursion is a little difficult with Emacs keyboard macros since the macro is executed before its definition is complete. So here's the recommended strategy: Create a "dummy macro" and assign it to a key with, e.g., Z K s. Now enter the true definition, using the z s command to call itself recursively, then assign it to the same key with Z K s. Now the z s command will run the complete recursive program. (Another way is to use Z E or C-x * m (`read-kbd-macro`) to read the whole macro at once, thus avoiding the "training" phase.) The task: Write a program that computes Stirling numbers of the first kind, given n and m on the stack. Test it with *small* inputs like $s(4, 2)$. (There is a built-in command for Stirling numbers, k s, which you can use to check your answers.) See Section 2.7.68 [Programming Answer 11], page 102. (•)

The programming commands we've seen in this part of the tutorial are low-level, general-purpose operations. Often you will find that a higher-level function, such as vector mapping or rewrite rules, will do the job much more easily than a detailed, step-by-step program can:

(•) **Exercise 12.** Write another program for computing Stirling numbers of the first kind, this time using rewrite rules. Once again, n and m should be taken from the stack. See Section 2.7.69 [Programming Answer 12], page 103. (•)

This ends the tutorial section of the Calc manual. Now you know enough about Calc to use it effectively for many kinds of calculations. But Calc has many features that were not even touched upon in this tutorial. The rest of this manual tells the whole story.

2.7 Answers to Exercises

This section includes answers to all the exercises in the Calc tutorial.

2.7.1 RPN Tutorial Exercise 1

*1 RET 2 RET 3 RET 4 + * -*

The result is $1 - (2 \times (3 + 4)) = -13$.

2.7.2 RPN Tutorial Exercise 2

$2 \times 4 + 7 \times 9.5 + \frac{5}{4} = 75.75$

After computing the intermediate term $2 \times 4 = 8$, you can leave that result on the stack while you compute the second term. With both of these results waiting on the stack you can then compute the final term, then press + + to add everything up.

```
2:  2           1:  8        3:  8        2:  8
1:  4                        2:  7        1:  66.5
    .               .        1:  9.5          .
                                 .

   2 RET 4          *       7 RET 9.5        *


4:  8           3:  8        2:  8        1:  75.75
3:  66.5        2:  66.5     1:  67.75        .
2:  5           1:  1.25         .
1:  4               .
    .

   5 RET 4          /            +            +
```

Alternatively, you could add the first two terms before going on with the third term.

```
2:  8           1:  74.5     3:  74.5     2:  74.5     1:  75.75
1:  66.5            .        2:  5        1:  1.25         .
    .                        1:  4            .
                                 .


   ...             +        5 RET 4          /            +
```

On an old-style RPN calculator this second method would have the advantage of using only three stack levels. But since Calc's stack can grow arbitrarily large this isn't really an issue. Which method you choose is purely a matter of taste.

2.7.3 RPN Tutorial Exercise 3

The TAB key provides a way to operate on the number in level 2.

```
3:  10          3:  10       4:  10       3:  10       3:  10
2:  20          2:  30       3:  30       2:  30       2:  21
1:  30          1:  20       2:  20       1:  21       1:  30
    .               .        1:  1            .            .
                                 .

                  TAB           1            +           TAB
```

Similarly, *M-TAB* gives you access to the number in level 3.

```
3:  10          3:  21          3:  21          3:  30          3:  11
2:  21          2:  30          2:  30          2:  11          2:  21
1:  30          1:  10          1:  11          1:  21          1:  30
    .               .               .               .               .

                M-TAB            1 +            M-TAB           M-TAB
```

2.7.4 RPN Tutorial Exercise 4

Either (*2 , 3*) or (*2 SPC 3*) would have worked, but using both the comma and the space at once yields:

```
1:  ( ...      2:  ( ...      1:  (2, ...    2:  (2, ...    2:  (2, ...
    .          1:  2              .          1:  (2, ...    1:  (2, 3)
                   .                             .              .

    (              2              ,              SPC           3 )
```

Joe probably tried to type *TAB DEL* to swap the extra incomplete object to the top of the stack and delete it. But a feature of Calc is that *DEL* on an incomplete object deletes just one component out of that object, so he had to press *DEL* twice to finish the job.

```
2:  (2, ...    2:  (2, 3)     2:  (2, 3)     1:  (2, 3)
1:  (2, 3)     1:  (2, ...    1:  ( ...          .
    .              .              .

                TAB            DEL            DEL
```

(As it turns out, deleting the second-to-top stack entry happens often enough that Calc provides a special key, *M-DEL*, to do just that. *M-DEL* is just like *TAB DEL*, except that it doesn't exhibit the "feature" that tripped poor Joe.)

2.7.5 Algebraic Entry Tutorial Exercise 1

Type ' *sqrt($) RET*.

If the *Q* key is broken, you could use ' *$^0.5 RET*. Or, RPN style, *0.5 ^*.

(Actually, '$^1:2', using the fraction one-half as the power, is a closer equivalent, since '9^0.5' yields 3.0 whereas 'sqrt(9)' and '9^1:2' yield the exact integer 3.)

2.7.6 Algebraic Entry Tutorial Exercise 2

In the formula '2 x (1+y)', 'x' was interpreted as a function name with '1+y' as its argument. Assigning a value to a variable has no relation to a function by the same name. Joe needed to use an explicit '*' symbol here: '2 x*(1+y)'.

2.7.7 Algebraic Entry Tutorial Exercise 3

The result from *1 RET 0 /* will be the formula 1/0. The "function" '/' cannot be evaluated when its second argument is zero, so it is left in symbolic form. When you now type *0 ∗*, the result will be zero because Calc uses the general rule that "zero times anything is zero."

The *m i* command enables an *Infinite mode* in which 1/0 results in a special symbol that represents "infinity." If you multiply infinity by zero, Calc uses another special new symbol to show that the answer is "indeterminate." See Section 4.5 [Infinities], page 119, for further discussion of infinite and indeterminate values.

2.7.8 Modes Tutorial Exercise 1

Calc always stores its numbers in decimal, so even though one-third has an exact base-3 representation ('3#0.1'), it is still stored as 0.3333333 (chopped off after 12 or however many decimal digits) inside the calculator's memory. When this inexact number is converted back to base 3 for display, it may still be slightly inexact. When we multiply this number by 3, we get 0.999999, also an inexact value.

When Calc displays a number in base 3, it has to decide how many digits to show. If the current precision is 12 (decimal) digits, that corresponds to '12 / log10(3) = 25.15' base-3 digits. Because 25.15 is not an exact integer, Calc shows only 25 digits, with the result that stored numbers carry a little bit of extra information that may not show up on the screen. When Joe entered '3#0.2', the stored number 0.666666 happened to round to a pleasing value when it lost that last 0.15 of a digit, but it was still inexact in Calc's memory. When he divided by 2, he still got the dreaded inexact value 0.333333. (Actually, he divided 0.666667 by 2 to get 0.333334, which is why he got something a little higher than 3#0.1 instead of a little lower.)

If Joe didn't want to be bothered with all this, he could have typed M-24 d n to display with one less digit than the default. (If you give d n a negative argument, it uses default-minus-that, so M-- d n would be an easier way to get the same effect.) Those inexact results would still be lurking there, but they would now be rounded to nice, natural-looking values for display purposes. (Remember, '0.022222' in base 3 is like '0.099999' in base 10; rounding off one digit will round the number up to '0.1'.) Depending on the nature of your work, this hiding of the inexactness may be a benefit or a danger. With the d n command, Calc gives you the choice.

Incidentally, another consequence of all this is that if you type M-30 d n to display more digits than are "really there," you'll see garbage digits at the end of the number. (In decimal display mode, with decimally-stored numbers, these garbage digits are always zero so they vanish and you don't notice them.) Because Calc rounds off that 0.15 digit, there is the danger that two numbers could be slightly different internally but still look the same. If you feel uneasy about this, set the d n precision to be a little higher than normal; you'll get ugly garbage digits, but you'll always be able to tell two distinct numbers apart.

An interesting side note is that most computers store their floating-point numbers in binary, and convert to decimal for display. Thus everyday programs have the same problem: Decimal 0.1 cannot be represented exactly in binary (try it: 0.1 d 2), so '0.1 * 10' comes out as an inexact approximation to 1 on some machines (though they generally arrange to hide it from you by rounding off one digit as we did above). Because Calc works in decimal instead of binary, you can be sure that numbers that look exact *are* exact as long as you stay in decimal display mode.

It's not hard to show that any number that can be represented exactly in binary, octal, or hexadecimal is also exact in decimal, so the kinds of problems we saw in this exercise are likely to be severe only when you use a relatively unusual radix like 3.

2.7.9 Modes Tutorial Exercise 2

If the radix is 15 or higher, we can't use the letter 'e' to mark the exponent because 'e' is interpreted as a digit. When Calc needs to display scientific notation in a high radix, it writes '16#F.E8F*16.^15'. You can enter a number like this as an algebraic entry. Also,

pressing *e* without any digits before it normally types *1e*, but in a high radix it types *16.^*
and puts you in algebraic entry: *16#f.e8f RET e 15 RET ** is another way to enter this
number.

The reason Calc puts a decimal point in the '16.^' is to prevent huge integers from
being generated if the exponent is large (consider '16#1.23*16^1000', where we compute
'16^1000' as a giant exact integer and then throw away most of the digits when we multiply it
by the floating-point '16#1.23'). While this wouldn't normally matter for display purposes,
it could give you a nasty surprise if you copied that number into a file and later moved it
back into Calc.

2.7.10 Modes Tutorial Exercise 3

The answer he got was 0.5000000000006399.

The problem is not that the square operation is inexact, but that the sine of 45 that was
already on the stack was accurate to only 12 places. Arbitrary-precision calculations still
only give answers as good as their inputs.

The real problem is that there is no 12-digit number which, when squared, comes out to
0.5 exactly. The *f [* and *f]* commands decrease or increase a number by one unit in the
last place (according to the current precision). They are useful for determining facts like
this.

```
1:  0.707106781187        1:  0.500000000001
    .                          .

    45 S                       2 ^

1:  0.707106781187        1:  0.707106781186        1:  0.499999999999
    .                          .                          .

    U  DEL                     f [                        2 ^
```

A high-precision calculation must be carried out in high precision all the way. The only
number in the original problem which was known exactly was the quantity 45 degrees, so
the precision must be raised before anything is done after the number 45 has been entered
in order for the higher precision to be meaningful.

2.7.11 Modes Tutorial Exercise 4

Many calculations involve real-world quantities, like the width and height of a piece of wood
or the volume of a jar. Such quantities can't be measured exactly anyway, and if the data
that is input to a calculation is inexact, doing exact arithmetic on it is a waste of time.

Fractions become unwieldy after too many calculations have been done with them. For
example, the sum of the reciprocals of the integers from 1 to 10 is 7381:2520. The sum from
1 to 30 is 9304682830147:2329089562800. After a point it will take a long time to add even
one more term to this sum, but a floating-point calculation of the sum will not have this
problem.

Also, rational numbers cannot express the results of all calculations. There is no fractional form for the square root of two, so if you type *2 Q*, Calc has no choice but to give
you a floating-point answer.

2.7.12 Arithmetic Tutorial Exercise 1

Dividing two integers that are larger than the current precision may give a floating-point result that is inaccurate even when rounded down to an integer. Consider 123456789/2 when the current precision is 6 digits. The true answer is 61728394.5, but with a precision of 6 this will be rounded to 12345700.0/2.0 = 61728500.0. The result, when converted to an integer, will be off by 106.

Here are two solutions: Raise the precision enough that the floating-point round-off error is strictly to the right of the decimal point. Or, convert to Fraction mode so that 123456789/2 produces the exact fraction 123456789:2, which can be rounded down by the *F* command without ever switching to floating-point format.

2.7.13 Arithmetic Tutorial Exercise 2

27 RET 9 B could give the exact result 3:2, but it does a floating-point calculation instead and produces 1.5.

Calc will find an exact result for a logarithm if the result is an integer or (when in Fraction mode) the reciprocal of an integer. But there is no efficient way to search the space of all possible rational numbers for an exact answer, so Calc doesn't try.

2.7.14 Vector Tutorial Exercise 1

Duplicate the vector, compute its length, then divide the vector by its length: *RET A /*.

```
1:  [1, 2, 3]   2:  [1, 2, 3]        1:  [0.27, 0.53, 0.80]   1:  1.
     .          1:  3.74165738677         .                        .


     r 1            RET A                  /                        A
```

The final *A* command shows that the normalized vector does indeed have unit length.

2.7.15 Vector Tutorial Exercise 2

The average position is equal to the sum of the products of the positions times their corresponding probabilities. This is the definition of the dot product operation. So all you need to do is to put the two vectors on the stack and press *.

2.7.16 Matrix Tutorial Exercise 1

The trick is to multiply by a vector of ones. Use *r 4 [1 1 1] *** to get the row sum. Similarly, use *[1 1] r 4 *** to get the column sum.

2.7.17 Matrix Tutorial Exercise 2

$$x + ay = 6$$
$$x + by = 10$$

Just enter the righthand side vector, then divide by the lefthand side matrix as usual.

```
1:  [6, 10]   2:  [6, 10]         1:  [4 a / (a - b) + 6, 4 / (b - a) ]
     .        1:  [ [ 1, a ]           .
                    [ 1, b ] ]


  ' [6 10] RET    ' [1 a; 1 b] RET       /
```

This can be made more readable using *d B* to enable Big display mode:

```
        4 a           4
 1:  [----- + 6, -----]
       a - b        b - a
```

Type *d N* to return to Normal display mode afterwards.

2.7.18 Matrix Tutorial Exercise 3

To solve $A^T A X = A^T B$, first we compute $A' = A^T A$ and $B' = A^T B$; now, we have a system $A'X = B'$ which we can solve using Calc's '/' command.

$$a + 2b + 3c = 6$$
$$4a + 5b + 6c = 2$$
$$7a + 6b \quad\quad = 3$$
$$2a + 4b + 6c = 11$$

The first step is to enter the coefficient matrix. We'll store it in quick variable number 7 for later reference. Next, we compute the B' vector.

```
 1:  [ [ 1, 2, 3 ]          2:  [ [ 1, 4, 7, 2 ]      1:  [57, 84, 96]
      [ 4, 5, 6 ]                [ 2, 5, 6, 4 ]            .
      [ 7, 6, 0 ]                [ 3, 6, 0, 6 ] ]
      [ 2, 4, 6 ] ]         1:  [6, 2, 3, 11]
      .                          .
```

```
  ' [1 2 3; 4 5 6; 7 6 0; 2 4 6] RET  s 7    v t   [6 2 3 11]     *
```

Now we compute the matrix A' and divide.

```
 2:  [57, 84, 96]           1:  [-11.64, 14.08, -3.64]
 1:  [ [ 70, 72, 39 ]           .
      [ 72, 81, 60 ]
      [ 39, 60, 81 ] ]
      .
```

```
      r 7 v t r 7 *                    /
```

(The actual computed answer will be slightly inexact due to round-off error.)

Notice that the answers are similar to those for the 3×3 system solved in the text. That's because the fourth equation that was added to the system is almost identical to the first one multiplied by two. (If it were identical, we would have gotten the exact same answer since the 4×3 system would be equivalent to the original 3×3 system.)

Since the first and fourth equations aren't quite equivalent, they can't both be satisfied at once. Let's plug our answers back into the original system of equations to see how well they match.

```
 2:  [-11.64, 14.08, -3.64]     1:  [5.6, 2., 3., 11.2]
 1:  [ [ 1, 2, 3 ]                  .
      [ 4, 5, 6 ]
      [ 7, 6, 0 ]
      [ 2, 4, 6 ] ]
      .
```

```
      r 7                              TAB *
```

This is reasonably close to our original B vector, $[6, 2, 3, 11]$.

2.7.19 List Tutorial Exercise 1

We can use **v x** to build a vector of integers. This needs to be adjusted to get the range of integers we desire. Mapping '-' across the vector will accomplish this, although it turns out the plain '-' key will work just as well.

```
2:  2                        2:  2
1:  [1, 2, 3, 4, 5, 6, 7, 8, 9]   1:  [-4, -3, -2, -1, 0, 1, 2, 3, 4]
    .                            .


    2  v x 9 RET              5 V M -   or   5 -
```

Now we use **V M ^** to map the exponentiation operator across the vector.

```
1:  [0.0625, 0.125, 0.25, 0.5, 1, 2, 4, 8, 16]
    .


    V M ^
```

2.7.20 List Tutorial Exercise 2

Given x and y vectors in quick variables 1 and 2 as before, the first job is to form the matrix that describes the problem.

$$m \times x + b \times 1 = y$$

Thus we want a 19×2 matrix with our x vector as one column and ones as the other column. So, first we build the column of ones, then we combine the two columns to form our A matrix.

```
2:  [1.34, 1.41, 1.49, ... ]   1:  [ [ 1.34, 1 ]
1:  [1, 1, 1, ...]                  [ 1.41, 1 ]
    .                                [ 1.49, 1 ]
                                     ...

    r 1 1 v b 19 RET           M-2 v p v t    s 3
```

Now we compute $A^T y$ and $A^T A$ and divide.

```
1:  [33.36554, 13.613]    2:  [33.36554, 13.613]
    .                     1:  [ [ 98.0003, 41.63 ]
                               [  41.63,   19   ] ]
                              .


    v t r 2 *                 r 3 v t r 3 *
```

(Hey, those numbers look familiar!)

```
1:  [0.52141679, -0.425978]
    .


    /
```

Since we were solving equations of the form $m \times x + b \times 1 = y$, these numbers should be m and b, respectively. Sure enough, they agree exactly with the result computed using **V M** and **V R**!

The moral of this story: **V M** and **V R** will probably solve your problem, but there is often an easier way using the higher-level arithmetic functions!

In fact, there is a built-in **a F** command that does least-squares fits. See Section 10.8 [Curve Fitting], page 275.

2.7.21 List Tutorial Exercise 3

Move to one end of the list and press `C-@` (or `C-SPC` or whatever) to set the mark, then move to the other end of the list and type `C-x * g`.

```
1:  [2.3, 6, 22, 15.1, 7, 15, 14, 7.5, 2.5]
    .
```

To make things interesting, let's assume we don't know at a glance how many numbers are in this list. Then we could type:

```
2:  [2.3, 6, 22, ... ]      2:  [2.3, 6, 22, ... ]
1:  [2.3, 6, 22, ... ]      1:  126356422.5
    .                           .


    RET                         V R *


2:  126356422.5             2:  126356422.5      1:  7.94652913734
1:  [2.3, 6, 22, ... ]      1:  9                    .
    .                           .


    TAB                         v l              I ^
```

(The `I ^` command computes the nth root of a number. You could also type `& ^` to take the reciprocal of 9 and then raise the number to that power.)

2.7.22 List Tutorial Exercise 4

A number j is a divisor of n if $n \% j = 0$. The first step is to get a vector that identifies the divisors.

```
2:  30                  2:  [0, 0, 0, 2, ...]    1:  [1, 1, 1, 0, ...]
1:  [1, 2, 3, 4, ...]   1:  0                        .
    .                       .


  30 RET v x 30 RET  s 1    V M % 0                 V M a = s 2
```

This vector has 1's marking divisors of 30 and 0's marking non-divisors.

The zeroth divisor function is just the total number of divisors. The first divisor function is the sum of the divisors.

```
1:  8       3:  8                    2:  8                 2:  8
            2:  [1, 2, 3, 4, ...]    1:  [1, 2, 3, 0, ...] 1:  72
            1:  [1, 1, 1, 0, ...]        .                     .


    V R +       r 1 r 2                 V M *                 V R +
```

Once again, the last two steps just compute a dot product for which a simple `*` would have worked equally well.

2.7.23 List Tutorial Exercise 5

The obvious first step is to obtain the list of factors with `k f`. This list will always be in sorted order, so if there are duplicates they will be right next to each other. A suitable method is to compare the list with a copy of itself shifted over by one.

```
1:  [3, 7, 7, 7, 19]    2:  [3, 7, 7, 7, 19]      2:  [3, 7, 7, 7, 19, 0]
    .                   1:  [3, 7, 7, 7, 19, 0]   1:  [0, 3, 7, 7, 7, 19]
                            .                         .


    19551 k f               RET 0 |                  TAB 0 TAB |
```

```
1:  [0, 0, 1, 1, 0, 0]    1:  2           1:  0
    .                         .               .

    V M a =                   V R +           0 a =
```

Note that we have to arrange for both vectors to have the same length so that the mapping operation works; no prime factor will ever be zero, so adding zeros on the left and right is safe. From then on the job is pretty straightforward.

Incidentally, Calc provides the *Möbius* μ function which is zero if and only if its argument is square-free. It would be a much more convenient way to do the above test in practice.

2.7.24 List Tutorial Exercise 6

First use *v x 6 RET* to get a list of integers, then *V M v x* to get a list of lists of integers!

2.7.25 List Tutorial Exercise 7

Here's one solution. First, compute the triangular list from the previous exercise and type *1 -* to subtract one from all the elements.

```
1:  [ [0],
      [0, 1],
      [0, 1, 2],
      . . .


    1 -
```

The numbers down the lefthand edge of the list we desire are called the "triangular numbers" (now you know why!). The nth triangular number is the sum of the integers from 1 to n, and can be computed directly by the formula $\frac{n(n+1)}{2}$.

```
2:  [ [0], [0, 1], ... ]    2:  [ [0], [0, 1], ... ]
1:  [0, 1, 2, 3, 4, 5]      1:  [0, 1, 3, 6, 10, 15]
    .                           .

    v x 6 RET 1 -               V M ' $ ($+1)/2 RET
```

Adding this list to the above list of lists produces the desired result:

```
1:  [ [0],
      [1, 2],
      [3, 4, 5],
      [6, 7, 8, 9],
      [10, 11, 12, 13, 14],
      [15, 16, 17, 18, 19, 20] ]
    .

    V M +
```

If we did not know the formula for triangular numbers, we could have computed them using a *V U +* command. We could also have gotten them the hard way by mapping a reduction across the original triangular list.

```
2:  [ [0], [0, 1], ... ]    2:  [ [0], [0, 1], ... ]
1:  [ [0], [0, 1], ... ]    1:  [0, 1, 3, 6, 10, 15]
    .                           .

    RET                         V M V R +
```

(This means "map a *V R +* command across the vector," and since each element of the main vector is itself a small vector, *V R +* computes the sum of its elements.)

2.7.26 List Tutorial Exercise 8

The first step is to build a list of values of x.

```
1:  [1, 2, 3, ..., 21]    1:  [0, 1, 2, ..., 20]    1:  [0, 0.25, 0.5, ..., 5]
    .                          .                          .


    v x 21 RET                 1 -                        4 / s 1
```

Next, we compute the Bessel function values.

```
1:  [0., 0.124, 0.242, ..., -0.328]
    .


    V M ' besJ(1,$) RET
```

(Another way to do this would be *1 TAB V M f j*.)

A way to isolate the maximum value is to compute the maximum using *V R X*, then compare all the Bessel values with that maximum.

```
2:  [0., 0.124, 0.242, ... ]    1:  [0, 0, 0, ... ]    2:  [0, 0, 0, ... ]
1:  0.5801562                       .                  1:  1
    .                                                      .


    RET V R X                       V M a =                RET V R +    DEL
```

It's a good idea to verify, as in the last step above, that only one value is equal to the maximum. (After all, a plot of $\sin x$ might have many points all equal to the maximum value, 1.)

The vector we have now has a single 1 in the position that indicates the maximum value of x. Now it is a simple matter to convert this back into the corresponding value itself.

```
2:  [0, 0, 0, ... ]         1:  [0, 0., 0., ... ]    1:  1.75
1:  [0, 0.25, 0.5, ... ]        .                        .
    .


    r 1                         V M *                    V R +
```

If **a =** had produced more than one 1 value, this method would have given the sum of all maximum x values; not very useful! In this case we could have used **v m** (`calc-mask-vector`) instead. This command deletes all elements of a "data" vector that correspond to zeros in a "mask" vector, leaving us with, in this example, a vector of maximum x values.

The built-in **a X** command maximizes a function using more efficient methods. Just for illustration, let's use **a X** to maximize 'besJ(1,x)' over this same interval.

```
2:  besJ(1, x)              1:  [1.84115, 0.581865]
1:  [0 .. 5]                    .
    .


    ' besJ(1,x), [0..5] RET      a X x RET
```

The output from **a X** is a vector containing the value of x that maximizes the function, and the function's value at that maximum. As you can see, our simple search got quite close to the right answer.

2.7.27 List Tutorial Exercise 9

Step one is to convert our integer into vector notation.

```
1:  25129925999              3:  25129925999
            .                 2:  10
                              1:  [11, 10, 9, ..., 1, 0]
                                        .


    25129925999 RET          10 RET 12 RET v x 12 RET -


1:  25129925999              1:  [0, 2, 25, 251, 2512, ... ]
2:  [100000000000, ... ]              .
          .


    V M ^   s 1                  V M \
```

(Recall, the \ command computes an integer quotient.)

```
1:  [0, 2, 5, 1, 2, 9, 9, 2, 5, 9, 9, 9]
          .


    10 V M %   s 2
```

Next we must increment this number. This involves adding one to the last digit, plus handling carries. There is a carry to the left out of a digit if that digit is a nine and all the digits to the right of it are nines.

```
1:  [0, 0, 0, 0, 0, 1, 1, 0, 0, 1, 1, 1]   1:  [1, 1, 1, 0, 0, 1, ... ]
          .                                           .


    9 V M a =                               v v


1:  [1, 1, 1, 0, 0, 0, ... ]   1:  [0, 0, 0, 0, 0, 0, 0, 0, 0, 1, 1, 1, 1]
          .                                 .


    V U *                       v v 1 |
```

Accumulating * across a vector of ones and zeros will preserve only the initial run of ones. These are the carries into all digits except the rightmost digit. Concatenating a one on the right takes care of aligning the carries properly, and also adding one to the rightmost digit.

```
2:  [0, 0, 0, 0, ... ]    1:  [0, 0, 2, 5, 1, 2, 9, 9, 2, 6, 0, 0, 0]
1:  [0, 0, 2, 5, ... ]              .
          .


    0 r 2 |                   V M + 10 V M %
```

Here we have concatenated 0 to the *left* of the original number; this takes care of shifting the carries by one with respect to the digits that generated them.

Finally, we must convert this list back into an integer.

```
3:  [0, 0, 2, 5, ... ]       2:  [0, 0, 2, 5, ... ]
2:  1000000000000            1:  [1000000000000, 100000000000, ... ]
1:  [100000000000, ... ]              .
          .


    10 RET 12 ^ r 1              |


1:  [0, 0, 20000000000, 5000000000, ... ]   1:  25129926000
          .                                       .


    V M *                       V R +
```

Another way to do this final step would be to reduce the formula '10 $$ + $' across the vector of digits.

```
1:  [0, 0, 2, 5, ... ]          1:  25129926000
    .                               .


                      V R ' 10 $$ + $ RET
```

2.7.28 List Tutorial Exercise 10

For the list $[a, b, c, d]$, the result is $((a = b) = c) = d$, which will compare a and b to produce a 1 or 0, which is then compared with c to produce another 1 or 0, which is then compared with d. This is not at all what Joe wanted.

Here's a more correct method:

```
1:  [7, 7, 7, 8, 7]       2:  [7, 7, 7, 8, 7]
    .                     1:  7
                              .


    ' [7,7,7,8,7] RET         RET v r 1 RET

1:  [1, 1, 1, 0, 1]       1:  0
    .                         .


    V M a =                   V R *
```

2.7.29 List Tutorial Exercise 11

The circle of unit radius consists of those points (x, y) for which $x^2 + y^2 < 1$. We start by generating a vector of x^2 and a vector of y^2.

We can make this go a bit faster by using the v . and t . commands.

```
2:  [2., 2., ..., 2.]      2:  [2., 2., ..., 2.]
1:  [2., 2., ..., 2.]      1:  [1.16, 1.98, ..., 0.81]
    .                          .


   v . t . 2. v b 100 RET RET    V M k r

2:  [2., 2., ..., 2.]      1:  [0.026, 0.96, ..., 0.036]
1:  [0.026, 0.96, ..., 0.036]  2:  [0.53, 0.81, ..., 0.094]
    .                          .


    1 - 2 V M ^                TAB V M k r 1 - 2 V M ^
```

Now we sum the x^2 and y^2 values, compare with 1 to get a vector of 1/0 truth values, then sum the truth values.

```
1:  [0.56, 1.78, ..., 0.13]    1:  [1, 0, ..., 1]    1:  84
    .                              .                     .


            +                      1 V M a <              V R +
```

The ratio 84/100 should approximate the ratio $\pi/4$.

```
1:  0.84        1:  3.36       2:  3.36        1:  1.0695
    .               .          1:  3.14159         .


    100 /           4 *            P                   /
```

Our estimate, 3.36, is off by about 7%. We could get a better estimate by taking more points (say, 1000), but it's clear that this method is not very efficient!

(Naturally, since this example uses random numbers your own answer will be slightly different from the one shown here!)

If you typed *v* . and *t* . before, type them again to return to full-sized display of vectors.

2.7.30 List Tutorial Exercise 12

This problem can be made a lot easier by taking advantage of some symmetries. First of all, after some thought it's clear that the y axis can be ignored altogether. Just pick a random x component for one end of the match, pick a random direction θ, and see if x and $x + \cos\theta$ (which is the x coordinate of the other endpoint) cross a line. The lines are at integer coordinates, so this happens when the two numbers surround an integer.

Since the two endpoints are equivalent, we may as well choose the leftmost of the two endpoints as x. Then *theta* is an angle pointing to the right, in the range -90 to 90 degrees. (We could use radians, but it would feel like cheating to refer to $\pi/2$ radians while trying to estimate π!)

In fact, since the field of lines is infinite we can choose the coordinates 0 and 1 for the lines on either side of the leftmost endpoint. The rightmost endpoint will be between 0 and 1 if the match does not cross a line, or between 1 and 2 if it does. So: Pick random x and θ, compute $x + \cos\theta$, and count how many of the results are greater than one. Simple!

We can make this go a bit faster by using the *v* . and *t* . commands.

```
1:  [0.52, 0.71, ..., 0.72]    2:  [0.52, 0.71, ..., 0.72]
          .                     1:  [78.4, 64.5, ..., -42.9]
                                          .


    v . t . 1. v b 100 RET  V M k r    180. v b 100 RET  V M k r  90 -
```

(The next step may be slow, depending on the speed of your computer.)

```
    2:  [0.52, 0.71, ..., 0.72]    1:  [0.72, 1.14, ..., 1.45]
    1:  [0.20, 0.43, ..., 0.73]              .
              .


        m d  V M C                          +


    1:  [0, 1, ..., 1]      1:  0.64          1:  3.125
              .                   .                .


        1 V M a >          V R + 100 /       2 TAB /
```

Let's try the third method, too. We'll use random integers up to one million. The *k r* command with an integer argument picks a random integer.

```
    2:  [1000000, 1000000, ..., 1000000]    2:  [78489, 527587, ..., 814975]
    1:  [1000000, 1000000, ..., 1000000]    1:  [324014, 358783, ..., 955450]
                  .                                       .


        1000000 v b 100 RET RET                 V M k r  TAB  V M k r


    1:  [1, 1, ..., 25]    1:  [1, 1, ..., 0]    1:  0.56
              .                     .                  .


        V M k g            1 V M a =            V R + 100 /
```

```
1:  10.714        1:  3.273
    .                 .


    6 TAB /           Q
```

For a proof of this property of the GCD function, see section 4.5.2, exercise 10, of Knuth's *Art of Computer Programming*, volume II.

If you typed *v* . and *t* . before, type them again to return to full-sized display of vectors.

2.7.31 List Tutorial Exercise 13

First, we put the string on the stack as a vector of ASCII codes.

```
1:  [84, 101, 115, ..., 51]
    .


    "Testing, 1, 2, 3 RET
```

Note that the " key, like *$*, initiates algebraic entry so there was no need to type an apostrophe. Also, Calc didn't mind that we omitted the closing ". (The same goes for all closing delimiters like) and *]* at the end of a formula.

We'll show two different approaches here. In the first, we note that if the input vector is $[a, b, c, d]$, then the hash code is $3(3(3a + b) + c) + d = 27a + 9b + 3c + d$. In other words, it's a sum of descending powers of three times the ASCII codes.

```
2:  [84, 101, 115, ..., 51]   2:  [84, 101, 115, ..., 51]
1:  16                        1:  [15, 14, 13, ..., 0]
    .                             .


    RET v 1                       v x 16 RET -


2:  [84, 101, 115, ..., 51]   1:  1960915098   1:  121
1:  [14348907, ..., 1]            .                .
    .


    3 TAB V M ^                   *              511 %
```

Once again, * elegantly summarizes most of the computation. But there's an even more elegant approach: Reduce the formula *3 $$ + $* across the vector. Recall that this represents a function of two arguments that computes its first argument times three plus its second argument.

```
1:  [84, 101, 115, ..., 51]   1:  1960915098
    .                             .


    "Testing, 1, 2, 3 RET          V R ' 3$$+$ RET
```

If you did the decimal arithmetic exercise, this will be familiar. Basically, we're turning a base-3 vector of digits into an integer, except that our "digits" are much larger than real digits.

Instead of typing *511 %* again to reduce the result, we can be cleverer still and notice that rather than computing a huge integer and taking the modulo at the end, we can take the modulo at each step without affecting the result. While this means there are more arithmetic operations, the numbers we operate on remain small so the operations are faster.

```
1:  [84, 101, 115, ..., 51]   1:  121
    .                             .


    "Testing, 1, 2, 3 RET          V R ' (3$$+$)%511 RET
```

Why does this work? Think about a two-step computation: $3(3a + b) + c$. Taking a result modulo 511 basically means subtracting off enough 511's to put the result in the desired range. So the result when we take the modulo after every step is,

$$3(3a + b - 511m) + c - 511n$$

for some suitable integers m and n. Expanding out by the distributive law yields

$$9a + 3b + c - 511 \times 3m - 511n$$

The m term in the latter formula is redundant because any contribution it makes could just as easily be made by the n term. So we can take it out to get an equivalent formula with $n' = 3m + n$,

$$9a + 3b + c - 511n'$$

which is just the formula for taking the modulo only at the end of the calculation. Therefore the two methods are essentially the same.

Later in the tutorial we will encounter *modulo forms*, which basically automate the idea of reducing every intermediate result modulo some value m.

2.7.32 List Tutorial Exercise 14

We want to use H V U to nest a function which adds a random step to an (x, y) coordinate. The function is a bit long, but otherwise the problem is quite straightforward.

```
2:  [0, 0]     1:  [ [    0,        0    ]
1:  50                [  0.4288, -0.1695 ]
     .                [ -0.4787, -0.9027 ]
                            . . .


    [0,0] 50       H V U ' <# + [random(2.0)-1, random(2.0)-1]> RET
```

Just as the text recommended, we used '< >' nameless function notation to keep the two **random** calls from being evaluated before nesting even begins.

We now have a vector of $[x, y]$ sub-vectors, which by Calc's rules acts like a matrix. We can transpose this matrix and unpack to get a pair of vectors, x and y, suitable for graphing.

```
2:  [ 0, 0.4288, -0.4787, ... ]
1:  [ 0, -0.1696, -0.9027, ... ]
     .


    v t   v u  g f
```

Incidentally, because the x and y are completely independent in this case, we could have done two separate commands to create our x and y vectors of numbers directly.

To make a random walk of unit steps, we note that **sincos** of a random direction exactly gives us an $[x, y]$ step of unit length; in fact, the new nesting function is even briefer, though we might want to lower the precision a bit for it.

```
2:  [0, 0]     1:  [ [    0,      0    ]
1:  50                [  0.1318, 0.9912 ]
     .                [ -0.5965, 0.3061 ]
                            . . .


    [0,0] 50   m d  p 6 RET   H V U ' <# + sincos(random(360.0))> RET
```

Another *v t v u g f* sequence will graph this new random walk.

An interesting twist on these random walk functions would be to use complex numbers instead of 2-vectors to represent points on the plane. In the first example, we'd use something like 'random + random*(0,1)', and in the second we could use polar complex numbers with random phase angles. (This exercise was first suggested in this form by Randal Schwartz.)

2.7.33 Types Tutorial Exercise 1

If the number is the square root of π times a rational number, then its square, divided by π, should be a rational number.

```
1:  1.26508260337    1:  0.509433962268    1:  2486645810:4881193627
    .                    .                     .


    2 ^ P /                                   c F
```

Technically speaking this is a rational number, but not one that is likely to have arisen in the original problem. More likely, it just happens to be the fraction which most closely represents some irrational number to within 12 digits.

But perhaps our result was not quite exact. Let's reduce the precision slightly and try again:

```
1:  0.509433962268    1:  27:53
    .                     .


    U p 10 RET            c F
```

Aha! It's unlikely that an irrational number would equal a fraction this simple to within ten digits, so our original number was probably $\sqrt{27\pi/53}$.

Notice that we didn't need to re-round the number when we reduced the precision. Remember, arithmetic operations always round their inputs to the current precision before they begin.

2.7.34 Types Tutorial Exercise 2

'inf / inf = nan'. Perhaps '1' is the "obvious" answer. But if '17 inf = inf', then '17 inf / inf = inf / inf = 17', too.

'exp(inf) = inf'. It's tempting to say that the exponential of infinity must be "bigger" than "regular" infinity, but as far as Calc is concerned all infinities are the same size. In other words, as x goes to infinity, e^x also goes to infinity, but the fact the e^x grows much faster than x is not relevant here.

'exp(-inf) = 0'. Here we have a finite answer even though the input is infinite.

'sqrt(-inf) = (0, 1) inf'. Remember that $(0,1)$ represents the imaginary number i. Here's a derivation: 'sqrt(-inf) = sqrt((-1) * inf) = sqrt(-1) * sqrt(inf)'. The first part is, by definition, i; the second is inf because, once again, all infinities are the same size.

'sqrt(uinf) = uinf'. In fact, we do know something about the direction because sqrt is defined to return a value in the right half of the complex plane. But Calc has no notation for this, so it settles for the conservative answer uinf.

'abs(uinf) = inf'. No matter which direction x points, 'abs(x)' always points along the positive real axis.

'ln(0) = -inf'. Here we have an infinite answer to a finite input. As in the 1/0 case, Calc will only use infinities here if you have turned on Infinite mode. Otherwise, it will treat 'ln(0)' as an error.

2.7.35 Types Tutorial Exercise 3

We can make 'inf - inf' be any real number we like, say, *a*, just by claiming that we added *a* to the first infinity but not to the second. This is just as true for complex values of *a*, so nan can stand for a complex number. (And, similarly, uinf can stand for an infinity that points in any direction in the complex plane, such as '(0, 1) inf'.)

In fact, we can multiply the first inf by two. Surely '2 inf - inf = inf', but also '2 inf - inf = inf - inf = nan'. So nan can even stand for infinity. Obviously it's just as easy to make it stand for minus infinity as for plus infinity.

The moral of this story is that "infinity" is a slippery fish indeed, and Calc tries to handle it by having a very simple model for infinities (only the direction counts, not the "size"); but Calc is careful to write nan any time this simple model is unable to tell what the true answer is.

2.7.36 Types Tutorial Exercise 4

```
2:  0@ 47' 26"            1:  0@ 2' 47.411765"
1:  17                        .
    .

    0@ 47' 26" RET 17              /
```
The average song length is two minutes and 47.4 seconds.
```
2:  0@ 2' 47.411765"    1:  0@ 3' 7.411765"    1:  0@ 53' 6.000005"
1:  0@ 0' 20"               .                      .
    .

    20"                         +                      17 *
```
The album would be 53 minutes and 6 seconds long.

2.7.37 Types Tutorial Exercise 5

Let's suppose it's January 14, 1991. The easiest thing to do is to keep trying 13ths of months until Calc reports a Friday. We can do this by manually entering dates, or by using *t I*:
```
1:  <Wed Feb 13, 1991>   1:  <Wed Mar 13, 1991>   1:  <Sat Apr 13, 1991>
    .                        .                        .


    ' <2/13> RET       DEL    ' <3/13> RET           t I
```
(Calc assumes the current year if you don't say otherwise.)

This is getting tedious—we can keep advancing the date by typing *t I* over and over again, but let's automate the job by using vector mapping. The *t I* command actually takes a second "how-many-months" argument, which defaults to one. This argument is exactly what we want to map over:
```
2:  <Sat Apr 13, 1991>   1:  [<Mon May 13, 1991>, <Thu Jun 13, 1991>,
1:  [1, 2, 3, 4, 5, 6]        <Sat Jul 13, 1991>, <Tue Aug 13, 1991>,
    .                         <Fri Sep 13, 1991>, <Sun Oct 13, 1991>]

                              .


    v x 6 RET                 V M t I
```

Et voilà, September 13, 1991 is a Friday.

```
1:  242
    .


'  <sep 13> - <jan 14> RET
```

And the answer to our original question: 242 days to go.

2.7.38 Types Tutorial Exercise 6

The full rule for leap years is that they occur in every year divisible by four, except that they don't occur in years divisible by 100, except that they *do* in years divisible by 400. We could work out the answer by carefully counting the years divisible by four and the exceptions, but there is a much simpler way that works even if we don't know the leap year rule.

Let's assume the present year is 1991. Years have 365 days, except that leap years (whenever they occur) have 366 days. So let's count the number of days between now and then, and compare that to the number of years times 365. The number of extra days we find must be equal to the number of leap years there were.

```
1:  <Mon Jan 1, 10001>    2:  <Mon Jan 1, 10001>    1:  2925593
    .                      1:  <Tue Jan 1, 1991>          .
                               .


'  <jan 1 10001> RET       '  <jan 1 1991> RET            -


3:  2925593      2:  2925593      2:  2925593      1:  1943
2:  10001        1:  8010         1:  2923650          .
1:  1991             .                .
    .


10001 RET 1991       -               365 *             -
```

There will be 1943 leap years before the year 10001. (Assuming, of course, that the algorithm for computing leap years remains unchanged for that long. See Section 4.9 [Date Forms], page 122, for some interesting background information in that regard.)

2.7.39 Types Tutorial Exercise 7

The relative errors must be converted to absolute errors so that '+/-' notation may be used.

```
1:  1.              2:  1.
    .               1:  0.2
                        .


20 RET .05 *        4 RET .05 *
```

Now we simply chug through the formula.

```
1:  19.7392088022    1:  394.78 +/- 19.739    1:  6316.5 +/- 706.21
    .                    .                        .


2 P 2 ^ *            20 p 1 *                 4 p .2 RET 2 ^ *
```

It turns out the *v u* command will unpack an error form as well as a vector. This saves us some retyping of numbers.

```
3:  6316.5 +/- 706.21      2:  6316.5 +/- 706.21
2:  6316.5                 1:  0.1118
1:  706.21                     .
    .


    RET v u                    TAB /
```

Thus the volume is 6316 cubic centimeters, within about 11 percent.

2.7.40 Types Tutorial Exercise 8

The first answer is pretty simple: '1 / (0 .. 10) = (0.1 .. inf)'. Since a number in the interval '(0 .. 10)' can get arbitrarily close to zero, its reciprocal can get arbitrarily large, so the answer is an interval that effectively means, "any number greater than 0.1" but with no upper bound.

The second answer, similarly, is '1 / (-10 .. 0) = (-inf .. -0.1)'.

Calc normally treats division by zero as an error, so that the formula '1 / 0' is left unsimplified. Our third problem, '1 / [0 .. 10]', also (potentially) divides by zero because zero is now a member of the interval. So Calc leaves this one unevaluated, too.

If you turn on Infinite mode by pressing m i, you will instead get the answer '[0.1 .. inf]', which includes infinity as a possible value.

The fourth calculation, '1 / (-10 .. 10)', has the same problem. Zero is buried inside the interval, but it's still a possible value. It's not hard to see that the actual result of '1 / (-10 .. 10)' will be either greater than 0.1, or less than −0.1. Thus the interval goes from minus infinity to plus infinity, with a "hole" in it from −0.1 to 0.1. Calc doesn't have any way to represent this, so it just reports '[-inf .. inf]' as the answer. It may be disappointing to hear "the answer lies somewhere between minus infinity and plus infinity, inclusive," but that's the best that interval arithmetic can do in this case.

2.7.41 Types Tutorial Exercise 9

```
1:  [-3 .. 3]       2:  [-3 .. 3]       2:  [0 .. 9]
    .               1:  [0 .. 9]        1:  [-9 .. 9]
                        .                   .


    [ 3 n .. 3 ]        RET 2 ^             TAB RET *
```

In the first case the result says, "if a number is between −3 and 3, its square is between 0 and 9." The second case says, "the product of two numbers each between −3 and 3 is between −9 and 9."

An interval form is not a number; it is a symbol that can stand for many different numbers. Two identical-looking interval forms can stand for different numbers.

The same issue arises when you try to square an error form.

2.7.42 Types Tutorial Exercise 10

Testing the first number, we might arbitrarily choose 17 for x.

```
1:  17 mod 811749613    2:  17 mod 811749613    1:  533694123 mod 811749613
    .                        811749612               .
                             .


    17 M 811749613 RET       811749612               ^
```

Since 533694123 is (considerably) different from 1, the number 811749613 must not be prime.

It's awkward to type the number in twice as we did above. There are various ways to avoid this, and algebraic entry is one. In fact, using a vector mapping operation we can perform several tests at once. Let's use this method to test the second number.

```
2:  [17, 42, 100000]              1:  [1 mod 15485863, 1 mod ... ]
1:  15485863                          .


    [17 42 100000] 15485863 RET        V M ' ($$ mod $)^($-1) RET
```

The result is three ones (modulo n), so it's very probable that 15485863 is prime. (In fact, this number is the millionth prime.)

Note that the functions '($$^($-1)) mod $' or '$$^($-1) % $' would have been hopelessly inefficient, since they would have calculated the power using full integer arithmetic.

Calc has a *k p* command that does primality testing. For small numbers it does an exact test; for large numbers it uses a variant of the Fermat test we used here. You can use *k p* repeatedly to prove that a large integer is prime with any desired probability.

2.7.43 Types Tutorial Exercise 11

There are several ways to insert a calculated number into an HMS form. One way to convert a number of seconds to an HMS form is simply to multiply the number by an HMS form representing one second:

```
1:  31415926.5359     2:  31415926.5359     1:  8726@ 38' 46.5359"
    .                  1:  0@ 0' 1"              .
                           .


    P 1e7 *                0@ 0' 1"                 *


2:  8726@ 38' 46.5359"           1:  6@ 6' 2.5359" mod 24@ 0' 0"
1:  15@ 27' 16" mod 24@ 0' 0"        .
    .


    x time RET                       +
```

It will be just after six in the morning.

The algebraic *hms* function can also be used to build an HMS form:

```
1:  hms(0, 0, 10000000. pi)     1:  8726@ 38' 46.5359"
    .                               .


    ' hms(0, 0, 1e7 pi) RET          =
```

The = key is necessary to evaluate the symbol 'pi' to the actual number 3.14159...

2.7.44 Types Tutorial Exercise 12

As we recall, there are 17 songs of about 2 minutes and 47 seconds each.

```
2:  0@ 2' 47"                    1:  [0@ 3' 7" .. 0@ 3' 47"]
1:  [0@ 0' 20" .. 0@ 1' 0"]          .
    .


    [ 0@ 20" .. 0@ 1' ]              +
```

```
1:  [0@ 52' 59." .. 1@ 4' 19."]

    .

    17 *
```

No matter how long it is, the album will fit nicely on one CD.

2.7.45 Types Tutorial Exercise 13

Type ' 1 yr RET u c s RET. The answer is 31557600 seconds.

2.7.46 Types Tutorial Exercise 14

How long will it take for a signal to get from one end of the computer to the other?

```
1:  m / c        1:  3.3356 ns

    .                .

    ' 1 m / c RET        u c ns RET
```

(Recall, 'c' is a "unit" corresponding to the speed of light.)

```
1:  3.3356 ns     1:  0.81356
2:  4.1 ns            .

    .

    ' 4.1 ns RET          /
```

Thus a signal could take up to 81 percent of a clock cycle just to go from one place to another inside the computer, assuming the signal could actually attain the full speed of light. Pretty tight!

2.7.47 Types Tutorial Exercise 15

The speed limit is 55 miles per hour on most highways. We want to find the ratio of Sam's speed to the US speed limit.

```
1:  55 mph       2:  55 mph          3:  11 hr mph / yd
    .            1:  5 yd / hr            .

                     .

    ' 55 mph RET     ' 5 yd/hr RET           /
```

The u s command cancels out these units to get a plain number. Now we take the logarithm base two to find the final answer, assuming that each successive pill doubles his speed.

```
1:  19360.       2:  19360.       1:  14.24
    .            1:  2               .

                     .

    u s              2                B
```

Thus Sam can take up to 14 pills without a worry.

2.7.48 Algebra Tutorial Exercise 1

The result 'sqrt(x)^2' is simplified back to x by the Calculator, but 'sqrt(x^2)' is not. (Consider what happens if $x = -4$.) If x is real, this formula could be simplified to 'abs(x)', but for general complex arguments even that is not safe. (See Section 6.6 [Declarations], page 143, for a way to tell Calc that x is known to be real.)

2.7.49 Algebra Tutorial Exercise 2

Suppose our roots are $[a, b, c]$. We want a polynomial which is zero when x is any of these values. The trivial polynomial $x - a$ is zero when $x = a$, so the product $(x-a)(x-b)(x-c)$ will do the job. We can use **a c x** to write this in a more familiar form.

```
1:  34 x - 24 x^3         1:  [1.19023, -1.19023, 0]
    .                         .


    r 2                       a P x RET


1:  [x - 1.19023, x + 1.19023, x]    1:  x*(x + 1.19023) (x - 1.19023)
    .                                    .


    V M ' x-$ RET                        V R *


1:  x^3 - 1.41666 x        1:  34 x - 24 x^3
    .                          .


    a c x RET                  24 n * a x
```

Sure enough, our answer (multiplied by a suitable constant) is the same as the original polynomial.

2.7.50 Algebra Tutorial Exercise 3

```
1:  x sin(pi x)           1:  sin(pi x) / pi^2 - x cos(pi x) / pi
    .                         .


    ' x sin(pi x) RET   m r   a i x RET


1:  [y, 1]
2:  sin(pi x) / pi^2 - x cos(pi x) / pi
    .


    ' [y,1] RET TAB


1:  [sin(pi y) / pi^2 - y cos(pi y) / pi, 1 / pi]
    .


    V M $ RET


1:  sin(pi y) / pi^2 - y cos(pi y) / pi - 1 / pi
    .


    V R -


1:  sin(3.14159 y) / 9.8696 - y cos(3.14159 y) / 3.14159 - 0.3183
    .


    =


1:  [0., -0.95493, 0.63662, -1.5915, 1.2732]
    .


    v x 5 RET  TAB  V M $ RET
```

2.7.51 Algebra Tutorial Exercise 4

The hard part is that V R + is no longer sufficient to add up all the contributions from the slices, since the slices have varying coefficients. So first we must come up with a vector of these coefficients. Here's one way:

```
2:  -1                    2:  3                     1:  [4, 2, ..., 4]
1:  [1, 2, ..., 9]        1:  [-1, 1, ..., -1]          .
    .                         .


   1 n v x 9 RET          V M ^  3 TAB              -


1:  [4, 2, ..., 4, 1]     1:  [1, 4, 2, ..., 4, 1]
    .                         .


    1 |                     1 TAB |
```

Now we compute the function values. Note that for this method we need eleven values, including both endpoints of the desired interval.

```
2:  [1, 4, 2, ..., 4, 1]
1:  [1, 1.1, 1.2,  ... , 1.8, 1.9, 2.]
    .


 11 RET 1 RET .1 RET  C-u v x


2:  [1, 4, 2, ..., 4, 1]
1:  [0., 0.084941, 0.16993, ... ]
    .


 ' sin(x) ln(x) RET   m r  p 5 RET   V M $ RET
```

Once again this calls for V M * V R +; a simple * does the same thing.

```
1:  11.22      1:  1.122      1:  0.374
    .              .              .


    *             .1 *          3 /
```

Wow! That's even better than the result from the Taylor series method.

2.7.52 Rewrites Tutorial Exercise 1

We'll use Big mode to make the formulas more readable.

```
                                         ---
                                         V 2  + 2
1:  (2 + sqrt(2)) / (1 + sqrt(2))    1:  ---------
    .                                        ---
                                         V 2  + 1


                                             .


 ' (2+sqrt(2)) / (1+sqrt(2)) RET         d B
```

Multiplying by the conjugate helps because $(a+b)(a-b) = a^2 - b^2$.

```
       ---       ---
1:  (2 + V 2 ) (V 2  - 1)
    .


 a r a/(b+c) := a*(b-c) / (b^2-c^2) RET
```

```
            ---
  1:  V 2

          .

       a r a*(b+c) := a*b + a*c
```

(We could have used `a x` instead of a rewrite rule for the second step.)

The multiply-by-conjugate rule turns out to be useful in many different circumstances, such as when the denominator involves sines and cosines or the imaginary constant `i`.

2.7.53 Rewrites Tutorial Exercise 2

Here is the rule set:

```
[ fib(n) := fib(n, 1, 1) :: integer(n) :: n >= 1,
  fib(1, x, y) := x,
  fib(n, x, y) := fib(n-1, y, x+y) ]
```

The first rule turns a one-argument `fib` that people like to write into a three-argument `fib` that makes computation easier. The second rule converts back from three-argument form once the computation is done. The third rule does the computation itself. It basically says that if x and y are two consecutive Fibonacci numbers, then y and $x + y$ are the next (overlapping) pair of Fibonacci numbers.

Notice that because the number n was "validated" by the conditions on the first rule, there is no need to put conditions on the other rules because the rule set would never get that far unless the input were valid. That further speeds computation, since no extra conditions need to be checked at every step.

Actually, a user with a nasty sense of humor could enter a bad three-argument `fib` call directly, say, '`fib(0, 1, 1)`', which would get the rules into an infinite loop. One thing that would help keep this from happening by accident would be to use something like '`ZzFib`' instead of `fib` as the name of the three-argument function.

2.7.54 Rewrites Tutorial Exercise 3

He got an infinite loop. First, Calc did as expected and rewrote '`2 + 3 x`' to '`f(2, 3, x)`'. Then it looked for ways to apply the rule again, and found that '`f(2, 3, x)`' looks like '`a + b x`' with '`a = 0`' and '`b = 1`', so it rewrote to '`f(0, 1, f(2, 3, x))`'. It then wrapped another '`f(0, 1, ...)`' around that, and so on, ad infinitum. Joe should have used `M-1 a r` to make sure the rule applied only once.

(Actually, even the first step didn't work as he expected. What Calc really gives for `M-1 a r` in this situation is '`f(3 x, 1, 2)`', treating 2 as the "variable," and '`3 x`' as a constant being added to it. While this may seem odd, it's just as valid a solution as the "obvious" one. One way to fix this would be to add the condition '`:: variable(x)`' to the rule, to make sure the thing that matches '`x`' is indeed a variable, or to change '`x`' to '`quote(x)`' on the lefthand side, so that the rule matches the actual variable '`x`' rather than letting '`x`' stand for something else.)

2.7.55 Rewrites Tutorial Exercise 4

Here is a suitable set of rules to solve the first part of the problem:

```
[ seq(n, c) := seq(n/2,  c+1) :: n%2 = 0,
  seq(n, c) := seq(3n+1, c+1) :: n%2 = 1 :: n > 1 ]
```

Given the initial formula 'seq(6, 0)', application of these rules produces the following
sequence of formulas:

```
seq( 3,  1)
seq(10,  2)
seq( 5,  3)
seq(16,  4)
seq( 8,  5)
seq( 4,  6)
seq( 2,  7)
seq( 1,  8)
```

whereupon neither of the rules match, and rewriting stops.

We can pretty this up a bit with a couple more rules:

```
[ seq(n) := seq(n, 0),
  seq(1, c) := c,
  ... ]
```

Now, given 'seq(6)' as the starting configuration, we get 8 as the result.

The change to return a vector is quite simple:

```
[ seq(n) := seq(n, []) :: integer(n) :: n > 0,
  seq(1, v) := v | 1,
  seq(n, v) := seq(n/2,  v | n) :: n%2 = 0,
  seq(n, v) := seq(3n+1, v | n) :: n%2 = 1 ]
```

Given 'seq(6)', the result is '[6, 3, 10, 5, 16, 8, 4, 2, 1]'.

Notice that the $n > 1$ guard is no longer necessary on the last rule since the $n = 1$ case
is now detected by another rule. But a guard has been added to the initial rule to make
sure the initial value is suitable before the computation begins.

While still a good idea, this guard is not as vitally important as it was for the `fib`
function, since calling, say, 'seq(x, [])' will not get into an infinite loop. Calc will not be
able to prove the symbol 'x' is either even or odd, so none of the rules will apply and the
rewrites will stop right away.

2.7.56 Rewrites Tutorial Exercise 5

If x is the sum $a + b$, then 'nterms(x)' must be 'nterms(a)' plus 'nterms(b)'. If x is not
a sum, then 'nterms(x)' $= 1$.

```
[ nterms(a + b) := nterms(a) + nterms(b),
  nterms(x)     := 1 ]
```

Here we have taken advantage of the fact that earlier rules always match before later rules;
'nterms(x)' will only be tried if we already know that 'x' is not a sum.

2.7.57 Rewrites Tutorial Exercise 6

Here is a rule set that will do the job:

```
[ a*(b + c)  := a*b + a*c,
  opt(a) O(x^n) + opt(b) O(x^m) := O(x^n) :: n <= m
     :: constant(a) :: constant(b),
  opt(a) O(x^n) + opt(b) x^m := O(x^n) :: n <= m
     :: constant(a) :: constant(b),
  a O(x^n) := O(x^n) :: constant(a),
  x^opt(m) O(x^n) := O(x^(n+m)),
  O(x^n) O(x^m) := O(x^(n+m)) ]
```

If we really want the + and * keys to operate naturally on power series, we should put these rules in `EvalRules`. For testing purposes, it is better to put them in a different variable, say, O, first.

The first rule just expands products of sums so that the rest of the rules can assume they have an expanded-out polynomial to work with. Note that this rule does not mention 'O' at all, so it will apply to any product-of-sum it encounters—this rule may surprise you if you put it into `EvalRules`!

In the second rule, the sum of two O's is changed to the smaller O. The optional constant coefficients are there mostly so that 'O(x^2) - O(x^3)' and 'O(x^3) - O(x^2)' are handled as well as 'O(x^2) + O(x^3)'.

The third rule absorbs higher powers of 'x' into O's.

The fourth rule says that a constant times a negligible quantity is still negligible. (This rule will also match 'O(x^3) / 4', with 'a = 1/4'.)

The fifth rule rewrites, for example, 'x^2 O(x^3)' to 'O(x^5)'. (It is easy to see that if one of these forms is negligible, the other is, too.) Notice the 'x^opt(m)' to pick up terms like 'x O(x^3)'. Optional powers will match 'x' as 'x^1' but not 1 as 'x^0'. This turns out to be exactly what we want here.

The sixth rule is the corresponding rule for products of two O's.

Another way to solve this problem would be to create a new "data type" that represents truncated power series. We might represent these as function calls 'series(*coefs*, *x*)' where *coefs* is a vector of coefficients for x^0, x^1, x^2, and so on. Rules would exist for sums and products of such `series` objects, and as an optional convenience could also know how to combine a `series` object with a normal polynomial. (With this, and with a rule that rewrites 'O(x^n)' to the equivalent `series` form, you could still enter power series in exactly the same notation as before.) Operations on such objects would probably be more efficient, although the objects would be a bit harder to read.

Some other symbolic math programs provide a power series data type similar to this. Mathematica, for example, has an object that looks like 'PowerSeries[*x*, *x0*, *coefs*, *nmin*, *nmax*, *den*]', where *x0* is the point about which the power series is taken (we've been assuming this was always zero), and *nmin*, *nmax*, and *den* allow pseudo-power-series with fractional or negative powers. Also, the `PowerSeries` objects have a special display format that makes them look like '2 x^2 + O(x^4)' when they are printed out. (See Section 6.8.10 [Compositions], page 168, for a way to do this in Calc, although for something as involved as this it would probably be better to write the formatting routine in Lisp.)

2.7.58 Programming Tutorial Exercise 1

Just enter the formula 'ninteg(sin(t)/t, t, 0, x)', type *Z F*, and answer the questions. Since this formula contains two variables, the default argument list will be '(t x)'. We want to change this to '(x)' since *t* is really a dummy variable to be used within `ninteg`.

The exact keystrokes are *Z F s Si RET RET C-b C-b DEL DEL RET y*. (The *C-b C-b DEL DEL* are what fix the argument list.)

2.7.59 Programming Tutorial Exercise 2

One way is to move the number to the top of the stack, operate on it, then move it back: *C-x (M-TAB n M-TAB M-TAB C-x)*.

Another way is to negate the top three stack entries, then negate again the top two stack entries: *C-x (M-3 n M-2 n C-x)*.

Finally, it turns out that a negative prefix argument causes a command like *n* to operate on the specified stack entry only, which is just what we want: *C-x (M-- 3 n C-x)*.

Just for kicks, let's also do it algebraically: *C-x (' -$$$, $$, $ RET C-x)*.

2.7.60 Programming Tutorial Exercise 3

Each of these functions can be computed using the stack, or using algebraic entry, whichever way you prefer:

Computing $\dfrac{\sin x}{x}$:

Using the stack: *C-x (RET S TAB / C-x)*.

Using algebraic entry: *C-x (' sin($)/$ RET C-x)*.

Computing the logarithm:

Using the stack: *C-x (TAB B C-x)*

Using algebraic entry: *C-x (' log($,$$) RET C-x)*.

Computing the vector of integers:

Using the stack: *C-x (1 RET 1 C-u v x C-x)*. (Recall that *C-u v x* takes the vector size, starting value, and increment from the stack.)

Alternatively: *C-x (~ v x C-x)*. (The ~ key pops a number from the stack and uses it as the prefix argument for the next command.)

Using algebraic entry: *C-x (' index($) RET C-x)*.

2.7.61 Programming Tutorial Exercise 4

Here's one way: *C-x (RET V R + TAB v l / C-x)*.

2.7.62 Programming Tutorial Exercise 5

```
2:  1              1:  1.61803398502       2:  1.61803398502
1:  20                 .                   1:  1.61803398875
    .                                          .


   1 RET 20         Z < & 1 + Z >            I H P
```

This answer is quite accurate.

2.7.63 Programming Tutorial Exercise 6

Here is the matrix:

```
[ [ 0, 1 ]    * [a, b] = [b, a + b]
  [ 1, 1 ] ]
```

Thus '[0, 1; 1, 1]^n * [1, 1]' computes Fibonacci numbers $n + 1$ and $n + 2$. Here's one program that does the job:

```
C-x ( ' [0, 1; 1, 1] ^ ($-1) * [1, 1] RET v u DEL C-x )
```

This program is quite efficient because Calc knows how to raise a matrix (or other value) to the power n in only $\log_2 n$ steps. For example, this program can compute the 1000th Fibonacci number (a 209-digit integer!) in about 10 steps; even though the *Z < ... Z >*

solution had much simpler steps, it would have required so many steps that it would not have been practical.

2.7.64 Programming Tutorial Exercise 7

The trick here is to compute the harmonic numbers differently, so that the loop counter itself accumulates the sum of reciprocals. We use a separate variable to hold the integer counter.

```
1:  1          2:  1        1:  .
    .          1:  4
                   .

    1 t 1        1 RET 4      Z ( t 2 r 1 1 + s 1 & Z )
```

The body of the loop goes as follows: First save the harmonic sum so far in variable 2. Then delete it from the stack; the for loop itself will take care of remembering it for us. Next, recall the count from variable 1, add one to it, and feed its reciprocal to the for loop to use as the step value. The for loop will increase the "loop counter" by that amount and keep going until the loop counter exceeds 4.

```
2:  31              3:  31
1:  3.99498713092   2:  3.99498713092
    .               1:  4.02724519544
                        .

    r 1 r 2             RET 31 & +
```

Thus we find that the 30th harmonic number is 3.99, and the 31st harmonic number is 4.02.

2.7.65 Programming Tutorial Exercise 8

The first step is to compute the derivative $f'(x)$ and thus the formula $x - \dfrac{f(x)}{f'(x)}$.

(Because this definition is long, it will be repeated in concise form below. You can use C-x * m to load it from there. While you are entering a Z ` Z ' body in a macro, Calc simply collects keystrokes without executing them. In the following diagrams we'll pretend Calc actually executed the keystrokes as you typed them, just for purposes of illustration.)

```
2:  sin(cos(x)) - 0.5        3:  4.5
1:  4.5                      2:  sin(cos(x)) - 0.5
    .                        1:  -(sin(x) cos(cos(x)))
                                 .

  ' sin(cos(x))-0.5 RET 4.5   m r  C-x ( Z `  TAB RET a d x RET


2:  4.5
1:  x + (sin(cos(x)) - 0.5) / sin(x) cos(cos(x))
    .

    /  ' x RET TAB -   t 1
```

Now, we enter the loop. We'll use a repeat loop with a 20-repetition limit just in case the method fails to converge for some reason. (Normally, the Z / command will stop the loop before all 20 repetitions are done.)

```
   1:  4.5              3:  4.5                       2:  4.5
         .              2:  x + (sin(cos(x)) ...      1:  5.24196456928
                        1:  4.5                             .
                              .

     20 Z <              RET r 1 TAB                   s l x RET
```

This is the new guess for x. Now we compare it with the old one to see if we've converged.

```
   3:  5.24196       2:  5.24196       1:  5.24196       1:  5.26345856348
   2:  5.24196       1:  0                   .                  .
   1:  4.5                 .
         .

     RET M-TAB          a =               Z /               Z > Z ' C-x )
```

The loop converges in just a few steps to this value. To check the result, we can simply substitute it back into the equation.

```
   2:  5.26345856348
   1:  0.499999999997
         .

     RET ' sin(cos($)) RET
```

Let's test the new definition again:

```
   2:  x^2 - 9            1:  3.
   1:  1                        .
         .

     ' x^2-9 RET 1           X
```

Once again, here's the full Newton's Method definition:

```
   C-x ( Z `  TAB RET a d x RET  /  ' x RET TAB -  t 1
            20 Z <  RET r 1 TAB  s l x RET
                    RET M-TAB  a =  Z /
               Z >
          Z '
   C-x )
```

It turns out that Calc has a built-in command for applying a formula repeatedly until it converges to a number. See Section 9.8.4 [Nesting and Fixed Points], page 239, to see how to use it.

Also, of course, a R is a built-in command that uses Newton's method (among others) to look for numerical solutions to any equation. See Section 10.7.1 [Root Finding], page 273.

2.7.66 Programming Tutorial Exercise 9

The first step is to adjust z to be greater than 5. A simple "for" loop will do the job here. If z is less than 5, we reduce the problem using $\psi(z) = \psi(z+1) - 1/z$. on to compute $\psi(z+1)$, and remember to add back a factor of $-1/z$ when we're done. This step is repeated until $z > 5$.

(Because this definition is long, it will be repeated in concise form below. You can use C-x * m to load it from there. While you are entering a Z ` Z ' body in a macro, Calc simply collects keystrokes without executing them. In the following diagrams we'll pretend Calc actually executed the keystrokes as you typed them, just for purposes of illustration.)

```
1:  1.              1:  1.
    .                   .

 1.0 RET      C-x ( Z `  s 1  0 t 2
```

Here, variable 1 holds z and variable 2 holds the adjustment factor. If $z < 5$, we use a loop to increase it.

(By the way, we started with '1.0' instead of the integer 1 because otherwise the calculation below will try to do exact fractional arithmetic, and will never converge because fractions compare equal only if they are exactly equal, not just equal to within the current precision.)

```
3:  1.      2:  1.      1:  6.
2:  1.      1:  1           .
1:  5           .
    .

   RET 5       a <     Z [  5 Z ( & s + 2  1 s + 1  1 Z ) r 1 Z ]
```

Now we compute the initial part of the sum: $\ln z - \frac{1}{2z}$ minus the adjustment factor.

```
2:  1.79175946923      2:  1.7084261359      1:  -0.57490719743
1:  0.0833333333333    1:  2.28333333333         .
    .                      .

   L  r 1 2 * &           - r 2                  -
```

Now we evaluate the series. We'll use another "for" loop counting up the value of $2n$. (Calc does have a summation command, a +, but we'll use loops just to get more practice with them.)

```
3:  -0.5749     3:  -0.5749     4:  -0.5749     2:  -0.5749
2:  2           2:  1:6         3:  1:6         1:  2.3148e-3
1:  40          1:  2          2:  2               .
    .               .          1:  36.
                                   .

   2 RET 40       Z ( RET k b TAB    RET r 1 TAB ^      * /
```

```
3:  -0.5749     3:  -0.5772     2:  -0.5772     1:  -0.577215664892
2:  -0.5749     2:  -0.5772     1:  0               .
1:  2.3148e-3   1:  -0.5749         .
    .               .

   TAB RET M-TAB     - RET M-TAB     a =     Z /    2 Z ) Z ' C-x )
```

This is the value of $-\gamma$, with a slight bit of roundoff error. To get a full 12 digits, let's use a higher precision:

```
2:  -0.577215664892    2:  -0.577215664892
1:  1.                 1:  -0.577215664901532

   1. RET                 p 16 RET X
```

Here's the complete sequence of keystrokes:

```
C-x ( Z ` s 1 0 t 2
        RET 5 a < Z [ 5 Z ( & s + 2 1 s + 1 1 Z ) r 1 Z ]
        L r 1 2 * & - r 2 -
        2 RET 40  Z (  RET k b TAB RET r 1 TAB ^ * /
                       TAB RET M-TAB - RET M-TAB a = Z /
                2  Z )
       Z '
C-x )
```

2.7.67 Programming Tutorial Exercise 10

Taking the derivative of a term of the form x^n will produce a term like nx^{n-1}. Taking the derivative of a constant produces zero. From this it is easy to see that the nth derivative of a polynomial, evaluated at $x = 0$, will equal the coefficient on the x^n term times $n!$.

(Because this definition is long, it will be repeated in concise form below. You can use C-x * m to load it from there. While you are entering a Z ` Z ' body in a macro, Calc simply collects keystrokes without executing them. In the following diagrams we'll pretend Calc actually executed the keystrokes as you typed them, just for purposes of illustration.)

```
2:  5 x^4 + (x + 1)^2        3:  5 x^4 + (x + 1)^2
1:  6                        2:  0
       .                     1:  6
                                    .
```

```
  ' 5 x^4 + (x+1)^2 RET 6       C-x ( Z ` [ ] t 1 0 TAB
```

Variable 1 will accumulate the vector of coefficients.

```
2:  0               3:  0               2:  5 x^4 + ...
1:  5 x^4 + ...     2:  5 x^4 + ...     1:  1
       .            1:  1                      .
                           .
```

```
    Z ( TAB        RET 0 s 1 x RET        M-TAB ! / s | 1
```

Note that s | 1 appends the top-of-stack value to the vector in a variable; it is completely analogous to s + 1. We could have written instead, r 1 TAB | t 1.

```
1:  20 x^3 + 2 x + 2     1:  0        1:  [1, 2, 1, 0, 5, 0, 0]
       .                       .             .
```

```
    a d x RET              1 Z )        DEL r 1 Z ' C-x )
```

To convert back, a simple method is just to map the coefficients against a table of powers of x.

```
2:  [1, 2, 1, 0, 5, 0, 0]     2:  [1, 2, 1, 0, 5, 0, 0]
1:  6                         1:  [0, 1, 2, 3, 4, 5, 6]
       .                             .
```

```
    6 RET                     1 + 0 RET 1 C-u v x
```

```
2:  [1, 2, 1, 0, 5, 0, 0]     2:  1 + 2 x + x^2 + 5 x^4
1:  [1, x, x^2, x^3, ... ]           .
       .
```

```
    ' x RET TAB V M ^              *
```

Once again, here are the whole polynomial to/from vector programs:

```
C-x ( Z ` [ ] t 1 0 TAB
          Z ( TAB RET 0 s 1 x RET M-TAB ! / s | 1
              a d x RET
          1 Z ) r 1
      Z '
C-x )


C-x ( 1 + 0 RET 1 C-u v x ' x RET TAB V M ^ *  C-x )
```

2.7.68 Programming Tutorial Exercise 11

First we define a dummy program to go on the *z s* key. The true *z s* key is supposed to take two numbers from the stack and return one number, so DEL as a dummy definition will make sure the stack comes out right.

```
2:  4              1:  4                          2:  4
1:  2                  .                          1:  2
    .                                                 .


    4 RET 2        C-x ( DEL C-x )  Z K s RET        2
```

The last step replaces the 2 that was eaten during the creation of the dummy *z s* command. Now we move on to the real definition. The recurrence needs to be rewritten slightly, to the form $s(n,m) = s(n-1, m-1) - (n-1)s(n-1, m)$.

(Because this definition is long, it will be repeated in concise form below. You can use *C-x * m* to load it from there.)

```
2:  4      4:  4      3:  4      2:  4
1:  2      3:  2      2:  2      1:  2
    .      2:  4      1:  0          .
           1:  2          .
               .


   C-x (       M-2 RET        a =        Z [  DEL DEL 1 Z :
```

```
4:  4      2:  4                2:  3      4:  3      4:  3      3:  3
3:  2      1:  2                1:  2      3:  2      3:  2      2:  2
2:  2          .                    .      2:  3      2:  3      1:  3
1:  0                                      1:  2      1:  1          .
    .                                          .          .


  RET 0   a = Z [  DEL DEL 0 Z :  TAB 1 - TAB   M-2 RET     1 -       z s
```

(Note that the value 3 that our dummy *z s* produces is not correct; it is merely a placeholder that will do just as well for now.)

```
3:  3              4:  3          3:  3      2:  3      1:  -6
2:  3              3:  3          2:  3      1:  9          .
1:  2              2:  3          1:  3          .
    .              1:  2              .
                       .


 M-TAB M-TAB      TAB RET M-TAB       z s          *          -
```

```
   1:  -6                          2:  4          1:  11      2:  11
       .                           1:  2              .       1:  11
                                       .                          .


     Z ] Z ] C-x )    Z K s RET      DEL 4 RET 2      z s      M-RET k s
```

Even though the result that we got during the definition was highly bogus, once the definition is complete the **z s** command gets the right answers.

Here's the full program once again:

```
C-x (  M-2 RET a =
       Z [  DEL DEL 1
       Z :  RET 0 a =
            Z [  DEL DEL 0
            Z :  TAB 1 - TAB M-2 RET 1 - z s
                 M-TAB M-TAB TAB RET M-TAB z s * -
            Z ]
       Z ]
C-x )
```

You can read this definition using *C-x * m* (read-kbd-macro) followed by *Z K s*, without having to make a dummy definition first, because **read-kbd-macro** doesn't need to execute the definition as it reads it in. For this reason, C-x * m is often the easiest way to create recursive programs in Calc.

2.7.69 Programming Tutorial Exercise 12

This turns out to be a much easier way to solve the problem. Let's denote Stirling numbers as calls of the function 's'.

First, we store the rewrite rules corresponding to the definition of Stirling numbers in a convenient variable:

```
s e StirlingRules RET
[ s(n,n) := 1  :: n >= 0,
  s(n,0) := 0  :: n > 0,
  s(n,m) := s(n-1,m-1) - (n-1) s(n-1,m) :: n >= m :: m >= 1 ]
C-c C-c
```

Now, it's just a matter of applying the rules:

```
   2:  4            1:  s(4, 2)              1:  11
   1:  2                .                        .
       .


     4 RET 2      C-x (  ' s($$,$) RET    a r StirlingRules RET  C-x )
```

As in the case of the **fib** rules, it would be useful to put these rules in **EvalRules** and to add a ':: remember' condition to the last rule.

3 Introduction

This chapter is the beginning of the Calc reference manual. It covers basic concepts such as the stack, algebraic and numeric entry, undo, numeric prefix arguments, etc.

3.1 Basic Commands

To start the Calculator in its standard interface, type M-x calc. By default this creates a pair of small windows, *Calculator* and *Calc Trail*. The former displays the contents of the Calculator stack and is manipulated exclusively through Calc commands. It is possible (though not usually necessary) to create several Calc mode buffers each of which has an independent stack, undo list, and mode settings. There is exactly one Calc Trail buffer; it records a list of the results of all calculations that have been done. The Calc Trail buffer uses a variant of Calc mode, so Calculator commands still work when the trail buffer's window is selected. It is possible to turn the trail window off, but the *Calc Trail* buffer itself still exists and is updated silently. See Section 5.3 [Trail Commands], page 135.

In most installations, the C-x * c key sequence is a more convenient way to start the Calculator. Also, C-x * * is a synonym for C-x * c unless you last used Calc in its Keypad mode.

Most Calc commands use one or two keystrokes. Lower- and upper-case letters are distinct. Commands may also be entered in full M-x form; for some commands this is the only form. As a convenience, the x key (calc-execute-extended-command) is like M-x except that it enters the initial string 'calc-' for you. For example, the following key sequences are equivalent: S, M-x calc-sin RET, x sin RET.

Although Calc is designed to be used from the keyboard, some of Calc's more common commands are available from a menu. In the menu, the arguments to the functions are given by referring to their stack level numbers.

The Calculator exists in many parts. When you type C-x * c, the Emacs "auto-load" mechanism will bring in only the first part, which contains the basic arithmetic functions. The other parts will be auto-loaded the first time you use the more advanced commands like trig functions or matrix operations. This is done to improve the response time of the Calculator in the common case when all you need to do is a little arithmetic. If for some reason the Calculator fails to load an extension module automatically, you can force it to load all the extensions by using the C-x * L (calc-load-everything) command. See Chapter 6 [Mode Settings], page 137.

If you type M-x calc or C-x * c with any numeric prefix argument, the Calculator is loaded if necessary, but it is not actually started. If the argument is positive, the calc-ext extensions are also loaded if necessary. User-written Lisp code that wishes to make use of Calc's arithmetic routines can use '(calc 0)' or '(calc 1)' to auto-load the Calculator.

If you type C-x * b, then next time you use C-x * c you will get a Calculator that uses the full height of the Emacs screen. When full-screen mode is on, C-x * c runs the full-calc command instead of calc. From the Unix shell you can type 'emacs -f full-calc' to start a new Emacs specifically for use as a calculator. When Calc is started from the Emacs command line like this, Calc's normal "quit" commands actually quit Emacs itself.

The C-x * o command is like C-x * c except that the Calc window is not actually selected. If you are already in the Calc window, C-x * o switches you out of it. (The regular

Emacs *C-x o* command would also work for this, but it has a tendency to drop you into the Calc Trail window instead, which *C-x * o* takes care not to do.)

For one quick calculation, you can type *C-x * q* (`quick-calc`) which prompts you for a formula (like '2+3/4'). The result is displayed at the bottom of the Emacs screen without ever creating any special Calculator windows. See Section 3.6 [Quick Calculator], page 110.

Finally, if you are using the X window system you may want to try *C-x * k* (`calc-keypad`) which runs Calc with a "calculator keypad" picture as well as a stack display. Click on the keys with the mouse to operate the calculator. See Chapter 15 [Keypad Mode], page 345.

The *q* key (`calc-quit`) exits Calc mode and closes the Calculator's window(s). It does not delete the Calculator buffers. If you type *M-x calc* again, the Calculator will reappear with the contents of the stack intact. Typing *C-x * c* or *C-x * * again from inside the Calculator buffer is equivalent to executing `calc-quit`; you can think of *C-x * * as toggling the Calculator on and off.

The *C-x * x* command also turns the Calculator off, no matter which user interface (standard, Keypad, or Embedded) is currently active. It also cancels `calc-edit` mode if used from there.

The *d SPC* key sequence (`calc-refresh`) redraws the contents of the Calculator buffer from memory. Use this if the contents of the buffer have been damaged somehow.

The *o* key (`calc-realign`) moves the cursor back to its "home" position at the bottom of the Calculator buffer.

The *<* and *>* keys are bound to `calc-scroll-left` and `calc-scroll-right`. These are just like the normal horizontal scrolling commands except that they scroll one half-screen at a time by default. (Calc formats its output to fit within the bounds of the window whenever it can.)

The *{* and *}* keys are bound to `calc-scroll-down` and `calc-scroll-up`. They scroll up or down by one-half the height of the Calc window.

The *C-x * 0* command (`calc-reset`; that's *C-x * followed by a zero) resets the Calculator to its initial state. This clears the stack, resets all the modes to their initial values (the values that were saved with *m m* (`calc-save-modes`)), clears the caches (see Section 3.11.3 [Caches], page 114), and so on. (It does *not* erase the values of any variables.) With an argument of 0, Calc will be reset to its default state; namely, the modes will be given their default values. With a positive prefix argument, *C-x * 0* preserves the contents of the stack but resets everything else to its initial state; with a negative prefix argument, *C-x * 0* preserves the contents of the stack but resets everything else to its default state.

3.2 Help Commands

The *?* key (`calc-help`) displays a series of brief help messages. Some keys (such as *b* and *d*) are prefix keys, like Emacs's *ESC* and *C-x* prefixes. You can type *?* after a prefix to see a list of commands beginning with that prefix. (If the message includes '[MORE]', press *?* again to see additional commands for that prefix.)

The *h h* (`calc-full-help`) command displays all the *?* responses at once. When printed, this makes a nice, compact (three pages) summary of Calc keystrokes.

In general, the *h* key prefix introduces various commands that provide help within Calc. Many of the *h* key functions are Calc-specific analogues to the *C-h* functions for Emacs help.

The *h i* (`calc-info`) command runs the Emacs Info system to read this manual on-line. This is basically the same as typing *C-h i* (the regular way to run the Info system), then, if Info is not already in the Calc manual, selecting the beginning of the manual. The *C-x * i* command is another way to read the Calc manual; it is different from *h i* in that it works any time, not just inside Calc. The plain *i* key is also equivalent to *h i*, though this key is obsolete and may be replaced with a different command in a future version of Calc.

The *h t* (`calc-tutorial`) command runs the Info system on the Tutorial section of the Calc manual. It is like *h i*, except that it selects the starting node of the tutorial rather than the beginning of the whole manual. (It actually selects the node "Interactive Tutorial" which tells a few things about using the Info system before going on to the actual tutorial.) The *C-x * t* key is equivalent to *h t* (but it works at all times).

The *h s* (`calc-info-summary`) command runs the Info system on the Summary node of the Calc manual. See Appendix E [Summary], page 443. The *C-x * s* key is equivalent to *h s*.

The *h k* (`calc-describe-key`) command looks up a key sequence in the Calc manual. For example, *h k H a S* looks up the documentation on the *H a S* (`calc-solve-for`) command. This works by looking up the textual description of the key(s) in the Key Index of the manual, then jumping to the node indicated by the index.

Most Calc commands do not have traditional Emacs documentation strings, since the *h k* command is both more convenient and more instructive. This means the regular Emacs *C-h k* (`describe-key`) command will not be useful for Calc keystrokes.

The *h c* (`calc-describe-key-briefly`) command reads a key sequence and displays a brief one-line description of it at the bottom of the screen. It looks for the key sequence in the Summary node of the Calc manual; if it doesn't find the sequence there, it acts just like its regular Emacs counterpart *C-h c* (`describe-key-briefly`). For example, *h c H a S* gives the description:

```
H a S runs calc-solve-for:  a `H a S' v  => fsolve(a,v)  (?=notes)
```

which means the command *H a S* or *H M-x calc-solve-for* takes a value *a* from the stack, prompts for a value *v*, then applies the algebraic function **fsolve** to these values. The '`?=notes`' message means you can now type *?* to see additional notes from the summary that apply to this command.

The *h f* (`calc-describe-function`) command looks up an algebraic function or a command name in the Calc manual. Enter an algebraic function name to look up that function in the Function Index or enter a command name beginning with '`calc-`' to look it up in the Command Index. This command will also look up operator symbols that can appear in algebraic formulas, like '`%`' and '`=>`'.

The *h v* (`calc-describe-variable`) command looks up a variable in the Calc manual. Enter a variable name like `pi` or `PlotRejects`.

The *h b* (`calc-describe-bindings`) command is just like *C-h b*, except that only local (Calc-related) key bindings are listed.

The *h n* or *h C-n* (`calc-view-news`) command displays the "news" or change history of Emacs, and jumps to the most recent portion concerning Calc (if present). For older history, see the file `etc/CALC-NEWS` in the Emacs distribution.

The *h C-c*, *h C-d*, and *h C-w* keys display copying, distribution, and warranty information about Calc. These work by pulling up the appropriate parts of the "Copying" or "Reporting Bugs" sections of the manual.

3.3 Stack Basics

Calc uses RPN notation. If you are not familiar with RPN, see Section 2.1.1 [RPN Tutorial], page 17.

To add the numbers 1 and 2 in Calc you would type the keys: *1 RET 2 +*. (RET corresponds to the ENTER key on most calculators.) The first three keystrokes "push" the numbers 1 and 2 onto the stack. The + key always "pops" the top two numbers from the stack, adds them, and pushes the result (3) back onto the stack. This number is ready for further calculations: *5 -* pushes 5 onto the stack, then pops the 3 and 5, subtracts them, and pushes the result (-2).

Note that the "top" of the stack actually appears at the *bottom* of the buffer. A line containing a single '.' character signifies the end of the buffer; Calculator commands operate on the number(s) directly above this line. The *d t* (calc-truncate-stack) command allows you to move the '.' marker up and down in the stack; see Section 6.7.8 [Truncating the Stack], page 157.

Stack elements are numbered consecutively, with number 1 being the top of the stack. These line numbers are ordinarily displayed on the lefthand side of the window. The *d l* (calc-line-numbering) command controls whether these numbers appear. (Line numbers may be turned off since they slow the Calculator down a bit and also clutter the display.)

The unshifted letter *o* (calc-realign) command repositions the cursor to its top-of-stack "home" position. It also undoes any horizontal scrolling in the window. If you give it a numeric prefix argument, it instead moves the cursor to the specified stack element.

The RET (or equivalent SPC) key is only required to separate two consecutive numbers. (After all, if you typed *1 2* by themselves the Calculator would enter the number 12.) If you press RET or SPC *not* right after typing a number, the key duplicates the number on the top of the stack. *RET ** is thus a handy way to square a number.

The DEL key pops and throws away the top number on the stack. The TAB key swaps the top two objects on the stack. See Chapter 5 [Stack and Trail], page 133, for descriptions of these and other stack-related commands.

3.4 Numeric Entry

Pressing a digit or other numeric key begins numeric entry using the minibuffer. The number is pushed on the stack when you press the RET or SPC keys. If you press any other non-numeric key, the number is pushed onto the stack and the appropriate operation is performed. If you press a numeric key which is not valid, the key is ignored.

There are three different concepts corresponding to the word "minus," typified by $a - b$ (subtraction), $-x$ (change-sign), and -5 (negative number). Calc uses three different keys for these operations, respectively: -, *n*, and _ (the underscore). The - key subtracts the two numbers on the top of the stack. The *n* key changes the sign of the number on the top of the stack or the number currently being entered. The _ key begins entry of a negative number or changes the sign of the number currently being entered. The following sequences all enter the number −5 onto the stack: *0 RET 5 -*, *5 n RET*, *5 RET n*, *_ 5 RET*, *5 _ RET*.

Some other keys are active during numeric entry, such as # for non-decimal numbers, : for fractions, and @ for HMS forms. These notations are described later in this manual with the corresponding data types. See Chapter 4 [Data Types], page 117.

During numeric entry, the only editing key available is DEL.

3.5 Algebraic Entry

The ' (`calc-algebraic-entry`) command can be used to enter calculations in algebraic form. This is accomplished by typing the apostrophe key, ', followed by the expression in standard format:

```
' 2+3*4 RET.
```

This will compute $2 + (3 \times 4) = 14$ and push it on the stack. If you wish you can ignore the RPN aspect of Calc altogether and simply enter algebraic expressions in this way. You may want to use DEL every so often to clear previous results off the stack.

You can press the apostrophe key during normal numeric entry to switch the half-entered number into Algebraic entry mode. One reason to do this would be to fix a typo, as the full Emacs cursor motion and editing keys are available during algebraic entry but not during numeric entry.

In the same vein, during either numeric or algebraic entry you can press ` (grave accent) to switch to `calc-edit` mode, where you complete your half-finished entry in a separate buffer. See Section 5.2 [Editing Stack Entries], page 134.

If you prefer algebraic entry, you can use the command *m a* (`calc-algebraic-mode`) to set Algebraic mode. In this mode, digits and other keys that would normally start numeric entry instead start full algebraic entry; as long as your formula begins with a digit you can omit the apostrophe. Open parentheses and square brackets also begin algebraic entry. You can still do RPN calculations in this mode, but you will have to press RET to terminate every number: *2 RET 3 RET * 4 RET +* would accomplish the same thing as *2*3+4 RET*.

If you give a numeric prefix argument like *C-u* to the *m a* command, it enables Incomplete Algebraic mode; this is like regular Algebraic mode except that it applies to the (and [keys only. Numeric keys still begin a numeric entry in this mode.

The *m t* (`calc-total-algebraic-mode`) gives you an even stronger algebraic-entry mode, in which *all* regular letter and punctuation keys begin algebraic entry. Use this if you prefer typing *sqrt( )* instead of *Q*, *factor( )* instead of *a f*, and so on. To type regular Calc commands when you are in Total Algebraic mode, hold down the META key. Thus *M-q* is the command to quit Calc, *M-p* sets the precision, and *M-m t* (or *M-m M-t*, if you prefer) turns Total Algebraic mode back off again. Meta keys also terminate algebraic entry, so that *2+3 M-S* is equivalent to *2+3 RET M-S*. The symbol 'Alg*' will appear in the mode line whenever you are in this mode.

Pressing ' (the apostrophe) a second time re-enters the previous algebraic formula. You can then use the normal Emacs editing keys to modify this formula to your liking before pressing RET.

Within a formula entered from the keyboard, the symbol $ represents the number on the top of the stack. If an entered formula contains any $ characters, the Calculator replaces the top of stack with that formula rather than simply pushing the formula onto the stack. Thus, ' *1+2 RET* pushes 3 on the stack, and *$*2 RET* replaces it with 6. Note that the $ key always initiates algebraic entry; the ' is unnecessary if $ is the first character in the new formula.

Higher stack elements can be accessed from an entered formula with the symbols *$$*, *$$$*, and so on. The number of stack elements removed (to be replaced by the entered values) equals the number of dollar signs in the longest such symbol in the formula. For example, '$$+$$$' adds the second and third stack elements, replacing the top three elements with the answer. (All information about the top stack element is thus lost since no single '$' appears in this formula.)

A slightly different way to refer to stack elements is with a dollar sign followed by a number: '$1', '$2', and so on are much like '$', '$$', etc., except that stack entries referred to numerically are not replaced by the algebraic entry. That is, while '$+1' replaces 5 on the stack with 6, '$1+1' leaves the 5 on the stack and pushes an additional 6.

If a sequence of formulas are entered separated by commas, each formula is pushed onto the stack in turn. For example, '1,2,3' pushes those three numbers onto the stack (leaving the 3 at the top), and '$+1,$-1' replaces a 5 on the stack with 4 followed by 6. Also, '$,$$' exchanges the top two elements of the stack, just like the TAB key.

You can finish an algebraic entry with *M-=* or *M-RET* instead of RET. This uses = to evaluate the variables in each formula that goes onto the stack. (Thus ' *pi RET* pushes the variable 'pi', but ' *pi M-RET* pushes 3.1415.)

If you finish your algebraic entry by pressing LFD (or *C-j*) instead of RET, Calc disables simplification (as if by *m 0*; see Section 6.5 [Simplification Modes], page 142) while the entry is being pushed on the stack. Thus ' *1+2 RET* pushes 3 on the stack, but ' *1+2 LFD* pushes the formula $1+2$; you might then press = when it is time to evaluate this formula.

3.6 "Quick Calculator" Mode

There is another way to invoke the Calculator if all you need to do is make one or two quick calculations. Type *C-x * q* (or *M-x quick-calc*), then type any formula as an algebraic entry. The Calculator will compute the result and display it in the echo area, without ever actually putting up a Calc window.

You can use the $ character in a Quick Calculator formula to refer to the previous Quick Calculator result. Older results are not retained; the Quick Calculator has no effect on the full Calculator's stack or trail. If you compute a result and then forget what it was, just run *C-x * q* again and enter '$' as the formula.

If this is the first time you have used the Calculator in this Emacs session, the *C-x * q* command will create the *Calculator* buffer and perform all the usual initializations; it simply will refrain from putting that buffer up in a new window. The Quick Calculator refers to the *Calculator* buffer for all mode settings. Thus, for example, to set the precision that the Quick Calculator uses, simply run the full Calculator momentarily and use the regular *p* command.

If you use *C-x * q* from inside the Calculator buffer, the effect is the same as pressing the apostrophe key (algebraic entry).

The result of a Quick calculation is placed in the Emacs "kill ring" as well as being displayed. A subsequent *C-y* command will yank the result into the editing buffer. You can also use this to yank the result into the next C-x * q input line as a more explicit alternative to $ notation, or to yank the result into the Calculator stack after typing C-x * c.

If you give a prefix argument to C-x * q or finish your formula by typing LFD (or C-j) instead of RET, the result is inserted immediately into the current buffer rather than going into the kill ring.

Quick Calculator results are actually evaluated as if by the = key (which replaces variable names by their stored values, if any). If the formula you enter is an assignment to a variable using the ':=' operator, say, 'foo := 2 + 3' or 'foo := foo + 1', then the result of the evaluation is stored in that Calc variable. See Chapter 12 [Store and Recall], page 323.

If the result is an integer and the current display radix is decimal, the number will also be displayed in hex, octal and binary formats. If the integer is in the range from 1 to 126, it will also be displayed as an ASCII character.

For example, the quoted character '"x"' produces the vector result '[120]' (because 120 is the ASCII code of the lower-case "x"; see Section 4.7 [Strings], page 120). Since this is a vector, not an integer, it is displayed only according to the current mode settings. But running Quick Calc again and entering '120' will produce the result '120 (16#78, 8#170, x)' which shows the number in its decimal, hexadecimal, octal, and ASCII forms.

Please note that the Quick Calculator is not any faster at loading or computing the answer than the full Calculator; the name "quick" merely refers to the fact that it's much less hassle to use for small calculations.

3.7 Numeric Prefix Arguments

Many Calculator commands use numeric prefix arguments. Some, such as d s (calc-sci-notation), set a parameter to the value of the prefix argument or use a default if you don't use a prefix. Others (like d f (calc-fix-notation)) require an argument and prompt for a number if you don't give one as a prefix.

As a rule, stack-manipulation commands accept a numeric prefix argument which is interpreted as an index into the stack. A positive argument operates on the top n stack entries; a negative argument operates on the nth stack entry in isolation; and a zero argument operates on the entire stack.

Most commands that perform computations (such as the arithmetic and scientific functions) accept a numeric prefix argument that allows the operation to be applied across many stack elements. For unary operations (that is, functions of one argument like absolute value or complex conjugate), a positive prefix argument applies that function to the top n stack entries simultaneously, and a negative argument applies it to the nth stack entry only. For binary operations (functions of two arguments like addition, GCD, and vector concatenation), a positive prefix argument "reduces" the function across the top n stack elements (for example, C-u 5 + sums the top 5 stack entries; see Section 9.8 [Reducing and Mapping], page 235), and a negative argument maps the next-to-top n stack elements with the top stack element as a second argument (for example, 7 c-u -5 + adds 7 to the top 5 stack elements). This feature is not available for operations which use the numeric prefix argument for some other purpose.

Numeric prefixes are specified the same way as always in Emacs: Press a sequence of META-digits, or press ESC followed by digits, or press C-u followed by digits. Some commands treat plain C-u (without any actual digits) specially.

You can type ~ (`calc-num-prefix`) to pop an integer from the top of the stack and enter it as the numeric prefix for the next command. For example, *C-u 16 p* sets the precision to 16 digits; an alternate (silly) way to do this would be *2 RET 4 ^ ~ p*, i.e., compute 2 to the fourth power and set the precision to that value.

Conversely, if you have typed a numeric prefix argument the ~ key pushes it onto the stack in the form of an integer.

3.8 Undoing Mistakes

The shift-*U* key (`calc-undo`) undoes the most recent operation. If that operation added or dropped objects from the stack, those objects are removed or restored. If it was a "store" operation, you are queried whether or not to restore the variable to its original value. The *U* key may be pressed any number of times to undo successively farther back in time; with a numeric prefix argument it undoes a specified number of operations. When the Calculator is quit, as with the *q* (`calc-quit`) command, the undo history will be truncated to the length of the customizable variable `calc-undo-length` (see Appendix C [Customizing Calc], page 435), which by default is 100. (Recall that *C-x * c* is synonymous with `calc-quit` while inside the Calculator; this also truncates the undo history.)

Currently the mode-setting commands (like `calc-precision`) are not undoable. You can undo past a point where you changed a mode, but you will need to reset the mode yourself.

The shift-*D* key (`calc-redo`) redoes an operation that was mistakenly undone. Pressing *U* with a negative prefix argument is equivalent to executing `calc-redo`. You can redo any number of times, up to the number of recent consecutive undo commands. Redo information is cleared whenever you give any command that adds new undo information, i.e., if you undo, then enter a number on the stack or make any other change, then it will be too late to redo.

The *M-RET* key (`calc-last-args`) is like undo in that it restores the arguments of the most recent command onto the stack; however, it does not remove the result of that command. Given a numeric prefix argument, this command applies to the *n*th most recent command which removed items from the stack; it pushes those items back onto the stack.

The *K* (`calc-keep-args`) command provides a related function to *M-RET*. See Chapter 5 [Stack and Trail], page 133.

It is also possible to recall previous results or inputs using the trail. See Section 5.3 [Trail Commands], page 135.

The standard Emacs *C-_* undo key is recognized as a synonym for *U*.

3.9 Error Messages

Many situations that would produce an error message in other calculators simply create unsimplified formulas in the Emacs Calculator. For example, *1 RET 0 /* pushes the formula 1/0; *0 L* pushes the formula '`ln(0)`'. Floating-point overflow and underflow are also reasons for this to happen.

When a function call must be left in symbolic form, Calc usually produces a message explaining why. Messages that are probably surprising or indicative of user errors are displayed automatically. Other messages are simply kept in Calc's memory and are displayed only if you type *w* (calc-why). You can also press *w* if the same computation results in several messages. (The first message will end with '[w=more]' in this case.)

The *d w* (calc-auto-why) command controls when error messages are displayed automatically. (Calc effectively presses *w* for you after your computation finishes.) By default, this occurs only for "important" messages. The other possible modes are to report *all* messages automatically, or to report none automatically (so that you must always press *w* yourself to see the messages).

3.10 Multiple Calculators

It is possible to have any number of Calc mode buffers at once. Usually this is done by executing *M-x another-calc*, which is similar to *C-x * c* except that if a *Calculator* buffer already exists, a new, independent one with a name of the form *Calculator*<n> is created. You can also use the command calc-mode to put any buffer into Calculator mode, but this would ordinarily never be done.

The *q* (calc-quit) command does not destroy a Calculator buffer; it only closes its window. Use *M-x kill-buffer* to destroy a Calculator buffer.

Each Calculator buffer keeps its own stack, undo list, and mode settings such as precision, angular mode, and display formats. In Emacs terms, variables such as calc-stack are buffer-local variables. The global default values of these variables are used only when a new Calculator buffer is created. The calc-quit command saves the stack and mode settings of the buffer being quit as the new defaults.

There is only one trail buffer, *Calc Trail*, used by all Calculator buffers.

3.11 Troubleshooting Commands

This section describes commands you can use in case a computation incorrectly fails or gives the wrong answer.

See Appendix D [Reporting Bugs], page 441, if you find a problem that appears to be due to a bug or deficiency in Calc.

3.11.1 Autoloading Problems

The Calc program is split into many component files; components are loaded automatically as you use various commands that require them. Occasionally Calc may lose track of when a certain component is necessary; typically this means you will type a command and it won't work because some function you've never heard of was undefined.

If this happens, the easiest workaround is to type *C-x * L* (calc-load-everything) to force all the parts of Calc to be loaded right away. This will cause Emacs to take up a lot more memory than it would otherwise, but it's guaranteed to fix the problem.

3.11.2 Recursion Depth

Calc uses recursion in many of its calculations. Emacs Lisp keeps a variable max-lisp-eval-depth which limits the amount of recursion possible in an attempt to recover from program bugs. If a calculation ever halts incorrectly with the message "Computation got stuck or ran too long," use the *M* command (calc-more-recursion-depth) to increase this limit. (Of course, this will not help if the calculation really did get stuck due to some problem inside Calc.)

The limit is always increased (multiplied) by a factor of two. There is also an *I M* (`calc-less-recursion-depth`) command which decreases this limit by a factor of two, down to a minimum value of 200. The default value is 1000.

These commands also double or halve `max-specpdl-size`, another internal Lisp recursion limit. The minimum value for this limit is 600.

3.11.3 Caches

Calc saves certain values after they have been computed once. For example, the *P* (`calc-pi`) command initially "knows" the constant π to about 20 decimal places; if the current precision is greater than this, it will recompute π using a series approximation. This value will not need to be recomputed ever again unless you raise the precision still further. Many operations such as logarithms and sines make use of similarly cached values such as $\pi/4$ and $\ln 2$. The visible effect of caching is that high-precision computations may seem to do extra work the first time. Other things cached include powers of two (for the binary arithmetic functions), matrix inverses and determinants, symbolic integrals, and data points computed by the graphing commands.

If you suspect a Calculator cache has become corrupt, you can use the `calc-flush-caches` command to reset all caches to the empty state. (This should only be necessary in the event of bugs in the Calculator.) The *C-x * 0* (with the zero key) command also resets caches along with all other aspects of the Calculator's state.

3.11.4 Debugging Calc

A few commands exist to help in the debugging of Calc commands. See Chapter 17 [Programming], page 363, to see the various ways that you can write your own Calc commands.

The *Z T* (`calc-timing`) command turns on and off a mode in which the timing of slow commands is reported in the Trail. Any Calc command that takes two seconds or longer writes a line to the Trail showing how many seconds it took. This value is accurate only to within one second.

All steps of executing a command are included; in particular, time taken to format the result for display in the stack and trail is counted. Some prompts also count time taken waiting for them to be answered, while others do not; this depends on the exact implementation of the command. For best results, if you are timing a sequence that includes prompts or multiple commands, define a keyboard macro to run the whole sequence at once. Calc's *X* command (see Section 17.2 [Keyboard Macros], page 364) will then report the time taken to execute the whole macro.

Another advantage of the *X* command is that while it is executing, the stack and trail are not updated from step to step. So if you expect the output of your test sequence to leave a result that may take a long time to format and you don't wish to count this formatting time, end your sequence with a `DEL` keystroke to clear the result from the stack. When you run the sequence with *X*, Calc will never bother to format the large result.

Another thing *Z T* does is to increase the Emacs variable `gc-cons-threshold` to a much higher value (two million; the usual default in Calc is 250,000) for the duration of each command. This generally prevents garbage collection during the timing of the command, though it may cause your Emacs process to grow abnormally large. (Garbage collection time is a major unpredictable factor in the timing of Emacs operations.)

Another command that is useful when debugging your own Lisp extensions to Calc is *M-x calc-pass-errors*, which disables the error handler that changes the "max-lisp-eval-depth exceeded" message to the much more friendly "Computation got stuck or ran too long." This handler interferes with the Emacs Lisp debugger's debug-on-error mode. Errors are reported in the handler itself rather than at the true location of the error. After you have executed calc-pass-errors, Lisp errors will be reported correctly but the user-friendly message will be lost.

4 Data Types

This chapter discusses the various types of objects that can be placed on the Calculator stack, how they are displayed, and how they are entered. (See Section 17.5.7.1 [Data Type Formats], page 385, for information on how these data types are represented as underlying Lisp objects.)

Integers, fractions, and floats are various ways of describing real numbers. HMS forms also for many purposes act as real numbers. These types can be combined to form complex numbers, modulo forms, error forms, or interval forms. (But these last four types cannot be combined arbitrarily: error forms may not contain modulo forms, for example.) Finally, all these types of numbers may be combined into vectors, matrices, or algebraic formulas.

4.1 Integers

The Calculator stores integers to arbitrary precision. Addition, subtraction, and multiplication of integers always yields an exact integer result. (If the result of a division or exponentiation of integers is not an integer, it is expressed in fractional or floating-point form according to the current Fraction mode. See Section 6.4.3 [Fraction Mode], page 140.)

A decimal integer is represented as an optional sign followed by a sequence of digits. Grouping (see Section 6.7.2 [Grouping Digits], page 149) can be used to insert a comma at every third digit for display purposes, but you must not type commas during the entry of numbers.

A non-decimal integer is represented as an optional sign, a radix between 2 and 36, a '#' symbol, and one or more digits. For radix 11 and above, the letters A through Z (upper- or lower-case) count as digits and do not terminate numeric entry mode. See Section 6.7.1 [Radix Modes], page 148, for how to set the default radix for display of integers. Numbers of any radix may be entered at any time. If you press # at the beginning of a number, the current display radix is used.

4.2 Fractions

A *fraction* is a ratio of two integers. Fractions are traditionally written "2/3" but Calc uses the notation '2:3'. (The / key performs RPN division; the following two sequences push the number '2:3' on the stack: *2 : 3 RET*, or *2 RET 3 /* assuming Fraction mode has been enabled.) When the Calculator produces a fractional result it always reduces it to simplest form, which may in fact be an integer.

Fractions may also be entered in a three-part form, where '2:3:4' represents two-and-three-quarters. See Section 6.7.5 [Fraction Formats], page 151, for fraction display formats.

Non-decimal fractions are entered and displayed as 'radix#num:denom' (or in the analogous three-part form). The numerator and denominator always use the same radix.

4.3 Floats

A floating-point number or *float* is a number stored in scientific notation. The number of significant digits in the fractional part is governed by the current floating precision (see Section 6.2 [Precision], page 138). The range of acceptable values is from $10^{-3999999}$ (inclusive) to $10^{4000000}$ (exclusive), plus the corresponding negative values and zero.

Calculations that would exceed the allowable range of values (such as '`exp(exp(20))`') are left in symbolic form by Calc. The messages "floating-point overflow" or "floating-point underflow" indicate that during the calculation a number would have been produced that was too large or too close to zero, respectively, to be represented by Calc. This does not necessarily mean the final result would have overflowed, just that an overflow occurred while computing the result. (In fact, it could report an underflow even though the final result would have overflowed!)

If a rational number and a float are mixed in a calculation, the result will in general be expressed as a float. Commands that require an integer value (such as `k g` [gcd]) will also accept integer-valued floats, i.e., floating-point numbers with nothing after the decimal point.

Floats are identified by the presence of a decimal point and/or an exponent. In general a float consists of an optional sign, digits including an optional decimal point, and an optional exponent consisting of an 'e', an optional sign, and up to seven exponent digits. For example, '`23.5e-2`' is 23.5 times ten to the minus-second power, or 0.235.

Floating-point numbers are normally displayed in decimal notation with all significant figures shown. Exceedingly large or small numbers are displayed in scientific notation. Various other display options are available. See Section 6.7.3 [Float Formats], page 150.

Floating-point numbers are stored in decimal, not binary. The result of each operation is rounded to the nearest value representable in the number of significant digits specified by the current precision, rounding away from zero in the case of a tie. Thus (in the default display mode) what you see is exactly what you get. Some operations such as square roots and transcendental functions are performed with several digits of extra precision and then rounded down, in an effort to make the final result accurate to the full requested precision. However, accuracy is not rigorously guaranteed. If you suspect the validity of a result, try doing the same calculation in a higher precision. The Calculator's arithmetic is not intended to be IEEE-conformant in any way.

While floats are always *stored* in decimal, they can be entered and displayed in any radix just like integers and fractions. Since a float that is entered in a radix other that 10 will be converted to decimal, the number that Calc stores may not be exactly the number that was entered, it will be the closest decimal approximation given the current precision. The notation '`radix#ddd.ddd`' is a floating-point number whose digits are in the specified radix. Note that the '`.`' is more aptly referred to as a "radix point" than as a decimal point in this case. The number '`8#123.4567`' is defined as '`8#1234567 * 8^-4`'. If the radix is 14 or less, you can use 'e' notation to write a non-decimal number in scientific notation. The exponent is written in decimal, and is considered to be a power of the radix: '`8#1234567e-4`'. If the radix is 15 or above, the letter 'e' is a digit, so scientific notation must be written out, e.g., '`16#123.4567*16^2`'. The first two exercises of the Modes Tutorial explore some of the properties of non-decimal floats.

4.4 Complex Numbers

There are two supported formats for complex numbers: rectangular and polar. The default format is rectangular, displayed in the form '`(real,imag)`' where *real* is the real part and *imag* is the imaginary part, each of which may be any real number. Rectangular complex numbers can also be displayed in 'a+bi' notation; see Section 6.7.4 [Complex Formats], page 150.

Polar complex numbers are displayed in the form '$(r;\theta)$' where r is the nonnegative magnitude and θ is the argument or phase angle. The range of θ depends on the current angular mode (see Section 6.4.1 [Angular Modes], page 139); it is generally between -180 and $+180$ degrees or the equivalent range in radians.

Complex numbers are entered in stages using incomplete objects. See Section 4.13 [Incomplete Objects], page 127.

Operations on rectangular complex numbers yield rectangular complex results, and similarly for polar complex numbers. Where the two types are mixed, or where new complex numbers arise (as for the square root of a negative real), the current *Polar mode* is used to determine the type. See Section 6.4.2 [Polar Mode], page 139.

A complex result in which the imaginary part is zero (or the phase angle is 0 or 180 degrees or π radians) is automatically converted to a real number.

4.5 Infinities

The word inf represents the mathematical concept of *infinity*. Calc actually has three slightly different infinity-like values: inf, uinf, and nan. These are just regular variable names (see Section 4.14 [Variables], page 128); you should avoid using these names for your own variables because Calc gives them special treatment. Infinities, like all variable names, are normally entered using algebraic entry.

Mathematically speaking, it is not rigorously correct to treat "infinity" as if it were a number, but mathematicians often do so informally. When they say that '1 / inf = 0', what they really mean is that $1/x$, as x becomes larger and larger, becomes arbitrarily close to zero. So you can imagine that if x got "all the way to infinity," then $1/x$ would go all the way to zero. Similarly, when they say that 'exp(inf) = inf', they mean that e^x grows without bound as x grows. The symbol '-inf' likewise stands for an infinitely negative real value; for example, we say that 'exp(-inf) = 0'. You can have an infinity pointing in any direction on the complex plane: 'sqrt(-inf) = i inf'.

The same concept of limits can be used to define 1/0. We really want the value that $1/x$ approaches as x approaches zero. But if all we have is 1/0, we can't tell which direction x was coming from. If x was positive and decreasing toward zero, then we should say that '1 / 0 = inf'. But if x was negative and increasing toward zero, the answer is '1 / 0 = -inf'. In fact, x could be an imaginary number, giving the answer 'i inf' or '-i inf'. Calc uses the special symbol 'uinf' to mean *undirected infinity*, i.e., a value which is infinitely large but with an unknown sign (or direction on the complex plane).

Calc actually has three modes that say how infinities are handled. Normally, infinities never arise from calculations that didn't already have them. Thus, 1/0 is treated simply as an error and left unevaluated. The m i (calc-infinite-mode) command (see Section 6.4.4 [Infinite Mode], page 140) enables a mode in which 1/0 evaluates to uinf instead. There is also an alternative type of infinite mode which says to treat zeros as if they were positive, so that '1 / 0 = inf'. While this is less mathematically correct, it may be the answer you want in some cases.

Since all infinities are "as large" as all others, Calc simplifies, e.g., '5 inf' to 'inf'. Another example is '5 - inf = -inf', where the '-inf' is so large that adding a finite number like five to it does not affect it. Note that 'a - inf' also results in '-inf'; Calc assumes that variables like a always stand for finite quantities. Just to show that infinities really are all the same size, note that 'sqrt(inf) = inf^2 = exp(inf) = inf' in Calc's notation.

It's not so easy to define certain formulas like '0 * inf' and 'inf / inf'. Depending on where these zeros and infinities came from, the answer could be literally anything. The latter formula could be the limit of x/x (giving a result of one), or $2x/x$ (giving two), or x^2/x (giving inf), or x/x^2 (giving zero). Calc uses the symbol nan to represent such an *indeterminate* value. (The name "nan" comes from analogy with the "NAN" concept of IEEE standard arithmetic; it stands for "Not A Number." This is somewhat of a misnomer, since nan *does* stand for some number or infinity, it's just that *which* number it stands for cannot be determined.) In Calc's notation, '0 * inf = nan' and 'inf / inf = nan'. A few other common indeterminate expressions are 'inf - inf' and 'inf ^ 0'. Also, '0 / 0 = nan' if you have turned on Infinite mode (as described above).

Infinities are especially useful as parts of *intervals*. See Section 4.12 [Interval Forms], page 126.

4.6 Vectors and Matrices

The *vector* data type is flexible and general. A vector is simply a list of zero or more data objects. When these objects are numbers, the whole is a vector in the mathematical sense. When these objects are themselves vectors of equal (nonzero) length, the whole is a *matrix*. A vector which is not a matrix is referred to here as a *plain vector*.

A vector is displayed as a list of values separated by commas and enclosed in square brackets: '[1, 2, 3]'. Thus the following is a 2 row by 3 column matrix: '[[1, 2, 3], [4, 5, 6]]'. Vectors, like complex numbers, are entered as incomplete objects. See Section 4.13 [Incomplete Objects], page 127. During algebraic entry, vectors are entered all at once in the usual brackets-and-commas form. Matrices may be entered algebraically as nested vectors, or using the shortcut notation '[1, 2, 3; 4, 5, 6]', with rows separated by semicolons. The commas may usually be omitted when entering vectors: '[1 2 3]'. Curly braces may be used in place of brackets: '{1, 2, 3}', but the commas are required in this case.

Traditional vector and matrix arithmetic is also supported; see Section 7.1 [Basic Arithmetic], page 185, and see Chapter 9 [Matrix Functions], page 221. Many other operations are applied to vectors element-wise. For example, the complex conjugate of a vector is a vector of the complex conjugates of its elements.

Algebraic functions for building vectors include 'vec(a, b, c)' to build '[a, b, c]', 'cvec(a, n, m)' to build an $n \times m$ matrix of 'a's, and 'index(n)' to build a vector of integers from 1 to 'n'.

4.7 Strings

Character strings are not a special data type in the Calculator. Rather, a string is represented simply as a vector all of whose elements are integers in the range 0 to 255 (ASCII codes). You can enter a string at any time by pressing the " key. Quotation marks and backslashes are written '\"' and '\\', respectively, inside strings. Other notations introduced by backslashes are:

\a	7	\^@	0
\b	8	\^a-z	1-26
\e	27	\^[	27
\f	12	\^\\	28
\n	10	\^]	29
\r	13	\^^	30
\t	9	\^_	31
		\^?	127

Finally, a backslash followed by three octal digits produces any character from its ASCII code.

Strings are normally displayed in vector-of-integers form. The d " (calc-display-strings) command toggles a mode in which any vectors of small integers are displayed as quoted strings instead.

The backslash notations shown above are also used for displaying strings. Characters 128 and above are not translated by Calc; unless you have an Emacs modified for 8-bit fonts, these will show up in backslash-octal-digits notation. For characters below 32, and for character 127, Calc uses the backslash-letter combination if there is one, or otherwise uses a '\^' sequence.

The only Calc feature that uses strings is *compositions*; see Section 6.8.10 [Compositions], page 168. Strings also provide a convenient way to do conversions between ASCII characters and integers.

There is a **string** function which provides a different display format for strings. Basically, 'string(s)', where s is a vector of integers in the proper range, is displayed as the corresponding string of characters with no surrounding quotation marks or other modifications. Thus 'string("ABC")' (or 'string([65 66 67])') will look like 'ABC' on the stack. This happens regardless of whether d " has been used. The only way to turn it off is to use d U (unformatted language mode) which will display 'string("ABC")' instead.

Control characters are displayed somewhat differently by **string**. Characters below 32, and character 127, are shown using '^' notation (same as shown above, but without the backslash). The quote and backslash characters are left alone, as are characters 128 and above.

The **bstring** function is just like **string** except that the resulting string is breakable across multiple lines if it doesn't fit all on one line. Potential break points occur at every space character in the string.

4.8 HMS Forms

HMS stands for Hours-Minutes-Seconds; when used as an angular argument, the interpretation is Degrees-Minutes-Seconds. All functions that operate on angles accept HMS forms. These are interpreted as degrees regardless of the current angular mode. It is also possible to use HMS as the angular mode so that calculated angles are expressed in degrees, minutes, and seconds.

The default format for HMS values is '*hours*@ *mins*' *secs*"'. During entry, the letters 'h' (for "hours") or 'o' (approximating the "degrees" symbol) are accepted as well as '@', 'm' is accepted in place of ''', and 's' is accepted in place of '"'. The *hours* value is an integer (or integer-valued float). The *mins* value is an integer or integer-valued float between 0 and 59. The *secs* value is a real number between 0 (inclusive) and 60 (exclusive). A positive HMS form is interpreted as *hours* + *mins*/60 + *secs*/3600. A negative HMS form is interpreted as −*hours* − *mins*/60 − *secs*/3600. Display format for HMS forms is quite flexible. See Section 6.7.6 [HMS Formats], page 151.

HMS forms can be added and subtracted. When they are added to numbers, the numbers are interpreted according to the current angular mode. HMS forms can also be multiplied and divided by real numbers. Dividing two HMS forms produces a real-valued ratio of the two angles.

Just for kicks, `M-x calc-time` pushes the current time of day on the stack as an HMS form.

4.9 Date Forms

A *date form* represents a date and possibly an associated time. Simple date arithmetic is supported: Adding a number to a date produces a new date shifted by that many days; adding an HMS form to a date shifts it by that many hours. Subtracting two date forms computes the number of days between them (represented as a simple number). Many other operations, such as multiplying two date forms, are nonsensical and are not allowed by Calc.

Date forms are entered and displayed enclosed in '< >' brackets. The default format is, e.g., '<Wed Jan 9, 1991>' for dates, or '<3:32:20pm Wed Jan 9, 1991>' for dates with times. Input is flexible; date forms can be entered in any of the usual notations for dates and times. See Section 6.7.7 [Date Formats], page 151.

Date forms are stored internally as numbers, specifically the number of days since midnight on the morning of December 31 of the year 1 BC. If the internal number is an integer, the form represents a date only; if the internal number is a fraction or float, the form represents a date and time. For example, '<6:00am Thu Jan 10, 1991>' is represented by the number 726842.25. The standard precision of 12 decimal digits is enough to ensure that a (reasonable) date and time can be stored without roundoff error.

If the current precision is greater than 12, date forms will keep additional digits in the seconds position. For example, if the precision is 15, the seconds will keep three digits after the decimal point. Decreasing the precision below 12 may cause the time part of a date form to become inaccurate. This can also happen if astronomically high years are used, though this will not be an issue in everyday (or even everymillennium) use. Note that date forms without times are stored as exact integers, so roundoff is never an issue for them.

You can use the `v p` (`calc-pack`) and `v u` (`calc-unpack`) commands to get at the numerical representation of a date form. See Section 9.1 [Packing and Unpacking], page 221.

Date forms can go arbitrarily far into the future or past. Negative year numbers represent years BC. There is no "year 0"; the day before '<Mon Jan 1, +1>' is '<Sun Dec 31, -1>'. These are days 1 and 0 respectively in Calc's internal numbering scheme. The Gregorian calendar is used for all dates, including dates before the Gregorian calendar was invented (although that can be configured; see below). Thus Calc's use of the day number −10000 to represent August 15, 28 BC should be taken with a grain of salt.

Some historical background: The Julian calendar was created by Julius Caesar in the year 46 BC as an attempt to fix the confusion caused by the irregular Roman calendar that was used before that time. The Julian calendar introduced an extra day in all years divisible by four. After some initial confusion, the calendar was adopted around the year we call 8 AD. Some centuries later it became apparent that the Julian year of 365.25 days was itself not quite right. In 1582 Pope Gregory XIII introduced the Gregorian calendar, which added the new rule that years divisible by 100, but not by 400, were not to be considered leap years despite being divisible by four. Many countries delayed adoption of the Gregorian calendar because of religious differences. For example, Great Britain and the British colonies switched to the Gregorian calendar in September 1752, when the Julian calendar was eleven days behind the Gregorian calendar. That year in Britain, the day after September 2 was September 14. To take another example, Russia did not adopt the Gregorian calendar until 1918, and that year in Russia the day after January 31 was February 14. Calc's reckoning therefore matches English practice starting in 1752 and Russian practice starting in 1918, but disagrees with earlier dates in both countries.

When the Julian calendar was introduced, it had January 1 as the first day of the year. By the Middle Ages, many European countries had changed the beginning of a new year to a different date, often to a religious festival. Almost all countries reverted to using January 1 as the beginning of the year by the time they adopted the Gregorian calendar.

Some calendars attempt to mimic the historical situation by using the Gregorian calendar for recent dates and the Julian calendar for older dates. The `cal` program in most Unix implementations does this, for example. While January 1 wasn't always the beginning of a calendar year, these hybrid calendars still use January 1 as the beginning of the year even for older dates. The customizable variable `calc-gregorian-switch` (see Appendix C [Customizing Calc], page 435) can be set to have Calc's date forms switch from the Julian to Gregorian calendar at any specified date.

Today's timekeepers introduce an occasional "leap second". These do not occur regularly and Calc does not take these minor effects into account. (If it did, it would have to report a non-integer number of days between, say, '`<12:00am Mon Jan 1, 1900>`' and '`<12:00am Sat Jan 1, 2000>`'.)

Another day counting system in common use is, confusingly, also called "Julian." Julian days go from noon to noon. The Julian day number is the numbers of days since 12:00 noon (GMT) on November 24, 4714 BC in the Gregorian calendar (i.e., January 1, 4713 BC in the Julian calendar). In Calc's scheme (in GMT) the Julian day origin is -1721422.5, because Calc starts at midnight instead of noon. Thus to convert a Calc date code obtained by unpacking a date form into a Julian day number, simply add 1721422.5 after compensating for the time zone difference. The built-in `t J` command performs this conversion for you.

The Julian day number is based on the Julian cycle, which was invented in 1583 by Joseph Justus Scaliger. Scaliger named it the Julian cycle since it involves the Julian calendar, but some have suggested that Scaliger named it in honor of his father, Julius Caesar Scaliger. The Julian cycle is based on three other cycles: the indiction cycle, the Metonic cycle, and the solar cycle. The indiction cycle is a 15 year cycle originally used by the Romans for tax purposes but later used to date medieval documents. The Metonic cycle is a 19 year cycle; 19 years is close to being a common multiple of a solar year and a lunar month, and so every 19 years the phases of the moon will occur on the same days of the year. The solar cycle is a 28 year cycle; the Julian calendar repeats itself every 28 years. The smallest time period which contains multiples of all three cycles is the least common multiple of 15 years, 19 years and 28 years, which (since they're pairwise relatively prime) is $15 \times 19 \times 28 = 7980$ years. This is the length of a Julian cycle. Working backwards, the previous year in which all three cycles began was 4713 BC, and so Scaliger chose that year as the beginning of a Julian cycle. Since at the time there were no historical records from before 4713 BC, using this year as a starting point had the advantage of avoiding negative year numbers. In 1849, the astronomer John Herschel (son of William Herschel) suggested using the number of days since the beginning of the Julian cycle as an astronomical dating system; this idea was taken up by other astronomers. (At the time, noon was the start of the astronomical day. Herschel originally suggested counting the days since Jan 1, 4713 BC at noon Alexandria time; this was later amended to noon GMT.) Julian day numbering is largely used in astronomy.

The Unix operating system measures time as an integer number of seconds since midnight, Jan 1, 1970. To convert a Calc date value into a Unix time stamp, first subtract 719163 (the code for '`<Jan 1, 1970>`'), then multiply by 86400 (the number of seconds in a day) and press `R` to round to the nearest integer. If you have a date form, you can simply subtract the day '`<Jan 1, 1970>`' instead of unpacking and subtracting 719163. Likewise, divide by 86400 and add '`<Jan 1, 1970>`' to convert from Unix time to a Calc date form. (Note that Unix normally maintains the time in the GMT time zone; you may need to subtract five hours to get New York time, or eight hours for California time. The same is usually true of Julian day counts.) The built-in `t U` command performs these conversions.

4.10 Modulo Forms

A *modulo form* is a real number which is taken modulo (i.e., within an integer multiple of) some value M. Arithmetic modulo M often arises in number theory. Modulo forms are written '`a mod M`', where a and M are real numbers or HMS forms, and $0 \le a < M$. In many applications a and M will be integers but this is not required.

To create a modulo form during numeric entry, press the shift-`M` key to enter the word '`mod`'. As a special convenience, pressing shift-`M` a second time automatically enters the value of M that was most recently used before. During algebraic entry, either type '`mod`' by hand or press `M-m` (that's `META-m`). Once again, pressing this a second time enters the current modulo.

Modulo forms are not to be confused with the modulo operator '`%`'. The expression '`27 % 10`' means to compute 27 modulo 10 to produce the result 7. Further computations treat this 7 as just a regular integer. The expression '`27 mod 10`' produces the result '`7 mod 10`'; further computations with this value are again reduced modulo 10 so that the result always lies in the desired range.

When two modulo forms with identical M's are added or multiplied, the Calculator simply adds or multiplies the values, then reduces modulo M. If one argument is a modulo form and the other a plain number, the plain number is treated like a compatible modulo form. It is also possible to raise modulo forms to powers; the result is the value raised to the power, then reduced modulo M. (When all values involved are integers, this calculation is done much more efficiently than actually computing the power and then reducing.)

Two modulo forms '`a mod M`' and '`b mod M`' can be divided if a, b, and M are all integers. The result is the modulo form which, when multiplied by '`b mod M`', produces '`a mod M`'. If there is no solution to this equation (which can happen only when M is non-prime), or if any of the arguments are non-integers, the division is left in symbolic form.

Other operations, such as square roots, are not yet supported for modulo forms. (Note that, although '(a mod M)^.5' will compute a "modulo square root" in the sense of reducing $\sqrt{a}$ modulo M, this is not a useful definition from the number-theoretical point of view.)

It is possible to mix HMS forms and modulo forms. For example, an HMS form modulo 24 could be used to manipulate clock times; an HMS form modulo 360 would be suitable for angles. Making the modulo M also be an HMS form eliminates troubles that would arise if the angular mode were inadvertently set to Radians, in which case '2@ 0' 0" mod 24' would be interpreted as two degrees modulo 24 radians!

Modulo forms cannot have variables or formulas for components. If you enter the formula '(x + 2) mod 5', Calc propagates the modulus to each of the coefficients: '(1 mod 5) x + (2 mod 5)'.

You can use v p and % to modify modulo forms. See Section 9.1 [Packing and Unpacking], page 221. See Section 7.1 [Basic Arithmetic], page 185.

The algebraic function 'makemod(a, m)' builds the modulo form 'a mod m'.

4.11 Error Forms

An *error form* is a number with an associated standard deviation, as in '2.3 +/- 0.12'. The notation 'x +/- σ' stands for an uncertain value which follows a normal or Gaussian distribution of mean x and standard deviation or "error" σ. Both the mean and the error can be either numbers or formulas. Generally these are real numbers but the mean may also be complex. If the error is negative or complex, it is changed to its absolute value. An error form with zero error is converted to a regular number by the Calculator.

All arithmetic and transcendental functions accept error forms as input. Operations on the mean-value part work just like operations on regular numbers. The error part for any function $f(x)$ (such as $\sin x$ is defined by the error of x times the derivative of f evaluated at the mean value of x. For a two-argument function $f(x, y)$ (such as addition) the error is the square root of the sum of the squares of the errors due to x and y.

$$f(x \text{ +/- } \sigma) = f(x) \text{ +/- } \sigma \left| \frac{df(x)}{dx} \right|$$
$$f(x \text{ +/- } \sigma_x, y \text{ +/- } \sigma_y) = f(x,y) \text{ +/- } \sqrt{\left(\sigma_x \left| \frac{\partial f(x,y)}{\partial x} \right|\right)^2 + \left(\sigma_y \left| \frac{\partial f(x,y)}{\partial y} \right|\right)^2}$$

Note that this definition assumes the errors in x and y are uncorrelated. A side effect of this definition is that '(2 +/- 1) * (2 +/- 1)' is not the same as '(2 +/- 1)^2'; the former represents the product of two independent values which happen to have the same probability distributions, and the latter is the product of one random value with itself. The former will produce an answer with less error, since on the average the two independent errors can be expected to cancel out.

Consult a good text on error analysis for a discussion of the proper use of standard deviations. Actual errors often are neither Gaussian-distributed nor uncorrelated, and the above formulas are valid only when errors are small. As an example, the error arising from 'sin(x +/- σ)' is 'σ abs(cos(x))'. When x is close to zero, $\cos x$ is close to one so the error in the sine is close to σ; this makes sense, since $\sin x$ is approximately x near zero, so a given error in x will produce about the same error in the sine. Likewise, near 90 degrees cos x is nearly zero and so the computed error is small: The sine curve is nearly flat in that region, so an error in x has relatively little effect on the value of sin x. However, consider '`sin(90 +/- 1000)`'. The cosine of 90 is zero, so Calc will report zero error! We get an obviously wrong result because we have violated the small-error approximation underlying the error analysis. If the error in x had been small, the error in sin x would indeed have been negligible.

To enter an error form during regular numeric entry, use the *p* ("plus-or-minus") key to type the '`+/-`' symbol. (If you try actually typing '`+/-`' the + key will be interpreted as the Calculator's + command!) Within an algebraic formula, you can press *M-+* to type the '`+/-`' symbol, or type it out by hand.

Error forms and complex numbers can be mixed; the formulas shown above are used for complex numbers, too; note that if the error part evaluates to a complex number its absolute value (or the square root of the sum of the squares of the absolute values of the two error contributions) is used. Mathematically, this corresponds to a radially symmetric Gaussian distribution of numbers on the complex plane. However, note that Calc considers an error form with real components to represent a real number, not a complex distribution around a real mean.

Error forms may also be composed of HMS forms. For best results, both the mean and the error should be HMS forms if either one is.

The algebraic function '`sdev(a, b)`' builds the error form '`a +/- b`'.

4.12 Interval Forms

An *interval* is a subset of consecutive real numbers. For example, the interval '`[2 .. 4]`' represents all the numbers from 2 to 4, inclusive. If you multiply it by the interval '`[0.5 .. 2]`' you obtain '`[1 .. 8]`'. This calculation represents the fact that if you multiply some number in the range '`[2 .. 4]`' by some other number in the range '`[0.5 .. 2]`', your result will lie in the range from 1 to 8. Interval arithmetic is used to get a worst-case estimate of the possible range of values a computation will produce, given the set of possible values of the input.

Calc supports several varieties of intervals, including *closed* intervals of the type shown above, *open* intervals such as '`(2 .. 4)`', which represents the range of numbers from 2 to 4 *exclusive*, and *semi-open* intervals in which one end uses a round parenthesis and the other a square bracket. In mathematical terms,

$$
\begin{aligned}
[2..4] \quad &\text{means} \quad 2 \le x \le 4 \\
[2..4) \quad &\text{means} \quad 2 \le x < 4 \\
(2..4] \quad &\text{means} \quad 2 < x \le 4 \\
(2..4) \quad &\text{means} \quad 2 < x < 4
\end{aligned}
$$

The lower and upper limits of an interval must be either real numbers (or HMS or date forms), or symbolic expressions which are assumed to be real-valued, or '`-inf`' and '`inf`'. In general the lower limit must be less than the upper limit. A closed interval containing only one value, '`[3 .. 3]`', is converted to a plain number (3) automatically. An interval containing no values at all (such as '`[3 .. 2]`' or '`[2 .. 2)`') can be represented but is not guaranteed to behave well when used in arithmetic. Note that the interval '`[3 .. inf)`' represents all real numbers greater than or equal to 3, and '(-inf .. inf)' represents all real numbers. In fact, '[-inf .. inf]' represents all real numbers including the real infinities.

Intervals are entered in the notation shown here, either as algebraic formulas, or using incomplete forms. (See Section 4.13 [Incomplete Objects], page 127.) In algebraic formulas, multiple periods in a row are collected from left to right, so that '1...1e2' is interpreted as '1.0 .. 1e2' rather than '1 .. 0.1e2'. Add spaces or zeros if you want to get the other interpretation. If you omit the lower or upper limit, a default of '-inf' or 'inf' (respectively) is furnished.

Infinite mode also affects operations on intervals (see Section 4.5 [Infinities], page 119). Calc will always introduce an open infinity, as in '1 / (0 .. 2] = [0.5 .. inf)'. But closed infinities, '1 / [0 .. 2] = [0.5 .. inf]', arise only in Infinite mode; otherwise they are left unevaluated. Note that the "direction" of a zero is not an issue in this case since the zero is always assumed to be continuous with the rest of the interval. For intervals that contain zero inside them Calc is forced to give the result, '1 / (-2 .. 2) = [-inf .. inf]'.

While it may seem that intervals and error forms are similar, they are based on entirely different concepts of inexact quantities. An error form 'x +/- σ' means a variable is random, and its value could be anything but is "probably" within one σ of the mean value x. An interval '[a .. b]' means a variable's value is unknown, but guaranteed to lie in the specified range. Error forms are statistical or "average case" approximations; interval arithmetic tends to produce "worst case" bounds on an answer.

Intervals may not contain complex numbers, but they may contain HMS forms or date forms.

See Section 9.6 [Set Operations], page 229, for commands that interpret interval forms as subsets of the set of real numbers.

The algebraic function 'intv(n, a, b)' builds an interval form from 'a' to 'b'; 'n' is an integer code which must be 0 for '(..)', 1 for '(..]', 2 for '[..)', or 3 for '[..]'.

Please note that in fully rigorous interval arithmetic, care would be taken to make sure that the computation of the lower bound rounds toward minus infinity, while upper bound computations round toward plus infinity. Calc's arithmetic always uses a round-to-nearest mode, which means that roundoff errors could creep into an interval calculation to produce intervals slightly smaller than they ought to be. For example, entering '[1..2]' and pressing Q 2 ^ should yield the interval '[1..2]' again, but in fact it yields the (slightly too small) interval '[1..1.9999999]' due to roundoff error.

4.13 Incomplete Objects

When (or [is typed to begin entering a complex number or vector, respectively, the effect is to push an *incomplete* complex number or vector onto the stack. The , key adds the value(s) at the top of the stack onto the current incomplete object. The) and] keys "close" the incomplete object after adding any values on the top of the stack in front of the incomplete object.

As a result, the sequence of keystrokes [2 , 3 RET 2 * , 9] pushes the vector '[2, 6, 9]' onto the stack. Likewise, (1 , 2 Q) pushes the complex number '(1, 1.414)' (approximately).

If several values lie on the stack in front of the incomplete object, all are collected and appended to the object. Thus the , key is redundant: *[2 RET 3 RET 2 * 9]*. Some people prefer the equivalent SPC key to RET.

As a special case, typing , immediately after *(*, *[*, or , adds a zero or duplicates the preceding value in the list being formed. Typing DEL during incomplete entry removes the last item from the list.

The ; key is used in the same way as , to create polar complex numbers: *(1 ; 2)*. When entering a vector, ; is useful for creating a matrix. In particular, *[[1 , 2 ; 3 , 4 ; 5 , 6]]* is equivalent to *[[1 , 2] , [3 , 4] , [5 , 6]]*.

Incomplete entry is also used to enter intervals. For example, *[2 .. 4)* enters a semi-open interval. Note that when you type the first period, it will be interpreted as a decimal point, but when you type a second period immediately afterward, it is re-interpreted as part of the interval symbol. Typing .. corresponds to executing the calc-dots command.

If you find incomplete entry distracting, you may wish to enter vectors and complex numbers as algebraic formulas by pressing the apostrophe key.

4.14 Variables

A *variable* is somewhere between a storage register on a conventional calculator, and a variable in a programming language. (In fact, a Calc variable is really just an Emacs Lisp variable that contains a Calc number or formula.) A variable's name is normally composed of letters and digits. Calc also allows apostrophes and # signs in variable names. (The Calc variable foo corresponds to the Emacs Lisp variable var-foo, but unless you access the variable from within Emacs Lisp, you don't need to worry about it. Variable names in algebraic formulas implicitly have 'var-' prefixed to their names. The '#' character in variable names used in algebraic formulas corresponds to a dash '-' in the Lisp variable name. If the name contains any dashes, the prefix 'var-' is *not* automatically added. Thus the two formulas 'foo + 1' and 'var#foo + 1' both refer to the same variable.)

In a command that takes a variable name, you can either type the full name of a variable, or type a single digit to use one of the special convenience variables q0 through q9. For example, *3 s s 2* stores the number 3 in variable q2, and *3 s s foo RET* stores that number in variable foo.

To push a variable itself (as opposed to the variable's value) on the stack, enter its name as an algebraic expression using the apostrophe (') key.

The = (calc-evaluate) key "evaluates" a formula by replacing all variables in the formula which have been given values by a calc-store or calc-let command by their stored values. Other variables are left alone. Thus a variable that has not been stored acts like an abstract variable in algebra; a variable that has been stored acts more like a register in a traditional calculator. With a positive numeric prefix argument, = evaluates the top n stack entries; with a negative argument, = evaluates the nth stack entry.

A few variables are called *special constants*. Their names are 'e', 'pi', 'i', 'phi', and 'gamma'. (See Chapter 8 [Scientific Functions], page 209.) When they are evaluated with =, their values are calculated if necessary according to the current precision or complex polar mode. If you wish to use these symbols for other purposes, simply undefine or redefine them using calc-store.

The variables 'inf', 'uinf', and 'nan' stand for infinite or indeterminate values. It's best not to use them as regular variables, since Calc uses special algebraic rules when it manipulates them. Calc displays a warning message if you store a value into any of these special variables.

See Chapter 12 [Store and Recall], page 323, for a discussion of commands dealing with variables.

4.15 Formulas

When you press the apostrophe key you may enter any expression or formula in algebraic form. (Calc uses the terms "expression" and "formula" interchangeably.) An expression is built up of numbers, variable names, and function calls, combined with various arithmetic operators. Parentheses may be used to indicate grouping. Spaces are ignored within formulas, except that spaces are not permitted within variable names or numbers. Arithmetic operators, in order from highest to lowest precedence, and with their equivalent function names, are:

'_' [subscr] (subscripts);

postfix '%' [percent] (as in '25% = 0.25');

prefix '!' [lnot] (logical "not," as in '!x');

'+/-' [sdev] (the standard deviation symbol) and 'mod' [makemod] (the symbol for modulo forms);

postfix '!' [fact] (factorial, as in 'n!') and postfix '!!' [dfact] (double factorial);

'^' [pow] (raised-to-the-power-of);

prefix '+' and '-' [neg] (as in '-x');

'*' [mul];

'/' [div], '%' [mod] (modulo), and '\' [idiv] (integer division);

infix '+' [add] and '-' [sub] (as in 'x-y');

'|' [vconcat] (vector concatenation);

relations '=' [eq], '!=' [neq], '<' [lt], '>' [gt], '<=' [leq], and '>=' [geq];

'&&' [land] (logical "and");

'||' [lor] (logical "or");

the C-style "if" operator 'a?b:c' [if];

'!!!' [pnot] (rewrite pattern "not");

'&&&' [pand] (rewrite pattern "and");

'|||' [por] (rewrite pattern "or");

':=' [assign] (for assignments and rewrite rules);

'::' [condition] (rewrite pattern condition);

'=>' [evalto].

Note that, unlike in usual computer notation, multiplication binds more strongly than division: 'a*b/c*d' is equivalent to $\frac{ab}{cd}$.

The multiplication sign '*' may be omitted in many cases. In particular, if the righthand side is a number, variable name, or parenthesized expression, the '*' may be omitted. Implicit multiplication has the same precedence as the explicit '*' operator. The one exception to the rule is that a variable name followed by a parenthesized expression, as in 'f(x)', is interpreted as a function call, not an implicit '*'. In many cases you must use a space if you omit the '*': '2a' is the same as '2*a', and 'a b' is the same as 'a*b', but 'ab' is a variable called ab, *not* the product of 'a' and 'b'! Also note that 'f (x)' is still a function call.

The rules are slightly different for vectors written with square brackets. In vectors, the space character is interpreted (like the comma) as a separator of elements of the vector. Thus '[2a b+c d]' is equivalent to '[2*a, b+c, d]', whereas '2a b+c d' is equivalent to '2*a*b + c*d'. Note that spaces around the brackets, and around explicit commas, are ignored. To force spaces to be interpreted as multiplication you can enclose a formula in parentheses as in '[(a b) 2(c d)]', which is interpreted as '[a*b, 2*c*d]'. An implicit comma is also inserted between '] [', as in the matrix '[[1 2] [3 4]]'.

Vectors that contain commas (not embedded within nested parentheses or brackets) do not treat spaces specially: '[a b, 2 c d]' is a vector of two elements. Also, if it would be an error to treat spaces as separators, but not otherwise, then Calc will ignore spaces: '[a - b]' is a vector of one element, but '[a -b]' is a vector of two elements. Finally, vectors entered with curly braces instead of square brackets do not give spaces any special treatment. When Calc displays a vector that does not contain any commas, it will insert parentheses if necessary to make the meaning clear: '[(a b)]'.

The expression '5%-2' is ambiguous; is this five-percent minus two, or five modulo minus-two? Calc always interprets the leftmost symbol as an infix operator preferentially (modulo, in this case), so you would need to write '(5%)-2' to get the former interpretation.

A function call is, e.g., 'sin(1+x)'. (The Calc algebraic function foo corresponds to the Emacs Lisp function calcFunc-foo, but unless you access the function from within Emacs Lisp, you don't need to worry about it.) Most mathematical Calculator commands like calc-sin have function equivalents like sin. If no Lisp function is defined for a function called by a formula, the call is left as it is during algebraic manipulation: 'f(x+y)' is left alone. Beware that many innocent-looking short names like in and re have predefined meanings which could surprise you; however, single letters or single letters followed by digits are always safe to use for your own function names. See [Function Index], page 477.

In the documentation for particular commands, the notation H S (calc-sinh) [sinh] means that the key sequence H S, the command M-x calc-sinh, and the algebraic function sinh(x) all represent the same operation.

Commands that interpret ("parse") text as algebraic formulas include algebraic entry ('), editing commands like ` which parse the contents of the editing buffer when you finish, the C-x * g and C-x * r commands, the C-y command, the X window system "paste" mouse operation, and Embedded mode. All of these operations use the same rules for parsing formulas; in particular, language modes (see Section 6.8 [Language Modes], page 158) affect them all in the same way.

When you read a large amount of text into the Calculator (say a vector which represents a big set of rewrite rules; see Section 10.11 [Rewrite Rules], page 291), you may wish to include comments in the text. Calc's formula parser ignores the symbol '%%' and anything following it on a line:

```
[ a + b,    %% the sum of "a" and "b"
  c + d,
  %% last line is coming up:
```

```
    e + f ]
```

This is parsed exactly the same as '[a + b, c + d, e + f]'.

See Section 6.8.11 [Syntax Tables], page 174, for a way to create your own operators and other input notations. See Section 6.8.10 [Compositions], page 168, for a way to create new display formats.

See Chapter 10 [Algebra], page 243, for commands for manipulating formulas symbolically.

5 Stack and Trail Commands

This chapter describes the Calc commands for manipulating objects on the stack and in the trail buffer. (These commands operate on objects of any type, such as numbers, vectors, formulas, and incomplete objects.)

5.1 Stack Manipulation Commands

To duplicate the top object on the stack, press RET or SPC (two equivalent keys for the calc-enter command). Given a positive numeric prefix argument, these commands duplicate several elements at the top of the stack. Given a negative argument, these commands duplicate the specified element of the stack. Given an argument of zero, they duplicate the entire stack. For example, with '10 20 30' on the stack, RET creates '10 20 30 30', *C-u 2 RET* creates '10 20 30 20 30', *C-u - 2 RET* creates '10 20 30 20', and *C-u 0 RET* creates '10 20 30 10 20 30'.

The LFD (calc-over) command (on a key marked Line-Feed if you have it, else on *C-j*) is like calc-enter except that the sign of the numeric prefix argument is interpreted oppositely. Also, with no prefix argument the default argument is 2. Thus with '10 20 30' on the stack, LFD and *C-u 2 LFD* are both equivalent to *C-u - 2 RET*, producing '10 20 30 20'.

To remove the top element from the stack, press DEL (calc-pop). The *C-d* key is a synonym for DEL. (If the top element is an incomplete object with at least one element, the last element is removed from it.) Given a positive numeric prefix argument, several elements are removed. Given a negative argument, the specified element of the stack is deleted. Given an argument of zero, the entire stack is emptied. For example, with '10 20 30' on the stack, DEL leaves '10 20', *C-u 2 DEL* leaves '10', *C-u - 2 DEL* leaves '10 30', and *C-u 0 DEL* leaves an empty stack.

The *M-DEL* (calc-pop-above) command is to DEL what LFD is to RET: It interprets the sign of the numeric prefix argument in the opposite way, and the default argument is 2. Thus *M-DEL* by itself removes the second-from-top stack element, leaving the first, third, fourth, and so on; *M-3 M-DEL* deletes the third stack element.

The above commands do not depend on the location of the cursor. If the customizable variable calc-context-sensitive-enter is non-nil (see Appendix C [Customizing Calc], page 435), these commands will become context sensitive. For example, instead of duplicating the top of the stack, RET will copy the element at the cursor to the top of the stack. With a positive numeric prefix, a copy of the element at the cursor and the appropriate number of preceding elements will be placed at the top of the stack. A negative prefix will still duplicate the specified element of the stack regardless of the cursor position. Similarly, DEL will remove the corresponding elements from the stack.

To exchange the top two elements of the stack, press TAB (calc-roll-down). Given a positive numeric prefix argument, the specified number of elements at the top of the stack are rotated downward. Given a negative argument, the entire stack is rotated downward the specified number of times. Given an argument of zero, the entire stack is reversed top-for-bottom. For example, with '10 20 30 40 50' on the stack, TAB creates '10 20 30 50 40', *C-u 3 TAB* creates '10 20 50 30 40', *C-u - 2 TAB* creates '40 50 10 20 30', and *C-u 0 TAB* creates '50 40 30 20 10'.

The command *M-TAB* (`calc-roll-up`) is analogous to `TAB` except that it rotates upward instead of downward. Also, the default with no prefix argument is to rotate the top 3 elements. For example, with '10 20 30 40 50' on the stack, *M-TAB* creates '10 20 40 50 30', *C-u 4 M-TAB* creates '10 30 40 50 20', *C-u - 2 M-TAB* creates '30 40 50 10 20', and *C-u 0 M-TAB* creates '50 40 30 20 10'.

A good way to view the operation of `TAB` and *M-TAB* is in terms of moving a particular element to a new position in the stack. With a positive argument n, `TAB` moves the top stack element down to level n, making room for it by pulling all the intervening stack elements toward the top. *M-TAB* moves the element at level n up to the top. (Compare with `LFD`, which copies instead of moving the element in level n.)

With a negative argument $-n$, `TAB` rotates the stack to move the object in level n to the deepest place in the stack, and the object in level $n + 1$ to the top. *M-TAB* rotates the deepest stack element to be in level n, also putting the top stack element in level $n + 1$.

See Section 10.1 [Selecting Subformulas], page 243, for a way to apply these commands to any portion of a vector or formula on the stack.

The command *C-x C-t* (`calc-transpose-lines`) will transpose the stack object determined by the point with the stack object at the next higher level. For example, with '10 20 30 40 50' on the stack and the point on the line containing '30', *C-x C-t* creates '10 20 40 30 50'. More generally, *C-x C-t* acts on the stack objects determined by the current point (and mark) similar to how the text-mode command `transpose-lines` acts on lines. With argument n, *C-x C-t* will move the stack object at the level above the current point and move it past N other objects; for example, with '10 20 30 40 50' on the stack and the point on the line containing '30', *C-u 2 C-x C-t* creates '10 40 20 30 50'. With an argument of 0, *C-x C-t* will switch the stack objects at the levels determined by the point and the mark.

5.2 Editing Stack Entries

The ` (`calc-edit`) command creates a temporary buffer (*Calc Edit*) for editing the top-of-stack value using regular Emacs commands. Note that ` is a grave accent, not an apostrophe. With a numeric prefix argument, it edits the specified number of stack entries at once. (An argument of zero edits the entire stack; a negative argument edits one specific stack entry.)

When you are done editing, press *C-c C-c* to finish and return to Calc. The `RET` and `LFD` keys also work to finish most sorts of editing, though in some cases Calc leaves `RET` with its usual meaning ("insert a newline") if it's a situation where you might want to insert new lines into the editing buffer.

When you finish editing, the Calculator parses the lines of text in the *Calc Edit* buffer as numbers or formulas, replaces the original stack elements in the original buffer with these new values, then kills the *Calc Edit* buffer. The original Calculator buffer continues to exist during editing, but for best results you should be careful not to change it until you have finished the edit. You can also cancel the edit by killing the buffer with *C-x k*.

The formula is normally reevaluated as it is put onto the stack. For example, editing 'a + 2' to '3 + 2' and pressing *C-c C-c* will push 5 on the stack. If you use `LFD` to finish, Calc will put the result on the stack without evaluating it.

If you give a prefix argument to *C-c C-c*, Calc will not kill the *Calc Edit* buffer. You can switch back to that buffer and continue editing if you wish. However, you should understand that if you initiated the edit with `, the *C-c C-c* operation will be programmed to replace the top of the stack with the new edited value, and it will do this even if you have rearranged the stack in the meanwhile. This is not so much of a problem with other editing commands, though, such as *s e* (`calc-edit-variable`; see Section 12.3 [Operations on Variables], page 325).

If the `calc-edit` command involves more than one stack entry, each line of the *Calc Edit* buffer is interpreted as a separate formula. Otherwise, the entire buffer is interpreted as one formula, with line breaks ignored. (You can use *C-o* or *C-q C-j* to insert a newline in the buffer without pressing RET.)

The ` key also works during numeric or algebraic entry. The text entered so far is moved to the *Calc Edit* buffer for more extensive editing than is convenient in the minibuffer.

5.3 Trail Commands

The commands for manipulating the Calc Trail buffer are two-key sequences beginning with the *t* prefix.

The *t d* (`calc-trail-display`) command turns display of the trail on and off. Normally the trail display is toggled on if it was off, off if it was on. With a numeric prefix of zero, this command always turns the trail off; with a prefix of one, it always turns the trail on. The other trail-manipulation commands described here automatically turn the trail on. Note that when the trail is off values are still recorded there; they are simply not displayed. To set Emacs to turn the trail off by default, type *t d* and then save the mode settings with *m m* (`calc-save-modes`).

The *t i* (`calc-trail-in`) and *t o* (`calc-trail-out`) commands switch the cursor into and out of the Calc Trail window. In practice they are rarely used, since the commands shown below are a more convenient way to move around in the trail, and they work "by remote control" when the cursor is still in the Calculator window.

There is a *trail pointer* which selects some entry of the trail at any given time. The trail pointer looks like a '>' symbol right before the selected number. The following commands operate on the trail pointer in various ways.

The *t y* (`calc-trail-yank`) command reads the selected value in the trail and pushes it onto the Calculator stack. It allows you to re-use any previously computed value without retyping. With a numeric prefix argument *n*, it yanks the value *n* lines above the current trail pointer.

The *t <* (`calc-trail-scroll-left`) and *t >* (`calc-trail-scroll-right`) commands horizontally scroll the trail window left or right by one half of its width.

The *t n* (`calc-trail-next`) and *t p* (`calc-trail-previous`) commands move the trail pointer down or up one line. The *t f* (`calc-trail-forward`) and *t b* (`calc-trail-backward`) commands move the trail pointer down or up one screenful at a time. All of these commands accept numeric prefix arguments to move several lines or screenfuls at a time.

The *t [* (`calc-trail-first`) and *t]* (`calc-trail-last`) commands move the trail pointer to the first or last line of the trail. The *t h* (`calc-trail-here`) command moves the trail pointer to the cursor position; unlike the other trail commands, *t h* works only when Calc Trail is the selected window.

The *t s* (`calc-trail-isearch-forward`) and *t r* (`calc-trail-isearch-backward`) commands perform an incremental search forward or backward through the trail. You can press RET to terminate the search; the trail pointer moves to the current line. If you cancel the search with *C-g*, the trail pointer stays where it was when the search began.

The *t m* (`calc-trail-marker`) command allows you to enter a line of text of your own choosing into the trail. The text is inserted after the line containing the trail pointer; this usually means it is added to the end of the trail. Trail markers are useful mainly as the targets for later incremental searches in the trail.

The *t k* (`calc-trail-kill`) command removes the selected line from the trail. The line is saved in the Emacs kill ring suitable for yanking into another buffer, but it is not easy to yank the text back into the trail buffer. With a numeric prefix argument, this command kills the *n* lines below or above the selected one.

The *t .* (`calc-full-trail-vectors`) command is described elsewhere; see Section 9.9 [Vector and Matrix Formats], page 240.

5.4 Keep Arguments

The *K* (`calc-keep-args`) command acts like a prefix for the following command. It prevents that command from removing its arguments from the stack. For example, after *2 RET 3 +*, the stack contains the sole number 5, but after *2 RET 3 K +*, the stack contains the arguments and the result: '2 3 5'.

With the exception of keyboard macros, this works for all commands that take arguments off the stack. (To avoid potentially unpleasant behavior, a *K* prefix before a keyboard macro will be ignored. A *K* prefix called *within* the keyboard macro will still take effect.) As another example, *K a s* simplifies a formula, pushing the simplified version of the formula onto the stack after the original formula (rather than replacing the original formula). Note that you could get the same effect by typing *RET a s*, copying the formula and then simplifying the copy. One difference is that for a very large formula the time taken to format the intermediate copy in *RET a s* could be noticeable; *K a s* would avoid this extra work.

Even stack manipulation commands are affected. TAB works by popping two values and pushing them back in the opposite order, so *2 RET 3 K TAB* produces '2 3 3 2'.

A few Calc commands provide other ways of doing the same thing. For example, *' sin($)* replaces the number on the stack with its sine using algebraic entry; to push the sine and keep the original argument you could use either *' sin($1)* or *K ' sin($)*. See Section 3.5 [Algebraic Entry], page 109. Also, the *s s* command is effectively the same as *K s t*. See Section 12.1 [Storing Variables], page 323.

If you execute a command and then decide you really wanted to keep the argument, you can press *M-RET* (`calc-last-args`). This command pushes the last arguments that were popped by any command onto the stack. Note that the order of things on the stack will be different than with *K*: *2 RET 3 + M-RET* leaves '5 2 3' on the stack instead of '2 3 5'. See Section 3.8 [Undo], page 112.

6 Mode Settings

This chapter describes commands that set modes in the Calculator. They do not affect the contents of the stack, although they may change the *appearance* or *interpretation* of the stack's contents.

6.1 General Mode Commands

You can save all of the current mode settings in your Calc init file (the file given by the variable `calc-settings-file`, typically `~/.emacs.d/calc.el`) with the `m m` (`calc-save-modes`) command. This will cause Emacs to reestablish these modes each time it starts up. The modes saved in the file include everything controlled by the `m` and `d` prefix keys, the current precision and binary word size, whether or not the trail is displayed, the current height of the Calc window, and more. The current interface (used when you type `C-x *` `*`) is also saved. If there were already saved mode settings in the file, they are replaced. Otherwise, the new mode information is appended to the end of the file.

The `m R` (`calc-mode-record-mode`) command tells Calc to record all the mode settings (as if by pressing `m m`) every time a mode setting changes. If the modes are saved this way, then this "automatic mode recording" mode is also saved. Type `m R` again to disable this method of recording the mode settings. To turn it off permanently, the `m m` command will also be necessary. (If Embedded mode is enabled, other options for recording the modes are available; see Section 16.4 [Mode Settings in Embedded Mode], page 358.)

The `m F` (`calc-settings-file-name`) command allows you to choose a different file than the current value of `calc-settings-file` for `m m`, `Z P`, and similar commands to save permanent information. You are prompted for a file name. All Calc modes are then reset to their default values, then settings from the file you named are loaded if this file exists, and this file becomes the one that Calc will use in the future for commands like `m m`. The default settings file name is `~/.emacs.d/calc.el`. You can see the current file name by giving a blank response to the `m F` prompt. See also the discussion of the `calc-settings-file` variable; see Appendix C [Customizing Calc], page 435.

If the file name you give is your user init file (typically `~/.emacs`), `m F` will not automatically load the new file. This is because your user init file may contain other things you don't want to reread. You can give a numeric prefix argument of 1 to `m F` to force it to read the file no matter what. Conversely, an argument of -1 tells `m F` *not* to read the new file. An argument of 2 or -2 tells `m F` not to reset the modes to their defaults beforehand, which is useful if you intend your new file to have a variant of the modes present in the file you were using before.

The `m x` (`calc-always-load-extensions`) command enables a mode in which the first use of Calc loads the entire program, including all extensions modules. Otherwise, the extensions modules will not be loaded until the various advanced Calc features are used. Since this mode only has effect when Calc is first loaded, `m x` is usually followed by `m m` to make the mode-setting permanent. To load all of Calc just once, rather than always in the future, you can press `C-x * L`.

The `m S` (`calc-shift-prefix`) command enables a mode in which all of Calc's letter prefix keys may be typed shifted as well as unshifted. If you are typing, say, `a S` (`calc-solve-for`) quite often you might find it easier to turn this mode on so that you can type `A S` instead. When this mode is enabled, the commands that used to be on those single shifted letters (e.g., *A* (`calc-abs`)) can now be invoked by pressing the shifted letter twice: *A A*. Note that the *v* prefix key always works both shifted and unshifted, and the *z* and *Z* prefix keys are always distinct. Also, the *h* prefix is not affected by this mode. Press *m S* again to disable shifted-prefix mode.

6.2 Precision

The *p* (`calc-precision`) command controls the precision to which floating-point calculations are carried. The precision must be at least 3 digits and may be arbitrarily high, within the limits of memory and time. This affects only floats: Integer and rational calculations are always carried out with as many digits as necessary.

The *p* key prompts for the current precision. If you wish you can instead give the precision as a numeric prefix argument.

Many internal calculations are carried to one or two digits higher precision than normal. Results are rounded down afterward to the current precision. Unless a special display mode has been selected, floats are always displayed with their full stored precision, i.e., what you see is what you get. Reducing the current precision does not round values already on the stack, but those values will be rounded down before being used in any calculation. The *c 0* through *c 9* commands (see Section 7.4 [Conversions], page 190) can be used to round an existing value to a new precision.

It is important to distinguish the concepts of *precision* and *accuracy*. In the normal usage of these words, the number 123.4567 has a precision of 7 digits but an accuracy of 4 digits. The precision is the total number of digits not counting leading or trailing zeros (regardless of the position of the decimal point). The accuracy is simply the number of digits after the decimal point (again not counting trailing zeros). In Calc you control the precision, not the accuracy of computations. If you were to set the accuracy instead, then calculations like 'exp(100)' would generate many more digits than you would typically need, while 'exp(-100)' would probably round to zero! In Calc, both these computations give you exactly 12 (or the requested number of) significant digits.

The only Calc features that deal with accuracy instead of precision are fixed-point display mode for floats (*d f*; see Section 6.7.3 [Float Formats], page 150), and the rounding functions like **floor** and **round** (see Section 7.2 [Integer Truncation], page 189). Also, *c 0* through *c 9* deal with both precision and accuracy depending on the magnitudes of the numbers involved.

If you need to work with a particular fixed accuracy (say, dollars and cents with two digits after the decimal point), one solution is to work with integers and an "implied" decimal point. For example, $8.99 divided by 6 would be entered *899 RET 6 /*, yielding 149.833 (actually $1.49833 with our implied decimal point); pressing *R* would round this to 150 cents, i.e., $1.50.

See Section 4.3 [Floats], page 117, for still more on floating-point precision and related issues.

6.3 Inverse and Hyperbolic Flags

There is no single-key equivalent to the `calc-arcsin` function. Instead, you must first press
I (`calc-inverse`) to set the *Inverse Flag*, then press *S* (`calc-sin`). The *I* key actually
toggles the Inverse Flag. When this flag is set, the word 'Inv' appears in the mode line.

Likewise, the *H* key (`calc-hyperbolic`) sets or clears the Hyperbolic Flag, which transforms `calc-sin` into `calc-sinh`. If both of these flags are set at once, the effect will be
`calc-arcsinh`. (The Hyperbolic flag is also used by some non-trigonometric commands;
for example *H L* computes a base-10, instead of base-*e*, logarithm.)

Command names like `calc-arcsin` are provided for completeness, and may be executed
with *x* or *M-x*. Their effect is simply to toggle the Inverse and/or Hyperbolic flags and then
execute the corresponding base command (`calc-sin` in this case).

The *O* key (`calc-option`) sets another flag, the *Option Flag*, which also can alter the
subsequent Calc command in various ways.

The Inverse, Hyperbolic and Option flags apply only to the next Calculator command,
after which they are automatically cleared. (They are also cleared if the next keystroke is
not a Calc command.) Digits you type after *I*, *H* or *O* (or *K*) are treated as prefix arguments
for the next command, not as numeric entries. The same is true of *C-u*, but not of the
minus sign (*K -* means to subtract and keep arguments).

Another Calc prefix flag, *K* (keep-arguments), is discussed elsewhere. See Section 5.4
[Keep Arguments], page 136.

6.4 Calculation Modes

The commands in this section are two-key sequences beginning with the *m* prefix. (That's
the letter *m*, not the META key.) The 'm a' (`calc-algebraic-mode`) command is described
elsewhere (see Section 3.5 [Algebraic Entry], page 109).

6.4.1 Angular Modes

The Calculator supports three notations for angles: radians, degrees, and degrees-minutes-
seconds. When a number is presented to a function like `sin` that requires an angle, the
current angular mode is used to interpret the number as either radians or degrees. If an
HMS form is presented to `sin`, it is always interpreted as degrees-minutes-seconds.

Functions that compute angles produce a number in radians, a number in degrees, or
an HMS form depending on the current angular mode. If the result is a complex number
and the current mode is HMS, the number is instead expressed in degrees. (Complex-
number calculations would normally be done in Radians mode, though. Complex numbers
are converted to degrees by calculating the complex result in radians and then multiplying
by 180 over π.)

The *m r* (`calc-radians-mode`), *m d* (`calc-degrees-mode`), and *m h* (`calc-hms-mode`)
commands control the angular mode. The current angular mode is displayed on the Emacs
mode line. The default angular mode is Degrees.

6.4.2 Polar Mode

The Calculator normally "prefers" rectangular complex numbers in the sense that rectangular form is used when the proper form can not be decided from the input. This might

happen by multiplying a rectangular number by a polar one, by taking the square root of a negative real number, or by entering (*2 SPC 3*).

The *m p* (`calc-polar-mode`) command toggles complex-number preference between rectangular and polar forms. In Polar mode, all of the above example situations would produce polar complex numbers.

6.4.3 Fraction Mode

Division of two integers normally yields a floating-point number if the result cannot be expressed as an integer. In some cases you would rather get an exact fractional answer. One way to accomplish this is to use the *:* (`calc-fdiv`) [`fdiv`] command, which divides the two integers on the top of the stack to produce a fraction: *6 RET 4 :* produces 3:2 even though *6 RET 4 /* produces 1.5.

To set the Calculator to produce fractional results for normal integer divisions, use the *m f* (`calc-frac-mode`) command. For example, 8/4 produces 2 in either mode, but 6/4 produces 3:2 in Fraction mode, 1.5 in Float mode.

At any time you can use *c f* (`calc-float`) to convert a fraction to a float, or *c F* (`calc-fraction`) to convert a float to a fraction. See Section 7.4 [Conversions], page 190.

6.4.4 Infinite Mode

The Calculator normally treats results like 1/0 as errors; formulas like this are left in unsimplified form. But Calc can be put into a mode where such calculations instead produce "infinite" results.

The *m i* (`calc-infinite-mode`) command turns this mode on and off. When the mode is off, infinities do not arise except in calculations that already had infinities as inputs. (One exception is that infinite open intervals like '[0 .. inf)' can be generated; however, intervals closed at infinity ('[0 .. inf]') will not be generated when Infinite mode is off.)

With Infinite mode turned on, '1 / 0' will generate `uinf`, an undirected infinity. See Section 4.5 [Infinities], page 119, for a discussion of the difference between `inf` and `uinf`. Also, 0/0 evaluates to `nan`, the "indeterminate" symbol. Various other functions can also return infinities in this mode; for example, 'ln(0) = -inf', and 'gamma(-7) = uinf'. Once again, note that 'exp(inf) = inf' regardless of Infinite mode because this calculation has infinity as an input.

The *m i* command with a numeric prefix argument of zero, i.e., *C-u 0 m i*, turns on a Positive Infinite mode in which zero is treated as positive instead of being directionless. Thus, '1 / 0 = inf' and '-1 / 0 = -inf' in this mode. Note that zero never actually has a sign in Calc; there are no separate representations for +0 and −0. Positive Infinite mode merely changes the interpretation given to the single symbol, '0'. One consequence of this is that, while you might expect '1 / -0 = -inf', actually '1 / -0' is equivalent to '1 / 0', which is equal to positive `inf`.

6.4.5 Symbolic Mode

Calculations are normally performed numerically wherever possible. For example, the `calc-sqrt` command, or `sqrt` function in an algebraic expression, produces a numeric answer if the argument is a number or a symbolic expression if the argument is an expression: *2 Q* pushes 1.4142 but *' x+1 RET Q* pushes 'sqrt(x+1)'.

In *Symbolic mode*, controlled by the *m s* (`calc-symbolic-mode`) command, functions which would produce inexact, irrational results are left in symbolic form. Thus *16 Q* pushes 4, but *2 Q* pushes '`sqrt(2)`'.

The shift-*N* (`calc-eval-num`) command evaluates numerically the expression at the top of the stack, by temporarily disabling `calc-symbolic-mode` and executing = (`calc-evaluate`). Given a numeric prefix argument, it also sets the floating-point precision to the specified value for the duration of the command.

To evaluate a formula numerically without expanding the variables it contains, you can use the key sequence *m s a v m s* (this uses `calc-alg-evaluate`, which resimplifies but doesn't evaluate variables.)

6.4.6 Matrix and Scalar Modes

Calc sometimes makes assumptions during algebraic manipulation that are awkward or incorrect when vectors and matrices are involved. Calc has two modes, *Matrix mode* and *Scalar mode*, which modify its behavior around vectors in useful ways.

Press *m v* (`calc-matrix-mode`) once to enter Matrix mode. In this mode, all objects are assumed to be matrices unless provably otherwise. One major effect is that Calc will no longer consider multiplication to be commutative. (Recall that in matrix arithmetic, '`A*B`' is not the same as '`B*A`'.) This assumption affects rewrite rules and algebraic simplification. Another effect of this mode is that calculations that would normally produce constants like 0 and 1 (e.g., $a - a$ and a/a, respectively) will now produce function calls that represent "generic" zero or identity matrices: '`idn(0)`', '`idn(1)`'. The `idn` function '`idn(a,n)`' returns a times an nxn identity matrix; if n is omitted, it doesn't know what dimension to use and so the `idn` call remains in symbolic form. However, if this generic identity matrix is later combined with a matrix whose size is known, it will be converted into a true identity matrix of the appropriate size. On the other hand, if it is combined with a scalar (as in '`idn(1) + 2`'), Calc will assume it really was a scalar after all and produce, e.g., 3.

Press *m v* a second time to get Scalar mode. Here, objects are assumed *not* to be vectors or matrices unless provably so. For example, normally adding a variable to a vector, as in '`[x, y, z] + a`', will leave the sum in symbolic form because as far as Calc knows, '`a`' could represent either a number or another 3-vector. In Scalar mode, '`a`' is assumed to be a non-vector, and the addition is evaluated to '`[x+a, y+a, z+a]`'.

Press *m v* a third time to return to the normal mode of operation.

If you press *m v* with a numeric prefix argument n, you get a special "dimensioned" Matrix mode in which matrices of unknown size are assumed to be nxn square matrices. Then, the function call '`idn(1)`' will expand into an actual matrix rather than representing a "generic" matrix. Simply typing *C-u m v* will get you a square Matrix mode, in which matrices of unknown size are assumed to be square matrices of unspecified size.

Of course these modes are approximations to the true state of affairs, which is probably that some quantities will be matrices and others will be scalars. One solution is to "declare" certain variables or functions to be scalar-valued. See Section 6.6 [Declarations], page 143, to see how to make declarations in Calc.

There is nothing stopping you from declaring a variable to be scalar and then storing a matrix in it; however, if you do, the results you get from Calc may not be valid. Suppose you let Calc get the result '`[x+a, y+a, z+a]`' shown above, and then stored '`[1, 2, 3]`' in 'a'. The result would not be the same as for '[x, y, z] + [1, 2, 3]', but that's because you have broken your earlier promise to Calc that 'a' would be scalar.

Another way to mix scalars and matrices is to use selections (see Section 10.1 [Selecting Subformulas], page 243). Use Matrix mode when operating on your formula normally; then, to apply Scalar mode to a certain part of the formula without affecting the rest just select that part, change into Scalar mode and press = to resimplify the part under this mode, then change back to Matrix mode before deselecting.

6.4.7 Automatic Recomputation

The *evaluates-to* operator, '=>', has the special property that any '=>' formulas on the stack are recomputed whenever variable values or mode settings that might affect them are changed. See Section 12.5 [Evaluates-To Operator], page 327.

The m C (calc-auto-recompute) command turns this automatic recomputation on and off. If you turn it off, Calc will not update '=>' operators on the stack (nor those in the attached Embedded mode buffer, if there is one). They will not be updated unless you explicitly do so by pressing = or until you press m C to turn recomputation back on. (While automatic recomputation is off, you can think of m C m C as a command to update all '=>' operators while leaving recomputation off.)

To update '=>' operators in an Embedded buffer while automatic recomputation is off, use C-x * u. See Chapter 16 [Embedded Mode], page 351.

6.4.8 Working Messages

Since the Calculator is written entirely in Emacs Lisp, which is not designed for heavy numerical work, many operations are quite slow. The Calculator normally displays the message 'Working...' in the echo area during any command that may be slow. In addition, iterative operations such as square roots and trigonometric functions display the intermediate result at each step. Both of these types of messages can be disabled if you find them distracting.

Type m w (calc-working) with a numeric prefix of 0 to disable all "working" messages. Use a numeric prefix of 1 to enable only the plain 'Working...' message. Use a numeric prefix of 2 to see intermediate results as well. With no numeric prefix this displays the current mode.

While it may seem that the "working" messages will slow Calc down considerably, experiments have shown that their impact is actually quite small. But if your terminal is slow you may find that it helps to turn the messages off.

6.5 Simplification Modes

The current *simplification mode* controls how numbers and formulas are "normalized" when being taken from or pushed onto the stack. Some normalizations are unavoidable, such as rounding floating-point results to the current precision, and reducing fractions to simplest form. Others, such as simplifying a formula like $a + a$ (or $2 + 3$), are done automatically but can be turned off when necessary.

When you press a key like + when 2 and 3 are on the stack, Calc pops these numbers, normalizes them, creates the formula $2 + 3$, normalizes it, and pushes the result. Of course the standard rules for normalizing $2 + 3$ will produce the result 5.

Simplification mode commands consist of the lower-case `m` prefix key followed by a shifted letter.

The `m O` (`calc-no-simplify-mode`) command turns off all optional simplifications. These would leave a formula like $2 + 3$ alone. In fact, nothing except simple numbers are ever affected by normalization in this mode. Explicit simplification commands, such as `=` or `a s`, can still be given to simplify any formulas. See Section 17.4 [Algebraic Definitions], page 369, for a sample use of No-Simplification mode.

The `m N` (`calc-num-simplify-mode`) command turns off simplification of any formulas except those for which all arguments are constants. For example, $1 + 2$ is simplified to 3, and $a + (2 - 2)$ is simplified to $a + 0$ but no further, since one argument of the sum is not a constant. Unfortunately, $(a + 2) - 2$ is *not* simplified because the top-level '-' operator's arguments are not both constant numbers (one of them is the formula $a + 2$). A constant is a number or other numeric object (such as a constant error form or modulo form), or a vector all of whose elements are constant.

The `m I` (`calc-basic-simplify-mode`) command does some basic simplifications for all formulas. This includes many easy and fast algebraic simplifications such as $a + 0$ to a, and $a + 2a$ to $3a$, as well as evaluating functions like $\mathtt{deriv}(x^2, x)$ to $2x$.

The `m B` (`calc-bin-simplify-mode`) mode applies the basic simplifications to a result and then, if the result is an integer, uses the `b c` (`calc-clip`) command to clip the integer according to the current binary word size. See Section 7.7 [Binary Functions], page 206. Real numbers are rounded to the nearest integer and then clipped; other kinds of results (after the basic simplifications) are left alone.

The `m A` (`calc-alg-simplify-mode`) mode does standard algebraic simplifications. See Section 10.3.2 [Algebraic Simplifications], page 257.

The `m E` (`calc-ext-simplify-mode`) mode does "extended", or "unsafe", algebraic simplification. See Section 10.3.3 [Unsafe Simplifications], page 260.

The `m U` (`calc-units-simplify-mode`) mode does units simplification. See Section 10.3.4 [Simplification of Units], page 261. These include the algebraic simplifications, plus variable names which are identifiable as unit names (like 'mm' for "millimeters") are simplified with their unit definitions in mind.

A common technique is to set the simplification mode down to the lowest amount of simplification you will allow to be applied automatically, then use manual commands like `a s` and `c c` (`calc-clean`) to perform higher types of simplifications on demand.

6.6 Declarations

A *declaration* is a statement you make that promises you will use a certain variable or function in a restricted way. This may give Calc the freedom to do things that it couldn't do if it had to take the fully general situation into account.

6.6.1 Declaration Basics

The `s d` (`calc-declare-variable`) command is the easiest way to make a declaration for a variable. This command prompts for the variable name, then prompts for the declaration. The default at the declaration prompt is the previous declaration, if any. You can edit this declaration, or press *C-k* to erase it and type a new declaration. (Or, erase it and press RET to clear the declaration, effectively "undeclaring" the variable.)

A declaration is in general a vector of *type symbols* and *range* values. If there is only one type symbol or range value, you can write it directly rather than enclosing it in a vector. For example, *s d foo RET real RET* declares foo to be a real number, and *s d bar RET [int, const, [1..6]] RET* declares bar to be a constant integer between 1 and 6. (Actually, you can omit the outermost brackets and Calc will provide them for you: *s d bar RET int, const, [1..6] RET*.)

Declarations in Calc are kept in a special variable called Decls. This variable encodes the set of all outstanding declarations in the form of a matrix. Each row has two elements: A variable or vector of variables declared by that row, and the declaration specifier as described above. You can use the *s D* command to edit this variable if you wish to see all the declarations at once. See Section 12.3 [Operations on Variables], page 325, for a description of this command and the *s p* command that allows you to save your declarations permanently if you wish.

Items being declared can also be function calls. The arguments in the call are ignored; the effect is to say that this function returns values of the declared type for any valid arguments. The *s d* command declares only variables, so if you wish to make a function declaration you will have to edit the Decls matrix yourself.

For example, the declaration matrix

```
[ [ foo,       real       ]
  [ [j, k, n], int        ]
  [ f(1,2,3),  [0 .. inf) ] ]
```

declares that foo represents a real number, j, k and n represent integers, and the function f always returns a real number in the interval shown.

If there is a declaration for the variable All, then that declaration applies to all variables that are not otherwise declared. It does not apply to function names. For example, using the row '[All, real]' says that all your variables are real unless they are explicitly declared without real in some other row. The *s d* command declares All if you give a blank response to the variable-name prompt.

6.6.2 Kinds of Declarations

The type-specifier part of a declaration (that is, the second prompt in the *s d* command) can be a type symbol, an interval, or a vector consisting of zero or more type symbols followed by zero or more intervals or numbers that represent the set of possible values for the variable.

```
[ [ a, [1, 2, 3, 4, 5] ]
  [ b, [1 .. 5]         ]
  [ c, [int, 1 .. 5]    ] ]
```

Here a is declared to contain one of the five integers shown; b is any number in the interval from 1 to 5 (any real number since we haven't specified), and c is any integer in that interval. Thus the declarations for a and c are nearly equivalent (see below).

The type-specifier can be the empty vector '[]' to say that nothing is known about a given variable's value. This is the same as not declaring the variable at all except that it overrides any All declaration which would otherwise apply.

The initial value of `Decls` is the empty vector '`[]`'. If `Decls` has no stored value or if the value stored in it is not valid, it is ignored and there are no declarations as far as Calc is concerned. (The *s d* command will replace such a malformed value with a fresh empty matrix, '`[]`', before recording the new declaration.) Unrecognized type symbols are ignored.

The following type symbols describe what sorts of numbers will be stored in a variable:

`int`   Integers.

`numint`   Numerical integers. (Integers or integer-valued floats.)

`frac`   Fractions. (Rational numbers which are not integers.)

`rat`   Rational numbers. (Either integers or fractions.)

`float`   Floating-point numbers.

`real`   Real numbers. (Integers, fractions, or floats. Actually, intervals and error forms with real components also count as reals here.)

`pos`   Positive real numbers. (Strictly greater than zero.)

`nonneg`   Nonnegative real numbers. (Greater than or equal to zero.)

`number`   Numbers. (Real or complex.)

Calc uses this information to determine when certain simplifications of formulas are safe. For example, '`(x^y)^z`' cannot be simplified to '`x^(y z)`' in general; for example, '`((-3)^2)^1:2`' is 3, but '`(-3)^(2*1:2) = (-3)^1`' is −3. However, this simplification *is* safe if `z` is known to be an integer, or if `x` is known to be a nonnegative real number. If you have given declarations that allow Calc to deduce either of these facts, Calc will perform this simplification of the formula.

Calc can apply a certain amount of logic when using declarations. For example, '`(x^y)^(2n+1)`' will be simplified if `n` has been declared `int`; Calc knows that an integer times an integer, plus an integer, must always be an integer. (In fact, Calc would simplify '`(-x)^(2n+1)`' to '`-(x^(2n+1))`' since it is able to determine that '`2n+1`' must be an odd integer.)

Similarly, '`(abs(x)^y)^z`' will be simplified to '`abs(x)^(y z)`' because Calc knows that the `abs` function always returns a nonnegative real. If you had a `myabs` function that also had this property, you could get Calc to recognize it by adding the row '`[myabs(), nonneg]`' to the `Decls` matrix.

One instance of this simplification is '`sqrt(x^2)`' (since the `sqrt` function is effectively a one-half power). Normally Calc leaves this formula alone. After the command *s d x RET real RET*, however, it can simplify the formula to '`abs(x)`'. And after *s d x RET nonneg RET*, Calc can simplify this formula all the way to '`x`'.

If there are any intervals or real numbers in the type specifier, they comprise the set of possible values that the variable or function being declared can have. In particular, the type symbol `real` is effectively the same as the range '`[-inf .. inf]`' (note that infinity is included in the range of possible values); `pos` is the same as '`(0 .. inf]`', and `nonneg` is the same as '`[0 .. inf]`'. Saying '`[real, [-5 .. 5]]`' is redundant because the fact that the variable is real can be deduced just from the interval, but '`[int, [-5 .. 5]]`' and '`[rat, [-5 .. 5]]`' are useful combinations.

Note that the vector of intervals or numbers is in the same format used by Calc's set-manipulation commands. See Section 9.6 [Set Operations], page 229.

The type specifier '[1, 2, 3]' is equivalent to '[numint, 1, 2, 3]', *not* to '[int, 1, 2, 3]'. In other words, the range of possible values means only that the variable's value must be numerically equal to a number in that range, but not that it must be equal in type as well. Calc's set operations act the same way; 'in(2, [1., 2., 3.])' and 'in(1.5, [1:2, 3:2, 5:2])' both report "true."

If you use a conflicting combination of type specifiers, the results are unpredictable. An example is '[pos, [0 .. 5]]', where the interval does not lie in the range described by the type symbol.

"Real" declarations mostly affect simplifications involving powers like the one described above. Another case where they are used is in the a P command which returns a list of all roots of a polynomial; if the variable has been declared real, only the real roots (if any) will be included in the list.

"Integer" declarations are used for simplifications which are valid only when certain values are integers (such as '(x^y)^z' shown above).

Calc's algebraic simplifications also make use of declarations when simplifying equations and inequalities. They will cancel x from both sides of 'a x = b x' only if it is sure x is non-zero, say, because it has a pos declaration. To declare specifically that x is real and non-zero, use '[[-inf .. 0), (0 .. inf]]'. (There is no way in the current notation to say that x is nonzero but not necessarily real.) The a e command does "unsafe" simplifications, including canceling 'x' from the equation when 'x' is not known to be nonzero.

Another set of type symbols distinguish between scalars and vectors.

scalar   The value is not a vector.

vector   The value is a vector.

matrix   The value is a matrix (a rectangular vector of vectors).

sqmatrix The value is a square matrix.

These type symbols can be combined with the other type symbols described above; '[int, matrix]' describes an object which is a matrix of integers.

Scalar/vector declarations are used to determine whether certain algebraic operations are safe. For example, '[a, b, c] + x' is normally not simplified to '[a + x, b + x, c + x]', but it will be if x has been declared scalar. On the other hand, multiplication is usually assumed to be commutative, but the terms in 'x y' will never be exchanged if both x and y are known to be vectors or matrices. (Calc currently never distinguishes between vector and matrix declarations.)

See Section 6.4.6 [Matrix Mode], page 141, for a discussion of Matrix mode and Scalar mode, which are similar to declaring '[All, matrix]' or '[All, scalar]' but much more convenient.

One more type symbol that is recognized is used with the H a d command for taking total derivatives of a formula. See Section 10.5 [Calculus], page 264.

const   The value is a constant with respect to other variables.

Calc does not check the declarations for a variable when you store a value in it. However, storing −3.5 in a variable that has been declared `pos`, `int`, or `matrix` may have unexpected effects; Calc may evaluate 'sqrt(x^2)' to 3.5 if it substitutes the value first, or to −3.5 if x was declared `pos` and the formula 'sqrt(x^2)' is simplified to 'x' before the value is substituted. Before using a variable for a new purpose, it is best to use *s d* or *s D* to check to make sure you don't still have an old declaration for the variable that will conflict with its new meaning.

6.6.3 Functions for Declarations

Calc has a set of functions for accessing the current declarations in a convenient manner. These functions return 1 if the argument can be shown to have the specified property, or 0 if the argument can be shown *not* to have that property; otherwise they are left unevaluated. These functions are suitable for use with rewrite rules (see Section 10.11.3 [Conditional Rewrite Rules], page 293) or programming constructs (see Section 17.2.2 [Conditionals in Macros], page 365). They can be entered only using algebraic notation. See Section 10.10 [Logical Operations], page 288, for functions that perform other tests not related to declarations.

For example, 'dint(17)' returns 1 because 17 is an integer, as do 'dint(n)' and 'dint(2 n - 3)' if n has been declared `int`, but 'dint(2.5)' and 'dint(n + 0.5)' return 0. Calc consults knowledge of its own built-in functions as well as your own declarations: 'dint(floor(x))' returns 1.

The `dint` function checks if its argument is an integer. The `dnatnum` function checks if its argument is a natural number, i.e., a nonnegative integer. The `dnumint` function checks if its argument is numerically an integer, i.e., either an integer or an integer-valued float. Note that these and the other data type functions also accept vectors or matrices composed of suitable elements, and that real infinities 'inf' and '-inf' are considered to be integers for the purposes of these functions.

The `drat` function checks if its argument is rational, i.e., an integer or fraction. Infinities count as rational, but intervals and error forms do not.

The `dreal` function checks if its argument is real. This includes integers, fractions, floats, real error forms, and intervals.

The `dimag` function checks if its argument is imaginary, i.e., is mathematically equal to a real number times i.

The `dpos` function checks for positive (but nonzero) reals. The `dneg` function checks for negative reals. The `dnonneg` function checks for nonnegative reals, i.e., reals greater than or equal to zero. Note that Calc's algebraic simplifications, which are effectively applied to all conditions in rewrite rules, can simplify an expression like $x > 0$ to 1 or 0 using `dpos`. So the actual functions `dpos`, `dneg`, and `dnonneg` are rarely necessary.

The `dnonzero` function checks that its argument is nonzero. This includes all nonzero real or complex numbers, all intervals that do not include zero, all nonzero modulo forms, vectors all of whose elements are nonzero, and variables or formulas whose values can be deduced to be nonzero. It does not include error forms, since they represent values which could be anything including zero. (This is also the set of objects considered "true" in conditional contexts.)

The **deven** function returns 1 if its argument is known to be an even integer (or integer-valued float); it returns 0 if its argument is known not to be even (because it is known to be odd or a non-integer). Calc's algebraic simplifications use this to simplify a test of the form 'x % 2 = 0'. There is also an analogous **dodd** function.

The **drange** function returns a set (an interval or a vector of intervals and/or numbers; see Section 9.6 [Set Operations], page 229) that describes the set of possible values of its argument. If the argument is a variable or a function with a declaration, the range is copied from the declaration. Otherwise, the possible signs of the expression are determined using a method similar to **dpos**, etc., and a suitable set like '[0 .. inf]' is returned. If the expression is not provably real, the **drange** function remains unevaluated.

The **dscalar** function returns 1 if its argument is provably scalar, or 0 if its argument is provably non-scalar. It is left unevaluated if this cannot be determined. (If Matrix mode or Scalar mode is in effect, this function returns 1 or 0, respectively, if it has no other information.) When Calc interprets a condition (say, in a rewrite rule) it considers an unevaluated formula to be "false." Thus, 'dscalar(a)' is "true" only if a is provably scalar, and '!dscalar(a)' is "true" only if a is provably non-scalar; both are "false" if there is insufficient information to tell.

6.7 Display Modes

The commands in this section are two-key sequences beginning with the *d* prefix. The *d 1* (`calc-line-numbering`) and *d b* (`calc-line-breaking`) commands are described elsewhere; see Section 3.3 [Stack Basics], page 108, and see Section 6.8.1 [Normal Language Modes], page 159, respectively. Display formats for vectors and matrices are also covered elsewhere; see Section 9.9 [Vector and Matrix Formats], page 240.

One thing all display modes have in common is their treatment of the *H* prefix. This prefix causes any mode command that would normally refresh the stack to leave the stack display alone. The word "Dirty" will appear in the mode line when Calc thinks the stack display may not reflect the latest mode settings.

The *d RET* (`calc-refresh-top`) command reformats the top stack entry according to all the current modes. Positive prefix arguments reformat the top *n* entries; negative prefix arguments reformat the specified entry, and a prefix of zero is equivalent to *d SPC* (`calc-refresh`), which reformats the entire stack. For example, *H d s M-2 d RET* changes to scientific notation but reformats only the top two stack entries in the new mode.

The *I* prefix has another effect on the display modes. The mode is set only temporarily; the top stack entry is reformatted according to that mode, then the original mode setting is restored. In other words, *I d s* is equivalent to *H d s d RET H d (old mode)*.

6.7.1 Radix Modes

Calc normally displays numbers in decimal (*base-10* or *radix-10*) notation. Calc can actually display in any radix from two (binary) to 36. When the radix is above 10, the letters A to Z are used as digits. When entering such a number, letter keys are interpreted as potential digits rather than terminating numeric entry mode.

The key sequences *d 2*, *d 8*, *d 6*, and *d 0* select binary, octal, hexadecimal, and decimal as the current display radix, respectively. Numbers can always be entered in any radix, though the current radix is used as a default if you press # without any initial digits. A number entered without a # is *always* interpreted as decimal.

To set the radix generally, use **d r** (`calc-radix`) and enter an integer from 2 to 36. You can specify the radix as a numeric prefix argument; otherwise you will be prompted for it.

Integers normally are displayed with however many digits are necessary to represent the integer and no more. The **d z** (`calc-leading-zeros`) command causes integers to be padded out with leading zeros according to the current binary word size. (See Section 7.7 [Binary Functions], page 206, for a discussion of word size.) If the absolute value of the word size is w, all integers are displayed with at least enough digits to represent $2^w - 1$ in the current radix. (Larger integers will still be displayed in their entirety.)

Calc can display w-bit integers using two's complement notation, although this is most useful with the binary, octal and hexadecimal display modes. This option is selected by using the *0* option prefix before setting the display radix, and a negative word size might be appropriate (see Section 7.7 [Binary Functions], page 206). In two's complement notation, the integers in the (nearly) symmetric interval from -2^{w-1} to $2^{w-1} - 1$ are represented by the integers from 0 to $2^w - 1$: the integers from 0 to $2^{w-1} - 1$ are represented by themselves and the integers from -2^{w-1} to -1 are represented by the integers from 2^{w-1} to $2^w - 1$ (the integer k is represented by $k + 2^w$). Calc will display a two's complement integer by the radix (either 2, 8 or 16), two # symbols, and then its representation (including any leading zeros necessary to include all w bits). In a two's complement display mode, numbers that are not displayed in two's complement notation (i.e., that aren't integers from -2^{w-1} to $2^{w-1} - 1$) will be represented using Calc's usual notation (in the appropriate radix).

6.7.2 Grouping Digits

Long numbers can be hard to read if they have too many digits. For example, the factorial of 30 is 33 digits long! Press **d g** (`calc-group-digits`) to enable *Grouping* mode, in which digits are displayed in clumps of 3 or 4 (depending on the current radix) separated by commas.

The **d g** command toggles grouping on and off. With a numeric prefix of 0, this command displays the current state of the grouping flag; with an argument of minus one it disables grouping; with a positive argument N it enables grouping on every N digits. For floating-point numbers, grouping normally occurs only before the decimal point. A negative prefix argument $-N$ enables grouping every N digits both before and after the decimal point.

The **d ,** (`calc-group-char`) command allows you to choose any character as the grouping separator. The default is the comma character. If you find it difficult to read vectors of large integers grouped with commas, you may wish to use spaces or some other character instead. This command takes the next character you type, whatever it is, and uses it as the digit separator. As a special case, **d , ** selects '\,' (TeX's thin-space symbol) as the digit separator.

Please note that grouped numbers will not generally be parsed correctly if re-read in textual form, say by the use of *C-x * y* and *C-x * g*. (See Chapter 14 [Kill and Yank], page 339, for details on these commands.) One exception is the '\,' separator, which doesn't interfere with parsing because it is ignored by TeX language mode.

6.7.3 Float Formats

Floating-point quantities are normally displayed in standard decimal form, with scientific notation used if the exponent is especially high or low. All significant digits are normally displayed. The commands in this section allow you to choose among several alternative display formats for floats.

The *d n* (`calc-normal-notation`) command selects the normal display format. All significant figures in a number are displayed. With a positive numeric prefix, numbers are rounded if necessary to that number of significant digits. With a negative numerix prefix, the specified number of significant digits less than the current precision is used. (Thus *C-u -2 d n* displays 10 digits if the current precision is 12.)

The *d f* (`calc-fix-notation`) command selects fixed-point notation. The numeric argument is the number of digits after the decimal point, zero or more. This format will relax into scientific notation if a nonzero number would otherwise have been rounded all the way to zero. Specifying a negative number of digits is the same as for a positive number, except that small nonzero numbers will be rounded to zero rather than switching to scientific notation.

The *d s* (`calc-sci-notation`) command selects scientific notation. A positive argument sets the number of significant figures displayed, of which one will be before and the rest after the decimal point. A negative argument works the same as for *d n* format. The default is to display all significant digits.

The *d e* (`calc-eng-notation`) command selects engineering notation. This is similar to scientific notation except that the exponent is rounded down to a multiple of three, with from one to three digits before the decimal point. An optional numeric prefix sets the number of significant digits to display, as for *d s*.

It is important to distinguish between the current *precision* and the current *display format*. After the commands *C-u 10 p* and *C-u 6 d n* the Calculator computes all results to ten significant figures but displays only six. (In fact, intermediate calculations are often carried to one or two more significant figures, but values placed on the stack will be rounded down to ten figures.) Numbers are never actually rounded to the display precision for storage, except by commands like *C-k* and *C-x * y* which operate on the actual displayed text in the Calculator buffer.

The *d .* (`calc-point-char`) command selects the character used as a decimal point. Normally this is a period; users in some countries may wish to change this to a comma. Note that this is only a display style; on entry, periods must always be used to denote floating-point numbers, and commas to separate elements in a list.

6.7.4 Complex Formats

There are three supported notations for complex numbers in rectangular form. The default is as a pair of real numbers enclosed in parentheses and separated by a comma: '(a,b)'. The *d c* (`calc-complex-notation`) command selects this style.

The other notations are *d i* (`calc-i-notation`), in which numbers are displayed in 'a+bi' form, and *d j* (`calc-j-notation`) which displays the form 'a+bj' preferred in some disciplines.

Complex numbers are normally entered in '(a,b)' format. If you enter '2+3i' as an algebraic formula, it will be stored as the formula '2 + 3 * i'. However, if you use = to evaluate this formula and you have not changed the variable 'i', the 'i' will be interpreted as '(0,1)' and the formula will be simplified to '(2,3)'. Other commands (like `calc-sin`) will *not* interpret the formula '2 + 3 * i' as a complex number. See Section 4.14 [Variables], page 128, under "special constants."

6.7.5 Fraction Formats

Display of fractional numbers is controlled by the *d o* (`calc-over-notation`) command. By default, a number like eight thirds is displayed in the form '8:3'. The *d o* command prompts for a one- or two-character format. If you give one character, that character is used as the fraction separator. Common separators are ':' and '/'. (During input of numbers, the : key must be used regardless of the display format; in particular, the / is used for RPN-style division, *not* for entering fractions.)

If you give two characters, fractions use "integer-plus-fractional-part" notation. For example, the format '+/' would display eight thirds as '2+2/3'. If two colons are present in a number being entered, the number is interpreted in this form (so that the entries *2:2:3* and *8:3* are equivalent).

It is also possible to follow the one- or two-character format with a number. For example: ':10' or '+/3'. In this case, Calc adjusts all fractions that are displayed to have the specified denominator, if possible. Otherwise it adjusts the denominator to be a multiple of the specified value. For example, in ':6' mode the fraction 1:6 will be unaffected, but 2:3 will be displayed as 4:6, 1:2 will be displayed as 3:6, and 1:8 will be displayed as 3:24. Integers are also affected by this mode: 3 is displayed as 18:6. Note that the format ':1' writes fractions the same as ':', but it writes integers as *n*:1.

The fraction format does not affect the way fractions or integers are stored, only the way they appear on the screen. The fraction format never affects floats.

6.7.6 HMS Formats

The *d h* (`calc-hms-notation`) command controls the display of HMS (hours-minutes-seconds) forms. It prompts for a string which consists basically of an "hours" marker, optional punctuation, a "minutes" marker, more optional punctuation, and a "seconds" marker. Punctuation is zero or more spaces, commas, or semicolons. The hours marker is one or more non-punctuation characters. The minutes and seconds markers must be single non-punctuation characters.

The default HMS format is '@ ' "', producing HMS values of the form '23@ 30' 15.75"'. The format 'deg, ms' would display this same value as '23deg, 30m15.75s'. During numeric entry, the *h* or *o* keys are recognized as synonyms for @ regardless of display format. The *m* and *s* keys are recognized as synonyms for ' and ", respectively, but only if an @ (or *h* or *o*) has already been typed; otherwise, they have their usual meanings (*m*- prefix and *s*-prefix). Thus, *5* ", *0 @ 5* ", and *0 h 5 s* are some of the ways to enter the quantity "five seconds." The ' key is recognized as "minutes" only if @ (or *h* or *o*) has already been pressed; otherwise it means to switch to algebraic entry.

6.7.7 Date Formats

The *d d* (`calc-date-notation`) command controls the display of date forms (see Section 4.9 [Date Forms], page 122). It prompts for a string which contains letters that represent the various parts of a date and time. To show which parts should be omitted when the form represents a pure date with no time, parts of the string can be enclosed in '< >' marks. If you don't include '< >' markers in the format, Calc guesses at which parts, if any, should be omitted when formatting pure dates.

The default format is: '<H:mm:SSpp >Www Mmm D, YYYY'. An example string in this format is '3:32pm Wed Jan 9, 1991'. If you enter a blank format string, this default format is reestablished.

Calc uses '< >' notation for nameless functions as well as for dates. See Section 9.8.1 [Specifying Operators], page 235. To avoid confusion with nameless functions, your date formats should avoid using the '#' character.

6.7.7.1 ISO 8601

The same date can be written down in different formats and Calc tries to allow you to choose your preferred format. Some common formats are ambiguous, however; for example, 10/11/2012 means October 11, 2012 in the United States but it means November 10, 2012 in Europe. To help avoid such ambiguities, the International Organization for Standardization (ISO) provides the ISO 8601 standard, which provides three different but easily distinguishable and unambiguous ways to represent a date.

The ISO 8601 calendar date representation is

    YYYY-MM-DD

where *YYYY* is the four digit year, *MM* is the two-digit month number (01 for January to 12 for December), and *DD* is the two-digit day of the month (01 to 31). (Note that *YYYY* does not correspond to Calc's date formatting code, which will be introduced later.) The year, which should be padded with zeros to ensure it has at least four digits, is the Gregorian year, except that the year before 0001 (1 AD) is the year 0000 (1 BC). The date October 11, 2012 is written 2012-10-11 in this representation and November 10, 2012 is written 2012-11-10.

The ISO 8601 ordinal date representation is

    YYYY-DDD

where *YYYY* is the year, as above, and *DDD* is the day of the year. The date December 31, 2011 is written 2011-365 in this representation and January 1, 2012 is written 2012-001.

The ISO 8601 week date representation is

    YYYY-Www-D

where *YYYY* is the ISO week-numbering year, *ww* is the two digit week number (preceded by a literal "W"), and *D* is the day of the week (1 for Monday through 7 for Sunday). The ISO week-numbering year is based on the Gregorian year but can differ slightly. The first week of an ISO week-numbering year is the week with the Gregorian year's first Thursday in it (equivalently, the week containing January 4); any day of that week (Monday through Sunday) is part of the same ISO week-numbering year, any day from the previous week is part of the previous year. For example, January 4, 2013 is on a Friday, and so the first week for the ISO week-numbering year 2013 starts on Monday, December 31, 2012. The day December 31, 2012 is then part of the Gregorian year 2012 but ISO week-numbering year 2013. In the week date representation, this week goes from 2013-W01-1 (December 31, 2012) to 2013-W01-7 (January 6, 2013).

All three ISO 8601 representations arrange the numbers from most significant to least significant; as well as being unambiguous representations, they are easy to sort since chronological order in this formats corresponds to lexicographical order. The hyphens are sometimes omitted.

The ISO 8601 standard uses a 24 hour clock; a particular time is represented by *hh:mm:ss* where *hh* is the two-digit hour (from 00 to 24), *mm* is the two-digit minute (from 00 to 59) and *ss* is the two-digit second. The seconds or minutes and seconds can be omitted, and decimals can be added. If a date with a time is represented, they should be separated by a literal "T", so noon on December 13, 2012 can be represented as 2012-12-13T12:00.

6.7.7.2 Date Formatting Codes

When displaying a date, the current date format is used. All characters except for letters and '<' and '>' are copied literally when dates are formatted. The portion between '< >' markers is omitted for pure dates, or included for date/time forms. Letters are interpreted according to the table below.

When dates are read in during algebraic entry, Calc first tries to match the input string to the current format either with or without the time part. The punctuation characters (including spaces) must match exactly; letter fields must correspond to suitable text in the input. If this doesn't work, Calc checks if the input is a simple number; if so, the number is interpreted as a number of days since Dec 31, 1 BC. Otherwise, Calc tries a much more relaxed and flexible algorithm which is described in the next section.

Weekday names are ignored during reading.

Two-digit year numbers are interpreted as lying in the range from 1941 to 2039. Years outside that range are always entered and displayed in full. Year numbers with a leading '+' sign are always interpreted exactly, allowing the entry and display of the years 1 through 99 AD.

Here is a complete list of the formatting codes for dates:

Y	Year: "91" for 1991, "7" for 2007, "+23" for 23 AD.
YY	Year: "91" for 1991, "07" for 2007, "+23" for 23 AD.
BY	Year: "91" for 1991, " 7" for 2007, "+23" for 23 AD.
YYY	Year: "1991" for 1991, "23" for 23 AD.
YYYY	Year: "1991" for 1991, "+23" for 23 AD.
ZYYY	Year: "1991" for 1991, "0023" for 23 AD, "0000" for 1 BC.
IYYY	Year: ISO 8601 week-numbering year.
aa	Year: "ad" or blank.
AA	Year: "AD" or blank.
aaa	Year: "ad " or blank. (Note trailing space.)
AAA	Year: "AD " or blank.
aaaa	Year: "a.d." or blank.
AAAA	Year: "A.D." or blank.

bb	Year: "bc" or blank.
BB	Year: "BC" or blank.
bbb	Year: " bc" or blank. (Note leading space.)
BBB	Year: " BC" or blank.
bbbb	Year: "b.c." or blank.
BBBB	Year: "B.C." or blank.
M	Month: "8" for August.
MM	Month: "08" for August.
BM	Month: " 8" for August.
MMM	Month: "AUG" for August.
Mmm	Month: "Aug" for August.
mmm	Month: "aug" for August.
MMMM	Month: "AUGUST" for August.
Mmmm	Month: "August" for August.
D	Day: "7" for 7th day of month.
DD	Day: "07" for 7th day of month.
BD	Day: " 7" for 7th day of month.
W	Weekday: "0" for Sunday, "6" for Saturday.
w	Weekday: "1" for Monday, "7" for Sunday.
WWW	Weekday: "SUN" for Sunday.
Www	Weekday: "Sun" for Sunday.
www	Weekday: "sun" for Sunday.
WWWW	Weekday: "SUNDAY" for Sunday.
Wwww	Weekday: "Sunday" for Sunday.
Iww	Week number: ISO 8601 week number, "W01" for week 1.
d	Day of year: "34" for Feb. 3.
ddd	Day of year: "034" for Feb. 3.
bdd	Day of year: " 34" for Feb. 3.
T	Letter: Literal "T".
h	Hour: "5" for 5 AM; "17" for 5 PM.
hh	Hour: "05" for 5 AM; "17" for 5 PM.
bh	Hour: " 5" for 5 AM; "17" for 5 PM.
H	Hour: "5" for 5 AM and 5 PM.

HH	Hour: "05" for 5 AM and 5 PM.
BH	Hour: " 5" for 5 AM and 5 PM.
p	AM/PM: "a" or "p".
P	AM/PM: "A" or "P".
pp	AM/PM: "am" or "pm".
PP	AM/PM: "AM" or "PM".
pppp	AM/PM: "a.m." or "p.m.".
PPPP	AM/PM: "A.M." or "P.M.".
m	Minutes: "7" for 7.
mm	Minutes: "07" for 7.
bm	Minutes: " 7" for 7.
s	Seconds: "7" for 7; "7.23" for 7.23.
ss	Seconds: "07" for 7; "07.23" for 7.23.
bs	Seconds: " 7" for 7; " 7.23" for 7.23.
SS	Optional seconds: "07" for 7; blank for 0.
BS	Optional seconds: " 7" for 7; blank for 0.
N	Numeric date/time: "726842.25" for 6:00am Wed Jan 9, 1991.
n	Numeric date: "726842" for any time on Wed Jan 9, 1991.
J	Julian date/time: "2448265.75" for 6:00am Wed Jan 9, 1991.
j	Julian date: "2448266" for any time on Wed Jan 9, 1991.
U	Unix time: "663400800" for 6:00am Wed Jan 9, 1991.
X	Brackets suppression. An "X" at the front of the format causes the surrounding '< >' delimiters to be omitted when formatting dates. Note that the brackets are still required for algebraic entry.

If "SS" or "BS" (optional seconds) is preceded by a colon, the colon is also omitted if the seconds part is zero.

If "bb," "bbb" or "bbbb" or their upper-case equivalents appear in the format, then negative year numbers are displayed without a minus sign. Note that "aa" and "bb" are mutually exclusive. Some typical usages would be 'YYYY AABB'; 'AAAYYYYBBB'; 'YYYYBBB'.

The formats "YY," "YYYY," "MM," "DD," "ddd," "hh," "HH," "mm," "ss," and "SS" actually match any number of digits during reading unless several of these codes are strung together with no punctuation in between, in which case the input must have exactly as many digits as there are letters in the format.

The "j," "J," and "U" formats do not make any time zone adjustment. They effectively use 'julian(x,0)' and 'unixtime(x,0)' to make the conversion; see Section 7.5 [Date Arithmetic], page 192.

6.7.7.3 Free-Form Dates

When reading a date form during algebraic entry, Calc falls back on the algorithm described here if the input does not exactly match the current date format. This algorithm generally "does the right thing" and you don't have to worry about it, but it is described here in full detail for the curious.

Calc does not distinguish between upper- and lower-case letters while interpreting dates.

First, the time portion, if present, is located somewhere in the text and then removed. The remaining text is then interpreted as the date.

A time is of the form 'hh:mm:ss', possibly with the seconds part omitted and possibly with an AM/PM indicator added to indicate 12-hour time. If the AM/PM is present, the minutes may also be omitted. The AM/PM part may be any of the words 'am', 'pm', 'noon', or 'midnight'; each of these may be abbreviated to one letter, and the alternate forms 'a.m.', 'p.m.', and 'mid' are also understood. Obviously 'noon' and 'midnight' are allowed only on 12:00:00. The words 'noon', 'mid', and 'midnight' are also recognized with no number attached. Midnight will represent the beginning of a day.

If there is no AM/PM indicator, the time is interpreted in 24-hour format.

When reading the date portion, Calc first checks to see if it is an ISO 8601 week-numbering date; if the string contains an integer representing the year, a "W" followed by two digits for the week number, and an integer from 1 to 7 representing the weekday (in that order), then all other characters are ignored and this information determines the date. Otherwise, all words and numbers are isolated from the string; other characters are ignored. All words must be either month names or day-of-week names (the latter of which are ignored). Names can be written in full or as three-letter abbreviations.

Large numbers, or numbers with '+' or '-' signs, are interpreted as years. If one of the other numbers is greater than 12, then that must be the day and the remaining number in the input is therefore the month. Otherwise, Calc assumes the month, day and year are in the same order that they appear in the current date format. If the year is omitted, the current year is taken from the system clock.

If there are too many or too few numbers, or any unrecognizable words, then the input is rejected.

If there are any large numbers (of five digits or more) other than the year, they are ignored on the assumption that they are something like Julian dates that were included along with the traditional date components when the date was formatted.

One of the words 'ad', 'a.d.', 'bc', or 'b.c.' may optionally be used; the latter two are equivalent to a minus sign on the year value.

If you always enter a four-digit year, and use a name instead of a number for the month, there is no danger of ambiguity.

6.7.7.4 Standard Date Formats

There are actually ten standard date formats, numbered 0 through 9. Entering a blank line at the *d d* command's prompt gives you format number 1, Calc's usual format. You can enter any digit to select the other formats.

To create your own standard date formats, give a numeric prefix argument from 0 to 9 to the *d d* command. The format you enter will be recorded as the new standard format of that number, as well as becoming the new current date format. You can save your formats permanently with the *m m* command (see Chapter 6 [Mode Settings], page 137).

0	'N' (Numerical format)
1	'<H:mm:SSpp >Www Mmm D, YYYY' (American format)
2	'D Mmm YYYY<, h:mm:SS>' (European format)
3	'Www Mmm BD< hh:mm:ss> YYYY' (Unix written date format)
4	'M/D/Y< H:mm:SSpp>' (American slashed format)
5	'D.M.Y< h:mm:SS>' (European dotted format)
6	'M-D-Y< H:mm:SSpp>' (American dashed format)
7	'D-M-Y< h:mm:SS>' (European dashed format)
8	'j<, h:mm:ss>' (Julian day plus time)
9	'YYddd< hh:mm:ss>' (Year-day format)
10	'ZYYYY-MM-DD Www< hh:mm>' (Org mode format)
11	'IYYYY-Iww-w<Thh:mm:ss>' (ISO 8601 week numbering format)

6.7.8 Truncating the Stack

The *d t* (calc-truncate-stack) command moves the '.' line that marks the top-of-stack up or down in the Calculator buffer. The number right above that line is considered to the be at the top of the stack. Any numbers below that line are "hidden" from all stack operations (although still visible to the user). This is similar to the Emacs "narrowing" feature, except that the values below the '.' are *visible*, just temporarily frozen. This feature allows you to keep several independent calculations running at once in different parts of the stack, or to apply a certain command to an element buried deep in the stack.

Pressing *d t* by itself moves the '.' to the line the cursor is on. Thus, this line and all those below it become hidden. To un-hide these lines, move down to the end of the buffer and press *d t*. With a positive numeric prefix argument n, *d t* hides the bottom n values in the buffer. With a negative argument, it hides all but the top n values. With an argument of zero, it hides zero values, i.e., moves the '.' all the way down to the bottom.

The *d [* (calc-truncate-up) and *d]* (calc-truncate-down) commands move the '.' up or down one line at a time (or several lines with a prefix argument).

6.7.9 Justification

Values on the stack are normally left-justified in the window. You can control this arrangement by typing *d <* (calc-left-justify), *d >* (calc-right-justify), or *d =* (calc-center-justify). For example, in Right-Justification mode, stack entries are displayed flush-right against the right edge of the window.

If you change the width of the Calculator window you may have to type *d SPC* (calc-refresh) to re-align right-justified or centered text.

Right-justification is especially useful together with fixed-point notation (see *d f*; calc-fix-notation). With these modes together, the decimal points on numbers will always line up.

With a numeric prefix argument, the justification commands give you a little extra control over the display. The argument specifies the horizontal "origin" of a display line. It is also possible to specify a maximum line width using the *d b* command (see Section 6.8.1 [Normal Language Modes], page 159). For reference, the precise rules for formatting and breaking lines are given below. Notice that the interaction between origin and line width is slightly different in each justification mode.

In Left-Justified mode, the line is indented by a number of spaces given by the origin (default zero). If the result is longer than the maximum line width, if given, or too wide to fit in the Calc window otherwise, then it is broken into lines which will fit; each broken line is indented to the origin.

In Right-Justified mode, lines are shifted right so that the rightmost character is just before the origin, or just before the current window width if no origin was specified. If the line is too long for this, then it is broken; the current line width is used, if specified, or else the origin is used as a width if that is specified, or else the line is broken to fit in the window.

In Centering mode, the origin is the column number of the center of each stack entry. If a line width is specified, lines will not be allowed to go past that width; Calc will either indent less or break the lines if necessary. If no origin is specified, half the line width or Calc window width is used.

Note that, in each case, if line numbering is enabled the display is indented an additional four spaces to make room for the line number. The width of the line number is taken into account when positioning according to the current Calc window width, but not when positioning by explicit origins and widths. In the latter case, the display is formatted as specified, and then uniformly shifted over four spaces to fit the line numbers.

6.7.10 Labels

The *d {* (`calc-left-label`) command prompts for a string, then displays that string to the left of every stack entry. If the entries are left-justified (see Section 6.7.9 [Justification], page 157), then they will appear immediately after the label (unless you specified an origin greater than the length of the label). If the entries are centered or right-justified, the label appears on the far left and does not affect the horizontal position of the stack entry.

Give a blank string (with *d {* RET) to turn the label off.

The *d }* (`calc-right-label`) command similarly adds a label on the righthand side. It does not affect positioning of the stack entries unless they are right-justified. Also, if both a line width and an origin are given in Right-Justified mode, the stack entry is justified to the origin and the righthand label is justified to the line width.

One application of labels would be to add equation numbers to formulas you are manipulating in Calc and then copying into a document (possibly using Embedded mode). The equations would typically be centered, and the equation numbers would be on the left or right as you prefer.

6.8 Language Modes

The commands in this section change Calc to use a different notation for entry and display of formulas, corresponding to the conventions of some other common language such as Pascal or LaTeX. Objects displayed on the stack or yanked from the Calculator to an editing buffer will be formatted in the current language; objects entered in algebraic entry or yanked from another buffer will be interpreted according to the current language.

The current language has no effect on things written to or read from the trail buffer, nor does it affect numeric entry. Only algebraic entry is affected. You can make even algebraic entry ignore the current language and use the standard notation by giving a numeric prefix, e.g., *C-u* '.

For example, suppose the formula '2*a[1] + atan(a[2])' occurs in a C program; elsewhere in the program you need the derivatives of this formula with respect to 'a[1]' and 'a[2]'. First, type *d C* to switch to C notation. Now use C-u C-x * g to grab the formula into the Calculator, *a d a[1] RET* to differentiate with respect to the first variable, and *C-x * y* to yank the formula for the derivative back into your C program. Press *U* to undo the differentiation and repeat with *a d a[2] RET* for the other derivative.

Without being switched into C mode first, Calc would have misinterpreted the brackets in 'a[1]' and 'a[2]', would not have known that atan was equivalent to Calc's built-in arctan function, and would have written the formula back with notations (like implicit multiplication) which would not have been valid for a C program.

As another example, suppose you are maintaining a C program and a LaTeX document, each of which needs a copy of the same formula. You can grab the formula from the program in C mode, switch to LaTeX mode, and yank the formula into the document in LaTeX math-mode format.

Language modes are selected by typing the letter *d* followed by a shifted letter key.

6.8.1 Normal Language Modes

The *d N* (calc-normal-language) command selects the usual notation for Calc formulas, as described in the rest of this manual. Matrices are displayed in a multi-line tabular format, but all other objects are written in linear form, as they would be typed from the keyboard.

The *d O* (calc-flat-language) command selects a language identical with the normal one, except that matrices are written in one-line form along with everything else. In some applications this form may be more suitable for yanking data into other buffers.

Even in one-line mode, long formulas or vectors will still be split across multiple lines if they exceed the width of the Calculator window. The *d b* (calc-line-breaking) command turns this line-breaking feature on and off. (It works independently of the current language.) If you give a numeric prefix argument of five or greater to the *d b* command, that argument will specify the line width used when breaking long lines.

The *d B* (calc-big-language) command selects a language which uses textual approximations to various mathematical notations, such as powers, quotients, and square roots:

```
   ------------
 | a + 1    2
 | ----- + c
\|   b
```

in place of 'sqrt((a+1)/b + c^2)'.

Subscripts like 'a_i' are displayed as actual subscripts in Big mode. Double subscripts, 'a_i_j' ('subscr(subscr(a, i), j)') are displayed as 'a' with subscripts separated by commas: 'i, j'. They must still be entered in the usual underscore notation.

One slight ambiguity of Big notation is that

```
    3
  - -
    4
```

can represent either the negative rational number −3:4, or the actual expression '−(3/4)'; but the latter formula would normally never be displayed because it would immediately be evaluated to −3:4 or −0.75, so this ambiguity is not a problem in typical use.

Non-decimal numbers are displayed with subscripts. Thus there is no way to tell the difference between '16#C2' and 'C2_16', though generally you will know which interpretation is correct. Logarithms 'log(x,b)' and 'log10(x)' also use subscripts in Big mode.

In Big mode, stack entries often take up several lines. To aid readability, stack entries are separated by a blank line in this mode. You may find it useful to expand the Calc window's height using C-x ^ (enlarge-window) or to make the Calc window the only one on the screen with C-x 1 (delete-other-windows).

Long lines are currently not rearranged to fit the window width in Big mode, so you may need to use the < and > keys to scroll across a wide formula. For really big formulas, you may even need to use { and } to scroll up and down.

The d U (calc-unformatted-language) command altogether disables the use of operator notation in formulas. In this mode, the formula shown above would be displayed:

```
sqrt(add(div(add(a, 1), b), pow(c, 2)))
```

These four modes differ only in display format, not in the format expected for algebraic entry. The standard Calc operators work in all four modes, and unformatted notation works in any language mode (except that Mathematica mode expects square brackets instead of parentheses).

6.8.2 C, FORTRAN, and Pascal Modes

The d C (calc-c-language) command selects the conventions of the C language for display and entry of formulas. This differs from the normal language mode in a variety of (mostly minor) ways. In particular, C language operators and operator precedences are used in place of Calc's usual ones. For example, 'a^b' means 'xor(a,b)' in C mode; a value raised to a power is written as a function call, 'pow(a,b)'.

In C mode, vectors and matrices use curly braces instead of brackets. Octal and hexadecimal values are written with leading '0' or '0x' rather than using the '#' symbol. Array subscripting is translated into subscr calls, so that 'a[i]' in C mode is the same as 'a_i' in Normal mode. Assignments turn into the assign function, which Calc normally displays using the ':=' symbol.

The variables pi and e would be displayed 'pi' and 'e' in Normal mode, but in C mode they are displayed as 'M_PI' and 'M_E', corresponding to the names of constants typically provided in the <math.h> header. Functions whose names are different in C are translated automatically for entry and display purposes. For example, entering 'asin(x)' will push the formula 'arcsin(x)' onto the stack; this formula will be displayed as 'asin(x)' as long as C mode is in effect.

The d P (calc-pascal-language) command selects Pascal conventions. Like C mode, Pascal mode interprets array brackets and uses a different table of operators. Hexadecimal numbers are entered and displayed with a preceding dollar sign. (Thus the regular meaning of $2 during algebraic entry does not work in Pascal mode, though $ (and $$, etc.) not followed by digits works the same as always.) No special provisions are made for other non-decimal numbers, vectors, and so on, since there is no universally accepted standard way of handling these in Pascal.

The `d F` (`calc-fortran-language`) command selects FORTRAN conventions. Various function names are transformed into FORTRAN equivalents. Vectors are written as '/1, 2, 3/', and may be entered this way or using square brackets. Since FORTRAN uses round parentheses for both function calls and array subscripts, Calc displays both in the same way; 'a(i)' is interpreted as a function call upon reading, and subscripts must be entered as 'subscr(a, i)'. If the variable `a` has been declared to have type `vector` or `matrix`, however, then 'a(i)' will be parsed as a subscript. (See Section 6.6 [Declarations], page 143.) Usually it doesn't matter, though; if you enter the subscript expression 'a(i)' and Calc interprets it as a function call, you'll never know the difference unless you switch to another language mode or replace `a` with an actual vector (or unless `a` happens to be the name of a built-in function!).

Underscores are allowed in variable and function names in all of these language modes. The underscore here is equivalent to the '#' in Normal mode, or to hyphens in the underlying Emacs Lisp variable names.

FORTRAN and Pascal modes normally do not adjust the case of letters in formulas. Most built-in Calc names use lower-case letters. If you use a positive numeric prefix argument with `d P` or `d F`, these modes will use upper-case letters exclusively for display, and will convert to lower-case on input. With a negative prefix, these modes convert to lower-case for display and input.

6.8.3 TEX and LATEX Language Modes

The `d T` (`calc-tex-language`) command selects the conventions of "math mode" in Donald Knuth's TEX typesetting language, and the `d L` (`calc-latex-language`) command selects the conventions of "math mode" in LATEX, a typesetting language that uses TEX as its formatting engine. Calc's LATEX language mode can read any formula that the TEX language mode can, although LATEX mode may display it differently.

Formulas are entered and displayed in the appropriate notation; $\sin(a/b)$ will appear as '\sin\left({a \over b} \right)' in TEX mode and '\sin\left(\frac{a}{b}\right)' in LATEX mode. Math formulas are often enclosed by '$ $' signs in TEX and LATEX; these should be omitted when interfacing with Calc. To Calc, the '$' sign has the same meaning it always does in algebraic formulas (a reference to an existing entry on the stack).

Complex numbers are displayed as in '3 + 4i'. Fractions and quotients are written using \over in TEX mode (as in {a \over b}) and \frac in LATEX mode (as in \frac{a}{b}); binomial coefficients are written with \choose in TEX mode (as in {a \choose b}) and \binom in LATEX mode (as in \binom{a}{b}). Interval forms are written with \ldots, and error forms are written with \pm. Absolute values are written as in '|x + 1|', and the floor and ceiling functions are written with \lfloor, \rfloor, etc. The words \left and \right are ignored when reading formulas in TEX and LATEX modes. Both inf and uinf are written as \infty; when read, \infty always translates to inf.

Function calls are written the usual way, with the function name followed by the arguments in parentheses. However, functions for which TEX and LATEX have special names (like

\sin) will use curly braces instead of parentheses for very simple arguments. During input, curly braces and parentheses work equally well for grouping, but when the document is formatted the curly braces will be invisible. Thus the printed result is sin 2x but sin(2 + x).

The TEX specific unit names (see Section 11.3 [Predefined Units], page 316) will not use the 'tex' prefix; the unit name for a TEX point will be 'pt' instead of 'texpt', for example.

Function and variable names not treated specially by TEX and LATEX are simply written out as-is, which will cause them to come out in italic letters in the printed document. If you invoke *d T* or *d L* with a positive numeric prefix argument, names of more than one character will instead be enclosed in a protective commands that will prevent them from being typeset in the math italics; they will be written '\hbox{*name*}' in TEX mode and '\text{*name*}' in LATEX mode. The '\hbox{ }' and '\text{ }' notations are ignored during reading. If you use a negative prefix argument, such function names are written '*name*', and function names that begin with \ during reading have the \ removed. (Note that in this mode, long variable names are still written with \hbox or \text. However, you can always make an actual variable name like \bar in any TEX mode.)

During reading, text of the form '\matrix{ ... }' is replaced by '[...]'. The same also applies to \pmatrix and \bmatrix. In LATEX mode this also applies to '\begin{matrix} ... \end{matrix}', '\begin{bmatrix} ... \end{bmatrix}', '\begin{pmatrix} ... \end{pmatrix}', as well as '\begin{smallmatrix} ... \end{smallmatrix}'. The symbol '&' is interpreted as a comma, and the symbols '\cr' and '\\' are interpreted as semicolons. During output, matrices are displayed in '\matrix{ a & b \\ c & d }' format in TEX mode and in '\begin{pmatrix} a & b \\ c & d \end{pmatrix}' format in LATEX mode; you may need to edit this afterwards to change to your preferred matrix form. If you invoke *d T* or *d L* with an argument of 2 or -2, then matrices will be displayed in two-dimensional form, such as

```
\begin{pmatrix}
a & b \\
c & d
\end{pmatrix}
```

This may be convenient for isolated matrices, but could lead to expressions being displayed like

```
\begin{pmatrix} \times x
a & b \\
c & d
\end{pmatrix}
```

While this wouldn't bother Calc, it is incorrect LATEX. (Similarly for TEX.)

Accents like \tilde and \bar translate into function calls internally ('tilde(x)', 'bar(x)'). The \underline sequence is treated as an accent. The \vec accent corresponds to the function name Vec, because vec is the name of a built-in Calc function. The following table shows the accents in Calc, TEX, LATEX and *eqn* (described in the next section):

Calc	TeX	LaTeX	eqn
----	---	-----	---
acute	\acute	\acute	
Acute		\Acute	

bar	\bar	\bar	bar
Bar		\Bar	
breve	\breve	\breve	
Breve		\Breve	
check	\check	\check	
Check		\Check	
dddot		\dddot	
ddddot		\ddddot	
dot	\dot	\dot	dot
Dot		\Dot	
dotdot	\ddot	\ddot	dotdot
DotDot		\Ddot	
dyad			dyad
grave	\grave	\grave	
Grave		\Grave	
hat	\hat	\hat	hat
Hat		\Hat	
Prime			prime
tilde	\tilde	\tilde	tilde
Tilde		\Tilde	
under	\underline	\underline	under
Vec	\vec	\vec	vec
VEC		\Vec	

The '=>' (evaluates-to) operator appears as a \to symbol: '{a \to b}'. TEX defines \to as an alias for \rightarrow. However, if the '=>' is the top-level expression being formatted, a slightly different notation is used: '\evalto a \to b'. The \evalto word is ignored by Calc's input routines, and is undefined in TEX. You will typically want to include one of the following definitions at the top of a TEX file that uses \evalto:

```
\def\evalto{}
\def\evalto#1\to{}
```

The first definition formats evaluates-to operators in the usual way. The second causes only the *b* part to appear in the printed document; the *a* part and the arrow are hidden. Another definition you may wish to use is '\let\to=\Rightarrow' which causes \to to appear more like Calc's '=>' symbol. See Section 12.5 [Evaluates-To Operator], page 327, for a discussion of evalto.

The complete set of TEX control sequences that are ignored during reading is:

```
\hbox  \mbox  \text  \left  \right
\,  \>  \:  \;  \!  \quad  \qquad  \hfil  \hfill
\displaystyle  \textstyle  \dsize  \tsize
\scriptstyle  \scriptscriptstyle  \ssize  \ssize
\rm  \bf  \it  \sl  \roman  \bold  \italic  \slanted
\cal  \mit  \Cal  \Bbb  \frak  \goth
\evalto
```

Note that, because these symbols are ignored, reading a TEX or LATEX formula into Calc and writing it back out may lose spacing and font information.

Also, the "discretionary multiplication sign" '*' is read the same as '*'.

Here are some examples of how various Calc formulas are formatted in TEX:

```
sin(a^2 / b_i)
\sin\left( a^2 \over b_i \right)
```

$$\sin\left(\frac{a^2}{b_i}\right)$$

```
[(3, 4), 3:4, 3 +/- 4, [3 .. inf)]
[3 + 4i, {3 \over 4}, 3 \pm 4, [3 \ldots \infty)]
```

$$[3 + 4i, \frac{3}{4}, 3 \pm 4, [3 \ldots \infty)]$$

```
[abs(a), abs(a / b), floor(a), ceil(a / b)]
[|a|, \left| a \over b \right|,
 \lfloor a \rfloor, \left\lceil a \over b \right\rceil]
```

$$[|a|, \left|\frac{a}{b}\right|, \lfloor a \rfloor, \left\lceil\frac{a}{b}\right\rceil]$$

```
[sin(a), sin(2 a), sin(2 + a), sin(a / b)]
[\sin{a}, \sin{2 a}, \sin(2 + a),
 \sin\left( {a \over b} \right)]
```

$$[\sin a, \sin 2a, \sin(2 + a), \sin\left(\frac{a}{b}\right)]$$

First with plain d T, then with C-u d T, then finally with C-u - d T (using the example definition '\def\foo#1{\tilde F(#1)}':

```
[f(a), foo(bar), sin(pi)]
[f(a), foo(bar), \sin\pi]
[f(a), \hbox{foo}(\hbox{bar}), \sin{\pi}]
[f(a), \foo{\hbox{bar}}, \sin{\pi}]
```

$$[f(a), foo(bar), \sin\pi]$$

$$[f(a), \mathrm{foo}(\mathrm{bar}), \sin\pi]$$

$$[f(a), \tilde{F}(\mathrm{bar}), \sin\pi]$$

First with '\def\evalto{}', then with '\def\evalto#1\to{}':

```
2 + 3 => 5
\evalto 2 + 3 \to 5
```

$$2 + 3 \to 5$$

$$5$$

First with standard `\to`, then with '`\let\to\Rightarrow`':

```
[2 + 3 => 5, a / 2 => (b + c) / 2]
[{2 + 3 \to 5}, {{a \over 2} \to {b + c \over 2}}]
```

$$[2 + 3 \to 5, \frac{a}{2} \to \frac{b+c}{2}]$$

$$[2 + 3 \Rightarrow 5, \frac{a}{2} \Rightarrow \frac{b+c}{2}]$$

Matrices normally, then changing `\matrix` to `\pmatrix`:

```
[ [ a / b, 0 ], [ 0, 2^(x + 1) ] ]
\matrix{ {a \over b} & 0 \\ 0 & 2^{(x + 1)} }
\pmatrix{ {a \over b} & 0 \\ 0 & 2^{(x + 1)} }
```

$$\begin{matrix} \frac{a}{b} & 0 \\ 0 & 2^{(x+1)} \end{matrix}$$

$$\begin{pmatrix} \frac{a}{b} & 0 \\ 0 & 2^{(x+1)} \end{pmatrix}$$

6.8.4 Eqn Language Mode

Eqn is another popular formatter for math formulas. It is designed for use with the TROFF text formatter, and comes standard with many versions of Unix. The *d E* (`calc-eqn-language`) command selects *eqn* notation.

The *eqn* language's main idiosyncrasy is that whitespace plays a significant part in the parsing of the language. For example, '`sqrt x+1 + y`' treats '`x+1`' as the argument of the `sqrt` operator. *Eqn* also understands more conventional grouping using curly braces: '`sqrt{x+1} + y`'. Braces are required only when the argument contains spaces.

In Calc's *eqn* mode, however, curly braces are required to delimit arguments of operators like `sqrt`. The first of the above examples would treat only the '`x`' as the argument of `sqrt`, and in fact '`sin x+1`' would be interpreted as '`sin * x + 1`', because `sin` is not a special operator in the *eqn* language. If you always surround the argument with curly braces, Calc will never misunderstand.

Calc also understands parentheses as grouping characters. Another peculiarity of *eqn*'s syntax makes it advisable to separate words with spaces from any surrounding characters that aren't curly braces, so Calc writes '`sin ( x + y )`' in *eqn* mode. (The spaces around `sin` are important to make *eqn* recognize that `sin` should be typeset in a roman font, and the spaces around `x` and `y` are a good idea just in case the *eqn* document has defined special meanings for these names, too.)

Powers and subscripts are written with the `sub` and `sup` operators, respectively. Note that the caret symbol '`^`' is treated the same as a space in *eqn* mode, as is the '`~`' symbol (these are used to introduce spaces of various widths into the typeset output of *eqn*).

As in LaTeX mode, Calc's formatter omits parentheses around the arguments of functions like `ln` and `sin` if they are "simple-looking"; in this case Calc surrounds the argument with braces, separated by a '`~`' from the function name: '`sin~{x}`'.

Font change codes (like '`roman x`') and positioning codes (like '`~`' and '`down n x`') are ignored by the *eqn* reader. Also ignored are the words `left`, `right`, `mark`, and `lineup`. Quotation marks in *eqn* mode input are treated the same as curly braces: '`sqrt "1+x"`' is equivalent to '`sqrt {1+x}`'; this is only an approximation to the true meaning of quotes in *eqn*, but it is good enough for most uses.

Accent codes ('`x dot`') are handled by treating them as function calls ('`dot(x)`') internally. See Section 6.8.3 [TeX and LaTeX Language Modes], page 161, for a table of these accent functions. The `prime` accent is treated specially if it occurs on a variable or function name: '`f prime prime ( x prime )`' is stored internally as '`f''(x')`'. For example, taking the derivative of '`f(2 x)`' with `a d x` will produce '`2 f'(2 x)`', which *eqn* mode will display as '`2 f prime ( 2 x )`'.

Assignments are written with the '`<-`' (left-arrow) symbol, and `evalto` operators are written with '`->`' or '`evalto ... ->`' (see Section 6.8.3 [TeX and LaTeX Language Modes], page 161, for a discussion of this). The regular Calc symbols '`:=`' and '`=>`' are also recognized for these operators during reading.

Vectors in *eqn* mode use regular Calc square brackets, but matrices are formatted as '`matrix { ccol { a above b } ... }`'. The words `lcol` and `rcol` are recognized as synonyms for `ccol` during input, and are generated instead of `ccol` if the matrix justification mode so specifies.

6.8.5 Yacas Language Mode

The *d Y* (`calc-yacas-language`) command selects the conventions of Yacas, a free computer algebra system. While the operators and functions in Yacas are similar to those of Calc, the names of built-in functions in Yacas are capitalized. The Calc formula '`sin(2 x)`', for example, is entered and displayed '`Sin(2 x)`' in Yacas mode, and "`arcsin(x^2)`' is '`ArcSin(x^2)`' in Yacas mode. Complex numbers are written are written '`3 + 4 I`'. The standard special constants are written `Pi`, `E`, `I`, `GoldenRatio` and `Gamma`. `Infinity` represents both `inf` and `uinf`, and `Undefined` represents `nan`.

Certain operators on functions, such as `D` for differentiation and `Integrate` for integration, take a prefix form in Yacas. For example, the derivative of '`e^x sin(x)`' can be computed with '`D(x) Exp(x)*Sin(x)`'.

Other notable differences between Yacas and standard Calc expressions are that vectors and matrices use curly braces in Yacas, and subscripts use square brackets. If, for example, '`A`' represents the list '`{a,2,c,4}`', then '`A[3]`' would equal '`c`'.

6.8.6 Maxima Language Mode

The *d X* (`calc-maxima-language`) command selects the conventions of Maxima, another free computer algebra system. The function names in Maxima are similar, but not always identical, to Calc. For example, instead of 'arcsin(x)', Maxima will use 'asin(x)'. Complex numbers are written '3 + 4 %i'. The standard special constants are written %pi, %e, %i, %phi and %gamma. In Maxima, inf means the same as in Calc, but infinity represents Calc's uinf.

Underscores as well as percent signs are allowed in function and variable names in Maxima mode. The underscore again is equivalent to the '#' in Normal mode, and the percent sign is equivalent to 'o'o'.

Maxima uses square brackets for lists and vectors, and matrices are written as calls to the function matrix, given the row vectors of the matrix as arguments. Square brackets are also used as subscripts.

6.8.7 Giac Language Mode

The *d A* (`calc-giac-language`) command selects the conventions of Giac, another free computer algebra system. The function names in Giac are similar to Maxima. Complex numbers are written '3 + 4 i'. The standard special constants in Giac are the same as in Calc, except that infinity represents both Calc's inf and uinf.

Underscores are allowed in function and variable names in Giac mode. Brackets are used for subscripts. In Giac, indexing of lists begins at 0, instead of 1 as in Calc. So if 'A' represents the list '[a,2,c,4]', then 'A[2]' would equal 'c'. In general, 'A[n]' in Giac mode corresponds to 'A_(n+1)' in Normal mode.

The Giac interval notation '2 .. 3' has no surrounding brackets; Calc reads '2 .. 3' as the closed interval '[2 .. 3]' and writes any kind of interval as '2 .. 3'. This means you cannot see the difference between an open and a closed interval while in Giac mode.

6.8.8 Mathematica Language Mode

The *d M* (`calc-mathematica-language`) command selects the conventions of Mathematica. Notable differences in Mathematica mode are that the names of built-in functions are capitalized, and function calls use square brackets instead of parentheses. Thus the Calc formula 'sin(2 x)' is entered and displayed 'Sin[2 x]' in Mathematica mode.

Vectors and matrices use curly braces in Mathematica. Complex numbers are written '3 + 4 I'. The standard special constants in Calc are written Pi, E, I, GoldenRatio, EulerGamma, Infinity, ComplexInfinity, and Indeterminate in Mathematica mode. Non-decimal numbers are written, e.g., '16^^7fff'. Floating-point numbers in scientific notation are written '1.23*10.^3'. Subscripts use double square brackets: 'a[[i]]'.

6.8.9 Maple Language Mode

The *d W* (`calc-maple-language`) command selects the conventions of Maple.

Maple's language is much like C. Underscores are allowed in symbol names; square brackets are used for subscripts; explicit '*'s for multiplications are required. Use either '^' or '**' to denote powers.

Maple uses square brackets for lists and curly braces for sets. Calc interprets both notations as vectors, and displays vectors with square brackets. This means Maple sets will be converted to lists when they pass through Calc. As a special case, matrices are written as calls to the function `matrix`, given a list of lists as the argument, and can be read in this form or with all-capitals `MATRIX`.

The Maple interval notation '2 .. 3' is like Giac's interval notation, and is handled the same by Calc.

Maple writes complex numbers as '3 + 4*I'. Its special constants are `Pi`, `E`, `I`, and `infinity` (all three of `inf`, `uinf`, and `nan` display as `infinity`). Floating-point numbers are written '1.23*10.^3'.

Among things not currently handled by Calc's Maple mode are the various quote symbols, procedures and functional operators, and inert ('`&`') operators.

6.8.10 Compositions

There are several *composition functions* which allow you to get displays in a variety of formats similar to those in Big language mode. Most of these functions do not evaluate to anything; they are placeholders which are left in symbolic form by Calc's evaluator but are recognized by Calc's display formatting routines.

Two of these, `string` and `bstring`, are described elsewhere. See Section 4.7 [Strings], page 120. For example, '`string("ABC")`' is displayed as '`ABC`'. When viewed on the stack it will be indistinguishable from the variable `ABC`, but internally it will be stored as '`string([65, 66, 67])`' and can still be manipulated this way; for example, the selection and vector commands *j 1 v v j u* would select the vector portion of this object and reverse the elements, then deselect to reveal a string whose characters had been reversed.

The composition functions do the same thing in all language modes (although their components will of course be formatted in the current language mode). The one exception is Unformatted mode (*d U*), which does not give the composition functions any special treatment. The functions are discussed here because of their relationship to the language modes.

6.8.10.1 Composition Basics

Compositions are generally formed by stacking formulas together horizontally or vertically in various ways. Those formulas are themselves compositions. TEX users will find this analogous to TEX's "boxes." Each multi-line composition has a *baseline*; horizontal compositions use the baselines to decide how formulas should be positioned relative to one another. For example, in the Big mode formula

```
         2
     a + b
17 + ------
       c
```

the second term of the sum is four lines tall and has line three as its baseline. Thus when the term is combined with 17, line three is placed on the same level as the baseline of 17.

Another important composition concept is *precedence*. This is an integer that represents the binding strength of various operators. For example, '`*`' has higher precedence (195) than '`+`' (180), which means that '`(a * b) + c`' will be formatted without the parentheses, but '`a * (b + c)`' will keep the parentheses.

The operator table used by normal and Big language modes has the following precedences:

_	1200	(subscripts)
%	1100	(as in n%)
!	1000	(as in !n)
mod	400	
+/-	300	
!!	210	(as in n!!)
!	210	(as in n!)
^	200	
-	197	(as in -n)
*	195	(or implicit multiplication)
/ % \	190	
+ -	180	(as in a+b)
|	170	
< =	160	(and other relations)
&&	110	
||	100	
? :	90	
!!!	85	
&&&	80	
|||	75	
:=	50	
::	45	
=>	40	

The general rule is that if an operator with precedence n occurs as an argument to an operator with precedence m, then the argument is enclosed in parentheses if $n < m$. Top-level expressions and expressions which are function arguments, vector components, etc., are formatted with precedence zero (so that they normally never get additional parentheses).

For binary left-associative operators like '+', the righthand argument is actually formatted with one-higher precedence than shown in the table. This makes sure '(a + b) + c' omits the parentheses, but the unnatural form 'a + (b + c)' keeps its parentheses. Right-associative operators like '^' format the lefthand argument with one-higher precedence.

The cprec function formats an expression with an arbitrary precedence. For example, 'cprec(abc, 185)' will combine into sums and products as follows: '7 + abc', '7 (abc)' (because this cprec form has higher precedence than addition, but lower precedence than multiplication).

A final composition issue is *line breaking*. Calc uses two different strategies for "flat" and "non-flat" compositions. A non-flat composition is anything that appears on multiple lines (not counting line breaking). Examples would be matrices and Big mode powers and quotients. Non-flat compositions are displayed exactly as specified. If they come out wider than the current window, you must use horizontal scrolling (< and >) to view them.

Flat compositions, on the other hand, will be broken across several lines if they are too wide to fit the window. Certain points in a composition are noted internally as *break points*. Calc's general strategy is to fill each line as much as possible, then to move down to the next line starting at the first break point that didn't fit. However, the line breaker understands the hierarchical structure of formulas. It will not break an "inner" formula if it can use an earlier break point from an "outer" formula instead. For example, a vector of sums might be formatted as:

```
[ a + b + c, d + e + f,
  g + h + i, j + k + l, m ]
```

If the 'm' can fit, then so, it seems, could the 'g'. But Calc prefers to break at the comma since the comma is part of a "more outer" formula. Calc would break at a plus sign only if it had to, say, if the very first sum in the vector had itself been too large to fit.

Of the composition functions described below, only `choriz` generates break points. The `bstring` function (see Section 4.7 [Strings], page 120) also generates breakable items: A break point is added after every space (or group of spaces) except for spaces at the very beginning or end of the string.

Composition functions themselves count as levels in the formula hierarchy, so a `choriz` that is a component of a larger `choriz` will be less likely to be broken. As a special case, if a `bstring` occurs as a component of a `choriz` or `choriz`-like object (such as a vector or a list of arguments in a function call), then the break points in that `bstring` will be on the same level as the break points of the surrounding object.

6.8.10.2 Horizontal Compositions

The `choriz` function takes a vector of objects and composes them horizontally. For example, '`choriz([17, a b/c, d])`' formats as '`17a b / cd`' in Normal language mode, or as

```
    a b
17---d
    c
```

in Big language mode. This is actually one case of the general function '`choriz(vec, sep, prec)`', where either or both of *sep* and *prec* may be omitted. *Prec* gives the *precedence* to use when formatting each of the components of *vec*. The default precedence is the precedence from the surrounding environment.

Sep is a string (i.e., a vector of character codes as might be entered with " " notation) which should separate components of the composition. Also, if *sep* is given, the line breaker will allow lines to be broken after each occurrence of *sep*. If *sep* is omitted, the composition will not be breakable (unless any of its component compositions are breakable).

For example, '`2 choriz([a, b c, d = e], " + ", 180)`' is formatted as '`2 a + b c + (d = e)`'. To get the `choriz` to have precedence 180 "outwards" as well as "inwards," enclose it in a `cprec` form: '`2 cprec(choriz(...), 180)`' formats as '`2 (a + b c + (d = e))`'.

The baseline of a horizontal composition is the same as the baselines of the component compositions, which are all aligned.

6.8.10.3 Vertical Compositions

The `cvert` function makes a vertical composition. Each component of the vector is centered in a column. The baseline of the result is by default the top line of the resulting composition. For example, '`f(cvert([a, bb, ccc]), cvert([a^2 + 1, b^2]))`' formats in Big mode as

```
f( a ,   2    )
   bb    a  + 1
   ccc      2
            b
```

There are several special composition functions that work only as components of a vertical composition. The `cbase` function controls the baseline of the vertical composition; the baseline will be the same as the baseline of whatever component is enclosed in `cbase`. Thus '`f(cvert([a, cbase(bb), ccc]), cvert([a^2 + 1, cbase(b^2)]))`' displays as

```
            2
           a  + 1
      a       2
  f(bb ,    b  )
     ccc
```

There are also `ctbase` and `cbbase` functions which make the baseline of the vertical composition equal to the top or bottom line (rather than the baseline) of that component. Thus '`cvert([cbase(a / b)]) + cvert([ctbase(a / b)]) + cvert([cbbase(a / b)])`' gives

```
            a
  a         -
  - + a + b
  b         -
            b
```

There should be only one `cbase`, `ctbase`, or `cbbase` function in a given vertical composition. These functions can also be written with no arguments: '`ctbase()`' is a zero-height object which means the baseline is the top line of the following item, and '`cbbase()`' means the baseline is the bottom line of the preceding item.

The `crule` function builds a "rule," or horizontal line, across a vertical composition. By itself '`crule()`' uses '–' characters to build the rule. You can specify any other character, e.g., '`crule("=")`'. The argument must be a character code or vector of exactly one character code. It is repeated to match the width of the widest item in the stack. For example, a quotient with a thick line is '`cvert([a + 1, cbase(crule("=")), b^2])`':

```
  a + 1
  =====
    2
    b
```

Finally, the functions `clvert` and `crvert` act exactly like `cvert` except that the items are left- or right-justified in the stack. Thus '`clvert([a, bb, ccc]) + crvert([a, bb, ccc])`' gives:

```
  a   +   a
  bb      bb
  ccc    ccc
```

Like `choriz`, the vertical compositions accept a second argument which gives the precedence to use when formatting the components. Vertical compositions do not support separator strings.

6.8.10.4 Other Compositions

The `csup` function builds a superscripted expression. For example, 'csup(a, b)' looks the same as 'a^b' does in Big language mode. This is essentially a horizontal composition of 'a' and 'b', where 'b' is shifted up so that its bottom line is one above the baseline.

Likewise, the `csub` function builds a subscripted expression. This shifts 'b' down so that its top line is one below the bottom line of 'a' (note that this is not quite analogous to `csup`). Other arrangements can be obtained by using `choriz` and `cvert` directly.

The `cflat` function formats its argument in "flat" mode, as obtained by 'd O', if the current language mode is normal or Big. It has no effect in other language modes. For example, 'a^(b/c)' is formatted by Big mode like 'csup(a, cflat(b/c))' to improve its readability.

The `cspace` function creates horizontal space. For example, 'cspace(4)' is effectively the same as 'string(" ")'. A second string (i.e., vector of characters) argument is repeated instead of the space character. For example, 'cspace(4, "ab")' looks like 'abababab'. If the second argument is not a string, it is formatted in the normal way and then several copies of that are composed together: 'cspace(4, a^2)' yields

```
 2 2 2
a a a a
```

If the number argument is zero, this is a zero-width object.

The `cvspace` function creates vertical space, or a vertical stack of copies of a certain string or formatted object. The baseline is the center line of the resulting stack. A numerical argument of zero will produce an object which contributes zero height if used in a vertical composition.

There are also `ctspace` and `cbspace` functions which create vertical space with the baseline the same as the baseline of the top or bottom copy, respectively, of the second argument. Thus 'cvspace(2, a/b) + ctspace(2, a/b) + cbspace(2, a/b)' displays as:

```
          a
          -
a         b
-   a     a
b + - + -
a   b   b
-   a
b   -
    b
```

6.8.10.5 Information about Compositions

The functions in this section are actual functions; they compose their arguments according to the current language and other display modes, then return a certain measurement of the composition as an integer.

The `cwidth` function measures the width, in characters, of a composition. For example, 'cwidth(a + b)' is 5, and 'cwidth(a / b)' is 5 in Normal mode, 1 in Big mode, and 11 in TEX mode (for '{a \over b}'). The argument may involve the composition functions described in this section.

The `cheight` function measures the height of a composition. This is the total number of lines in the argument's printed form.

The functions `cascent` and `cdescent` measure the amount of the height that is above (and including) the baseline, or below the baseline, respectively. Thus '`cascent(x) + cdescent(x)`' always equals '`cheight(x)`'. For a one-line formula like '`a + b`', `cascent` returns 1 and `cdescent` returns 0. For '`a / b`' in Big mode, `cascent` returns 2 and `cdescent` returns 1. The only formula for which `cascent` will return zero is '`cvspace(0)`' or equivalents.

6.8.10.6 User-Defined Compositions

The `Z C` (`calc-user-define-composition`) command lets you define the display format for any algebraic function. You provide a formula containing a certain number of argument variables on the stack. Any time Calc formats a call to the specified function in the current language mode and with that number of arguments, Calc effectively replaces the function call with that formula with the arguments replaced.

Calc builds the default argument list by sorting all the variable names that appear in the formula into alphabetical order. You can edit this argument list before pressing RET if you wish. Any variables in the formula that do not appear in the argument list will be displayed literally; any arguments that do not appear in the formula will not affect the display at all.

You can define formats for built-in functions, for functions you have defined with `Z F` (see Section 17.4 [Algebraic Definitions], page 369), or for functions which have no definitions but are being used as purely syntactic objects. You can define different formats for each language mode, and for each number of arguments, using a succession of `Z C` commands. When Calc formats a function call, it first searches for a format defined for the current language mode (and number of arguments); if there is none, it uses the format defined for the Normal language mode. If neither format exists, Calc uses its built-in standard format for that function (usually just '*func*(*args*)').

If you execute `Z C` with the number 0 on the stack instead of a formula, any defined formats for the function in the current language mode will be removed. The function will revert to its standard format.

For example, the default format for the binomial coefficient function '`choose(n, m)`' in the Big language mode is

```
n
( )
m
```

You might prefer the notation,

```
 C
n m
```

To define this notation, first make sure you are in Big mode, then put the formula

```
choriz([cvert([cvspace(1), n]), C, cvert([cvspace(1), m])])
```

on the stack and type `Z C`. Answer the first prompt with `choose`. The second prompt will be the default argument list of '`(C m n)`'. Edit this list to be '`(n m)`' and press RET. Now, try it out: For example, turn simplification off with `m 0` and enter '`choose(a,b) + choose(7,3)`' as an algebraic entry.

```
     C  +  C
    a b   7 3
```

As another example, let's define the usual notation for Stirling numbers of the first kind, 'stir1(n, m)'. This is just like the regular format for binomial coefficients but with square brackets instead of parentheses.

```
    choriz([string("["), cvert([n, cbase(cvspace(1)), m]), string("]")])
```

Now type *Z C stir1 RET*, edit the argument list to '(n m)', and type RET.

The formula provided to *Z C* usually will involve composition functions, but it doesn't have to. Putting the formula 'a + b + c' onto the stack and typing *Z C foo RET RET* would define the function 'foo(x,y,z)' to display like 'x + y + z'. This "sum" will act exactly like a real sum for all formatting purposes (it will be parenthesized the same, and so on). However it will be computationally unrelated to a sum. For example, the formula '2 * foo(1, 2, 3)' will display as '2 (1 + 2 + 3)'. Operator precedences have caused the "sum" to be written in parentheses, but the arguments have not actually been summed. (Generally a display format like this would be undesirable, since it can easily be confused with a real sum.)

The special function eval can be used inside a *Z C* composition formula to cause all or part of the formula to be evaluated at display time. For example, if the formula is 'a + eval(b + c)', then 'foo(1, 2, 3)' will be displayed as '1 + 5'. Evaluation will use the default simplifications, regardless of the current simplification mode. There are also evalsimp and evalextsimp which simplify as if by *a s* and *a e* (respectively). Note that these "functions" operate only in the context of composition formulas (and also in rewrite rules, where they serve a similar purpose; see Section 10.11 [Rewrite Rules], page 291). On the stack, a call to eval will be left in symbolic form.

It is not a good idea to use eval except as a last resort. It can cause the display of formulas to be extremely slow. For example, while 'eval(a + b)' might seem quite fast and simple, there are several situations where it could be slow. For example, 'a' and/or 'b' could be polar complex numbers, in which case doing the sum requires trigonometry. Or, 'a' could be the factorial 'fact(100)' which is unevaluated because you have typed *m O*; eval will evaluate it anyway to produce a large, unwieldy integer.

You can save your display formats permanently using the *Z P* command (see Section 17.1 [Creating User Keys], page 363).

6.8.11 Syntax Tables

Syntax tables do for input what compositions do for output: They allow you to teach custom notations to Calc's formula parser. Calc keeps a separate syntax table for each language mode.

(Note that the Calc "syntax tables" discussed here are completely unrelated to the syntax tables described in the Emacs manual.)

The *Z S* (calc-edit-user-syntax) command edits the syntax table for the current language mode. If you want your syntax to work in any language, define it in the Normal language mode. Type *C-c C-c* to finish editing the syntax table, or *C-x k* to cancel the edit. The *m m* command saves all the syntax tables along with the other mode settings; see Section 6.1 [General Mode Commands], page 137.

6.8.11.1 Syntax Table Basics

Parsing is the process of converting a raw string of characters, such as you would type in during algebraic entry, into a Calc formula. Calc's parser works in two stages. First, the input is broken down into *tokens*, such as words, numbers, and punctuation symbols like '+', ':=', and '+/-'. Space between tokens is ignored (except when it serves to separate adjacent words). Next, the parser matches this string of tokens against various built-in syntactic patterns, such as "an expression followed by '+' followed by another expression" or "a name followed by '(', zero or more expressions separated by commas, and ')'."

A *syntax table* is a list of user-defined *syntax rules*, which allow you to specify new patterns to define your own favorite input notations. Calc's parser always checks the syntax table for the current language mode, then the table for the Normal language mode, before it uses its built-in rules to parse an algebraic formula you have entered. Each syntax rule should go on its own line; it consists of a *pattern*, a ':=' symbol, and a Calc formula with an optional *condition*. (Syntax rules resemble algebraic rewrite rules, but the notation for patterns is completely different.)

A syntax pattern is a list of tokens, separated by spaces. Except for a few special symbols, tokens in syntax patterns are matched literally, from left to right. For example, the rule,

```
foo ( ) := 2+3
```

would cause Calc to parse the formula '4+foo()*5' as if it were '4+(2+3)*5'. Notice that the parentheses were written as two separate tokens in the rule. As a result, the rule works for both 'foo()' and 'foo ( )'. If we had written the rule as 'foo () := 2+3', then Calc would treat '()' as a single, indivisible token, so that 'foo( )' would not be recognized by the rule. (It would be parsed as a regular zero-argument function call instead.) In fact, this rule would also make trouble for the rest of Calc's parser: An unrelated formula like 'bar()' would now be tokenized into 'bar ()' instead of 'bar ( )', so that the standard parser for function calls would no longer recognize it!

While it is possible to make a token with a mixture of letters and punctuation symbols, this is not recommended. It is better to break it into several tokens, as we did with 'foo()' above.

The symbol '#' in a syntax pattern matches any Calc expression. On the righthand side, the things that matched the '#'s can be referred to as '#1', '#2', and so on (where '#1' matches the leftmost '#' in the pattern). For example, these rules match a user-defined function, prefix operator, infix operator, and postfix operator, respectively:

```
foo ( # ) := myfunc(#1)
foo # := myprefix(#1)
# foo # := myinfix(#1,#2)
# foo := mypostfix(#1)
```

Thus 'foo(3)' will parse as 'myfunc(3)', and '2+3 foo' will parse as 'mypostfix(2+3)'.

It is important to write the first two rules in the order shown, because Calc tries rules in order from first to last. If the pattern 'foo #' came first, it would match anything that could match the 'foo (#)' rule, since an expression in parentheses is itself a valid expression. Thus the 'foo (#)' rule would never get to match anything. Likewise, the last two rules must be written in the order shown or else '3 foo 4' will be parsed as 'mypostfix(3) * 4'.

(Of course, the best way to avoid these ambiguities is not to use the same symbol in more than one way at the same time! In case you're not convinced, try the following exercise: How will the above rules parse the input 'foo(3,4)', if at all? Work it out for yourself, then try it in Calc and see.)

Calc is quite flexible about what sorts of patterns are allowed. The only rule is that every pattern must begin with a literal token (like 'foo' in the first two patterns above), or with a '#' followed by a literal token (as in the last two patterns). After that, any mixture is allowed, although putting two '#'s in a row will not be very useful since two expressions with nothing between them will be parsed as one expression that uses implicit multiplication.

As a more practical example, Maple uses the notation 'sum(a(i), i=1..10)' for sums, which Calc's Maple mode doesn't recognize at present. To handle this syntax, we simply add the rule,

```
sum ( # , # = # .. # ) := sum(#1,#2,#3,#4)
```

to the Maple mode syntax table. As another example, C mode can't read assignment operators like '++' and '*='. We can define these operators quite easily:

```
# *= # := muleq(#1,#2)
# ++ := postinc(#1)
++ # := preinc(#1)
```

To complete the job, we would use corresponding composition functions and Z C to cause these functions to display in their respective Maple and C notations. (Note that the C example ignores issues of operator precedence, which are discussed in the next section.)

You can enclose any token in quotes to prevent its usual interpretation in syntax patterns:

```
# ":=" # := becomes(#1,#2)
```

Quotes also allow you to include spaces in a token, although once again it is generally better to use two tokens than one token with an embedded space. To include an actual quotation mark in a quoted token, precede it with a backslash. (This also works to include backslashes in tokens.)

```
# "bad token" # "/\"\\" # := silly(#1,#2,#3)
```

This will parse '3 bad token 4 /"\ 5' to 'silly(3,4,5)'.

The token # has a predefined meaning in Calc's formula parser; it is not valid to use '"#"' in a syntax rule. However, longer tokens that include the '#' character are allowed. Also, while '"$"' and '"\""' are allowed as tokens, their presence in the syntax table will prevent those characters from working in their usual ways (referring to stack entries and quoting strings, respectively).

Finally, the notation '%%' anywhere in a syntax table causes the rest of the line to be ignored as a comment.

6.8.11.2 Precedence

Different operators are generally assigned different *precedences*. By default, an operator defined by a rule like

```
# foo # := foo(#1,#2)
```

will have an extremely low precedence, so that '2*3+4 foo 5 == 6' will be parsed as '(2*3+4) foo (5 == 6)'. To change the precedence of an operator, use the notation '#/*p*' in place of

'#', where p is an integer precedence level. For example, 185 lies between the precedences for '+' and '*', so if we change this rule to

```
#/185 foo #/186 := foo(#1,#2)
```

then '2+3 foo 4*5' will be parsed as '2+(3 foo (4*5))'. Also, because we've given the righthand expression slightly higher precedence, our new operator will be left-associative: '1 foo 2 foo 3' will be parsed as '(1 foo 2) foo 3'. By raising the precedence of the lefthand expression instead, we can create a right-associative operator.

See Section 6.8.10.1 [Composition Basics], page 168, for a table of precedences of the standard Calc operators. For the precedences of operators in other language modes, look in the Calc source file `calc-lang.el`.

6.8.11.3 Advanced Syntax Patterns

To match a function with a variable number of arguments, you could write

```
foo ( # ) := myfunc(#1)
foo ( # , # ) := myfunc(#1,#2)
foo ( # , # , # ) := myfunc(#1,#2,#3)
```

but this isn't very elegant. To match variable numbers of items, Calc uses some notations inspired regular expressions and the "extended BNF" style used by some language designers.

```
foo ( { # }*, ) := apply(myfunc,#1)
```

The token '{' introduces a repeated or optional portion. One of the three tokens '}*', '}+', or '}?' ends the portion. These will match zero or more, one or more, or zero or one copies of the enclosed pattern, respectively. In addition, '}*' and '}+' can be followed by a separator token (with no space in between, as shown above). Thus '{ # }*,' matches nothing, or one expression, or several expressions separated by commas.

A complete '{ ... }' item matches as a vector of the items that matched inside it. For example, the above rule will match 'foo(1,2,3)' to get 'apply(myfunc,[1,2,3])'. The Calc `apply` function takes a function name and a vector of arguments and builds a call to the function with those arguments, so the net result is the formula 'myfunc(1,2,3)'.

If the body of a '{ ... }' contains several '#'s (or nested '{ ... }' constructs), then the items will be strung together into the resulting vector. If the body does not contain anything but literal tokens, the result will always be an empty vector.

```
foo ( { # , # }+, ) := bar(#1)
foo ( { { # }*, }*; ) := matrix(#1)
```

will parse 'foo(1, 2, 3, 4)' as 'bar([1, 2, 3, 4])', and 'foo(1, 2; 3, 4)' as 'matrix([[1, 2], [3, 4]])'. Also, after some thought it's easy to see how this pair of rules will parse 'foo(1, 2, 3)' as 'matrix([[1, 2, 3]])', since the first rule will only match an even number of arguments. The rule

```
foo ( # { , # , # }? ) := bar(#1,#2)
```

will parse 'foo(2,3,4)' as 'bar(2,[3,4])', and 'foo(2)' as 'bar(2,[])'.

The notation '{ ... }?.' (note the trailing period) works just the same as regular '{ ... }?', except that it does not count as an argument; the following two rules are equivalent:

```
foo ( # , { also }? # ) := bar(#1,#3)
foo ( # , { also }?. # ) := bar(#1,#2)
```

Note that in the first case the optional text counts as '#2', which will always be an empty vector, but in the second case no empty vector is produced.

Another variant is '{ ... }?$', which means the body is optional only at the end of the input formula. All built-in syntax rules in Calc use this for closing delimiters, so that during algebraic entry you can type *[sqrt(2), sqrt(3 RET*, omitting the closing parenthesis and bracket. Calc does this automatically for trailing ')', ']', and '>' tokens in syntax rules, but you can use '{ ... }?$' explicitly to get this effect with any token (such as '"}"' or 'end'). Like '{ ... }?.', this notation does not count as an argument. Conversely, you can use quotes, as in '")"', to prevent a closing-delimiter token from being automatically treated as optional.

Calc's parser does not have full backtracking, which means some patterns will not work as you might expect:

```
foo ( { # , }? # , # ) := bar(#1,#2,#3)
```

Here we are trying to make the first argument optional, so that 'foo(2,3)' parses as 'bar([],2,3)'. Unfortunately, Calc first tries to match '2,' against the optional part of the pattern, finds a match, and so goes ahead to match the rest of the pattern. Later on it will fail to match the second comma, but it doesn't know how to go back and try the other alternative at that point. One way to get around this would be to use two rules:

```
foo ( # , # , # ) := bar([#1],#2,#3)
foo ( # , # ) := bar([],#1,#2)
```

More precisely, when Calc wants to match an optional or repeated part of a pattern, it scans forward attempting to match that part. If it reaches the end of the optional part without failing, it "finalizes" its choice and proceeds. If it fails, though, it backs up and tries the other alternative. Thus Calc has "partial" backtracking. A fully backtracking parser would go on to make sure the rest of the pattern matched before finalizing the choice.

6.8.11.4 Conditional Syntax Rules

It is possible to attach a *condition* to a syntax rule. For example, the rules

```
foo ( # ) := ifoo(#1) :: integer(#1)
foo ( # ) := gfoo(#1)
```

will parse 'foo(3)' as 'ifoo(3)', but will parse 'foo(3.5)' and 'foo(x)' as calls to gfoo. Any number of conditions may be attached; all must be true for the rule to succeed. A condition is "true" if it evaluates to a nonzero number. See Section 10.10 [Logical Operations], page 288, for a list of Calc functions like integer that perform logical tests.

The exact sequence of events is as follows: When Calc tries a rule, it first matches the pattern as usual. It then substitutes '#1', '#2', etc., in the conditions, if any. Next, the conditions are simplified and evaluated in order from left to right, using the algebraic simplifications (see Section 10.3 [Simplifying Formulas], page 253). Each result is true if it is a nonzero number, or an expression that can be proven to be nonzero (see Section 6.6 [Declarations], page 143). If the results of all conditions are true, the expression (such as 'ifoo(#1)') has its '#'s substituted, and that is the result of the parse. If the result of any condition is false, Calc goes on to try the next rule in the syntax table.

Syntax rules also support let conditions, which operate in exactly the same way as they do in algebraic rewrite rules. See Section 10.11.5 [Other Features of Rewrite Rules], page 298, for details. A `let` condition is always true, but as a side effect it defines a variable which can be used in later conditions, and also in the expression after the ':=' sign:

```
foo ( # ) := hifoo(x) :: let(x := #1 + 0.5) :: dnumint(x)
```

The `dnumint` function tests if a value is numerically an integer, i.e., either a true integer or an integer-valued float. This rule will parse `foo` with a half-integer argument, like 'foo(3.5)', to a call like 'hifoo(4.)'.

The lefthand side of a syntax rule `let` must be a simple variable, not the arbitrary pattern that is allowed in rewrite rules.

The `matches` function is also treated specially in syntax rule conditions (again, in the same way as in rewrite rules). See Section 10.11.10 [Matching Commands], page 308. If the matching pattern contains meta-variables, then those meta-variables may be used in later conditions and in the result expression. The arguments to `matches` are not evaluated in this situation.

```
sum ( # , # ) := sum(#1,a,b,c) :: matches(#2, a=[b..c])
```

This is another way to implement the Maple mode `sum` notation. In this approach, we allow '#2' to equal the whole expression 'i=1..10'. Then, we use `matches` to break it apart into its components. If the expression turns out not to match the pattern, the syntax rule will fail. Note that *Z S* always uses Calc's Normal language mode for editing expressions in syntax rules, so we must use regular Calc notation for the interval '[b..c]' that will correspond to the Maple mode interval '1..10'.

6.9 The `Modes` Variable

The *m g* (`calc-get-modes`) command pushes onto the stack a vector of numbers that describes the various mode settings that are in effect. With a numeric prefix argument, it pushes only the nth mode, i.e., the nth element of this vector. Keyboard macros can use the *m g* command to modify their behavior based on the current mode settings.

The modes vector is also available in the special variable `Modes`. In other words, *m g* is like *s r Modes RET*. It will not work to store into this variable; in fact, if you do, `Modes` will cease to track the current modes. (The *m g* command will continue to work, however.)

In general, each number in this vector is suitable as a numeric prefix argument to the associated mode-setting command. (Recall that the ~ key takes a number from the stack and gives it as a numeric prefix to the next command.)

The elements of the modes vector are as follows:

1. Current precision. Default is 12; associated command is *p*.

2. Binary word size. Default is 32; associated command is *b w*.

3. Stack size (not counting the value about to be pushed by *m g*). This is zero if *m g* is executed with an empty stack.

4. Number radix. Default is 10; command is *d r*.

5. Floating-point format. This is the number of digits, plus the constant 0 for normal notation, 10000 for scientific notation, 20000 for engineering notation, or 30000 for fixed-point notation. These codes are acceptable as prefix arguments to the *d n* command, but note that this may lose information: For example, *d s* and *C-u 12 d s* have similar (but not quite identical) effects if the current precision is 12, but they both

produce a code of 10012, which will be treated by *d n* as *C-u 12 d s*. If the precision then changes, the float format will still be frozen at 12 significant figures.

6. Angular mode. Default is 1 (degrees). Other values are 2 (radians) and 3 (HMS). The *m d* command accepts these prefixes.

7. Symbolic mode. Value is 0 or 1; default is 0. Command is *m s*.

8. Fraction mode. Value is 0 or 1; default is 0. Command is *m f*.

9. Polar mode. Value is 0 (rectangular) or 1 (polar); default is 0. Command is *m p*.

10. Matrix/Scalar mode. Default value is −1. Value is 0 for Scalar mode, −2 for Matrix mode, −3 for square Matrix mode, or N for $N \times N$ Matrix mode. Command is *m v*.

11. Simplification mode. Default is 1. Value is −1 for off (*m O*), 0 for *m N*, 2 for *m B*, 3 for *m A*, 4 for *m E*, or 5 for *m U*. The *m D* command accepts these prefixes.

12. Infinite mode. Default is −1 (off). Value is 1 if the mode is on, or 0 if the mode is on with positive zeros. Command is *m i*.

For example, the sequence *M-1 m g RET 2 + ~ p* increases the precision by two, leaving a copy of the old precision on the stack. Later, *~ p* will restore the original precision using that stack value. (This sequence might be especially useful inside a keyboard macro.)

As another example, *M-3 m g 1 - ~ DEL* deletes all but the oldest (bottommost) stack entry.

Yet another example: The HP-48 "round" command rounds a number to the current displayed precision. You could roughly emulate this in Calc with the sequence *M-5 m g 10000 % ~ c c*. (This would not work for fixed-point mode, but it wouldn't be hard to do a full emulation with the help of the *Z [* and *Z]* programming commands. See Section 17.2.2 [Conditionals in Macros], page 365.)

6.10 The Calc Mode Line

This section is a summary of all symbols that can appear on the Calc mode line, the highlighted bar that appears under the Calc stack window (or under an editing window in Embedded mode).

The basic mode line format is:

```
--%*-Calc: 12 Deg other modes        (Calculator)
```

The '%*' indicates that the buffer is "read-only"; it shows that regular Emacs commands are not allowed to edit the stack buffer as if it were text.

The word 'Calc:' changes to 'CalcEmbed:' if Embedded mode is enabled. The words after this describe the various Calc modes that are in effect.

The first mode is always the current precision, an integer. The second mode is always the angular mode, either Deg, Rad, or Hms.

Here is a complete list of the remaining symbols that can appear on the mode line:

Alg   Algebraic mode (*m a*; see Section 3.5 [Algebraic Entry], page 109).

Alg[(Incomplete algebraic mode (*C-u m a*).

Alg*   Total algebraic mode (*m t*).

Symb   Symbolic mode (*m s*; see Section 6.4.5 [Symbolic Mode], page 140).

Matrix	Matrix mode (*m v*; see Section 6.4.6 [Matrix Mode], page 141).
Matrixn	Dimensioned Matrix mode (*C-u n m v*; see Section 6.4.6 [Matrix Mode], page 141).
SqMatrix	Square Matrix mode (*C-u m v*; see Section 6.4.6 [Matrix Mode], page 141).
Scalar	Scalar mode (*m v*; see Section 6.4.6 [Matrix Mode], page 141).
Polar	Polar complex mode (*m p*; see Section 6.4.2 [Polar Mode], page 139).
Frac	Fraction mode (*m f*; see Section 6.4.3 [Fraction Mode], page 140).
Inf	Infinite mode (*m i*; see Section 6.4.4 [Infinite Mode], page 140).
+Inf	Positive Infinite mode (*C-u 0 m i*).
NoSimp	Default simplifications off (*m 0*; see Section 6.5 [Simplification Modes], page 142).
NumSimp	Default simplifications for numeric arguments only (*m N*).
BinSimp*w*	Binary-integer simplification mode; word size *w* (*m B*, *b w*).
BasicSimp	
	Basic simplification mode (*m I*).
ExtSimp	Extended algebraic simplification mode (*m E*).
UnitSimp	Units simplification mode (*m U*).
Bin	Current radix is 2 (*d 2*; see Section 6.7.1 [Radix Modes], page 148).
Oct	Current radix is 8 (*d 8*).
Hex	Current radix is 16 (*d 6*).
Radix*n*	Current radix is *n* (*d r*).
Zero	Leading zeros (*d z*; see Section 6.7.1 [Radix Modes], page 148).
Big	Big language mode (*d B*; see Section 6.8.1 [Normal Language Modes], page 159).
Flat	One-line normal language mode (*d 0*).
Unform	Unformatted language mode (*d U*).
C	C language mode (*d C*; see Section 6.8.2 [C FORTRAN Pascal], page 160).
Pascal	Pascal language mode (*d P*).
Fortran	FORTRAN language mode (*d F*).
TeX	TeX language mode (*d T*; see Section 6.8.3 [TeX and LaTeX Language Modes], page 161).
LaTeX	LaTeX language mode (*d L*; see Section 6.8.3 [TeX and LaTeX Language Modes], page 161).
Eqn	*Eqn* language mode (*d E*; see Section 6.8.4 [Eqn Language Mode], page 165).
Math	Mathematica language mode (*d M*; see Section 6.8.8 [Mathematica Language Mode], page 167).

Maple	Maple language mode (d W; see Section 6.8.9 [Maple Language Mode], page 167).
Normn	Normal float mode with n digits (d n; see Section 6.7.3 [Float Formats], page 150).
Fixn	Fixed point mode with n digits after the point (d f).
Sci	Scientific notation mode (d s).
Scin	Scientific notation with n digits (d s).
Eng	Engineering notation mode (d e).
Engn	Engineering notation with n digits (d e).
Leftn	Left-justified display indented by n (d <; see Section 6.7.9 [Justification], page 157).
Right	Right-justified display (d >).
Rightn	Right-justified display with width n (d >).
Center	Centered display (d =).
Centern	Centered display with center column n (d =).
Widn	Line breaking with width n (d b; see Section 6.8.1 [Normal Language Modes], page 159).
Wide	No line breaking (d b).
Break	Selections show deep structure (j b; see Section 10.1.1 [Making Selections], page 243).
Save	Record modes in ~/.emacs.d/calc.el (m R; see Section 6.1 [General Mode Commands], page 137).
Local	Record modes in Embedded buffer (m R).
LocEdit	Record modes as editing-only in Embedded buffer (m R).
LocPerm	Record modes as permanent-only in Embedded buffer (m R).
Global	Record modes as global in Embedded buffer (m R).
Manual	Automatic recomputation turned off (m C; see Section 6.4.7 [Automatic Recomputation], page 142).
Graph	GNUPLOT process is alive in background (see Chapter 13 [Graphics], page 329).
Sel	Top-of-stack has a selection (Embedded only; see Section 10.1.1 [Making Selections], page 243).
Dirty	The stack display may not be up-to-date (see Section 6.7 [Display Modes], page 148).
Inv	"Inverse" prefix was pressed (I; see Section 6.3 [Inverse and Hyperbolic], page 139).
Hyp	"Hyperbolic" prefix was pressed (H).

Keep   "Keep-arguments" prefix was pressed (*K*).

Narrow   Stack is truncated (*d t*; see Section 6.7.8 [Truncating the Stack], page 157).

In addition, the symbols `Active` and `~Active` can appear as minor modes on an Embedded buffer's mode line. See Chapter 16 [Embedded Mode], page 351.

7 Arithmetic Functions

This chapter describes the Calc commands for doing simple calculations on numbers, such as addition, absolute value, and square roots. These commands work by removing the top one or two values from the stack, performing the desired operation, and pushing the result back onto the stack. If the operation cannot be performed, the result pushed is a formula instead of a number, such as '2/0' (because division by zero is invalid) or 'sqrt(x)' (because the argument 'x' is a formula).

Most of the commands described here can be invoked by a single keystroke. Some of the more obscure ones are two-letter sequences beginning with the *f* ("functions") prefix key.

See Section 3.7 [Prefix Arguments], page 111, for a discussion of the effect of numeric prefix arguments on commands in this chapter which do not otherwise interpret a prefix argument.

7.1 Basic Arithmetic

The + (`calc-plus`) command adds two numbers. The numbers may be any of the standard Calc data types. The resulting sum is pushed back onto the stack.

If both arguments of + are vectors or matrices (of matching dimensions), the result is a vector or matrix sum. If one argument is a vector and the other a scalar (i.e., a non-vector), the scalar is added to each of the elements of the vector to form a new vector. If the scalar is not a number, the operation is left in symbolic form: Suppose you added 'x' to the vector '[1,2]'. You may want the result '[1+x,2+x]', or you may plan to substitute a 2-vector for 'x' in the future. Since the Calculator can't tell which interpretation you want, it makes the safest assumption. See Section 9.8 [Reducing and Mapping], page 235, for a way to add 'x' to every element of a vector.

If either argument of + is a complex number, the result will in general be complex. If one argument is in rectangular form and the other polar, the current Polar mode determines the form of the result. If Symbolic mode is enabled, the sum may be left as a formula if the necessary conversions for polar addition are non-trivial.

If both arguments of + are HMS forms, the forms are added according to the usual conventions of hours-minutes-seconds notation. If one argument is an HMS form and the other is a number, that number is converted from degrees or radians (depending on the current Angular mode) to HMS format and then the two HMS forms are added.

If one argument of + is a date form, the other can be either a real number, which advances the date by a certain number of days, or an HMS form, which advances the date by a certain amount of time. Subtracting two date forms yields the number of days between them. Adding two date forms is meaningless, but Calc interprets it as the subtraction of one date form and the negative of the other. (The negative of a date form can be understood by remembering that dates are stored as the number of days before or after Jan 1, 1 AD.)

If both arguments of + are error forms, the result is an error form with an appropriately computed standard deviation. If one argument is an error form and the other is a number, the number is taken to have zero error. Error forms may have symbolic formulas as their mean and/or error parts; adding these will produce a symbolic error form result. However, adding an error form to a plain symbolic formula (as in '(a +/- b) + c') will not work, for the same reasons just mentioned for vectors. Instead you must write '(a +/- b) + (c +/- 0)'.

If both arguments of + are modulo forms with equal values of M, or if one argument is a modulo form and the other a plain number, the result is a modulo form which represents the sum, modulo M, of the two values.

If both arguments of + are intervals, the result is an interval which describes all possible sums of the possible input values. If one argument is a plain number, it is treated as the interval '[x .. x]'.

If one argument of + is an infinity and the other is not, the result is that same infinity. If both arguments are infinite and in the same direction, the result is the same infinity, but if they are infinite in different directions the result is **nan**.

The - (`calc-minus`) command subtracts two values. The top number on the stack is subtracted from the one behind it, so that the computation *5 RET 2* - produces 3, not -3. All options available for + are available for - as well.

The * (`calc-times`) command multiplies two numbers. If one argument is a vector and the other a scalar, the scalar is multiplied by the elements of the vector to produce a new vector. If both arguments are vectors, the interpretation depends on the dimensions of the vectors: If both arguments are matrices, a matrix multiplication is done. If one argument is a matrix and the other a plain vector, the vector is interpreted as a row vector or column vector, whichever is dimensionally correct. If both arguments are plain vectors, the result is a single scalar number which is the dot product of the two vectors.

If one argument of * is an HMS form and the other a number, the HMS form is multiplied by that amount. It is an error to multiply two HMS forms together, or to attempt any multiplication involving date forms. Error forms, modulo forms, and intervals can be multiplied; see the comments for addition of those forms. When two error forms or intervals are multiplied they are considered to be statistically independent; thus, '[-2 .. 3] * [-2 .. 3]' is '[-6 .. 9]', whereas '[-2 .. 3] ^ 2' is '[0 .. 9]'.

The / (`calc-divide`) command divides two numbers.

When combining multiplication and division in an algebraic formula, it is good style to use parentheses to distinguish between possible interpretations; the expression 'a/b*c' should be written '(a/b)*c' or 'a/(b*c)', as appropriate. Without the parentheses, Calc will interpret 'a/b*c' as 'a/(b*c)', since in algebraic entry Calc gives division a lower precedence than multiplication. (This is not standard across all computer languages, and Calc may change the precedence depending on the language mode being used. See Section 6.8 [Language Modes], page 158.) This default ordering can be changed by setting the customizable variable `calc-multiplication-has-precedence` to `nil` (see Appendix C [Customizing Calc], page 435); this will give multiplication and division equal precedences. Note that Calc's default choice of precedence allows 'a b / c d' to be used as a shortcut for

```
a b
---.
c d
```

When dividing a scalar B by a square matrix A, the computation performed is B times the inverse of A. This also occurs if B is itself a vector or matrix, in which case the effect is to solve the set of linear equations represented by B. If B is a matrix with the same number of rows as A, or a plain vector (which is interpreted here as a column vector), then the equation $AX = B$ is solved for the vector or matrix X. Otherwise, if B is a non-square matrix with the same number of *columns* as A, the equation $XA = B$ is solved. If you wish a vector B to be interpreted as a row vector to be solved as $XA = B$, make it into a one-row matrix with `C-u 1 v p` first. To force a left-handed solution with a square matrix B, transpose A and B before dividing, then transpose the result.

HMS forms can be divided by real numbers or by other HMS forms. Error forms can be divided in any combination of ways. Modulo forms where both values and the modulo are integers can be divided to get an integer modulo form result. Intervals can be divided; dividing by an interval that encompasses zero or has zero as a limit will result in an infinite interval.

The `^` (`calc-power`) command raises a number to a power. If the power is an integer, an exact result is computed using repeated multiplications. For non-integer powers, Calc uses Newton's method or logarithms and exponentials. Square matrices can be raised to integer powers. If either argument is an error (or interval or modulo) form, the result is also an error (or interval or modulo) form.

If you press the `I` (inverse) key first, the `I ^` command computes an Nth root: `125 RET 3 I ^` computes the number 5. (This is entirely equivalent to `125 RET 1:3 ^`.)

The `\` (`calc-idiv`) command divides two numbers on the stack to produce an integer result. It is equivalent to dividing with `/`, then rounding down with `F` (`calc-floor`), only a bit more convenient and efficient. Also, since it is an all-integer operation when the arguments are integers, it avoids problems that `/ F` would have with floating-point roundoff.

The `%` (`calc-mod`) command performs a "modulo" (or "remainder") operation. Mathematically, '`a%b = a - (a\b)*b`', and is defined for all real numbers a and b (except $b = 0$). For positive b, the result will always be between 0 (inclusive) and b (exclusive). Modulo does not work for HMS forms and error forms. If a is a modulo form, its modulo is changed to b, which must be positive real number.

The `:` (`calc-fdiv`) [`fdiv`] command divides the two integers on the top of the stack to produce a fractional result. This is a convenient shorthand for enabling Fraction mode (with `m f`) temporarily and using '`/`'. Note that during numeric entry the `:` key is interpreted as a fraction separator, so to divide 8 by 6 you would have to type `8 RET 6 RET :`. (Of course, in this case, it would be much easier simply to enter the fraction directly as `8:6 RET`!)

The `n` (`calc-change-sign`) command negates the number on the top of the stack. It works on numbers, vectors and matrices, HMS forms, date forms, error forms, intervals, and modulo forms.

The `A` (`calc-abs`) [`abs`] command computes the absolute value of a number. The result of `abs` is always a nonnegative real number: With a complex argument, it computes the complex magnitude. With a vector or matrix argument, it computes the Frobenius norm, i.e., the square root of the sum of the squares of the absolute values of the elements. The absolute value of an error form is defined by replacing the mean part with its absolute value and leaving the error part the same. The absolute value of a modulo form is undefined. The absolute value of an interval is defined in the obvious way.

The `f A` (`calc-abssqr`) [`abssqr`] command computes the absolute value squared of a number, vector or matrix, or error form.

The `f s` (`calc-sign`) [`sign`] command returns 1 if its argument is positive, -1 if its argument is negative, or 0 if its argument is zero. In algebraic form, you can also write 'sign(a,x)' which evaluates to 'x * sign(a)', i.e., either 'x', '-x', or zero depending on the sign of 'a'.

The & (calc-inv) [inv] command computes the reciprocal of a number, i.e., $1/x$. Operating on a square matrix, it computes the inverse of that matrix.

The Q (calc-sqrt) [sqrt] command computes the square root of a number. For a negative real argument, the result will be a complex number whose form is determined by the current Polar mode.

The f h (calc-hypot) [hypot] command computes the square root of the sum of the squares of two numbers. That is, 'hypot(a,b)' is the length of the hypotenuse of a right triangle with sides a and b. If the arguments are complex numbers, their squared magnitudes are used.

The f Q (calc-isqrt) [isqrt] command computes the integer square root of an integer. This is the true square root of the number, rounded down to an integer. For example, 'isqrt(10)' produces 3. Note that, like \ [idiv], this uses exact integer arithmetic throughout to avoid roundoff problems. If the input is a floating-point number or other non-integer value, this is exactly the same as 'floor(sqrt(x))'.

The f n (calc-min) [min] and f x (calc-max) [max] commands take the minimum or maximum of two real numbers, respectively. These commands also work on HMS forms, date forms, intervals, and infinities. (In algebraic expressions, these functions take any number of arguments and return the maximum or minimum among all the arguments.)

The f M (calc-mant-part) [mant] function extracts the "mantissa" part m of its floating-point argument; f X (calc-xpon-part) [xpon] extracts the "exponent" part e. The original number is equal to $m \times 10^e$, where m is in the interval '[1.0 .. 10.0]' except that $m = e = 0$ if the original number is zero. For integers and fractions, mant returns the number unchanged and xpon returns zero. The v u (calc-unpack) command can also be used to "unpack" a floating-point number; this produces an integer mantissa and exponent, with the constraint that the mantissa is not a multiple of ten (again except for the $m = e = 0$ case).

The f S (calc-scale-float) [scf] function scales a number by a given power of ten. Thus, 'scf(mant(x), xpon(x)) = x' for any real 'x'. The second argument must be an integer, but the first may actually be any numeric value. For example, 'scf(5,-2) = 0.05' or '1:20' depending on the current Fraction mode.

The f [(calc-decrement) [decr] and f] (calc-increment) [incr] functions decrease or increase a number by one unit. For integers, the effect is obvious. For floating-point numbers, the change is by one unit in the last place. For example, incrementing '12.3456' when the current precision is 6 digits yields '12.3457'. If the current precision had been 8 digits, the result would have been '12.345601'. Incrementing '0.0' produces 10^{-p}, where p is the current precision. These operations are defined only on integers and floats. With numeric prefix arguments, they change the number by n units.

Note that incrementing followed by decrementing, or vice-versa, will almost but not quite always cancel out. Suppose the precision is 6 digits and the number '9.99999' is on the stack. Incrementing will produce '10.0000'; decrementing will produce '9.9999'. One digit has been dropped. This is an unavoidable consequence of the way floating-point numbers work.

Incrementing a date/time form adjusts it by a certain number of seconds. Incrementing a pure date form adjusts it by a certain number of days.

7.2 Integer Truncation

There are four commands for truncating a real number to an integer, differing mainly in their treatment of negative numbers. All of these commands have the property that if the argument is an integer, the result is the same integer. An integer-valued floating-point argument is converted to integer form.

If you press *H* (`calc-hyperbolic`) first, the result will be expressed as an integer-valued floating-point number.

The *F* (`calc-floor`) [`floor` or `ffloor`] command truncates a real number to the next lower integer, i.e., toward minus infinity. Thus *3.6 F* produces 3, but *_3.6 F* produces −4.

The *I F* (`calc-ceiling`) [`ceil` or `fceil`] command truncates toward positive infinity. Thus *3.6 I F* produces 4, and *_3.6 I F* produces −3.

The *R* (`calc-round`) [`round` or `fround`] command rounds to the nearest integer. When the fractional part is .5 exactly, this command rounds away from zero. (All other rounding in the Calculator uses this convention as well.) Thus *3.5 R* produces 4 but *3.4 R* produces 3; *_3.5 R* produces −4.

The *I R* (`calc-trunc`) [`trunc` or `ftrunc`] command truncates toward zero. In other words, it "chops off" everything after the decimal point. Thus *3.6 I R* produces 3 and *_3.6 I R* produces −3.

These functions may not be applied meaningfully to error forms, but they do work for intervals. As a convenience, applying `floor` to a modulo form floors the value part of the form. Applied to a vector, these functions operate on all elements of the vector one by one. Applied to a date form, they operate on the internal numerical representation of dates, converting a date/time form into a pure date.

There are two more rounding functions which can only be entered in algebraic notation. The `roundu` function is like `round` except that it rounds up, toward plus infinity, when the fractional part is .5. This distinction matters only for negative arguments. Also, `rounde` rounds to an even number in the case of a tie, rounding up or down as necessary. For example, 'round(3.5)' and 'round(4.5)' both return 4, but 'round(5.5)' returns 6. The advantage of round-to-even is that the net error due to rounding after a long calculation tends to cancel out to zero. An important subtle point here is that the number being fed to `rounde` will already have been rounded to the current precision before `rounde` begins. For example, 'rounde(2.500001)' with a current precision of 6 will incorrectly, or at least surprisingly, yield 2 because the argument will first have been rounded down to 2.5 (which `rounde` sees as an exact tie between 2 and 3).

Each of these functions, when written in algebraic formulas, allows a second argument which specifies the number of digits after the decimal point to keep. For example, 'round(123.4567, 2)' will produce the answer 123.46, and 'round(123.4567, -1)' will produce 120 (i.e., the cutoff is one digit to the *left* of the decimal point). A second argument of zero is equivalent to no second argument at all.

To compute the fractional part of a number (i.e., the amount which, when added to 'floor(n)', will produce n) just take n modulo 1 using the % command.

Note also the \ (integer quotient), *f I* (integer logarithm), and *f Q* (integer square root) commands, which are analogous to /, *B*, and *Q*, respectively, except that they take integer arguments and return the result rounded down to an integer.

7.3 Complex Number Functions

The *J* (calc-conj) [conj] command computes the complex conjugate of a number. For complex number $a + bi$, the complex conjugate is $a - bi$. If the argument is a real number, this command leaves it the same. If the argument is a vector or matrix, this command replaces each element by its complex conjugate.

The *G* (calc-argument) [arg] command computes the "argument" or polar angle of a complex number. For a number in polar notation, this is simply the second component of the pair '$(r; \theta)$'. The result is expressed according to the current angular mode and will be in the range −180 degrees (exclusive) to +180 degrees (inclusive), or the equivalent range in radians.

The calc-imaginary command multiplies the number on the top of the stack by the imaginary number $i = (0, 1)$. This command is not normally bound to a key in Calc, but it is available on the IMAG button in Keypad mode.

The *f r* (calc-re) [re] command replaces a complex number by its real part. This command has no effect on real numbers. (As an added convenience, re applied to a modulo form extracts the value part.)

The *f i* (calc-im) [im] command replaces a complex number by its imaginary part; real numbers are converted to zero. With a vector or matrix argument, these functions operate element-wise.

The *v p* (calc-pack) command can pack the top two numbers on the stack into a composite object such as a complex number. With a prefix argument of −1, it produces a rectangular complex number; with an argument of −2, it produces a polar complex number. (Also, see Section 9.2 [Building Vectors], page 223.)

The *v u* (calc-unpack) command takes the complex number (or other composite object) on the top of the stack and unpacks it into its separate components.

7.4 Conversions

The commands described in this section convert numbers from one form to another; they are two-key sequences beginning with the letter *c*.

The *c f* (calc-float) [pfloat] command converts the number on the top of the stack to floating-point form. For example, 23 is converted to 23.0, 3:2 is converted to 1.5, and 2.3 is left the same. If the value is a composite object such as a complex number or vector, each of the components is converted to floating-point. If the value is a formula, all numbers in the formula are converted to floating-point. Note that depending on the current floating-point precision, conversion to floating-point format may lose information.

As a special exception, integers which appear as powers or subscripts are not floated by *c f*. If you really want to float a power, you can use a *j s* command to select the power followed by *c f*. Because *c f* cannot examine the formula outside of the selection, it does not notice that the thing being floated is a power. See Section 10.1 [Selecting Subformulas], page 243.

The normal `c f` command is "pervasive" in the sense that it applies to all numbers throughout the formula. The `pfloat` algebraic function never stays around in a formula; 'pfloat(a + 1)' changes to 'a + 1.0' as soon as it is evaluated.

With the Hyperbolic flag, `H c f` [float] operates only on the number or vector of numbers at the top level of its argument. Thus, 'float(1)' is 1.0, but 'float(a + 1)' is left unevaluated because its argument is not a number.

You should use `H c f` if you wish to guarantee that the final value, once all the variables have been assigned, is a float; you would use `c f` if you wish to do the conversion on the numbers that appear right now.

The `c F` (`calc-fraction`) [pfrac] command converts a floating-point number into a fractional approximation. By default, it produces a fraction whose decimal representation is the same as the input number, to within the current precision. You can also give a numeric prefix argument to specify a tolerance, either directly, or, if the prefix argument is zero, by using the number on top of the stack as the tolerance. If the tolerance is a positive integer, the fraction is correct to within that many significant figures. If the tolerance is a non-positive integer, it specifies how many digits fewer than the current precision to use. If the tolerance is a floating-point number, the fraction is correct to within that absolute amount.

The `pfrac` function is pervasive, like `pfloat`. There is also a non-pervasive version, `H c F` [frac], which is analogous to `H c f` discussed above.

The `c d` (`calc-to-degrees`) [deg] command converts a number into degrees form. The value on the top of the stack may be an HMS form (interpreted as degrees-minutes-seconds), or a real number which will be interpreted in radians regardless of the current angular mode.

The `c r` (`calc-to-radians`) [rad] command converts an HMS form or angle in degrees into an angle in radians.

The `c h` (`calc-to-hms`) [hms] command converts a real number, interpreted according to the current angular mode, to an HMS form describing the same angle. In algebraic notation, the `hms` function also accepts three arguments: 'hms(h, m, s)'. (The three-argument version is independent of the current angular mode.)

The `calc-from-hms` command converts the HMS form on the top of the stack into a real number according to the current angular mode.

The `c p` (`calc-polar`) command converts the complex number on the top of the stack from polar to rectangular form, or from rectangular to polar form, whichever is appropriate. Real numbers are left the same. This command is equivalent to the `rect` or `polar` functions in algebraic formulas, depending on the direction of conversion. (It uses `polar`, except that if the argument is already a polar complex number, it uses `rect` instead. The `I c p` command always uses `rect`.)

The `c c` (`calc-clean`) [pclean] command "cleans" the number on the top of the stack. Floating point numbers are re-rounded according to the current precision. Polar numbers whose angular components have strayed from the −180 to +180 degree range are normalized. (Note that results will be undesirable if the current angular mode is different from the one under which the number was produced!) Integers and fractions are generally unaffected by this operation. Vectors and formulas are cleaned by cleaning each component number (i.e., pervasively).

If the simplification mode is set below basic simplification, it is raised for the purposes of this command. Thus, *c c* applies the basic simplifications even if their automatic application is disabled. See Section 6.5 [Simplification Modes], page 142.

A numeric prefix argument to *c c* sets the floating-point precision to that value for the duration of the command. A positive prefix (of at least 3) sets the precision to the specified value; a negative or zero prefix decreases the precision by the specified amount.

The keystroke sequences *c 0* through *c 9* are equivalent to *c c* with the corresponding negative prefix argument. If roundoff errors have changed 2.0 into 1.999999, typing *c 1* to clip off one decimal place often conveniently does the trick.

The *c c* command with a numeric prefix argument, and the *c 0* through *c 9* commands, also "clip" very small floating-point numbers to zero. If the exponent is less than or equal to the negative of the specified precision, the number is changed to 0.0. For example, if the current precision is 12, then *c 2* changes the vector '[1e-8, 1e-9, 1e-10, 1e-11]' to '[1e-8, 1e-9, 0, 0]'. Numbers this small generally arise from roundoff noise.

If the numbers you are using really are legitimately this small, you should avoid using the *c 0* through *c 9* commands. (The plain *c c* command rounds to the current precision but does not clip small numbers.)

One more property of *c 0* through *c 9*, and of *c c* with a prefix argument, is that integer-valued floats are converted to plain integers, so that *c 1* on '[1., 1.5, 2., 2.5, 3.]' produces '[1, 1.5, 2, 2.5, 3]'. This is not done for huge numbers ('1e100' is technically an integer-valued float, but you wouldn't want it automatically converted to a 100-digit integer).

With the Hyperbolic flag, *H c c* and *H c 0* through *H c 9* operate non-pervasively [clean].

7.5 Date Arithmetic

The commands described in this section perform various conversions and calculations involving date forms (see Section 4.9 [Date Forms], page 122). They use the *t* (for time/date) prefix key followed by shifted letters.

The simplest date arithmetic is done using the regular + and – commands. In particular, adding a number to a date form advances the date form by a certain number of days; adding an HMS form to a date form advances the date by a certain amount of time; and subtracting two date forms produces a difference measured in days. The commands described here provide additional, more specialized operations on dates.

Many of these commands accept a numeric prefix argument; if you give plain *C-u* as the prefix, these commands will instead take the additional argument from the top of the stack.

7.5.1 Date Conversions

The *t D* (calc-date) [date] command converts a date form into a number, measured in days since Jan 1, 1 AD. The result will be an integer if *date* is a pure date form, or a fraction or float if *date* is a date/time form. Or, if its argument is a number, it converts this number into a date form.

With a numeric prefix argument, *t D* takes that many objects (up to six) from the top of the stack and interprets them in one of the following ways:

The 'date(*year*, *month*, *day*)' function builds a pure date form out of the specified year, month, and day, which must all be integers. *Year* is a year number, such as 1991 (*not* the same as 91!*). *Month* must be an integer in the range 1 to 12; *day* must be in the range 1 to 31. If the specified month has fewer than 31 days and *day* is too large, the equivalent day in the following month will be used.

The 'date(*month*, *day*)' function builds a pure date form using the current year, as determined by the real-time clock.

The 'date(*year*, *month*, *day*, *hms*)' function builds a date/time form using an *hms* form.

The 'date(*year*, *month*, *day*, *hour*, *minute*, *second*)' function builds a date/time form. *hour* should be an integer in the range 0 to 23; *minute* should be an integer in the range 0 to 59; *second* should be any real number in the range '[0 .. 60)'. The last two arguments default to zero if omitted.

The *t J* (calc-julian) [julian] command converts a date form into a Julian day count, which is the number of days since noon (GMT) on Jan 1, 4713 BC. A pure date is converted to an integer Julian count representing noon of that day. A date/time form is converted to an exact floating-point Julian count, adjusted to interpret the date form in the current time zone but the Julian day count in Greenwich Mean Time. A numeric prefix argument allows you to specify the time zone; see Section 7.5.4 [Time Zones], page 197. Use a prefix of zero to suppress the time zone adjustment. Note that pure date forms are never time-zone adjusted.

This command can also do the opposite conversion, from a Julian day count (either an integer day, or a floating-point day and time in the GMT zone), into a pure date form or a date/time form in the current or specified time zone.

The *t U* (calc-unix-time) [unixtime] command converts a date form into a Unix time value, which is the number of seconds since midnight on Jan 1, 1970, or vice-versa. The numeric result will be an integer if the current precision is 12 or less; for higher precision, the result may be a float with (*precision*−12) digits after the decimal. Just as for *t J*, the numeric time is interpreted in the GMT time zone and the date form is interpreted in the current or specified zone. Some systems use Unix-like numbering but with the local time zone; give a prefix of zero to suppress the adjustment if so.

The *t C* (calc-convert-time-zones) [tzconv] command converts a date form from one time zone to another. You are prompted for each time zone name in turn; you can answer with any suitable Calc time zone expression (see Section 7.5.4 [Time Zones], page 197). If you answer either prompt with a blank line, the local time zone is used for that prompt. You can also answer the first prompt with $ to take the two time zone names from the stack (and the date to be converted from the third stack level).

7.5.2 Date Functions

The *t N* (calc-now) [now] command pushes the current date and time on the stack as a date form. The time is reported in terms of the specified time zone; with no numeric prefix argument, *t N* reports for the current time zone.

The *t P* (calc-date-part) command extracts one part of a date form. The prefix argument specifies the part; with no argument, this command prompts for a part code from 1 to 9. The various part codes are described in the following paragraphs.

The *M-1 t P* [year] function extracts the year number from a date form as an integer, e.g., 1991. This and the following functions will also accept a real number for an argument, which is interpreted as a standard Calc day number. Note that this function will never return zero, since the year 1 BC immediately precedes the year 1 AD.

The *M-2 t P* [month] function extracts the month number from a date form as an integer in the range 1 to 12.

The *M-3 t P* [day] function extracts the day number from a date form as an integer in the range 1 to 31.

The *M-4 t P* [hour] function extracts the hour from a date form as an integer in the range 0 (midnight) to 23. Note that 24-hour time is always used. This returns zero for a pure date form. This function (and the following two) also accept HMS forms as input.

The *M-5 t P* [minute] function extracts the minute from a date form as an integer in the range 0 to 59.

The *M-6 t P* [second] function extracts the second from a date form. If the current precision is 12 or less, the result is an integer in the range 0 to 59. For higher precision, the result may instead be a floating-point number.

The *M-7 t P* [weekday] function extracts the weekday number from a date form as an integer in the range 0 (Sunday) to 6 (Saturday).

The *M-8 t P* [yearday] function extracts the day-of-year number from a date form as an integer in the range 1 (January 1) to 366 (December 31 of a leap year).

The *M-9 t P* [time] function extracts the time portion of a date form as an HMS form. This returns '0@ 0' 0"' for a pure date form.

The *t M* (`calc-new-month`) [newmonth] command computes a new date form that represents the first day of the month specified by the input date. The result is always a pure date form; only the year and month numbers of the input are retained. With a numeric prefix argument n in the range from 1 to 31, *t M* computes the nth day of the month. (If n is greater than the actual number of days in the month, or if n is zero, the last day of the month is used.)

The *t Y* (`calc-new-year`) [newyear] command computes a new pure date form that represents the first day of the year specified by the input. The month, day, and time of the input date form are lost. With a numeric prefix argument n in the range from 1 to 366, *t Y* computes the nth day of the year (366 is treated as 365 in non-leap years). A prefix argument of 0 computes the last day of the year (December 31). A negative prefix argument from −1 to −12 computes the first day of the nth month of the year.

The *t W* (`calc-new-week`) [newweek] command computes a new pure date form that represents the Sunday on or before the input date. With a numeric prefix argument, it can be made to use any day of the week as the starting day; the argument must be in the range from 0 (Sunday) to 6 (Saturday). This function always subtracts between 0 and 6 days from the input date.

Here's an example use of `newweek`: Find the date of the next Wednesday after a given date. Using *M-3 t W* or '`newweek(d, 3)`' will give you the *preceding* Wednesday, so '`newweek(d+7, 3)`' will give you the following Wednesday. A further look at the definition of `newweek` shows that if the input date is itself a Wednesday, this formula will return the Wednesday one week in the future. An exercise for the reader is to modify this formula to yield the same day if the input is already a Wednesday. Another interesting exercise is to preserve the time-of-day portion of the input (newweek resets the time to midnight; hint: how can newweek be defined in terms of the weekday function?).

The 'pwday(date)' function (not on any key) computes the day-of-month number of the Sunday on or before *date*. With two arguments, 'pwday(date, day)' computes the day number of the Sunday on or before day number *day* of the month specified by *date*. The *day* must be in the range from 7 to 31; if the day number is greater than the actual number of days in the month, the true number of days is used instead. Thus 'pwday(date, 7)' finds the first Sunday of the month, and 'pwday(date, 31)' finds the last Sunday of the month. With a third *weekday* argument, pwday can be made to look for any day of the week instead of Sunday.

The *t I* (calc-inc-month) [incmonth] command increases a date form by one month, or by an arbitrary number of months specified by a numeric prefix argument. The time portion, if any, of the date form stays the same. The day also stays the same, except that if the new month has fewer days the day number may be reduced to lie in the valid range. For example, 'incmonth(<Jan 31, 1991>)' produces '<Feb 28, 1991>'. Because of this, *t I t I* and *M-2 t I* do not always give the same results ('<Mar 28, 1991>' versus '<Mar 31, 1991>' in this case).

The 'incyear(date, step)' function increases a date form by the specified number of years, which may be any positive or negative integer. Note that 'incyear(d, n)' is equivalent to 'incmonth(d, 12*n)', but these do not have simple equivalents in terms of day arithmetic because months and years have varying lengths. If the *step* argument is omitted, 1 year is assumed. There is no keyboard command for this function; use *C-u 12 t I* instead.

There is no newday function at all because *F* [floor] serves this purpose. Similarly, instead of incday and incweek simply use $d + n$ or $d + 7n$.

See Section 7.1 [Basic Arithmetic], page 185, for the *f]* [incr] command which can adjust a date/time form by a certain number of seconds.

7.5.3 Business Days

Often time is measured in "business days" or "working days," where weekends and holidays are skipped. Calc's normal date arithmetic functions use calendar days, so that subtracting two consecutive Mondays will yield a difference of 7 days. By contrast, subtracting two consecutive Mondays would yield 5 business days (assuming two-day weekends and the absence of holidays).

The *t +* (calc-business-days-plus) [badd] and *t -* (calc-business-days-minus) [bsub] commands perform arithmetic using business days. For *t +*, one argument must be a date form and the other must be a real number (positive or negative). If the number is not an integer, then a certain amount of time is added as well as a number of days; for example, adding 0.5 business days to a time in Friday evening will produce a time in Monday morning. It is also possible to add an HMS form; adding '12@ 0' 0"' also adds half a business day. For *t -*, the arguments are either a date form and a number or HMS form, or two date forms, in which case the result is the number of business days between the two dates.

By default, Calc considers any day that is not a Saturday or Sunday to be a business day. You can define any number of additional holidays by editing the variable `Holidays`. (There is an `s H` convenience command for editing this variable.) Initially, `Holidays` contains the vector '`[sat, sun]`'. Entries in the `Holidays` vector may be any of the following kinds of objects:

- Date forms (pure dates, not date/time forms). These specify particular days which are to be treated as holidays.

- Intervals of date forms. These specify a range of days, all of which are holidays (e.g., Christmas week). See Section 4.12 [Interval Forms], page 126.

- Nested vectors of date forms. Each date form in the vector is considered to be a holiday.

- Any Calc formula which evaluates to one of the above three things. If the formula involves the variable y, it stands for a yearly repeating holiday; y will take on various year numbers like 1992. For example, '`date(y, 12, 25)`' specifies Christmas day, and '`newweek(date(y, 11, 7), 4) + 21`' specifies Thanksgiving (which is held on the fourth Thursday of November). If the formula involves the variable m, that variable takes on month numbers from 1 to 12: '`date(y, m, 15)`' is a holiday that takes place on the 15th of every month.

- A weekday name, such as `sat` or `sun`. This is really a variable whose name is a three-letter, lower-case day name.

- An interval of year numbers (integers). This specifies the span of years over which this holiday list is to be considered valid. Any business-day arithmetic that goes outside this range will result in an error message. Use this if you are including an explicit list of holidays, rather than a formula to generate them, and you want to make sure you don't accidentally go beyond the last point where the holidays you entered are complete. If there is no limiting interval in the `Holidays` vector, the default '`[1 .. 2737]`' is used. (This is the absolute range of years for which Calc's business-day algorithms will operate.)

- An interval of HMS forms. This specifies the span of hours that are to be considered one business day. For example, if this range is '`[9@ 0' 0" .. 17@ 0' 0"]`' (i.e., 9am to 5pm), then the business day is only eight hours long, so that `1.5 t +` on '`<4:00pm Fri Dec 13, 1991>`' will add one business day and four business hours to produce '`<12:00pm Tue Dec 17, 1991>`'. Likewise, `t -` will now express differences in time as fractions of an eight-hour day. Times before 9am will be treated as 9am by business date arithmetic, and times at or after 5pm will be treated as 4:59:59pm. If there is no HMS interval in `Holidays`, the full 24-hour day '`[0 0' 0" .. 24 0' 0"]`' is assumed. (Regardless of the type of bounds you specify, the interval is treated as inclusive on the low end and exclusive on the high end, so that the work day goes from 9am up to, but not including, 5pm.)

If the `Holidays` vector is empty, then `t +` and `t -` will act just like `+` and `-` because there will then be no difference between business days and calendar days.

Calc expands the intervals and formulas you give into a complete list of holidays for internal use. This is done mainly to make sure it can detect multiple holidays. (For example, '`<Jan 1, 1989>`' is both New Year's Day and a Sunday, but Calc's algorithms take care to count it only once when figuring the number of holidays between two dates.)

Since the complete list of holidays for all the years from 1 to 2737 would be huge, Calc actually computes only the part of the list between the smallest and largest years that have been involved in business-day calculations so far. Normally, you won't have to worry about this. Keep in mind, however, that if you do one calculation for 1992, and another for 1792, even if both involve only a small range of years, Calc will still work out all the holidays that fall in that 200-year span.

If you add a (positive) number of days to a date form that falls on a weekend or holiday, the date form is treated as if it were the most recent business day. (Thus adding one business day to a Friday, Saturday, or Sunday will all yield the following Monday.) If you subtract a number of days from a weekend or holiday, the date is effectively on the following business day. (So subtracting one business day from Saturday, Sunday, or Monday yields the preceding Friday.) The difference between two dates one or both of which fall on holidays equals the number of actual business days between them. These conventions are consistent in the sense that, if you add n business days to any date, the difference between the result and the original date will come out to n business days. (It can't be completely consistent though; a subtraction followed by an addition might come out a bit differently, since $t +$ is incapable of producing a date that falls on a weekend or holiday.)

There is a `holiday` function, not on any keys, that takes any date form and returns 1 if that date falls on a weekend or holiday, as defined in `Holidays`, or 0 if the date is a business day.

7.5.4 Time Zones

Time zones and daylight saving time are a complicated business. The conversions to and from Julian and Unix-style dates automatically compute the correct time zone and daylight saving adjustment to use, provided they can figure out this information. This section describes Calc's time zone adjustment algorithm in detail, in case you want to do conversions in different time zones or in case Calc's algorithms can't determine the right correction to use.

Adjustments for time zones and daylight saving time are done by t U, t J, t N, and t C, but not by any other commands. In particular, '<may 1 1991> − <apr 1 1991>' evaluates to exactly 30 days even though there is a daylight-saving transition in between. This is also true for Julian pure dates: 'julian(<may 1 1991>) − julian(<apr 1 1991>)'. But Julian and Unix date/times will adjust for daylight saving time: using Calc's default daylight saving time rule (see the explanation below), 'julian(<12am may 1 1991>) − julian(<12am apr 1 1991>)' evaluates to '29.95833' (that's 29 days and 23 hours) because one hour was lost when daylight saving commenced on April 7, 1991.

In brief, the idiom 'julian(*date1*) − julian(*date2*)' computes the actual number of 24-hour periods between two dates, whereas '*date1* − *date2*' computes the number of calendar days between two dates without taking daylight saving into account.

The `calc-time-zone` [tzone] command converts the time zone specified by its numeric prefix argument into a number of seconds difference from Greenwich mean time (GMT). If the argument is a number, the result is simply that value multiplied by 3600. Typical arguments for North America are 5 (Eastern) or 8 (Pacific). If Daylight Saving time is in effect, one hour should be subtracted from the normal difference.

If you give a prefix of plain *C-u*, `calc-time-zone` (like other date arithmetic commands that include a time zone argument) takes the zone argument from the top of the stack.

(In the case of *t J* and *t U*, the normal argument is then taken from the second-to-top stack position.) This allows you to give a non-integer time zone adjustment. The time-zone argument can also be an HMS form, or it can be a variable which is a time zone name in upper- or lower-case. For example 'tzone(PST) = tzone(8)' and 'tzone(pdt) = tzone(7)' (for Pacific standard and daylight saving times, respectively).

North American and European time zone names are defined as follows; note that for each time zone there is one name for standard time, another for daylight saving time, and a third for "generalized" time in which the daylight saving adjustment is computed from context.

YST	PST	MST	CST	EST	AST	NST	GMT	WET	MET	MEZ
9	8	7	6	5	4	3.5	0	-1	-2	-2

YDT	PDT	MDT	CDT	EDT	ADT	NDT	BST	WETDST	METDST	MESZ
8	7	6	5	4	3	2.5	-1	-2	-3	-3

YGT	PGT	MGT	CGT	EGT	AGT	NGT	BGT	WEGT	MEGT	MEGZ
9/8	8/7	7/6	6/5	5/4	4/3	3.5/2.5	0/-1	-1/-2	-2/-3	-2/-3

To define time zone names that do not appear in the above table, you must modify the Lisp variable `math-tzone-names`. This is a list of lists describing the different time zone names; its structure is best explained by an example. The three entries for Pacific Time look like this:

```
( ( "PST" 8 0 )    ; Name as an upper-case string, then standard
  ( "PDT" 8 -1 )   ; adjustment, then daylight saving adjustment.
  ( "PGT" 8 "PST" "PDT" ) )   ; Generalized time zone.
```

With no arguments, `calc-time-zone` or 'tzone()' will by default get the time zone and daylight saving information from the calendar (see Section "The Calendar and the Diary" in *The GNU Emacs Manual*). To use a different time zone, or if the calendar does not give the desired result, you can set the Calc variable `TimeZone` (which is by default `nil`) to an appropriate time zone name. (The easiest way to do this is to edit the `TimeZone` variable using Calc's *s T* command, then use the *s p* (`calc-permanent-variable`) command to save the value of `TimeZone` permanently.) If the time zone given by `TimeZone` is a generalized time zone, e.g., `EGT`, Calc examines the date being converted to tell whether to use standard or daylight saving time. But if the current time zone is explicit, e.g., `EST` or `EDT`, then that adjustment is used exactly and Calc's daylight saving algorithm is not consulted. The special time zone name `local` is equivalent to no argument; i.e., it uses the information obtained from the calendar.

The *t J* and *t U* commands with no numeric prefix arguments do the same thing as 'tzone()'; namely, use the information from the calendar if `TimeZone` is `nil`, otherwise use the time zone given by `TimeZone`.

When Calc computes the daylight saving information itself (i.e., when the `TimeZone` variable is set), it will by default consider daylight saving time to begin at 2 a.m. on the second Sunday of March (for years from 2007 on) or on the last Sunday in April (for years before 2007), and to end at 2 a.m. on the first Sunday of November. (for years from 2007 on) or the last Sunday in October (for years before 2007). These are the rules that have been in effect in much of North America since 1966 and take into account the rule change that began in 2007. If you are in a country that uses different rules for computing daylight saving time, you have two choices: Write your own daylight saving hook, or control time zones explicitly by setting the `TimeZone` variable and/or always giving a time-zone argument for the conversion functions.

The Lisp variable `math-daylight-savings-hook` holds the name of a function that is used to compute the daylight saving adjustment for a given date. The default is `math-std-daylight-savings`, which computes an adjustment (either 0 or -1) using the North American rules given above.

The daylight saving hook function is called with four arguments: The date, as a floating-point number in standard Calc format; a six-element list of the date decomposed into year, month, day, hour, minute, and second, respectively; a string which contains the generalized time zone name in upper-case, e.g., `"WEGT"`; and a special adjustment to be applied to the hour value when converting into a generalized time zone (see below).

The Lisp function `math-prev-weekday-in-month` is useful for daylight saving computations. This is an internal version of the user-level `pwday` function described in the previous section. It takes four arguments: The floating-point date value, the corresponding six-element date list, the day-of-month number, and the weekday number (0–6).

The default daylight saving hook ignores the time zone name, but a more sophisticated hook could use different algorithms for different time zones. It would also be possible to use different algorithms depending on the year number, but the default hook always uses the algorithm for 1987 and later. Here is a listing of the default daylight saving hook:

```
(defun math-std-daylight-savings (date dt zone bump)
  (cond ((< (nth 1 dt) 4) 0)
        ((= (nth 1 dt) 4)
         (let ((sunday (math-prev-weekday-in-month date dt 7 0)))
           (cond ((< (nth 2 dt) sunday) 0)
                 ((= (nth 2 dt) sunday)
                  (if (>= (nth 3 dt) (+ 3 bump)) -1 0))
                 (t -1))))
        ((< (nth 1 dt) 10) -1)
        ((= (nth 1 dt) 10)
         (let ((sunday (math-prev-weekday-in-month date dt 31 0)))
           (cond ((< (nth 2 dt) sunday) -1)
                 ((= (nth 2 dt) sunday)
                  (if (>= (nth 3 dt) (+ 2 bump)) 0 -1))
                 (t 0))))
        (t 0))
)
```

The `bump` parameter is equal to zero when Calc is converting from a date form in a generalized time zone into a GMT date value. It is -1 when Calc is converting in the other direction. The adjustments shown above ensure that the conversion behaves correctly and reasonably around the 2 a.m. transition in each direction.

There is a "missing" hour between 2 a.m. and 3 a.m. at the beginning of daylight saving time; converting a date/time form that falls in this hour results in a time value for the following hour, from 3 a.m. to 4 a.m. At the end of daylight saving time, the hour from 1 a.m. to 2 a.m. repeats itself; converting a date/time form that falls in this hour results in a time value for the first manifestation of that time (*not* the one that occurs one hour later).

If `math-daylight-savings-hook` is `nil`, then the daylight saving adjustment is always taken to be zero.

In algebraic formulas, '`tzone(zone, date)`' computes the time zone adjustment for a given zone name at a given date. The *date* is ignored unless *zone* is a generalized time zone.

If *date* is a date form, the daylight saving computation is applied to it as it appears. If *date* is a numeric date value, it is adjusted for the daylight-saving version of *zone* before being given to the daylight saving hook. This odd-sounding rule ensures that the daylight-saving computation is always done in local time, not in the GMT time that a numeric *date* is typically represented in.

The '`dsadj(date, zone)`' function computes the daylight saving adjustment that is appropriate for *date* in time zone *zone*. If *zone* is explicitly in or not in daylight saving time (e.g., `PDT` or `PST`) the *date* is ignored. If *zone* is a generalized time zone, the algorithms described above are used. If *zone* is omitted, the computation is done for the current time zone.

7.6 Financial Functions

Calc's financial or business functions use the *b* prefix key followed by a shifted letter. (The *b* prefix followed by a lower-case letter is used for operations on binary numbers.)

Note that the rate and the number of intervals given to these functions must be on the same time scale, e.g., both months or both years. Mixing an annual interest rate with a time expressed in months will give you very wrong answers!

It is wise to compute these functions to a higher precision than you really need, just to make sure your answer is correct to the last penny; also, you may wish to check the definitions at the end of this section to make sure the functions have the meaning you expect.

7.6.1 Percentages

The `M-%` (`calc-percent`) command takes a percentage value, say 5.4, and converts it to an equivalent actual number. For example, *5.4 M-%* enters 0.054 on the stack. (That's the `META` or `ESC` key combined with `%`.)

Actually, `M-%` creates a formula of the form '`5.4%`'. You can enter '`5.4%`' yourself during algebraic entry. The '`%`' operator simply means, "the preceding value divided by 100." The '`%`' operator has very high precedence, so that '`1+8%`' is interpreted as '`1+(8%)`', not as '`(1+8)%`'. (The '`%`' operator is just a postfix notation for the `percent` function, just like '`20!`' is the notation for '`fact(20)`', or twenty-factorial.)

The formula '`5.4%`' would normally evaluate immediately to 0.054, but the `M-%` command suppresses evaluation as it puts the formula onto the stack. However, the next Calc command that uses the formula '`5.4%`' will evaluate it as its first step. The net effect is that you get to look at '`5.4%`' on the stack, but Calc commands see it as '`0.054`', which is what they expect.

In particular, '`5.4%`' and '`0.054`' are suitable values for the *rate* arguments of the various financial functions, but the number '`5.4`' is probably *not* suitable—it represents a rate of 540 percent!

The key sequence `M-% *` effectively means "percent-of." For example, *68 RET 25 M-% ** computes 17, which is 25% of 68 (and also 68% of 25, which comes out to the same thing).

The *c %* (`calc-convert-percent`) command converts the value on the top of the stack from numeric to percentage form. For example, if 0.08 is on the stack, *c %* converts it to '`8%`'. The quantity is the same, it's just represented differently. (Contrast this with `M-%`, which would convert this number to '0.08%'.) The = key is a convenient way to convert a formula like '8%' back to numeric form, 0.08.

To compute what percentage one quantity is of another quantity, use / c %. For example, *17 RET 68 / c %* displays '25%'.

The *b %* (calc-percent-change) [relch] command calculates the percentage change from one number to another. For example, *40 RET 50 b %* produces the answer '25%', since 50 is 25% larger than 40. A negative result represents a decrease: *50 RET 40 b %* produces '-20%', since 40 is 20% smaller than 50. (The answers are different in magnitude because, in the first case, we're increasing by 25% of 40, but in the second case, we're decreasing by 20% of 50.) The effect of *40 RET 50 b %* is to compute $(50 - 40)/40$, converting the answer to percentage form as if by *c %*.

7.6.2 Future Value

The *b F* (calc-fin-fv) [fv] command computes the future value of an investment. It takes three arguments from the stack: 'fv(*rate, n, payment*)'. If you give payments of *payment* every year for *n* years, and the money you have paid earns interest at *rate* per year, then this function tells you what your investment would be worth at the end of the period. (The actual interval doesn't have to be years, as long as *n* and *rate* are expressed in terms of the same intervals.) This function assumes payments occur at the *end* of each interval.

The *I b F* [fvb] command does the same computation, but assuming your payments are at the beginning of each interval. Suppose you plan to deposit $1000 per year in a savings account earning 5.4% interest, starting right now. How much will be in the account after five years? fvb(5.4%, 5, 1000) = 5870.73. Thus you will have earned $870 worth of interest over the years. Using the stack, this calculation would have been *5.4 M-% 5 RET 1000 I b F*. Note that the rate is expressed as a number between 0 and 1, *not* as a percentage.

The *H b F* [fvl] command computes the future value of an initial lump sum investment. Suppose you could deposit those five thousand dollars in the bank right now; how much would they be worth in five years? fvl(5.4%, 5, 5000) = 6503.89.

The algebraic functions fv and fvb accept an optional fourth argument, which is used as an initial lump sum in the sense of fvl. In other words, fv(*rate, n, payment, initial*) = fv(*rate, n, payment*) + fvl(*rate, n, initial*).

To illustrate the relationships between these functions, we could do the fvb calculation "by hand" using fvl. The final balance will be the sum of the contributions of our five deposits at various times. The first deposit earns interest for five years: fvl(5.4%, 5, 1000) = 1300.78. The second deposit only earns interest for four years: fvl(5.4%, 4, 1000) = 1234.13. And so on down to the last deposit, which earns one year's interest: fvl(5.4%, 1, 1000) = 1054.00. The sum of these five values is, sure enough, $5870.73, just as was computed by fvb directly.

What does fv(5.4%, 5, 1000) = 5569.96 mean? The payments are now at the ends of the periods. The end of one year is the same as the beginning of the next, so what this really means is that we've lost the payment at year zero (which contributed $1300.78), but we're now counting the payment at year five (which, since it didn't have a chance to earn interest, counts as $1000). Indeed, $5569.96 = 5870.73 - 1300.78 + 1000$ (give or take a bit of roundoff error).

7.6.3 Present Value

The `b P` (`calc-fin-pv`) [pv] command computes the present value of an investment. Like `fv`, it takes three arguments: `pv(rate, n, payment)`. It computes the present value of a series of regular payments. Suppose you have the chance to make an investment that will pay $2000 per year over the next four years; as you receive these payments you can put them in the bank at 9% interest. You want to know whether it is better to make the investment, or to keep the money in the bank where it earns 9% interest right from the start. The calculation `pv(9%, 4, 2000)` gives the result 6479.44. If your initial investment must be less than this, say, $6000, then the investment is worthwhile. But if you had to put up $7000, then it would be better just to leave it in the bank.

Here is the interpretation of the result of `pv`: You are trying to compare the return from the investment you are considering, which is `fv(9%, 4, 2000) = 9146.26`, with the return from leaving the money in the bank, which is `fvl(9%, 4, x)` where x is the amount of money you would have to put up in advance. The `pv` function finds the break-even point, $x = 6479.44$, at which `fvl(9%, 4, 6479.44)` is also equal to 9146.26. This is the largest amount you should be willing to invest.

The `I b P` [pvb] command solves the same problem, but with payments occurring at the beginning of each interval. It has the same relationship to `fvb` as `pv` has to `fv`. For example `pvb(9%, 4, 2000) = 7062.59`, a larger number than `pv` produced because we get to start earning interest on the return from our investment sooner.

The `H b P` [pvl] command computes the present value of an investment that will pay off in one lump sum at the end of the period. For example, if we get our $8000 all at the end of the four years, `pvl(9%, 4, 8000) = 5667.40`. This is much less than `pv` reported, because we don't earn any interest on the return from this investment. Note that `pvl` and `fvl` are simple inverses: `fvl(9%, 4, 5667.40) = 8000`.

You can give an optional fourth lump-sum argument to `pv` and `pvb`; this is handled in exactly the same way as the fourth argument for `fv` and `fvb`.

The `b N` (`calc-fin-npv`) [npv] command computes the net present value of a series of irregular investments. The first argument is the interest rate. The second argument is a vector which represents the expected return from the investment at the end of each interval. For example, if the rate represents a yearly interest rate, then the vector elements are the return from the first year, second year, and so on.

Thus, `npv(9%, [2000,2000,2000,2000]) = pv(9%, 4, 2000) = 6479.44`. Obviously this function is more interesting when the payments are not all the same!

The `npv` function can actually have two or more arguments. Multiple arguments are interpreted in the same way as for the vector statistical functions like `vsum`. See Section 9.7.1 [Single-Variable Statistics], page 232. Basically, if there are several payment arguments, each either a vector or a plain number, all these values are collected left-to-right into the complete list of payments. A numeric prefix argument on the `b N` command says how many payment values or vectors to take from the stack.

The `I b N` [npvb] command computes the net present value where payments occur at the beginning of each interval rather than at the end.

7.6.4 Related Financial Functions

The functions in this section are basically inverses of the present value functions with respect to the various arguments.

The *b M* (calc-fin-pmt) [pmt] command computes the amount of periodic payment necessary to amortize a loan. Thus pmt(rate, n, amount) equals the value of *payment* such that pv(rate, n, payment) = amount.

The *I b M* [pmtb] command does the same computation but using pvb instead of pv. Like pv and pvb, these functions can also take a fourth argument which represents an initial lump-sum investment.

The *H b M* key just invokes the fvl function, which is the inverse of pvl. There is no explicit pmtl function.

The *b #* (calc-fin-nper) [nper] command computes the number of regular payments necessary to amortize a loan. Thus nper(rate, payment, amount) equals the value of *n* such that pv(rate, n, payment) = amount. If *payment* is too small ever to amortize a loan for *amount* at interest rate *rate*, the nper function is left in symbolic form.

The *I b #* [nperb] command does the same computation but using pvb instead of pv. You can give a fourth lump-sum argument to these functions, but the computation will be rather slow in the four-argument case.

The *H b #* [nperl] command does the same computation using pvl. By exchanging *payment* and *amount* you can also get the solution for fvl. For example, nperl(8%, 2000, 1000) = 9.006, so if you place $1000 in a bank account earning 8%, it will take nine years to grow to $2000.

The *b T* (calc-fin-rate) [rate] command computes the rate of return on an investment. This is also an inverse of pv: rate(n, payment, amount) computes the value of *rate* such that pv(rate, n, payment) = amount. The result is expressed as a formula like '6.3%'.

The *I b T* [rateb] and *H b T* [ratel] commands solve the analogous equations with pvb or pvl in place of pv. Also, rate and rateb can accept an optional fourth argument just like pv and pvb. To redo the above example from a different perspective, ratel(9, 2000, 1000) = 8.00597%, which says you will need an interest rate of 8% in order to double your account in nine years.

The *b I* (calc-fin-irr) [irr] command is the analogous function to rate but for net present value. Its argument is a vector of payments. Thus irr(payments) computes the *rate* such that npv(rate, payments) = 0; this rate is known as the *internal rate of return*.

The *I b I* [irrb] command computes the internal rate of return assuming payments occur at the beginning of each period.

7.6.5 Depreciation Functions

The functions in this section calculate *depreciation*, which is the amount of value that a possession loses over time. These functions are characterized by three parameters: *cost*, the original cost of the asset; *salvage*, the value the asset will have at the end of its expected "useful life"; and *life*, the number of years (or other periods) of the expected useful life.

There are several methods for calculating depreciation that differ in the way they spread the depreciation over the lifetime of the asset.

The *b S* (`calc-fin-sln`) [sln] command computes the "straight-line" depreciation. In this method, the asset depreciates by the same amount every year (or period). For example, 'sln(12000, 2000, 5)' returns 2000. The asset costs $12000 initially and will be worth $2000 after five years; it loses $2000 per year.

The *b Y* (`calc-fin-syd`) [syd] command computes the accelerated "sum-of-years'-digits" depreciation. Here the depreciation is higher during the early years of the asset's life. Since the depreciation is different each year, *b Y* takes a fourth *period* parameter which specifies which year is requested, from 1 to *life*. If *period* is outside this range, the syd function will return zero.

The *b D* (`calc-fin-ddb`) [ddb] command computes an accelerated depreciation using the double-declining balance method. It also takes a fourth *period* parameter.

For symmetry, the sln function will accept a *period* parameter as well, although it will ignore its value except that the return value will as usual be zero if *period* is out of range.

For example, pushing the vector $[1, 2, 3, 4, 5]$ (perhaps with *v x 5*) and then mapping *V M* ' *[sln(12000,2000,5,$), syd(12000,2000,5,$), ddb(12000,2000,5,$)]* RET produces a matrix that allows us to compare the three depreciation methods:

```
[ [ 2000, 3333, 4800 ]
  [ 2000, 2667, 2880 ]
  [ 2000, 2000, 1728 ]
  [ 2000, 1333,  592 ]
  [ 2000,  667,    0 ] ]
```

(Values have been rounded to nearest integers in this figure.) We see that sln depreciates by the same amount each year, *syd* depreciates more at the beginning and less at the end, and *ddb* weights the depreciation even more toward the beginning.

Summing columns with *V R : +* yields $[10000, 10000, 10000]$; the total depreciation in any method is (by definition) the difference between the cost and the salvage value.

7.6.6 Definitions

For your reference, here are the actual formulas used to compute Calc's financial functions.

Calc will not evaluate a financial function unless the *rate* or *n* argument is known. However, *payment* or *amount* can be a variable. Calc expands these functions according to the formulas below for symbolic arguments only when you use the *a "* (`calc-expand-formula`) command, or when taking derivatives or integrals or solving equations involving the functions.

$$\text{fv}(r, n, p) = p\frac{(1+r)^n - 1}{r}$$

$$\text{fvb}(r, n, p) = p\frac{((1+r)^n - 1)(1+r)}{r}$$

$$\text{fvl}(r, n, p) = p(1+r)^n$$

$$\text{pv}(r, n, p) = p\frac{1 - (1+r)^{-n}}{r}$$

$$\text{pvb}(r, n, p) = p\frac{(1 - (1+r)^{-n})(1+r)}{r}$$

$$\mathtt{pvl}(r, n, p) = p(1 + r)^{-n}$$

$$\mathtt{npv}(r, [a, b, c]) = a(1 + r)^{-1} + b(1 + r)^{-2} + c(1 + r)^{-3}$$

$$\mathtt{npvb}(r, [a, b, c]) = a + b(1 + r)^{-1} + c(1 + r)^{-2}$$

$$\mathtt{pmt}(r, n, a, x) = \frac{(a - x(1 + r)^{-n})r}{1 - (1 + r)^{-n}}$$

$$\mathtt{pmtb}(r, n, a, x) = \frac{(a - x(1 + r)^{-n})r}{(1 - (1 + r)^{-n})(1 + r)}$$

$$\mathtt{nper}(r, p, a) = -\mathtt{log}(1 - \frac{ar}{p}, 1 + r)$$

$$\mathtt{nperb}(r, p, a) = -\mathtt{log}(1 - \frac{ar}{p(1 + r)}, 1 + r)$$

$$\mathtt{nperl}(r, p, a) = -\mathtt{log}(\frac{a}{p}, 1 + r)$$

$$\mathtt{ratel}(n, p, a) = \frac{p^{1/n}}{a^{1/n}} - 1$$

$$\mathtt{sln}(c, s, l) = \frac{c - s}{l}$$

$$\mathtt{syd}(c, s, l, p) = \frac{(c - s)(l - p + 1)}{l(l + 1)/2}$$

$$\mathtt{ddb}(c, s, l, p) = \frac{2(c - \text{depreciation so far})}{l}$$

In `pmt` and `pmtb`, $x = 0$ if omitted.

These functions accept any numeric objects, including error forms, intervals, and even (though not very usefully) complex numbers. The above formulas specify exactly the behavior of these functions with all sorts of inputs.

Note that if the first argument to the `log` in `nper` is negative, `nper` leaves itself in symbolic form rather than returning a (financially meaningless) complex number.

'`rate(num, pmt, amt)`' solves the equation '`pv(rate, num, pmt) = amt`' for '`rate`' using *H a R* (calc-find-root), with the interval '`[.01% .. 100%]`' for an initial guess. The `rateb` function is the same except that it uses `pvb`. Note that `ratel` can be solved directly; its formula is shown in the above list.

Similarly, '`irr(pmts)`' solves the equation '`npv(rate, pmts) = 0`' for '`rate`'.

If you give a fourth argument to `nper` or `nperb`, Calc will also use *H a R* to solve the equation using an initial guess interval of '`[0 .. 100]`'.

A fourth argument to `fv` simply sums the two components calculated from the above formulas for `fv` and `fvl`. The same is true of `fvb`, `pv`, and `pvb`.

The *ddb* function is computed iteratively; the "book" value starts out equal to *cost*, and decreases according to the above formula for the specified number of periods. If the book value would decrease below *salvage*, it only decreases to *salvage* and the depreciation is zero for all subsequent periods. The `ddb` function returns the amount the book value decreased in the specified period.

7.7 Binary Number Functions

The commands in this chapter all use two-letter sequences beginning with the *b* prefix.

The "binary" operations actually work regardless of the currently displayed radix, although their results make the most sense in a radix like 2, 8, or 16 (as obtained by the *d 2*, *d 8*, or *d 6* commands, respectively). You may also wish to enable display of leading zeros with *d z*. See Section 6.7.1 [Radix Modes], page 148.

The Calculator maintains a current *word size* w, an arbitrary positive or negative integer. For a positive word size, all of the binary operations described here operate modulo 2^w. In particular, negative arguments are converted to positive integers modulo 2^w by all binary functions.

If the word size is negative, binary operations produce twos-complement integers from -2^{-w-1} to $2^{-w-1} - 1$ inclusive. Either mode accepts inputs in any range; the sign of w affects only the results produced.

The *b c* (`calc-clip`) [clip] command can be used to clip a number by reducing it modulo 2^w. The commands described in this chapter automatically clip their results to the current word size. Note that other operations like addition do not use the current word size, since integer addition generally is not "binary." (However, see Section 6.5 [Simplification Modes], page 142, `calc-bin-simplify-mode`.) For example, with a word size of 8 bits *b c* converts a number to the range 0 to 255; with a word size of -8 *b c* converts to the range -128 to 127.

The default word size is 32 bits. All operations except the shifts and rotates allow you to specify a different word size for that one operation by giving a numeric prefix argument: *C-u 8 b c* clips the top of stack to the range 0 to 255 regardless of the current word size. To set the word size permanently, use *b w* (`calc-word-size`). This command displays a prompt with the current word size; press RET immediately to keep this word size, or type a new word size at the prompt.

When the binary operations are written in symbolic form, they take an optional second (or third) word-size parameter. When a formula like '`and(a,b)`' is finally evaluated, the word size current at that time will be used, but when '`and(a,b,-8)`' is evaluated, a word size of -8 will always be used. A symbolic binary function will be left in symbolic form unless the all of its argument(s) are integers or integer-valued floats.

If either or both arguments are modulo forms for which M is a power of two, that power of two is taken as the word size unless a numeric prefix argument overrides it. The current word size is never consulted when modulo-power-of-two forms are involved.

The *b a* (`calc-and`) [and] command computes the bitwise AND of the two numbers on the top of the stack. In other words, for each of the w binary digits of the two numbers (pairwise), the corresponding bit of the result is 1 if and only if both input bits are 1: '`and(2#1100, 2#1010) = 2#1000`'.

The *b o* (`calc-or`) [or] command computes the bitwise inclusive OR of two numbers. A bit is 1 if either of the input bits, or both, are 1: '`or(2#1100, 2#1010) = 2#1110`'.

The *b x* (`calc-xor`) [xor] command computes the bitwise exclusive OR of two numbers. A bit is 1 if exactly one of the input bits is 1: '`xor(2#1100, 2#1010) = 2#0110`'.

The *b d* (`calc-diff`) [diff] command computes the bitwise difference of two numbers; this is defined by 'diff(a,b) = and(a,not(b))', so that 'diff(2#1100, 2#1010) = 2#0100'.

The *b n* (`calc-not`) [not] command computes the bitwise NOT of a number. A bit is 1 if the input bit is 0 and vice-versa.

The *b l* (`calc-lshift-binary`) [lsh] command shifts a number left by one bit, or by the number of bits specified in the numeric prefix argument. A negative prefix argument performs a logical right shift, in which zeros are shifted in on the left. In symbolic form, 'lsh(a)' is short for 'lsh(a,1)', which in turn is short for 'lsh(a,n,w)'. Bits shifted "off the end," according to the current word size, are lost.

The *H b l* command also does a left shift, but it takes two arguments from the stack (the value to shift, and, at top-of-stack, the number of bits to shift). This version interprets the prefix argument just like the regular binary operations, i.e., as a word size. The Hyperbolic flag has a similar effect on the rest of the binary shift and rotate commands.

The *b r* (`calc-rshift-binary`) [rsh] command shifts a number right by one bit, or by the number of bits specified in the numeric prefix argument: 'rsh(a,n) = lsh(a,-n)'.

The *b L* (`calc-lshift-arith`) [ash] command shifts a number left. It is analogous to lsh, except that if the shift is rightward (the prefix argument is negative), an arithmetic shift is performed as described below.

The *b R* (`calc-rshift-arith`) [rash] command performs an "arithmetic" shift to the right, in which the leftmost bit (according to the current word size) is duplicated rather than shifting in zeros. This corresponds to dividing by a power of two where the input is interpreted as a signed, twos-complement number. (The distinction between the 'rsh' and 'rash' operations is totally independent from whether the word size is positive or negative.) With a negative prefix argument, this performs a standard left shift.

The *b t* (`calc-rotate-binary`) [rot] command rotates a number one bit to the left. The leftmost bit (according to the current word size) is dropped off the left and shifted in on the right. With a numeric prefix argument, the number is rotated that many bits to the left or right.

See Section 9.6 [Set Operations], page 229, for the *b p* and *b u* commands that pack and unpack binary integers into sets. (For example, *b u* unpacks the number '2#11001' to the set of bit-numbers '[0, 3, 4]'.) Type *b u V #* to count the number of "1" bits in a binary integer.

Another interesting use of the set representation of binary integers is to reverse the bits in, say, a 32-bit integer. Type *b u* to unpack; type *31 TAB -* to replace each bit-number in the set with 31 minus that bit-number; type *b p* to pack the set back into a binary integer.

8 Scientific Functions

The functions described here perform trigonometric and other transcendental calculations. They generally produce floating-point answers correct to the full current precision. The *H* (Hyperbolic) and *I* (Inverse) flag keys must be used to get some of these functions from the keyboard.

One miscellaneous command is shift-*P* (`calc-pi`), which pushes the value of π (at the current precision) onto the stack. With the Hyperbolic flag, it pushes the value e, the base of natural logarithms. With the Inverse flag, it pushes Euler's constant γ (about 0.5772). With both Inverse and Hyperbolic, it pushes the "golden ratio" ϕ (about 1.618). (At present, Euler's constant is not available to unlimited precision; Calc knows only the first 100 digits.) In Symbolic mode, these commands push the actual variables 'pi', 'e', 'gamma', and 'phi', respectively, instead of their values; see Section 6.4.5 [Symbolic Mode], page 140.

The *Q* (`calc-sqrt`) [sqrt] function is described elsewhere; see Section 7.1 [Basic Arithmetic], page 185. With the Inverse flag [sqr], this command computes the square of the argument.

See Section 3.7 [Prefix Arguments], page 111, for a discussion of the effect of numeric prefix arguments on commands in this chapter which do not otherwise interpret a prefix argument.

8.1 Logarithmic Functions

The shift-*L* (`calc-ln`) [ln] command computes the natural logarithm of the real or complex number on the top of the stack. With the Inverse flag it computes the exponential function instead, although this is redundant with the *E* command.

The shift-*E* (`calc-exp`) [exp] command computes the exponential, i.e., e raised to the power of the number on the stack. The meanings of the Inverse and Hyperbolic flags follow from those for the `calc-ln` command.

The *H L* (`calc-log10`) [log10] command computes the common (base-10) logarithm of a number. (With the Inverse flag [exp10], it raises ten to a given power.) Note that the common logarithm of a complex number is computed by taking the natural logarithm and dividing by ln 10.

The *B* (`calc-log`) [log] command computes a logarithm to any base. For example, *1024 RET 2 B* produces 10, since $2^{10} = 1024$. In certain cases like 'log(3,9)', the result will be either 1:2 or 0.5 depending on the current Fraction mode setting. With the Inverse flag [alog], this command is similar to ^ except that the order of the arguments is reversed.

The *f I* (`calc-ilog`) [ilog] command computes the integer logarithm of a number to any base. The number and the base must themselves be positive integers. This is the true logarithm, rounded down to an integer. Thus *ilog(x,10)* is 3 for all x in the range from 1000 to 9999. If both arguments are positive integers, exact integer arithmetic is used; otherwise, this is equivalent to 'floor(log(x,b))'.

The *f E* (`calc-expm1`) [expm1] command computes $e^x - 1$, but using an algorithm that produces a more accurate answer when the result is close to zero, i.e., when e^x is close to one.

The f L (calc-lnp1) [lnp1] command computes $\ln(x + 1)$, producing a more accurate answer when x is close to zero.

8.2 Trigonometric/Hyperbolic Functions

The shift-S (calc-sin) [sin] command computes the sine of an angle or complex number. If the input is an HMS form, it is interpreted as degrees-minutes-seconds; otherwise, the input is interpreted according to the current angular mode. It is best to use Radians mode when operating on complex numbers.

Calc's "units" mechanism includes angular units like deg, rad, and grad. While 'sin(45 deg)' is not evaluated all the time, the u s (calc-simplify-units) command will simplify 'sin(45 deg)' by taking the sine of 45 degrees, regardless of the current angular mode. See Section 11.1 [Basic Operations on Units], page 313.

Also, the symbolic variable pi is not ordinarily recognized in arguments to trigonometric functions, as in 'sin(3 pi / 4)', but the default algebraic simplifications recognize many such formulas when the current angular mode is Radians *and* Symbolic mode is enabled; this example would be replaced by 'sqrt(2) / 2'. See Section 6.4.5 [Symbolic Mode], page 140. Beware, this simplification occurs even if you have stored a different value in the variable 'pi'; this is one reason why changing built-in variables is a bad idea. Arguments of the form x plus a multiple of $\pi/2$ are also simplified. Calc includes similar formulas for cos and tan.

Calc's algebraic simplifications know all angles which are integer multiples of $\pi/12$, $\pi/10$, or $\pi/8$ radians. In Degrees mode, analogous simplifications occur for integer multiples of 15 or 18 degrees, and for arguments plus multiples of 90 degrees.

With the Inverse flag, calc-sin computes an arcsine. This is also available as the calc-arcsin command or arcsin algebraic function. The returned argument is converted to degrees, radians, or HMS notation depending on the current angular mode.

With the Hyperbolic flag, calc-sin computes the hyperbolic sine, also available as calc-sinh [sinh]. With the Hyperbolic and Inverse flags, it computes the hyperbolic arcsine (calc-arcsinh) [arcsinh].

The shift-C (calc-cos) [cos] command computes the cosine of an angle or complex number, and shift-T (calc-tan) [tan] computes the tangent, along with all the various inverse and hyperbolic variants of these functions.

The f T (calc-arctan2) [arctan2] command takes two numbers from the stack and computes the arc tangent of their ratio. The result is in the full range from -180 (exclusive) to $+180$ (inclusive) degrees, or the analogous range in radians. A similar result would be obtained with / followed by I T, but the value would only be in the range from -90 to $+90$ degrees since the division loses information about the signs of the two components, and an error might result from an explicit division by zero which arctan2 would avoid. By (arbitrary) definition, 'arctan2(0,0)=0'.

The calc-sincos [sincos] command computes the sine and cosine of a number, returning them as a vector of the form '[cos, sin]'. With the Inverse flag [arcsincos], this command takes a two-element vector as an argument and computes arctan2 of the elements. (This command does not accept the Hyperbolic flag.)

The remaining trigonometric functions, calc-sec [sec], calc-csc [csc] and calc-cot [cot], are also available. With the Hyperbolic flag, these compute their hyperbolic counterparts, which are also available separately as `calc-sech` [sech], `calc-csch` [csch] and `calc-coth` [coth]. (These commands do not accept the Inverse flag.)

8.3 Advanced Mathematical Functions

Calc can compute a variety of less common functions that arise in various branches of mathematics. All of the functions described in this section allow arbitrary complex arguments and, except as noted, will work to arbitrarily large precision. They can not at present handle error forms or intervals as arguments.

NOTE: These functions are still experimental. In particular, their accuracy is not guaranteed in all domains. It is advisable to set the current precision comfortably higher than you actually need when using these functions. Also, these functions may be impractically slow for some values of the arguments.

The `f g` (calc-gamma) [gamma] command computes the Euler gamma function. For positive integer arguments, this is related to the factorial function: '`gamma(n+1) = fact(n)`'. For general complex arguments the gamma function can be defined by the following definite integral: $\Gamma(a) = \int_0^\infty t^{a-1} e^t dt$. (The actual implementation uses far more efficient computational methods.)

The `f G` (calc-inc-gamma) [gammaP] command computes the incomplete gamma function, denoted '`P(a,x)`'. This is defined by the integral, $P(a, x) = \left(\int_0^x t^{a-1} e^t dt \right) / \Gamma(a)$. This implies that '`gammaP(a,inf) = 1`' for any a (see the definition of the normal gamma function).

Several other varieties of incomplete gamma function are defined. The complement of $P(a, x)$, called $Q(a, x) = 1 - P(a, x)$ by some authors, is computed by the `I f G` [gammaQ] command. You can think of this as taking the other half of the integral, from x to infinity.

The functions corresponding to the integrals that define $P(a, x)$ and $Q(a, x)$ but without the normalizing $1/\Gamma(a)$ factor are called $\gamma(a, x)$ and $\Gamma(a, x)$, respectively. You can obtain these using the `H f G` [gammag] and `I H f G` [gammaG] commands.

The `f b` (calc-beta) [beta] command computes the Euler beta function, which is defined in terms of the gamma function as $B(a, b) = \Gamma(a)\Gamma(b)/\Gamma(a + b)$, or by $B(a, b) = \int_0^1 t^{a-1}(1 - t)^{b-1} dt$.

The `f B` (calc-inc-beta) [betaI] command computes the incomplete beta function $I(x, a, b)$. It is defined by $I(x, a, b) = \left(\int_0^x t^{a-1}(1 - t)^{b-1} dt \right) / B(a, b)$. Once again, the `H` (hyperbolic) prefix gives the corresponding un-normalized version [betaB].

The `f e` (calc-erf) [erf] command computes the error function $\text{erf}(x) = \frac{2}{\sqrt{\pi}} \int_0^x e^{-t^2} dt$. The complementary error function `I f e` (calc-erfc) [erfc] is the corresponding integral from '`x`' to infinity; the sum $\text{erf}(x) + \text{erfc}(x) = 1$.

The `f j` (calc-bessel-J) [besJ] and `f y` (calc-bessel-Y) [besY] commands compute the Bessel functions of the first and second kinds, respectively. In '`besJ(n,x)`' and '`besY(n,x)`' the "order" parameter n is often an integer, but is not required to be one. Calc's implementation of the Bessel functions currently limits the precision to 8 digits, and may not be exact even to that precision. Use with care!

8.4 Branch Cuts and Principal Values

All of the logarithmic, trigonometric, and other scientific functions are defined for complex numbers as well as for reals. This section describes the values returned in cases where the general result is a family of possible values. Calc follows section 12.5.3 of Steele's *Common Lisp, the Language*, second edition, in these matters. This section will describe each function briefly; for a more detailed discussion (including some nifty diagrams), consult Steele's book.

Note that the branch cuts for `arctan` and `arctanh` were changed between the first and second editions of Steele. Recent versions of Calc follow the second edition.

The new branch cuts exactly match those of the HP-28/48 calculators. They also match those of Mathematica 1.2, except that Mathematica's `arctan` cut is always in the right half of the complex plane, and its `arctanh` cut is always in the top half of the plane. Calc's cuts are continuous with quadrants I and III for `arctan`, or II and IV for `arctanh`.

Note: The current implementations of these functions with complex arguments are designed with proper behavior around the branch cuts in mind, *not* efficiency or accuracy. You may need to increase the floating precision and wait a while to get suitable answers from them.

For 'sqrt(a+bi)': When $a < 0$ and b is small but positive or zero, the result is close to the $+i$ axis. For b small and negative, the result is close to the $-i$ axis. The result always lies in the right half of the complex plane.

For 'ln(a+bi)': The real part is defined as 'ln(abs(a+bi))'. The imaginary part is defined as 'arg(a+bi) = arctan2(b,a)'. Thus the branch cuts for `sqrt` and `ln` both lie on the negative real axis.

The following table describes these branch cuts in another way. If the real and imaginary parts of z are as shown, then the real and imaginary parts of $f(z)$ will be as shown. Here `eps` stands for a small positive value; each occurrence of `eps` may stand for a different small value.

```
       z              sqrt(z)        ln(z)
-------------------------------------------------
    +,   0            +,   0         any, 0
    -,   0            0,   +         any, pi
    -, +eps          +eps, +         +eps, +
    -, -eps          +eps, -         +eps, -
```

For 'z1^z2': This is defined by 'exp(ln(z1)*z2)'. One interesting consequence of this is that '(-8)^1:3' does not evaluate to -2 as you might expect, but to the complex number $(1., 1.732)$. Both of these are valid cube roots of -8 (as is $(1., -1.732)$); Calc chooses a perhaps less-obvious root for the sake of mathematical consistency.

For 'arcsin(z)': This is defined by '-i*ln(i*z + sqrt(1-z^2))'. The branch cuts are on the real axis, less than -1 and greater than 1.

For 'arccos(z)': This is defined by '-i*ln(z + i*sqrt(1-z^2))', or equivalently by 'pi/2 - arcsin(z)'. The branch cuts are on the real axis, less than -1 and greater than 1.

For 'arctan(z)': This is defined by '(ln(1+i*z) - ln(1-i*z)) / (2*i)'. The branch cuts are on the imaginary axis, below $-i$ and above i.

For 'arcsinh(z)': This is defined by 'ln(z + sqrt(1+z^2))'. The branch cuts are on the imaginary axis, below $-i$ and above i.

For 'arccosh(z)': This is defined by 'ln(z + (z+1)*sqrt((z-1)/(z+1)))'. The branch cut is on the real axis less than 1.

For 'arctanh(z)': This is defined by '(ln(1+z) - ln(1-z)) / 2'. The branch cuts are on the real axis, less than −1 and greater than 1.

The following tables for arcsin, arccos, and arctan assume the current angular mode is Radians. The hyperbolic functions operate independently of the angular mode.

```
      z              arcsin(z)            arccos(z)
-----------------------------------------------------------
 (-1..1),  0     (-pi/2..pi/2),  0      (0..pi),  0
 (-1..1), +eps   (-pi/2..pi/2), +eps    (0..pi), -eps
 (-1..1), -eps   (-pi/2..pi/2), -eps    (0..pi), +eps
   <-1,    0        -pi/2,       +          pi,    -
   <-1,  +eps     -pi/2 + eps,   +       pi - eps, -
   <-1,  -eps     -pi/2 + eps,   -       pi - eps, +
   >1,     0        pi/2,        -           0,    +
   >1,   +eps     pi/2 - eps,    +        +eps,    -
   >1,   -eps     pi/2 - eps,    -        +eps,    +

      z              arccosh(z)           arctanh(z)
-----------------------------------------------------------
 (-1..1),  0       0,  (0..pi)         any,       0
 (-1..1), +eps   +eps, (0..pi)         any,     +eps
 (-1..1), -eps   +eps, (-pi..0)        any,     -eps
   <-1,    0       +,    pi             -,      pi/2
   <-1,  +eps      +,  pi - eps         -,   pi/2 - eps
   <-1,  -eps      +, -pi + eps         -,  -pi/2 + eps
   >1,     0       +,    0              +,     -pi/2
   >1,   +eps      +,   +eps            +,   pi/2 - eps
   >1,   -eps      +,   -eps            +,  -pi/2 + eps

      z              arcsinh(z)           arctan(z)
-----------------------------------------------------------
   0, (-1..1)     0, (-pi/2..pi/2)        0,       any
   0,   <-1         -,    -pi/2         -pi/2,      -
 +eps,  <-1        +, -pi/2 + eps      pi/2 - eps,  -
 -eps,  <-1        -, -pi/2 + eps     -pi/2 + eps,  -
   0,   >1          +,    pi/2          pi/2,       +
 +eps,  >1         +,  pi/2 - eps      pi/2 - eps,  +
 -eps,  >1         -,  pi/2 - eps     -pi/2 + eps,  +
```

Finally, the following identities help to illustrate the relationship between the complex trigonometric and hyperbolic functions. They are valid everywhere, including on the branch cuts.

```
sin(i*z)  = i*sinh(z)      arcsin(i*z)  = i*arcsinh(z)
cos(i*z)  =   cosh(z)      arcsinh(i*z) = i*arcsin(z)
tan(i*z)  = i*tanh(z)      arctan(i*z)  = i*arctanh(z)
sinh(i*z) = i*sin(z)       cosh(i*z)    =   cos(z)
```

The "advanced math" functions (gamma, Bessel, etc.) are also defined for general complex arguments, but their branch cuts and principal values are not rigorously specified at present.

8.5 Random Numbers

The k r (calc-random) [random] command produces random numbers of various sorts.

Given a positive numeric prefix argument M, it produces a random integer N in the range $0 \le N < M$. Each possible value N appears with equal probability.

With no numeric prefix argument, the k r command takes its argument from the stack instead. Once again, if this is a positive integer M the result is a random integer less than M. However, note that while numeric prefix arguments are limited to six digits or so, an M taken from the stack can be arbitrarily large. If M is negative, the result is a random integer in the range $M < N \leq 0$.

If the value on the stack is a floating-point number M, the result is a random floating-point number N in the range $0 \leq N < M$ or $M < N \leq 0$, according to the sign of M.

If M is zero, the result is a Gaussian-distributed random real number; the distribution has a mean of zero and a standard deviation of one. The algorithm used generates random numbers in pairs; thus, every other call to this function will be especially fast.

If M is an error form m +/- σ where m and σ are both real numbers, the result uses a Gaussian distribution with mean m and standard deviation σ.

If M is an interval form, the lower and upper bounds specify the acceptable limits of the random numbers. If both bounds are integers, the result is a random integer in the specified range. If either bound is floating-point, the result is a random real number in the specified range. If the interval is open at either end, the result will be sure not to equal that end value. (This makes a big difference for integer intervals, but for floating-point intervals it's relatively minor: with a precision of 6, 'random([1.0..2.0))' will return any of one million numbers from 1.00000 to 1.99999; 'random([1.0..2.0])' may additionally return 2.00000, but the probability of this happening is extremely small.)

If M is a vector, the result is one element taken at random from the vector. All elements of the vector are given equal probabilities.

The sequence of numbers produced by k r is completely random by default, i.e., the sequence is seeded each time you start Calc using the current time and other information. You can get a reproducible sequence by storing a particular "seed value" in the Calc variable RandSeed. Any integer will do for a seed; integers of from 1 to 12 digits are good. If you later store a different integer into RandSeed, Calc will switch to a different pseudo-random sequence. If you "unstore" RandSeed, Calc will re-seed itself from the current time. If you store the same integer that you used before back into RandSeed, you will get the exact same sequence of random numbers as before.

The calc-rrandom command (not on any key) produces a random real number between zero and one. It is equivalent to 'random(1.0)'.

The k a (calc-random-again) command produces another random number, re-using the most recent value of M. With a numeric prefix argument n, it produces n more random numbers using that value of M.

The k h (calc-shuffle) command produces a vector of several random values with no duplicates. The value on the top of the stack specifies the set from which the random values are drawn, and may be any of the M formats described above. The numeric prefix argument gives the length of the desired list. (If you do not provide a numeric prefix argument, the length of the list is taken from the top of the stack, and M from second-to-top.)

If M is a floating-point number, zero, or an error form (so that the random values are being drawn from the set of real numbers) there is little practical difference between using k h and using k r several times. But if the set of possible values consists of just a few integers, or the elements of a vector, then there is a very real chance that multiple k r's will produce the same number more than once. The *k h* command produces a vector whose elements are always distinct. (Actually, there is a slight exception: If M is a vector, no given vector element will be drawn more than once, but if several elements of M are equal, they may each make it into the result vector.)

One use of *k h* is to rearrange a list at random. This happens if the prefix argument is equal to the number of values in the list: *[1, 1.5, 2, 2.5, 3] 5 k h* might produce the permuted list '*[2.5, 1, 1.5, 3, 2]*'. As a convenient feature, if the argument n is negative it is replaced by the size of the set represented by M. Naturally, this is allowed only when M specifies a small discrete set of possibilities.

To do the equivalent of *k h* but with duplications allowed, given M on the stack and with n just entered as a numeric prefix, use *v b* to build a vector of copies of M, then use *V M k r* to "map" the normal *k r* function over the elements of this vector. See Chapter 9 [Matrix Functions], page 221.

8.5.1 Random Number Generator

Calc's random number generator uses several methods to ensure that the numbers it produces are highly random. Knuth's *Art of Computer Programming*, Volume II, contains a thorough description of the theory of random number generators and their measurement and characterization.

If `RandSeed` has no stored value, Calc calls Emacs's built-in `random` function to get a stream of random numbers, which it then treats in various ways to avoid problems inherent in the simple random number generators that many systems use to implement `random`.

When Calc's random number generator is first invoked, it "seeds" the low-level random sequence using the time of day, so that the random number sequence will be different every time you use Calc.

Since Emacs Lisp doesn't specify the range of values that will be returned by its `random` function, Calc exercises the function several times to estimate the range. When Calc subsequently uses the `random` function, it takes only 10 bits of the result near the most-significant end. (It avoids at least the bottom four bits, preferably more, and also tries to avoid the top two bits.) This strategy works well with the linear congruential generators that are typically used to implement `random`.

If `RandSeed` contains an integer, Calc uses this integer to seed an "additive congruential" method (Knuth's algorithm 3.2.2A, computing $X_{n-55} - X_{n-24}$. This method expands the seed value into a large table which is maintained internally; the variable `RandSeed` is changed from, e.g., 42 to the vector [42] to indicate that the seed has been absorbed into this table. When `RandSeed` contains a vector, *k r* and related commands continue to use the same internal table as last time. There is no way to extract the complete state of the random number generator so that you can restart it from any point; you can only restart it from the same initial seed value. A simple way to restart from the same seed is to type *s r RandSeed* to get the seed vector, *v u* to unpack it back into a number, then *s t RandSeed* to reseed the generator with that number.

Calc uses a "shuffling" method as described in algorithm 3.2.2B of Knuth. It fills a table with 13 random 10-bit numbers. Then, to generate a new random number, it uses the previous number to index into the table, picks the value it finds there as the new random number, then replaces that table entry with a new value obtained from a call to the base random number generator (either the additive congruential generator or the `random` function supplied by the system). If there are any flaws in the base generator, shuffling will tend to even them out. But if the system provides an excellent `random` function, shuffling will not damage its randomness.

To create a random integer of a certain number of digits, Calc builds the integer three decimal digits at a time. For each group of three digits, Calc calls its 10-bit shuffling random number generator (which returns a value from 0 to 1023); if the random value is 1000 or more, Calc throws it out and tries again until it gets a suitable value.

To create a random floating-point number with precision p, Calc simply creates a random p-digit integer and multiplies by 10^{-p}. The resulting random numbers should be very clean, but note that relatively small numbers will have few significant random digits. In other words, with a precision of 12, you will occasionally get numbers on the order of 10^{-9} or 10^{-10}, but those numbers will only have two or three random digits since they correspond to small integers times 10^{-12}.

To create a random integer in the interval '`[0 .. m)`', Calc counts the digits in m, creates a random integer with three additional digits, then reduces modulo m. Unless m is a power of ten the resulting values will be very slightly biased toward the lower numbers, but this bias will be less than 0.1%. (For example, if m is 42, Calc will reduce a random integer less than 100000 modulo 42 to get a result less than 42. It is easy to show that the numbers 40 and 41 will be only 2380/2381 as likely to result from this modulo operation as numbers 39 and below.) If m is a power of ten, however, the numbers should be completely unbiased.

The Gaussian random numbers generated by '`random(0.0)`' use the "polar" method described in Knuth section 3.4.1C. This method generates a pair of Gaussian random numbers at a time, so only every other call to '`random(0.0)`' will require significant calculations.

8.6 Combinatorial Functions

Commands relating to combinatorics and number theory begin with the `k` key prefix.

The `k g` (`calc-gcd`) [`gcd`] command computes the Greatest Common Divisor of two integers. It also accepts fractions; the GCD of two fractions is defined by taking the GCD of the numerators, and the LCM of the denominators. This definition is consistent with the idea that '`a / gcd(a,x)`' should yield an integer for any '`a`' and '`x`'. For other types of arguments, the operation is left in symbolic form.

The `k l` (`calc-lcm`) [`lcm`] command computes the Least Common Multiple of two integers or fractions. The product of the LCM and GCD of two numbers is equal to the product of the numbers.

The `k E` (`calc-extended-gcd`) [`egcd`] command computes the GCD of two integers x and y and returns a vector $[g, a, b]$ where $g = \gcd(x, y) = ax + by$.

The `!` (`calc-factorial`) [`fact`] command computes the factorial of the number at the top of the stack. If the number is an integer, the result is an exact integer. If the number is an integer-valued float, the result is a floating-point approximation. If the number is a non-integral real number, the generalized factorial is used, as defined by the Euler Gamma function. Please note that computation of large factorials can be slow; using floating-point format will help since fewer digits must be maintained. The same is true of many of the commands in this section.

The *k d* (`calc-double-factorial`) [`dfact`] command computes the "double factorial" of an integer. For an even integer, this is the product of even integers from 2 to N. For an odd integer, this is the product of odd integers from 3 to N. If the argument is an integer-valued float, the result is a floating-point approximation. This function is undefined for negative even integers. The notation $N!!$ is also recognized for double factorials.

The *k c* (`calc-choose`) [`choose`] command computes the binomial coefficient N-choose-M, where M is the number on the top of the stack and N is second-to-top. If both arguments are integers, the result is an exact integer. Otherwise, the result is a floating-point approximation. The binomial coefficient is defined for all real numbers by $\frac{N!}{M!(N-M)!}$.

The *H k c* (`calc-perm`) [`perm`] command computes the number-of-permutations function $\frac{N!}{(N-M)!}$.

The *k b* (`calc-bernoulli-number`) [`bern`] command computes a given Bernoulli number. The value at the top of the stack is a nonnegative integer n that specifies which Bernoulli number is desired. The *H k b* command computes a Bernoulli polynomial, taking n from the second-to-top position and x from the top of the stack. If x is a variable or formula the result is a polynomial in x; if x is a number the result is a number.

The *k e* (`calc-euler-number`) [`euler`] command similarly computes an Euler number, and *H k e* computes an Euler polynomial. Bernoulli and Euler numbers occur in the Taylor expansions of several functions.

The *k s* (`calc-stirling-number`) [`stir1`] command computes a Stirling number of the first kind $\begin{bmatrix} n \\ m \end{bmatrix}$, given two integers n and m on the stack. The *H k s* [`stir2`] command computes a Stirling number of the second kind $\begin{Bmatrix} n \\ m \end{Bmatrix}$. These are the number of m-cycle permutations of n objects, and the number of ways to partition n objects into m non-empty sets, respectively.

The *k p* (`calc-prime-test`) command checks if the integer on the top of the stack is prime. For integers less than eight million, the answer is always exact and reasonably fast. For larger integers, a probabilistic method is used (see Knuth vol. II, section 4.5.4, algorithm P). The number is first checked against small prime factors (up to 13). Then, any number of iterations of the algorithm are performed. Each step either discovers that the number is non-prime, or substantially increases the certainty that the number is prime. After a few steps, the chance that a number was mistakenly described as prime will be less than one percent. (Indeed, this is a worst-case estimate of the probability; in practice even a single iteration is quite reliable.) After the *k p* command, the number will be reported as definitely prime or non-prime if possible, or otherwise "probably" prime with a certain probability of error.

The normal *k p* command performs one iteration of the primality test. Pressing *k p* repeatedly for the same integer will perform additional iterations. Also, *k p* with a numeric prefix performs the specified number of iterations. There is also an algebraic function 'prime(n)' or 'prime(n,iters)' which returns 1 if n is (probably) prime and 0 if not.

The *k f* (`calc-prime-factors`) [`prfac`] command attempts to decompose an integer into its prime factors. For numbers up to 25 million, the answer is exact although it may take some time. The result is a vector of the prime factors in increasing order. For larger inputs, prime factors above 5000 may not be found, in which case the last number in the vector will be an unfactored integer greater than 25 million (with a warning message). For negative integers, the first element of the list will be −1. For inputs −1, 0, and 1, the result is a list of the same number.

The *k n* (`calc-next-prime`) [nextprime] command finds the next prime above a given number. Essentially, it searches by calling `calc-prime-test` on successive integers until it finds one that passes the test. This is quite fast for integers less than eight million, but once the probabilistic test comes into play the search may be rather slow. Ordinarily this command stops for any prime that passes one iteration of the primality test. With a numeric prefix argument, a number must pass the specified number of iterations before the search stops. (This only matters when searching above eight million.) You can always use additional *k p* commands to increase your certainty that the number is indeed prime.

The *I k n* (`calc-prev-prime`) [prevprime] command analogously finds the next prime less than a given number.

The *k t* (`calc-totient`) [totient] command computes the Euler "totient" function $\phi(n)$, the number of integers less than n which are relatively prime to n.

The *k m* (`calc-moebius`) [moebius] command computes the Möbius μ function. If the input number is a product of k distinct factors, this is $(-1)^k$. If the input number has any duplicate factors (i.e., can be divided by the same prime more than once), the result is zero.

8.7 Probability Distribution Functions

The functions in this section compute various probability distributions. For continuous distributions, this is the integral of the probability density function from x to infinity. (These are the "upper tail" distribution functions; there are also corresponding "lower tail" functions which integrate from minus infinity to x.) For discrete distributions, the upper tail function gives the sum from x to infinity; the lower tail function gives the sum from minus infinity up to, but not including, x.

To integrate from x to y, just use the distribution function twice and subtract. For example, the probability that a Gaussian random variable with mean 2 and standard deviation 1 will lie in the range from 2.5 to 2.8 is 'utpn(2.5,2,1) - utpn(2.8,2,1)' ("the probability that it is greater than 2.5, but not greater than 2.8"), or equivalently 'ltpn(2.8,2,1) - ltpn(2.5,2,1)'.

The *k B* (`calc-utpb`) [utpb] function uses the binomial distribution. Push the parameters n, p, and then x onto the stack; the result ('utpb(x,n,p)') is the probability that an event will occur x or more times out of n trials, if its probability of occurring in any given trial is p. The *I k B* [ltpb] function is the probability that the event will occur fewer than x times.

The other probability distribution functions similarly take the form *k X* (`calc-utpx`) [utpx] and *I k X* [ltpx], for various letters x. The arguments to the algebraic functions are the value of the random variable first, then whatever other parameters define the distribution. Note these are among the few Calc functions where the order of the arguments in algebraic form differs from the order of arguments as found on the stack. (The random variable comes last on the stack, so that you can type, e.g., *2 RET 1 RET 2.5 k N M-RET DEL 2.8 k N -*, using *M-RET DEL* to recover the original arguments but substitute a new value for x.)

The 'utpc(x,v)' function uses the chi-square distribution with ν degrees of freedom. It is the probability that a model is correct if its chi-square statistic is x.

The 'utpf(F,v1,v2)' function uses the F distribution, used in various statistical tests. The parameters ν_1 and ν_2 are the degrees of freedom in the numerator and denominator, respectively, used in computing the statistic F.

The 'utpn(x,m,s)' function uses a normal (Gaussian) distribution with mean m and standard deviation σ. It is the probability that such a normal-distributed random variable would exceed x.

The 'utpp(n,x)' function uses a Poisson distribution with mean x. It is the probability that n or more such Poisson random events will occur.

The 'utpt(t,v)' function uses the Student's "t" distribution with ν degrees of freedom. It is the probability that a t-distributed random variable will be greater than t. (Note: This computes the distribution function $A(t|\nu)$ where $A(0|\nu) = 1$ and $A(\infty|\nu) \to 0$. The UTPT operation on the HP-48 uses a different definition which returns half of Calc's value: 'UTPT(t,v) = .5*utpt(t,v)'.)

While Calc does not provide inverses of the probability distribution functions, the a R command can be used to solve for the inverse. Since the distribution functions are monotonic, a R is guaranteed to be able to find a solution given any initial guess. See Section 10.7 [Numerical Solutions], page 272.

9 Vector/Matrix Functions

Many of the commands described here begin with the *v* prefix. (For convenience, the shift-*V* prefix is equivalent to *v*.) The commands usually apply to both plain vectors and matrices; some apply only to matrices or only to square matrices. If the argument has the wrong dimensions the operation is left in symbolic form.

Vectors are entered and displayed using '[a,b,c]' notation. Matrices are vectors of which all elements are vectors of equal length. (Though none of the standard Calc commands use this concept, a three-dimensional matrix or rank-3 tensor could be defined as a vector of matrices, and so on.)

9.1 Packing and Unpacking

Calc's "pack" and "unpack" commands collect stack entries to build composite objects such as vectors and complex numbers. They are described in this chapter because they are most often used to build vectors.

The *v p* (`calc-pack`) [pack] command collects several elements from the stack into a matrix, complex number, HMS form, error form, etc. It uses a numeric prefix argument to specify the kind of object to be built; this argument is referred to as the "packing mode." If the packing mode is a nonnegative integer, a vector of that length is created. For example, *C-u 5 v p* will pop the top five stack elements and push back a single vector of those five elements. (*C-u 0 v p* simply creates an empty vector.)

The same effect can be had by pressing *[* to push an incomplete vector on the stack, using TAB (`calc-roll-down`) to sneak the incomplete object up past a certain number of elements, and then pressing *]* to complete the vector.

Negative packing modes create other kinds of composite objects:

-1   Two values are collected to build a complex number. For example, *5 RET 7 C-u -1 v p* creates the complex number (5, 7). The result is always a rectangular complex number. The two input values must both be real numbers, i.e., integers, fractions, or floats. If they are not, Calc will instead build a formula like 'a + (0, 1) b'. (The other packing modes also create a symbolic answer if the components are not suitable.)

-2   Two values are collected to build a polar complex number. The first is the magnitude; the second is the phase expressed in either degrees or radians according to the current angular mode.

-3   Three values are collected into an HMS form. The first two values (hours and minutes) must be integers or integer-valued floats. The third value may be any real number.

-4   Two values are collected into an error form. The inputs may be real numbers or formulas.

-5   Two values are collected into a modulo form. The inputs must be real numbers.

-6   Two values are collected into the interval '[a .. b]'. The inputs may be real numbers, HMS or date forms, or formulas.

-7   Two values are collected into the interval '`[a .. b)`'.

-8   Two values are collected into the interval '`(a .. b]`'.

-9   Two values are collected into the interval '`(a .. b)`'.

-10   Two integer values are collected into a fraction.

-11   Two values are collected into a floating-point number. The first is the mantissa;
              the second, which must be an integer, is the exponent. The result is the mantissa
              times ten to the power of the exponent.

-12   This is treated the same as −11 by the *v p* command. When unpacking, −12
              specifies that a floating-point mantissa is desired.

-13   A real number is converted into a date form.

-14   Three numbers (year, month, day) are packed into a pure date form.

-15   Six numbers are packed into a date/time form.

With any of the two-input negative packing modes, either or both of the inputs may
be vectors. If both are vectors of the same length, the result is another vector made by
packing corresponding elements of the input vectors. If one input is a vector and the other
is a plain number, the number is packed along with each vector element to produce a new
vector. For example, *C-u -4 v p* could be used to convert a vector of numbers and a vector
of errors into a single vector of error forms; *C-u -5 v p* could convert a vector of numbers
and a single number M into a vector of numbers modulo M.

If you don't give a prefix argument to *v p*, it takes the packing mode from the top of the
stack. The elements to be packed then begin at stack level 2. Thus *1 RET 2 RET 4 n v p* is
another way to enter the error form '`1 +/- 2`'.

If the packing mode taken from the stack is a vector, the result is a matrix with the
dimensions specified by the elements of the vector, which must each be integers. For example, if the packing mode is '`[2, 3]`', then six numbers will be taken from the stack and
returned in the form '`[[a, b, c], [d, e, f]]`'.

If any elements of the vector are negative, other kinds of packing are done at that level
as described above. For example, '`[2, 3, -4]`' takes 12 objects and creates a 2×3 matrix
of error forms: '`[[a +/- b, c +/- d ... ]]`'. Also, '`[-4, -10]`' will convert four integers
into an error form consisting of two fractions: '`a:b +/- c:d`'.

There is an equivalent algebraic function, '`pack(mode, items)`' where *mode* is a packing
mode (an integer or a vector of integers) and *items* is a vector of objects to be packed (re-
packed, really) according to that mode. For example, '`pack([3, -4], [a,b,c,d,e,f])`'
yields '`[a +/- b, c +/- d, e +/- f]`'. The function is left in symbolic form if the packing
mode is invalid, or if the number of data items does not match the number of items required
by the mode.

The *v u* (`calc-unpack`) command takes the vector, complex number, HMS form, or other
composite object on the top of the stack and "unpacks" it, pushing each of its elements
onto the stack as separate objects. Thus, it is the "inverse" of *v p*. If the value at the top
of the stack is a formula, *v u* unpacks it by pushing each of the arguments of the top-level
operator onto the stack.

You can optionally give a numeric prefix argument to *v u* to specify an explicit (un)packing mode. If the packing mode is negative and the input is actually a vector or matrix, the result will be two or more similar vectors or matrices of the elements. For example, given the vector '[a +/- b, c^2, d +/- 7]', the result of *C-u -4 v u* will be the two vectors '[a, c^2, d]' and '[b, 0, 7]'.

Note that the prefix argument can have an effect even when the input is not a vector. For example, if the input is the number −5, then *c-u -1 v u* yields −5 and 0 (the components of −5 when viewed as a rectangular complex number); *C-u -2 v u* yields 5 and 180 (assuming Degrees mode); and *C-u -10 v u* yields −5 and 1 (the numerator and denominator of −5, viewed as a rational number). Plain *v u* with this input would complain that the input is not a composite object.

Unpacking mode −11 converts a float into an integer mantissa and an integer exponent, where the mantissa is not divisible by 10 (except that 0.0 is represented by a mantissa and exponent of 0). Unpacking mode −12 converts a float into a floating-point mantissa and integer exponent, where the mantissa (for non-zero numbers) is guaranteed to lie in the range [1 .. 10). In both cases, the mantissa is shifted left or right (and the exponent adjusted to compensate) in order to satisfy these constraints.

Positive unpacking modes are treated differently than for *v p*. A mode of 1 is much like plain *v u* with no prefix argument, except that in addition to the components of the input object, a suitable packing mode to re-pack the object is also pushed. Thus, *C-u 1 v u* followed by *v p* will re-build the original object.

A mode of 2 unpacks two levels of the object; the resulting re-packing mode will be a vector of length 2. This might be used to unpack a matrix, say, or a vector of error forms. Higher unpacking modes unpack the input even more deeply.

There are two algebraic functions analogous to *v u*. The 'unpack(*mode*, *item*)' function unpacks the *item* using the given *mode*, returning the result as a vector of components. Here the *mode* must be an integer, not a vector. For example, 'unpack(-4, a +/- b)' returns '[a, b]', as does 'unpack(1, a +/- b)'.

The **unpackt** function is like **unpack** but instead of returning a simple vector of items, it returns a vector of two things: The mode, and the vector of items. For example, 'unpackt(1, 2:3 +/- 1:4)' returns '[-4, [2:3, 1:4]]', and 'unpackt(2, 2:3 +/- 1:4)' returns '[[-4, -10], [2, 3, 1, 4]]'. The identity for re-building the original object is 'apply(pack, unpackt(n, x)) = x'. (The **apply** function builds a function call given the function name and a vector of arguments.)

Subscript notation is a useful way to extract a particular part of an object. For example, to get the numerator of a rational number, you can use 'unpack(-10, x)_1'.

9.2 Building Vectors

Vectors and matrices can be added, subtracted, multiplied, and divided; see Section 7.1 [Basic Arithmetic], page 185.

The | (calc-concat) [vconcat] command "concatenates" two vectors into one. For example, after *[1 , 2] [3 , 4] |*, the stack will contain the single vector '[1, 2, 3, 4]'. If the arguments are matrices, the rows of the first matrix are concatenated with the rows of the second. (In other words, two matrices are just two vectors of row-vectors as far as | is concerned.)

If either argument to | is a scalar (a non-vector), it is treated like a one-element vector for purposes of concatenation: *1 [2 , 3]* | produces the vector '[1, 2, 3]'. Likewise, if one argument is a matrix and the other is a plain vector, the vector is treated as a one-row matrix.

The *H* | (`calc-append`) [`append`] command concatenates two vectors without any special cases. Both inputs must be vectors. Whether or not they are matrices is not taken into account. If either argument is a scalar, the `append` function is left in symbolic form. See also `cons` and `rcons` below.

The *I* | and *H I* | commands are similar, but they use their two stack arguments in the opposite order. Thus *I* | is equivalent to *TAB* |, but possibly more convenient and also a bit faster.

The *v d* (`calc-diag`) [`diag`] function builds a diagonal square matrix. The optional numeric prefix gives the number of rows and columns in the matrix. If the value at the top of the stack is a vector, the elements of the vector are used as the diagonal elements; the prefix, if specified, must match the size of the vector. If the value on the stack is a scalar, it is used for each element on the diagonal, and the prefix argument is required.

To build a constant square matrix, e.g., a 3×3 matrix filled with ones, use *0 M-3 v d 1 +*, i.e., build a zero matrix first and then add a constant value to that matrix. (Another alternative would be to use *v b* and *v a*; see below.)

The *v i* (`calc-ident`) [`idn`] function builds an identity matrix of the specified size. It is a convenient form of *v d* where the diagonal element is always one. If no prefix argument is given, this command prompts for one.

In algebraic notation, 'idn(a,n)' acts much like 'diag(a,n)', except that *a* is required to be a scalar (non-vector) quantity. If *n* is omitted, 'idn(a)' represents *a* times an identity matrix of unknown size. Calc can operate algebraically on such generic identity matrices, and if one is combined with a matrix whose size is known, it is converted automatically to an identity matrix of a suitable matching size. The *v i* command with an argument of zero creates a generic identity matrix, 'idn(1)'. Note that in dimensioned Matrix mode (see Section 6.4.6 [Matrix Mode], page 141), generic identity matrices are immediately expanded to the current default dimensions.

The *v x* (`calc-index`) [`index`] function builds a vector of consecutive integers from 1 to *n*, where *n* is the numeric prefix argument. If you do not provide a prefix argument, you will be prompted to enter a suitable number. If *n* is negative, the result is a vector of negative integers from *n* to -1.

With a prefix argument of just *C-u*, the *v x* command takes three values from the stack: *n*, *start*, and *incr* (with *incr* at top-of-stack). Counting starts at *start* and increases by *incr* for successive vector elements. If *start* or *n* is in floating-point format, the resulting vector elements will also be floats. Note that *start* and *incr* may in fact be any kind of numbers or formulas.

When *start* and *incr* are specified, a negative *n* has a different interpretation: It causes a geometric instead of arithmetic sequence to be generated. For example, 'index(-3, a, b)' produces '[a, a b, a b^2]'. If you omit *incr* in the algebraic form, 'index(n, start)', the default value for *incr* is one for positive *n* or two for negative *n*.

The *v b* (`calc-build-vector`) [`cvec`] function builds a vector of *n* copies of the value on the top of the stack, where *n* is the numeric prefix argument. In algebraic formulas, 'cvec(x,n,m)' can also be used to build an n-by-m matrix of copies of x. (Interactively, just use *v b* twice: once to build a row, then again to build a matrix of copies of that row.)

The *v h* (calc-head) [head] function returns the first element of a vector. The *I v h* (calc-tail) [tail] function returns the vector with its first element removed. In both cases, the argument must be a non-empty vector.

The *v k* (calc-cons) [cons] function takes a value h and a vector t from the stack, and produces the vector whose head is h and whose tail is t. This is similar to |, except if h is itself a vector, | will concatenate the two vectors whereas cons will insert h at the front of the vector t.

Each of these three functions also accepts the Hyperbolic flag [rhead, rtail, rcons] in which case t instead represents the *last* single element of the vector, with h representing the remainder of the vector. Thus the vector '[a, b, c, d] = cons(a, [b, c, d]) = rcons([a, b, c], d)'. Also, 'head([a, b, c, d]) = a', 'tail([a, b, c, d]) = [b, c, d]', 'rhead([a, b, c, d]) = [a, b, c]', and 'rtail([a, b, c, d]) = d'.

9.3 Extracting Vector Elements

The *v r* (calc-mrow) [mrow] command extracts one row of the matrix on the top of the stack, or one element of the plain vector on the top of the stack. The row or element is specified by the numeric prefix argument; the default is to prompt for the row or element number. The matrix or vector is replaced by the specified row or element in the form of a vector or scalar, respectively.

With a prefix argument of *C-u* only, *v r* takes the index of the element or row from the top of the stack, and the vector or matrix from the second-to-top position. If the index is itself a vector of integers, the result is a vector of the corresponding elements of the input vector, or a matrix of the corresponding rows of the input matrix. This command can be used to obtain any permutation of a vector.

With *C-u*, if the index is an interval form with integer components, it is interpreted as a range of indices and the corresponding subvector or submatrix is returned.

Subscript notation in algebraic formulas ('a_b') stands for the Calc function subscr, which is synonymous with mrow. Thus, '[x, y, z]_k' produces x, y, or z if k is one, two, or three, respectively. A double subscript ('M_i_j', equivalent to 'subscr(subscr(M, i), j)') will access the element at row i, column j of a matrix. The *a _* (calc-subscript) command creates a subscript formula 'a_b' out of two stack entries. (It is on the *a* "algebra" prefix because subscripted variables are often used purely as an algebraic notation.)

Given a negative prefix argument, *v r* instead deletes one row or element from the matrix or vector on the top of the stack. Thus *C-u 2 v r* replaces a matrix with its second row, but *C-u -2 v r* replaces the matrix with the same matrix with its second row removed. In algebraic form this function is called mrrow.

Given a prefix argument of zero, *v r* extracts the diagonal elements of a square matrix in the form of a vector. In algebraic form this function is called getdiag.

The *v c* (calc-mcol) [mcol or mrcol] command is the analogous operation on columns of a matrix. Given a plain vector it extracts (or removes) one element, just like *v r*. If the index in *C-u v c* is an interval or vector and the argument is a matrix, the result is a submatrix with only the specified columns retained (and possibly permuted in the case of a vector index).

To extract a matrix element at a given row and column, use v r to extract the row as a vector, then v c to extract the column element from that vector. In algebraic formulas, it is often more convenient to use subscript notation: 'm_i_j' gives row i, column j of matrix m.

The v s (calc-subvector) [subvec] command extracts a subvector of a vector. The arguments are the vector, the starting index, and the ending index, with the ending index in the top-of-stack position. The starting index indicates the first element of the vector to take. The ending index indicates the first element *past* the range to be taken. Thus, 'subvec([a, b, c, d, e], 2, 4)' produces the subvector '[b, c]'. You could get the same result using 'mrow([a, b, c, d, e], [2 .. 4))'.

If either the start or the end index is zero or negative, it is interpreted as relative to the end of the vector. Thus 'subvec([a, b, c, d, e], 2, -2)' also produces '[b, c]'. In the algebraic form, the end index can be omitted in which case it is taken as zero, i.e., elements from the starting element to the end of the vector are used. The infinity symbol, inf, also has this effect when used as the ending index.

With the Inverse flag, I v s [rsubvec] removes a subvector from a vector. The arguments are interpreted the same as for the normal v s command. Thus, 'rsubvec([a, b, c, d, e], 2, 4)' produces '[a, d, e]'. It is always true that subvec and rsubvec return complementary parts of the input vector.

See Section 10.1 [Selecting Subformulas], page 243, for an alternative way to operate on vectors one element at a time.

9.4 Manipulating Vectors

The v l (calc-vlength) [vlen] command computes the length of a vector. The length of a non-vector is considered to be zero. Note that matrices are just vectors of vectors for the purposes of this command.

With the Hyperbolic flag, H v l [mdims] computes a vector of the dimensions of a vector, matrix, or higher-order object. For example, 'mdims([[a,b,c],[d,e,f]])' returns '[2, 3]' since its argument is a 2×3 matrix.

The v f (calc-vector-find) [find] command searches along a vector for the first element equal to a given target. The target is on the top of the stack; the vector is in the second-to-top position. If a match is found, the result is the index of the matching element. Otherwise, the result is zero. The numeric prefix argument, if given, allows you to select any starting index for the search.

The v a (calc-arrange-vector) [arrange] command rearranges a vector to have a certain number of columns and rows. The numeric prefix argument specifies the number of columns; if you do not provide an argument, you will be prompted for the number of columns. The vector or matrix on the top of the stack is *flattened* into a plain vector. If the number of columns is nonzero, this vector is then formed into a matrix by taking successive groups of n elements. If the number of columns does not evenly divide the number of elements in the vector, the last row will be short and the result will not be suitable for use as a matrix. For example, with the matrix '[[1, 2], [3, 4]]' on the stack, v a 4 produces

'[[1, 2, 3, 4]]' (a 1×4 matrix), v a 1 produces '[[1], [2], [3], [4]]' (a 4×1 matrix), v a 2 produces '[[1, 2], [3, 4]]' (the original 2×2 matrix), v a 3 produces '[[1, 2, 3], [4]]' (not a matrix), and v a 0 produces the flattened list '[1, 2, 3, 4]'.

The V S (calc-sort) [sort] command sorts the elements of a vector into increasing order. Real numbers, real infinities, and constant interval forms come first in this ordering; next come other kinds of numbers, then variables (in alphabetical order), then finally come formulas and other kinds of objects; these are sorted according to a kind of lexicographic ordering with the useful property that one vector is less or greater than another if the first corresponding unequal elements are less or greater, respectively. Since quoted strings are stored by Calc internally as vectors of ASCII character codes (see Section 4.7 [Strings], page 120), this means vectors of strings are also sorted into alphabetical order by this command.

The I V S [rsort] command sorts a vector into decreasing order.

The V G (calc-grade) [grade, rgrade] command produces an index table or permutation vector which, if applied to the input vector (as the index of C-u v r, say), would sort the vector. A permutation vector is just a vector of integers from 1 to n, where each integer occurs exactly once. One application of this is to sort a matrix of data rows using one column as the sort key; extract that column, grade it with V G, then use the result to reorder the original matrix with C-u v r. Another interesting property of the V G command is that, if the input is itself a permutation vector, the result will be the inverse of the permutation. The inverse of an index table is a rank table, whose kth element says where the kth original vector element will rest when the vector is sorted. To get a rank table, just use V G V G.

With the Inverse flag, I V G produces an index table that would sort the input into decreasing order. Note that V S and V G use a "stable" sorting algorithm, i.e., any two elements which are equal will not be moved out of their original order. Generally there is no way to tell with V S, since two elements which are equal look the same, but with V G this can be an important issue. In the matrix-of-rows example, suppose you have names and telephone numbers as two columns and you wish to sort by phone number primarily, and by name when the numbers are equal. You can sort the data matrix by names first, and then again by phone numbers. Because the sort is stable, any two rows with equal phone numbers will remain sorted by name even after the second sort.

The V H (calc-histogram) [histogram] command builds a histogram of a vector of numbers. Vector elements are assumed to be integers or real numbers in the range $[0..n)$ for some "number of bins" n, which is the numeric prefix argument given to the command. The result is a vector of n counts of how many times each value appeared in the original vector. Non-integers in the input are rounded down to integers. Any vector elements outside the specified range are ignored. (You can tell if elements have been ignored by noting that the counts in the result vector don't add up to the length of the input vector.)

If no prefix is given, then you will be prompted for a vector which will be used to determine the bins. (If a positive integer is given at this prompt, it will be still treated as if it were given as a prefix.) Each bin will consist of the interval of numbers closest to the corresponding number of this new vector; if the vector $[a, b, c, ...]$ is entered at the prompt, the bins will be $(-inf, (a + b)/2]$, $((a + b)/2, (b + c)/2]$, etc. The result of this command will be a vector counting how many elements of the original vector are in each bin.

The result will then be a vector with the same length as this new vector; each element of the new vector will be replaced by the number of elements of the original vector which are closest to it.

With the Hyperbolic flag, `H V H` pulls two vectors from the stack. The second-to-top vector is the list of numbers as before. The top vector is an equal-sized list of "weights" to attach to the elements of the data vector. For example, if the first data element is 4.2 and the first weight is 10, then 10 will be added to bin 4 of the result vector. Without the hyperbolic flag, every element has a weight of one.

The `v t` (`calc-transpose`) [`trn`] command computes the transpose of the matrix at the top of the stack. If the argument is a plain vector, it is treated as a row vector and transposed into a one-column matrix.

The `v v` (`calc-reverse-vector`) [`rev`] command reverses a vector end-for-end. Given a matrix, it reverses the order of the rows. (To reverse the columns instead, just use `v t v v v t`. The same principle can be used to apply other vector commands to the columns of a matrix.)

The `v m` (`calc-mask-vector`) [`vmask`] command uses one vector as a mask to extract elements of another vector. The mask is in the second-to-top position; the target vector is on the top of the stack. These vectors must have the same length. The result is the same as the target vector, but with all elements which correspond to zeros in the mask vector deleted. Thus, for example, 'vmask([1, 0, 1, 0, 1], [a, b, c, d, e])' produces '[a, c, e]'. See Section 10.10 [Logical Operations], page 288.

The `v e` (`calc-expand-vector`) [`vexp`] command expands a vector according to another mask vector. The result is a vector the same length as the mask, but with nonzero elements replaced by successive elements from the target vector. The length of the target vector is normally the number of nonzero elements in the mask. If the target vector is longer, its last few elements are lost. If the target vector is shorter, the last few nonzero mask elements are left unreplaced in the result. Thus 'vexp([2, 0, 3, 0, 7], [a, b])' produces '[a, 0, b, 0, 7]'.

With the Hyperbolic flag, `H v e` takes a filler value from the top of the stack; the mask and target vectors come from the third and second elements of the stack. This filler is used where the mask is zero: 'vexp([2, 0, 3, 0, 7], [a, b], z)' produces '[a, z, c, z, 7]'. If the filler value is itself a vector, then successive values are taken from it, so that the effect is to interleave two vectors according to the mask: 'vexp([2, 0, 3, 7, 0, 0], [a, b], [x, y])' produces '[a, x, b, 7, y, 0]'.

Another variation on the masking idea is to combine '[a, b, c, d, e]' with the mask '[1, 0, 1, 0, 1]' to produce '[a, 0, c, 0, e]'. You can accomplish this with `V M a &`, mapping the logical "and" operation across the two vectors. See Section 10.10 [Logical Operations], page 288. Note that the `? :` operation also discussed there allows other types of masking using vectors.

9.5 Vector and Matrix Arithmetic

Basic arithmetic operations like addition and multiplication are defined for vectors and matrices as well as for numbers. Division of matrices, in the sense of multiplying by the inverse, is supported. (Division by a matrix actually uses LU-decomposition for greater accuracy and speed.) See Section 7.1 [Basic Arithmetic], page 185.

The following functions are applied element-wise if their arguments are vectors or matrices: `change-sign`, `conj`, `arg`, `re`, `im`, `polar`, `rect`, `clean`, `float`, `frac`. See [Function Index], page 477.

The V J (`calc-conj-transpose`) [`ctrn`] command computes the conjugate transpose of its argument, i.e., '`conj(trn(x))`'.

The A (`calc-abs`) [`abs`] command computes the Frobenius norm of a vector or matrix argument. This is the square root of the sum of the squares of the absolute values of the elements of the vector or matrix. If the vector is interpreted as a point in two- or three-dimensional space, this is the distance from that point to the origin.

The v n (`calc-rnorm`) [`rnorm`] command computes the infinity-norm of a vector, or the row norm of a matrix. For a plain vector, this is the maximum of the absolute values of the elements. For a matrix, this is the maximum of the row-absolute-value-sums, i.e., of the sums of the absolute values of the elements along the various rows.

The V N (`calc-cnorm`) [`cnorm`] command computes the one-norm of a vector, or column norm of a matrix. For a plain vector, this is the sum of the absolute values of the elements. For a matrix, this is the maximum of the column-absolute-value-sums. General k-norms for k other than one or infinity are not provided. However, the 2-norm (or Frobenius norm) is provided for vectors by the A (`calc-abs`) command.

The V C (`calc-cross`) [`cross`] command computes the right-handed cross product of two vectors, each of which must have exactly three elements.

The & (`calc-inv`) [`inv`] command computes the inverse of a square matrix. If the matrix is singular, the inverse operation is left in symbolic form. Matrix inverses are recorded so that once an inverse (or determinant) of a particular matrix has been computed, the inverse and determinant of the matrix can be recomputed quickly in the future.

If the argument to & is a plain number x, this command simply computes $1/x$. This is okay, because the '`/`' operator also does a matrix inversion when dividing one by a matrix.

The V D (`calc-mdet`) [`det`] command computes the determinant of a square matrix.

The V L (`calc-mlud`) [`lud`] command computes the LU decomposition of a matrix. The result is a list of three matrices which, when multiplied together left-to-right, form the original matrix. The first is a permutation matrix that arises from pivoting in the algorithm, the second is lower-triangular with ones on the diagonal, and the third is upper-triangular.

The V T (`calc-mtrace`) [`tr`] command computes the trace of a square matrix. This is defined as the sum of the diagonal elements of the matrix.

The V K (`calc-kron`) [`kron`] command computes the Kronecker product of two matrices.

9.6 Set Operations using Vectors

Calc includes several commands which interpret vectors as *sets* of objects. A set is a collection of objects; any given object can appear only once in the set. Calc stores sets as vectors of objects in sorted order. Objects in a Calc set can be any of the usual things, such as numbers, variables, or formulas. Two set elements are considered equal if they are identical, except that numerically equal numbers like the integer 4 and the float 4.0 are considered equal even though they are not "identical." Variables are treated like plain symbols without attached values by the set operations; subtracting the set '`[b]`' from '`[a,` b]' always yields the set '[a]' even though if the variables 'a' and 'b' both equaled 17, you might expect the answer '[]'.

If a set contains interval forms, then it is assumed to be a set of real numbers. In this case, all set operations require the elements of the set to be only things that are allowed in intervals: Real numbers, plus and minus infinity, HMS forms, and date forms. If there are variables or other non-real objects present in a real set, all set operations on it will be left in unevaluated form.

If the input to a set operation is a plain number or interval form a, it is treated like the one-element vector '[a]'. The result is always a vector, except that if the set consists of a single interval, the interval itself is returned instead.

See Section 10.10 [Logical Operations], page 288, for the in function which tests if a certain value is a member of a given set. To test if the set A is a subset of the set B, use 'vdiff(A, B) = []'.

The V + (calc-remove-duplicates) [rdup] command converts an arbitrary vector into set notation. It works by sorting the vector as if by V S, then removing duplicates. (For example, [a, 5, 4, a, 4.0] is sorted to '[4, 4.0, 5, a, a]' and then reduced to '[4, 5, a]'). Overlapping intervals are merged as necessary. You rarely need to use V + explicitly, since all the other set-based commands apply V + to their inputs before using them.

The V V (calc-set-union) [vunion] command computes the union of two sets. An object is in the union of two sets if and only if it is in either (or both) of the input sets. (You could accomplish the same thing by concatenating the sets with |, then using V +.)

The V ^ (calc-set-intersect) [vint] command computes the intersection of two sets. An object is in the intersection if and only if it is in both of the input sets. Thus if the input sets are disjoint, i.e., if they share no common elements, the result will be the empty vector '[]'. Note that the characters V and ^ were chosen to be close to the conventional mathematical notation for set union $(A \cup B)$ and intersection $(A \cap B)$.

The V − (calc-set-difference) [vdiff] command computes the difference between two sets. An object is in the difference $A − B$ if and only if it is in A but not in B. Thus subtracting '[y,z]' from a set will remove the elements 'y' and 'z' if they are present. You can also think of this as a general *set complement* operator; if A is the set of all possible values, then $A − B$ is the "complement" of B. Obviously this is only practical if the set of all possible values in your problem is small enough to list in a Calc vector (or simple enough to express in a few intervals).

The V X (calc-set-xor) [vxor] command computes the "exclusive-or," or "symmetric difference" of two sets. An object is in the symmetric difference of two sets if and only if it is in one, but *not* both, of the sets. Objects that occur in both sets "cancel out."

The V ~ (calc-set-complement) [vcompl] command computes the complement of a set with respect to the real numbers. Thus 'vcompl(x)' is equivalent to 'vdiff([-inf .. inf], x)'. For example, 'vcompl([2, (3 .. 4]])' evaluates to '[[-inf .. 2), (2 .. 3], (4 .. inf]]'.

The V F (calc-set-floor) [vfloor] command reinterprets a set as a set of integers. Any non-integer values, and intervals that do not enclose any integers, are removed. Open intervals are converted to equivalent closed intervals. Successive integers are converted into intervals of integers. For example, the complement of the set '[2, 6, 7, 8]' is messy, but if you wanted the complement with respect to the set of integers you could type *V* ~ *V F* to get '[[-inf .. 1], [3 .. 5], [9 .. inf]]'.

The *V E* (calc-set-enumerate) [venum] command converts a set of integers into an explicit vector. Intervals in the set are expanded out to lists of all integers encompassed by the intervals. This only works for finite sets (i.e., sets which do not involve '-inf' or 'inf').

The *V :* (calc-set-span) [vspan] command converts any set of reals into an interval form that encompasses all its elements. The lower limit will be the smallest element in the set; the upper limit will be the largest element. For an empty set, 'vspan([])' returns the empty interval '[0 .. 0]'.

The *V #* (calc-set-cardinality) [vcard] command counts the number of integers in a set. The result is the length of the vector that would be produced by *V E*, although the computation is much more efficient than actually producing that vector.

Another representation for sets that may be more appropriate in some cases is binary numbers. If you are dealing with sets of integers in the range 0 to 49, you can use a 50-bit binary number where a particular bit is 1 if the corresponding element is in the set. See Section 7.7 [Binary Functions], page 206, for a list of commands that operate on binary numbers. Note that many of the above set operations have direct equivalents in binary arithmetic: *b o* (calc-or), *b a* (calc-and), *b d* (calc-diff), *b x* (calc-xor), and *b n* (calc-not), respectively. You can use whatever representation for sets is most convenient to you.

The *b u* (calc-unpack-bits) [vunpack] command converts an integer that represents a set in binary into a set in vector/interval notation. For example, 'vunpack(67)' returns '[[0 .. 1], 6]'. If the input is negative, the set it represents is semi-infinite: 'vunpack(-4) = [2 .. inf)'. Use *V E* afterwards to expand intervals to individual values if you wish. Note that this command uses the *b* (binary) prefix key.

The *b p* (calc-pack-bits) [vpack] command converts the other way, from a vector or interval representing a set of nonnegative integers into a binary integer describing the same set. The set may include positive infinity, but must not include any negative numbers. The input is interpreted as a set of integers in the sense of *V F* (vfloor). Beware that a simple input like '[100]' can result in a huge integer representation (2^{100}, a 31-digit integer, in this case).

9.7 Statistical Operations on Vectors

The commands in this section take vectors as arguments and compute various statistical measures on the data stored in the vectors. The references used in the definitions of these functions are Bevington's *Data Reduction and Error Analysis for the Physical Sciences*, and *Numerical Recipes* by Press, Flannery, Teukolsky and Vetterling.

The statistical commands use the *u* prefix key followed by a shifted letter or other character.

See Section 9.4 [Manipulating Vectors], page 226, for a description of *V H* (calc-histogram).

See Section 10.8 [Curve Fitting], page 275, for the *a F* command for doing least-squares fits to statistical data.

See Section 8.7 [Probability Distribution Functions], page 218, for several common probability distribution functions.

9.7.1 Single-Variable Statistics

These functions do various statistical computations on single vectors. Given a numeric prefix argument, they actually pop n objects from the stack and combine them into a data vector. Each object may be either a number or a vector; if a vector, any sub-vectors inside it are "flattened" as if by v a 0; see Section 9.4 [Manipulating Vectors], page 226. By default one object is popped, which (in order to be useful) is usually a vector.

If an argument is a variable name, and the value stored in that variable is a vector, then the stored vector is used. This method has the advantage that if your data vector is large, you can avoid the slow process of manipulating it directly on the stack.

These functions are left in symbolic form if any of their arguments are not numbers or vectors, e.g., if an argument is a formula, or a non-vector variable. However, formulas embedded within vector arguments are accepted; the result is a symbolic representation of the computation, based on the assumption that the formula does not itself represent a vector. All varieties of numbers such as error forms and interval forms are acceptable.

Some of the functions in this section also accept a single error form or interval as an argument. They then describe a property of the normal or uniform (respectively) statistical distribution described by the argument. The arguments are interpreted in the same way as the M argument of the random number function k r. In particular, an interval with integer limits is considered an integer distribution, so that '[2 .. 6)' is the same as '[2 .. 5]'. An interval with at least one floating-point limit is a continuous distribution: '[2.0 .. 6.0)' is *not* the same as '[2.0 .. 5.0]'!

The u # (calc-vector-count) [vcount] command computes the number of data values represented by the inputs. For example, 'vcount(1, [2, 3], [[4, 5], [], x, y])' returns 7. If the argument is a single vector with no sub-vectors, this simply computes the length of the vector.

The u + (calc-vector-sum) [vsum] command computes the sum of the data values. The u * (calc-vector-prod) [vprod] command computes the product of the data values. If the input is a single flat vector, these are the same as V R + and V R * (see Section 9.8 [Reducing and Mapping], page 235).

The u X (calc-vector-max) [vmax] command computes the maximum of the data values, and the u N (calc-vector-min) [vmin] command computes the minimum. If the argument is an interval, this finds the minimum or maximum value in the interval. (Note that 'vmax([2..6)) = 5' as described above.) If the argument is an error form, this returns plus or minus infinity.

The u M (calc-vector-mean) [vmean] command computes the average (arithmetic mean) of the data values. If the inputs are error forms $x \pm \sigma$, this is the weighted mean of the x values with weights $1/\sigma^2$.

$$\mu = \frac{\sum \dfrac{x_i}{\sigma_i^2}}{\sum \dfrac{1}{\sigma_i^2}}$$

If the inputs are not error forms, this is simply the sum of the values divided by the count of the values.

Note that a plain number can be considered an error form with error $\sigma = 0$. If the input to u M is a mixture of plain numbers and error forms, the result is the mean of the plain numbers, ignoring all values with non-zero errors. (By the above definitions it's clear that a plain number effectively has an infinite weight, next to which an error form with a finite weight is completely negligible.)

This function also works for distributions (error forms or intervals). The mean of an error form 'a +/- b' is simply a. The mean of an interval is the mean of the minimum and maximum values of the interval.

The I u M (calc-vector-mean-error) [vmeane] command computes the mean of the data points expressed as an error form. This includes the estimated error associated with the mean. If the inputs are error forms, the error is the square root of the reciprocal of the sum of the reciprocals of the squares of the input errors. (I.e., the variance is the reciprocal of the sum of the reciprocals of the variances.)

$$\sigma_\mu^2 = \frac{1}{\sum \frac{1}{\sigma_i^2}}$$

If the inputs are plain numbers, the error is equal to the standard deviation of the values divided by the square root of the number of values. (This works out to be equivalent to calculating the standard deviation and then assuming each value's error is equal to this standard deviation.)

$$\sigma_\mu^2 = \frac{\sigma^2}{N}$$

The H u M (calc-vector-median) [vmedian] command computes the median of the data values. The values are first sorted into numerical order; the median is the middle value after sorting. (If the number of data values is even, the median is taken to be the average of the two middle values.) The median function is different from the other functions in this section in that the arguments must all be real numbers; variables are not accepted even when nested inside vectors. (Otherwise it is not possible to sort the data values.) If any of the input values are error forms, their error parts are ignored.

The median function also accepts distributions. For both normal (error form) and uniform (interval) distributions, the median is the same as the mean.

The H I u M (calc-vector-harmonic-mean) [vhmean] command computes the harmonic mean of the data values. This is defined as the reciprocal of the arithmetic mean of the reciprocals of the values.

$$\frac{N}{\sum \frac{1}{x_i}}$$

The u G (calc-vector-geometric-mean) [vgmean] command computes the geometric mean of the data values. This is the nth root of the product of the values. This is also equal to the exp of the arithmetic mean of the logarithms of the data values.

$$\exp\left(\sum \ln x_i\right) = \left(\prod x_i\right)^{1/N}$$

The *H u G* [agmean] command computes the "arithmetic-geometric mean" of two numbers taken from the stack. This is computed by replacing the two numbers with their arithmetic mean and geometric mean, then repeating until the two values converge.

$$a_{i+1} = \frac{a_i + b_i}{2}, \qquad b_{i+1} = \sqrt{a_i b_i}$$

The *u R* (calc-vector-rms) [rms] command computes the RMS (root-mean-square) of the data values. As its name suggests, this is the square root of the mean of the squares of the data values.

The *u S* (calc-vector-sdev) [vsdev] command computes the standard deviation σ of the data values. If the values are error forms, the errors are used as weights just as for *u M*. This is the *sample* standard deviation, whose value is the square root of the sum of the squares of the differences between the values and the mean of the N values, divided by $N - 1$.

$$\sigma^2 = \frac{1}{N-1} \sum (x_i - \mu)^2$$

This function also applies to distributions. The standard deviation of a single error form is simply the error part. The standard deviation of a continuous interval happens to equal the difference between the limits, divided by $\sqrt{12}$. The standard deviation of an integer interval is the same as the standard deviation of a vector of those integers.

The *I u S* (calc-vector-pop-sdev) [vpsdev] command computes the *population* standard deviation. It is defined by the same formula as above but dividing by N instead of by $N - 1$. The population standard deviation is used when the input represents the entire set of data values in the distribution; the sample standard deviation is used when the input represents a sample of the set of all data values, so that the mean computed from the input is itself only an estimate of the true mean.

$$\sigma^2 = \frac{1}{N} \sum (x_i - \mu)^2$$

For error forms and continuous intervals, vpsdev works exactly like vsdev. For integer intervals, it computes the population standard deviation of the equivalent vector of integers.

The *H u S* (calc-vector-variance) [vvar] and *H I u S* (calc-vector-pop-variance) [vpvar] commands compute the variance of the data values. The variance is the square σ^2 of the standard deviation, i.e., the sum of the squares of the deviations of the data values from the mean. (This definition also applies when the argument is a distribution.)

The vflat algebraic function returns a vector of its arguments, interpreted in the same way as the other functions in this section. For example, 'vflat(1, [2, [3, 4]], 5)' returns '[1, 2, 3, 4, 5]'.

9.7.2 Paired-Sample Statistics

The functions in this section take two arguments, which must be vectors of equal size. The vectors are each flattened in the same way as by the single-variable statistical functions. Given a numeric prefix argument of 1, these functions instead take one object from the stack, which must be an $N \times 2$ matrix of data values. Once again, variable names can be used in place of actual vectors and matrices.

The u C (`calc-vector-covariance`) [vcov] command computes the sample covariance of two vectors. The covariance of vectors x and y is the sum of the products of the differences between the elements of x and the mean of x times the differences between the corresponding elements of y and the mean of y, all divided by $N-1$. Note that the variance of a vector is just the covariance of the vector with itself. Once again, if the inputs are error forms the errors are used as weight factors. If both x and y are composed of error forms, the error for a given data point is taken as the square root of the sum of the squares of the two input errors.

$$\sigma_{xy}^2 = \frac{1}{N-1} \sum (x_i - \mu_x)(y_i - \mu_y)$$

$$\sigma_{xy}^2 = \frac{\dfrac{1}{N-1} \sum \dfrac{(x_i - \mu_x)(y_i - \mu_y)}{\sigma_i^2}}{\dfrac{1}{N} \sum \dfrac{1}{\sigma_i^2}}$$

The I u C (`calc-vector-pop-covariance`) [vpcov] command computes the population covariance, which is the same as the sample covariance computed by u C except dividing by N instead of $N-1$.

The H u C (`calc-vector-correlation`) [vcorr] command computes the linear correlation coefficient of two vectors. This is defined by the covariance of the vectors divided by the product of their standard deviations. (There is no difference between sample or population statistics here.)

$$r_{xy} = \frac{\sigma_{xy}^2}{\sigma_x^2 \sigma_y^2}$$

9.8 Reducing and Mapping Vectors

The commands in this section allow for more general operations on the elements of vectors.

The simplest of these operations is V A (`calc-apply`) [apply], which applies a given operator to the elements of a vector. For example, applying the hypothetical function f to the vector '[1, 2, 3]' would produce the function call 'f(1, 2, 3)'. Applying the + function to the vector '[a, b]' gives 'a + b'. Applying + to the vector '[a, b, c]' is an error, since the + function expects exactly two arguments.

While V A is useful in some cases, you will usually find that either V R or V M, described below, is closer to what you want.

9.8.1 Specifying Operators

Commands in this section (like V A) prompt you to press the key corresponding to the desired operator. Press ? for a partial list of the available operators. Generally, an operator is any key or sequence of keys that would normally take one or more arguments from the stack and replace them with a result. For example, V A H C uses the hyperbolic cosine operator, cosh. (Since cosh expects one argument, V A H C requires a vector with a single element as its argument.)

You can press x at the operator prompt to select any algebraic function by name to use as the operator. This includes functions you have defined yourself using the Z F command. (See Section 17.4 [Algebraic Definitions], page 369.) If you give a name for which no function has been defined, the result is left in symbolic form, as in 'f(1, 2, 3)'. Calc will prompt for the number of arguments the function takes if it can't figure it out on its own (say, because you named a function that is currently undefined). It is also possible to type a digit key before the function name to specify the number of arguments, e.g., *V M 3 x f RET* calls f with three arguments even if it looks like it ought to have only two. This technique may be necessary if the function allows a variable number of arguments. For example, the *v e* [vexp] function accepts two or three arguments; if you want to map with the three-argument version, you will have to type *V M 3 v e*.

It is also possible to apply any formula to a vector by treating that formula as a function. When prompted for the operator to use, press ' (the apostrophe) and type your formula as an algebraic entry. You will then be prompted for the argument list, which defaults to a list of all variables that appear in the formula, sorted into alphabetic order. For example, suppose you enter the formula 'x + 2y^x'. The default argument list would be '(x y)', which means that if this function is applied to the arguments '[3, 10]' the result will be '3 + 2*10^3'. (If you plan to use a certain formula in this way often, you might consider defining it as a function with *Z F*.)

Another way to specify the arguments to the formula you enter is with $, $$, and so on. For example, *V A ' $$ + 2$^$$* has the same effect as the previous example. The argument list is automatically taken to be '($$ $)'. (The order of the arguments may seem backwards, but it is analogous to the way normal algebraic entry interacts with the stack.)

If you press $ at the operator prompt, the effect is similar to the apostrophe except that the relevant formula is taken from top-of-stack instead. The actual vector arguments of the *V A $* or related command then start at the second-to-top stack position. You will still be prompted for an argument list.

A function can be written without a name using the notation '<#1 - #2>', which means "a function of two arguments that computes the first argument minus the second argument." The symbols '#1' and '#2' are placeholders for the arguments. You can use any names for these placeholders if you wish, by including an argument list followed by a colon: '<x, y : x - y>'. When you type *V A ' $$ + 2$^$$ RET*, Calc builds the nameless function '<#1 + 2 #2^#1>' as the function to map across the vectors. When you type *V A ' x + 2y^x RET RET*, Calc builds the nameless function '<x, y : x + 2 y^x>'. In both cases, Calc also writes the nameless function to the Trail so that you can get it back later if you wish.

If there is only one argument, you can write '#' in place of '#1'. (Note that '< >' notation is also used for date forms. Calc tells that '<*stuff*>' is a nameless function by the presence of '#' signs inside *stuff*, or by the fact that *stuff* begins with a list of variables followed by a colon.)

You can type a nameless function directly to *V A '*, or put one on the stack and use it with *V A $*. Calc will not prompt for an argument list in this case, since the nameless function specifies the argument list as well as the function itself. In *V A '*, you can omit the '< >' marks if you use '#' notation for the arguments, so that *V A ' #1+#2 RET* is the same as *V A ' <#1+#2> RET*, which in turn is the same as *V A ' $$+$ RET*.

The internal format for '<x, y : x + y>' is 'lambda(x, y, x + y)'. (The word lambda derives from Lisp notation and the theory of functions.) The internal format for '<#1 + #2>' is 'lambda(ArgA, ArgB, ArgA + ArgB)'. Note that there is no actual Calc function called lambda; the whole point is that the lambda expression is used in its symbolic form, not evaluated for an answer until it is applied to specific arguments by a command like *V A* or *V M*.

(Actually, `lambda` does have one special property: Its arguments are never evaluated; for example, putting '`<(2/3) #>`' on the stack will not simplify the '2/3' until the nameless function is actually called.)

As usual, commands like *V A* have algebraic function name equivalents. For example, *V A k g* with an argument of 'v' is equivalent to '`apply(gcd, v)`'. The first argument specifies the operator name, and is either a variable whose name is the same as the function name, or a nameless function like '`<#^3+1>`'. Operators that are normally written as algebraic symbols have the names `add`, `sub`, `mul`, `div`, `pow`, `neg`, `mod`, and `vconcat`.

The `call` function builds a function call out of several arguments: '`call(gcd, x, y)`' is the same as '`apply(gcd, [x, y])`', which in turn is the same as '`gcd(x, y)`'. The first argument of `call`, like the other functions described here, may be either a variable naming a function, or a nameless function ('`call(<#1+2#2>, x, y)`' is the same as 'x + 2y').

(Experts will notice that it's not quite proper to use a variable to name a function, since the name `gcd` corresponds to the Lisp variable `var-gcd` but to the Lisp function `calcFunc-gcd`. Calc automatically makes this translation, so you don't have to worry about it.)

9.8.2 Mapping

The *V M* (`calc-map`) [map] command applies a given operator elementwise to one or more vectors. For example, mapping A [abs] produces a vector of the absolute values of the elements in the input vector. Mapping + pops two vectors from the stack, which must be of equal length, and produces a vector of the pairwise sums of the elements. If either argument is a non-vector, it is duplicated for each element of the other vector. For example, *[1,2,3] 2 V M ^* squares the elements of the specified vector. With the 2 listed first, it would have computed a vector of powers of two. Mapping a user-defined function pops as many arguments from the stack as the function requires. If you give an undefined name, you will be prompted for the number of arguments to use.

If any argument to *V M* is a matrix, the operator is normally mapped across all elements of the matrix. For example, given the matrix $[[1, -2, 3], [-4, 5, -6]]$, *V M A* takes six absolute values to produce another 3×2 matrix, $[[1, 2, 3], [4, 5, 6]]$.

The command *V M _* [mapr] (i.e., type an underscore at the operator prompt) maps by rows instead. For example, *V M _ A* views the above matrix as a vector of two 3-element row vectors. It produces a new vector which contains the absolute values of those row vectors, namely $[3.74, 8.77]$. (Recall, the absolute value of a vector is defined as the square root of the sum of the squares of the elements.) Some operators accept vectors and return new vectors; for example, *v v* reverses a vector, so *V M _ v v* would reverse each row of the matrix to get a new matrix, $[[3, -2, 1], [-6, 5, -4]]$.

Sometimes a vector of vectors (representing, say, strings, sets, or lists) happens to look like a matrix. If so, remember to use *V M _* if you want to map a function across the whole strings or sets rather than across their individual elements.

The command *V M :* [mapc] maps by columns. Basically, it transposes the input matrix, maps by rows, and then, if the result is a matrix, transposes again. For example, *V M : A* takes the absolute values of the three columns of the matrix, treating each as a 2-vector, and *V M : v v* reverses the columns to get the matrix $[[-4, 5, -6], [1, -2, 3]]$.

(The symbols _ and : were chosen because they had row-like and column-like appearances, and were not already taken by useful operators. Also, they appear shifted on most keyboards so they are easy to type after *V M*.)

The _ and : modifiers have no effect on arguments that are not matrices (so if none of the arguments are matrices, they have no effect at all). If some of the arguments are matrices and others are plain numbers, the plain numbers are held constant for all rows of the matrix (so that *2 V M _ ^* squares every row of a matrix; squaring a vector takes a dot product of the vector with itself).

If some of the arguments are vectors with the same lengths as the rows (for *V M _*) or columns (for *V M :*) of the matrix arguments, those vectors are also held constant for every row or column.

Sometimes it is useful to specify another mapping command as the operator to use with *V M*. For example, *V M _ V A +* applies *V A +* to each row of the input matrix, which in turn adds the two values on that row. If you give another vector-operator command as the operator for *V M*, it automatically uses map-by-rows mode if you don't specify otherwise; thus *V M V A +* is equivalent to *V M _ V A +*. (If you really want to map-by-elements another mapping command, you can use a triple-nested mapping command: *V M V M V A +* means to map *V M V A +* over the rows of the matrix; in turn, *V A +* is mapped over the elements of each row.)

Previous versions of Calc had "map across" and "map down" modes that are now considered obsolete; the old "map across" is now simply *V M V A*, and "map down" is now *V M : V A*. The algebraic functions `mapa` and `mapd` are still supported, though. Note also that, while the old mapping modes were persistent (once you set the mode, it would apply to later mapping commands until you reset it), the new : and _ modifiers apply only to the current mapping command. The default *V M* always means map-by-elements.

See Section 10.2 [Algebraic Manipulation], page 251, for the *a M* command, which is like *V M* but for equations and inequalities instead of vectors. See Section 12.1 [Storing Variables], page 323, for the *s m* command which modifies a variable's stored value using a *V M*-like operator.

9.8.3 Reducing

The *V R* (`calc-reduce`) [reduce] command applies a given binary operator across all the elements of a vector. A binary operator is a function such as + or `max` which takes two arguments. For example, reducing + over a vector computes the sum of the elements of the vector. Reducing − computes the first element minus each of the remaining elements. Reducing `max` computes the maximum element and so on. In general, reducing f over the vector '[a, b, c, d]' produces 'f(f(f(a, b), c), d)'.

The *I V R* [rreduce] command is similar to *V R* except that works from right to left through the vector. For example, plain *V R −* on the vector '[a, b, c, d]' produces 'a − b − c − d' but *I V R −* on the same vector produces 'a − (b − (c − d))', or 'a − b + c − d'. This "alternating sum" occurs frequently in power series expansions.

The *V U* (`calc-accumulate`) [accum] command does an accumulation operation. Here Calc does the corresponding reduction operation, but instead of producing only the final result, it produces a vector of all the intermediate results. Accumulating + over the vector '[a, b, c, d]' produces the vector '[a, a + b, a + b + c, a + b + c + d]'.

The I V U [raccum] command does a right-to-left accumulation. For example, I V U - on the vector '[a, b, c, d]' produces the vector '[a - b + c - d, b - c + d, c - d, d]'.

As for V M, V R normally reduces a matrix elementwise. For example, given the matrix $[[a, b, c], [d, e, f]]$, V R + will compute $a + b + c + d + e + f$. You can type V R _ or V R : to modify this behavior. The V R _ [reducea] command reduces "across" the matrix; it reduces each row of the matrix as a vector, then collects the results. Thus V R _ + of this matrix would produce $[a + b + c, d + e + f]$. Similarly, V R : [reduced] reduces down; V R : + would produce $[a + d, b + e, c + f]$.

There is a third "by rows" mode for reduction that is occasionally useful; V R = [reducer] simply reduces the operator over the rows of the matrix themselves. Thus V R = + on the above matrix would get the same result as V R : +, since adding two row vectors is equivalent to adding their elements. But V R = * would multiply the two rows (to get a single number, their dot product), while V R : * would produce a vector of the products of the columns.

These three matrix reduction modes work with V R and I V R, but they are not currently supported with V U or I V U.

The obsolete reduce-by-columns function, reducec, is still supported but there is no way to get it through the V R command.

The commands C-x * : and C-x * _ are equivalent to typing C-x * r to grab a rectangle of data into Calc, and then typing V R : + or V R _ +, respectively, to sum the columns or rows of the matrix. See Section 14.5 [Grabbing From Buffers], page 340.

9.8.4 Nesting and Fixed Points

The H V R [nest] command applies a function to a given argument repeatedly. It takes two values, 'a' and 'n', from the stack, where 'n' must be an integer. It then applies the function nested 'n' times; if the function is 'f' and 'n' is 3, the result is 'f(f(f(a)))'. The number 'n' may be negative if Calc knows an inverse for the function 'f'; for example, 'nest(sin, a, -2)' returns 'arcsin(arcsin(a))'.

The H V U [anest] command is an accumulating version of nest: It returns a vector of 'n+1' values, e.g., '[a, f(a), f(f(a)), f(f(f(a)))]'. If 'n' is negative and 'F' is the inverse of 'f', then the result is of the form '[a, F(a), F(F(a)), F(F(F(a)))]'.

The H I V R [fixp] command is like H V R, except that it takes only an 'a' value from the stack; the function is applied until it reaches a "fixed point," i.e., until the result no longer changes.

The H I V U [afixp] command is an accumulating fixp. The first element of the return vector will be the initial value 'a'; the last element will be the final result that would have been returned by fixp.

For example, 0.739085 is a fixed point of the cosine function (in radians): 'cos(0.739085) = 0.739085'. You can find this value by putting, say, 1.0 on the stack and typing H I V U C. (We use the accumulating version so we can see the intermediate results: '[1, 0.540302, 0.857553, 0.65329, ...]'. With a precision of six, this command will take 36 steps to converge to 0.739085.)

Newton's method for finding roots is a classic example of iteration to a fixed point. To find the square root of five starting with an initial guess, Newton's method would look for a fixed point of the function '(x + 5/x) / 2'. Putting a guess of 1 on the stack and typing *H I V R ' ($ + 5/$)/2 RET* quickly yields the result 2.23607. This is equivalent to using the a *R* (`calc-find-root`) command to find a root of the equation 'x^2 = 5'.

These examples used numbers for 'a' values. Calc keeps applying the function until two successive results are equal to within the current precision. For complex numbers, both the real parts and the imaginary parts must be equal to within the current precision. If 'a' is a formula (say, a variable name), then the function is applied until two successive results are exactly the same formula. It is up to you to ensure that the function will eventually converge; if it doesn't, you may have to press *C-g* to stop the Calculator.

The algebraic `fixp` function takes two optional arguments, 'n' and 'tol'. The first is the maximum number of steps to be allowed, and must be either an integer or the symbol 'inf' (infinity, the default). The second is a convergence tolerance. If a tolerance is specified, all results during the calculation must be numbers, not formulas, and the iteration stops when the magnitude of the difference between two successive results is less than or equal to the tolerance. (This implies that a tolerance of zero iterates until the results are exactly equal.)

Putting it all together, 'fixp(<(# + A/#)/2>, B, 20, 1e-10)' computes the square root of 'A' given the initial guess 'B', stopping when the result is correct within the specified tolerance, or when 20 steps have been taken, whichever is sooner.

9.8.5 Generalized Products

The *V O* (`calc-outer-product`) [outer] command applies a given binary operator to all possible pairs of elements from two vectors, to produce a matrix. For example, *V O* * with '[a, b]' and '[x, y, z]' on the stack produces a multiplication table: '[[a x, a y, a z], [b x, b y, b z]]'. Element *r,c* of the result matrix is obtained by applying the operator to element *r* of the lefthand vector and element *c* of the righthand vector.

The *V I* (`calc-inner-product`) [inner] command computes the generalized inner product of two vectors or matrices, given a "multiplicative" operator and an "additive" operator. These can each actually be any binary operators; if they are '*' and '+', respectively, the result is a standard matrix multiplication. Element *r,c* of the result matrix is obtained by mapping the multiplicative operator across row *r* of the lefthand matrix and column *c* of the righthand matrix, and then reducing with the additive operator. Just as for the standard * command, this can also do a vector-matrix or matrix-vector inner product, or a vector-vector generalized dot product.

Since *V I* requires two operators, it prompts twice. In each case, you can use any of the usual methods for entering the operator. If you use $ twice to take both operator formulas from the stack, the first (multiplicative) operator is taken from the top of the stack and the second (additive) operator is taken from second-to-top.

9.9 Vector and Matrix Display Formats

Commands for controlling vector and matrix display use the *v* prefix instead of the usual *d* prefix. But they are display modes; in particular, they are influenced by the *I* and *H* prefix keys in the same way (see Section 6.7 [Display Modes], page 148). Matrix display is also influenced by the *d O* (`calc-flat-language`) mode; see Section 6.8.1 [Normal Language Modes], page 159.

The commands *v* < (calc-matrix-left-justify), *v* > (calc-matrix-right-justify), and *v* = (calc-matrix-center-justify) control whether matrix elements are justified to the left, right, or center of their columns.

The *v* [(calc-vector-brackets) command turns the square brackets that surround vectors and matrices displayed in the stack on and off. The *v* { (calc-vector-braces) and *v* ((calc-vector-parens) commands use curly braces or parentheses, respectively, instead of square brackets. For example, *v* { might be used in preparation for yanking a matrix into a buffer running Mathematica. (In fact, the Mathematica language mode uses this mode; see Section 6.8.8 [Mathematica Language Mode], page 167.) Note that, regardless of the display mode, either brackets or braces may be used to enter vectors, and parentheses may never be used for this purpose.

The *v*] (calc-matrix-brackets) command controls the "big" style display of matrices, for matrices which have more than one row. It prompts for a string of code letters; currently implemented letters are R, which enables brackets on each row of the matrix; O, which enables outer brackets in opposite corners of the matrix; and C, which enables commas or semicolons at the ends of all rows but the last. The default format is 'RO'. (Before Calc 2.00, the format was fixed at 'ROC'.) Here are some example matrices:

```
[ [ 123,   0,    0  ]          [ [ 123,   0,    0  ],
  [  0,  123,    0  ]            [  0,  123,    0  ],
  [  0,    0,  123 ] ]           [  0,    0,  123 ] ]


          RO                              ROC


[ 123,   0,    0               [ 123,   0,    0 ;
    0,  123,   0                    0,  123,   0 ;
    0,    0,  123 ]                 0,    0,  123 ]


           O                              OC


[ 123,   0,    0  ]             123,   0,    0
[  0,  123,    0  ]               0,  123,    0
[  0,    0,  123 ]                0,    0,  123


           R                            blank
```

Note that of the formats shown here, 'RO', 'ROC', and 'OC' are all recognized as matrices during reading, while the others are useful for display only.

The *v* , (calc-vector-commas) command turns commas on and off in vector and matrix display.

In vectors of length one, and in all vectors when commas have been turned off, Calc adds extra parentheses around formulas that might otherwise be ambiguous. For example, '[a b]' could be a vector of the one formula 'a b', or it could be a vector of two variables with commas turned off. Calc will display the former case as '[(a b)]'. You can disable these extra parentheses (to make the output less cluttered at the expense of allowing some ambiguity) by adding the letter P to the control string you give to *v*] (as described above).

The `v .` (`calc-full-vectors`) command turns abbreviated display of long vectors on and off. In this mode, vectors of six or more elements, or matrices of six or more rows or columns, will be displayed in an abbreviated form that displays only the first three elements and the last element: '`[a, b, c, ..., z]`'. When very large vectors are involved this will substantially improve Calc's display speed.

The `t .` (`calc-full-trail-vectors`) command controls a similar mode for recording vectors in the Trail. If you turn on this mode, vectors of six or more elements and matrices of six or more rows or columns will be abbreviated when they are put in the Trail. The `t y` (`calc-trail-yank`) command will be unable to recover those vectors. If you are working with very large vectors, this mode will improve the speed of all operations that involve the trail.

The `v /` (`calc-break-vectors`) command turns multi-line vector display on and off. Normally, matrices are displayed with one row per line but all other types of vectors are displayed in a single line. This mode causes all vectors, whether matrices or not, to be displayed with a single element per line. Sub-vectors within the vectors will still use the normal linear form.

10 Algebra

This section covers the Calc features that help you work with algebraic formulas. First, the general sub-formula selection mechanism is described; this works in conjunction with any Calc commands. Then, commands for specific algebraic operations are described. Finally, the flexible *rewrite rule* mechanism is discussed.

The algebraic commands use the a key prefix; selection commands use the j (for "just a letter that wasn't used for anything else") prefix.

See Section 5.2 [Editing Stack Entries], page 134, to see how to manipulate formulas using regular Emacs editing commands.

When doing algebraic work, you may find several of the Calculator's modes to be helpful, including Algebraic Simplification mode (m A) or No-Simplification mode (m 0), Algebraic entry mode (m a), Fraction mode (m f), and Symbolic mode (m s). See Chapter 6 [Mode Settings], page 137, for discussions of these modes. You may also wish to select Big display mode (d B). See Section 6.8.1 [Normal Language Modes], page 159.

10.1 Selecting Sub-Formulas

When working with an algebraic formula it is often necessary to manipulate a portion of the formula rather than the formula as a whole. Calc allows you to "select" a portion of any formula on the stack. Commands which would normally operate on that stack entry will now operate only on the sub-formula, leaving the surrounding part of the stack entry alone.

One common non-algebraic use for selection involves vectors. To work on one element of a vector in-place, simply select that element as a "sub-formula" of the vector.

10.1.1 Making Selections

To select a sub-formula, move the Emacs cursor to any character in that sub-formula, and press j s (calc-select-here). Calc will highlight the smallest portion of the formula that contains that character. By default the sub-formula is highlighted by blanking out all of the rest of the formula with dots. Selection works in any display mode but is perhaps easiest in Big mode (d B). Suppose you enter the following formula:

```
            3     ___
      (a + b)  + V c
   1: ------------------
          2 x + 1
```

(by typing ' ((a+b)^3 + sqrt(c)) / (2x+1)). If you move the cursor to the letter 'b' and press j s, the display changes to

```
            .     ...
      ... b.  . . .
   1* ..............
          . . . .
```

Every character not part of the sub-formula 'b' has been changed to a dot. (If the customizable variable calc-highlight-selections-with-faces is non-nil, then the characters not part of the sub-formula are de-emphasized by using a less noticeable face instead of using dots. see Section 10.1.3 [Displaying Selections], page 246.) The '*' next to the line number is to remind you that the formula has a portion of it selected. (In this case, it's very obvious, but it might not always be. If Embedded mode is enabled, the word 'Sel' also appears in the mode line because the stack may not be visible. see Chapter 16 [Embedded Mode], page 351.)

If you had instead placed the cursor on the parenthesis immediately to the right of the 'b', the selection would have been:

```
            .    . . .
     (a + b)  .  .  .
  1* . . . . . . . . . . . . . .
            .  .  .  .
```

The portion selected is always large enough to be considered a complete formula all by itself, so selecting the parenthesis selects the whole formula that it encloses. Putting the cursor on the '+' sign would have had the same effect.

(Strictly speaking, the Emacs cursor is really the manifestation of the Emacs "point," which is a position *between* two characters in the buffer. So purists would say that Calc selects the smallest sub-formula which contains the character to the right of "point.")

If you supply a numeric prefix argument n, the selection is expanded to the nth enclosing sub-formula. Thus, positioning the cursor on the 'b' and typing $C-u$ 1 j s will select 'a + b'; typing $C-u$ 2 j s will select '(a + b)^3', and so on.

If the cursor is not on any part of the formula, or if you give a numeric prefix that is too large, the entire formula is selected.

If the cursor is on the '.' line that marks the top of the stack (i.e., its normal "rest position"), this command selects the entire formula at stack level 1. Most selection commands similarly operate on the formula at the top of the stack if you haven't positioned the cursor on any stack entry.

The j a (calc-select-additional) command enlarges the current selection to encompass the cursor. To select the smallest sub-formula defined by two different points, move to the first and press j s, then move to the other and press j a. This is roughly analogous to using $C-@$ (set-mark-command) to select the two ends of a region of text during normal Emacs editing.

The j o (calc-select-once) command selects a formula in exactly the same way as j s, except that the selection will last only as long as the next command that uses it. For example, j o 1 + is a handy way to add one to the sub-formula indicated by the cursor.

(A somewhat more precise definition: The j o command sets a flag such that the next command involving selected stack entries will clear the selections on those stack entries afterwards. All other selection commands except j a and j O clear this flag.)

The j S (calc-select-here-maybe) and j O (calc-select-once-maybe) commands are equivalent to j s and j o, respectively, except that if the formula already has a selection they have no effect. This is analogous to the behavior of some commands such as j r (calc-rewrite-selection; see Section 10.11.9 [Selections with Rewrite Rules], page 307) and is mainly intended to be used in keyboard macros that implement your own selection-oriented commands.

Selection of sub-formulas normally treats associative terms like 'a + b - c + d' and 'x * y * z' as single levels of the formula. If you place the cursor anywhere inside 'a + b - c + d' except on one of the variable names and use j s, you will select the entire four-term sum.

The *j b* (`calc-break-selections`) command controls a mode in which the "deep structure" of these associative formulas shows through. Calc actually stores the above formulas as '`((a + b) - c) + d`' and '`x * (y * z)`'. (Note that for certain obscure reasons, by default Calc treats multiplication as right-associative.) Once you have enabled *j b* mode, selecting with the cursor on the '`-`' sign would only select the '`a + b - c`' portion, which makes sense when the deep structure of the sum is considered. There is no way to select the '`b - c + d`' portion; although this might initially look like just as legitimate a sub-formula as '`a + b - c`', the deep structure shows that it isn't. The *d U* command can be used to view the deep structure of any formula (see Section 6.8.1 [Normal Language Modes], page 159).

When *j b* mode has not been enabled, the deep structure is generally hidden by the selection commands—what you see is what you get.

The *j u* (`calc-unselect`) command unselects the formula that the cursor is on. If there was no selection in the formula, this command has no effect. With a numeric prefix argument, it unselects the *n*th stack element rather than using the cursor position.

The *j c* (`calc-clear-selections`) command unselects all stack elements.

10.1.2 Changing Selections

Once you have selected a sub-formula, you can expand it using the *j m* (`calc-select-more`) command. If '`a + b`' is selected, pressing *j m* repeatedly works as follows:

```
          3    ...              3    ___              3    ___
      (a + b) . . .         (a + b)  + V c        (a + b)  + V c
   1* ..............     1* ..............     1* ---------------
          . . . .               . . . .               2 x + 1
```

In the last example, the entire formula is selected. This is roughly the same as having no selection at all, but because there are subtle differences the '`*`' character is still there on the line number.

With a numeric prefix argument *n*, *j m* expands *n* times (or until the entire formula is selected). Note that *j s* with argument *n* is equivalent to plain *j s* followed by *j m* with argument *n*. If *j m* is used when there is no current selection, it is equivalent to *j s*.

Even though *j m* does not explicitly use the location of the cursor within the formula, it nevertheless uses the cursor to determine which stack element to operate on. As usual, *j m* when the cursor is not on any stack element operates on the top stack element.

The *j l* (`calc-select-less`) command reduces the current selection around the cursor position. That is, it selects the immediate sub-formula of the current selection which contains the cursor, the opposite of *j m*. If the cursor is not inside the current selection, the command de-selects the formula.

The *j 1* through *j 9* (`calc-select-part`) commands select the *n*th sub-formula of the current selection. They are like *j l* (`calc-select-less`) except they use counting rather than the cursor position to decide which sub-formula to select. For example, if the current selection is `a + b + c` or `f(a, b, c)` or `[a, b, c]`, then *j 1* selects '`a`', *j 2* selects '`b`', and *j 3* selects '`c`'; in each of these cases, *j 4* through *j 9* would be errors.

If there is no current selection, *j 1* through *j 9* select the *n*th top-level sub-formula. (In other words, they act as if the entire stack entry were selected first.) To select the *n*th sub-formula where *n* is greater than nine, you must instead invoke *j 1* with *n* as a numeric prefix argument.

The *j n* (`calc-select-next`) and *j p* (`calc-select-previous`) commands change the current selection to the next or previous sub-formula at the same level. For example, if 'b' is selected in '2 + a*b*c + x', then *j n* selects 'c'. Further *j n* commands would be in error because, even though there is something to the right of 'c' (namely, 'x'), it is not at the same level; in this case, it is not a term of the same product as 'b' and 'c'. However, *j m* (to select the whole product 'a*b*c' as a term of the sum) followed by *j n* would successfully select the 'x'.

Similarly, *j p* moves the selection from the 'b' in this sample formula to the 'a'. Both commands accept numeric prefix arguments to move several steps at a time.

It is interesting to compare Calc's selection commands with the Emacs Info system's commands for navigating through hierarchically organized documentation. Calc's *j n* command is completely analogous to Info's *n* command. Likewise, *j p* maps to *p*, *j 2* maps to 2, and Info's *u* is like *j m*. (Note that *j u* stands for `calc-unselect`, not "up".) The Info *m* command is somewhat similar to Calc's *j s* and *j l*; in each case, you can jump directly to a sub-component of the hierarchy simply by pointing to it with the cursor.

10.1.3 Displaying Selections

The *j d* (`calc-show-selections`) command controls how selected sub-formulas are displayed. One of the alternatives is illustrated in the above examples; if we press *j d* we switch to the other style in which the selected portion itself is obscured by '#' signs:

```
         3    ...                    #     ___
      (a + b)  . . .              ## # ##  + V c
  1*  . . . . . . . . . . . . .    1* ---------------
            . . . .                      2 x + 1
```

If the customizable variable `calc-highlight-selections-with-faces` is non-nil, then the non-selected portion of the formula will be de-emphasized by using a less noticeable face (`calc-nonselected-face`) instead of dots and the selected sub-formula will be highlighted by using a more noticeable face (`calc-selected-face`) instead of '#' signs. (see Appendix C [Customizing Calc], page 435.)

10.1.4 Operating on Selections

Once a selection is made, all Calc commands that manipulate items on the stack will operate on the selected portions of the items instead. (Note that several stack elements may have selections at once, though there can be only one selection at a time in any given stack element.)

The *j e* (`calc-enable-selections`) command disables the effect that selections have on Calc commands. The current selections still exist, but Calc commands operate on whole stack elements anyway. This mode can be identified by the fact that the '*' markers on the line numbers are gone, even though selections are visible. To reactivate the selections, press *j e* again.

To extract a sub-formula as a new formula, simply select the sub-formula and press RET. This normally duplicates the top stack element; here it duplicates only the selected portion of that element.

To replace a sub-formula with something different, you can enter the new value onto the stack and press TAB. This normally exchanges the top two stack elements; here it swaps the value you entered into the selected portion of the formula, returning the old selected portion to the top of the stack.

```
          3    ...                        ...                      ---
      (a + b)  ...            17 x y . . .            17 x y + V c
   2* .............        2* ............        2: -------------
          . . . .                 . . . .              2 x + 1

                                       3                      3
   1:  17 x y             1:  (a + b)            1:  (a + b)
```

In this example we select a sub-formula of our original example, enter a new formula, TAB it into place, then deselect to see the complete, edited formula.

If you want to swap whole formulas around even though they contain selections, just use *j e* before and after.

The *j '* (calc-enter-selection) command is another way to replace a selected sub-formula. This command does an algebraic entry just like the regular ' key. When you press RET, the formula you type replaces the original selection. You can use the '$' symbol in the formula to refer to the original selection. If there is no selection in the formula under the cursor, the cursor is used to make a temporary selection for the purposes of the command. Thus, to change a term of a formula, all you have to do is move the Emacs cursor to that term and press *j '*.

The *j `* (calc-edit-selection) command is a similar analogue of the ` (calc-edit) command. It edits the selected sub-formula in a separate buffer. If there is no selection, it edits the sub-formula indicated by the cursor.

To delete a sub-formula, press DEL. This generally replaces the sub-formula with the constant zero, but in a few suitable contexts it uses the constant one instead. The DEL key automatically deselects and re-simplifies the entire formula afterwards. Thus:

```
             ###
      17 x y + # #            17 x y            17 # y           17 y
   1* -------------     1:  -------     1*  -------     1:  -------
         2 x + 1             2 x + 1           2 x + 1          2 x + 1
```

In this example, we first delete the 'sqrt(c)' term; Calc accomplishes this by replacing 'sqrt(c)' with zero and resimplifying. We then delete the *x* in the numerator; since this is part of a product, Calc replaces it with '1' and resimplifies.

If you select an element of a vector and press DEL, that element is deleted from the vector. If you delete one side of an equation or inequality, only the opposite side remains.

The *j DEL* (calc-del-selection) command is like DEL but with the auto-selecting behavior of *j '* and *j `*. It deletes the selected portion of the formula indicated by the cursor, or, in the absence of a selection, it deletes the sub-formula indicated by the cursor position.

(There is also an auto-selecting *j RET* (calc-copy-selection) command.)

Normal arithmetic operations also apply to sub-formulas. Here we select the denominator, press *5 -* to subtract five from the denominator, press *n* to negate the denominator, then press *Q* to take the square root.

```
        . . .            . . .            . . .            . . .
   1* .......     1* .......     1* .......     1* .........
       2 x + 1          2 x - 4          4 - 2 x
                                                     ---------
                                                      V 4 - 2 x
```

Certain types of operations on selections are not allowed. For example, for an arithmetic function like − no more than one of the arguments may be a selected sub-formula. (As the above example shows, the result of the subtraction is spliced back into the argument which had the selection; if there were more than one selection involved, this would not be well-defined.) If you try to subtract two selections, the command will abort with an error message.

Operations on sub-formulas sometimes leave the formula as a whole in an "un-natural" state. Consider negating the '2 x' term of our sample formula by selecting it and pressing n (`calc-change-sign`).

```
         . . .                    . . .
1*  ..........         1*  ..........
    ..........             ..........
    . . . 2 x             . . . -2 x
```

Unselecting the sub-formula reveals that the minus sign, which would normally have canceled out with the subtraction automatically, has not been able to do so because the subtraction was not part of the selected portion. Pressing = (`calc-evaluate`) or doing any other mathematical operation on the whole formula will cause it to be simplified.

```
         17 y                     17 y
1:    -----------       1:    ----------

      -----------             ----------
    V 4 - -2 x               V 4 + 2 x
```

10.1.5 Rearranging Formulas using Selections

The j R (`calc-commute-right`) command moves the selected sub-formula to the right in its surrounding formula. Generally the selection is one term of a sum or product; the sum or product is rearranged according to the commutative laws of algebra.

As with j ' and j DEL, the term under the cursor is used if there is no selection in the current formula. All commands described in this section share this property. In this example, we place the cursor on the 'a' and type j R, then repeat.

```
1:  a + b - c         1:  b + a - c         1:  b - c + a
```

Note that in the final step above, the 'a' is switched with the 'c' but the signs are adjusted accordingly. When moving terms of sums and products, j R will never change the mathematical meaning of the formula.

The selected term may also be an element of a vector or an argument of a function. The term is exchanged with the one to its right. In this case, the "meaning" of the vector or function may of course be drastically changed.

```
1:  [a, b, c]         1:  [b, a, c]         1:  [b, c, a]

1:  f(a, b, c)        1:  f(b, a, c)        1:  f(b, c, a)
```

The j L (`calc-commute-left`) command is like j R except that it swaps the selected term with the one to its left.

With numeric prefix arguments, these commands move the selected term several steps at a time. It is an error to try to move a term left or right past the end of its enclosing formula. With numeric prefix arguments of zero, these commands move the selected term as far as possible in the given direction.

The j D (`calc-sel-distribute`) command mixes the selected sum or product into the surrounding formula using the distributive law. For example, in 'a * (b - c)' with the 'b - c' selected, the result is 'a b - a c'. This also distributes products or quotients into surrounding powers, and can also do transformations like 'exp(a + b)' to 'exp(a) exp(b)', where 'a + b' is the selected term, and 'ln(a ^ b)' to 'ln(a) b', where 'a ^ b' is the selected term.

For multiple-term sums or products, $j\ D$ takes off one term at a time: 'a * (b + c - d)' goes to 'a * (c - d) + a b' with the 'c - d' selected so that you can type $j\ D$ repeatedly to expand completely. The $j\ D$ command allows a numeric prefix argument which specifies the maximum number of times to expand at once; the default is one time only.

The $j\ D$ command is implemented using rewrite rules. See Section 10.11.9 [Selections with Rewrite Rules], page 307. The rules are stored in the Calc variable `DistribRules`. A convenient way to view these rules is to use $s\ e$ (`calc-edit-variable`) which displays and edits the stored value of a variable. Press $C\text{-}c\ C\text{-}c$ to return from editing mode; be careful not to make any actual changes or else you will affect the behavior of future $j\ D$ commands!

To extend $j\ D$ to handle new cases, just edit `DistribRules` as described above. You can then use the $s\ p$ command to save this variable's value permanently for future Calc sessions. See Section 12.3 [Operations on Variables], page 325.

The $j\ M$ (`calc-sel-merge`) command is the complement of $j\ D$; given 'a b - a c' with either 'a b' or 'a c' selected, the result is 'a * (b - c)'. Once again, $j\ M$ can also merge calls to functions like `exp` and `ln`; examine the variable `MergeRules` to see all the relevant rules.

The $j\ C$ (`calc-sel-commute`) command swaps the arguments of the selected sum, product, or equation. It always behaves as if $j\ b$ mode were in effect, i.e., the sum 'a + b + c' is treated as the nested sums '(a + b) + c' by this command. If you put the cursor on the first '+', the result is '(b + a) + c'; if you put the cursor on the second '+', the result is 'c + (a + b)' (which the default simplifications will rearrange to '(c + a) + b'). The relevant rules are stored in the variable `CommuteRules`.

You may need to turn default simplifications off (with the $m\ O$ command) in order to get the full benefit of $j\ C$. For example, commuting 'a - b' produces '-b + a', but the default simplifications will "simplify" this right back to 'a - b' if you don't turn them off. The same is true of some of the other manipulations described in this section.

The $j\ N$ (`calc-sel-negate`) command replaces the selected term with the negative of that term, then adjusts the surrounding formula in order to preserve the meaning. For example, given 'exp(a - b)' where 'a - b' is selected, the result is '1 / exp(b - a)'. By contrast, selecting a term and using the regular n (`calc-change-sign`) command negates the term without adjusting the surroundings, thus changing the meaning of the formula as a whole. The rules variable is `NegateRules`.

The $j\ \&$ (`calc-sel-invert`) command is similar to $j\ N$ except it takes the reciprocal of the selected term. For example, given 'a - ln(b)' with 'b' selected, the result is 'a + ln(1/b)'. The rules variable is `InvertRules`.

The $j\ E$ (`calc-sel-jump-equals`) command moves the selected term from one side of an equation to the other. Given 'a + b = c + d' with 'c' selected, the result is 'a + b - c = d'. This command also works if the selected term is part of a '*', '/', or '^' formula. The relevant rules variable is `JumpRules`.

The $j\ I$ (`calc-sel-isolate`) command isolates the selected term on its side of an equation. It uses the $a\ S$ (`calc-solve-for`) command to solve the equation, and the Hyperbolic flag affects it in the same way. See Section 10.6 [Solving Equations], page 268. When it applies, *j I* is often easier to use than *j E*. It understands more rules of algebra, and works for inequalities as well as equations.

The *j ** (calc-sel-mult-both-sides) command prompts for a formula using algebraic entry, then multiplies both sides of the selected quotient or equation by that formula. It performs the default algebraic simplifications before re-forming the quotient or equation. You can suppress this simplification by providing a prefix argument: *C-u j **. There is also a *j /* (calc-sel-div-both-sides) which is similar to *j ** but dividing instead of multiplying by the factor you enter.

If the selection is a quotient with numerator 1, then Calc's default simplifications would normally cancel the new factors. To prevent this, when the *j ** command is used on a selection whose numerator is 1 or -1, the denominator is expanded at the top level using the distributive law (as if using the *C-u 1 a x* command). Suppose the formula on the stack is '1 / (a + 1)' and you wish to multiplying the top and bottom by 'a - 1'. Calc's default simplifications would normally change the result '(a - 1) /(a + 1) (a - 1)' back to the original form by cancellation; when *j ** is used, Calc expands the denominator to 'a (a - 1) + a - 1' to prevent this.

If you wish the *j ** command to completely expand the denominator of a quotient you can call it with a zero prefix: *C-u 0 j **. For example, if the formula on the stack is '1 / (sqrt(a) + 1)', you may wish to eliminate the square root in the denominator by multiplying the top and bottom by 'sqrt(a) - 1'. If you did this simply by using a simple *j ** command, you would get '(sqrt(a)-1)/ (sqrt(a) (sqrt(a) - 1) + sqrt(a) - 1)'. Instead, you would probably want to use *C-u 0 j **, which would expand the bottom and give you the desired result '(sqrt(a)-1)/(a-1)'. More generally, if *j ** is called with an argument of a positive integer n, then the denominator of the expression will be expanded n times (as if with the *C-u n a x* command).

If the selection is an inequality, *j ** and *j /* will accept any factor, but will warn unless they can prove the factor is either positive or negative. (In the latter case the direction of the inequality will be switched appropriately.) See Section 6.6 [Declarations], page 143, for ways to inform Calc that a given variable is positive or negative. If Calc can't tell for sure what the sign of the factor will be, it will assume it is positive and display a warning message.

For selections that are not quotients, equations, or inequalities, these commands pull out a multiplicative factor: They divide (or multiply) by the entered formula, simplify, then multiply (or divide) back by the formula.

The *j +* (calc-sel-add-both-sides) and *j -* (calc-sel-sub-both-sides) commands analogously add to or subtract from both sides of an equation or inequality. For other types of selections, they extract an additive factor. A numeric prefix argument suppresses simplification of the intermediate results.

The *j U* (calc-sel-unpack) command replaces the selected function call with its argument. For example, given 'a + sin(x^2)' with 'sin(x^2)' selected, the result is 'a + x^2'. (The 'x^2' will remain selected; if you wanted to change the sin to cos, just press *C* now to take the cosine of the selected part.)

The *j v* (calc-sel-evaluate) command performs the basic simplifications on the selected sub-formula. These simplifications would normally be done automatically on all results, but may have been partially inhibited by previous selection-related operations, or turned off altogether by the *m 0* command. This command is just an auto-selecting version of the *a v* command (see Section 10.2 [Algebraic Manipulation], page 251).

With a numeric prefix argument of 2, *C-u 2 j v* applies the default algebraic simplifications to the selected sub-formula. With a prefix argument of 3 or more, e.g., *C-u j v* applies the *a e* (`calc-simplify-extended`) command. See Section 10.3 [Simplifying Formulas], page 253. With a negative prefix argument it simplifies at the top level only, just as with *a v*. Here the "top" level refers to the top level of the selected sub-formula.

The *j "* (`calc-sel-expand-formula`) command is to *a "* (see Section 10.2 [Algebraic Manipulation], page 251) what *j v* is to *a v*.

You can use the *j r* (`calc-rewrite-selection`) command to define other algebraic operations on sub-formulas. See Section 10.11 [Rewrite Rules], page 291.

10.2 Algebraic Manipulation

The commands in this section perform general-purpose algebraic manipulations. They work on the whole formula at the top of the stack (unless, of course, you have made a selection in that formula).

Many algebra commands prompt for a variable name or formula. If you answer the prompt with a blank line, the variable or formula is taken from top-of-stack, and the normal argument for the command is taken from the second-to-top stack level.

The *a v* (`calc-alg-evaluate`) command performs the normal default simplifications on a formula; for example, 'a - -b' is changed to 'a + b'. These simplifications are normally done automatically on all Calc results, so this command is useful only if you have turned default simplifications off with an *m 0* command. See Section 6.5 [Simplification Modes], page 142.

It is often more convenient to type =, which is like *a v* but which also substitutes stored values for variables in the formula. Use *a v* if you want the variables to ignore their stored values.

If you give a numeric prefix argument of 2 to *a v*, it simplifies using Calc's algebraic simplifications; see Section 10.3 [Simplifying Formulas], page 253. If you give a numeric prefix of 3 or more, it uses Extended Simplification mode (*a e*).

If you give a negative prefix argument -1, -2, or -3, it simplifies in the corresponding mode but only works on the top-level function call of the formula. For example, '(2 + 3) * (2 + 3)' will simplify to '(2 + 3)^2', without simplifying the sub-formulas '2 + 3'. As another example, typing *V R +* to sum the vector '[1, 2, 3, 4]' produces the formula 'reduce(add, [1, 2, 3, 4])' in No-Simplify mode. Using *a v* will evaluate this all the way to 10; using *C-u - a v* will evaluate it only to '1 + 2 + 3 + 4'. (See Section 9.8 [Reducing and Mapping], page 235.)

The = command corresponds to the `evalv` function, and the related *N* command, which is like = but temporarily disables Symbolic mode (*m s*) during the evaluation, corresponds to the `evalvn` function. (These commands interpret their prefix arguments differently than *a v*; = treats the prefix as the number of stack elements to evaluate at once, and *N* treats it as a temporary different working precision.)

The `evalvn` function can take an alternate working precision as an optional second argument. This argument can be either an integer, to set the precision absolutely, or a vector containing a single integer, to adjust the precision relative to the current precision. Note that `evalvn` with a larger than current precision will do the calculation at this higher precision, but the result will as usual be rounded back down to the current precision afterward. For example, '`evalvn(pi - 3.1415)`' at a precision of 12 will return '`9.265359e-5`'; '`evalvn(pi - 3.1415, 30)`' will return '`9.26535897932e-5`' (computing a 25-digit result which is then rounded down to 12); and '`evalvn(pi - 3.1415, [-2])`' will return '`9.2654e-5`'.

The a " (`calc-expand-formula`) command expands functions into their defining formulas wherever possible. For example, '`deg(x^2)`' is changed to '`180 x^2 / pi`'. Most functions, like `sin` and `gcd`, are not defined by simple formulas and so are unaffected by this command. One important class of functions which *can* be expanded is the user-defined functions created by the *Z F* command. See Section 17.4 [Algebraic Definitions], page 369. Other functions which a " can expand include the probability distribution functions, most of the financial functions, and the hyperbolic and inverse hyperbolic functions. A numeric prefix argument affects a " in the same way as it does a *v*: A positive argument expands all functions in the formula and then simplifies in various ways; a negative argument expands and simplifies only the top-level function call.

The a *M* (`calc-map-equation`) [mapeq] command applies a given function or operator to one or more equations. It is analogous to *V M*, which operates on vectors instead of equations. see Section 9.8 [Reducing and Mapping], page 235. For example, a *M S* changes '`x = y+1`' to '`sin(x) = sin(y+1)`', and a *M +* with '`x = y+1`' and 6 on the stack produces '`x+6 = y+7`'. With two equations on the stack, a *M +* would add the lefthand sides together and the righthand sides together to get the two respective sides of a new equation.

Mapping also works on inequalities. Mapping two similar inequalities produces another inequality of the same type. Mapping an inequality with an equation produces an inequality of the same type. Mapping a '`<=`' with a '`<`' or '`!=`' (not-equal) produces a '`<`'. If inequalities with opposite direction (e.g., '`<`' and '`>`') are mapped, the direction of the second inequality is reversed to match the first: Using a *M +* on '`a < b`' and '`a > 2`' reverses the latter to get '`2 < a`', which then allows the combination '`a + 2 < b + a`', which the algebraic simplifications can reduce to '`2 < b`'.

Using a *M **, a *M /*, a *M n*, or a *M &* to negate or invert an inequality will reverse the direction of the inequality. Other adjustments to inequalities are *not* done automatically; a *M S* will change '`x < y`' to '`sin(x) < sin(y)`' even though this is not true for all values of the variables.

With the Hyperbolic flag, *H a M* [mapeqp] does a plain mapping operation without reversing the direction of any inequalities. Thus, *H a M &* would change *x > 2* to *1/x > 0.5*. (This change is mathematically incorrect, but perhaps you were fixing an inequality which was already incorrect.)

With the Inverse flag, *I a M* [mapeqr] always reverses the direction of the inequality. You might use *I a M C* to change '`x < y`' to '`cos(x) > cos(y)`' if you know you are working with small positive angles.

The a *b* (`calc-substitute`) [subst] command substitutes all occurrences of some variable or sub-expression of an expression with a new sub-expression. For example, substituting '`sin(x)`' with '`cos(y)`' in '`2 sin(x)^2 + x sin(x) + sin(2 x)`' produces '`2 cos(y)^2 + x cos(y) + sin(2 x)`'. Note that this is a purely structural substitution; the lone '`x`' and the 'sin(2 x)' stayed the same because they did not look like 'sin(x)'. See Section 10.11 [Rewrite Rules], page 291, for a more general method for doing substitutions.

The **a b** command normally prompts for two formulas, the old one and the new one. If you enter a blank line for the first prompt, all three arguments are taken from the stack (new, then old, then target expression). If you type an old formula but then enter a blank line for the new one, the new formula is taken from top-of-stack and the target from second-to-top. If you answer both prompts, the target is taken from top-of-stack as usual.

Note that **a b** has no understanding of commutativity or associativity. The pattern 'x+y' will not match the formula 'y+x'. Also, 'y+z' will not match inside the formula 'x+y+z' because the '+' operator is left-associative, so the "deep structure" of that formula is '(x+y) + z'. Use *d U* (`calc-unformatted-language`) mode to see the true structure of a formula. The rewrite rule mechanism, discussed later, does not have these limitations.

As an algebraic function, `subst` takes three arguments: Target expression, old, new. Note that `subst` is always evaluated immediately, even if its arguments are variables, so if you wish to put a call to `subst` onto the stack you must turn the default simplifications off first (with *m 0*).

10.3 Simplifying Formulas

The sections below describe all the various kinds of simplifications Calc provides in full detail. None of Calc's simplification commands are designed to pull rabbits out of hats; they simply apply certain specific rules to put formulas into less redundant or more pleasing forms. Serious algebra in Calc must be done manually, usually with a combination of selections and rewrite rules. See Section 10.1.5 [Rearranging with Selections], page 248. See Section 10.11 [Rewrite Rules], page 291.

See Section 6.5 [Simplification Modes], page 142, for commands to control what level of simplification occurs automatically. Normally the algebraic simplifications described below occur. If you have turned on a simplification mode which does not do these algebraic simplifications, you can still apply them to a formula with the **a s** (`calc-simplify`) [simplify] command.

There are some simplifications that, while sometimes useful, are never done automatically. For example, the *I* prefix can be given to **a s**; the *I* **a s** command will change any trigonometric function to the appropriate combination of 'sin's and 'cos's before simplifying. This can be useful in simplifying even mildly complicated trigonometric expressions. For example, while the algebraic simplifications can reduce 'sin(x) csc(x)' to '1', they will not simplify 'sin(x)^2 csc(x)'. The command *I* **a s** can be used to simplify this latter expression; it will transform 'sin(x)^2 csc(x)' into 'sin(x)'. However, *I* **a s** will also perform some "simplifications" which may not be desired; for example, it will transform 'tan(x)^2' into 'sin(x)^2 / cos(x)^2'. The Hyperbolic prefix *H* can be used similarly; the *H* **a s** will replace any hyperbolic functions in the formula with the appropriate combinations of 'sinh's and 'cosh's before simplifying.

10.3.1 Basic Simplifications

This section describes basic simplifications which Calc performs in many situations. For example, both binary simplifications and algebraic simplifications begin by performing these basic simplifications. You can type `m I` to restrict the simplifications done on the stack to these simplifications.

The most basic simplification is the evaluation of functions. For example, $2 + 3$ is evaluated to 5, and `sqrt(9)` is evaluated to 3. Evaluation does not occur if the arguments to a function are somehow of the wrong type `tan([2, 3, 4]))`, range (`tan(90)`), or number (`tan(3, 5)`), or if the function name is not recognized (`f(5)`), or if Symbolic mode (see Section 6.4.5 [Symbolic Mode], page 140) prevents evaluation (`sqrt(2)`).

Calc simplifies (evaluates) the arguments to a function before it simplifies the function itself. Thus `sqrt(5 + 4)` is simplified to `sqrt(9)` before the `sqrt` function itself is applied. There are very few exceptions to this rule: `quote`, `lambda`, and `condition` (the :: operator) do not evaluate their arguments, `if` (the ? : operator) does not evaluate all of its arguments, and `evalto` does not evaluate its lefthand argument.

Most commands apply at least these basic simplifications to all arguments they take from the stack, perform a particular operation, then simplify the result before pushing it back on the stack. In the common special case of regular arithmetic commands like `+` and `Q` [`sqrt`], the arguments are simply popped from the stack and collected into a suitable function call, which is then simplified (the arguments being simplified first as part of the process, as described above).

Even the basic set of simplifications are too numerous to describe completely here, but this section will describe the ones that apply to the major arithmetic operators. This list will be rather technical in nature, and will probably be interesting to you only if you are a serious user of Calc's algebra facilities.

As well as the simplifications described here, if you have stored any rewrite rules in the variable `EvalRules` then these rules will also be applied before any of the basic simplifications. See Section 10.11.11 [Automatic Rewrites], page 309, for details.

And now, on with the basic simplifications:

Arithmetic operators like `+` and `*` always take two arguments in Calc's internal form. Sums and products of three or more terms are arranged by the associative law of algebra into a left-associative form for sums, $((a + b) + c) + d$, and (by default) a right-associative form for products, $a * (b * (c * d))$. Formulas like $(a + b) + (c + d)$ are rearranged to left-associative form, though this rarely matters since Calc's algebra commands are designed to hide the inner structure of sums and products as much as possible. Sums and products in their proper associative form will be written without parentheses in the examples below.

Sums and products are *not* rearranged according to the commutative law $(a + b$ to $b + a)$ except in a few special cases described below. Some algebra programs always rearrange terms into a canonical order, which enables them to see that $ab + ba$ can be simplified to $2ab$. If you are using Basic Simplification mode, Calc assumes you have put the terms into the order you want and generally leaves that order alone, with the consequence that formulas like the above will only be simplified if you explicitly give the `a s` command. See Section 10.3.2 [Algebraic Simplifications], page 257.

Differences $a - b$ are treated like sums $a + (-b)$ for purposes of simplification; one of the default simplifications is to rewrite $a + (-b)$ or $(-b) + a$, where $-b$ represents a "negative-looking" term, into $a - b$ form. "Negative-looking" means negative numbers, negated formulas like $-x$, and products or quotients in which either term is negative-looking.

Other simplifications involving negation are $-(-x)$ to x; $-(ab)$ or $-(a/b)$ where either a or b is negative-looking, simplified by negating that term, or else where a or b is any number, by negating that number; $-(a + b)$ to $-a - b$, and $-(b - a)$ to $a - b$. (This, and rewriting $(-b) + a$ to $a - b$, are the only cases where the order of terms in a sum is changed by the default simplifications.)

The distributive law is used to simplify sums in some cases: $ax + bx$ to $(a + b)x$, where a represents a number or an implicit 1 or -1 (as in x or $-x$) and similarly for b. Use the **a c**, **a f**, or **j M** commands to merge sums with non-numeric coefficients using the distributive law.

The distributive law is only used for sums of two terms, or for adjacent terms in a larger sum. Thus $a+b+b+c$ is simplified to $a+2b+c$, but $a+b+c+b$ is not simplified. The reason is that comparing all terms of a sum with one another would require time proportional to the square of the number of terms; Calc omits potentially slow operations like this in basic simplification mode.

Finally, $a + 0$ and $0 + a$ are simplified to a. A consequence of the above rules is that $0 - a$ is simplified to $-a$.

The products $1a$ and $a1$ are simplified to a; $(-1)a$ and $a(-1)$ are simplified to $-a$; $0a$ and $a0$ are simplified to 0, except that in Matrix mode where a is not provably scalar the result is the generic zero matrix 'idn(0)', and that if a is infinite the result is 'nan'.

Also, $(-a)b$ and $a(-b)$ are simplified to $-(ab)$, where this occurs for negated formulas but not for regular negative numbers.

Products are commuted only to move numbers to the front: $ab2$ is commuted to $2ab$.

The product $a(b + c)$ is distributed over the sum only if a and at least one of b and c are numbers: $2(x + 3)$ goes to $2x + 6$. The formula $(-a)(b - c)$, where $-a$ is a negative number, is rewritten to $a(c - b)$.

The distributive law of products and powers is used for adjacent terms of the product: $x^a x^b$ goes to x^{a+b} where a is a number, or an implicit 1 (as in x), or the implicit one-half of $\mathrm{sqrt}(x)$, and similarly for b. The result is written using 'sqrt' or '1/sqrt' if the sum of the powers is $1/2$ or $-1/2$, respectively. If the sum of the powers is zero, the product is simplified to 1 or to 'idn(1)' if Matrix mode is enabled.

The product of a negative power times anything but another negative power is changed to use division: $x^{-2}y$ goes to y/x^2 unless Matrix mode is in effect and neither x nor y are scalar (in which case it is considered unsafe to rearrange the order of the terms).

Finally, $a(b/c)$ is rewritten to $(ab)/c$, and also $(a/b)c$ is changed to $(ac)/b$ unless in Matrix mode.

Simplifications for quotients are analogous to those for products. The quotient $0/x$ is simplified to 0, with the same exceptions that were noted for $0x$. Likewise, $x/1$ and $x/(-1)$ are simplified to x and $-x$, respectively.

The quotient $x/0$ is left unsimplified or changed to an infinite quantity, as directed by the current infinite mode. See Section 6.4.4 [Infinite Mode], page 140.

The expression a/b^{-c} is changed to ab^c, where $-c$ is any negative-looking power. Also, $1/b^c$ is changed to b^{-c} for any power c.

Also, $(-a)/b$ and $a/(-b)$ go to $-(a/b)$; $(a/b)/c$ goes to $a/(bc)$; and $a/(b/c)$ goes to $(ac)/b$ unless Matrix mode prevents this rearrangement. Similarly, $a/(b{:}c)$ is simplified to $(c{:}b)a$ for any fraction $b{:}c$.

The distributive law is applied to $(a+b)/c$ only if c and at least one of a and b are numbers. Quotients of powers and square roots are distributed just as described for multiplication.

Quotients of products cancel only in the leading terms of the numerator and denominator. In other words, axb/ayb is canceled to xb/yb but not to x/y. Once again this is because full cancellation can be slow; use `a s` to cancel all terms of the quotient.

Quotients of negative-looking values are simplified according to $(-a)/(-b)$ to a/b, $(-a)/(b-c)$ to $a/(c-b)$, and $(a-b)/(-c)$ to $(b-a)/c$.

The formula x^0 is simplified to 1, or to `idn(1)` in Matrix mode. The formula 0^x is simplified to 0 unless x is a negative number, complex number or zero. If x is negative, complex or 0.0, 0^x is an infinity or an unsimplified formula according to the current infinite mode. The expression 0^0 is simplified to 1.

Powers of products or quotients $(ab)^c$, $(a/b)^c$ are distributed to $a^c b^c$, a^c/b^c only if c is an integer, or if either a or b are nonnegative real numbers. Powers of powers $(a^b)^c$ are simplified to a^{bc} only when c is an integer and bc also evaluates to an integer. Without these restrictions these simplifications would not be safe because of problems with principal values. (In other words, $((-3)^{1/2})^2$ is safe to simplify, but $((-3)^2)^{1/2}$ is not.) See Section 6.6 [Declarations], page 143, for ways to inform Calc that your variables satisfy these requirements.

As a special case of this rule, $\mathtt{sqrt}(x)^n$ is simplified to $x^{n/2}$ only for even integers n.

If a is known to be real, b is an even integer, and c is a half- or quarter-integer, then $(a^b)^c$ is simplified to $\mathtt{abs}(a^{(}bc))$.

Also, $(-a)^b$ is simplified to a^b if b is an even integer, or to $-(a^b)$ if b is an odd integer, for any negative-looking expression $-a$.

Square roots $\mathtt{sqrt}(x)$ generally act like one-half powers $x^{1{:}2}$ for the purposes of the above-listed simplifications.

Also, note that $1/x^{1{:}2}$ is changed to $x^{-1{:}2}$, but $1/\mathtt{sqrt}(x)$ is left alone.

Generic identity matrices (see Section 6.4.6 [Matrix Mode], page 141) are simplified by the following rules: $\mathtt{idn}(a)+b$ to $a+b$ if b is provably scalar, or expanded out if b is a matrix; $\mathtt{idn}(a)+\mathtt{idn}(b)$ to $\mathtt{idn}(a+b)$; $-\mathtt{idn}(a)$ to $\mathtt{idn}(-a)$; $a\,\mathtt{idn}(b)$ to $\mathtt{idn}(ab)$ if a is provably scalar, or to ab if a is provably non-scalar; $\mathtt{idn}(a)\mathtt{idn}(b)$ to $\mathtt{idn}(ab)$; analogous simplifications for quotients involving $\mathtt{idn}$; and $\mathtt{idn}(a)^n$ to $\mathtt{idn}(a^n)$ where n is an integer.

The `floor` function and other integer truncation functions vanish if the argument is provably integer-valued, so that $\mathtt{floor}(\mathtt{round}(x))$ simplifies to $\mathtt{round}(x)$. Also, combinations of `float`, `floor` and its friends, and `ffloor` and its friends, are simplified in appropriate ways. See Section 7.2 [Integer Truncation], page 189.

The expression $\mathtt{abs}(-x)$ changes to $\mathtt{abs}(x)$. The expression $\mathtt{abs}(\mathtt{abs}(x))$ changes to $\mathtt{abs}(x)$; in fact, $\mathtt{abs}(x)$ changes to x or $-x$ if x is provably nonnegative or nonpositive (see Section 6.6 [Declarations], page 143).

While most functions do not recognize the variable i as an imaginary number, the `arg` function does handle the two cases `arg(i)` and `arg(-i)` just for convenience.

The expression `conj(conj(x))` simplifies to x. Various other expressions involving `conj`, `re`, and `im` are simplified, especially if some of the arguments are provably real or involve the constant i. For example, $\text{conj}(a + bi)$ is changed to $\text{conj}(a) - \text{conj}(b)i$, or to $a - bi$ if a and b are known to be real.

Functions like `sin` and `arctan` generally don't have any default simplifications beyond simply evaluating the functions for suitable numeric arguments and infinity. The algebraic simplifications described in the next section do provide some simplifications for these functions, though.

One important simplification that does occur is that `ln(e)` is simplified to 1, and $\text{ln}(e^x)$ is simplified to x for any x. This occurs even if you have stored a different value in the Calc variable 'e'; but this would be a bad idea in any case if you were also using natural logarithms!

Among the logical functions, `!(a <= b)` changes to `a > b` and so on. Equations and inequalities where both sides are either negative-looking or zero are simplified by negating both sides and reversing the inequality. While it might seem reasonable to simplify `!!x` to x, this would not be valid in general because `!!2` is 1, not 2.

Most other Calc functions have few if any basic simplifications defined, aside of course from evaluation when the arguments are suitable numbers.

10.3.2 Algebraic Simplifications

This section describes all simplifications that are performed by the algebraic simplification mode, which is the default simplification mode. If you have switched to a different simplification mode, you can switch back with the `m A` command. Even in other simplification modes, the `a s` command will use these algebraic simplifications to simplify the formula.

There is a variable, `AlgSimpRules`, in which you can put rewrites to be applied. Its use is analogous to `EvalRules`, but without the special restrictions. Basically, the simplifier does 'a r AlgSimpRules' with an infinite repeat count on the whole expression being simplified, then it traverses the expression applying the built-in rules described below. If the result is different from the original expression, the process repeats with the basic simplifications (including `EvalRules`), then `AlgSimpRules`, then the built-in simplifications, and so on.

Sums are simplified in two ways. Constant terms are commuted to the end of the sum, so that $a + 2 + b$ changes to $a + b + 2$. The only exception is that a constant will not be commuted away from the first position of a difference, i.e., $2 - x$ is not commuted to $-x + 2$.

Also, terms of sums are combined by the distributive law, as in $x + y + 2x$ to $y + 3x$. This always occurs for adjacent terms, but Calc's algebraic simplifications compare all pairs of terms including non-adjacent ones.

Products are sorted into a canonical order using the commutative law. For example, bca is commuted to abc. This allows easier comparison of products; for example, the basic simplifications will not change $xy + yx$ to $2xy$, but the algebraic simplifications; it first rewrites the sum to $xy + xy$ which can then be recognized as a sum of identical terms.

The canonical ordering used to sort terms of products has the property that real-valued numbers, interval forms and infinities come first, and are sorted into increasing order. The *V S* command uses the same ordering when sorting a vector.

Sorting of terms of products is inhibited when Matrix mode is turned on; in this case, Calc will never exchange the order of two terms unless it knows at least one of the terms is a scalar.

Products of powers are distributed by comparing all pairs of terms, using the same method that the default simplifications use for adjacent terms of products.

Even though sums are not sorted, the commutative law is still taken into account when terms of a product are being compared. Thus $(x+y)(y+x)$ will be simplified to $(x+y)^2$. A subtle point is that $(x-y)(y-x)$ will *not* be simplified to $-(x-y)^2$; Calc does not notice that one term can be written as a constant times the other, even if that constant is -1.

A fraction times any expression, $(a{:}b)x$, is changed to a quotient involving integers: ax/b. This is not done for floating-point numbers like 0.5, however. This is one reason why you may find it convenient to turn Fraction mode on while doing algebra; see Section 6.4.3 [Fraction Mode], page 140.

Quotients are simplified by comparing all terms in the numerator with all terms in the denominator for possible cancellation using the distributive law. For example, ax^2b/cx^3d will cancel x^2 from the top and bottom to get ab/cxd. (The terms in the denominator will then be rearranged to cdx as described above.) If there is any common integer or fractional factor in the numerator and denominator, it is canceled out; for example, $(4x+6)/8x$ simplifies to $(2x+3)/4x$.

Non-constant common factors are not found even by algebraic simplifications. To cancel the factor a in $(ax+a)/a^2$ you could first use *j M* on the product ax to Merge the numerator to $a(1+x)$, which can then be simplified successfully.

Integer powers of the variable i are simplified according to the identity $i^2 = -1$. If you store a new value other than the complex number $(0,1)$ in i, this simplification will no longer occur. This is not done by the basic simplifications; in case someone (unwisely) wants to use the name i for a variable unrelated to complex numbers, they can use basic simplification mode.

Square roots of integer or rational arguments are simplified in several ways. (Note that these will be left unevaluated only in Symbolic mode.) First, square integer or rational factors are pulled out so that $\mathtt{sqrt}(8)$ is rewritten as $2\,\mathtt{sqrt}(2)$. Conceptually speaking this implies factoring the argument into primes and moving pairs of primes out of the square root, but for reasons of efficiency Calc only looks for primes up to 29.

Square roots in the denominator of a quotient are moved to the numerator: $1/\mathtt{sqrt}(3)$ changes to $\mathtt{sqrt}(3)/3$. The same effect occurs for the square root of a fraction: $\mathtt{sqrt}(2{:}3)$ changes to $\mathtt{sqrt}(6)/3$.

The % (modulo) operator is simplified in several ways when the modulus M is a positive real number. First, if the argument is of the form $x+n$ for some real number n, then n is itself reduced modulo M. For example, '(x - 23) % 10' is simplified to '(x + 7) % 10'.

If the argument is multiplied by a constant, and this constant has a common integer divisor with the modulus, then this factor is canceled out. For example, '12 x % 15' is changed to '3 (4 x % 5)' by factoring out 3. Also, '(12 x + 1) % 15' is changed to '3 ((4 x + 1:3) % 5)'. While these forms may not seem "simpler," they allow Calc to discover useful information about modulo forms in the presence of declarations.

If the modulus is 1, then Calc can use $\mathtt{int}$ declarations to evaluate the expression. For example, the idiom 'x % 2' is often used to check whether a number is odd or even. As described above, '2 n % 2' and '(2 n + 1) % 2' are simplified to '2 (n % 1)' and '2 ((n + 1:2) % 1)', respectively; Calc can simplify these to 0 and 1 (respectively) if $\mathtt{n}$ has been declared to be an integer.

Trigonometric functions are simplified in several ways. Whenever a products of two trigonometric functions can be replaced by a single function, the replacement is made; for example, $\mathtt{tan}(x)\mathtt{cos}(x)$ is simplified to $\mathtt{sin}(x)$. Reciprocals of trigonometric functions are replaced by their reciprocal function; for example, $1/\mathtt{sec}(x)$ is simplified to $\mathtt{cos}(x)$. The corresponding simplifications for the hyperbolic functions are also handled.

Trigonometric functions of their inverse functions are simplified. The expression $\mathtt{sin}(\mathtt{arcsin}(x))$ is simplified to x, and similarly for $\mathtt{cos}$ and $\mathtt{tan}$. Trigonometric functions of inverses of different trigonometric functions can also be simplified, as in $\mathtt{sin}(\mathtt{arccos}(x))$ to $\mathtt{sqrt}(1 - x^2)$.

If the argument to $\mathtt{sin}$ is negative-looking, it is simplified to $-\mathtt{sin}(x)$, and similarly for $\mathtt{cos}$ and $\mathtt{tan}$. Finally, certain special values of the argument are recognized; see Section 8.2 [Trigonometric and Hyperbolic Functions], page 210.

Hyperbolic functions of their inverses and of negative-looking arguments are also handled, as are exponentials of inverse hyperbolic functions.

No simplifications for inverse trigonometric and hyperbolic functions are known, except for negative arguments of $\mathtt{arcsin}$, $\mathtt{arctan}$, $\mathtt{arcsinh}$, and $\mathtt{arctanh}$. Note that $\mathtt{arcsin}(\mathtt{sin}(x))$ can *not* safely change to x, since this only correct within an integer multiple of 2π radians or 360 degrees. However, $\mathtt{arcsinh}(\mathtt{sinh}(x))$ is simplified to x if x is known to be real.

Several simplifications that apply to logarithms and exponentials are that $\mathtt{exp}(\mathtt{ln}(x))$, $\mathtt{e}^{\mathtt{ln}(x)}$, and $10^{\log 10(x)}$ all reduce to x. Also, $\mathtt{ln}(\mathtt{exp}(x))$, etc., can reduce to x if x is provably real. The form $\mathtt{exp}(x)^y$ is simplified to $\mathtt{exp}(xy)$. If x is a suitable multiple of πi (as described above for the trigonometric functions), then $\mathtt{exp}(x)$ or e^x will be expanded. Finally, $\mathtt{ln}(x)$ is simplified to a form involving $\mathtt{pi}$ and $\mathtt{i}$ where x is provably negative, positive imaginary, or negative imaginary.

The error functions $\mathtt{erf}$ and $\mathtt{erfc}$ are simplified when their arguments are negative-looking or are calls to the $\mathtt{conj}$ function.

Equations and inequalities are simplified by canceling factors of products, quotients, or sums on both sides. Inequalities change sign if a negative multiplicative factor is canceled. Non-constant multiplicative factors as in $ab = ac$ are canceled from equations only if they are provably nonzero (generally because they were declared so; see Section 6.6 [Declarations], page 143). Factors are canceled from inequalities only if they are nonzero and their sign is known.

Simplification also replaces an equation or inequality with 1 or 0 ("true" or "false") if it can through the use of declarations. If x is declared to be an integer greater than 5, then $x < 3$, $x = 3$, and $x = 7.5$ are all simplified to 0, but $x > 3$ is simplified to 1. By a similar analysis, $abs(x) >= 0$ is simplified to 1, as is $x^2 >= 0$ if x is known to be real.

10.3.3 "Unsafe" Simplifications

Calc is capable of performing some simplifications which may sometimes be desired but which are not "safe" in all cases. The a e (`calc-simplify-extended`) [esimplify] command applies the algebraic simplifications as well as these extended, or "unsafe", simplifications. Use this only if you know the values in your formula lie in the restricted ranges for which these simplifications are valid. You can use Extended Simplification mode (m E) to have these simplifications done automatically.

The symbolic integrator uses these extended simplifications; one effect of this is that the integrator's results must be used with caution. Where an integral table will often attach conditions like "for positive a only," Calc (like most other symbolic integration programs) will simply produce an unqualified result.

Because a e's simplifications are unsafe, it is sometimes better to type C-u -3 a v, which does extended simplification only on the top level of the formula without affecting the sub-formulas. In fact, C-u -3 j v allows you to target extended simplification to any specific part of a formula.

The variable `ExtSimpRules` contains rewrites to be applied when the extended simplifications are used. These are applied in addition to `EvalRules` and `AlgSimpRules`. (The a r `AlgSimpRules` step described above is simply followed by an a r `ExtSimpRules` step.)

Following is a complete list of the "unsafe" simplifications.

Inverse trigonometric or hyperbolic functions, called with their corresponding non-inverse functions as arguments, are simplified. For example, $\texttt{arcsin}(\texttt{sin}(x))$ changes to x. Also, $\texttt{arcsin}(\texttt{cos}(x))$ and $\texttt{arccos}(\texttt{sin}(x))$ both change to $\texttt{pi}/2 - x$. These simplifications are unsafe because they are valid only for values of x in a certain range; outside that range, values are folded down to the 360-degree range that the inverse trigonometric functions always produce.

Powers of powers $(x^a)^b$ are simplified to x^{ab} for all a and b. These results will be valid only in a restricted range of x; for example, in $(x^2)^{1:2}$ the powers cancel to get x, which is valid for positive values of x but not for negative or complex values.

Similarly, $\texttt{sqrt}(x^a)$ and $\texttt{sqrt}(x)^a$ are both simplified (possibly unsafely) to $x^{a/2}$.

Forms like $\texttt{sqrt}(1 - sin(x)^2)$ are simplified to, e.g., $\texttt{cos}(x)$. Calc has identities of this sort for $\texttt{sin}$, $\texttt{cos}$, $\texttt{tan}$, $\texttt{sinh}$, and $\texttt{cosh}$.

Arguments of square roots are partially factored to look for squared terms that can be extracted. For example, $\texttt{sqrt}(a^2 b^3 + a^3 b^2)$ simplifies to $ab \texttt{sqrt}(a + b)$.

The simplifications of $\texttt{ln}(\texttt{exp}(x))$, $\texttt{ln}(e^x)$, and $\texttt{log10}(10^x)$ to x are also unsafe because of problems with principal values (although these simplifications are safe if x is known to be real).

Common factors are canceled from products on both sides of an equation, even if those factors may be zero: ax/bx to a/b. Such factors are never canceled from inequalities: Even the extended simplifications are not bold enough to reduce $ax < bx$ to $a < b$ (or $a > b$, depending on whether you believe x is positive or negative). The `a M /` command can be used to divide a factor out of both sides of an inequality.

10.3.4 Simplification of Units

The simplifications described in this section (as well as the algebraic simplifications) are applied when units need to be simplified. They can be applied using the `u s` (`calc-simplify-units`) command, or will be done automatically in Units Simplification mode (`m U`). See Section 11.1 [Basic Operations on Units], page 313.

The variable `UnitSimpRules` contains rewrites to be applied by units simplifications. These are applied in addition to `EvalRules` and `AlgSimpRules`.

Scalar mode is automatically put into effect when simplifying units. See Section 6.4.6 [Matrix Mode], page 141.

Sums $a + b$ involving units are simplified by extracting the units of a as if by the `u x` command (call the result u_a), then simplifying the expression b/u_a using `u b` and `u s`. If the result has units then the sum is inconsistent and is left alone. Otherwise, it is rewritten in terms of the units u_a.

If units auto-ranging mode is enabled, products or quotients in which the first argument is a number which is out of range for the leading unit are modified accordingly.

When canceling and combining units in products and quotients, Calc accounts for unit names that differ only in the prefix letter. For example, '2 km m' is simplified to '2000 m^2'. However, compatible but different units like `ft` and `in` are not combined in this way.

Quotients a/b are simplified in three additional ways. First, if b is a number or a product beginning with a number, Calc computes the reciprocal of this number and moves it to the numerator.

Second, for each pair of unit names from the numerator and denominator of a quotient, if the units are compatible (e.g., they are both units of area) then they are replaced by the ratio between those units. For example, in '3 s in N / kg cm' the units 'in / cm' will be replaced by 2.54.

Third, if the units in the quotient exactly cancel out, so that a `u b` command on the quotient would produce a dimensionless number for an answer, then the quotient simplifies to that number.

For powers and square roots, the "unsafe" simplifications $(ab)^c$ to $a^c b^c$, $(a/b)^c$ to a^c/b^c, and $(a^b)^c$ to a^{bc} are done if the powers are real numbers. (These are safe in the context of units because all numbers involved can reasonably be assumed to be real.)

Also, if a unit name is raised to a fractional power, and the base units in that unit name all occur to powers which are a multiple of the denominator of the power, then the unit name is expanded out into its base units, which can then be simplified according to the previous paragraph. For example, 'acre^1.5' is simplified by noting that $1.5 = 3:2$, that 'acre' is defined in terms of 'm^2', and that the 2 in the power of `m` is a multiple of 2 in $3:2$. Thus, `acre^1.5` is replaced by approximately $(4046m^2)^{1.5}$ which is then changed to $4046^{1.5} (m^2)^{1.5}$, then to $257440m^3$.

The functions `float`, `frac`, `clean`, `abs`, as well as `floor` and the other integer truncation functions, applied to unit names or products or quotients involving units, are simplified.

For example, 'round(1.6 in)' is changed to 'round(1.6) round(in)'; the lefthand term evaluates to 2, and the righthand term simplifies to in.

The functions sin, cos, and tan with arguments that have angular units like rad or arcmin are simplified by converting to base units (radians), then evaluating with the angular mode temporarily set to radians.

10.4 Polynomials

A *polynomial* is a sum of terms which are coefficients times various powers of a "base" variable. For example, $2x^2 + 3x - 4$ is a polynomial in x. Some formulas can be considered polynomials in several different variables: $1 + 2x + 3y + 4xy^2$ is a polynomial in both x and y. Polynomial coefficients are often numbers, but they may in general be any formulas not involving the base variable.

The a f (calc-factor) [factor] command factors a polynomial into a product of terms. For example, the polynomial $x^3 + 2x^2 + x$ is factored into 'x*(x+1)^2'. As another example, $ac + bd + bc + ad$ is factored into the product $(a + b)(c + d)$.

Calc currently has three algorithms for factoring. Formulas which are linear in several variables, such as the second example above, are merged according to the distributive law. Formulas which are polynomials in a single variable, with constant integer or fractional coefficients, are factored into irreducible linear and/or quadratic terms. The first example above factors into three linear terms (x, $x + 1$, and $x + 1$ again). Finally, formulas which do not fit the above criteria are handled by the algebraic rewrite mechanism.

Calc's polynomial factorization algorithm works by using the general root-finding command (a P) to solve for the roots of the polynomial. It then looks for roots which are rational numbers or complex-conjugate pairs, and converts these into linear and quadratic terms, respectively. Because it uses floating-point arithmetic, it may be unable to find terms that involve large integers (whose number of digits approaches the current precision). Also, irreducible factors of degree higher than quadratic are not found, and polynomials in more than one variable are not treated. (A more robust factorization algorithm may be included in a future version of Calc.)

The rewrite-based factorization method uses rules stored in the variable FactorRules. See Section 10.11 [Rewrite Rules], page 291, for a discussion of the operation of rewrite rules. The default FactorRules are able to factor quadratic forms symbolically into two linear terms, $(ax + b)(cx + d)$. You can edit these rules to include other cases if you wish. To use the rules, Calc builds the formula 'thecoefs(x, [a, b, c, ...])' where x is the polynomial base variable and a, b, etc., are polynomial coefficients (which may be numbers or formulas). The constant term is written first, i.e., in the a position. When the rules complete, they should have changed the formula into the form 'thefactors(x, [f1, f2, f3, ...])' where each fi should be a factored term, e.g., 'x - ai'. Calc then multiplies these terms together to get the complete factored form of the polynomial. If the rules do not change the thecoefs call to a thefactors call, a f leaves the polynomial alone on the assumption that it is unfactorable. (Note that the function names thecoefs and thefactors are used only as placeholders; there are no actual Calc functions by those names.)

The H a f [factors] command also factors a polynomial, but it returns a list of factors instead of an expression which is the product of the factors. Each factor is represented by a sub-vector of the factor, and the power with which it appears. For example, $x^5 + x^4 - 33x^3 + 63x^2$ factors to $(x + 7)x^2(x - 3)^2$ in `a f`, or to $[[x, 2], [x + 7, 1], [x - 3, 2]]$ in `H a f`. If there is an overall numeric factor, it always comes first in the list. The functions `factor` and `factors` allow a second argument when written in algebraic form; '`factor(x,v)`' factors x with respect to the specific variable v. The default is to factor with respect to all the variables that appear in x.

The `a c` (`calc-collect`) [collect] command rearranges a formula as a polynomial in a given variable, ordered in decreasing powers of that variable. For example, given $1 + 2x + 3y + 4xy^2$ on the stack, `a c x` would produce $(2 + 4y^2)x + (1 + 3y)$, and `a c y` would produce $(4x)y^2 + 3y + (1 + 2x)$. The polynomial will be expanded out using the distributive law as necessary: Collecting x in $(x - 1)^3$ produces $x^3 - 3x^2 + 3x - 1$. Terms not involving x will not be expanded.

The "variable" you specify at the prompt can actually be any expression: `a c ln(x+1)` will collect together all terms multiplied by '`ln(x+1)`' or integer powers thereof. If '`x`' also appears in the formula in a context other than '`ln(x+1)`', `a c` will treat those occurrences as unrelated to '`ln(x+1)`', i.e., as constants.

The `a x` (`calc-expand`) [expand] command expands an expression by applying the distributive law everywhere. It applies to products, quotients, and powers involving sums. By default, it fully distributes all parts of the expression. With a numeric prefix argument, the distributive law is applied only the specified number of times, then the partially expanded expression is left on the stack.

The `a x` and `j D` commands are somewhat redundant. Use `a x` if you want to expand all products of sums in your formula. Use `j D` if you want to expand a particular specified term of the formula. There is an exactly analogous correspondence between `a f` and `j M`. (The `j D` and `j M` commands also know many other kinds of expansions, such as '`exp(a + b) = exp(a) exp(b)`', which `a x` and `a f` do not do.)

Calc's automatic simplifications will sometimes reverse a partial expansion. For example, the first step in expanding $(x + 1)^3$ is to write $(x + 1)(x + 1)^2$. If `a x` stops there and tries to put this formula onto the stack, though, Calc will automatically simplify it back to $(x + 1)^3$ form. The solution is to turn simplification off first (see Section 6.5 [Simplification Modes], page 142), or to run `a x` without a numeric prefix argument so that it expands all the way in one step.

The `a a` (`calc-apart`) [apart] command expands a rational function by partial fractions. A rational function is the quotient of two polynomials; `apart` pulls this apart into a sum of rational functions with simple denominators. In algebraic notation, the `apart` function allows a second argument that specifies which variable to use as the "base"; by default, Calc chooses the base variable automatically.

The `a n` (`calc-normalize-rat`) [nrat] command attempts to arrange a formula into a quotient of two polynomials. For example, given $1 + (a + b/c)/d$, the result would be $(b + ac + cd)/cd$. The quotient is reduced, so that `a n` will simplify $(x^2 + 2x + 1)/(x^2 - 1)$ by dividing out the common factor $x + 1$, yielding $(x + 1)/(x - 1)$.

The `a \` (`calc-poly-div`) [pdiv] command divides two polynomials u and v, yielding a new polynomial q. If several variables occur in the inputs, the inputs are considered multivariate polynomials. (Calc divides by the variable with the largest power in u first, or, in the case of equal powers, chooses the variables in alphabetical order.) For example, dividing $x^2 + 3x + 2$ by $x + 2$ yields $x + 1$. The remainder from the division, if any, is reported at the bottom of the screen and is also placed in the Trail along with the quotient.

Using `pdiv` in algebraic notation, you can specify the particular variable to be used as the base: `pdiv(a,b,x)`. If `pdiv` is given only two arguments (as is always the case with the `a \` command), then it does a multivariate division as outlined above.

The `a %` (`calc-poly-rem`) [`prem`] command divides two polynomials and keeps the remainder r. The quotient q is discarded. For any formulas a and b, the results of `a \` and `a %` satisfy $a = qb + r$. (This is analogous to plain `\` and `%`, which compute the integer quotient and remainder from dividing two numbers.)

The `a /` (`calc-poly-div-rem`) [`pdivrem`] command divides two polynomials and reports both the quotient and the remainder as a vector $[q, r]$. The `H a /` [`pdivide`] command divides two polynomials and constructs the formula $q + r/b$ on the stack. (Naturally if the remainder is zero, this will immediately simplify to q.)

The `a g` (`calc-poly-gcd`) [`pgcd`] command computes the greatest common divisor of two polynomials. (The GCD actually is unique only to within a constant multiplier; Calc attempts to choose a GCD which will be unsurprising.) For example, the `a n` command uses `a g` to take the GCD of the numerator and denominator of a quotient, then divides each by the result using `a \`. (The definition of GCD ensures that this division can take place without leaving a remainder.)

While the polynomials used in operations like `a /` and `a g` often have integer coefficients, this is not required. Calc can also deal with polynomials over the rationals or floating-point reals. Polynomials with modulo-form coefficients are also useful in many applications; if you enter '`(x^2 + 3 x - 1) mod 5`', Calc automatically transforms this into a polynomial over the field of integers mod 5: '`(1 mod 5) x^2 + (3 mod 5) x + (4 mod 5)`'.

Congratulations and thanks go to Ove Ewerlid (`ewerlid@mizar.DoCS.UU.SE`), who contributed many of the polynomial routines used in the above commands.

See Section 10.6.3 [Decomposing Polynomials], page 271, for several useful functions for extracting the individual coefficients of a polynomial.

10.5 Calculus

The following calculus commands do not automatically simplify their inputs or outputs using `calc-simplify`. You may find it helps to do this by hand by typing `a s` or `a e`. It may also help to use `a x` and/or `a c` to arrange a result in the most readable way.

10.5.1 Differentiation

The `a d` (`calc-derivative`) [`deriv`] command computes the derivative of the expression on the top of the stack with respect to some variable, which it will prompt you to enter. Normally, variables in the formula other than the specified differentiation variable are considered constant, i.e., '`deriv(y,x)`' is reduced to zero. With the Hyperbolic flag, the `tderiv` (total derivative) operation is used instead, in which derivatives of variables are not reduced to zero unless those variables are known to be "constant," i.e., independent of any other variables. (The built-in special variables like `pi` are considered constant, as are variables that have been declared `const`; see Section 6.6 [Declarations], page 143.)

With a numeric prefix argument n, this command computes the nth derivative.

When working with trigonometric functions, it is best to switch to Radians mode first (with `m r`). The derivative of 'sin(x)' in degrees is '(pi/180) cos(x)', probably not the expected answer!

If you use the `deriv` function directly in an algebraic formula, you can write 'deriv(f,x,x0)' which represents the derivative of f with respect to x, evaluated at the point $x = x_0$.

If the formula being differentiated contains functions which Calc does not know, the derivatives of those functions are produced by adding primes (apostrophe characters). For example, 'deriv(f(2x), x)' produces '2 f'(2 x)', where the function f' represents the derivative of f.

For functions you have defined with the *Z F* command, Calc expands the functions according to their defining formulas unless you have also defined f' suitably. For example, suppose we define 'sinc(x) = sin(x)/x' using *Z F*. If we then differentiate the formula 'sinc(2 x)', the formula will be expanded to 'sin(2 x) / (2 x)' and differentiated. However, if we also define 'sinc'(x) = dsinc(x)', say, then Calc will write the result as '2 dsinc(2 x)'. See Section 17.4 [Algebraic Definitions], page 369.

For multi-argument functions 'f(x,y,z)', the derivative with respect to the first argument is written 'f'(x,y,z)'; derivatives with respect to the other arguments are 'f'2(x,y,z)' and 'f'3(x,y,z)'. Various higher-order derivatives can be formed in the obvious way, e.g., 'f''(x)' (the second derivative of f) or 'f''2'3(x,y,z)' (f differentiated with respect to each argument once).

10.5.2 Integration

The `a i` (calc-integral) [integ] command computes the indefinite integral of the expression on the top of the stack with respect to a prompted-for variable. The integrator is not guaranteed to work for all integrable functions, but it is able to integrate several large classes of formulas. In particular, any polynomial or rational function (a polynomial divided by a polynomial) is acceptable. (Rational functions don't have to be in explicit quotient form, however; $x/(1 + x^{-2})$ is not strictly a quotient of polynomials, but it is equivalent to $x^3/(x^2 + 1)$, which is.) Also, square roots of terms involving x and x^2 may appear in rational functions being integrated. Finally, rational functions involving trigonometric or hyperbolic functions can be integrated.

With an argument (`C-u a i`), this command will compute the definite integral of the expression on top of the stack. In this case, the command will again prompt for an integration variable, then prompt for a lower limit and an upper limit.

If you use the `integ` function directly in an algebraic formula, you can also write 'integ(f,x,v)' which expresses the resulting indefinite integral in terms of variable v instead of x. With four arguments, 'integ(f(x),x,a,b)' represents a definite integral $\int_a^b f(x)\, dx$.

Please note that the current implementation of Calc's integrator sometimes produces results that are significantly more complex than they need to be. For example, the integral Calc finds for $1/(x+\sqrt{x^2+1})$ is several times more complicated than the answer Mathematica returns for the same input, although the two forms are numerically equivalent. Also, any indefinite integral should be considered to have an arbitrary constant of integration added to it, although Calc does not write an explicit constant of integration in its result.

For example, Calc's solution for $1/(1 + \tan x)$ differs from the solution given in the *CRC Math Tables* by a constant factor of $\pi i/2$ due to a different choice of constant of integration.

The Calculator remembers all the integrals it has done. If conditions change in a way that would invalidate the old integrals, say, a switch from Degrees to Radians mode, then they will be thrown out. If you suspect this is not happening when it should, use the `calc-flush-caches` command; see Section 3.11.3 [Caches], page 114.

Calc normally will pursue integration by substitution or integration by parts up to 3 nested times before abandoning an approach as fruitless. If the integrator is taking too long, you can lower this limit by storing a number (like 2) in the variable `IntegLimit`. (The `s I` command is a convenient way to edit `IntegLimit`.) If this variable has no stored value or does not contain a nonnegative integer, a limit of 3 is used. The lower this limit is, the greater the chance that Calc will be unable to integrate a function it could otherwise handle. Raising this limit allows the Calculator to solve more integrals, though the time it takes may grow exponentially. You can monitor the integrator's actions by creating an Emacs buffer called `*Trace*`. If such a buffer exists, the `a i` command will write a log of its actions there.

If you want to manipulate integrals in a purely symbolic way, you can set the integration nesting limit to 0 to prevent all but fast table-lookup solutions of integrals. You might then wish to define rewrite rules for integration by parts, various kinds of substitutions, and so on. See Section 10.11 [Rewrite Rules], page 291.

10.5.3 Customizing the Integrator

Calc has two built-in rewrite rules called `IntegRules` and `IntegAfterRules` which you can edit to define new integration methods. See Section 10.11 [Rewrite Rules], page 291. At each step of the integration process, Calc wraps the current integrand in a call to the fictitious function '`integtry(expr,var)`', where *expr* is the integrand and *var* is the integration variable. If your rules rewrite this to be a plain formula (not a call to `integtry`), then Calc will use this formula as the integral of *expr*. For example, the rule '`integtry(mysin(x),x) := -mycos(x)`' would define a rule to integrate a function `mysin` that acts like the sine function. Then, putting '`4 mysin(2y+1)`' on the stack and typing `a i y` will produce the integral '`-2 mycos(2y+1)`'. Note that Calc has automatically made various transformations on the integral to allow it to use your rule; integral tables generally give rules for '`mysin(a x + b)`', but you don't need to use this much generality in your `IntegRules`.

As a more serious example, the expression '`exp(x)/x`' cannot be integrated in terms of the standard functions, so the "exponential integral" function $\text{Ei}(x)$ was invented to describe it. We can get Calc to do this integral in terms of a made-up `Ei` function by adding the rule '`[integtry(exp(x)/x, x) := Ei(x)]`' to `IntegRules`. Now entering '`exp(2x)/x`' on the stack and typing `a i x` yields '`Ei(2 x)`'. This new rule will work with Calc's various built-in integration methods (such as integration by substitution) to solve a variety of other problems involving `Ei`: For example, now Calc will also be able to integrate '`exp(exp(x))`' and '`ln(ln(x))`' (to get '`Ei(exp(x))`' and '`x ln(ln(x)) - Ei(ln(x))`', respectively).

Your rule may do further integration by calling `integ`. For example, '`integtry(twice(u),x) := twice(integ(u))`' allows Calc to integrate '`twice(sin(x))`' to get '`twice(-cos(x))`'. Note that `integ` was called with only one argument. This notation is allowed only within `IntegRules`; it means "integrate this with respect to the same integration variable." If Calc is unable to integrate `u`, the integration that invoked `IntegRules` also fails. Thus integrating '`twice(f(x))`' fails, returning the unevaluated integral '`integ(twice(f(x)), x)`'. It is still valid to call `integ` with two or more arguments, however; in this case, if `u` is not integrable, `twice` itself will still be integrated: If the above rule is changed to '`... := twice(integ(u,x))`', then integrating '`twice(f(x))`' will yield '`twice(integ(f(x),x))`'.

If a rule instead produces the formula '`integsubst(`*sexpr*`, `*svar*`)`', either replacing the top-level `integtry` call or nested anywhere inside the expression, then Calc will apply the substitution '`u = `*sexpr*`(`*svar*`)`' to try to integrate the original *expr*. For example, the rule '`sqrt(a) := integsubst(sqrt(x),x)`' says that if Calc ever finds a square root in the integrand, it should attempt the substitution '`u = sqrt(x)`'. (This particular rule is unnecessary because Calc always tries "obvious" substitutions where *sexpr* actually appears in the integrand.) The variable *svar* may be the same as the *var* that appeared in the call to `integtry`, but it need not be.

When integrating according to an `integsubst`, Calc uses the equation solver to find the inverse of *sexpr* (if the integrand refers to *var* anywhere except in subexpressions that exactly match *sexpr*). It uses the differentiator to find the derivative of *sexpr* and/or its inverse (it has two methods that use one derivative or the other). You can also specify these items by adding extra arguments to the `integsubst` your rules construct; the general form is '`integsubst(`*sexpr*`, `*svar*`, `*sinv*`, `*sprime*`)`', where *sinv* is the inverse of *sexpr* (still written as a function of *svar*), and *sprime* is the derivative of *sexpr* with respect to *svar*. If you don't specify these things, and Calc is not able to work them out on its own with the information it knows, then your substitution rule will work only in very specific, simple cases.

Calc applies `IntegRules` as if by *C-u 1 a r IntegRules*; in other words, Calc stops rewriting as soon as any rule in your rule set succeeds. (If it weren't for this, the '`integsubst(sqrt(x),x)`' example above would keep on adding layers of `integsubst` calls forever!)

Another set of rules, stored in `IntegSimpRules`, are applied every time the integrator uses algebraic simplifications to simplify an intermediate result. For example, putting the rule '`twice(x) := 2 x`' into `IntegSimpRules` would tell Calc to convert the `twice` function into a form it knows whenever integration is attempted.

One more way to influence the integrator is to define a function with the *Z F* command (see Section 17.4 [Algebraic Definitions], page 369). Calc's integrator automatically expands such functions according to their defining formulas, even if you originally asked for the function to be left unevaluated for symbolic arguments. (Certain other Calc systems, such as the differentiator and the equation solver, also do this.)

Sometimes Calc is able to find a solution to your integral, but it expresses the result in a way that is unnecessarily complicated. If this happens, you can either use `integsubst` as described above to try to hint at a more direct path to the desired result, or you can use `IntegAfterRules`. This is an extra rule set that runs after the main integrator returns its result; basically, Calc does an *a r IntegAfterRules* on the result before showing it to you. (It also does algebraic simplifications, without `IntegSimpRules`, after that to further simplify the result.) For example, Calc's integrator sometimes produces expressions of the form '`ln(1+x) - ln(1-x)`'; the default `IntegAfterRules` rewrite this into the more readable form '`2 arctanh(x)`'. Note that, unlike `IntegRules`, `IntegSimpRules` and

`IntegAfterRules` are applied any number of times until no further changes are possible. Rewriting by `IntegAfterRules` occurs only after the main integrator has finished, not at every step as for `IntegRules` and `IntegSimpRules`.

10.5.4 Numerical Integration

If you want a purely numerical answer to an integration problem, you can use the `a I` (`calc-num-integral`) [`ninteg`] command. This command prompts for an integration variable, a lower limit, and an upper limit. Except for the integration variable, all other variables that appear in the integrand formula must have stored values. (A stored value, if any, for the integration variable itself is ignored.)

Numerical integration works by evaluating your formula at many points in the specified interval. Calc uses an "open Romberg" method; this means that it does not evaluate the formula actually at the endpoints (so that it is safe to integrate '`sin(x)/x`' from zero, for example). Also, the Romberg method works especially well when the function being integrated is fairly smooth. If the function is not smooth, Calc will have to evaluate it at quite a few points before it can accurately determine the value of the integral.

Integration is much faster when the current precision is small. It is best to set the precision to the smallest acceptable number of digits before you use `a I`. If Calc appears to be taking too long, press `C-g` to halt it and try a lower precision. If Calc still appears to need hundreds of evaluations, check to make sure your function is well-behaved in the specified interval.

It is possible for the lower integration limit to be '`-inf`' (minus infinity). Likewise, the upper limit may be plus infinity. Calc internally transforms the integral into an equivalent one with finite limits. However, integration to or across singularities is not supported: The integral of '`1/sqrt(x)`' from 0 to 1 exists (it can be found by Calc's symbolic integrator, for example), but `a I` will fail because the integrand goes to infinity at one of the endpoints.

10.5.5 Taylor Series

The `a t` (`calc-taylor`) [`taylor`] command computes a power series expansion or Taylor series of a function. You specify the variable and the desired number of terms. You may give an expression of the form '`var = a`' or '`var - a`' instead of just a variable to produce a Taylor expansion about the point a. You may specify the number of terms with a numeric prefix argument; otherwise the command will prompt you for the number of terms. Note that many series expansions have coefficients of zero for some terms, so you may appear to get fewer terms than you asked for.

If the `a i` command is unable to find a symbolic integral for a function, you can get an approximation by integrating the function's Taylor series.

10.6 Solving Equations

The `a S` (`calc-solve-for`) [`solve`] command rearranges an equation to solve for a specific variable. An equation is an expression of the form $L = R$. For example, the command `a S x` will rearrange $y = 3x + 6$ to the form, $x = y/3 - 2$. If the input is not an equation, it is treated like an equation of the form $X = 0$.

This command also works for inequalities, as in $y < 3x + 6$. Some inequalities cannot be solved where the analogous equation could be; for example, solving $a < b\,c$ for b is impossible without knowing the sign of c. In this case, a S will produce the result $b \mathrel{!=} a/c$ (using the not-equal-to operator) to signify that the direction of the inequality is now unknown. The inequality $a \leq bc$ is not even partially solved. See Section 6.6 [Declarations], page 143, for a way to tell Calc that the signs of the variables in a formula are in fact known.

Two useful commands for working with the result of a S are a . (see Section 10.10 [Logical Operations], page 288), which converts $x = y/3 - 2$ to $y/3 - 2$, and s l (see Section 12.4 [Let Command], page 327) which evaluates another formula with x set equal to $y/3 - 2$.

10.6.1 Multiple Solutions

Some equations have more than one solution. The Hyperbolic flag (H a S) [fsolve] tells the solver to report the fully general family of solutions. It will invent variables n1, n2, ..., which represent independent arbitrary integers, and s1, s2, ..., which represent independent arbitrary signs (either $+1$ or -1). If you don't use the Hyperbolic flag, Calc will use zero in place of all arbitrary integers, and plus one in place of all arbitrary signs. Note that variables like n1 and s1 are not given any special interpretation in Calc except by the equation solver itself. As usual, you can use the s l (calc-let) command to obtain solutions for various actual values of these variables.

For example, ' x^2 = y RET H a S x RET solves to get 'x = s1 sqrt(y)', indicating that the two solutions to the equation are 'sqrt(y)' and '-sqrt(y)'. Another way to think about it is that the square-root operation is really a two-valued function; since every Calc function must return a single result, sqrt chooses to return the positive result. Then H a S doctors this result using s1 to indicate the full set of possible values of the mathematical square-root.

There is a similar phenomenon going the other direction: Suppose we solve 'sqrt(y) = x' for y. Calc squares both sides to get 'y = x^2'. This is correct, except that it introduces some dubious solutions. Consider solving 'sqrt(y) = -3': Calc will report $y = 9$ as a valid solution, which is true in the mathematical sense of square-root, but false (there is no solution) for the actual Calc positive-valued sqrt. This happens for both a S and H a S.

If you store a positive integer in the Calc variable GenCount, then Calc will generate formulas of the form 'as(n)' for arbitrary signs, and 'an(n)' for arbitrary integers, where n represents successive values taken by incrementing GenCount by one. While the normal arbitrary sign and integer symbols start over at s1 and n1 with each new Calc command, the GenCount approach will give each arbitrary value a name that is unique throughout the entire Calc session. Also, the arbitrary values are function calls instead of variables, which is advantageous in some cases. For example, you can make a rewrite rule that recognizes all arbitrary signs using a pattern like 'as(n)'. The s l command only works on variables, but you can use the a b (calc-substitute) command to substitute actual values for function calls like 'as(3)'.

The s G (calc-edit-GenCount) command is a convenient way to create or edit this variable. Press C-c C-c to finish.

If you have not stored a value in GenCount, or if the value in that variable is not a positive integer, the regular s1/n1 notation is used.

With the Inverse flag, I a S [finv] treats the expression on top of the stack as a function of the specified variable and solves to find the inverse function, written in terms of the same variable. For example, *I a S x* inverts $2x + 6$ to $x/2 - 3$. You can use both Inverse and Hyperbolic [ffinv] to obtain a fully general inverse, as described above.

Some equations, specifically polynomials, have a known, finite number of solutions. The *a P* (`calc-poly-roots`) [roots] command uses *H a S* to solve an equation in general form, then, for all arbitrary-sign variables like `s1`, and all arbitrary-integer variables like `n1` for which `n1` only usefully varies over a finite range, it expands these variables out to all their possible values. The results are collected into a vector, which is returned. For example, 'roots(x^4 = 1, x)' returns the four solutions '[1, -1, (0, 1), (0, -1)]'. Generally an *n*th degree polynomial will always have *n* roots on the complex plane. (If you have given a **real** declaration for the solution variable, then only the real-valued solutions, if any, will be reported; see Section 6.6 [Declarations], page 143.)

Note that because *a P* uses *H a S*, it is able to deliver symbolic solutions if the polynomial has symbolic coefficients. Also note that Calc's solver is not able to get exact symbolic solutions to all polynomials. Polynomials containing powers up to x^4 can always be solved exactly; polynomials of higher degree sometimes can be: $x^6 + x^3 + 1$ is converted to $(x^3)^2 + (x^3) + 1$, which can be solved for x^3 using the quadratic equation, and then for x by taking cube roots. But in many cases, like $x^6 + x + 1$, Calc does not know how to rewrite the polynomial into a form it can solve. The *a P* command can still deliver a list of numerical roots, however, provided that Symbolic mode (*m s*) is not turned on. (If you work with Symbolic mode on, recall that the *N* (`calc-eval-num`) key is a handy way to reevaluate the formula on the stack with Symbolic mode temporarily off.) Naturally, *a P* can only provide numerical roots if the polynomial coefficients are all numbers (real or complex).

10.6.2 Solving Systems of Equations

You can also use the commands described above to solve systems of simultaneous equations. Just create a vector of equations, then specify a vector of variables for which to solve. (You can omit the surrounding brackets when entering the vector of variables at the prompt.)

For example, putting '[x + y = a, x - y = b]' on the stack and typing *a S x,y RET* produces the vector of solutions '[x = a - (a-b)/2, y = (a-b)/2]'. The result vector will have the same length as the variables vector, and the variables will be listed in the same order there. Note that the solutions are not always simplified as far as possible; the solution for *x* here could be improved by an application of the *a n* command.

Calc's algorithm works by trying to eliminate one variable at a time by solving one of the equations for that variable and then substituting into the other equations. Calc will try all the possibilities, but you can speed things up by noting that Calc first tries to eliminate the first variable with the first equation, then the second variable with the second equation, and so on. It also helps to put the simpler (e.g., more linear) equations toward the front of the list. Calc's algorithm will solve any system of linear equations, and also many kinds of nonlinear systems.

Normally there will be as many variables as equations. If you give fewer variables than equations (an "over-determined" system of equations), Calc will find a partial solution. For example, typing *a S y RET* with the above system of equations would produce '[y = a - x]'. There are now several ways to express this solution in terms of the original variables; Calc uses the first one that it finds. You can control the choice by adding variable specifiers of the form 'elim(v)' to the variables list. This says that *v* should be eliminated from the equations; the variable will not appear at all in the solution. For example, typing `a S y,elim(x)` would yield '`[y = a - (b+a)/2]`'.

If the variables list contains only `elim` specifiers, Calc simply eliminates those variables from the equations and then returns the resulting set of equations. For example, `a S elim(x)` produces '`[a - 2 y = b]`'. Every variable eliminated will reduce the number of equations in the system by one.

Again, `a S` gives you one solution to the system of equations. If there are several solutions, you can use `H a S` to get a general family of solutions, or, if there is a finite number of solutions, you can use `a P` to get a list. (In the latter case, the result will take the form of a matrix where the rows are different solutions and the columns correspond to the variables you requested.)

Another way to deal with certain kinds of overdetermined systems of equations is the `a F` command, which does least-squares fitting to satisfy the equations. See Section 10.8 [Curve Fitting], page 275.

10.6.3 Decomposing Polynomials

The `poly` function takes a polynomial and a variable as arguments, and returns a vector of polynomial coefficients (constant coefficient first). For example, '`poly(x^3 + 2 x, x)`' returns $[0, 2, 0, 1]$. If the input is not a polynomial in x, the call to `poly` is left in symbolic form. If the input does not involve the variable x, the input is returned in a list of length one, representing a polynomial with only a constant coefficient. The call '`poly(x, x)`' returns the vector $[0, 1]$. The last element of the returned vector is guaranteed to be nonzero; note that '`poly(0, x)`' returns the empty vector $[]$. Note also that x may actually be any formula; for example, '`poly(sin(x)^2 - sin(x) + 3, sin(x))`' returns $[3, -1, 1]$.

To get the x^k coefficient of polynomial p, use '`poly(p, x)_(k+1)`'. To get the degree of polynomial p, use '`vlen(poly(p, x)) - 1`'. For example, '`poly((x+1)^4, x)`' returns '`[1, 4, 6, 4, 1]`', so '`poly((x+1)^4, x)_(2+1)`' gives the x^2 coefficient of this polynomial, 6.

One important feature of the solver is its ability to recognize formulas which are "essentially" polynomials. This ability is made available to the user through the `gpoly` function, which is used just like `poly`: '`gpoly(expr, var)`'. If expr is a polynomial in some term which includes var, then this function will return a vector '`[x, c, a]`' where x is the term that depends on var, c is a vector of polynomial coefficients (like the one returned by `poly`), and a is a multiplier which is usually 1. Basically, '`expr = a*(c_1 + c_2 x + c_3 x^2 + ...)`'. The last element of c is guaranteed to be non-zero, and c will not equal '`[1]`' (i.e., the trivial decomposition expr = x is not considered a polynomial). One side effect is that '`gpoly(x, x)`' and '`gpoly(6, x)`', both of which might be expected to recognize their arguments as polynomials, will not because the decomposition is considered trivial.

For example, '`gpoly((x-2)^2, x)`' returns '`[x, [4, -4, 1], 1]`', since the expanded form of this polynomial is $4 - 4x + x^2$.

The term x may itself be a polynomial in var. This is done to reduce the size of the c vector. For example, '`gpoly(x^4 + x^2 - 1, x)`' returns '`[x^2, [-1, 1, 1], 1]`', since a quadratic polynomial in x^2 is easier to solve than a quartic polynomial in x.

A few more examples of the kinds of polynomials `gpoly` can discover:

```
sin(x) - 1          [sin(x), [-1, 1], 1]
x + 1/x - 1         [x, [1, -1, 1], 1/x]
```

```
x + 1/x                      [x^2, [1, 1], 1/x]
x^3 + 2 x                    [x^2, [2, 1], x]
x + x^2:3 + sqrt(x)          [x^1:6, [1, 1, 0, 1], x^1:2]
x^(2a) + 2 x^a + 5           [x^a, [5, 2, 1], 1]
(exp(-x) + exp(x)) / 2       [e^(2 x), [0.5, 0.5], e^-x]
```

The `poly` and `gpoly` functions accept a third integer argument which specifies the largest degree of polynomial that is acceptable. If this is n, then only c vectors of length $n + 1$ or less will be returned. Otherwise, the `poly` or `gpoly` call will remain in symbolic form. For example, the equation solver can handle quartics and smaller polynomials, so it calls 'gpoly(*expr*, *var*, 4)' to discover whether *expr* can be treated by its linear, quadratic, cubic, or quartic formulas.

The `pdeg` function computes the degree of a polynomial; 'pdeg(p,x)' is the highest power of x that appears in p. This is the same as 'vlen(poly(p,x))-1', but is much more efficient. If p is constant with respect to x, then 'pdeg(p,x) = 0'. If p is not a polynomial in x (e.g., 'pdeg(2 cos(x), x)', the function remains unevaluated. It is possible to omit the second argument x, in which case 'pdeg(p)' returns the highest total degree of any term of the polynomial, counting all variables that appear in p. Note that pdeg(c) = pdeg(c,x) = 0 for any nonzero constant c; the degree of the constant zero is considered to be `-inf` (minus infinity).

The `plead` function finds the leading term of a polynomial. Thus 'plead(p,x)' is equivalent to 'poly(p,x)_vlen(poly(p,x))', though again more efficient. In particular, 'plead((2x+1)^10, x)' returns 1024 without expanding out the list of coefficients. The value of `plead(p,x)` will be zero only if $p = 0$.

The `pcont` function finds the *content* of a polynomial. This is the greatest common divisor of all the coefficients of the polynomial. With two arguments, `pcont(p,x)` effectively uses 'poly(p,x)' to get a list of coefficients, then uses `pgcd` (the polynomial GCD function) to combine these into an answer. For example, 'pcont(4 x y^2 + 6 x^2 y, x)' is '2 y'. The content is basically the "biggest" polynomial that can be divided into p exactly. The sign of the content is the same as the sign of the leading coefficient.

With only one argument, 'pcont(p)' computes the numerical content of the polynomial, i.e., the `gcd` of the numerical coefficients of all the terms in the formula. Note that `gcd` is defined on rational numbers as well as integers; it computes the `gcd` of the numerators and the `lcm` of the denominators. Thus 'pcont(4:3 x y^2 + 6 x^2 y)' returns 2:3. Dividing the polynomial by this number will clear all the denominators, as well as dividing by any common content in the numerators. The numerical content of a polynomial is negative only if all the coefficients in the polynomial are negative.

The `pprim` function finds the *primitive part* of a polynomial, which is simply the polynomial divided (using `pdiv` if necessary) by its content. If the input polynomial has rational coefficients, the result will have integer coefficients in simplest terms.

10.7 Numerical Solutions

Not all equations can be solved symbolically. The commands in this section use numerical algorithms that can find a solution to a specific instance of an equation to any desired accuracy. Note that the numerical commands are slower than their algebraic cousins; it is a good idea to try a S before resorting to these commands.

(See Section 10.8 [Curve Fitting], page 275, for some other, more specialized, operations on numerical data.)

10.7.1 Root Finding

The `a R` (`calc-find-root`) [root] command finds a numerical solution (or *root*) of an equation. (This command treats inequalities the same as equations. If the input is any other kind of formula, it is interpreted as an equation of the form $X = 0$.)

The `a R` command requires an initial guess on the top of the stack, and a formula in the second-to-top position. It prompts for a solution variable, which must appear in the formula. All other variables that appear in the formula must have assigned values, i.e., when a value is assigned to the solution variable and the formula is evaluated with `=`, it should evaluate to a number. Any assigned value for the solution variable itself is ignored and unaffected by this command.

When the command completes, the initial guess is replaced on the stack by a vector of two numbers: The value of the solution variable that solves the equation, and the difference between the lefthand and righthand sides of the equation at that value. Ordinarily, the second number will be zero or very nearly zero. (Note that Calc uses a slightly higher precision while finding the root, and thus the second number may be slightly different from the value you would compute from the equation yourself.)

The `v h` (`calc-head`) command is a handy way to extract the first element of the result vector, discarding the error term.

The initial guess can be a real number, in which case Calc searches for a real solution near that number, or a complex number, in which case Calc searches the whole complex plane near that number for a solution, or it can be an interval form which restricts the search to real numbers inside that interval.

Calc tries to use `a d` to take the derivative of the equation. If this succeeds, it uses Newton's method. If the equation is not differentiable Calc uses a bisection method. (If Newton's method appears to be going astray, Calc switches over to bisection if it can, or otherwise gives up. In this case it may help to try again with a slightly different initial guess.) If the initial guess is a complex number, the function must be differentiable.

If the formula (or the difference between the sides of an equation) is negative at one end of the interval you specify and positive at the other end, the root finder is guaranteed to find a root. Otherwise, Calc subdivides the interval into small parts looking for positive and negative values to bracket the root. When your guess is an interval, Calc will not look outside that interval for a root.

The `H a R` [wroot] command is similar to `a R`, except that if the initial guess is an interval for which the function has the same sign at both ends, then rather than subdividing the interval Calc attempts to widen it to enclose a root. Use this mode if you are not sure if the function has a root in your interval.

If the function is not differentiable, and you give a simple number instead of an interval as your initial guess, Calc uses this widening process even if you did not type the Hyperbolic flag. (If the function *is* differentiable, Calc uses Newton's method which does not require a bounding interval in order to work.)

If Calc leaves the `root` or `wroot` function in symbolic form on the stack, it will normally display an explanation for why no root was found. If you miss this explanation, press `w` (`calc-why`) to get it back.

10.7.2 Minimization

The `a N` (`calc-find-minimum`) [`minimize`] command finds a minimum value for a formula. It is very similar in operation to `a R` (`calc-find-root`): You give the formula and an initial guess on the stack, and are prompted for the name of a variable. The guess may be either a number near the desired minimum, or an interval enclosing the desired minimum. The function returns a vector containing the value of the variable which minimizes the formula's value, along with the minimum value itself.

Note that this command looks for a *local* minimum. Many functions have more than one minimum; some, like $x \sin x$, have infinitely many. In fact, there is no easy way to define the "global" minimum of $x \sin x$ but Calc can still locate any particular local minimum for you. Calc basically goes downhill from the initial guess until it finds a point at which the function's value is greater both to the left and to the right. Calc does not use derivatives when minimizing a function.

If your initial guess is an interval and it looks like the minimum occurs at one or the other endpoint of the interval, Calc will return that endpoint only if that endpoint is closed; thus, minimizing $17x$ over [2..3] will return [2, 38], but minimizing over (2..3] would report no minimum found. In general, you should use closed intervals to find literally the minimum value in that range of x, or open intervals to find the local minimum, if any, that happens to lie in that range.

Most functions are smooth and flat near their minimum values. Because of this flatness, if the current precision is, say, 12 digits, the variable can only be determined meaningfully to about six digits. Thus you should set the precision to twice as many digits as you need in your answer.

The `H a N` [`wminimize`] command, analogously to `H a R`, expands the guess interval to enclose a minimum rather than requiring that the minimum lie inside the interval you supply.

The `a X` (`calc-find-maximum`) [`maximize`] and `H a X` [`wmaximize`] commands effectively minimize the negative of the formula you supply.

The formula must evaluate to a real number at all points inside the interval (or near the initial guess if the guess is a number). If the initial guess is a complex number the variable will be minimized over the complex numbers; if it is real or an interval it will be minimized over the reals.

10.7.3 Systems of Equations

The `a R` command can also solve systems of equations. In this case, the equation should instead be a vector of equations, the guess should instead be a vector of numbers (intervals are not supported), and the variable should be a vector of variables. You can omit the brackets while entering the list of variables. Each equation must be differentiable by each variable for this mode to work. The result will be a vector of two vectors: The variable values that solved the system of equations, and the differences between the sides of the equations with those variable values. There must be the same number of equations as variables. Since only plain numbers are allowed as guesses, the Hyperbolic flag has no effect when solving a system of equations.

It is also possible to minimize over many variables with a N (or maximize with a X). Once again the variable name should be replaced by a vector of variables, and the initial guess should be an equal-sized vector of initial guesses. But, unlike the case of multidimensional a R, the formula being minimized should still be a single formula, *not* a vector. Beware that multidimensional minimization is currently *very* slow.

10.8 Curve Fitting

The a F command fits a set of data to a *model formula*, such as $y = mx + b$ where m and b are parameters to be determined. For a typical set of measured data there will be no single m and b that exactly fit the data; in this case, Calc chooses values of the parameters that provide the closest possible fit. The model formula can be entered in various ways after the key sequence a F is pressed.

If the letter P is pressed after a F but before the model description is entered, the data as well as the model formula will be plotted after the formula is determined. This will be indicated by a "P" in the minibuffer after the help message.

10.8.1 Linear Fits

The a F (`calc-curve-fit`) [fit] command attempts to fit a set of data (x and y vectors of numbers) to a straight line, polynomial, or other function of x. For the moment we will consider only the case of fitting to a line, and we will ignore the issue of whether or not the model was in fact a good fit for the data.

In a standard linear least-squares fit, we have a set of (x, y) data points that we wish to fit to the model $y = mx + b$ by adjusting the parameters m and b to make the y values calculated from the formula be as close as possible to the actual y values in the data set. (In a polynomial fit, the model is instead, say, $y = ax^3 + bx^2 + cx + d$. In a multilinear fit, we have data points of the form (x_1, x_2, x_3, y) and our model is $y = ax_1 + bx_2 + cx_3 + d$. These will be discussed later.)

In the model formula, variables like x and x_2 are called the *independent variables*, and y is the *dependent variable*. Variables like m, a, and b are called the *parameters* of the model.

The a F command takes the data set to be fitted from the stack. By default, it expects the data in the form of a matrix. For example, for a linear or polynomial fit, this would be a $2 \times N$ matrix where the first row is a list of x values and the second row has the corresponding y values. For the multilinear fit shown above, the matrix would have four rows (x_1, x_2, x_3, and y, respectively).

If you happen to have an $N \times 2$ matrix instead of a $2 \times N$ matrix, just press v t first to transpose the matrix.

After you type a F, Calc prompts you to select a model. For a linear fit, press the digit 1.

Calc then prompts for you to name the variables. By default it chooses high letters like x and y for independent variables and low letters like a and b for parameters. (The dependent variable doesn't need a name.) The two kinds of variables are separated by a semicolon.

Since you generally care more about the names of the independent variables than of the parameters, Calc also allows you to name only those and let the parameters use default names.

For example, suppose the data matrix

$$\begin{pmatrix} 1 & 2 & 3 & 4 & 5 \\ 5 & 7 & 9 & 11 & 13 \end{pmatrix}$$

is on the stack and we wish to do a simple linear fit. Type a F, then 1 for the model, then RET to use the default names. The result will be the formula $3. + 2.x$ on the stack. Calc has created the model expression a + b x, then found the optimal values of a and b to fit the data. (In this case, it was able to find an exact fit.) Calc then substituted those values for a and b in the model formula.

The a F command puts two entries in the trail. One is, as always, a copy of the result that went to the stack; the other is a vector of the actual parameter values, written as equations: $[a = 3, b = 2]$, in case you'd rather read them in a list than pick them out of the formula. (You can type t y to move this vector to the stack; see Section 5.3 [Trail Commands], page 135.

Specifying a different independent variable name will affect the resulting formula: a F 1 k RET produces 3 + 2 k. Changing the parameter names (say, a F 1 k;b,m RET) will affect the equations that go into the trail.

To see what happens when the fit is not exact, we could change the number 13 in the data matrix to 14 and try the fit again. The result is:

    2.6 + 2.2 x

Evaluating this formula, say with v x 5 RET TAB V M $ RET, shows a reasonably close match to the y-values in the data.

    [4.8, 7., 9.2, 11.4, 13.6]

Since there is no line which passes through all the n data points, Calc has chosen a line that best approximates the data points using the method of least squares. The idea is to define the *chi-square* error measure

$$\chi^2 = \sum_{i=1}^{N}(y_i - (a + bx_i))^2$$

which is clearly zero if $a+bx$ exactly fits all data points, and increases as various $a+bx_i$ values fail to match the corresponding y_i values. There are several reasons why the summand is squared, one of them being to ensure that $\chi^2 \geq 0$. Least-squares fitting simply chooses the values of a and b for which the error χ^2 is as small as possible.

Other kinds of models do the same thing but with a different model formula in place of $a + bx_i$.

A numeric prefix argument causes the a F command to take the data in some other form than one big matrix. A positive argument n will take N items from the stack, corresponding to the n rows of a data matrix. In the linear case, n must be 2 since there is always one independent variable and one dependent variable.

A prefix of zero or plain C-u is a compromise; Calc takes two items from the stack, an n-row matrix of x values, and a vector of y values. If there is only one independent variable, the x values can be either a one-row matrix or a plain vector, in which case the C-u prefix is the same as a C-u 2 prefix.

10.8.2 Polynomial and Multilinear Fits

To fit the data to higher-order polynomials, just type one of the digits 2 through 9 when prompted for a model. For example, we could fit the original data matrix from the previous section (with 13, not 14) to a parabola instead of a line by typing a F 2 RET.

      2.00000000001 x - 1.5e-12 x^2 + 2.99999999999

Note that since the constant and linear terms are enough to fit the data exactly, it's no surprise that Calc chose a tiny contribution for x^2. (The fact that it's not exactly zero is due only to roundoff error. Since our data are exact integers, we could get an exact answer by typing m f first to get Fraction mode. Then the x^2 term would vanish altogether. Usually, though, the data being fitted will be approximate floats so Fraction mode won't help.)

Doing the a F 2 fit on the data set with 14 instead of 13 gives a much larger x^2 contribution, as Calc bends the line slightly to improve the fit.

      0.142857142855 x^2 + 1.34285714287 x + 3.59999999998

An important result from the theory of polynomial fitting is that it is always possible to fit n data points exactly using a polynomial of degree $n-1$, sometimes called an *interpolating polynomial*. Using the modified (14) data matrix, a model number of 4 gives a polynomial that exactly matches all five data points:

      0.04167 x^4 - 0.4167 x^3 + 1.458 x^2 - 0.08333 x + 4.

The actual coefficients we get with a precision of 12, like 0.0416666663588, clearly suffer from loss of precision. It is a good idea to increase the working precision to several digits beyond what you need when you do a fitting operation. Or, if your data are exact, use Fraction mode to get exact results.

You can type i instead of a digit at the model prompt to fit the data exactly to a polynomial. This just counts the number of columns of the data matrix to choose the degree of the polynomial automatically.

Fitting data "exactly" to high-degree polynomials is not always a good idea, though. High-degree polynomials have a tendency to wiggle uncontrollably in between the fitting data points. Also, if the exact-fit polynomial is going to be used to interpolate or extrapolate the data, it is numerically better to use the a p command described below. See Section 10.8.6 [Interpolation], page 285.

Another generalization of the linear model is to assume the y values are a sum of linear contributions from several x values. This is a *multilinear* fit, and it is also selected by the 1 digit key. (Calc decides whether the fit is linear or multilinear by counting the rows in the data matrix.)

Given the data matrix,

      [[1,   2,   3,   4,   5]
        [7,   2,   3,   5,   2]
        [14.5, 15, 18.5, 22.5, 24]]

the command a F 1 RET will call the first row x and the second row y, and will fit the values in the third row to the model $a + bx + cy$.

      8. + 3. x + 0.5 y

Calc can do multilinear fits with any number of independent variables (i.e., with any number of data rows).

Yet another variation is *homogeneous* linear models, in which the constant term is known to be zero. In the linear case, this means the model formula is simply ax; in the multilinear case, the model might be $ax + by + cz$; and in the polynomial case, the model could be $ax + bx^2 + cx^3$. You can get a homogeneous linear or multilinear model by pressing the letter *h* followed by a regular model key, like *1* or *2*. This will be indicated by an "h" in the minibuffer after the help message.

It is certainly possible to have other constrained linear models, like $2.3 + ax$ or $a - 4x$. While there is no single key to select models like these, a later section shows how to enter any desired model by hand. In the first case, for example, you would enter a F ' 2.3 + a x.

Another class of models that will work but must be entered by hand are multinomial fits, e.g., $a + bx + cy + dx^2 + ey^2 + fxy$.

10.8.3 Error Estimates for Fits

With the Hyperbolic flag, H a F [`efit`] performs the same fitting operation as a F, but reports the coefficients as error forms instead of plain numbers. Fitting our two data matrices (first with 13, then with 14) to a line with H a F gives the results,

```
3. + 2. x
2.6 +/- 0.382970843103 + 2.2 +/- 0.115470053838 x
```

In the first case the estimated errors are zero because the linear fit is perfect. In the second case, the errors are nonzero but moderately small, because the data are still very close to linear.

It is also possible for the *input* to a fitting operation to contain error forms. The data values must either all include errors or all be plain numbers. Error forms can go anywhere but generally go on the numbers in the last row of the data matrix. If the last row contains error forms 'y_i +/- σ_i', then the χ^2 statistic is now,

$$\chi^2 = \sum_{i=1}^{N} \left(\frac{y_i - (a + bx_i)}{\sigma_i} \right)^2$$

so that data points with larger error estimates contribute less to the fitting operation.

If there are error forms on other rows of the data matrix, all the errors for a given data point are combined; the square root of the sum of the squares of the errors forms the σ_i used for the data point.

Both a F and H a F can accept error forms in the input matrix, although if you are concerned about error analysis you will probably use H a F so that the output also contains error estimates.

If the input contains error forms but all the σ_i values are the same, it is easy to see that the resulting fitted model will be the same as if the input did not have error forms at all (χ^2 is simply scaled uniformly by $1/\sigma^2$, which doesn't affect where it has a minimum). But there *will* be a difference in the estimated errors of the coefficients reported by H a F.

Consult any text on statistical modeling of data for a discussion of where these error estimates come from and how they should be interpreted.

With the Inverse flag, *I a F* [xfit] produces even more information. The result is a vector of six items:

1. The model formula with error forms for its coefficients or parameters. This is the result that *H a F* would have produced.

2. A vector of "raw" parameter values for the model. These are the polynomial coefficients or other parameters as plain numbers, in the same order as the parameters appeared in the final prompt of the *I a F* command. For polynomials of degree d, this vector will have length $M = d + 1$ with the constant term first.

3. The covariance matrix C computed from the fit. This is an mxm symmetric matrix; the diagonal elements C_{jj} are the variances σ_j^2 of the parameters. The other elements are covariances σ_{ij}^2 that describe the correlation between pairs of parameters. (A related set of numbers, the *linear correlation coefficients* r_{ij}, are defined as $\sigma_{ij}^2 / \sigma_i \sigma_j$.)

4. A vector of M "parameter filter" functions whose meanings are described below. If no filters are necessary this will instead be an empty vector; this is always the case for the polynomial and multilinear fits described so far.

5. The value of χ^2 for the fit, calculated by the formulas shown above. This gives a measure of the quality of the fit; statisticians consider $\chi^2 \approx N - M$ to indicate a moderately good fit (where again N is the number of data points and M is the number of parameters).

6. A measure of goodness of fit expressed as a probability Q. This is computed from the `utpc` probability distribution function using χ^2 with $N - M$ degrees of freedom. A value of 0.5 implies a good fit; some texts recommend that often $Q = 0.1$ or even 0.001 can signify an acceptable fit. In particular, χ^2 statistics assume the errors in your inputs follow a normal (Gaussian) distribution; if they don't, you may have to accept smaller values of Q.

   The Q value is computed only if the input included error estimates. Otherwise, Calc will report the symbol `nan` for Q. The reason is that in this case the χ^2 value has effectively been used to estimate the original errors in the input, and thus there is no redundant information left over to use for a confidence test.

10.8.4 Standard Nonlinear Models

The *a F* command also accepts other kinds of models besides lines and polynomials. Some common models have quick single-key abbreviations; others must be entered by hand as algebraic formulas.

Here is a complete list of the standard models recognized by *a F*:

1	Linear or multilinear. $a + bx + cy + dz$.
2-9	Polynomials. $a + bx + cx^2 + dx^3$.
e	Exponential. $a \exp(bx) \exp(cy)$.
E	Base-10 exponential. $a\ 10\verb|^|(bx)\ 10\verb|^|(cy)$.
x	Exponential (alternate notation). $\exp(a + bx + cy)$.
X	Base-10 exponential (alternate). $10\verb|^|(a + bx + cy)$.
l	Logarithmic. $a + b \ln(x) + c \ln(y)$.

L   Base-10 logarithmic. $a + b\ \mathtt{log10}(x) + c\ \mathtt{log10}(y)$.

^   General exponential. $ab^x c^y$.

p   Power law. $ax^b y^c$.

q   Quadratic. $a + b(x-c)^2 + d(x-e)^2$.

g   Gaussian. $\frac{a}{b\sqrt{2\pi}} \exp\left(-\frac{1}{2}\left(\frac{x-c}{b}\right)^2\right)$.

s   Logistic s curve. $a/(1 + e^{b(x-c)})$.

b   Logistic bell curve. $ae^{b(x-c)}/(1 + e^{b(x-c)})^2$.

o   Hubbert linearization. $\frac{y}{x} = a(1 - x/b)$.

All of these models are used in the usual way; just press the appropriate letter at the model prompt, and choose variable names if you wish. The result will be a formula as shown in the above table, with the best-fit values of the parameters substituted. (You may find it easier to read the parameter values from the vector that is placed in the trail.)

All models except Gaussian, logistics, Hubbert and polynomials can generalize as shown to any number of independent variables. Also, all the built-in models except for the logistic and Hubbert curves have an additive or multiplicative parameter shown as a in the above table which can be replaced by zero or one, as appropriate, by typing h before the model key.

Note that many of these models are essentially equivalent, but express the parameters slightly differently. For example, ab^x and the other two exponential models are all algebraic rearrangements of each other. Also, the "quadratic" model is just a degree-2 polynomial with the parameters expressed differently. Use whichever form best matches the problem.

The HP-28/48 calculators support four different models for curve fitting, called LIN, LOG, EXP, and PWR. These correspond to Calc models 'a + b x', 'a + b ln(x)', 'a exp(b x)', and 'a x^b', respectively. In each case, a is what the HP-48 identifies as the "intercept," and b is what it calls the "slope."

If the model you want doesn't appear on this list, press ' (the apostrophe key) at the model prompt to enter any algebraic formula, such as m x - b, as the model. (Not all models will work, though—see the next section for details.)

The model can also be an equation like $y = mx + b$. In this case, Calc thinks of all the rows of the data matrix on equal terms; this model effectively has two parameters (m and b) and two independent variables (x and y), with no "dependent" variables. Model equations do not need to take this $y =$ form. For example, the implicit line equation $ax + by = 1$ works fine as a model.

When you enter a model, Calc makes an alphabetical list of all the variables that appear in the model. These are used for the default parameters, independent variables, and dependent variable (in that order). If you enter a plain formula (not an equation), Calc assumes the dependent variable does not appear in the formula and thus does not need a name.

For example, if the model formula has the variables $a, mu, sigma, t, x$, and the data matrix has three rows (meaning two independent variables), Calc will use $a, mu, sigma$ as the default parameters, and the data rows will be named t and x, respectively. If you enter an equation instead of a plain formula, Calc will use a, mu as the parameters, and $sigma, t, x$ as the three independent variables.

You can, of course, override these choices by entering something different at the prompt. If you leave some variables out of the list, those variables must have stored values and those stored values will be used as constants in the model. (Stored values for the parameters and independent variables are ignored by the a F command.) If you list only independent variables, all the remaining variables in the model formula will become parameters.

If there are $ signs in the model you type, they will stand for parameters and all other variables (in alphabetical order) will be independent. Use $ for one parameter, $$ for another, and so on. Thus $ x + $$ is another way to describe a linear model.

If you type a $ instead of ' at the model prompt itself, Calc will take the model formula from the stack. (The data must then appear at the second stack level.) The same conventions are used to choose which variables in the formula are independent by default and which are parameters.

Models taken from the stack can also be expressed as vectors of two or three elements, [model, vars] or [model, vars, params]. Each of vars and params may be either a variable or a vector of variables. (If params is omitted, all variables in model except those listed as vars are parameters.)

When you enter a model manually with ', Calc puts a 3-vector describing the model in the trail so you can get it back if you wish.

Finally, you can store a model in one of the Calc variables Model1 or Model2, then use this model by typing a F u or a F U (respectively). The value stored in the variable can be any of the formats that a F $ would accept for a model on the stack.

Calc uses the principal values of inverse functions like ln and arcsin when doing fits. For example, when you enter the model 'y = sin(a t + b)' Calc actually uses the easier form 'arcsin(y) = a t + b'. The arcsin function always returns results in the range from −90 to 90 degrees (or the equivalent range in radians). Suppose you had data that you believed to represent roughly three oscillations of a sine wave, so that the argument of the sine might go from zero to 3×360 degrees. The above model would appear to be a good way to determine the true frequency and phase of the sine wave, but in practice it would fail utterly. The righthand side of the actual model 'arcsin(y) = a t + b' will grow smoothly with t, but the lefthand side will bounce back and forth between −90 and 90. No values of a and b can make the two sides match, even approximately.

There is no good solution to this problem at present. You could restrict your data to small enough ranges so that the above problem doesn't occur (i.e., not straddling any peaks in the sine wave). Or, in this case, you could use a totally different method such as Fourier analysis, which is beyond the scope of the a F command. (Unfortunately, Calc does not currently have any facilities for taking Fourier and related transforms.)

10.8.5 Curve Fitting Details

Calc's internal least-squares fitter can only handle multilinear models. More precisely, it can handle any model of the form $af(x, y, z) + bg(x, y, z) + ch(x, y, z)$, where a, b, c are the parameters and x, y, z are the independent variables (of course there can be any number of each, not just three).

In a simple multilinear or polynomial fit, it is easy to see how to convert the model into this form. For example, if the model is $a + bx + cx^2$, then $f(x) = 1$, $g(x) = x$, and $h(x) = x^2$ are suitable functions.

For most other models, Calc uses a variety of algebraic manipulations to try to put the problem into the form

```
Y(x,y,z) = A(a,b,c) F(x,y,z) + B(a,b,c) G(x,y,z) + C(a,b,c) H(x,y,z)
```

where Y, A, B, C, F, G, H are arbitrary functions. It computes Y, F, G, and H for all the data points, does a standard linear fit to find the values of A, B, and C, then uses the equation solver to solve for a, b, c in terms of A, B, C.

A remarkable number of models can be cast into this general form. We'll look at two examples here to see how it works. The power-law model $y = ax^b$ with two independent variables and two parameters can be rewritten as follows:

```
y = a x^b
y = a exp(b ln(x))
y = exp(ln(a) + b ln(x))
ln(y) = ln(a) + b ln(x)
```

which matches the desired form with $Y = \ln(y)$, $A = \ln(a)$, $F = 1$, $B = b$, and $G = \ln(x)$. Calc thus computes the logarithms of your y and x values, does a linear fit for A and B, then solves to get $a = \exp(A)$ and $b = B$.

Another interesting example is the "quadratic" model, which can be handled by expanding according to the distributive law.

```
y = a + b*(x - c)^2
y = a + b c^2 - 2 b c x + b x^2
```

which matches with $Y = y$, $A = a + bc^2$, $F = 1$, $B = -2bc$, $G = x$ (the -2 factor could just as easily have been put into G instead of B), $C = b$, and $H = x^2$.

The Gaussian model looks quite complicated, but a closer examination shows that it's actually similar to the quadratic model but with an exponential that can be brought to the top and moved into Y.

The logistic models cannot be put into general linear form. For these models, and the Hubbert linearization, Calc computes a rough approximation for the parameters, then uses the Levenberg-Marquardt iterative method to refine the approximations.

Another model that cannot be put into general linear form is a Gaussian with a constant background added on, i.e., d + the regular Gaussian formula. If you have a model like this, your best bet is to replace enough of your parameters with constants to make the model linearizable, then adjust the constants manually by doing a series of fits. You can compare the fits by graphing them, by examining the goodness-of-fit measures returned by `I a F`, or by some other method suitable to your application. Note that some models can be linearized in several ways. The Gaussian-plus-d model can be linearized by setting d (the background) to a constant, or by setting b (the standard deviation) and c (the mean) to constants.

To fit a model with constants substituted for some parameters, just store suitable values in those parameter variables, then omit them from the list of parameters when you answer the variables prompt.

A last desperate step would be to use the general-purpose `minimize` function rather than `fit`. After all, both functions solve the problem of minimizing an expression (the χ^2 sum) by adjusting certain parameters in the expression. The `a F` command is able to use a vastly more efficient algorithm due to its special knowledge about linear chi-square sums, but the `a N` command can do the same thing by brute force.

A compromise would be to pick out a few parameters without which the fit is linearizable, and use `minimize` on a call to `fit` which efficiently takes care of the rest of the parameters. The thing to be minimized would be the value of χ^2 returned as the fifth result of the `xfit` function:

```
minimize(xfit(gaus(a,b,c,d,x), x, [a,b,c], data)_5, d, guess)
```

where `gaus` represents the Gaussian model with background, `data` represents the data matrix, and `guess` represents the initial guess for d that `minimize` requires. This operation will only be, shall we say, extraordinarily slow rather than astronomically slow (as would be the case if `minimize` were used by itself to solve the problem).

The `I a F` [`xfit`] command is somewhat trickier when nonlinear models are used. The second item in the result is the vector of "raw" parameters A, B, C. The covariance matrix is written in terms of those raw parameters. The fifth item is a vector of *filter* expressions. This is the empty vector '`[]`' if the raw parameters were the same as the requested parameters, i.e., if $A = a$, $B = b$, and so on (which is always true if the model is already linear in the parameters as written, e.g., for polynomial fits). If the parameters had to be rearranged, the fifth item is instead a vector of one formula per parameter in the original model. The raw parameters are expressed in these "filter" formulas as '`fitdummy(1)`' for A, '`fitdummy(2)`' for B, and so on.

When Calc needs to modify the model to return the result, it replaces '`fitdummy(1)`' in all the filters with the first item in the raw parameters list, and so on for the other raw parameters, then evaluates the resulting filter formulas to get the actual parameter values to be substituted into the original model. In the case of `H a F` and `I a F` where the parameters must be error forms, Calc uses the square roots of the diagonal entries of the covariance matrix as error values for the raw parameters, then lets Calc's standard error-form arithmetic take it from there.

If you use `I a F` with a nonlinear model, be sure to remember that the covariance matrix is in terms of the raw parameters, *not* the actual requested parameters. It's up to you to figure out how to interpret the covariances in the presence of nontrivial filter functions.

Things are also complicated when the input contains error forms. Suppose there are three independent and dependent variables, x, y, and z, one or more of which are error forms in the data. Calc combines all the error values by taking the square root of the sum of the squares of the errors. It then changes x and y to be plain numbers, and makes z into an error form with this combined error. The $Y(x, y, z)$ part of the linearized model is evaluated, and the result should be an error form. The error part of that result is used for σ_i for the data point. If for some reason $Y(x, y, z)$ does not return an error form, the combined error from z is used directly for σ_i. Finally, z is also stripped of its error for use in computing $F(x, y, z)$, $G(x, y, z)$ and so on; the righthand side of the linearized model is computed in regular arithmetic with no error forms.

(While these rules may seem complicated, they are designed to do the most reasonable thing in the typical case that $Y(x, y, z)$ depends only on the dependent variable z, and in fact is often simply equal to z. For common cases like polynomials and multilinear models, the combined error is simply used as the σ for the data point with no further ado.)

It may be the case that the model you wish to use is linearizable, but Calc's built-in rules are unable to figure it out. Calc uses its algebraic rewrite mechanism to linearize a model. The rewrite rules are kept in the variable `FitRules`. You can edit this variable using the *s e FitRules* command; in fact, there is a special *s F* command just for editing `FitRules`. See Section 12.3 [Operations on Variables], page 325.

See Section 10.11 [Rewrite Rules], page 291, for a discussion of rewrite rules.

Calc uses `FitRules` as follows. First, it converts the model to an equation if necessary and encloses the model equation in a call to the function `fitmodel` (which is not actually a defined function in Calc; it is only used as a placeholder by the rewrite rules). Parameter variables are renamed to function calls 'fitparam(1)', 'fitparam(2)', and so on, and independent variables are renamed to 'fitvar(1)', 'fitvar(2)', etc. The dependent variable is the highest-numbered `fitvar`. For example, the power law model ax^b is converted to $y = ax^b$, then to

```
fitmodel(fitvar(2) = fitparam(1) fitvar(1)^fitparam(2))
```

Calc then applies the rewrites as if by 'C-u 0 a r FitRules'. (The zero prefix means that rewriting should continue until no further changes are possible.)

When rewriting is complete, the `fitmodel` call should have been replaced by a `fitsystem` call that looks like this:

```
fitsystem(Y, FGH, abc)
```

where Y is a formula that describes the function $Y(x, y, z)$, FGH is the vector of formulas $[F(x, y, z), G(x, y, z), H(x, y, z)]$, and abc is the vector of parameter filters which refer to the raw parameters as 'fitdummy(1)' for A, 'fitdummy(2)' for B, etc. While the number of raw parameters (the length of the FGH vector) is usually the same as the number of original parameters (the length of the abc vector), this is not required.

The power law model eventually boils down to

```
fitsystem(ln(fitvar(2)),
          [1, ln(fitvar(1))],
          [exp(fitdummy(1)), fitdummy(2)])
```

The actual implementation of `FitRules` is complicated; it proceeds in four phases. First, common rearrangements are done to try to bring linear terms together and to isolate functions like `exp` and `ln` either all the way "out" (so that they can be put into Y) or all the way "in" (so that they can be put into abc or FGH). In particular, all non-constant powers are converted to logs-and-exponentials form, and the distributive law is used to expand products of sums. Quotients are rewritten to use the 'fitinv' function, where 'fitinv(x)' represents $1/x$ while the `FitRules` are operating. (The use of `fitinv` makes recognition of linear-looking forms easier.) If you modify `FitRules`, you will probably only need to modify the rules for this phase.

Phase two, whose rules can actually also apply during phases one and three, first rewrites `fitmodel` to a two-argument form 'fitmodel(Y, model)', where Y is initially zero and *model* has been changed from $a = b$ to $a - b$ form. It then tries to peel off invertible functions from the outside of *model* and put them into Y instead, calling the equation solver to invert the functions. Finally, when this is no longer possible, the `fitmodel` is changed to a four-argument `fitsystem`, where the fourth argument is *model* and the FGH and abc vectors are initially empty. (The last vector is really ABC, corresponding to raw parameters, for now.)

Phase three converts a sum of items in the *model* to a sum of 'fitpart(a, b, c)' terms which represent terms 'a*b*c' of the sum, where *a* is all factors that do not involve any variables, *b* is all factors that involve only parameters, and *c* is the factors that involve only independent variables. (If this decomposition is not possible, the rule set will not complete and Calc will complain that the model is too complex.) Then fitparts with equal *b* or *c* components are merged back together using the distributive law in order to minimize the number of raw parameters needed.

Phase four moves the fitpart terms into the *FGH* and *ABC* vectors. Also, some of the algebraic expansions that were done in phase 1 are undone now to make the formulas more computationally efficient. Finally, it calls the solver one more time to convert the *ABC* vector to an *abc* vector, and removes the fourth *model* argument (which by now will be zero) to obtain the three-argument fitsystem that the linear least-squares solver wants to see.

Two functions which are useful in connection with FitRules are 'hasfitparams(x)' and 'hasfitvars(x)', which check whether *x* refers to any parameters or independent variables, respectively. Specifically, these functions return "true" if the argument contains any fitparam (or fitvar) function calls, and "false" otherwise. (Recall that "true" means a nonzero number, and "false" means zero. The actual nonzero number returned is the largest *n* from all the 'fitparam(n)'s or 'fitvar(n)'s, respectively, that appear in the formula.)

The fit function in algebraic notation normally takes four arguments, 'fit(*model*, *vars*, *params*, *data*)', where *model* is the model formula as it would be typed after a F ', *vars* is the independent variable or a vector of independent variables, *params* likewise gives the parameter(s), and *data* is the data matrix. Note that the length of *vars* must be equal to the number of rows in *data* if *model* is an equation, or one less than the number of rows if *model* is a plain formula. (Actually, a name for the dependent variable is allowed but will be ignored in the plain-formula case.)

If *params* is omitted, the parameters are all variables in *model* except those that appear in *vars*. If *vars* is also omitted, Calc sorts all the variables that appear in *model* alphabetically and uses the higher ones for *vars* and the lower ones for *params*.

Alternatively, 'fit(*modelvec*, *data*)' is allowed where *modelvec* is a 2- or 3-vector describing the model and variables, as discussed previously.

If Calc is unable to do the fit, the fit function is left in symbolic form, ordinarily with an explanatory message. The message will be "Model expression is too complex" if the linearizer was unable to put the model into the required form.

The efit (corresponding to *H* a *F*) and xfit (for *I* a *F*) functions are completely analogous.

10.8.6 Polynomial Interpolation

The a p (calc-poly-interp) [polint] command does a polynomial interpolation at a particular *x* value. It takes two arguments from the stack: A data matrix of the sort used by a F, and a single number which represents the desired *x* value. Calc effectively does an exact polynomial fit as if by a F i, then substitutes the *x* value into the result in order to get an approximate *y* value based on the fit. (Calc does not actually use a F i, however; it uses a direct method which is both more efficient and more numerically stable.)

The result of **a p** is actually a vector of two values: The y value approximation, and an error measure dy that reflects Calc's estimation of the probable error of the approximation at that value of x. If the input x is equal to any of the x values in the data matrix, the output y will be the corresponding y value from the matrix, and the output dy will be exactly zero.

A prefix argument of 2 causes **a p** to take separate x- and y-vectors from the stack instead of one data matrix.

If x is a vector of numbers, **a p** will return a matrix of interpolated results for each of those x values. (The matrix will have two columns, the y values and the dy values.) If x is a formula instead of a number, the `polint` function remains in symbolic form; use the **a "** command to expand it out to a formula that describes the fit in symbolic terms.

In all cases, the **a p** command leaves the data vectors or matrix on the stack. Only the x value is replaced by the result.

The *H* **a p** [`ratint`] command does a rational function interpolation. It is used exactly like **a p**, except that it uses as its model the quotient of two polynomials. If there are N data points, the numerator and denominator polynomials will each have degree $N/2$ (if N is odd, the denominator will have degree one higher than the numerator).

Rational approximations have the advantage that they can accurately describe functions that have poles (points at which the function's value goes to infinity, so that the denominator polynomial of the approximation goes to zero). If x corresponds to a pole of the fitted rational function, then the result will be a division by zero. If Infinite mode is enabled, the result will be '`[uinf, uinf]`'.

There is no way to get the actual coefficients of the rational function used by *H* **a p**. (The algorithm never generates these coefficients explicitly, and quotients of polynomials are beyond **a F**'s capabilities to fit.)

10.9 Summations

The **a +** (`calc-summation`) [`sum`] command computes the sum of a formula over a certain range of index values. The formula is taken from the top of the stack; the command prompts for the name of the summation index variable, the lower limit of the sum (any formula), and the upper limit of the sum. If you enter a blank line at any of these prompts, that prompt and any later ones are answered by reading additional elements from the stack. Thus, **'** *k^2 RET* **'** *k RET 1 RET 5 RET* **a +** *RET* produces the result 55.

$$\sum_{k=1}^{5} k^2 = 55$$

The choice of index variable is arbitrary, but it's best not to use a variable with a stored value. In particular, while *i* is often a favorite index variable, it should be avoided in Calc because *i* has the imaginary constant $(0, 1)$ as a value. If you pressed = on a sum over *i*, it would be changed to a nonsensical sum over the "variable" $(0, 1)$! If you really want to use *i* as an index variable, use **s u** *i RET* first to "unstore" this variable. (See Section 12.1 [Storing Variables], page 323.)

A numeric prefix argument steps the index by that amount rather than by one. Thus **'** *a_k RET C-u –2* **a +** *k RET 10 RET 0 RET* yields '`a_10 + a_8 + a_6 + a_4 + a_2 + a_0`'. A prefix argument of plain *C-u* causes a + to prompt for the step value, in which case you can enter any formula or enter a blank line to take the step value from the stack. With the *C-u* prefix, a + can take up to five arguments from the stack: The formula, the variable, the lower limit, the upper limit, and (at the top of the stack), the step value.

Calc knows how to do certain sums in closed form. For example, 'sum(6 k^2, k, 1, n) = 2 n^3 + 3 n^2 + n'. In particular, this is possible if the formula being summed is polynomial or exponential in the index variable. Sums of logarithms are transformed into logarithms of products. Sums of trigonometric and hyperbolic functions are transformed to sums of exponentials and then done in closed form. Also, of course, sums in which the lower and upper limits are both numbers can always be evaluated just by grinding them out, although Calc will use closed forms whenever it can for the sake of efficiency.

The notation for sums in algebraic formulas is 'sum(*expr, var, low, high, step*)'. If *step* is omitted, it defaults to one. If *high* is omitted, *low* is actually the upper limit and the lower limit is one. If *low* is also omitted, the limits are '-inf' and 'inf', respectively.

Infinite sums can sometimes be evaluated: 'sum(.5^k, k, 1, inf)' returns 1. This is done by evaluating the sum in closed form (to '1. - 0.5^n' in this case), then evaluating this formula with n set to inf. Calc's usual rules for "infinite" arithmetic can find the answer from there. If infinite arithmetic yields a 'nan', or if the sum cannot be solved in closed form, Calc leaves the **sum** function in symbolic form. See Section 4.5 [Infinities], page 119.

As a special feature, if the limits are infinite (or omitted, as described above) but the formula includes vectors subscripted by expressions that involve the iteration variable, Calc narrows the limits to include only the range of integers which result in valid subscripts for the vector. For example, the sum 'sum(k [a,b,c,d,e,f,g]_(2k),k)' evaluates to 'b + 2 d + 3 f'.

The limits of a sum do not need to be integers. For example, 'sum(a_k, k, 0, 2 n, n)' produces 'a_0 + a_n + a_(2 n)'. Calc computes the number of iterations using the formula '1 + (*high – low*) / *step*', which must, after algebraic simplification, evaluate to an integer.

If the number of iterations according to the above formula does not come out to an integer, the sum is invalid and will be left in symbolic form. However, closed forms are still supplied, and you are on your honor not to misuse the resulting formulas by substituting mismatched bounds into them. For example, 'sum(k, k, 1, 10, 2)' is invalid, but Calc will go ahead and evaluate the closed form solution for the limits 1 and 10 to get the rather dubious answer, 29.25.

If the lower limit is greater than the upper limit (assuming a positive step size), the result is generally zero. However, Calc only guarantees a zero result when the upper limit is exactly one step less than the lower limit, i.e., if the number of iterations is −1. Thus 'sum(f(k), k, n, n-1)' is zero but the sum from 'n' to 'n-2' may report a nonzero value if Calc used a closed form solution.

Calc's logical predicates like $a < b$ return 1 for "true" and 0 for "false." See Section 10.10 [Logical Operations], page 288. This can be used to advantage for building conditional sums. For example, 'sum(prime(k)*k^2, k, 1, 20)' is the sum of the squares of all prime numbers from 1 to 20; the **prime** predicate returns 1 if its argument is prime and 0 otherwise. You can read this expression as "the sum of k^2, where k is prime." Indeed, 'sum(prime(k)*k^2, k)' would represent the sum of *all* primes squared, since the limits default to plus and minus infinity, but there are no such sums that Calc's built-in rules can do in closed form.

As another example, 'sum((k != k_0) * f(k), k, 1, n)' is the sum of $f(k)$ for all k from 1 to n, excluding one value k_0. Slightly more tricky is the summand '(k != k_0) / (k - k_0)', which is an attempt to describe the sum of all $1/(k - k_0)$ except at $k = k_0$, where this would be a division by zero. But at $k = k_0$, this formula works out to the indeterminate form $0/0$, which Calc will not assume is zero. Better would be to use '(k != k_0) ? 1/(k-k_0) : 0'; the '? :' operator does an "if-then-else" test: This expression says, "if $k \neq k_0$, then $1/(k - k_0)$, else zero." Now the formula $1/(k - k_0)$ will not even be evaluated by Calc when $k = k_0$.

The a - (calc-alt-summation) [asum] command computes an alternating sum. Successive terms of the sequence are given alternating signs, with the first term (corresponding to the lower index value) being positive. Alternating sums are converted to normal sums with an extra term of the form '(-1)^(k-*low*)'. This formula is adjusted appropriately if the step value is other than one. For example, the Taylor series for the sine function is 'asum(x^k / k!, k, 1, inf, 2)'. (Calc cannot evaluate this infinite series, but it can approximate it if you replace inf with any particular odd number.) Calc converts this series to a regular sum with a step of one, namely 'sum((-1)^k x^(2k+1) / (2k+1)!, k, 0, inf)'.

The a * (calc-product) [prod] command is the analogous way to take a product of many terms. Calc also knows some closed forms for products, such as 'prod(k, k, 1, n) = n!'. Conditional products can be written 'prod(k^prime(k), k, 1, n)' or 'prod(prime(k) ? k : 1, k, 1, n)'.

The a T (calc-tabulate) [table] command evaluates a formula at a series of iterated index values, just like sum and prod, but its result is simply a vector of the results. For example, 'table(a_i, i, 1, 7, 2)' produces '[a_1, a_3, a_5, a_7]'.

10.10 Logical Operations

The following commands and algebraic functions return true/false values, where 1 represents "true" and 0 represents "false." In cases where a truth value is required (such as for the condition part of a rewrite rule, or as the condition for a Z [Z] control structure), any nonzero value is accepted to mean "true." (Specifically, anything for which **dnonzero** returns 1 is "true," and anything for which **dnonzero** returns 0 or cannot decide is assumed "false." Note that this means that Z [Z] will execute the "then" portion if its condition is provably true, but it will execute the "else" portion for any condition like $a = b$ that is not provably true, even if it might be true. Algebraic functions that have conditions as arguments, like ? : and &&, remain unevaluated if the condition is neither provably true nor provably false. See Section 6.6 [Declarations], page 143.)

The a = (calc-equal-to) command, or 'eq(a,b)' function (which can also be written 'a = b' or 'a == b' in an algebraic formula) is true if a and b are equal, either because they are identical expressions, or because they are numbers which are numerically equal. (Thus the integer 1 is considered equal to the float 1.0.) If the equality of a and b cannot be determined, the comparison is left in symbolic form. Note that as a command, this operation pops two values from the stack and pushes back either a 1 or a 0, or a formula 'a = b' if the values' equality cannot be determined.

Many Calc commands use '=' formulas to represent *equations*. For example, the a S (calc-solve-for) command rearranges an equation to solve for a given variable. The a M (calc-map-equation) command can be used to apply any function to both sides of an equation; for example, 2 a M * multiplies both sides of the equation by two. Note that just 2 * would not do the same thing; it would produce the formula '2 (a = b)' which represents 2 if the equality is true or zero if not.

The eq function with more than two arguments (e.g., C-u 3 a = or 'a = b = c') tests if all of its arguments are equal. In algebraic notation, the '=' operator is unusual in that it is neither left- nor right-associative: 'a = b = c' is not the same as '(a = b) = c' or 'a = (b = c)' (which each compare one variable with the 1 or 0 that results from comparing two other variables).

The a # (calc-not-equal-to) command, or 'neq(a,b)' or 'a != b' function, is true if a and b are not equal. This also works with more than two arguments; 'a != b != c != d' tests that all four of a, b, c, and d are distinct numbers.

The a < (calc-less-than) ['lt(a,b)' or 'a < b'] operation is true if a is less than b. Similar functions are a > (calc-greater-than) ['gt(a,b)' or 'a > b'], a [(calc-less-equal) ['leq(a,b)' or 'a <= b'], and a] (calc-greater-equal) ['geq(a,b)' or 'a >= b'].

While the inequality functions like lt do not accept more than two arguments, the syntax 'a <= b < c' is translated to an equivalent expression involving intervals: 'b in [a .. c)'. (See the description of in below.) All four combinations of '<' and '<=' are allowed, or any of the four combinations of '>' and '>='. Four-argument constructions like 'a < b < c < d', and mixtures like 'a < b = c' that involve both equations and inequalities, are not allowed.

The a . (calc-remove-equal) [rmeq] command extracts the righthand side of the equation or inequality on the top of the stack. It also works elementwise on vectors. For example, if '[x = 2.34, y = z / 2]' is on the stack, then a . produces '[2.34, z / 2]'. As a special case, if the righthand side is a variable and the lefthand side is a number (as in '2.34 = x'), then Calc keeps the lefthand side instead. Finally, this command works with assignments 'x := 2.34' as well as equations, always taking the righthand side, and for '=>' (evaluates-to) operators, always taking the lefthand side.

The a & (calc-logical-and) ['land(a,b)' or 'a && b'] function is true if both of its arguments are true, i.e., are non-zero numbers. In this case, the result will be either a or b, chosen arbitrarily. If either argument is zero, the result is zero. Otherwise, the formula is left in symbolic form.

The a | (calc-logical-or) ['lor(a,b)' or 'a || b'] function is true if either or both of its arguments are true (nonzero). The result is whichever argument was nonzero, choosing arbitrarily if both are nonzero. If both a and b are zero, the result is zero.

The a ! (calc-logical-not) ['lnot(a)' or '! a'] function is true if a is false (zero), or false if a is true (nonzero). It is left in symbolic form if a is not a number.

The a : (calc-logical-if) ['if(a,b,c)' or 'a ? b : c'] function is equal to either b or c if a is a nonzero number or zero, respectively. If a is not a number, the test is left in symbolic form and neither b nor c is evaluated in any way. In algebraic formulas, this is one of the few Calc functions whose arguments are not automatically evaluated when the function itself is evaluated. The others are lambda, quote, and condition.

One minor surprise to watch out for is that the formula 'a?3:4' will not work because the '3:4' is parsed as a fraction instead of as three separate symbols. Type something like 'a ? 3 : 4' or 'a?(3):4' instead.

As a special case, if a evaluates to a vector, then both b and c are evaluated; the result is a vector of the same length as a whose elements are chosen from corresponding elements of b and c according to whether each element of a is zero or nonzero. Each of b and c must be either a vector of the same length as a, or a non-vector which is matched with all elements of a.

The a { (calc-in-set) ['in(a,b)'] function is true if the number a is in the set of numbers represented by b. If b is an interval form, a must be one of the values encompassed by the interval. If b is a vector, a must be equal to one of the elements of the vector. (If any vector elements are intervals, a must be in any of the intervals.) If b is a plain number, a must be numerically equal to b. See Section 9.6 [Set Operations], page 229, for a group of commands that manipulate sets of this sort.

The 'typeof(a)' function produces an integer or variable which characterizes a. If a is a number, vector, or variable, the result will be one of the following numbers:

```
  1    Integer
  2    Fraction
  3    Floating-point number
  4    HMS form
  5    Rectangular complex number
  6    Polar complex number
  7    Error form
  8    Interval form
  9    Modulo form
 10    Date-only form
 11    Date/time form
 12    Infinity (inf, uinf, or nan)
100    Variable
101    Vector (but not a matrix)
102    Matrix
```

Otherwise, a is a formula, and the result is a variable which represents the name of the top-level function call.

The 'integer(a)' function returns true if a is an integer. The 'real(a)' function is true if a is a real number, either integer, fraction, or float. The 'constant(a)' function returns true if a is any of the objects for which typeof would produce an integer code result except for variables, and provided that the components of an object like a vector or error form are themselves constant. Note that infinities do not satisfy any of these tests, nor do special constants like pi and e.

See Section 6.6 [Declarations], page 143, for a set of similar functions that recognize formulas as well as actual numbers. For example, 'dint(floor(x))' is true because 'floor(x)' is provably integer-valued, but 'integer(floor(x))' does not because 'floor(x)' is not literally an integer constant.

The 'refers(a,b)' function is true if the variable (or sub-expression) b appears in a, or false otherwise. Unlike the other tests described here, this function returns a definite "no" answer even if its arguments are still in symbolic form. The only case where `refers` will be left unevaluated is if a is a plain variable (different from b).

The '`negative(a)`' function returns true if a "looks" negative, because it is a negative number, because it is of the form $-x$, or because it is a product or quotient with a term that looks negative. This is most useful in rewrite rules. Beware that '`negative(a)`' evaluates to 1 or 0 for *any* argument a, so it can only be stored in a formula if the default simplifications are turned off first with `m O` (or if it appears in an unevaluated context such as a rewrite rule condition).

The '`variable(a)`' function is true if a is a variable, or false if not. If a is a function call, this test is left in symbolic form. Built-in variables like `pi` and `inf` are considered variables like any others by this test.

The '`nonvar(a)`' function is true if a is a non-variable. If its argument is a variable it is left unsimplified; it never actually returns zero. However, since Calc's condition-testing commands consider "false" anything not provably true, this is often good enough.

The functions `lin`, `linnt`, `islin`, and `islinnt` check if an expression is "linear," i.e., can be written in the form $a+bx$ for some constants a and b, and some variable or subformula x. The function '`islin(f,x)`' checks if formula f is linear in x, returning 1 if so. For example, '`islin(x,x)`', '`islin(-x,x)`', '`islin(3,x)`', and '`islin(x y / 3 - 2, x)`' all return 1. The '`lin(f,x)`' function is similar, except that instead of returning 1 it returns the vector $[a, b, x]$. For the above examples, this vector would be $[0, 1, x]$, $[0, -1, x]$, $[3, 0, x]$, and $[-2, y/3, x]$, respectively. Both `lin` and `islin` generally remain unevaluated for expressions which are not linear, e.g., '`lin(2 x^2, x)`' and '`lin(sin(x), x)`'. The second argument can also be a formula; '`islin(2 + 3 sin(x), sin(x))`' returns true.

The `linnt` and `islinnt` functions perform a similar check, but require a "non-trivial" linear form, which means that the b coefficient must be non-zero. For example, '`lin(2,x)`' returns $[2, 0, x]$ and '`lin(y,x)`' returns $[y, 0, x]$, but '`linnt(2,x)`' and '`linnt(y,x)`' are left unevaluated (in other words, these formulas are considered to be only "trivially" linear in x).

All four linearity-testing functions allow you to omit the second argument, in which case the input may be linear in any non-constant formula. Here, the $a = 0$, $b = 1$ case is also considered trivial, and only constant values for a and b are recognized. Thus, '`lin(2 x y)`' returns $[0, 2, xy]$, '`lin(2 - x y)`' returns $[2, -1, xy]$, and '`lin(x y)`' returns $[0, 1, xy]$. The `linnt` function would allow the first two cases but not the third. Also, neither `lin` nor `linnt` accept plain constants as linear in the one-argument case: '`islin(2,x)`' is true, but '`islin(2)`' is false.

The '`istrue(a)`' function returns 1 if a is a nonzero number or provably nonzero formula, or 0 if a is anything else. Calls to `istrue` can only be manipulated if `m O` mode is used to make sure they are not evaluated prematurely. (Note that declarations are used when deciding whether a formula is true; `istrue` returns 1 when `dnonzero` would return 1, and it returns 0 when `dnonzero` would return 0 or leave itself in symbolic form.)

10.11 Rewrite Rules

The `a r` (`calc-rewrite`) [`rewrite`] command makes substitutions in a formula according to a specified pattern or patterns known as *rewrite rules*. Whereas `a b` (`calc-substitute`) matches literally, so that substituting '`sin(x)`' with '`cos(x)`' matches only the `sin` function applied to the variable x, rewrite rules match general kinds of formulas; rewriting using the rule 'sin(x) := cos(x)' matches sin of any argument and replaces it with cos of that same argument. The only significance of the name x is that the same name is used on both sides of the rule.

Rewrite rules rearrange formulas already in Calc's memory. See Section 6.8.11 [Syntax Tables], page 174, to read about *syntax rules*, which are similar to algebraic rewrite rules but operate when new algebraic entries are being parsed, converting strings of characters into Calc formulas.

10.11.1 Entering Rewrite Rules

Rewrite rules normally use the "assignment" operator 'old := new'. This operator is equivalent to the function call 'assign(old, new)'. The assign function is undefined by itself in Calc, so an assignment formula such as a rewrite rule will be left alone by ordinary Calc commands. But certain commands, like the rewrite system, interpret assignments in special ways.

For example, the rule 'sin(x)^2 := 1-cos(x)^2' says to replace every occurrence of the sine of something, squared, with one minus the square of the cosine of that same thing. All by itself as a formula on the stack it does nothing, but when given to the **a r** command it turns that command into a sine-squared-to-cosine-squared converter.

To specify a set of rules to be applied all at once, make a vector of rules.

When **a r** prompts you to enter the rewrite rules, you can answer in several ways:

1. With a rule: *f(x) := g(x) RET*.

2. With a vector of rules: *[f1(x) := g1(x), f2(x) := g2(x)] RET*. (You can omit the enclosing square brackets if you wish.)

3. With the name of a variable that contains the rule or rules vector: *myrules RET*.

4. With any formula except a rule, a vector, or a variable name; this will be interpreted as the *old* half of a rewrite rule, and you will be prompted a second time for the *new* half: *f(x) RET g(x) RET*.

5. With a blank line, in which case the rule, rules vector, or variable will be taken from the top of the stack (and the formula to be rewritten will come from the second-to-top position).

If you enter the rules directly (as opposed to using rules stored in a variable), those rules will be put into the Trail so that you can retrieve them later. See Section 5.3 [Trail Commands], page 135.

It is most convenient to store rules you use often in a variable and invoke them by giving the variable name. The **s e** (calc-edit-variable) command is an easy way to create or edit a rule set stored in a variable. You may also wish to use **s p** (calc-permanent-variable) to save your rules permanently; see Section 12.3 [Operations on Variables], page 325.

Rewrite rules are compiled into a special internal form for faster matching. If you enter a rule set directly it must be recompiled every time. If you store the rules in a variable and refer to them through that variable, they will be compiled once and saved away along with the variable for later reference. This is another good reason to store your rules in a variable.

Calc also accepts an obsolete notation for rules, as vectors '[old, new]'. But because it is easily confused with a vector of two rules, the use of this notation is no longer recommended.

10.11.2 Basic Rewrite Rules

To match a particular formula x with a particular rewrite rule 'old := new', Calc compares the structure of x with the structure of old. Variables that appear in old are treated as meta-variables; the corresponding positions in x may contain any sub-formulas. For example, the pattern 'f(x,y)' would match the expression 'f(12, a+1)' with the meta-variable 'x' corresponding to 12 and with 'y' corresponding to 'a+1'. However, this pattern would not match 'f(12)' or 'g(12, a+1)', since there is no assignment of the meta-variables that will make the pattern match these expressions. Notice that if the pattern is a single meta-variable, it will match any expression.

If a given meta-variable appears more than once in old, the corresponding sub-formulas of x must be identical. Thus the pattern 'f(x,x)' would match 'f(12, 12)' and 'f(a+1, a+1)' but not 'f(12, a+1)' or 'f(a+b, b+a)'. (See Section 10.11.3 [Conditional Rewrite Rules], page 293, for a way to match the latter.)

Things other than variables must match exactly between the pattern and the target formula. To match a particular variable exactly, use the pseudo-function 'quote(v)' in the pattern. For example, the pattern 'x+quote(y)' matches 'x+y', '2+y', or 'sin(a)+y'.

The special variable names 'e', 'pi', 'i', 'phi', 'gamma', 'inf', 'uinf', and 'nan' always match literally. Thus the pattern 'sin(d + e + f)' acts exactly like 'sin(d + quote(e) + f)'.

If the old pattern is found to match a given formula, that formula is replaced by new, where any occurrences in new of meta-variables from the pattern are replaced with the sub-formulas that they matched. Thus, applying the rule 'f(x,y) := g(y+x,x)' to 'f(12, a+1)' would produce 'g(a+13, 12)'.

The normal **a r** command applies rewrite rules over and over throughout the target formula until no further changes are possible (up to a limit of 100 times). Use *C-u 1 a r* to make only one change at a time.

10.11.3 Conditional Rewrite Rules

A rewrite rule can also be *conditional*, written in the form 'old := new :: cond'. (There is also the obsolete form '[old, new, cond]'.) If a cond part is present in the rule, this is an additional condition that must be satisfied before the rule is accepted. Once old has been successfully matched to the target expression, cond is evaluated (with all the meta-variables substituted for the values they matched) and simplified with Calc's algebraic simplifications. If the result is a nonzero number or any other object known to be nonzero (see Section 6.6 [Declarations], page 143), the rule is accepted. If the result is zero or if it is a symbolic formula that is not known to be nonzero, the rule is rejected. See Section 10.10 [Logical Operations], page 288, for a number of functions that return 1 or 0 according to the results of various tests.

For example, the formula 'n > 0' simplifies to 1 or 0 if n is replaced by a positive or nonpositive number, respectively (or if n has been declared to be positive or nonpositive). Thus, the rule 'f(x,y) := g(y+x,x) :: x+y > 0' would apply to 'f(0, 4)' but not to 'f(-3, 2)' or 'f(12, a+1)' (assuming no outstanding declarations for a). In the case of 'f(-3, 2)', the condition can be shown not to be satisfied; in the case of 'f(12, a+1)', the condition merely cannot be shown to be satisfied, but that is enough to reject the rule.

While Calc will use declarations to reason about variables in the formula being rewritten, declarations do not apply to meta-variables. For example, the rule 'f(a) := g(a+1)' will match for any values of 'a', such as complex numbers, vectors, or formulas, even if 'a' has been declared to be real or scalar. If you want the meta-variable 'a' to match only literal real numbers, use 'f(a) := g(a+1) :: real(a)'. If you want 'a' to match only reals and formulas which are provably real, use 'dreal(a)' as the condition.

The ':::' operator is a shorthand for the `condition` function; '*old* := *new* :: *cond*' is equivalent to the formula 'condition(assign(*old*, *new*), *cond*)'.

If you have several conditions, you can use '... :: c1 :: c2 :: c3' or '... :: c1 && c2 && c3'. The two are entirely equivalent.

It is also possible to embed conditions inside the pattern: 'f(x :: x>0, y) := g(y+x, x)'. This is purely a notational convenience, though; where a condition appears in a rule has no effect on when it is tested. The rewrite-rule compiler automatically decides when it is best to test each condition while a rule is being matched.

Certain conditions are handled as special cases by the rewrite rule system and are tested very efficiently: Where x is any meta-variable, these conditions are 'integer(x)', 'real(x)', 'constant(x)', 'negative(x)', 'x >= y' where y is either a constant or another meta-variable and '>=' may be replaced by any of the six relational operators, and 'x % a = b' where a and b are constants. Other conditions, like 'x >= y+1' or 'dreal(x)', will be less efficient to check since Calc must bring the whole evaluator and simplifier into play.

An interesting property of '::' is that neither of its arguments will be touched by Calc's default simplifications. This is important because conditions often are expressions that cannot safely be evaluated early. For example, the `typeof` function never remains in symbolic form; entering 'typeof(a)' will put the number 100 (the type code for variables like 'a') on the stack. But putting the condition '... :: typeof(a) = 6' on the stack is safe since '::' prevents the `typeof` from being evaluated until the condition is actually used by the rewrite system.

Since '::' protects its lefthand side, too, you can use a dummy condition to protect a rule that must itself not evaluate early. For example, it's not safe to put 'a(f,x) := apply(f, [x])' on the stack because it will immediately evaluate to 'a(f,x) := f(x)', where the meta-variable-ness of f on the righthand side has been lost. But 'a(f,x) := apply(f, [x]) :: 1' is safe, and of course the condition '1' is always true (nonzero) so it has no effect on the functioning of the rule. (The rewrite compiler will ensure that it doesn't even impact the speed of matching the rule.)

10.11.4 Algebraic Properties of Rewrite Rules

The rewrite mechanism understands the algebraic properties of functions like '+' and '*'. In particular, pattern matching takes the associativity and commutativity of the following functions into account:

```
+ - *  = != && ||  and or xor  vint vunion vxor  gcd lcm  max min  beta
```

For example, the rewrite rule:

```
a x + b x  :=  (a + b) x
```

will match formulas of the form,

         a x + b x,   x a + x b,   a x + x b,   x a + b x

Rewrites also understand the relationship between the '+' and '-' operators. The above
rewrite rule will also match the formulas,

         a x - b x,   x a - x b,   a x - x b,   x a - b x

by matching 'b' in the pattern to '-b' from the formula.

Applied to a sum of many terms like 'r + a x + s + b x + t', this pattern will check all
pairs of terms for possible matches. The rewrite will take whichever suitable pair it discovers
first.

In general, a pattern using an associative operator like 'a + b' will try *2 n* different ways
to match a sum of *n* terms like 'x + y + z - w'. First, 'a' is matched against each of 'x',
'y', 'z', and '-w' in turn, with 'b' being matched to the remainders 'y + z - w', 'x + z - w',
etc. If none of these succeed, then 'b' is matched against each of the four terms with 'a'
matching the remainder. Half-and-half matches, like '(x + y) + (z - w)', are not tried.

Note that '*' is not commutative when applied to matrices, but rewrite rules pretend that
it is. If you type *m v* to enable Matrix mode (see Section 6.4.6 [Matrix Mode], page 141),
rewrite rules will match '*' literally, ignoring its usual commutativity property. (In the
current implementation, the associativity also vanishes—it is as if the pattern had been
enclosed in a **plain** marker; see below.) If you are applying rewrites to formulas with
matrices, it's best to enable Matrix mode first to prevent algebraically incorrect rewrites
from occurring.

The pattern '-x' will actually match any expression. For example, the rule

         f(-x)   :=   -f(x)

will rewrite 'f(a)' to '-f(-a)'. To avoid this, either use a **plain** marker as described below,
or add a 'negative(x)' condition. The **negative** function is true if its argument "looks"
negative, for example, because it is a negative number or because it is a formula like '-x'.
The new rule using this condition is:

         f(x)   :=   -f(-x)   :: negative(x)   or, equivalently,
         f(-x)   :=   -f(x)   :: negative(-x)

In the same way, the pattern 'x - y' will match the sum 'a + b' by matching 'y' to '-b'.

The pattern 'a b' will also match the formula 'x/y' if 'y' is a number. Thus the rule 'a x +
b x := (a+b) x' will also convert 'a x + x / 2' to '(a + 0.5) x' (or '(a + 1:2) x', depending
on the current fraction mode).

Calc will *not* take other liberties with '*', '/', and '^'. For example, the pattern 'f(a b)'
will not match 'f(x^2)', and 'f(a + b)' will not match 'f(2 x)', even though conceivably
these patterns could match with 'a = b = x'. Nor will 'f(a b)' match 'f(x / y)' if 'y' is not
a constant, even though it could be considered to match with 'a = x' and 'b = 1/y'. The
reasons are partly for efficiency, and partly because while few mathematical operations are
substantively different for addition and subtraction, often it is preferable to treat the cases
of multiplication, division, and integer powers separately.

Even more subtle is the rule set

         [f(a) + f(b) := f(a + b),   -f(a) := f(-a)]

attempting to match 'f(x) - f(y)'. You might think that Calc will view this subtraction as
'f(x) + (-f(y))' and then apply the above two rules in turn, but actually this will not work
because Calc only does this when considering rules for '+' (like the first rule in this set). So
it will see first that 'f(x) + (-f(y))' does not match 'f(a) + f(b)' for any assignments of
the meta-variables, and then it will see that 'f(x) - f(y)' does not match '-f(a)' for any
assignment of 'a'. Because Calc tries only one rule at a time, it will not be able to rewrite
'f(x) - f(y)' with this rule set. An explicit 'f(a) - f(b)' rule will have to be added.

Another thing patterns will *not* do is break up complex numbers. The pattern 'myconj(a
+ b i) := a - b i' will work for formulas involving the special constant 'i' (such as '3 - 4
i'), but it will not match actual complex numbers like '(3, -4)'. A version of the above
rule for complex numbers would be

        myconj(a) := re(a) - im(a) (0,1) :: im(a) != 0

(Because the re and im functions understand the properties of the special constant 'i',
this rule will also work for '3 - 4 i'. In fact, this particular rule would probably be better
without the 'im(a) != 0' condition, since if 'im(a) = 0' the righthand side of the rule will
still give the correct answer for the conjugate of a real number.)

It is also possible to specify optional arguments in patterns. The rule

        opt(a) x + opt(b) (x^opt(c) + opt(d)) := f(a, b, c, d)

will match the formula

        5 (x^2 - 4) + 3 x

in a fairly straightforward manner, but it will also match reduced formulas like

        x + x^2,   2(x + 1) - x,   x + x

producing, respectively,

        f(1, 1, 2, 0),   f(-1, 2, 1, 1),   f(1, 1, 1, 0)

(The latter two formulas can be entered only if default simplifications have been turned
off with m 0.)

The default value for a term of a sum is zero. The default value for a part of a product,
for a power, or for the denominator of a quotient, is one. Also, '-x' matches the pattern
'opt(a) b' with 'a = -1'.

In particular, the distributive-law rule can be refined to

        opt(a) x + opt(b) x := (a + b) x

so that it will convert, e.g., 'a x - x', to '(a - 1) x'.

The pattern 'opt(a) + opt(b) x' matches almost any formulas which are linear in 'x'.
You can also use the lin and islin functions with rewrite conditions to test for this; see
Section 10.10 [Logical Operations], page 288. These functions are not as convenient to use
in rewrite rules, but they recognize more kinds of formulas as linear: 'x/z' is considered
linear with $b = 1/z$ by lin, but it will not match the above pattern because that pattern
calls for a multiplication, not a division.

As another example, the obvious rule to replace 'sin(x)^2 + cos(x)^2' by 1,

        sin(x)^2 + cos(x)^2 := 1

misses many cases because the sine and cosine may both be multiplied by an equal factor.
Here's a more successful rule:

        opt(a) sin(x)^2 + opt(a) cos(x)^2 := a

Note that this rule will *not* match 'sin(x)^2 + 6 cos(x)^2' because one *a* would have "matched" 1 while the other matched 6.

Calc automatically converts a rule like

```
f(x-1, x)   :=  g(x)
```

into the form

```
f(temp, x)   :=  g(x)   ::  temp = x-1
```

(where `temp` stands for a new, invented meta-variable that doesn't actually have a name). This modified rule will successfully match 'f(6, 7)', binding 'temp' and 'x' to 6 and 7, respectively, then verifying that they differ by one even though '6' does not superficially look like 'x-1'.

However, Calc does not solve equations to interpret a rule. The following rule,

```
f(x-1, x+1)   :=  g(x)
```

will not work. That is, it will match 'f(a − 1 + b, a + 1 + b)' but not 'f(6, 8)'. Calc always interprets at least one occurrence of a variable by literal matching. If the variable appears "isolated" then Calc is smart enough to use it for literal matching. But in this last example, Calc is forced to rewrite the rule to 'f(x-1, temp) := g(x) :: temp = x+1' where the 'x-1' term must correspond to an actual "something-minus-one" in the target formula.

A successful way to write this would be 'f(x, x+2) := g(x+1)'. You could make this resemble the original form more closely by using `let` notation, which is described in the next section:

```
f(xm1, x+1)   :=  g(x)   ::  let(x := xm1+1)
```

Calc does this rewriting or "conditionalizing" for any sub-pattern which involves only the functions in the following list, operating only on constants and meta-variables which have already been matched elsewhere in the pattern. When matching a function call, Calc is careful to match arguments which are plain variables before arguments which are calls to any of the functions below, so that a pattern like 'f(x-1, x)' can be conditionalized even though the isolated 'x' comes after the 'x-1'.

```
+ - * / \ % ^  abs sign  round rounde roundu trunc floor ceil
max min  re im conj arg
```

You can suppress all of the special treatments described in this section by surrounding a function call with a `plain` marker. This marker causes the function call which is its argument to be matched literally, without regard to commutativity, associativity, negation, or conditionalization. When you use `plain`, the "deep structure" of the formula being matched can show through. For example,

```
plain(a - a b)   :=  f(a, b)
```

will match only literal subtractions. However, the `plain` marker does not affect its arguments' arguments. In this case, commutativity and associativity is still considered while matching the 'a b' sub-pattern, so the whole pattern will match 'x − y x' as well as 'x − x y'. We could go still further and use

```
plain(a - plain(a b))   :=  f(a, b)
```

which would do a completely strict match for the pattern.

By contrast, the `quote` marker means that not only the function name but also the arguments must be literally the same. The above pattern will match 'x − x y' but

```
quote(a - a b)   :=  f(a, b)
```

will match only the single formula 'a − a b'. Also,

```
quote(a - quote(a b))  :=  f(a, b)
```

will match only 'a − quote(a b)'—probably not the desired effect!

A certain amount of algebra is also done when substituting the meta-variables on the righthand side of a rule. For example, in the rule

```
a + f(b)  :=  f(a + b)
```

matching 'f(x) − y' would produce 'f((−y) + x)' if taken literally, but the rewrite mechanism will simplify the righthand side to 'f(x − y)' automatically. (Of course, the default simplifications would do this anyway, so this special simplification is only noticeable if you have turned the default simplifications off.) This rewriting is done only when a meta-variable expands to a "negative-looking" expression. If this simplification is not desirable, you can use a plain marker on the righthand side:

```
a + f(b)  :=  f(plain(a + b))
```

In this example, we are still allowing the pattern-matcher to use all the algebra it can muster, but the righthand side will always simplify to a literal addition like 'f((−y) + x)'.

10.11.5 Other Features of Rewrite Rules

Certain "function names" serve as markers in rewrite rules. Here is a complete list of these markers. First are listed the markers that work inside a pattern; then come the markers that work in the righthand side of a rule.

One kind of marker, 'import(x)', takes the place of a whole rule. Here x is the name of a variable containing another rule set; those rules are "spliced into" the rule set that imports them. For example, if '[f(a+b) := f(a) + f(b), f(a b) := a f(b) :: real(a)]' is stored in variable 'linearF', then the rule set '[f(0) := 0, import(linearF)]' will apply all three rules. It is possible to modify the imported rules slightly: 'import(x, v1, x1, v2, x2, ...)' imports the rule set x with all occurrences of v_1, as either a variable name or a function name, replaced with x_1 and so on. (If v_1 is used as a function name, then x_1 must be either a function name itself or a '< >' nameless function; see Section 9.8.1 [Specifying Operators], page 235.) For example, '[g(0) := 0, import(linearF, f, g)]' applies the linearity rules to the function 'g' instead of 'f'. Imports can be nested, but the import-with-renaming feature may fail to rename sub-imports properly.

The special functions allowed in patterns are:

'quote(x)'

> This pattern matches exactly x; variable names in x are not interpreted as meta-variables. The only flexibility is that numbers are compared for numeric equality, so that the pattern 'f(quote(12))' will match both 'f(12)' and 'f(12.0)'. (Numbers are always treated this way by the rewrite mechanism: The rule 'f(x,x) := g(x)' will match 'f(12, 12.0)'. The rewrite may produce either 'g(12)' or 'g(12.0)' as a result in this case.)

'plain(x)'

> Here x must be a function call 'f(x1,x2,...)'. This pattern matches a call to function f with the specified argument patterns. No special knowledge of the properties of the function f is used in this case; '+' is not commutative or associative. Unlike quote, the arguments 'x1,x2,...' are treated as patterns.

If you wish them to be treated "plainly" as well, you must enclose them with more plain markers: 'plain(plain(-a) + plain(b c))'.

'opt(x,def)'

Here x must be a variable name. This must appear as an argument to a function or an element of a vector; it specifies that the argument or element is optional. As an argument to '+', '-', '*', '&&', or '||', or as the second argument to '/' or '^', the value *def* may be omitted. The pattern 'x + opt(y)' matches a sum by binding one summand to x and the other to y, and it matches anything else by binding the whole expression to x and zero to y. The other operators above work similarly.

For general miscellaneous functions, the default value def must be specified. Optional arguments are dropped starting with the rightmost one during matching. For example, the pattern 'f(opt(a,0), b, opt(c,b))' will match 'f(b)', 'f(a,b)', or 'f(a,b,c)'. Default values of zero and b are supplied in this example for the omitted arguments. Note that the literal variable b will be the default in the latter case, *not* the value that matched the meta-variable b. In other words, the default *def* is effectively quoted.

'condition(x,c)'

This matches the pattern x, with the attached condition c. It is the same as 'x :: c'.

'pand(x,y)'

This matches anything that matches both pattern x and pattern y. It is the same as 'x &&& y'. see Section 10.11.6 [Composing Patterns in Rewrite Rules], page 303.

'por(x,y)'

This matches anything that matches either pattern x or pattern y. It is the same as 'x ||| y'.

'pnot(x)' This matches anything that does not match pattern x. It is the same as '!!! x'.

'cons(h,t)'

This matches any vector of one or more elements. The first element is matched to h; a vector of the remaining elements is matched to t. Note that vectors of fixed length can also be matched as actual vectors: The rule 'cons(a,cons(b,[])) := cons(a+b,[])' is equivalent to the rule '[a,b] := [a+b]'.

'rcons(t,h)'

This is like cons, except that the *last* element is matched to h, with the remaining elements matched to t.

'apply(f,args)'

This matches any function call. The name of the function, in the form of a variable, is matched to f. The arguments of the function, as a vector of zero or more objects, are matched to 'args'. Constants, variables, and vectors do *not* match an apply pattern. For example, 'apply(f,x)' matches any function call, 'apply(quote(f),x)' matches any call to the function 'f', 'apply(f,[a,b])' matches any function call with exactly two arguments, and 'apply(quote(f), cons(a,cons(b,x)))' matches any call to the function 'f' with two or more arguments. Another way to implement the latter, if the rest of the rule does not need to refer to the first two arguments of 'f' by name, would be 'apply(quote(f), x :: vlen(x) >= 2)'. Here's a more interesting sample use of apply:

```
apply(f,[x+n])   :=  n + apply(f,[x])
   :: in(f, [floor,ceil,round,trunc]) :: integer(n)
```

Note, however, that this will be slower to match than a rule set with four separate rules. The reason is that Calc sorts the rules of a rule set according to top-level function name; if the top-level function is apply, Calc must try the rule for every single formula and sub-formula. If the top-level function in the pattern is, say, floor, then Calc invokes the rule only for sub-formulas which are calls to floor.

Formulas normally written with operators like + are still considered function calls: apply(f,x) matches 'a+b' with 'f = add', 'x = [a,b]'.

You must use apply for meta-variables with function names on both sides of a rewrite rule: 'apply(f, [x]) := f(x+1)' is *not* correct, because it rewrites 'spam(6)' into 'f(7)'. The righthand side should be 'apply(f, [x+1])'. Also note that you will have to use No-Simplify mode (*m 0*) when entering this rule so that the apply isn't evaluated immediately to get the new rule 'f(x) := f(x+1)'. Or, use *s e* to enter the rule without going through the stack, or enter the rule as 'apply(f, [x]) := apply(f, [x+1]) :: 1'. See Section 10.11.3 [Conditional Rewrite Rules], page 293.

'select(x)'

This is used for applying rules to formulas with selections; see Section 10.11.9 [Selections with Rewrite Rules], page 307.

Special functions for the righthand sides of rules are:

'quote(x)'

The notation 'quote(x)' is changed to 'x' when the righthand side is used. As far as the rewrite rule is concerned, quote is invisible. However, quote has the special property in Calc that its argument is not evaluated. Thus, while it will not work to put the rule 't(a) := typeof(a)' on the stack because 'typeof(a)' is evaluated immediately to produce 't(a) := 100', you can use quote to protect the righthand side: 't(a) := quote(typeof(a))'. (See Section 10.11.3 [Conditional Rewrite Rules], page 293, for another trick for protecting rules from evaluation.)

'plain(x)'

Special properties of and simplifications for the function call x are not used. One interesting case where plain is useful is the rule, 'q(x) := quote(x)', trying to expand a shorthand notation for the quote function. This rule will not work as shown; instead of replacing 'q(foo)' with 'quote(foo)', it will replace it with 'foo'! The correct rule would be 'q(x) := plain(quote(x))'.

'cons(h,t)'

>   Where *t* is a vector, this is converted into an expanded vector during rewrite processing. Note that cons is a regular Calc function which normally does this anyway; the only way cons is treated specially by rewrites is that cons on the righthand side of a rule will be evaluated even if default simplifications have been turned off.

'rcons(t,h)'

>   Analogous to cons except putting *h* at the *end* of the vector *t*.

'apply(f,args)'

>   Where *f* is a variable and *args* is a vector, this is converted to a function call. Once again, note that apply is also a regular Calc function.

'eval(x)'   The formula *x* is handled in the usual way, then the default simplifications are applied to it even if they have been turned off normally. This allows you to treat any function similarly to the way cons and apply are always treated. However, there is a slight difference: 'cons(2+3, [])' with default simplifications off will be converted to '[2+3]', whereas 'eval(cons(2+3, []))' will be converted to '[5]'.

'evalsimp(x)'

>   The formula *x* has meta-variables substituted in the usual way, then algebraically simplified.

'evalextsimp(x)'

>   The formula *x* has meta-variables substituted in the normal way, then "extendedly" simplified as if by the **a e** command.

'select(x)'

>   See Section 10.11.9 [Selections with Rewrite Rules], page 307.

There are also some special functions you can use in conditions.

'let(v := x)'

>   The expression *x* is evaluated with meta-variables substituted. The algebraic simplifications are *not* applied by default, but *x* can include calls to evalsimp or evalextsimp as described above to invoke higher levels of simplification. The result of *x* is then bound to the meta-variable *v*. As usual, if this meta-variable has already been matched to something else the two values must be equal; if the meta-variable is new then it is bound to the result of the expression. This variable can then appear in later conditions, and on the righthand side of the rule. In fact, *v* may be any pattern in which case the result of evaluating *x* is matched to that pattern, binding any meta-variables that appear in that pattern. Note that let can only appear by itself as a condition, or as one term of an '&&' which is a whole condition: It cannot be inside an '||' term or otherwise buried.

>   The alternate, equivalent form 'let(v, x)' is also recognized. Note that the use of ':=' by let, while still being assignment-like in character, is unrelated to the use of ':=' in the main part of a rewrite rule.

As an example, 'f(a) := g(ia) :: let(ia := 1/a) :: constant(ia)' replaces 'f(a)' with 'g' of the inverse of 'a', if that inverse exists and is constant. For example, if 'a' is a singular matrix the operation '1/a' is left unsimplified and 'constant(ia)' fails, but if 'a' is an invertible matrix then the rule succeeds. Without let there would be no way to express this rule that didn't have to invert the matrix twice. Note that, because the meta-variable 'ia' is otherwise unbound in this rule, the let condition itself always "succeeds" because no matter what '1/a' evaluates to, it can successfully be bound to ia.

Here's another example, for integrating cosines of linear terms: 'myint(cos(y),x) := sin(y)/b :: let([a,b,x] := lin(y,x))'. The lin function returns a 3-vector if its argument is linear, or leaves itself unevaluated if not. But an unevaluated lin call will not match the 3-vector on the lefthand side of the let, so this let both verifies that y is linear, and binds the coefficients a and b for use elsewhere in the rule. (It would have been possible to use 'sin(a x + b)/b' for the righthand side instead, but using 'sin(y)/b' avoids gratuitous rearrangement of the argument of the sine.)

Similarly, here is a rule that implements an inverse-erf function. It uses root to search for a solution. If root succeeds, it will return a vector of two numbers where the first number is the desired solution. If no solution is found, root remains in symbolic form. So we use let to check that the result was indeed a vector.

        ierf(x) := y :: let([y,z] := root(erf(a) = x, a, .5))

'matches(v,p)'

> The meta-variable v, which must already have been matched to something elsewhere in the rule, is compared against pattern p. Since matches is a standard Calc function, it can appear anywhere in a condition. But if it appears alone or as a term of a top-level '&&', then you get the special extra feature that meta-variables which are bound to things inside p can be used elsewhere in the surrounding rewrite rule.

> The only real difference between 'let(p := v)' and 'matches(v, p)' is that the former evaluates 'v' using the default simplifications, while the latter does not.

'remember'

> This is actually a variable, not a function. If remember appears as a condition in a rule, then when that rule succeeds the original expression and rewritten expression are added to the front of the rule set that contained the rule. If the rule set was not stored in a variable, remember is ignored. The lefthand side is enclosed in quote in the added rule if it contains any variables.

> For example, the rule 'f(n) := n f(n-1) :: remember' applied to 'f(7)' will add the rule 'f(7) := 7 f(6)' to the front of the rule set. The rule set EvalRules works slightly differently: There, the evaluation of 'f(6)' will complete before the result is added to the rule set, in this case as 'f(7) := 5040'. Thus remember is most useful inside EvalRules.

> It is up to you to ensure that the optimization performed by remember is safe. For example, the rule 'foo(n) := n :: evalv(eatfoo) > 0 :: remember' is a bad idea (evalv is the function equivalent of the = command); if the variable

eatfoo ever contains 1, rules like 'foo(7) := 7' will be added to the rule set and will continue to operate even if eatfoo is later changed to 0.

'remember(c)'

Remember the match as described above, but only if condition *c* is true. For example, 'remember(n % 4 = 0)' in the above factorial rule remembers only every fourth result. Note that 'remember(1)' is equivalent to 'remember', and 'remember(0)' has no effect.

10.11.6 Composing Patterns in Rewrite Rules

There are three operators, '&&&', '|||', and '!!!', that combine rewrite patterns to make larger patterns. The combinations are "and," "or," and "not," respectively, and these operators are the pattern equivalents of '&&', '||' and '!' (which operate on zero-or-nonzero logical values).

Note that '&&&', '|||', and '!!!' are left in symbolic form by all regular Calc features; they have special meaning only in the context of rewrite rule patterns.

The pattern '*p1* &&& *p2*' matches anything that matches both *p1* and *p2*. One especially useful case is when one of *p1* or *p2* is a meta-variable. For example, here is a rule that operates on error forms:

    f(x &&& a +/- b, x)   :=   g(x)

This does the same thing, but is arguably simpler than, the rule

    f(a +/- b, a +/- b)   :=   g(a +/- b)

Here's another interesting example:

    ends(cons(a, x) &&& rcons(y, b))   :=   [a, b]

which effectively clips out the middle of a vector leaving just the first and last elements. This rule will change a one-element vector '[a]' to '[a, a]'. The similar rule

    ends(cons(a, rcons(y, b)))   :=   [a, b]

would do the same thing except that it would fail to match a one-element vector.

The pattern '*p1* ||| *p2*' matches anything that matches either *p1* or *p2*. Calc first tries matching against *p1*; if that fails, it goes on to try *p2*.

A simple example of '|||' is

    curve(inf ||| -inf)   :=   0

which converts both 'curve(inf)' and 'curve(-inf)' to zero.

Here is a larger example:

    log(a, b) ||| (ln(a) :: let(b := e))   :=   mylog(a, b)

This matches both generalized and natural logarithms in a single rule. Note that the '::' term must be enclosed in parentheses because that operator has lower precedence than '|||' or ':='.

(In practice this rule would probably include a third alternative, omitted here for brevity, to take care of log10.)

While Calc generally treats interior conditions exactly the same as conditions on the outside of a rule, it does guarantee that if all the variables in the condition are special names like e, or already bound in the pattern to which the condition is attached (say, if 'a' had appeared in this condition), then Calc will process this condition right after matching the pattern to the left of the '::'. Thus, we know that 'b' will be bound to 'e' only if the ln branch of the '|||' was taken.

Note that this rule was careful to bind the same set of meta-variables on both sides of the '|||'. Calc does not check this, but if you bind a certain meta-variable only in one branch and then use that meta-variable elsewhere in the rule, results are unpredictable:

    f(a,b) ||| g(b) := h(a,b)

Here if the pattern matches 'g(17)', Calc makes no promises about the value that will be substituted for 'a' on the righthand side.

The pattern '!!! *pat*' matches anything that does not match *pat*. Any meta-variables that are bound while matching *pat* remain unbound outside of *pat*.

For example,

    f(x &&& !!! a +/- b, !!![]) := g(x)

converts f whose first argument is anything *except* an error form, and whose second argument is not the empty vector, into a similar call to g (but without the second argument).

If we know that the second argument will be a vector (empty or not), then an equivalent rule would be:

    f(x, y) := g(x) :: typeof(x) != 7 :: vlen(y) > 0

where of course 7 is the typeof code for error forms. Another final condition, that works for any kind of 'y', would be '!istrue(y == [])'. (The istrue function returns an explicit 0 if its argument was left in symbolic form; plain '!(y == [])' or 'y != []' would not work to replace '!!![]' since these would be left unsimplified, and thus cause the rule to fail, if 'y' was something like a variable name.)

It is possible for a '!!!' to refer to meta-variables bound elsewhere in the pattern. For example,

    f(a, !!!a) := g(a)

matches any call to f with different arguments, changing this to g with only the first argument.

If a function call is to be matched and one of the argument patterns contains a '!!!' somewhere inside it, that argument will be matched last. Thus

    f(!!!a, a) := g(a)

will be careful to bind 'a' to the second argument of f before testing the first argument. If Calc had tried to match the first argument of f first, the results would have been disastrous: since a was unbound so far, the pattern 'a' would have matched anything at all, and the pattern '!!!a' therefore would *not* have matched anything at all!

10.11.7 Nested Formulas with Rewrite Rules

When a r (calc-rewrite) is used, it takes an expression from the top of the stack and attempts to match any of the specified rules to any part of the expression, starting with the whole expression and then, if that fails, trying deeper and deeper sub-expressions. For each part of the expression, the rules are tried in the order they appear in the rules vector.

The first rule to match the first sub-expression wins; it replaces the matched sub-expression according to the *new* part of the rule.

Often, the rule set will match and change the formula several times. The top-level formula is first matched and substituted repeatedly until it no longer matches the pattern; then, sub-formulas are tried, and so on. Once every part of the formula has gotten its chance, the rewrite mechanism starts over again with the top-level formula (in case a substitution of one of its arguments has caused it again to match). This continues until no further matches can be made anywhere in the formula.

It is possible for a rule set to get into an infinite loop. The most obvious case, replacing a formula with itself, is not a problem because a rule is not considered to "succeed" unless the righthand side actually comes out to something different than the original formula or sub-formula that was matched. But if you accidentally had both 'ln(a b) := ln(a) + ln(b)' and the reverse 'ln(a) + ln(b) := ln(a b)' in your rule set, Calc would run forever switching a formula back and forth between the two forms.

To avoid disaster, Calc normally stops after 100 changes have been made to the formula. This will be enough for most multiple rewrites, but it will keep an endless loop of rewrites from locking up the computer forever. (On most systems, you can also type *C-g* to halt any Emacs command prematurely.)

To change this limit, give a positive numeric prefix argument. In particular, *M-1 a r* applies only one rewrite at a time, useful when you are first testing your rule (or just if repeated rewriting is not what is called for by your application).

You can also put a "function call" 'iterations(*n*)' in place of a rule anywhere in your rules vector (but usually at the top). Then, *n* will be used instead of 100 as the default number of iterations for this rule set. You can use 'iterations(inf)' if you want no iteration limit by default. A prefix argument will override the iterations limit in the rule set.

```
[ iterations(1),
  f(x) := f(x+1) ]
```

More precisely, the limit controls the number of "iterations," where each iteration is a successful matching of a rule pattern whose righthand side, after substituting meta-variables and applying the default simplifications, is different from the original sub-formula that was matched.

A prefix argument of zero sets the limit to infinity. Use with caution!

Given a negative numeric prefix argument, *a r* will match and substitute the top-level expression up to that many times, but will not attempt to match the rules to any sub-expressions.

In a formula, **rewrite(***expr*, *rules*, *n***)** does a rewriting operation. Here *expr* is the expression being rewritten, *rules* is the rule, vector of rules, or variable containing the rules, and *n* is the optional iteration limit, which may be a positive integer, a negative integer, or 'inf' or '-inf'. If *n* is omitted the **iterations** value from the rule set is used; if both are omitted, 100 is used.

10.11.8 Multi-Phase Rewrite Rules

It is possible to separate a rewrite rule set into several *phases*. During each phase, certain rules will be enabled while certain others will be disabled. A *phase schedule* controls the order in which phases occur during the rewriting process.

If a call to the marker function `phase` appears in the rules vector in place of a rule, all rules following that point will be members of the phase(s) identified in the arguments to `phase`. Phases are given integer numbers. The markers 'phase()' and 'phase(all)' both mean the following rules belong to all phases; this is the default at the start of the rule set.

If you do not explicitly schedule the phases, Calc sorts all phase numbers that appear in the rule set and executes the phases in ascending order. For example, the rule set

```
[ f0(x) := g0(x),
  phase(1),
  f1(x) := g1(x),
  phase(2),
  f2(x) := g2(x),
  phase(3),
  f3(x) := g3(x),
  phase(1,2),
  f4(x) := g4(x) ]
```

has three phases, 1 through 3. Phase 1 consists of the `f0`, `f1`, and `f4` rules (in that order). Phase 2 consists of `f0`, `f2`, and `f4`. Phase 3 consists of `f0` and `f3`.

When Calc rewrites a formula using this rule set, it first rewrites the formula using only the phase 1 rules until no further changes are possible. Then it switches to the phase 2 rule set and continues until no further changes occur, then finally rewrites with phase 3. When no more phase 3 rules apply, rewriting finishes. (This is assuming `a r` with a large enough prefix argument to allow the rewriting to run to completion; the sequence just described stops early if the number of iterations specified in the prefix argument, 100 by default, is reached.)

During each phase, Calc descends through the nested levels of the formula as described previously. (See Section 10.11.7 [Nested Formulas with Rewrite Rules], page 304.) Rewriting starts at the top of the formula, then works its way down to the parts, then goes back to the top and works down again. The phase 2 rules do not begin until no phase 1 rules apply anywhere in the formula.

A `schedule` marker appearing in the rule set (anywhere, but conventionally at the top) changes the default schedule of phases. In the simplest case, `schedule` has a sequence of phase numbers for arguments; each phase number is invoked in turn until the arguments to `schedule` are exhausted. Thus adding 'schedule(3,2,1)' at the top of the above rule set would reverse the order of the phases; 'schedule(1,2,3)' would have no effect since this is the default schedule; and 'schedule(1,2,1,3)' would give phase 1 a second chance after phase 2 has completed, before moving on to phase 3.

Any argument to `schedule` can instead be a vector of phase numbers (or even of sub-vectors). Then the sub-sequence of phases described by the vector are tried repeatedly until no change occurs in any phase in the sequence. For example, 'schedule([1, 2], 3)' tries phase 1, then phase 2, then, if either phase made any changes to the formula, repeats these two phases until they can make no further progress. Finally, it goes on to phase 3 for finishing touches.

Also, items in `schedule` can be variable names as well as numbers. A variable name is interpreted as the name of a function to call on the whole formula. For example, 'schedule(1, simplify)' says to apply the phase-1 rules (presumably, all of them), then to call `simplify` which is the function name equivalent of *a s*. Likewise, 'schedule([1, simplify])' says to alternate between phase 1 and *a s* until no further changes occur.

Phases can be used purely to improve efficiency; if it is known that a certain group of rules will apply only at the beginning of rewriting, and a certain other group will apply only at the end, then rewriting will be faster if these groups are identified as separate phases. Once the phase 1 rules are done, Calc can put them aside and no longer spend any time on them while it works on phase 2.

There are also some problems that can only be solved with several rewrite phases. For a real-world example of a multi-phase rule set, examine the set `FitRules`, which is used by the curve-fitting command to convert a model expression to linear form. See Section 10.8.5 [Curve Fitting Details], page 281. This set is divided into four phases. The first phase rewrites certain kinds of expressions to be more easily linearizable, but less computationally efficient. After the linear components have been picked out, the final phase includes the opposite rewrites to put each component back into an efficient form. If both sets of rules were included in one big phase, Calc could get into an infinite loop going back and forth between the two forms.

Elsewhere in `FitRules`, the components are first isolated, then recombined where possible to reduce the complexity of the linear fit, then finally packaged one component at a time into vectors. If the packaging rules were allowed to begin before the recombining rules were finished, some components might be put away into vectors before they had a chance to recombine. By putting these rules in two separate phases, this problem is neatly avoided.

10.11.9 Selections with Rewrite Rules

If a sub-formula of the current formula is selected (as by *j s*; see Section 10.1 [Selecting Subformulas], page 243), the *a r* (`calc-rewrite`) command applies only to that sub-formula. Together with a negative prefix argument, you can use this fact to apply a rewrite to one specific part of a formula without affecting any other parts.

The *j r* (`calc-rewrite-selection`) command allows more sophisticated operations on selections. This command prompts for the rules in the same way as *a r*, but it then applies those rules to the whole formula in question even though a sub-formula of it has been selected. However, the selected sub-formula will first have been surrounded by a 'select( )' function call. (Calc's evaluator does not understand the function name `select`; this is only a tag used by the *j r* command.)

For example, suppose the formula on the stack is '2 (a + b)^2' and the sub-formula 'a + b' is selected. This formula will be rewritten to '2 select(a + b)^2' and then the rewrite rules will be applied in the usual way. The rewrite rules can include references to `select` to tell where in the pattern the selected sub-formula should appear.

If there is still exactly one 'select( )' function call in the formula after rewriting is done, it indicates which part of the formula should be selected afterwards. Otherwise, the formula will be unselected.

You can make *j r* act much like **a r** by enclosing both parts of the rewrite rule with
'`select()`'. However, *j r* allows you to use the current selection in more flexible ways.
Suppose you wished to make a rule which removed the exponent from the selected term;
the rule '`select(a)^x := select(a)`' would work. In the above example, it would rewrite
'`2 select(a + b)^2`' to '`2 select(a + b)`'. This would then be returned to the stack as '`2
(a + b)`' with the '`a + b`' selected.

The *j r* command uses one iteration by default, unlike **a r** which defaults to 100 iterations. A numeric prefix argument affects *j r* in the same way as **a r**. See Section 10.11.7
[Nested Formulas with Rewrite Rules], page 304.

As with other selection commands, *j r* operates on the stack entry that contains the
cursor. (If the cursor is on the top-of-stack '`.`' marker, it works as if the cursor were on the
formula at stack level 1.)

If you don't specify a set of rules, the rules are taken from the top of the stack, just as
with **a r**. In this case, the cursor must indicate stack entry 2 or above as the formula to
be rewritten (otherwise the same formula would be used as both the target and the rewrite
rules).

If the indicated formula has no selection, the cursor position within the formula temporarily selects a sub-formula for the purposes of this command. If the cursor is not on any
sub-formula (e.g., it is in the line-number area to the left of the formula), the '`select( )`'
markers are ignored by the rewrite mechanism and the rules are allowed to apply anywhere
in the formula.

As a special feature, the normal **a r** command also ignores '`select( )`' calls in rewrite
rules. For example, if you used the above rule '`select(a)^x := select(a)`' with **a r**, it
would apply the rule as if it were '`a^x := a`'. Thus, you can write general purpose rules
with '`select( )`' hints inside them so that they will "do the right thing" in both **a r** and *j
r*, both with and without selections.

10.11.10 Matching Commands

The **a m** (`calc-match`) [`match`] function takes a vector of formulas and a rewrite-rule-style
pattern, and produces a vector of all formulas which match the pattern. The command
prompts you to enter the pattern; as for **a r**, you can enter a single pattern (i.e., a formula
with meta-variables), or a vector of patterns, or a variable which contains patterns, or you
can give a blank response in which case the patterns are taken from the top of the stack.
The pattern set will be compiled once and saved if it is stored in a variable. If there are
several patterns in the set, vector elements are kept if they match any of the patterns.

For example, '`match(a+b, [x, x+y, x-y, 7, x+y+z])`' will return '`[x+y, x-y, x+y+z]`'.

The `import` mechanism is not available for pattern sets.

The **a m** command can also be used to extract all vector elements which satisfy any
condition: The pattern '`x :: x>0`' will select all the positive vector elements.

With the Inverse flag [`matchnot`], this command extracts all vector elements which do
not match the given pattern.

There is also a function '`matches(x, p)`' which evaluates to 1 if expression *x* matches
pattern *p*, or to 0 otherwise. This is sometimes useful for including into the conditional
clauses of other rewrite rules.

The function `vmatches` is just like `matches`, except that if the match succeeds it returns a vector of assignments to the meta-variables instead of the number 1. For example, 'vmatches(f(1,2), f(a,b))' returns '[a := 1, b := 2]'. If the match fails, the function returns the number 0.

10.11.11 Automatic Rewrites

It is possible to get Calc to apply a set of rewrite rules on all results, effectively adding to the built-in set of default simplifications. To do this, simply store your rule set in the variable `EvalRules`. There is a convenient *s E* command for editing `EvalRules`; see Section 12.3 [Operations on Variables], page 325.

For example, suppose you want 'sin(a + b)' to be expanded out to 'sin(b) cos(a) + cos(b) sin(a)' wherever it appears, and similarly for 'cos(a + b)'. The corresponding rewrite rule set would be,

```
[ sin(a + b)  :=  cos(a) sin(b) + sin(a) cos(b),
  cos(a + b)  :=  cos(a) cos(b) - sin(a) sin(b) ]
```

To apply these manually, you could put them in a variable called `trigexp` and then use *a r trigexp* every time you wanted to expand trig functions. But if instead you store them in the variable `EvalRules`, they will automatically be applied to all sines and cosines of sums. Then, with '2 x' and '45' on the stack, typing + *S* will (assuming Degrees mode) result in '0.7071 sin(2 x) + 0.7071 cos(2 x)' automatically.

As each level of a formula is evaluated, the rules from `EvalRules` are applied before the default simplifications. Rewriting continues until no further `EvalRules` apply. Note that this is different from the usual order of application of rewrite rules: `EvalRules` works from the bottom up, simplifying the arguments to a function before the function itself, while *a r* applies rules from the top down.

Because the `EvalRules` are tried first, you can use them to override the normal behavior of any built-in Calc function.

It is important not to write a rule that will get into an infinite loop. For example, the rule set '[f(0) := 1, f(n) := n f(n-1)]' appears to be a good definition of a factorial function, but it is unsafe. Imagine what happens if 'f(2.5)' is simplified. Calc will continue to subtract 1 from this argument forever without reaching zero. A safer second rule would be 'f(n) := n f(n-1) :: n>0'. Another dangerous rule is 'g(x, y) := g(y, x)'. Rewriting 'g(2, 4)', this would bounce back and forth between that and 'g(4, 2)' forever. If an infinite loop in `EvalRules` occurs, Emacs will eventually stop with a "Computation got stuck or ran too long" message.

Another subtle difference between `EvalRules` and regular rewrites concerns rules that rewrite a formula into an identical formula. For example, 'f(n) := f(floor(n))' "fails to match" when n is already an integer. But in `EvalRules` this case is detected only if the righthand side literally becomes the original formula before any further simplification. This means that 'f(n) := f(floor(n))' will get into an infinite loop if it occurs in `EvalRules`. Calc will replace 'f(6)' with 'f(floor(6))', which is different from 'f(6)', so it will consider the rule to have matched and will continue simplifying that formula; first the argument is simplified to get 'f(6)', then the rule matches again to get 'f(floor(6))' again, ad infinitum. A much safer rule would check its argument first, say, with 'f(n) := f(floor(n)) :: !dint(n)'.

(What really happens is that the rewrite mechanism substitutes the meta-variables in the righthand side of a rule, compares to see if the result is the same as the original formula and fails if so, then uses the default simplifications to simplify the result and compares again (and again fails if the formula has simplified back to its original form). The only special wrinkle for the `EvalRules` is that the same rules will come back into play when the default simplifications are used. What Calc wants to do is build '`f(floor(6))`', see that this is different from the original formula, simplify to '`f(6)`', see that this is the same as the original formula, and thus halt the rewriting. But while simplifying, '`f(6)`' will again trigger the same `EvalRules` rule and Calc will get into a loop inside the rewrite mechanism itself.)

The `phase`, `schedule`, and `iterations` markers do not work in `EvalRules`. If the rule set is divided into phases, only the phase 1 rules are applied, and the schedule is ignored. The rules are always repeated as many times as possible.

The `EvalRules` are applied to all function calls in a formula, but not to numbers (and other number-like objects like error forms), nor to vectors or individual variable names. (Though they will apply to *components* of vectors and error forms when appropriate.) You might try to make a variable `phihat` which automatically expands to its definition without the need to press = by writing the rule '`quote(phihat) := (1-sqrt(5))/2`', but unfortunately this rule will not work as part of `EvalRules`.

Finally, another limitation is that Calc sometimes calls its built-in functions directly rather than going through the default simplifications. When it does this, `EvalRules` will not be able to override those functions. For example, when you take the absolute value of the complex number $(2, 3)$, Calc computes '`sqrt(2*2 + 3*3)`' by calling the multiplication, addition, and square root functions directly rather than applying the default simplifications to this formula. So an `EvalRules` rule that (perversely) rewrites '`sqrt(13) := 6`' would not apply. (However, if you put Calc into Symbolic mode so that '`sqrt(13)`' will be left in symbolic form by the built-in square root function, your rule will be able to apply. But if the complex number were $(3, 4)$, so that '`sqrt(25)`' must be calculated, then Symbolic mode will not help because '`sqrt(25)`' can be evaluated exactly to 5.)

One subtle restriction that normally only manifests itself with `EvalRules` is that while a given rewrite rule is in the process of being checked, that same rule cannot be recursively applied. Calc effectively removes the rule from its rule set while checking the rule, then puts it back once the match succeeds or fails. (The technical reason for this is that compiled pattern programs are not reentrant.) For example, consider the rule '`foo(x) := x :: foo(x/2) > 0`' attempting to match '`foo(8)`'. This rule will be inactive while the condition '`foo(4) > 0`' is checked, even though it might be an integral part of evaluating that condition. Note that this is not a problem for the more usual recursive type of rule, such as '`foo(x) := foo(x/2)`', because there the rule has succeeded and been reactivated by the time the righthand side is evaluated.

If `EvalRules` has no stored value (its default state), or if anything but a vector is stored in it, then it is ignored.

Even though Calc's rewrite mechanism is designed to compare rewrite rules to formulas as quickly as possible, storing rules in `EvalRules` may make Calc run substantially slower. This is particularly true of rules where the top-level call is a commonly used function, or is not fixed. The rule '`f(n) := n f(n-1) :: n>0`' will only activate the rewrite mechanism for calls to the function `f`, but '`lg(n) + lg(m) := lg(n m)`' will check every '`+`' operator.

```
apply(f, [a*b]) := apply(f, [a]) + apply(f, [b]) :: in(f, [ln, log10])
```

may seem more "efficient" than two separate rules for `ln` and `log10`, but actually it is vastly less efficient because rules with `apply` as the top-level pattern must be tested against *every* function call that is simplified.

Suppose you want 'sin(a + b)' to be expanded out not all the time, but only when algebraic simplifications are used to simplify the formula. The variable `AlgSimpRules` holds rules for this purpose. The `a s` command will apply `EvalRules` and `AlgSimpRules` to the formula, as well as all of its built-in simplifications.

Most of the special limitations for `EvalRules` don't apply to `AlgSimpRules`. Calc simply does an `a r AlgSimpRules` command with an infinite repeat count as the first step of algebraic simplifications. It then applies its own built-in simplifications throughout the formula, and then repeats these two steps (along with applying the default simplifications) until no further changes are possible.

There are also `ExtSimpRules` and `UnitSimpRules` variables that are used by `a e` and `u s`, respectively; these commands also apply `EvalRules` and `AlgSimpRules`. The variable `IntegSimpRules` contains simplification rules that are used only during integration by `a i`.

10.11.12 Debugging Rewrites

If a buffer named `*Trace*` exists, the rewrite mechanism will record some useful information there as it operates. The original formula is written there, as is the result of each successful rewrite, and the final result of the rewriting. All phase changes are also noted.

Calc always appends to `*Trace*`. You must empty this buffer yourself periodically if it is in danger of growing unwieldy.

Note that the rewriting mechanism is substantially slower when the `*Trace*` buffer exists, even if the buffer is not visible on the screen. Once you are done, you will probably want to kill this buffer (with `C-x k *Trace* RET`). If you leave it in existence and forget about it, all your future rewrite commands will be needlessly slow.

10.11.13 Examples of Rewrite Rules

Returning to the example of substituting the pattern 'sin(x)^2 + cos(x)^2' with 1, we saw that the rule 'opt(a) sin(x)^2 + opt(a) cos(x)^2 := a' does a good job of finding suitable cases. Another solution would be to use the rule 'cos(x)^2 := 1 - sin(x)^2', followed by algebraic simplification if necessary. This rule will be the most effective way to do the job, but at the expense of making some changes that you might not desire.

Another algebraic rewrite rule is 'exp(x+y) := exp(x) exp(y)'. To make this work with the *j r* command so that it can be easily targeted to a particular exponential in a large formula, you might wish to write the rule as 'select(exp(x+y)) := select(exp(x) exp(y))'. The 'select' markers will be ignored by the regular *a r* command (see Section 10.11.9 [Selections with Rewrite Rules], page 307).

A surprisingly useful rewrite rule is 'a/(b-c) := a*(b+c)/(b^2-c^2)'. This will simplify the formula whenever *b* and/or *c* can be made simpler by squaring. For example, applying this rule to '2 / (sqrt(2) + 3)' yields '6:7 - 2:7 sqrt(2)' (assuming Symbolic mode has been enabled to keep the square root from being evaluated to a floating-point approximation). This rule is also useful when working with symbolic complex numbers, e.g., '(a + b i) / (c + d i)'.

As another example, we could define our own "triangular numbers" function with the rules '[tri(0) := 0, tri(n) := n + tri(n-1) :: n>0]'. Enter this vector and store it in a variable: *s t trirules*. Now, given a suitable formula like 'tri(5)' on the stack, type 'a r trirules' to apply these rules repeatedly. After six applications, a r will stop with 15 on the stack. Once these rules are debugged, it would probably be most useful to add them to EvalRules so that Calc will evaluate the new tri function automatically. We could then use *Z K* on the keyboard macro ' *tri($) RET* to make a command that applies tri to the value on the top of the stack. See Chapter 17 [Programming], page 363.

The following rule set, contributed by François Pinard, implements *quaternions*, a generalization of the concept of complex numbers. Quaternions have four components, and are here represented by function calls 'quat(w, [x, y, z])' with "real part" w and the three "imaginary" parts collected into a vector. Various arithmetical operations on quaternions are supported. To use these rules, either add them to EvalRules, or create a command based on a r for simplifying quaternion formulas. A convenient way to enter quaternions would be a command defined by a keyboard macro containing: ' *quat($$$$, [$$$, $$, $]) RET*.

```
[ quat(w, x, y, z) := quat(w, [x, y, z]),
  quat(w, [0, 0, 0]) := w,
  abs(quat(w, v)) := hypot(w, v),
  -quat(w, v) := quat(-w, -v),
  r + quat(w, v) := quat(r + w, v) :: real(r),
  r - quat(w, v) := quat(r - w, -v) :: real(r),
  quat(w1, v1) + quat(w2, v2) := quat(w1 + w2, v1 + v2),
  r * quat(w, v) := quat(r * w, r * v) :: real(r),
  plain(quat(w1, v1) * quat(w2, v2))
      := quat(w1 * w2 - v1 * v2, w1 * v2 + w2 * v1 + cross(v1, v2)),
  quat(w1, v1) / r := quat(w1 / r, v1 / r) :: real(r),
  z / quat(w, v) := z * quatinv(quat(w, v)),
  quatinv(quat(w, v)) := quat(w, -v) / (w^2 + v^2),
  quatsqr(quat(w, v)) := quat(w^2 - v^2, 2 * w * v),
  quat(w, v)^k := quatsqr(quat(w, v)^(k / 2))
                  :: integer(k) :: k > 0 :: k % 2 = 0,
  quat(w, v)^k := quatsqr(quat(w, v)^((k - 1) / 2)) * quat(w, v)
                  :: integer(k) :: k > 2,
  quat(w, v)^-k := quatinv(quat(w, v)^k) :: integer(k) :: k > 0 ]
```

Quaternions, like matrices, have non-commutative multiplication. In other words, $q1 * q2 = q2 * q1$ is not necessarily true if $q1$ and $q2$ are quat forms. The 'quat*quat' rule above uses plain to prevent Calc from rearranging the product. It may also be wise to add the line '[quat(), matrix]' to the Decls matrix, to ensure that Calc's other algebraic operations will not rearrange a quaternion product. See Section 6.6 [Declarations], page 143.

These rules also accept a four-argument quat form, converting it to the preferred form in the first rule. If you would rather see results in the four-argument form, just append the two items 'phase(2), quat(w, [x, y, z]) := quat(w, x, y, z)' to the end of the rule set. (But remember that multi-phase rule sets don't work in EvalRules.)

11 Operating on Units

One special interpretation of algebraic formulas is as numbers with units. For example, the formula '5 m / s^2' can be read "five meters per second squared." The commands in this chapter help you manipulate units expressions in this form. Units-related commands begin with the u prefix key.

11.1 Basic Operations on Units

A *units expression* is a formula which is basically a number multiplied and/or divided by one or more *unit names*, which may optionally be raised to integer powers. Actually, the value part need not be a number; any product or quotient involving unit names is a units expression. Many of the units commands will also accept any formula, where the command applies to all units expressions which appear in the formula.

A unit name is a variable whose name appears in the *unit table*, or a variable whose name is a prefix character like 'k' (for "kilo") or 'u' (for "micro") followed by a name in the unit table. A substantial table of built-in units is provided with Calc; see Section 11.3 [Predefined Units], page 316. You can also define your own unit names; see Section 11.4 [User-Defined Units], page 317.

Note that if the value part of a units expression is exactly '1', it will be removed by the Calculator's automatic algebra routines: The formula '1 mm' is "simplified" to 'mm'. This is only a display anomaly, however; 'mm' will work just fine as a representation of one millimeter.

You may find that Algebraic mode (see Section 3.5 [Algebraic Entry], page 109) makes working with units expressions easier. Otherwise, you will have to remember to hit the apostrophe key every time you wish to enter units.

The u s (calc-simplify-units) [usimplify] command simplifies a units expression. It uses Calc's algebraic simplifications to simplify the expression first as a regular algebraic formula; it then looks for features that can be further simplified by converting one object's units to be compatible with another's. For example, '5 m + 23 mm' will simplify to '5.023 m'. When different but compatible units are added, the righthand term's units are converted to match those of the lefthand term. See Section 6.5 [Simplification Modes], page 142, for a way to have this done automatically at all times.

Units simplification also handles quotients of two units with the same dimensionality, as in '2 in s/L cm' to '5.08 s/L'; fractional powers of unit expressions, as in 'sqrt(9 mm^2)' to '3 mm' and 'sqrt(9 acre)' to a quantity in meters; and floor, ceil, round, rounde, roundu, trunc, float, frac, abs, and clean applied to units expressions, in which case the operation in question is applied only to the numeric part of the expression. Finally, trigonometric functions of quantities with units of angle are evaluated, regardless of the current angular mode.

The u c (calc-convert-units) command converts a units expression to new, compatible units. For example, given the units expression '55 mph', typing u c m/s RET produces '24.5872 m/s'. If you have previously converted a units expression with the same type of units (in this case, distance over time), you will be offered the previous choice of new units as a default. Continuing the above example, entering the units expression '100 km/hr' and typing u c RET (without specifying new units) produces '27.7777777778 m/s'.

The *u c* command treats temperature units (like 'degC' and 'K') as relative temperatures. For example, *u c* converts '10 degC' to '18 degF': A change of 10 degrees Celsius corresponds to a change of 18 degrees Fahrenheit. To convert absolute temperatures, you can use the *u t* (`calc-convert-temperature`) command. The value on the stack must be a simple units expression with units of temperature only. This command would convert '10 degC' to '50 degF', the equivalent temperature on the Fahrenheit scale.

While many of Calc's conversion factors are exact, some are necessarily approximate. If Calc is in fraction mode (see Section 6.4.3 [Fraction Mode], page 140), then unit conversions will try to give exact, rational conversions, but it isn't always possible. Given '55 mph' in fraction mode, typing *u c m/s RET* produces '15367:625 m/s', for example, while typing *u c au/yr RET* produces '5.18665819999e-3 au/yr'.

If the units you request are inconsistent with the original units, the number will be converted into your units times whatever "remainder" units are left over. For example, converting '55 mph' into acres produces '6.08e-3 acre / (m s)'. Remainder units are expressed in terms of "fundamental" units like 'm' and 's', regardless of the input units.

If you intend that your new units be consistent with the original units, the *u n* (`calc-convert-exact-units`) command will check the units before the conversion. For example, to change 'mi/hr' to 'km/hr', you could type *u c km RET*, but *u n km RET* would signal an error. You would need to type *u n km/hr RET*.

One special exception is that if you specify a single unit name, and a compatible unit appears somewhere in the units expression, then that compatible unit will be converted to the new unit and the remaining units in the expression will be left alone. For example, given the input '980 cm/s^2', the command *u c ms* will change the 's' to 'ms' to get '9.8e-4 cm/ms^2'. The "remainder unit" 'cm' is left alone rather than being changed to the base unit 'm'.

You can use explicit unit conversion instead of the *u s* command to gain more control over the units of the result of an expression. For example, given '5 m + 23 mm', you can type *u c m* or *u c mm* to express the result in either meters or millimeters. (For that matter, you could type *u c fath* to express the result in fathoms, if you preferred!)

In place of a specific set of units, you can also enter one of the units system names si, mks (equivalent), or cgs. For example, *u c si RET* converts the expression into International System of Units (SI) base units. Also, *u c base* converts to Calc's base units, which are the same as si units except that base uses 'g' as the fundamental unit of mass whereas si uses 'kg'.

The *u c* command also accepts *composite units*, which are expressed as the sum of several compatible unit names. For example, converting '30.5 in' to units 'mi+ft+in' (miles, feet, and inches) produces '2 ft + 6.5 in'. Calc first sorts the unit names into order of decreasing relative size. It then accounts for as much of the input quantity as it can using an integer number times the largest unit, then moves on to the next smaller unit, and so on. Only the smallest unit may have a non-integer amount attached in the result. A few standard unit names exist for common combinations, such as mfi for 'mi+ft+in', and tpo for 'ton+lb+oz'. Composite units are expanded as if by *a x*, so that '(ft+in)/hr' is first converted to 'ft/hr+in/hr'.

If the value on the stack does not contain any units, *u c* will prompt first for the old units which this value should be considered to have, then for the new units. (If the value on the stack can be simplified so that it doesn't contain any units, like 'ft/in' can be simplified to 12, then u c will still prompt for both old units and new units. Assuming the old and new units you give are consistent with each other, the result also will not contain any units. For example, u c cm RET in RET converts the number 2 on the stack to 5.08.

The u b (calc-base-units) command is shorthand for u c base; it converts the units expression on the top of the stack into base units. If u s does not simplify a units expression as far as you would like, try u b.

Like the u c command, the u b command treats temperature units as relative temperatures.

The u r (calc-remove-units) command removes units from the formula at the top of the stack. The u x (calc-extract-units) command extracts only the units portion of a formula. These commands essentially replace every term of the formula that does or doesn't (respectively) look like a unit name by the constant 1, then resimplify the formula.

The u a (calc-autorange-units) command turns on and off a mode in which unit prefixes like k ("kilo") are automatically applied to keep the numeric part of a units expression in a reasonable range. This mode affects u s and all units conversion commands except u b. For example, with autoranging on, '12345 Hz' will be simplified to '12.345 kHz'. Autoranging is useful for some kinds of units (like Hz and m), but is probably undesirable for non-metric units like ft and tbsp. (Composite units are more appropriate for those; see above.)

Autoranging always applies the prefix to the leftmost unit name. Calc chooses the largest prefix that causes the number to be greater than or equal to 1.0. Thus an increasing sequence of adjusted times would be '1 ms, 10 ms, 100 ms, 1 s, 10 s, 100 s, 1 ks'. Generally the rule of thumb is that the number will be adjusted to be in the interval '[1 .. 1000)', although there are several exceptions to this rule. First, if the unit has a power then this is not possible; '0.1 s^2' simplifies to '100000 ms^2'. Second, the "centi-" prefix is allowed to form cm (centimeters), but will not apply to other units. The "deci-," "deka-," and "hecto-" prefixes are never used. Thus the allowable interval is '[1 .. 10)' for millimeters and '[1 .. 100)' for centimeters. Finally, a prefix will not be added to a unit if the resulting name is also the actual name of another unit; '1e-15 t' would normally be considered a "femto-ton," but it is written as '1000 at' (1000 atto-tons) instead because ft would be confused with feet.

11.2 The Units Table

The u v (calc-enter-units-table) command displays the units table in another buffer called *Units Table*. Each entry in this table gives the unit name as it would appear in an expression, the definition of the unit in terms of simpler units, and a full name or description of the unit. Fundamental units are defined as themselves; these are the units produced by the u b command. The fundamental units are meters, seconds, grams, kelvins, amperes, candelas, moles, radians, and steradians.

The Units Table buffer also displays the Unit Prefix Table. Note that two prefixes, "kilo" and "hecto," accept either upper- or lower-case prefix letters. 'Meg' is also accepted as a synonym for the 'M' prefix. Whenever a unit name can be interpreted as either a built-in name or a prefix followed by another built-in name, the former interpretation wins. For example, '2 pt' means two pints, not two pico-tons.

The Units Table buffer, once created, is not rebuilt unless you define new units. To force the buffer to be rebuilt, give any numeric prefix argument to *u v*.

The *u V* (`calc-view-units-table`) command is like *u v* except that the cursor is not moved into the Units Table buffer. You can type *u V* again to remove the Units Table from the display. To return from the Units Table buffer after a *u v*, type *C-x * c* again or use the regular Emacs *C-x o* (`other-window`) command. You can also kill the buffer with *C-x k* if you wish; the actual units table is safely stored inside the Calculator.

The *u g* (`calc-get-unit-definition`) command retrieves a unit's defining expression and pushes it onto the Calculator stack. For example, *u g in* will produce the expression '2.54 cm'. This is the same definition for the unit that would appear in the Units Table buffer. Note that this command works only for actual unit names; *u g km* will report that no such unit exists, for example, because km is really the unit m with a k ("kilo") prefix. To see a definition of a unit in terms of base units, it is easier to push the unit name on the stack and then reduce it to base units with *u b*.

The *u e* (`calc-explain-units`) command displays an English description of the units of the expression on the stack. For example, for the expression '62 km^2 g / s^2 mol K', the description is "Square-Kilometer Gram per (Second-squared Mole Degree-Kelvin)." This command uses the English descriptions that appear in the righthand column of the Units Table.

11.3 Predefined Units

The definitions of many units have changed over the years. For example, the meter was originally defined in 1791 as one ten-millionth of the distance from the Equator to the North Pole. In order to be more precise, the definition was adjusted several times, and now a meter is defined as the distance that light will travel in a vacuum in 1/299792458 of a second; consequently, the speed of light in a vacuum is exactly 299792458 m/s. Many other units have been redefined in terms of fundamental physical processes; a second, for example, is currently defined as 9192631770 periods of a certain radiation related to the cesium-133 atom. The only SI unit that is not based on a fundamental physical process (although there are efforts to change this) is the kilogram, which was originally defined as the mass of one liter of water, but is now defined as the mass of the international prototype of the kilogram (IPK), a cylinder of platinum-iridium kept at the Bureau international des poids et mesures in Sèvres, France. (There are several copies of the IPK throughout the world.) The British imperial units, once defined in terms of physical objects, were redefined in 1963 in terms of SI units. The US customary units, which were the same as British units until the British imperial system was created in 1824, were also defined in terms of the SI units in 1893. Because of these redefinitions, conversions between metric, British Imperial, and US customary units can often be done precisely.

Since the exact definitions of many kinds of units have evolved over the years, and since certain countries sometimes have local differences in their definitions, it is a good idea to examine Calc's definition of a unit before depending on its exact value. For example, there are three different units for gallons, corresponding to the US (`gal`), Canadian (`galC`), and British (`galUK`) definitions. Also, note that `oz` is a standard ounce of mass, `ozt` is a Troy ounce, and `ozfl` is a fluid ounce.

The temperature units corresponding to degrees Kelvin and Centigrade (Celsius) are the same in this table, since most units commands treat temperatures as being relative. The `calc-convert-temperature` command has special rules for handling the different absolute magnitudes of the various temperature scales.

The unit of volume "liters" can be referred to by either the lower-case `l` or the upper-case `L`.

The unit `A` stands for amperes; the name `Ang` is used for angstroms.

The unit `pt` stands for pints; the name `point` stands for a typographical point, defined by '72 point = 1 in'. This is slightly different than the point defined by the American Typefounder's Association in 1886, but the point used by Calc has become standard largely due to its use by the PostScript page description language. There is also `texpt`, which stands for a printer's point as defined by the TeX typesetting system: '72.27 texpt = 1 in'. Other units used by TeX are available; they are `texpc` (a pica), `texbp` (a "big point", equal to a standard point which is larger than the point used by TeX), `texdd` (a Didot point), `texcc` (a Cicero) and `texsp` (a scaled TeX point, all dimensions representable in TeX are multiples of this value).

When Calc is using the TeX or LaTeX language mode (see Section 6.8.3 [TeX and LaTeX Language Modes], page 161), the TeX specific unit names will not use the 'tex' prefix; the unit name for a TeX point will be 'pt' instead of 'texpt', for example. To avoid conflicts, the unit names for pint and parsec will simply be 'pint' and 'parsec' instead of 'pt' and 'pc'.

The unit `e` stands for the elementary (electron) unit of charge; because algebra command could mistake this for the special constant e, Calc provides the alternate unit name `ech` which is preferable to `e`.

The name `g` stands for one gram of mass; there is also `gf`, one gram of force. (Likewise for `lb`, pounds, and `lbf`.) Meanwhile, one "g" of acceleration is denoted `ga`.

The unit `ton` is a U.S. ton of '2000 lb', and `t` is a metric ton of '1000 kg'.

The names `s` (or `sec`) and `min` refer to units of time; `arcsec` and `arcmin` are units of angle.

Some "units" are really physical constants; for example, `c` represents the speed of light, and `h` represents Planck's constant. You can use these just like other units: converting '.5 c' to 'm/s' expresses one-half the speed of light in meters per second. You can also use this merely as a handy reference; the `u g` command gets the definition of one of these constants in its normal terms, and `u b` expresses the definition in base units.

Two units, `pi` and `alpha` (the fine structure constant, approximately 1/137) are dimensionless. The units simplification commands simply treat these names as equivalent to their corresponding values. However you can, for example, use `u c` to convert a pure number into multiples of the fine structure constant, or `u b` to convert this back into a pure number. (When `u c` prompts for the "old units," just enter a blank line to signify that the value really is unitless.)

11.4 User-Defined Units

Calc provides ways to get quick access to your selected "favorite" units, as well as ways to define your own new units.

To select your favorite units, store a vector of unit names or expressions in the Calc variable `Units`. The `u 1` through `u 9` commands (`calc-quick-units`) provide access to these units. If the value on the top of the stack is a plain number (with no units attached), then `u 1` gives it the specified units. (Basically, it multiplies the number by the first item in the `Units` vector.) If the number on the stack *does* have units, then `u 1` converts that number to the new units. For example, suppose the vector '[in, ft]' is stored in `Units`. Then *30 u 1* will create the expression '30 in', and *u 2* will convert that expression to '2.5 ft'.

The *u 0* command accesses the tenth element of `Units`. Only ten quick units may be defined at a time. If the `Units` variable has no stored value (the default), or if its value is not a vector, then the quick-units commands will not function. The *s U* command is a convenient way to edit the `Units` variable; see Section 12.3 [Operations on Variables], page 325.

The *u d* (`calc-define-unit`) command records the units expression on the top of the stack as the definition for a new, user-defined unit. For example, putting '16.5 ft' on the stack and typing *u d rod* defines the new unit 'rod' to be equivalent to 16.5 feet. The unit conversion and simplification commands will now treat `rod` just like any other unit of length. You will also be prompted for an optional English description of the unit, which will appear in the Units Table. If you wish the definition of this unit to be displayed in a special way in the Units Table buffer (such as with an asterisk to indicate an approximate value), then you can call this command with an argument, *C-u u d*; you will then also be prompted for a string that will be used to display the definition.

The *u u* (`calc-undefine-unit`) command removes a user-defined unit. It is not possible to remove one of the predefined units, however.

If you define a unit with an existing unit name, your new definition will replace the original definition of that unit. If the unit was a predefined unit, the old definition will not be replaced, only "shadowed." The built-in definition will reappear if you later use *u u* to remove the shadowing definition.

To create a new fundamental unit, use either 1 or the unit name itself as the defining expression. Otherwise the expression can involve any other units that you like (except for composite units like 'mfi'). You can create a new composite unit with a sum of other units as the defining expression. The next unit operation like *u c* or *u v* will rebuild the internal unit table incorporating your modifications. Note that erroneous definitions (such as two units defined in terms of each other) will not be detected until the unit table is next rebuilt; *u v* is a convenient way to force this to happen.

Temperature units are treated specially inside the Calculator; it is not possible to create user-defined temperature units.

The *u p* (`calc-permanent-units`) command stores the user-defined units in your Calc init file (the file given by the variable `calc-settings-file`, typically `~/.emacs.d/calc.el`), so that the units will still be available in subsequent Emacs sessions. If there was already a set of user-defined units in your Calc init file, it is replaced by the new set. (See Section 6.1 [General Mode Commands], page 137, for a way to tell Calc to use a different file for the Calc init file.)

11.5 Logarithmic Units

The units dB (decibels) and Np (nepers) are logarithmic units which are manipulated differ-ently than standard units. Calc provides commands to work with these logarithmic units.

Decibels and nepers are used to measure power quantities as well as field quantities (quantities whose squares are proportional to power); these two types of quantities are handled slightly different from each other. By default the Calc commands work as if power quantities are being used; with the H prefix the Calc commands work as if field quantities are being used.

The decibel level of a power P_1, relative to a reference power P_0, is defined to be $10\log_{10}(P_1/P_0)$dB. (The factor of 10 is because a decibel, as its name implies, is one-tenth of a bel. The bel, named after Alexander Graham Bell, was considered to be too large of a unit and was effectively replaced by the decibel.) If F is a field quantity with power $P = kF^2$, then a reference quantity of F_0 would correspond to a power of $P_0 = kF_0^2$. If $P_1 = kF_1^2$, then

$$10\log_{10}(P_1/P_0) = 10\log_{10}(F_1^2/F_0^2) = 20\log_{10}(F_1/F_0)$$

In order to get the same decibel level regardless of whether a field quantity or the correspond-ing power quantity is used, the decibel level of a field quantity F_1, relative to a reference F_0, is defined as $20\log_{10}(F_1/F_0)$dB. For example, the decibel value of a sound pressure level of 60μPa relative to 20μPa (the threshold of human hearing) is $20\log_{10}(60\mu\text{Pa}/20\mu\text{Pa})$dB $= 20\log_{10}(3)$dB, which is about 9.54dB. Note that in taking the ratio, the original units cancel and so these logarithmic units are dimensionless.

Nepers (named after John Napier, who is credited with inventing the logarithm) are similar to bels except they use natural logarithms instead of common logarithms. The neper level of a power P_1, relative to a reference power P_0, is $(1/2)\ln(P_1/P_0)$Np. The neper level of a field F_1, relative to a reference field F_0, is $\ln(F_1/F_0)$Np.

For power quantities, Calc uses 1mW as the default reference quantity; this default can be changed by changing the value of the customizable variable `calc-lu-power-reference` (see Appendix C [Customizing Calc], page 435). For field quantities, Calc uses 20μPa as the default reference quantity; this is the value used in acoustics which is where decibels are commonly encountered. This default can be changed by changing the value of the customiz-able variable `calc-lu-field-reference` (see Appendix C [Customizing Calc], page 435). A non-default reference quantity will be read from the stack if the capital O prefix is used.

The l q (`calc-lu-quant`) [lupquant] command computes the power quantity corre-sponding to a given number of logarithmic units. With the capital O prefix, O l q, the reference level will be read from the top of the stack. (In an algebraic formula, lupquant can be given an optional second argument which will be used for the reference level.) For example, 20 dB RET l q will return 100 mW; 20 dB RET 4 W RET O l q will return 400 W. The H l q [lufquant] command behaves like l q but computes field quantities instead of power quantities.

The l d (`calc-db`) [dbpower] command will compute the decibel level of a power quan-tity using the default reference level; H l d [dbfield] will compute the decibel level of a field quantity. The commands l n (`calc-np`) [nppower] and H l n [npfield] will similarly compute neper levels. With the capital O prefix these commands will read a reference level from the stack; in an algebraic formula the reference level can be given as an optional second argument.

The sum of two power or field quantities doesn't correspond to the sum of the corresponding decibel or neper levels. If the powers corresponding to decibel levels D_1 and D_2 are added, the corresponding decibel level "sum" will be

$$10 \log_{10}(10^{D_1/10} + 10^{D_2/10}) \text{dB}.$$

When field quantities are combined, it often means the corresponding powers are added and so the above formula might be used. In acoustics, for example, the sound pressure level is a field quantity and so the decibels are often defined using the field formula, but the sound pressure levels are combined as the sound power levels, and so the above formula should be used. If two field quantities themselves are added, the new decibel level will be

$$20 \log_{10}(10^{D_1/20} + 10^{D_2/20}) \text{dB}.$$

If the power corresponding to D dB is multiplied by a number N, then the corresponding decibel level will be

$$D + 10 \log_{10}(N) \text{dB},$$

if a field quantity is multiplied by N the corresponding decibel level will be

$$D + 20 \log_{10}(N) \text{dB}.$$

There are similar formulas for combining nepers. The `l +` (`calc-lu-plus`) [`lupadd`] command will "add" two logarithmic unit power levels this way; with the `H` prefix, `H l +` [`lufadd`] will add logarithmic unit field levels. Similarly, logarithmic units can be "subtracted" with `l -` (`calc-lu-minus`) [`lupsub`] or `H l -` [`lufsub`]. The `l *` (`calc-lu-times`) [`lupmul`] and `H l *` [`lufmul`] commands will "multiply" a logarithmic unit by a number; the `l /` (`calc-lu-divide`) [`lupdiv`] and `H l /` [`lufdiv`] commands will "divide" a logarithmic unit by a number. Note that the reference quantities don't play a role in this arithmetic.

11.6 Musical Notes

Calc can convert between musical notes and their associated frequencies. Notes can be given using either scientific pitch notation or midi numbers. Since these note systems are basically logarithmic scales, Calc uses the `l` prefix for functions operating on notes.

Scientific pitch notation refers to a note by giving a letter A through G, possibly followed by a flat or sharp) with a subscript indicating an octave number. Each octave starts with C and ends with B and the octave numbered 0 was chosen to correspond to the lowest audible frequency. Using this system, middle C (about 261.625 Hz) corresponds to the note C in octave 4 and is denoted C_4. Any frequency can be described by giving a note plus an offset in cents (where a cent is a ratio of frequencies so that a semitone consists of 100 cents).

The midi note number system assigns numbers to notes so that $C_{(-1)}$ corresponds to the midi note number 0 and G_9 corresponds to the midi note number 127. A midi controller can have up to 128 keys and each midi note number from 0 to 127 corresponds to a possible key.

The `l s` (`calc-spn`) [spn] command converts either a frequency or a midi number to scientific pitch notation. For example, 500 Hz gets converted to `B_4 + 21.3094853649 cents` and 84 to `C_6`.

The `l m` (`calc-midi`) [midi] command converts either a frequency or a note given in scientific pitch notation to the corresponding midi number. For example, `C_6` gets converted to 84 and 440 Hz to 69.

The `l f` (`calc-freq`) [freq] command converts either either a midi number or a note given in scientific pitch notation to the corresponding frequency. For example, `Asharp_2 + 30 cents` gets converted to `118.578040134 Hz` and 55 to `195.99771799 Hz`.

Since the frequencies of notes are not usually given exactly (and are typically irrational), the customizable variable `calc-note-threshold` determines how close (in cents) a frequency needs to be to a note to be recognized as that note (see Appendix C [Customizing Calc], page 435). This variable has a default value of 1. For example, middle C is approximately $261.625565302 Hz$; this frequency is often shortened to $261.625 Hz$. Without `calc-note-threshold` (or a value of 0), Calc would convert `261.625 Hz` to scientific pitch notation `B_3 + 99.9962592773 cents`; with the default value of 1, Calc converts `261.625 Hz` to `C_4`.

12 Storing and Recalling

Calculator variables are really just Lisp variables that contain numbers or formulas in a form that Calc can understand. The commands in this section allow you to manipulate variables conveniently. Commands related to variables use the *s* prefix key.

12.1 Storing Variables

The *s s* (calc-store) command stores the value at the top of the stack into a specified variable. It prompts you to enter the name of the variable. If you press a single digit, the value is stored immediately in one of the "quick" variables q0 through q9. Or you can enter any variable name.

The *s s* command leaves the stored value on the stack. There is also an *s t* (calc-store-into) command, which removes a value from the stack and stores it in a variable.

If the top of stack value is an equation 'a = 7' or assignment 'a := 7' with a variable on the lefthand side, then Calc will assign that variable with that value by default, i.e., if you type *s s RET* or *s t RET*. In this example, the value 7 would be stored in the variable 'a'. (If you do type a variable name at the prompt, the top-of-stack value is stored in its entirety, even if it is an equation: 's s b RET' with 'a := 7' on the stack stores 'a := 7' in b.)

In fact, the top of stack value can be a vector of equations or assignments with different variables on their lefthand sides; the default will be to store all the variables with their corresponding righthand sides simultaneously.

It is also possible to type an equation or assignment directly at the prompt for the *s s* or *s t* command: *s s foo = 7*. In this case the expression to the right of the = or := symbol is evaluated as if by the = command, and that value is stored in the variable. No value is taken from the stack; *s s* and *s t* are equivalent when used in this way.

The prefix keys *s* and *t* may be followed immediately by a digit; *s 9* is equivalent to *s s 9*, and *t 9* is equivalent to *s t 9*. (The *t* prefix is otherwise used for trail and time/date commands.)

There are also several "arithmetic store" commands. For example, *s +* removes a value from the stack and adds it to the specified variable. The other arithmetic stores are *s -*, *s **, *s /*, *s ^*, and *s |* (vector concatenation), plus *s n* and *s &* which negate or invert the value in a variable, and *s [* and *s]* which decrease or increase a variable by one.

All the arithmetic stores accept the Inverse prefix to reverse the order of the operands. If v represents the contents of the variable, and a is the value drawn from the stack, then regular *s -* assigns $v := v - a$, but *I s -* assigns $v := a - v$. While *I s ** might seem pointless, it is useful if matrix multiplication is involved. Actually, all the arithmetic stores use formulas designed to behave usefully both forwards and backwards:

```
s +          v := v + a              v := a + v
s -          v := v - a              v := a - v
s *          v := v * a              v := a * v
s /          v := v / a              v := a / v
s ^          v := v ^ a              v := a ^ v
s |          v := v | a              v := a | v
s n          v := v / (-1)           v := (-1) / v
s &          v := v ^ (-1)           v := (-1) ^ v
s [          v := v - 1              v := 1 - v
s ]          v := v - (-1)           v := (-1) - v
```

In the last four cases, a numeric prefix argument will be used in place of the number one. (For example, *M-2 s]* increases a variable by 2, and *M-2 I s]* replaces a variable by minus-two minus the variable.

The first six arithmetic stores can also be typed *s t +*, *s t -*, etc. The commands *s s +*, *s s -*, and so on are analogous arithmetic stores that don't remove the value *a* from the stack.

All arithmetic stores report the new value of the variable in the Trail for your information. They signal an error if the variable previously had no stored value. If default simplifications have been turned off, the arithmetic stores temporarily turn them on for numeric arguments only (i.e., they temporarily do an *m N* command). See Section 6.5 [Simplification Modes], page 142. Large vectors put in the trail by these commands always use abbreviated (*t .*) mode.

The *s m* command is a general way to adjust a variable's value using any Calc function. It is a "mapping" command analogous to *V M*, *V R*, etc. See Section 9.8 [Reducing and Mapping], page 235, to see how to specify a function for a mapping command. Basically, all you do is type the Calc command key that would invoke that function normally. For example, *s m n* applies the *n* key to negate the contents of the variable, so *s m n* is equivalent to *s n*. Also, *s m Q* takes the square root of the value stored in a variable, *s m v v* uses *v v* to reverse the vector stored in the variable, and *s m H I S* takes the hyperbolic arcsine of the variable contents.

If the mapping function takes two or more arguments, the additional arguments are taken from the stack; the old value of the variable is provided as the first argument. Thus *s m -* with *a* on the stack computes $v - a$, just like *s -*. With the Inverse prefix, the variable's original value becomes the *last* argument instead of the first. Thus *I s m -* is also equivalent to *I s -*.

The *s x* (`calc-store-exchange`) command exchanges the value of a variable with the value on the top of the stack. Naturally, the variable must already have a stored value for this to work.

You can type an equation or assignment at the *s x* prompt. The command *s x a=6* takes no values from the stack; instead, it pushes the old value of 'a' on the stack and stores 'a = 6'.

Until you store something in them, most variables are "void," that is, they contain no value at all. If they appear in an algebraic formula they will be left alone even if you press = (`calc-evaluate`). The *s u* (`calc-unstore`) command returns a variable to the void state.

The *s c* (`calc-copy-variable`) command copies the stored value of one variable to another. One way it differs from a simple *s r* followed by an *s t* (aside from saving keystrokes) is that the value never goes on the stack and thus is never rounded, evaluated, or simplified in any way; it is not even rounded down to the current precision.

The only variables with predefined values are the "special constants" `pi`, `e`, `i`, `phi`, and `gamma`. You are free to unstore these variables or to store new values into them if you like, although some of the algebraic-manipulation functions may assume these variables represent their standard values. Calc displays a warning if you change the value of one of these variables, or of one of the other special variables `inf`, `uinf`, and `nan` (which are normally void).

Note that `pi` doesn't actually have 3.14159265359 stored in it, but rather a special magic value that evaluates to π at the current precision. Likewise `e`, `i`, and `phi` evaluate according to the current precision or polar mode. If you recall a value from `pi` and store it back, this magic property will be lost. The magic property is preserved, however, when a variable is copied with *s c*.

If one of the "special constants" is redefined (or undefined) so that it no longer has its magic property, the property can be restored with *s k* (`calc-copy-special-constant`). This command will prompt for a special constant and a variable to store it in, and so a special constant can be stored in any variable. Here, the special constant that you enter doesn't depend on the value of the corresponding variable; `pi` will represent 3.14159... regardless of what is currently stored in the Calc variable `pi`. If one of the other special variables, `inf`, `uinf` or `nan`, is given a value, its original behavior can be restored by voiding it with *s u*.

12.2 Recalling Variables

The most straightforward way to extract the stored value from a variable is to use the *s r* (`calc-recall`) command. This command prompts for a variable name (similarly to `calc-store`), looks up the value of the specified variable, and pushes that value onto the stack. It is an error to try to recall a void variable.

It is also possible to recall the value from a variable by evaluating a formula containing that variable. For example, *' a RET =* is the same as *s r a RET* except that if the variable is void, the former will simply leave the formula 'a' on the stack whereas the latter will produce an error message.

The *r* prefix may be followed by a digit, so that *r 9* is equivalent to *s r 9*.

12.3 Other Operations on Variables

The *s e* (`calc-edit-variable`) command edits the stored value of a variable without ever putting that value on the stack or simplifying or evaluating the value. It prompts for the name of the variable to edit. If the variable has no stored value, the editing buffer will start out empty. If the editing buffer is empty when you press *C-c C-c* to finish, the variable will be made void. See Section 5.2 [Editing Stack Entries], page 134, for a general description of editing.

The *s e* command is especially useful for creating and editing rewrite rules which are stored in variables. Sometimes these rules contain formulas which must not be evaluated until the rules are actually used. (For example, they may refer to 'deriv(x,y)', where x will someday become some expression involving y; if you let Calc evaluate the rule while you are defining it, Calc will replace 'deriv(x,y)' with 0 because the formula x does not itself refer to y.) By contrast, recalling the variable, editing with `, and storing will evaluate the variable's value as a side effect of putting the value on the stack.

There are several special-purpose variable-editing commands that use the *s* prefix followed by a shifted letter:

s A   Edit `AlgSimpRules`. See Section 10.3.2 [Algebraic Simplifications], page 257.

s D   Edit `Decls`. See Section 6.6 [Declarations], page 143.

s E   Edit `EvalRules`. See Section 10.3.1 [Basic Simplifications], page 253.

s F   Edit `FitRules`. See Section 10.8 [Curve Fitting], page 275.

s G   Edit `GenCount`. See Section 10.6 [Solving Equations], page 268.

s H   Edit `Holidays`. See Section 7.5.3 [Business Days], page 195.

s I   Edit `IntegLimit`. See Section 10.5 [Calculus], page 264.

s L   Edit `LineStyles`. See Chapter 13 [Graphics], page 329.

s P   Edit `PointStyles`. See Chapter 13 [Graphics], page 329.

s R   Edit `PlotRejects`. See Chapter 13 [Graphics], page 329.

s T   Edit `TimeZone`. See Section 7.5.4 [Time Zones], page 197.

s U   Edit `Units`. See Section 11.4 [User-Defined Units], page 317.

s X   Edit `ExtSimpRules`. See Section 10.3.3 [Unsafe Simplifications], page 260.

These commands are just versions of *s e* that use fixed variable names rather than prompting for the variable name.

The *s p* (`calc-permanent-variable`) command saves a variable's value permanently in your Calc init file (the file given by the variable `calc-settings-file`, typically `~/.emacs.d/calc.el`), so that its value will still be available in future Emacs sessions. You can re-execute *s p* later on to update the saved value, but the only way to remove a saved variable is to edit your calc init file by hand. (See Section 6.1 [General Mode Commands], page 137, for a way to tell Calc to use a different file for the Calc init file.)

If you do not specify the name of a variable to save (i.e., *s p RET*), all Calc variables with defined values are saved except for the special constants `pi`, `e`, `i`, `phi`, and `gamma`; the variables `TimeZone` and `PlotRejects`; `FitRules`, `DistribRules`, and other built-in rewrite rules; and `PlotDatan` variables generated by the graphics commands. (You can still save these variables by explicitly naming them in an *s p* command.)

The *s i* (`calc-insert-variables`) command writes the values of all Calc variables into a specified buffer. The variables are written with the prefix `var-` in the form of Lisp `setq` commands which store the values in string form. You can place these commands in your Calc init file (or `.emacs`) if you wish, though in this case it would be easier to use *s p RET*. (Note that *s i* omits the same set of variables as *s p RET*; the difference is that *s i* will store the variables in any buffer, and it also stores in a more human-readable format.)

12.4 The Let Command

If you have an expression like 'a+b^2' on the stack and you wish to compute its value where $b = 3$, you can simply store 3 in b and then press = to reevaluate the formula. This has the side-effect of leaving the stored value of 3 in b for future operations.

The *s l* (calc-let) command evaluates a formula under a *temporary* assignment of a variable. It stores the value on the top of the stack into the specified variable, then evaluates the second-to-top stack entry, then restores the original value (or lack of one) in the variable. Thus after ' a+b^2 RET 3 s l b RET, the stack will contain the formula 'a + 9'. The subsequent command *5 s l a RET* will replace this formula with the number 14. The variables 'a' and 'b' are not permanently affected in any way by these commands.

The value on the top of the stack may be an equation or assignment, or a vector of equations or assignments, in which case the default will be analogous to the case of *s t RET*. See Section 12.1 [Storing Variables], page 323.

Also, you can answer the variable-name prompt with an equation or assignment: *s l b=3 RET* is the same as storing 3 on the stack and typing *s l b RET*.

The *a b* (calc-substitute) command is another way to substitute a variable with a value in a formula. It does an actual substitution rather than temporarily assigning the variable and evaluating. For example, letting $n = 2$ in 'f(n pi)' with *a b* will produce 'f(2 pi)', whereas *s l* would give 'f(6.28)' since the evaluation step will also evaluate pi.

12.5 The Evaluates-To Operator

The special algebraic symbol '=>' is known as the *evaluates-to operator*. (It will show up as an evalto function call in other language modes like Pascal and LaTeX.) This is a binary operator, that is, it has a lefthand and a righthand argument, although it can be entered with the righthand argument omitted.

A formula like 'a => b' is evaluated by Calc as follows: First, a is not simplified or modified in any way. The previous value of argument b is thrown away; the formula a is then copied and evaluated as if by the = command according to all current modes and stored variable values, and the result is installed as the new value of b.

For example, suppose you enter the algebraic formula '2 + 3 => 17'. The number 17 is ignored, and the lefthand argument is left in its unevaluated form; the result is the formula '2 + 3 => 5'.

You can enter an '=>' formula either directly using algebraic entry (in which case the righthand side may be omitted since it is going to be replaced right away anyhow), or by using the *s =* (calc-evalto) command, which takes a from the stack and replaces it with 'a => b'.

Calc keeps track of all '=>' operators on the stack, and recomputes them whenever anything changes that might affect their values, i.e., a mode setting or variable value. This occurs only if the '=>' operator is at the top level of the formula, or if it is part of a top-level vector. In other words, pushing '2 + (a => 17)' will change the 17 to the actual value of 'a' when you enter the formula, but the result will not be dynamically updated when 'a' is changed later because the '=>' operator is buried inside a sum. However, a vector of '=>' operators will be recomputed, since it is convenient to push a vector like '[a =>, b =>, c =>]' on the stack to make a concise display of all the variables in your problem. (Another way to do this would be to use '[a, b, c] =>', which provides a slightly different format of display. You can use whichever you find easiest to read.)

The *m C* (`calc-auto-recompute`) command allows you to turn this automatic recomputation on or off. If you turn recomputation off, you must explicitly recompute an '=>' operator on the stack in one of the usual ways, such as by pressing =. Turning recomputation off temporarily can save a lot of time if you will be changing several modes or variables before you look at the '=>' entries again.

Most commands are not especially useful with '=>' operators as arguments. For example, given 'x + 2 => 17', it won't work to type *1 +* to get 'x + 3 => 18'. If you want to operate on the lefthand side of the '=>' operator on the top of the stack, type *j 1* (that's the digit "one") to select the lefthand side, execute your commands, then type *j u* to unselect.

All current modes apply when an '=>' operator is computed, including the current simplification mode. Recall that the formula 'arcsin(sin(x))' will not be handled by Calc's algebraic simplifications, but Calc's unsafe simplifications will reduce it to 'x'. If you enter 'arcsin(sin(x)) =>' normally, the result will be 'arcsin(sin(x)) => arcsin(sin(x))'. If you change to Extended Simplification mode, the result will be 'arcsin(sin(x)) => x'. However, just pressing *a e* once will have no effect on 'arcsin(sin(x)) => arcsin(sin(x))', because the righthand side depends only on the lefthand side and the current mode settings, and the lefthand side is not affected by commands like *a e*.

The "let" command (*s l*) has an interesting interaction with the '=>' operator. The *s l* command evaluates the second-to-top stack entry with the top stack entry supplying a temporary value for a given variable. As you might expect, if that stack entry is an '=>' operator its righthand side will temporarily show this value for the variable. In fact, all '=>'s on the stack will be updated if they refer to that variable. But this change is temporary in the sense that the next command that causes Calc to look at those stack entries will make them revert to the old variable value.

```
2:  a => a           2:  a => 17         2:  a => a
1:  a + 1 => a + 1    1:  a + 1 => 18     1:  a + 1 => a + 1
    .                     .                   .

        17 s l a RET          p 8 RET
```

Here the *p 8* command changes the current precision, thus causing the '=>' forms to be recomputed after the influence of the "let" is gone. The *d SPC* command (`calc-refresh`) is a handy way to force the '=>' operators on the stack to be recomputed without any other side effects.

Embedded mode also uses '=>' operators. In Embedded mode, the lefthand side of an '=>' operator can refer to variables assigned elsewhere in the file by ':=' operators. The assignment operator 'a := 17' does not actually do anything by itself. But Embedded mode recognizes it and marks it as a sort of file-local definition of the variable. You can enter ':=' operators in Algebraic mode, or by using the *s :* (`calc-assign`) [assign] command which takes a variable and value from the stack and replaces them with an assignment.

See Section 6.8.3 [TeX and LaTeX Language Modes], page 161, for the way '=>' appears in TeX language output. The *eqn* mode gives similar treatment to '=>'.

13 Graphics

The commands for graphing data begin with the *g* prefix key. Calc uses GNUPLOT 2.0 or later to do graphics. These commands will only work if GNUPLOT is available on your system. (While GNUPLOT sounds like a relative of GNU Emacs, it is actually completely unrelated. However, it is free software. It can be obtained from 'http://www.gnuplot.info'.)

If you have GNUPLOT installed on your system but Calc is unable to find it, you may need to set the `calc-gnuplot-name` variable in your Calc init file or .emacs. You may also need to set some Lisp variables to show Calc how to run GNUPLOT on your system; these are described under *g D* and *g O* below. If you are using the X window system or MS-Windows, Calc will configure GNUPLOT for you automatically. If you have GNUPLOT 3.0 or later and you are using a Unix or GNU system without X, Calc will configure GNUPLOT to display graphs using simple character graphics that will work on any Posix-compatible terminal.

13.1 Basic Graphics

The easiest graphics command is *g f* (`calc-graph-fast`). This command takes two vectors of equal length from the stack. The vector at the top of the stack represents the "y" values of the various data points. The vector in the second-to-top position represents the corresponding "x" values. This command runs GNUPLOT (if it has not already been started by previous graphing commands) and displays the set of data points. The points will be connected by lines, and there will also be some kind of symbol to indicate the points themselves.

The "x" entry may instead be an interval form, in which case suitable "x" values are interpolated between the minimum and maximum values of the interval (whether the interval is open or closed is ignored).

The "x" entry may also be a number, in which case Calc uses the sequence of "x" values x, $x + 1$, $x + 2$, etc. (Generally the number 0 or 1 would be used for x in this case.)

The "y" entry may be any formula instead of a vector. Calc effectively uses *N* (`calc-eval-num`) to evaluate variables in the formula; the result of this must be a formula in a single (unassigned) variable. The formula is plotted with this variable taking on the various "x" values. Graphs of formulas by default use lines without symbols at the computed data points. Note that if neither "x" nor "y" is a vector, Calc guesses at a reasonable number of data points to use. See the *g N* command below. (The "x" values must be either a vector or an interval if "y" is a formula.)

If "y" is (or evaluates to) a formula of the form 'xy(x, y)' then the result is a parametric plot. The two arguments of the fictitious xy function are used as the "x" and "y" coordinates of the curve, respectively. In this case the "x" vector or interval you specified is not directly visible in the graph. For example, if "x" is the interval '[0..360]' and "y" is the formula 'xy(sin(t), cos(t))', the resulting graph will be a circle.

Also, "x" and "y" may each be variable names, in which case Calc looks for suitable vectors, intervals, or formulas stored in those variables.

The "x" and "y" values for the data points (as pulled from the vectors, calculated from the formulas, or interpolated from the intervals) should be real numbers (integers, fractions, or floats). One exception to this is that the "y" entry can consist of a vector of numbers combined with error forms, in which case the points will be plotted with the appropriate error bars. Other than this, if either the "x" value or the "y" value of a given data point is not a real number, that data point will be omitted from the graph. The points on either side of the invalid point will *not* be connected by a line.

See the documentation for *g* **a** below for a description of the way numeric prefix arguments affect *g* **f**.

If you store an empty vector in the variable `PlotRejects` (i.e., `[ ] s t PlotRejects`), Calc will append information to this vector for every data point which was rejected because its "x" or "y" values were not real numbers. The result will be a matrix where each row holds the curve number, data point number, "x" value, and "y" value for a rejected data point. See Section 12.5 [Evaluates-To Operator], page 327, for a handy way to keep tabs on the current value of `PlotRejects`. See Section 12.3 [Operations on Variables], page 325, for the *s* **R** command which is another easy way to examine `PlotRejects`.

To clear the graphics display, type *g* **c** (`calc-graph-clear`). If the GNUPLOT output device is an X window, the window will go away. Effects on other kinds of output devices will vary. You don't need to use *g* **c** if you don't want to—if you give another *g* **f** or *g* **p** command later on, it will reuse the existing graphics window if there is one.

13.2 Three-Dimensional Graphics

The *g* **F** (`calc-graph-fast-3d`) command makes a three-dimensional graph. It works only if you have GNUPLOT 3.0 or later; with GNUPLOT 2.0, you will see a GNUPLOT error message if you try this command.

The *g* **F** command takes three values from the stack, called "x", "y", and "z", respectively. As was the case for 2D graphs, there are several options for these values.

In the first case, "x" and "y" are each vectors (not necessarily of the same length); either or both may instead be interval forms. The "z" value must be a matrix with the same number of rows as elements in "x", and the same number of columns as elements in "y". The result is a surface plot where z_{ij} is the height of the point at coordinate (x_i, y_j) on the surface. The 3D graph will be displayed from a certain default viewpoint; you can change this viewpoint by adding a '`set view`' to the *Gnuplot Commands* buffer as described later. See the GNUPLOT documentation for a description of the '`set view`' command.

Each point in the matrix will be displayed as a dot in the graph, and these points will be connected by a grid of lines (*isolines*).

In the second case, "x", "y", and "z" are all vectors of equal length. The resulting graph displays a 3D line instead of a surface, where the coordinates of points along the line are successive triplets of values from the input vectors.

In the third case, "x" and "y" are vectors or interval forms, and "z" is any formula involving two variables (not counting variables with assigned values). These variables are sorted into alphabetical order; the first takes on values from "x" and the second takes on values from "y" to form a matrix of results that are graphed as a 3D surface.

If the "z" formula evaluates to a call to the fictitious function '`xyz(x, y, z)`', then the result is a "parametric surface." In this case, the axes of the graph are taken from the x and *y* values in these calls, and the "x" and "y" values from the input vectors or intervals are used only to specify the range of inputs to the formula. For example, plotting '[0..360], [0..180], xyz(sin(x)*sin(y), cos(x)*sin(y), cos(y))' will draw a sphere. (Since the default resolution for 3D plots is 5 steps in each of "x" and "y", this will draw a very crude sphere. You could use the *g N* command, described below, to increase this resolution, or specify the "x" and "y" values as vectors with more than 5 elements.

It is also possible to have a function in a regular *g f* plot evaluate to an xyz call. Since *g f* plots a line, not a surface, the result will be a 3D parametric line. For example, '[[0..720], xyz(sin(x), cos(x), x)]' will plot two turns of a helix (a three-dimensional spiral).

As for *g f*, each of "x", "y", and "z" may instead be variables containing the relevant data.

13.3 Managing Curves

The *g f* command is really shorthand for the following commands: *C-u g d g a g p*. Likewise, *g F* is shorthand for *C-u g d g A g p*. You can gain more control over your graph by using these commands directly.

The *g a* (calc-graph-add) command adds the "curve" represented by the two values on the top of the stack to the current graph. You can have any number of curves in the same graph. When you give the *g p* command, all the curves will be drawn superimposed on the same axes.

The *g a* command (and many others that affect the current graph) will cause a special buffer, *Gnuplot Commands*, to be displayed in another window. This buffer is a template of the commands that will be sent to GNUPLOT when it is time to draw the graph. The first *g a* command adds a plot command to this buffer. Succeeding *g a* commands add extra curves onto that plot command. Other graph-related commands put other GNUPLOT commands into this buffer. In normal usage you never need to work with this buffer directly, but you can if you wish. The only constraint is that there must be only one plot command, and it must be the last command in the buffer. If you want to save and later restore a complete graph configuration, you can use regular Emacs commands to save and restore the contents of the *Gnuplot Commands* buffer.

If the values on the stack are not variable names, *g a* will invent variable names for them (of the form 'PlotData*n*') and store the values in those variables. The "x" and "y" variables are what go into the plot command in the template. If you add a curve that uses a certain variable and then later change that variable, you can replot the graph without having to delete and re-add the curve. That's because the variable name, not the vector, interval or formula itself, is what was added by *g a*.

A numeric prefix argument on *g a* or *g f* changes the way stack entries are interpreted as curves. With a positive prefix argument *n*, the top *n* stack entries are "y" values for *n* different curves which share a common "x" value in the *n* + 1st stack entry. (Thus *g a* with no prefix argument is equivalent to *C-u 1 g a*.)

A prefix of zero or plain *C-u* means to take two stack entries, "x" and "y" as usual, but to interpret "y" as a vector of "y" values for several curves that share a common "x".

A negative prefix argument tells Calc to read *n* vectors from the stack; each vector [*x*, *y*] describes an independent curve. This is the only form of *g a* that creates several curves at once that don't have common "x" values. (Of course, the range of "x" values covered by all the curves ought to be roughly the same if they are to look nice on the same graph.)

For example, to plot $\sin nx$ for integers n from 1 to 5, you could use `v x` to create a vector of integers (n), then `V M '` or `V M $` to map `'sin(n x)'` across this vector. The resulting vector of formulas is suitable for use as the "y" argument to a `C-u g a` or `C-u g f` command.

The `g A` (`calc-graph-add-3d`) command adds a 3D curve to the graph. It is not valid to intermix 2D and 3D curves in a single graph. This command takes three arguments, "x", "y", and "z", from the stack. With a positive prefix n, it takes $n + 2$ arguments (common "x" and "y", plus n separate "z"s). With a zero prefix, it takes three stack entries but the "z" entry is a vector of curve values. With a negative prefix $-n$, it takes n vectors of the form $[x, y, z]$. The `g A` command works by adding a `splot` (surface-plot) command to the `*Gnuplot Commands*` buffer.

(Although `g a` adds a 2D `plot` command to the `*Gnuplot Commands*` buffer, Calc changes this to `splot` before sending it to GNUPLOT if it notices that the data points are evaluating to `xyz` calls. It will not work to mix 2D and 3D `g a` curves in a single graph, although Calc does not currently check for this.)

The `g d` (`calc-graph-delete`) command deletes the most recently added curve from the graph. It has no effect if there are no curves in the graph. With a numeric prefix argument of any kind, it deletes all of the curves from the graph.

The `g H` (`calc-graph-hide`) command "hides" or "unhides" the most recently added curve. A hidden curve will not appear in the actual plot, but information about it such as its name and line and point styles will be retained.

The `g j` (`calc-graph-juggle`) command moves the curve at the end of the list (the "most recently added curve") to the front of the list. The next-most-recent curve is thus exposed for `g d` or similar commands to use. With `g j` you can work with any curve in the graph even though curve-related commands only affect the last curve in the list.

The `g p` (`calc-graph-plot`) command uses GNUPLOT to draw the graph described in the `*Gnuplot Commands*` buffer. Any GNUPLOT parameters which are not defined by commands in this buffer are reset to their default values. The variables named in the `plot` command are written to a temporary data file and the variable names are then replaced by the file name in the template. The resulting plotting commands are fed to the GNUPLOT program. See the documentation for the GNUPLOT program for more specific information. All temporary files are removed when Emacs or GNUPLOT exits.

If you give a formula for "y", Calc will remember all the values that it calculates for the formula so that later plots can reuse these values. Calc throws out these saved values when you change any circumstances that may affect the data, such as switching from Degrees to Radians mode, or changing the value of a parameter in the formula. You can force Calc to recompute the data from scratch by giving a negative numeric prefix argument to `g p`.

Calc uses a fairly rough step size when graphing formulas over intervals. This is to ensure quick response. You can "refine" a plot by giving a positive numeric prefix argument to `g p`. Calc goes through the data points it has computed and saved from previous plots of the function, and computes and inserts a new data point midway between each of the existing points. You can refine a plot any number of times, but beware that the amount of calculation involved doubles each time.

Calc does not remember computed values for 3D graphs. This means the numerix prefix argument, if any, to *g p* is effectively ignored if the current graph is three-dimensional.

The *g P* (`calc-graph-print`) command is like *g p*, except that it sends the output to a printer instead of to the screen. More precisely, *g p* looks for '`set terminal`' or '`set output`' commands in the `*Gnuplot Commands*` buffer; lacking these it uses the default settings. However, *g P* ignores '`set terminal`' and '`set output`' commands and uses a different set of default values. All of these values are controlled by the *g D* and *g O* commands discussed below. Provided everything is set up properly, *g p* will plot to the screen unless you have specified otherwise and *g P* will always plot to the printer.

13.4 Graphics Options

The *g g* (`calc-graph-grid`) command turns the "grid" on and off. It is off by default; tick marks appear only at the edges of the graph. With the grid turned on, dotted lines appear across the graph at each tick mark. Note that this command only changes the setting in `*Gnuplot Commands*`; to see the effects of the change you must give another *g p* command.

The *g b* (`calc-graph-border`) command turns the border (the box that surrounds the graph) on and off. It is on by default. This command will only work with GNUPLOT 3.0 and later versions.

The *g k* (`calc-graph-key`) command turns the "key" on and off. The key is a chart in the corner of the graph that shows the correspondence between curves and line styles. It is off by default, and is only really useful if you have several curves on the same graph.

The *g N* (`calc-graph-num-points`) command allows you to select the number of data points in the graph. This only affects curves where neither "x" nor "y" is specified as a vector. Enter a blank line to revert to the default value (initially 15). With no prefix argument, this command affects only the current graph. With a positive prefix argument this command changes or, if you enter a blank line, displays the default number of points used for all graphs created by *g a* that don't specify the resolution explicitly. With a negative prefix argument, this command changes or displays the default value (initially 5) used for 3D graphs created by *g A*. Note that a 3D setting of 5 means that a total of $5^2 = 25$ points will be computed for the surface.

Data values in the graph of a function are normally computed to a precision of five digits, regardless of the current precision at the time. This is usually more than adequate, but there are cases where it will not be. For example, plotting $1+x$ with x in the interval '`[0 .. 1e-6]`' will round all the data points down to 1.0! Putting the command '`set precision n`' in the `*Gnuplot Commands*` buffer will cause the data to be computed at precision n instead of 5. Since this is such a rare case, there is no keystroke-based command to set the precision.

The *g h* (`calc-graph-header`) command sets the title for the graph. This will show up centered above the graph. The default title is blank (no title).

The *g n* (`calc-graph-name`) command sets the title of an individual curve. Like the other curve-manipulating commands, it affects the most recently added curve, i.e., the last curve on the list in the `*Gnuplot Commands*` buffer. To set the title of the other curves you must first juggle them to the end of the list with *g j*, or edit the `*Gnuplot Commands*` buffer by hand. Curve titles appear in the key; if the key is turned off they are not used.

The *g t* (`calc-graph-title-x`) and *g T* (`calc-graph-title-y`) commands set the titles on the "x" and "y" axes, respectively. These titles appear next to the tick marks on the left and bottom edges of the graph, respectively. Calc does not have commands to control the tick marks themselves, but you can edit them into the `*Gnuplot Commands*` buffer if you wish. See the GNUPLOT documentation for details.

The *g r* (`calc-graph-range-x`) and *g R* (`calc-graph-range-y`) commands set the range of values on the "x" and "y" axes, respectively. You are prompted to enter a suitable range. This should be either a pair of numbers of the form, '`min:max`', or a blank line to revert to the default behavior of setting the range based on the range of values in the data, or '`$`' to take the range from the top of the stack. Ranges on the stack can be represented as either interval forms or vectors: '`[min .. max]`' or '`[min, max]`'.

The *g l* (`calc-graph-log-x`) and *g L* (`calc-graph-log-y`) commands allow you to set either or both of the axes of the graph to be logarithmic instead of linear.

For 3D plots, *g C-t*, *g C-r*, and *g C-l* (those are letters with the Control key held down) are the corresponding commands for the "z" axis.

The *g z* (`calc-graph-zero-x`) and *g Z* (`calc-graph-zero-y`) commands control whether a dotted line is drawn to indicate the "x" and/or "y" zero axes. (These are the same dotted lines that would be drawn there anyway if you used *g g* to turn the "grid" feature on.) Zero-axis lines are on by default, and may be turned off only in GNUPLOT 3.0 and later versions. They are not available for 3D plots.

The *g s* (`calc-graph-line-style`) command turns the connecting lines on or off for the most recently added curve, and optionally selects the style of lines to be used for that curve. Plain *g s* simply toggles the lines on and off. With a numeric prefix argument, *g s* turns lines on and sets a particular line style. Line style numbers start at one and their meanings vary depending on the output device. GNUPLOT guarantees that there will be at least six different line styles available for any device.

The *g S* (`calc-graph-point-style`) command similarly turns the symbols at the data points on or off, or sets the point style. If you turn both lines and points off, the data points will show as tiny dots. If the "y" values being plotted contain error forms and the connecting lines are turned off, then this command will also turn the error bars on or off.

Another way to specify curve styles is with the `LineStyles` and `PointStyles` variables. These variables initially have no stored values, but if you store a vector of integers in one of these variables, the *g a* and *g f* commands will use those style numbers instead of the defaults for new curves that are added to the graph. An entry should be a positive integer for a specific style, or 0 to let the style be chosen automatically, or -1 to turn off lines or points altogether. If there are more curves than elements in the vector, the last few curves will continue to have the default styles. Of course, you can later use *g s* and *g S* to change any of these styles.

For example, '`[2 -1 3] RET s t LineStyles`' causes the first curve to have lines in style number 2, the second curve to have no connecting lines, and the third curve to have lines in style 3. Point styles will still be assigned automatically, but you could store another vector in `PointStyles` to define them, too.

13.5 Graphical Devices

The *g D* (`calc-graph-device`) command sets the device name (or "terminal name" in GNUPLOT lingo) to be used by *g p* commands on this graph. It does not affect the permanent default device name. If you enter a blank name, the device name reverts to the default. Enter '?' to see a list of supported devices.

With a positive numeric prefix argument, *g D* instead sets the default device name, used by all plots in the future which do not override it with a plain *g D* command. If you enter a blank line this command shows you the current default. The special name `default` signifies that Calc should choose `x11` if the X window system is in use (as indicated by the presence of a `DISPLAY` environment variable), `windows` on MS-Windows, or otherwise `dumb` under GNUPLOT 3.0 and later, or `postscript` under GNUPLOT 2.0. This is the initial default value.

The `dumb` device is an interface to "dumb terminals," i.e., terminals with no special graphics facilities. It writes a crude picture of the graph composed of characters like - and | to a buffer called *Gnuplot Trail*, which Calc then displays. The graph is made the same size as the Emacs screen, which on most dumb terminals will be 80 × 24 characters. The graph is displayed in an Emacs "recursive edit"; type q or C-c C-c to exit the recursive edit and return to Calc. Note that the `dumb` device is present only in GNUPLOT 3.0 and later versions.

The word `dumb` may be followed by two numbers separated by spaces. These are the desired width and height of the graph in characters. Also, the device name `big` is like `dumb` but creates a graph four times the width and height of the Emacs screen. You will then have to scroll around to view the entire graph. In the *Gnuplot Trail* buffer, SPC, DEL, <, and > are defined to scroll by one screenful in each of the four directions.

With a negative numeric prefix argument, *g D* sets or displays the device name used by *g P* (`calc-graph-print`). This is initially `postscript`. If you don't have a PostScript printer, you may decide once again to use `dumb` to create a plot on any text-only printer.

The *g O* (`calc-graph-output`) command sets the name of the output file used by GNUPLOT. For some devices, notably `x11` and `windows`, there is no output file and this information is not used. Many other "devices" are really file formats like `postscript`; in these cases the output in the desired format goes into the file you name with *g O*. Type *g O stdout RET* to set GNUPLOT to write to its standard output stream, i.e., to *Gnuplot Trail*. This is the default setting.

Another special output name is `tty`, which means that GNUPLOT is going to write graphics commands directly to its standard output, which you wish Emacs to pass through to your terminal. Tektronix graphics terminals, among other devices, operate this way. Calc does this by telling GNUPLOT to write to a temporary file, then running a sub-shell executing the command `cat tempfile >/dev/tty`. On typical Unix systems, this will copy the temporary file directly to the terminal, bypassing Emacs entirely. You will have to type C-l to Emacs afterwards to refresh the screen.

Once again, *g O* with a positive or negative prefix argument sets the default or printer output file names, respectively. In each case you can specify `auto`, which causes Calc to invent a temporary file name for each *g p* (or *g P*) command. This temporary file will be deleted once it has been displayed or printed. If the output file name is not `auto`, the file is not automatically deleted.

The default and printer devices and output files can be saved permanently by the m m (`calc-save-modes`) command. The default number of data points (see g N) and the X geometry (see g X) are also saved. Other graph information is *not* saved; you can save a graph's configuration simply by saving the contents of the *Gnuplot Commands* buffer.

You may wish to configure the default and printer devices and output files for the whole system. The relevant Lisp variables are `calc-gnuplot-default-device` and `-output`, and `calc-gnuplot-print-device` and `-output`. The output file names must be either strings as described above, or Lisp expressions which are evaluated on the fly to get the output file names.

Other important Lisp variables are `calc-gnuplot-plot-command` and `calc-gnuplot-print-command`, which give the system commands to display or print the output of GNU-PLOT, respectively. These may be `nil` if no command is necessary, or strings which can include '%s' to signify the name of the file to be displayed or printed. Or, these variables may contain Lisp expressions which are evaluated to display or print the output. These variables are customizable (see Appendix C [Customizing Calc], page 435).

The g x (`calc-graph-display`) command lets you specify on which X window system display your graphs should be drawn. Enter a blank line to see the current display name. This command has no effect unless the current device is x11.

The g X (`calc-graph-geometry`) command is a similar command for specifying the position and size of the X window. The normal value is `default`, which generally means your window manager will let you place the window interactively. Entering '800x500+0+0' would create an 800-by-500 pixel window in the upper-left corner of the screen. This command has no effect if the current device is `windows`.

The buffer called *Gnuplot Trail* holds a transcript of the session with GNUPLOT. This shows the commands Calc has "typed" to GNUPLOT and the responses it has received. Calc tries to notice when an error message has appeared here and display the buffer for you when this happens. You can check this buffer yourself if you suspect something has gone wrong[1].

The g C (`calc-graph-command`) command prompts you to enter any line of text, then simply sends that line to the current GNUPLOT process. The *Gnuplot Trail* buffer looks deceptively like a Shell buffer but you can't type commands in it yourself. Instead, you must use g C for this purpose.

The g v (`calc-graph-view-commands`) and g V (`calc-graph-view-trail`) commands display the *Gnuplot Commands* and *Gnuplot Trail* buffers, respectively, in another window. This happens automatically when Calc thinks there is something you will want to see in either of these buffers. If you type g v or g V when the relevant buffer is already displayed, the buffer is hidden again. (Note that on MS-Windows, the *Gnuplot Trail* buffer will usually show nothing of interest, because GNUPLOT's responses are not communicated back to Calc.)

One reason to use g v is to add your own commands to the *Gnuplot Commands* buffer. Press g v, then use C-x o to switch into that window. For example, GNUPLOT has 'set label' and 'set arrow' commands that allow you to annotate your plots. Since Calc doesn't

---

[1] On MS-Windows, due to the peculiarities of how the Windows version of GNUPLOT (called `wgnuplot`) works, the GNUPLOT responses are not communicated back to Calc. Instead, you need to look them up in the GNUPLOT command window that is displayed as in normal interactive usage of GNUPLOT.

understand these commands, you have to add them to the *Gnuplot Commands* buffer yourself, then use *g p* to replot using these new commands. Note that your commands must appear *before* the `plot` command. To get help on any GNUPLOT feature, type, e.g., *g C help set label*. You may have to type *g C RET* a few times to clear the "press return for more" or "subtopic of . . ." requests. Note that Calc always sends commands (like 'set nolabel') to reset all plotting parameters to the defaults before each plot, so to delete a label all you need to do is delete the 'set label' line you added (or comment it out with '#') and then replot with *g p*.

You can use *g q* (`calc-graph-quit`) to kill the GNUPLOT process that is running. The next graphing command you give will start a fresh GNUPLOT process. The word 'Graph' appears in the Calc window's mode line whenever a GNUPLOT process is currently running. The GNUPLOT process is automatically killed when you exit Emacs if you haven't killed it manually by then.

The *g K* (`calc-graph-kill`) command is like *g q* except that it also views the *Gnuplot Trail* buffer so that you can see the process being killed. This is better if you are killing GNUPLOT because you think it has gotten stuck.

14 Kill and Yank Functions

The commands in this chapter move information between the Calculator and other Emacs editing buffers.

In many cases Embedded mode is an easier and more natural way to work with Calc from a regular editing buffer. See Chapter 16 [Embedded Mode], page 351.

14.1 Killing from the Stack

Kill commands are Emacs commands that insert text into the "kill ring," from which it can later be "yanked" by a C-y command. Three common kill commands in normal Emacs are C-k, which kills one line, C-w, which kills the region between mark and point, and M-w, which puts the region into the kill ring without actually deleting it. All of these commands work in the Calculator, too, although in the Calculator they operate on whole stack entries, so they "round up" the specified region to encompass full lines. (To copy only parts of lines, the M-C-w command in the Calculator will copy the region to the kill ring without any "rounding up", just like the M-w command in normal Emacs.) Also, M-k has been provided to complete the set; it puts the current line into the kill ring without deleting anything.

The kill commands are unusual in that they pay attention to the location of the cursor in the Calculator buffer. If the cursor is on or below the bottom line, the kill commands operate on the top of the stack. Otherwise, they operate on whatever stack element the cursor is on. The text is copied into the kill ring exactly as it appears on the screen, including line numbers if they are enabled.

A numeric prefix argument to C-k or M-k affects the number of lines killed. A positive argument kills the current line and $n - 1$ lines below it. A negative argument kills the $-n$ lines above the current line. Again this mirrors the behavior of the standard Emacs C-k command. Although a whole line is always deleted, C-k with no argument copies only the number itself into the kill ring, whereas C-k with a prefix argument of 1 copies the number with its trailing newline.

14.2 Yanking into the Stack

The C-y command yanks the most recently killed text back into the Calculator. It pushes this value onto the top of the stack regardless of the cursor position. In general it re-parses the killed text as a number or formula (or a list of these separated by commas or newlines). However if the thing being yanked is something that was just killed from the Calculator itself, its full internal structure is yanked. For example, if you have set the floating-point display mode to show only four significant digits, then killing and re-yanking 3.14159 (which displays as 3.142) will yank the full 3.14159, even though yanking it into any other buffer would yank the number in its displayed form, 3.142. (Since the default display modes show all objects to their full precision, this feature normally makes no difference.)

The C-y command can be given a prefix, which will interpret the text being yanked with a different radix. If the text being yanked can be interpreted as a binary, octal, hexadecimal, or decimal number, then a prefix of 2, 8, 6 or 0 will have Calc interpret the yanked text as a number in the appropriate base. For example, if '111' has just been killed and is yanked into Calc with a command of C-2 C-y, then the number '7' will be put on the stack. If you use the plain prefix `C-u`, then you will be prompted for a base to use, which can be any integer from 2 to 36. If Calc doesn't allow the text being yanked to be read in a different base (such as if the text is an algebraic expression), then the prefix will have no effect.

14.3 Saving into Registers

An alternative to killing and yanking stack entries is using registers in Calc. Saving stack entries in registers is like saving text in normal Emacs registers; although, like Calc's kill commands, register commands always operate on whole stack entries.

Registers in Calc are places to store stack entries for later use; each register is indexed by a single character. To store the current region (rounded up, of course, to include full stack entries) into a register, use the command `r s` (`calc-copy-to-register`). You will then be prompted for a register to use, the next character you type will be the index for the register. To store the region in register *r*, the full command will be `r s r`. With an argument, `C-u r s r`, the region being copied to the register will be deleted from the Calc buffer.

It is possible to add additional stack entries to a register. The command `M-x calc-append-to-register` will prompt for a register, then add the stack entries in the region to the end of the register contents. The command `M-x calc-prepend-to-register` will similarly prompt for a register and add the stack entries in the region to the beginning of the register contents. Both commands take `C-u` arguments, which will cause the region to be deleted after being added to the register.

14.4 Inserting from Registers

The command `r i` (`calc-insert-register`) will prompt for a register, then insert the contents of that register into the Calculator. If the contents of the register were placed there from within Calc, then the full internal structure of the contents will be inserted into the Calculator, otherwise whatever text is in the register is reparsed and then inserted into the Calculator.

14.5 Grabbing from Other Buffers

The `C-x * g` (`calc-grab-region`) command takes the text between point and mark in the current buffer and attempts to parse it as a vector of values. Basically, it wraps the text in vector brackets '`[ ]`' unless the text already is enclosed in vector brackets, then reads the text as if it were an algebraic entry. The contents of the vector may be numbers, formulas, or any other Calc objects. If the `C-x * g` command works successfully, it does an automatic `C-x * c` to enter the Calculator buffer.

A numeric prefix argument grabs the specified number of lines around point, ignoring the mark. A positive prefix grabs from point to the *n*th following newline (so that `M-1 C-x * g` grabs from point to the end of the current line); a negative prefix grabs from point back to the $n+1$st preceding newline. In these cases the text that is grabbed is exactly the same as the text that `C-k` would delete given that prefix argument.

A prefix of zero grabs the current line; point may be anywhere on the line.

A plain `C-u` prefix interprets the region between point and mark as a single number or formula rather than a vector. For example, `C-x * g` on the text '2 a b' produces the vector of three values '[2, a, b]', but *C-u C-x * g* on the same region reads a formula which is a product of three things: '2 a b'. (The text 'a + b', on the other hand, will be grabbed as a vector of one element by plain *C-x * g* because the interpretation '[a, +, b]' would be a syntax error.)

If a different language has been specified (see Section 6.8 [Language Modes], page 158), the grabbed text will be interpreted according to that language.

The *C-x * r* (`calc-grab-rectangle`) command takes the text between point and mark and attempts to parse it as a matrix. If point and mark are both in the leftmost column, the lines in between are parsed in their entirety. Otherwise, point and mark define the corners of a rectangle whose contents are parsed.

Each line of the grabbed area becomes a row of the matrix. The result will actually be a vector of vectors, which Calc will treat as a matrix only if every row contains the same number of values.

If a line contains a portion surrounded by square brackets (or curly braces), that portion is interpreted as a vector which becomes a row of the matrix. Any text surrounding the bracketed portion on the line is ignored.

Otherwise, the entire line is interpreted as a row vector as if it were surrounded by square brackets. Leading line numbers (in the format used in the Calc stack buffer) are ignored. If you wish to force this interpretation (even if the line contains bracketed portions), give a negative numeric prefix argument to the *C-x * r* command.

If you give a numeric prefix argument of zero or plain *C-u*, each line is instead interpreted as a single formula which is converted into a one-element vector. Thus the result of *C-u C-x * r* will be a one-column matrix. For example, suppose one line of the data is the expression '2 a'. A plain *C-x * r* will interpret this as '[2 a]', which in turn is read as a two-element vector that forms one row of the matrix. But a *C-u C-x * r* will interpret this row as '[2*a]'.

If you give a positive numeric prefix argument *n*, then each line will be split up into columns of width *n*; each column is parsed separately as a matrix element. If a line contained '2 +/- 3 4 +/- 5', then grabbing with a prefix argument of 8 would correctly split the line into two error forms.

See Chapter 9 [Matrix Functions], page 221, to see how to pull the matrix apart into its constituent rows and columns. (If it is a 1×1 matrix, just hit *v u* (`calc-unpack`) twice.)

The *C-x * :* (`calc-grab-sum-down`) command is a handy way to grab a rectangle of data and sum its columns. It is equivalent to typing *C-x * r*, followed by *V R : +* (the vector reduction command that sums the columns of a matrix; see Section 9.8.3 [Reducing], page 238). The result of the command will be a vector of numbers, one for each column in the input data. The *C-x * _* (`calc-grab-sum-across`) command similarly grabs a rectangle and sums its rows by executing *V R _ +*.

As well as being more convenient, *C-x * :* and *C-x * _* are also much faster because they don't actually place the grabbed vector on the stack. In a *C-x * r V R : +* sequence, formatting the vector for display on the stack takes a large fraction of the total time (unless you have planned ahead and used *v .* and *t .* modes).

For example, suppose we have a column of numbers in a file which we wish to sum. Go to one corner of the column and press *C-@* to set the mark; go to the other corner and type

C-x * :. Since there is only one column, the result will be a vector of one number, the sum. (You can type *v u* to unpack this vector into a plain number if you want to do further arithmetic with it.)

To compute the product of the column of numbers, we would have to do it "by hand" since there's no special grab-and-multiply command. Use *C-x* * *r* to grab the column of numbers into the calculator in the form of a column matrix. The statistics command *u* * is a handy way to find the product of a vector or matrix of numbers. See Section 9.7 [Statistical Operations], page 231. Another approach would be to use an explicit column reduction command, *V R : *.

14.6 Yanking into Other Buffers

The plain *y* (`calc-copy-to-buffer`) command inserts the number at the top of the stack into the most recently used normal editing buffer. (More specifically, this is the most recently used buffer which is displayed in a window and whose name does not begin with '*'. If there is no such buffer, this is the most recently used buffer except for Calculator and Calc Trail buffers.) The number is inserted exactly as it appears and without a newline. (If line-numbering is enabled, the line number is normally not included.) The number is *not* removed from the stack.

With a prefix argument, *y* inserts several numbers, one per line. A positive argument inserts the specified number of values from the top of the stack. A negative argument inserts the *n*th value from the top of the stack. An argument of zero inserts the entire stack. Note that *y* with an argument of 1 is slightly different from *y* with no argument; the former always copies full lines, whereas the latter strips off the trailing newline.

With a lone *C-u* as a prefix argument, *y* *replaces* the region in the other buffer with the yanked text, then quits the Calculator, leaving you in that buffer. A typical use would be to use *C-x* * *g* to read a region of data into the Calculator, operate on the data to produce a new matrix, then type *C-u y* to replace the original data with the new data. One might wish to alter the matrix display style (see Section 9.9 [Vector and Matrix Formats], page 240) or change the current display language (see Section 6.8 [Language Modes], page 158) before doing this. Also, note that this command replaces a linear region of text (as grabbed by *C-x* * *g*), not a rectangle (as grabbed by *C-x* * *r*).

If the editing buffer is in overwrite (as opposed to insert) mode, and the *C-u* prefix was not used, then the yanked number will overwrite the characters following point rather than being inserted before those characters. The usual conventions of overwrite mode are observed; for example, characters will be inserted at the end of a line rather than overflowing onto the next line. Yanking a multi-line object such as a matrix in overwrite mode overwrites the next *n* lines in the buffer, lengthening or shortening each line as necessary. Finally, if the thing being yanked is a simple integer or floating-point number (like '`-1.2345e-3`') and the characters following point also make up such a number, then Calc will replace that number with the new number, lengthening or shortening as necessary. The concept of "overwrite mode" has thus been generalized from overwriting characters to overwriting one complete number with another.

The *C-x* * *y* key sequence is equivalent to *y* except that it can be typed anywhere, not just in Calc. This provides an easy way to guarantee that Calc knows which editing buffer you want to use!

14.7 X Cut and Paste

If you are using Emacs with the X window system, there is an easier way to move small amounts of data into and out of the calculator: Use the mouse-oriented cut and paste facilities of X.

The default bindings for a three-button mouse cause the left button to move the Emacs cursor to the given place, the right button to select the text between the cursor and the clicked location, and the middle button to yank the selection into the buffer at the clicked location. So, if you have a Calc window and an editing window on your Emacs screen, you can use left-click/right-click to select a number, vector, or formula from one window, then middle-click to paste that value into the other window. When you paste text into the Calc window, Calc interprets it as an algebraic entry. It doesn't matter where you click in the Calc window; the new value is always pushed onto the top of the stack.

The `xterm` program that is typically used for general-purpose shell windows in X interprets the mouse buttons in the same way. So you can use the mouse to move data between Calc and any other Unix program. One nice feature of `xterm` is that a double left-click selects one word, and a triple left-click selects a whole line. So you can usually transfer a single number into Calc just by double-clicking on it in the shell, then middle-clicking in the Calc window.

15 Keypad Mode

The `C-x * k` (`calc-keypad`) command starts the Calculator and displays a picture of a calculator-style keypad. If you are using the X window system, you can click on any of the "keys" in the keypad using the left mouse button to operate the calculator. The original window remains the selected window; in Keypad mode you can type in your file while simultaneously performing calculations with the mouse.

If you have used `C-x * b` first, `C-x * k` instead invokes the `full-calc-keypad` command, which takes over the whole Emacs screen and displays the keypad, the Calc stack, and the Calc trail all at once. This mode would normally be used when running Calc standalone (see Section 1.5.5 [Standalone Operation], page 9).

If you aren't using the X window system, you must switch into the `*Calc Keypad*` window, place the cursor on the desired "key," and type SPC or RET. If you think this is easier than using Calc normally, go right ahead.

Calc commands are more or less the same in Keypad mode. Certain keypad keys differ slightly from the corresponding normal Calc keystrokes; all such deviations are described below.

Keypad mode includes many more commands than will fit on the keypad at once. Click the right mouse button [`calc-keypad-menu`] to switch to the next menu. The bottom five rows of the keypad stay the same; the top three rows change to a new set of commands. To return to earlier menus, click the middle mouse button [`calc-keypad-menu-back`] or simply advance through the menus until you wrap around. Typing TAB inside the keypad window is equivalent to clicking the right mouse button there.

You can always click the EXEC button and type any normal Calc key sequence. This is equivalent to switching into the Calc buffer, typing the keys, then switching back to your original buffer.

15.1 Main Menu

```
|----+----+--Calc---+----+----1
|FLR |CEIL|RND |TRNC|CLN2|FLT |
|----+----+----+----+----+----|
| LN |EXP |    |ABS |IDIV|MOD |
|----+----+----+----+----+----|
|SIN |COS |TAN |SQRT|y^x |1/x |
|----+----+----+----+----+----|
|  ENTER  |+/- |EEX |UNDO| <- |
|-----+---+-+--+---+-+----++----|
| INV |  7  |  8  |  9  |  /  |
|-----+-----+-----+-----+-----|
| HYP |  4  |  5  |  6  |  *  |
|-----+-----+-----+-----+-----|
|EXEC |  1  |  2  |  3  |  -  |
|-----+-----+-----+-----+-----|
| OFF |  0  |  .  | PI  |  +  |
|-----+-----+-----+-----+-----+
```

This is the menu that appears the first time you start Keypad mode. It will show up in a vertical window on the right side of your screen. Above this menu is the traditional Calc stack display. On a 24-line screen you will be able to see the top three stack entries.

The ten digit keys, decimal point, and EEX key are used for entering numbers in the obvious way. EEX begins entry of an exponent in scientific notation. Just as with regular Calc, the number is pushed onto the stack as soon as you press ENTER or any other function key.

The +/- key corresponds to normal Calc's *n* key. During numeric entry it changes the sign of the number or of the exponent. At other times it changes the sign of the number on the top of the stack.

The INV and HYP keys modify other keys. As well as having the effects described elsewhere in this manual, Keypad mode defines several other "inverse" operations. These are described below and in the following sections.

The ENTER key finishes the current numeric entry, or otherwise duplicates the top entry on the stack.

The UNDO key undoes the most recent Calc operation. *INV UNDO* is the "redo" command, and *HYP UNDO* is "last arguments" (*M-RET*).

The <- key acts as a "backspace" during numeric entry. At other times it removes the top stack entry. *INV* <- clears the entire stack. *HYP* <- takes an integer from the stack, then removes that many additional stack elements.

The EXEC key prompts you to enter any keystroke sequence that would normally work in Calc mode. This can include a numeric prefix if you wish. It is also possible simply to switch into the Calc window and type commands in it; there is nothing "magic" about this window when Keypad mode is active.

The other keys in this display perform their obvious calculator functions. CLN2 rounds the top-of-stack by temporarily reducing the precision by 2 digits. FLT converts an integer or fraction on the top of the stack to floating-point.

The INV and HYP keys combined with several of these keys give you access to some common functions even if the appropriate menu is not displayed. Obviously you don't need to learn these keys unless you find yourself wasting time switching among the menus.

INV +/-	is the same as 1/x.
INV +	is the same as SQRT.
INV -	is the same as CONJ.
INV *	is the same as y^x.
INV /	is the same as INV y^x (the *x*th root of *y*).
HYP/INV 1	are the same as SIN / *INV SIN*.
HYP/INV 2	are the same as COS / *INV COS*.
HYP/INV 3	are the same as TAN / *INV TAN*.
INV/HYP 4	are the same as LN / *HYP LN*.
INV/HYP 5	are the same as EXP / *HYP EXP*.
INV 6	is the same as ABS.
INV 7	is the same as RND (calc-round).

INV 8   is the same as CLN2.

INV 9   is the same as FLT (`calc-float`).

INV 0   is the same as IMAG.

INV .   is the same as PREC.

INV ENTER is the same as SWAP.

HYP ENTER is the same as RLL3.

INV HYP ENTER

        is the same as OVER.

HYP +/-   packs the top two stack entries as an error form.

HYP EEX   packs the top two stack entries as a modulo form.

INV EEX   creates an interval form; this removes an integer which is one of 0 '[]', 1 '[)',
2 '(]' or 3 '()', followed by the two limits of the interval.

The *OFF* key turns Calc off; typing *C-x * k* or *C-x * * * again has the same effect. This is analogous to typing *q* or hitting *C-x * c* again in the normal calculator. If Calc is running standalone (the `full-calc-keypad` command appeared in the command line that started Emacs), then *OFF* is replaced with *EXIT*; clicking on this actually exits Emacs itself.

15.2 Functions Menu

```
|----+----+----+----+----+----2
|IGAM|BETA|IBET|ERF |BESJ|BESY|
|----+----+----+----+----+----|
|IMAG|CONJ| RE |ATN2|RAND|RAGN|
|----+----+----+----+----+----|
|GCD |FACT|DFCT|BNOM|PERM|NXTP|
|----+----+----+----+----+----|
```

This menu provides various operations from the *f* and *k* prefix keys.

IMAG multiplies the number on the stack by the imaginary number $i = (0, 1)$.

RE extracts the real part a complex number. *INV RE* extracts the imaginary part.

RAND takes a number from the top of the stack and computes a random number greater than or equal to zero but less than that number. (See Section 8.5 [Random Numbers], page 213.) RAGN is the "random again" command; it computes another random number using the same limit as last time.

INV GCD computes the LCM (least common multiple) function.

INV FACT is the gamma function. $\Gamma(x) = (x - 1)!$.

PERM is the number-of-permutations function, which is on the *H k c* key in normal Calc.

NXTP finds the next prime after a number. *INV NXTP* finds the previous prime.

15.3 Binary Menu

```
|----+----+----+----+----+----3
|AND | OR |XOR |NOT |LSH |RSH |
|----+----+----+----+----+----|
|DEC |HEX |OCT |BIN |WSIZ|ARSH|
|----+----+----+----+----+----|
| A  | B  | C  | D  | E  | F  |
|----+----+----+----+----+----|
```

The keys in this menu perform operations on binary integers. Note that both logical and arithmetic right-shifts are provided. `INV LSH` rotates one bit to the left.

The "difference" function (normally on *b d*) is on `INV AND`. The "clip" function (normally on *b c*) is on `INV NOT`.

The `DEC`, `HEX`, `OCT`, and `BIN` keys select the current radix for display and entry of numbers: Decimal, hexadecimal, octal, or binary. The six letter keys `A` through `F` are used for entering hexadecimal numbers.

The `WSIZ` key displays the current word size for binary operations and allows you to enter a new word size. You can respond to the prompt using either the keyboard or the digits and `ENTER` from the keypad. The initial word size is 32 bits.

15.4 Vectors Menu

```
|----+----+----+----+----+----4
|SUM |PROD|MAX |MAP*|MAP^|MAP$|
|----+----+----+----+----+----|
|MINV|MDET|MTRN|IDNT|CRSS|"x" |
|----+----+----+----+----+----|
|PACK|UNPK|INDX|BLD |LEN |... |
|----+----+----+----+----+----|
```

The keys in this menu operate on vectors and matrices.

`PACK` removes an integer *n* from the top of the stack; the next *n* stack elements are removed and packed into a vector, which is replaced onto the stack. Thus the sequence *1 ENTER 3 ENTER 5 ENTER 3 PACK* enters the vector '[1, 3, 5]' onto the stack. To enter a matrix, build each row on the stack as a vector, then use a final `PACK` to collect the rows into a matrix.

`UNPK` unpacks the vector on the stack, pushing each of its components separately.

`INDX` removes an integer *n*, then builds a vector of integers from 1 to *n*. *INV INDX* takes three numbers from the stack: The vector size *n*, the starting number, and the increment. *BLD* takes an integer *n* and any value *x* and builds a vector of *n* copies of *x*.

`IDNT` removes an integer *n*, then builds an *n*-by-*n* identity matrix.

`LEN` replaces a vector by its length, an integer.

`...` turns on or off "abbreviated" display mode for large vectors.

`MINV`, `MDET`, `MTRN`, and `CROSS` are the matrix inverse, determinant, and transpose, and vector cross product.

`SUM` replaces a vector by the sum of its elements. It is equivalent to `u +` in normal Calc (see Section 9.7 [Statistical Operations], page 231). `PROD` computes the product of the elements of a vector, and `MAX` computes the maximum of all the elements of a vector.

`INV SUM` computes the alternating sum of the first element minus the second, plus the third, minus the fourth, and so on. `INV MAX` computes the minimum of the vector elements.

`HYP SUM` computes the mean of the vector elements. `HYP PROD` computes the sample standard deviation. `HYP MAX` computes the median.

`MAP*` multiplies two vectors elementwise. It is equivalent to the *V M * * command. `MAP^` computes powers elementwise. The arguments must be vectors of equal length, or one must be a vector and the other must be a plain number. For example, *2 MAP^* squares all the elements of a vector.

`MAP$` maps the formula on the top of the stack across the vector in the second-to-top position. If the formula contains several variables, Calc takes that many vectors starting at the second-to-top position and matches them to the variables in alphabetical order. The result is a vector of the same size as the input vectors, whose elements are the formula evaluated with the variables set to the various sets of numbers in those vectors. For example, you could simulate `MAP^` using `MAP$` with the formula `'x^y'`.

The `"x"` key pushes the variable name x onto the stack. To build the formula $x^2 + 6$, you would use the key sequence `"x"` *2 y^x 6 +*. This formula would then be suitable for use with the `MAP$` key described above. With `INV`, `HYP`, or `INV` and `HYP`, the `"x"` key pushes the variable names y, z, and t, respectively.

15.5 Modes Menu

```
|----+----+----+----+----+----5
|FLT |FIX |SCI |ENG |GRP |    |
|----+----+----+----+----+----|
|RAD |DEG |FRAC|POLR|SYMB|PREC|
|----+----+----+----+----+----|
|SWAP|RLL3|RLL4|OVER|STO |RCL |
|----+----+----+----+----+----|
```

The keys in this menu manipulate modes, variables, and the stack.

The `FLT`, `FIX`, `SCI`, and `ENG` keys select floating-point, fixed-point, scientific, or engineering notation. `FIX` displays two digits after the decimal by default; the others display full precision. With the `INV` prefix, these keys pop a number-of-digits argument from the stack.

The `GRP` key turns grouping of digits with commas on or off. *INV GRP* enables grouping to the right of the decimal point as well as to the left.

The `RAD` and `DEG` keys switch between radians and degrees for trigonometric functions.

The `FRAC` key turns Fraction mode on or off. This affects whether commands like `/` with integer arguments produce fractional or floating-point results.

The `POLR` key turns Polar mode on or off, determining whether polar or rectangular complex numbers are used by default.

The `SYMB` key turns Symbolic mode on or off, in which operations that would produce inexact floating-point results are left unevaluated as algebraic formulas.

The `PREC` key selects the current precision. Answer with the keyboard or with the keypad digit and `ENTER` keys.

The `SWAP` key exchanges the top two stack elements. The `RLL3` key rotates the top three stack elements upwards. The `RLL4` key rotates the top four stack elements upwards. The `OVER` key duplicates the second-to-top stack element.

The STO and RCL keys are analogous to *s t* and *s r* in regular Calc. See Chapter 12 [Store and Recall], page 323. Click the STO or RCL key, then one of the ten digits. (Named variables are not available in Keypad mode.) You can also use, for example, *STO + 3* to add to register 3.

16 Embedded Mode

Embedded mode in Calc provides an alternative to copying numbers and formulas back and forth between editing buffers and the Calc stack. In Embedded mode, your editing buffer becomes temporarily linked to the stack and this copying is taken care of automatically.

16.1 Basic Embedded Mode

To enter Embedded mode, position the Emacs point (cursor) on a formula in any buffer and press `C-x * e` (`calc-embedded`). Note that `C-x * e` is not to be used in the Calc stack buffer like most Calc commands, but rather in regular editing buffers that are visiting your own files.

Calc will try to guess an appropriate language based on the major mode of the editing buffer. (See Section 6.8 [Language Modes], page 158.) If the current buffer is in `latex-mode`, for example, Calc will set its language to LaTeX. Similarly, Calc will use TeX language for `tex-mode`, `plain-tex-mode` and `context-mode`, C language for `c-mode` and `c++-mode`, FORTRAN language for `fortran-mode` and `f90-mode`, Pascal for `pascal-mode`, and eqn for `nroff-mode` (see Appendix C [Customizing Calc], page 435). These can be overridden with Calc's mode changing commands (see Section 16.4 [Mode Settings in Embedded Mode], page 358). If no suitable language is available, Calc will continue with its current language.

Calc normally scans backward and forward in the buffer for the nearest opening and closing *formula delimiters*. The simplest delimiters are blank lines. Other delimiters that Embedded mode understands are:

1. The TeX and LaTeX math delimiters '$ $', '$$ $$', '\[\]', and '\(\)';
2. Lines beginning with '\begin' and '\end' (except matrix delimiters);
3. Lines beginning with '@' (Texinfo delimiters).
4. Lines beginning with '.EQ' and '.EN' (*eqn* delimiters);
5. Lines containing a single '%' or '.\"' symbol and nothing else.

See Section 16.5 [Customizing Embedded Mode], page 360, to see how to make Calc recognize your own favorite delimiters. Delimiters like '$ $' can appear on their own separate lines or in-line with the formula.

If you give a positive or negative numeric prefix argument, Calc instead uses the current point as one end of the formula, and includes that many lines forward or backward (respectively, including the current line). Explicit delimiters are not necessary in this case.

With a prefix argument of zero, Calc uses the current region (delimited by point and mark) instead of formula delimiters. With a prefix argument of `C-u` only, Calc uses the current line as the formula.

The `C-x * w` (`calc-embedded-word`) command will start Embedded mode on the current "word"; in this case Calc will scan for the first non-numeric character (i.e., the first character that is not a digit, sign, decimal point, or upper- or lower-case 'e') forward and backward to delimit the formula.

When you enable Embedded mode for a formula, Calc reads the text between the delimiters and tries to interpret it as a Calc formula. Calc can generally identify TeX formulas and Big-style formulas even if the language mode is wrong. If Calc can't make sense of the formula, it beeps and refuses to enter Embedded mode. But if the current language is wrong, Calc can sometimes parse the formula successfully (but incorrectly); for example, the C expression 'atan(a[1])' can be parsed in Normal language mode, but the atan won't correspond to the built-in arctan function, and the 'a[1]' will be interpreted as 'a' times the vector '[1]'!

If you press C-x * e or C-x * w to activate an embedded formula which is blank, say with the cursor on the space between the two delimiters '$ $', Calc will immediately prompt for an algebraic entry.

Only one formula in one buffer can be enabled at a time. If you move to another area of the current buffer and give Calc commands, Calc turns Embedded mode off for the old formula and then tries to restart Embedded mode at the new position. Other buffers are not affected by Embedded mode.

When Embedded mode begins, Calc pushes the current formula onto the stack. No Calc stack window is created; however, Calc copies the top-of-stack position into the original buffer at all times. You can create a Calc window by hand with C-x * o if you find you need to see the entire stack.

For example, typing C-x * e while somewhere in the formula 'n>2' in the following line enables Embedded mode on that inequality:

```
We define $F_n = F_(n-1)+F_(n-2)$ for all $n>2$.
```

The formula $n > 2$ will be pushed onto the Calc stack, and the top of stack will be copied back into the editing buffer. This means that spaces will appear around the '>' symbol to match Calc's usual display style:

```
We define $F_n = F_(n-1)+F_(n-2)$ for all $n > 2$.
```

No spaces have appeared around the '+' sign because it's in a different formula, one which we have not yet touched with Embedded mode.

Now that Embedded mode is enabled, keys you type in this buffer are interpreted as Calc commands. At this point we might use the "commute" command j C to reverse the inequality. This is a selection-based command for which we first need to move the cursor onto the operator ('>' in this case) that needs to be commuted.

```
We define $F_n = F_(n-1)+F_(n-2)$ for all $2 < n$.
```

The C-x * o command is a useful way to open a Calc window without actually selecting that window. Giving this command verifies that '2 < n' is also on the Calc stack. Typing 17 RET would produce:

```
We define $F_n = F_(n-1)+F_(n-2)$ for all $17$.
```

with '2 < n' and '17' on the stack; typing TAB at this point will exchange the two stack values and restore '2 < n' to the embedded formula. Even though you can't normally see the stack in Embedded mode, it is still there and it still operates in the same way. But, as with old-fashioned RPN calculators, you can only see the value at the top of the stack at any given time (unless you use C-x * o).

Typing C-x * e again turns Embedded mode off. The Calc window reveals that the formula '2 < n' is automatically removed from the stack, but the '17' is not. Entering Embedded mode always pushes one thing onto the stack, and leaving Embedded mode always removes one thing. Anything else that happens on the stack is entirely your business as far as Embedded mode is concerned.

If you press *C-x * e* in the wrong place by accident, it is possible that Calc will be able to parse the nearby text as a formula and will mangle that text in an attempt to redisplay it "properly" in the current language mode. If this happens, press *C-x * e* again to exit Embedded mode, then give the regular Emacs "undo" command (*C-_* or *C-x u*) to put the text back the way it was before Calc edited it. Note that Calc's own Undo command (typed before you turn Embedded mode back off) will not do you any good, because as far as Calc is concerned you haven't done anything with this formula yet.

16.2 More About Embedded Mode

When Embedded mode "activates" a formula, i.e., when it examines the formula for the first time since the buffer was created or loaded, Calc tries to sense the language in which the formula was written. If the formula contains any LaTeX-like '\' sequences, it is parsed (i.e., read) in LaTeX mode. If the formula appears to be written in multi-line Big mode, it is parsed in Big mode. Otherwise, it is parsed according to the current language mode.

Note that Calc does not change the current language mode according the formula it reads in. Even though it can read a LaTeX formula when not in LaTeX mode, it will immediately rewrite this formula using whatever language mode is in effect.

Calc's parser is unable to read certain kinds of formulas. For example, with *v J* (calc-matrix-brackets) you can specify matrix display styles which the parser is unable to recognize as matrices. The *d p* (calc-show-plain) command turns on a mode in which a "plain" version of a formula is placed in front of the fully-formatted version. When Calc reads a formula that has such a plain version in front, it reads the plain version and ignores the formatted version.

Plain formulas are preceded and followed by '%%%' signs by default. This notation has the advantage that the '%' character begins a comment in TeX and LaTeX, so if your formula is embedded in a TeX or LaTeX document its plain version will be invisible in the final printed copy. Certain major modes have different delimiters to ensure that the "plain" version will be in a comment for those modes, also. See Section 16.5 [Customizing Embedded Mode], page 360, to see how to change the "plain" formula delimiters.

There are several notations which Calc's parser for "big" formatted formulas can't yet recognize. In particular, it can't read the large symbols for sum, prod, and integ, and it can't handle '=>' with the righthand argument omitted. Also, Calc won't recognize special formats you have defined with the *Z C* command (see Section 6.8.10.6 [User-Defined Compositions], page 173). In these cases it is important to use "plain" mode to make sure Calc will be able to read your formula later.

Another example where "plain" mode is important is if you have specified a float mode with few digits of precision. Normally any digits that are computed but not displayed will simply be lost when you save and re-load your embedded buffer, but "plain" mode allows you to make sure that the complete number is present in the file as well as the rounded-down number.

Embedded buffers remember active formulas for as long as they exist in Emacs memory. Suppose you have an embedded formula which is π to the normal 12 decimal places, and then type *C-u 5 d n* to display only five decimal places. If you then type *d n*, all 12 places reappear because the full number is still there on the Calc stack. More surprisingly, even if you exit Embedded mode and later re-enter it for that formula, typing d n will restore all 12 places because each buffer remembers all its active formulas. However, if you save the buffer in a file and reload it in a new Emacs session, all non-displayed digits will have been lost unless you used "plain" mode.

In some applications of Embedded mode, you will want to have a sequence of copies of a formula that show its evolution as you work on it. For example, you might want to have a sequence like this in your file (elaborating here on the example from the "Getting Started" chapter):

```
The derivative of
```

$$\ln(\ln(x))$$

```
is
```

$$(\text{the derivative of } \ln(\ln(x)))$$

```
whose value at x = 2 is
```

$$(\text{the value})$$

```
and at x = 3 is
```

$$(\text{the value})$$

The C-x * d (calc-embedded-duplicate) command is a handy way to make sequences like this. If you type C-x * d, the formula under the cursor (which may or may not have Embedded mode enabled for it at the time) is copied immediately below and Embedded mode is then enabled for that copy.

For this example, you would start with just

```
The derivative of
```

$$\ln(\ln(x))$$

and press C-x * d with the cursor on this formula. The result is

```
The derivative of
```

$$\ln(\ln(x))$$

$$\ln(\ln(x))$$

with the second copy of the formula enabled in Embedded mode. You can now press a d x RET to take the derivative, and C-x * d C-x * d to make two more copies of the derivative. To complete the computations, type 3 s l x RET to evaluate the last formula, then move up to the second-to-last formula and type 2 s l x RET.

Finally, you would want to press C-x * e to exit Embedded mode, then go up and insert the necessary text in between the various formulas and numbers.

The C-x * f (calc-embedded-new-formula) command creates a new embedded formula at the current point. It inserts some default delimiters, which are usually just blank lines, and then does an algebraic entry to get the formula (which is then enabled for Embedded mode). This is just shorthand for typing the delimiters yourself, positioning the cursor between the new delimiters, and pressing *C-x * e*. The key sequence *C-x * '* is equivalent to *C-x * f*.

The *C-x * n* (calc-embedded-next) and *C-x * p* (calc-embedded-previous) commands move the cursor to the next or previous active embedded formula in the buffer. They can take positive or negative prefix arguments to move by several formulas. Note that these commands do not actually examine the text of the buffer looking for formulas; they only see formulas which have previously been activated in Embedded mode. In fact, *C-x * n* and *C-x * p* are a useful way to tell which embedded formulas are currently active. Also, note that these commands do not enable Embedded mode on the next or previous formula, they just move the cursor.

The *C-x * `* (calc-embedded-edit) command edits the embedded formula at the current point as if by ` (calc-edit). Embedded mode does not have to be enabled for this to work. Press *C-c C-c* to finish the edit, or *C-x k* to cancel.

16.3 Assignments in Embedded Mode

The ':=' (assignment) and '=>' ("evaluates-to") operators are especially useful in Embedded mode. They allow you to make a definition in one formula, then refer to that definition in other formulas embedded in the same buffer.

An embedded formula which is an assignment to a variable, as in

    foo := 5

records 5 as the stored value of foo for the purposes of Embedded mode operations in the current buffer. It does *not* actually store 5 as the "global" value of foo, however. Regular Calc operations, and Embedded formulas in other buffers, will not see this assignment.

One way to use this assigned value is simply to create an Embedded formula elsewhere that refers to foo, and to press = in that formula. However, this permanently replaces the foo in the formula with its current value. More interesting is to use '=>' elsewhere:

    foo + 7 => 12

See Section 12.5 [Evaluates-To Operator], page 327, for a general discussion of '=>'.

If you move back and change the assignment to foo, any '=>' formulas which refer to it are automatically updated.

    foo := 17

    foo + 7 => 24

The obvious question then is, *how* can one easily change the assignment to foo? If you simply select the formula in Embedded mode and type 17, the assignment itself will be replaced by the 17. The effect on the other formula will be that the variable foo becomes unassigned:

    17

    foo + 7 => foo + 7

The right thing to do is first to use a selection command (*j 2* will do the trick) to select the righthand side of the assignment. Then, *17 TAB DEL* will swap the 17 into place (see Section 10.1 [Selecting Subformulas], page 243, to see how this works).

The *C-x * j* (`calc-embedded-select`) command provides an easy way to operate on assignments. It is just like *C-x * e*, except that if the enabled formula is an assignment, it uses *j 2* to select the righthand side. If the enabled formula is an evaluates-to, it uses *j 1* to select the lefthand side. A formula can also be a combination of both:

        bar := foo + 3 => 20

in which case *C-x * j* will select the middle part ('foo + 3').

The formula is automatically deselected when you leave Embedded mode.

Another way to change the assignment to `foo` would simply be to edit the number using regular Emacs editing rather than Embedded mode. Then, we have to find a way to get Embedded mode to notice the change. The *C-x * u* (`calc-embedded-update-formula`) command is a convenient way to do this.

        foo := 6

        foo + 7 => 13

Pressing *C-x * u* is much like pressing *C-x * e = C-x * e*, that is, temporarily enabling Embedded mode for the formula under the cursor and then evaluating it with =. But *C-x * u* does not actually use *C-x * e*, and in fact another formula somewhere else can be enabled in Embedded mode while you use *C-x * u* and that formula will not be disturbed.

With a numeric prefix argument, *C-x * u* updates all active '=>' formulas in the buffer. Formulas which have not yet been activated in Embedded mode, and formulas which do not have '=>' as their top-level operator, are not affected by this. (This is useful only if you have used *m C*; see below.)

With a plain *C-u* prefix, *C-u C-x * u* updates only in the region between mark and point rather than in the whole buffer.

*C-x * u* is also a handy way to activate a formula, such as an '=>' formula that has freshly been typed in or loaded from a file.

The *C-x * a* (`calc-embedded-activate`) command scans through the current buffer and activates all embedded formulas that contain ':=' or '=>' symbols. This does not mean that Embedded mode is actually turned on, but only that the formulas' positions are registered with Embedded mode so that the '=>' values can be properly updated as assignments are changed.

It is a good idea to type *C-x * a* right after loading a file that uses embedded '=>' operators. Emacs includes a nifty "buffer-local variables" feature that you can use to do this automatically. The idea is to place near the end of your file a few lines that look like this:

        --- Local Variables: ---
        --- eval:(calc-embedded-activate) ---
        --- End: ---

where the leading and trailing '---' can be replaced by any suitable strings (which must be the same on all three lines) or omitted altogether; in a TeX or LaTeX file, '%' would be a good leading string and no trailing string would be necessary. In a C program, '/*' and '*/' would be good leading and trailing strings.

When Emacs loads a file into memory, it checks for a Local Variables section like this one at the end of the file. If it finds this section, it does the specified things (in this case, running C-x * a automatically) before editing of the file begins. The Local Variables section must be within 3000 characters of the end of the file for Emacs to find it, and it must be in the last page of the file if the file has any page separators. See Section "Local Variables in Files" in *the Emacs manual*.

Note that C-x * a does not update the formulas it finds. To do this, type, say, M-1 C-x * u after C-x * a. Generally this should not be a problem, though, because the formulas will have been up-to-date already when the file was saved.

Normally, C-x * a activates all the formulas it finds, but any previous active formulas remain active as well. With a positive numeric prefix argument, C-x * a first deactivates all current active formulas, then actives the ones it finds in its scan of the buffer. With a negative prefix argument, C-x * a simply deactivates all formulas.

Embedded mode has two symbols, 'Active' and '~Active', which it puts next to the major mode name in a buffer's mode line. It puts 'Active' if it has reason to believe that all formulas in the buffer are active, because you have typed C-x * a and Calc has not since had to deactivate any formulas (which can happen if Calc goes to update an '=>' formula somewhere because a variable changed, and finds that the formula is no longer there due to some kind of editing outside of Embedded mode). Calc puts '~Active' in the mode line if some, but probably not all, formulas in the buffer are active. This happens if you activate a few formulas one at a time but never use C-x * a, or if you used C-x * a but then Calc had to deactivate a formula because it lost track of it. If neither of these symbols appears in the mode line, no embedded formulas are active in the buffer (e.g., before Embedded mode has been used, or after a M-- C-x * a).

Embedded formulas can refer to assignments both before and after them in the buffer. If there are several assignments to a variable, the nearest preceding assignment is used if there is one, otherwise the following assignment is used.

```
x => 1

x := 1

x => 1

x := 2

x => 2
```

As well as simple variables, you can also assign to subscript expressions of the form 'var_number' (as in x_0), or 'var_var' (as in x_max). Assignments to other kinds of objects can be represented by Calc, but the automatic linkage between assignments and references works only for plain variables and these two kinds of subscript expressions.

If there are no assignments to a given variable, the global stored value for the variable is used (see Section 12.1 [Storing Variables], page 323), or, if no value is stored, the variable is left in symbolic form. Note that global stored values will be lost when the file is saved and loaded in a later Emacs session, unless you have used the s p (calc-permanent-variable) command to save them; see Section 12.3 [Operations on Variables], page 325.

The m C (calc-auto-recompute) command turns automatic recomputation of '=>' forms on and off. If you turn automatic recomputation off, you will have to use C-x * u to update these formulas manually after an assignment has been changed. If you plan to change several assignments at once, it may be more efficient to type *m C*, change all the assignments, then use *M-1 C-x * u* to update the entire buffer afterwards. The *m C* command also controls '=>' formulas on the stack; see Section 12.5 [Evaluates-To Operator], page 327. When you turn automatic recomputation back on, the stack will be updated but the Embedded buffer will not; you must use *C-x * u* to update the buffer by hand.

16.4 Mode Settings in Embedded Mode

The mode settings can be changed while Calc is in embedded mode, but by default they will revert to their original values when embedded mode is ended. However, the modes saved when the mode-recording mode is `Save` (see below) and the modes in effect when the *m e* (`calc-embedded-preserve-modes`) command is given will be preserved when embedded mode is ended.

Embedded mode has a rather complicated mechanism for handling mode settings in Embedded formulas. It is possible to put annotations in the file that specify mode settings either global to the entire file or local to a particular formula or formulas. In the latter case, different modes can be specified for use when a formula is the enabled Embedded mode formula.

When you give any mode-setting command, like *m f* (for Fraction mode) or *d s* (for scientific notation), Embedded mode adds a line like the following one to the file just before the opening delimiter of the formula.

```
% [calc-mode: fractions: t]
% [calc-mode: float-format: (sci 0)]
```

When Calc interprets an embedded formula, it scans the text before the formula for mode-setting annotations like these and sets the Calc buffer to match these modes. Modes not explicitly described in the file are not changed. Calc scans all the way to the top of the file, or up to a line of the form

```
% [calc-defaults]
```

which you can insert at strategic places in the file if this backward scan is getting too slow, or just to provide a barrier between one "zone" of mode settings and another.

If the file contains several annotations for the same mode, the closest one before the formula is used. Annotations after the formula are never used (except for global annotations, described below).

The scan does not look for the leading '% ', only for the square brackets and the text they enclose. In fact, the leading characters are different for different major modes. You can edit the mode annotations to a style that works better in context if you wish. See Section 16.5 [Customizing Embedded Mode], page 360, to see how to change the style that Calc uses when it generates the annotations. You can write mode annotations into the file yourself if you know the syntax; the easiest way to find the syntax for a given mode is to let Calc write the annotation for it once and see what it does.

If you give a mode-changing command for a mode that already has a suitable annotation just above the current formula, Calc will modify that annotation rather than generating a new, conflicting one.

Mode annotations have three parts, separated by colons. (Spaces after the colons are optional.) The first identifies the kind of mode setting, the second is a name for the mode itself, and the third is the value in the form of a Lisp symbol, number, or list. Annotations with unrecognizable text in the first or second parts are ignored. The third part is not checked to make sure the value is of a valid type or range; if you write an annotation by hand, be sure to give a proper value or results will be unpredictable. Mode-setting annotations are case-sensitive.

While Embedded mode is enabled, the word `Local` appears in the mode line. This is to show that mode setting commands generate annotations that are "local" to the current formula or set of formulas. The `m R` (`calc-mode-record-mode`) command causes Calc to generate different kinds of annotations. Pressing `m R` repeatedly cycles through the possible modes.

`LocEdit` and `LocPerm` modes generate annotations that look like this, respectively:

```
% [calc-edit-mode: float-format: (sci 0)]
% [calc-perm-mode: float-format: (sci 5)]
```

The first kind of annotation will be used only while a formula is enabled in Embedded mode. The second kind will be used only when the formula is *not* enabled. (Whether the formula is "active" or not, i.e., whether Calc has seen this formula yet, is not relevant here.)

`Global` mode generates an annotation like this at the end of the file:

```
% [calc-global-mode: fractions t]
```

Global mode annotations affect all formulas throughout the file, and may appear anywhere in the file. This allows you to tuck your mode annotations somewhere out of the way, say, on a new page of the file, as long as those mode settings are suitable for all formulas in the file.

Enabling a formula with `C-x * e` causes a fresh scan for local mode annotations; you will have to use this after adding annotations above a formula by hand to get the formula to notice them. Updating a formula with `C-x * u` will also re-scan the local modes, but global modes are only re-scanned by `C-x * a`.

Another way that modes can get out of date is if you add a local mode annotation to a formula that has another formula after it. In this example, we have used the `d s` command while the first of the two embedded formulas is active. But the second formula has not changed its style to match, even though by the rules of reading annotations the '`(sci 0)`' applies to it, too.

```
% [calc-mode: float-format: (sci 0)]
1.23e2

456.
```

We would have to go down to the other formula and press `C-x * u` on it in order to get it to notice the new annotation.

Two more mode-recording modes selectable by `m R` are available which are also available outside of Embedded mode. (see Section 6.1 [General Mode Commands], page 137.) They are `Save`, in which mode settings are recorded permanently in your Calc init file (the file given by the variable `calc-settings-file`, typically `~/.emacs.d/calc.el`) rather than by annotating the current document, and no-recording mode (where there is no symbol like `Save` or `Local` in the mode line), in which mode-changing commands do not leave any annotations at all.

When Embedded mode is not enabled, mode-recording modes except for `Save` have no effect.

16.5 Customizing Embedded Mode

You can modify Embedded mode's behavior by setting various Lisp variables described here. These variables are customizable (see Appendix C [Customizing Calc], page 435), or you can use *M-x set-variable* or *M-x edit-options* to adjust a variable on the fly. (Another possibility would be to use a file-local variable annotation at the end of the file; see Section "Local Variables in Files" in *the Emacs manual*.) Many of the variables given mentioned here can be set to depend on the major mode of the editing buffer (see Appendix C [Customizing Calc], page 435).

The `calc-embedded-open-formula` variable holds a regular expression for the opening delimiter of a formula. See Section "Regular Expression Search" in *the Emacs manual*, to see how regular expressions work. Basically, a regular expression is a pattern that Calc can search for. A regular expression that considers blank lines, '$', and '$$' to be opening delimiters is `"\\`\\|^\n\\|\\$\\$?"`. Just in case the meaning of this regular expression is not completely plain, let's go through it in detail.

The surrounding '" "' marks quote the text between them as a Lisp string. If you left them off, `set-variable` or `edit-options` would try to read the regular expression as a Lisp program.

The most obvious property of this regular expression is that it contains indecently many backslashes. There are actually two levels of backslash usage going on here. First, when Lisp reads a quoted string, all pairs of characters beginning with a backslash are interpreted as special characters. Here, \n changes to a new-line character, and \\ changes to a single backslash. So the actual regular expression seen by Calc is '\\`\|^ (newline) \|\$\$?'.

Regular expressions also consider pairs beginning with backslash to have special meanings. Sometimes the backslash is used to quote a character that otherwise would have a special meaning in a regular expression, like '$', which normally means "end-of-line," or '?', which means that the preceding item is optional. So '\$\$?' matches either one or two dollar signs.

The other codes in this regular expression are '^', which matches "beginning-of-line," '\|', which means "or," and '\`', which matches "beginning-of-buffer." So the whole pattern means that a formula begins at the beginning of the buffer, or on a newline that occurs at the beginning of a line (i.e., a blank line), or at one or two dollar signs.

The default value of `calc-embedded-open-formula` looks just like this example, with several more alternatives added on to recognize various other common kinds of delimiters.

By the way, the reason to use '^\n' rather than '^$' or '\n\n', which also would appear to match blank lines, is that the former expression actually "consumes" only one newline character as *part of* the delimiter, whereas the latter expressions consume zero or two newlines, respectively. The former choice gives the most natural behavior when Calc must operate on a whole formula including its delimiters.

See the Emacs manual for complete details on regular expressions. But just for your convenience, here is a list of all characters which must be quoted with backslash (like '\$')

to avoid some special interpretation: '. * + ? [ ] ^ $ \'. (Note the backslash in this list; for example, to match '\[' you must use "\\\\\\[". An exercise for the reader is to account for each of these six backslashes!)

The `calc-embedded-close-formula` variable holds a regular expression for the closing delimiter of a formula. A closing regular expression to match the above example would be "\\'\\|\n$\\|\\$\\$?". This is almost the same as the other one, except it now uses '\'' ("end-of-buffer") and '\n$' (newline occurring at end of line, yet another way of describing a blank line that is more appropriate for this case).

The `calc-embedded-word-regexp` variable holds a regular expression used to define an expression to look for (a "word") when you type *C-x * w* to enable Embedded mode.

The `calc-embedded-open-plain` variable is a string which begins a "plain" formula written in front of the formatted formula when *d p* mode is turned on. Note that this is an actual string, not a regular expression, because Calc must be able to write this string into a buffer as well as to recognize it. The default string is "%%% " (note the trailing space), but may be different for certain major modes.

The `calc-embedded-close-plain` variable is a string which ends a "plain" formula. The default is " %%%\n", but may be different for different major modes. Without the trailing newline here, the first line of a Big mode formula that followed might be shifted over with respect to the other lines.

The `calc-embedded-open-new-formula` variable is a string which is inserted at the front of a new formula when you type *C-x * f*. Its default value is "\n\n". If this string begins with a newline character and the *C-x * f* is typed at the beginning of a line, *C-x * f* will skip this first newline to avoid introducing unnecessary blank lines in the file.

The `calc-embedded-close-new-formula` variable is the corresponding string which is inserted at the end of a new formula. Its default value is also "\n\n". The final newline is omitted by *C-x * f* if typed at the end of a line. (It follows that if *C-x * f* is typed on a blank line, both a leading opening newline and a trailing closing newline are omitted.)

The `calc-embedded-announce-formula` variable is a regular expression which is sure to be followed by an embedded formula. The *C-x * a* command searches for this pattern as well as for '=>' and ':=' operators. Note that *C-x * a* will not activate just anything surrounded by formula delimiters; after all, blank lines are considered formula delimiters by default! But if your language includes a delimiter which can only occur actually in front of a formula, you can take advantage of it here. The default pattern is "%Embed\n\\(% .*\n\\)*", but may be different for different major modes. This pattern will check for '%Embed' followed by any number of lines beginning with '%' and a space. This last is important to make Calc consider mode annotations part of the pattern, so that the formula's opening delimiter really is sure to follow the pattern.

The `calc-embedded-open-mode` variable is a string (not a regular expression) which should precede a mode annotation. Calc never scans for this string; Calc always looks for the annotation itself. But this is the string that is inserted before the opening bracket when Calc adds an annotation on its own. The default is "% ", but may be different for different major modes.

The `calc-embedded-close-mode` variable is a string which follows a mode annotation written by Calc. Its default value is simply a newline, "\n", but may be different for different major modes. If you change this, it is a good idea still to end with a newline so that mode annotations will appear on lines by themselves.

17 Programming

There are several ways to "program" the Emacs Calculator, depending on the nature of the problem you need to solve.

1. *Keyboard macros* allow you to record a sequence of keystrokes and play them back at a later time. This is just the standard Emacs keyboard macro mechanism, dressed up with a few more features such as loops and conditionals.

2. *Algebraic definitions* allow you to use any formula to define a new function. This function can then be used in algebraic formulas or as an interactive command.

3. *Rewrite rules* are discussed in the section on algebra commands. See Section 10.11 [Rewrite Rules], page 291. If you put your rewrite rules in the variable `EvalRules`, they will be applied automatically to all Calc results in just the same way as an internal "rule" is applied to evaluate '`sqrt(9)`' to 3 and so on. See Section 10.11.11 [Automatic Rewrites], page 309.

4. *Lisp* is the programming language that Calc (and most of Emacs) is written in. If the above techniques aren't powerful enough, you can write Lisp functions to do anything that built-in Calc commands can do. Lisp code is also somewhat faster than keyboard macros or rewrite rules.

Programming features are available through the *z* and *Z* prefix keys. New commands that you define are two-key sequences beginning with *z*. Commands for managing these definitions use the shift-*Z* prefix. (The *Z T* (`calc-timing`) command is described elsewhere; see Section 3.11 [Troubleshooting Commands], page 113. The *Z C* (`calc-user-define-composition`) command is also described elsewhere; see Section 6.8.10.6 [User-Defined Compositions], page 173.)

17.1 Creating User Keys

Any Calculator command may be bound to a key using the *Z D* (`calc-user-define`) command. Actually, it is bound to a two-key sequence beginning with the lower-case *z* prefix.

The *Z D* command first prompts for the key to define. For example, press *Z D a* to define the new key sequence *z a*. You are then prompted for the name of the Calculator command that this key should run. For example, the `calc-sincos` command is not normally available on a key. Typing *Z D s sincos RET* programs the *z s* key sequence to run `calc-sincos`. This definition will remain in effect for the rest of this Emacs session, or until you redefine *z s* to be something else.

You can actually bind any Emacs command to a *z* key sequence by backspacing over the '`calc-`' when you are prompted for the command name.

As with any other prefix key, you can type *z ?* to see a list of all the two-key sequences you have defined that start with *z*. Initially, no *z* sequences (except *z ?* itself) are defined.

User keys are typically letters, but may in fact be any key. (META-keys are not permitted, nor are a terminal's special function keys which generate multi-character sequences when pressed.) You can define different commands on the shifted and unshifted versions of a letter if you wish.

The *Z U* (`calc-user-undefine`) command unbinds a user key. For example, the key sequence *Z U s* will undefine the `sincos` key we defined above.

The *Z P* (`calc-user-define-permanent`) command makes a key binding permanent so that it will remain in effect even in future Emacs sessions. (It does this by adding a suitable bit of Lisp code into your Calc init file; that is, the file given by the variable `calc-settings-file`, typically `~/.emacs.d/calc.el`.) For example, *Z P s* would register our `sincos` command permanently. If you later wish to unregister this command you must edit your Calc init file by hand. (See Section 6.1 [General Mode Commands], page 137, for a way to tell Calc to use a different file for the Calc init file.)

The *Z P* command also saves the user definition, if any, for the command bound to the key. After *Z F* and *Z C*, a given user key could invoke a command, which in turn calls an algebraic function, which might have one or more special display formats. A single *Z P* command will save all of these definitions. To save an algebraic function, type ' (the apostrophe) when prompted for a key, and type the function name. To save a command without its key binding, type *M-x* and enter a function name. (The 'calc-' prefix will automatically be inserted for you.) (If the command you give implies a function, the function will be saved, and if the function has any display formats, those will be saved, but not the other way around: Saving a function will not save any commands or key bindings associated with the function.)

The *Z E* (`calc-user-define-edit`) command edits the definition of a user key. This works for keys that have been defined by either keyboard macros or formulas; further details are contained in the relevant following sections.

17.2 Programming with Keyboard Macros

The easiest way to "program" the Emacs Calculator is to use standard keyboard macros. Press *C-x (* to begin recording a macro. From this point on, keystrokes you type will be saved away as well as performing their usual functions. Press *C-x)* to end recording. Press shift-*X* (or the standard Emacs key sequence *C-x e*) to execute your keyboard macro by replaying the recorded keystrokes. See Section "Keyboard Macros" in *the Emacs Manual*, for further information.

When you use *X* to invoke a keyboard macro, the entire macro is treated as a single command by the undo and trail features. The stack display buffer is not updated during macro execution, but is instead fixed up once the macro completes. Thus, commands defined with keyboard macros are convenient and efficient. The *C-x e* command, on the other hand, invokes the keyboard macro with no special treatment: Each command in the macro will record its own undo information and trail entry, and update the stack buffer accordingly. If your macro uses features outside of Calc's control to operate on the contents of the Calc stack buffer, or if it includes Undo, Redo, or last-arguments commands, you must use *C-x e* to make sure the buffer and undo list are up-to-date at all times. You could also consider using *K* (`calc-keep-args`) instead of *M-RET* (`calc-last-args`).

Calc extends the standard Emacs keyboard macros in several ways. Keyboard macros can be used to create user-defined commands. Keyboard macros can include conditional and iteration structures, somewhat analogous to those provided by a traditional programmable calculator.

17.2.1 Naming Keyboard Macros

Once you have defined a keyboard macro, you can bind it to a *z* key sequence with the *Z K* (`calc-user-define-kbd-macro`) command. This command prompts first for a key, then for a command name. For example, if you type *C-x (n TAB n TAB C-x)* you will define a keyboard macro which negates the top two numbers on the stack (*TAB* swaps the top two stack elements). Now you can type *Z K n RET* to define this keyboard macro onto the *z n* key sequence. The default command name (if you answer the second prompt with just the *RET* key as in this example) will be something like '`calc-User-n`'. The keyboard macro will now be available as both *z n* and *M-x calc-User-n*. You can backspace and enter a more descriptive command name if you wish.

Macros defined by *Z K* act like single commands; they are executed in the same way as by the *X* key. If you wish to define the macro as a standard no-frills Emacs macro (to be executed as if by *C-x e*), give a negative prefix argument to *Z K*.

Once you have bound your keyboard macro to a key, you can use *Z P* to register it permanently with Emacs. See Section 17.1 [Creating User Keys], page 363.

The *Z E* (`calc-user-define-edit`) command on a key that has been defined by a keyboard macro tries to use the `edmacro` package edit the macro. Type *C-c C-c* to finish editing and update the definition stored on the key, or, to cancel the edit, kill the buffer with *C-x k*. The special characters RET, LFD, TAB, SPC, DEL, and NUL must be entered as these three character sequences, written in all uppercase, as must the prefixes C- and M-. Spaces and line breaks are ignored. Other characters are copied verbatim into the keyboard macro. Basically, the notation is the same as is used in all of this manual's examples, except that the manual takes some liberties with spaces: When we say *' [1 2 3] RET*, we take it for granted that it is clear we really mean *' [1 SPC 2 SPC 3] RET*.

The *C-x * m* (`read-kbd-macro`) command reads an Emacs "region" of spelled-out keystrokes and defines it as the current keyboard macro. It is a convenient way to define a keyboard macro that has been stored in a file, or to define a macro without executing it at the same time.

17.2.2 Conditionals in Keyboard Macros

The *Z [* (`calc-kbd-if`) and *Z]* (`calc-kbd-end-if`) commands allow you to put simple tests in a keyboard macro. When Calc sees the *Z [*, it pops an object from the stack and, if the object is a non-zero value, continues executing keystrokes. But if the object is zero, or if it is not provably nonzero, Calc skips ahead to the matching *Z]* keystroke. See Section 10.10 [Logical Operations], page 288, for a set of commands for performing tests which conveniently produce 1 for true and 0 for false.

For example, *RET 0 a < Z [n Z]* implements an absolute-value function in the form of a keyboard macro. This macro duplicates the number on the top of the stack, pushes zero and compares using *a <* (`calc-less-than`), then, if the number was less than zero, executes *n* (`calc-change-sign`). Otherwise, the change-sign command is skipped.

To program this macro, type *C-x (*, type the above sequence of keystrokes, then type *C-x)*. Note that the keystrokes will be executed while you are making the definition as well as when you later re-execute the macro by typing *X*. Thus you should make sure a suitable number is on the stack before defining the macro so that you don't get a stack-underflow error during the definition process.

Conditionals can be nested arbitrarily. However, there should be exactly one Z] for each Z [in a keyboard macro.

The Z : (calc-kbd-else) command allows you to choose between two keystroke sequences. The general format is *cond Z [then-part Z : else-part Z]*. If *cond* is true (i.e., if the top of stack contains a non-zero number after *cond* has been executed), the *then-part* will be executed and the *else-part* will be skipped. Otherwise, the *then-part* will be skipped and the *else-part* will be executed.

The Z | (calc-kbd-else-if) command allows you to choose between any number of alternatives. For example, *cond1 Z [part1 Z : cond2 Z | part2 Z : part3 Z]* will execute *part1* if *cond1* is true, otherwise it will execute *part2* if *cond2* is true, otherwise it will execute *part3*.

More precisely, Z [pops a number and conditionally skips to the next matching Z : or Z] key. Z] has no effect when actually executed. Z : skips to the next matching Z]. Z | pops a number and conditionally skips to the next matching Z : or Z]; thus, Z [and Z | are functionally equivalent except that Z [participates in nesting but Z | does not.

Calc's conditional and looping constructs work by scanning the keyboard macro for occurrences of character sequences like 'Z:' and 'Z]'. One side-effect of this is that if you use these constructs you must be careful that these character pairs do not occur by accident in other parts of the macros. Since Calc rarely uses shift-Z for any purpose except as a prefix character, this is not likely to be a problem. Another side-effect is that it will not work to define your own custom key bindings for these commands. Only the standard shift-Z bindings will work correctly.

If Calc gets stuck while skipping characters during the definition of a macro, type Z C-g to cancel the definition. (Typing plain C-g actually adds a C-g keystroke to the macro.)

17.2.3 Loops in Keyboard Macros

The Z < (calc-kbd-repeat) and Z > (calc-kbd-end-repeat) commands pop a number from the stack, which must be an integer, then repeat the keystrokes between the brackets the specified number of times. If the integer is zero or negative, the body is skipped altogether. For example, *1 TAB Z < 2 * Z >* computes two to a nonnegative integer power. First, we push 1 on the stack and then swap the integer argument back to the top. The Z < pops that argument leaving the 1 back on top of the stack. Then, we repeat a multiply-by-two step however many times.

Once again, the keyboard macro is executed as it is being entered. In this case it is especially important to set up reasonable initial conditions before making the definition: Suppose the integer 1000 just happened to be sitting on the stack before we typed the above definition! Another approach is to enter a harmless dummy definition for the macro, then go back and edit in the real one with a Z E command. Yet another approach is to type the macro as written-out keystroke names in a buffer, then use C-x * m (read-kbd-macro) to read the macro.

The Z / (calc-kbd-break) command allows you to break out of a keyboard macro loop prematurely. It pops an object from the stack; if that object is true (a non-zero number), control jumps out of the innermost enclosing Z < ... Z > loop and continues after the Z >. If the object is false, the Z / has no effect. Thus *cond Z /* is similar to 'if (cond) break;' in the C language.

The Z ((`calc-kbd-for`) and Z) (`calc-kbd-end-for`) commands are similar to $Z <$ and $Z >$, except that they make the value of the counter available inside the loop. The general layout is *init final Z (body step Z)*. The Z (command pops initial and final values from the stack. It then creates a temporary internal counter and initializes it with the value *init*. The Z (command then repeatedly pushes the counter value onto the stack and executes *body* and *step*, adding *step* to the counter each time until the loop finishes.

By default, the loop finishes when the counter becomes greater than (or less than) *final*, assuming *initial* is less than (greater than) *final*. If *initial* is equal to *final*, the body executes exactly once. The body of the loop always executes at least once. For example, *0 1 10 Z (* *2 ^ + 1 Z)* computes the sum of the squares of the integers from 1 to 10, in steps of 1.

If you give a numeric prefix argument of 1 to Z (, the loop is forced to use upward-counting conventions. In this case, if *initial* is greater than *final* the body will not be executed at all. Note that *step* may still be negative in this loop; the prefix argument merely constrains the loop-finished test. Likewise, a prefix argument of -1 forces downward-counting conventions.

The Z { (`calc-kbd-loop`) and Z } (`calc-kbd-end-loop`) commands are similar to $Z <$ and $Z >$, except that they do not pop a count from the stack—they effectively create an infinite loop. Every Z { ... Z } loop ought to include at least one Z / to make sure the loop doesn't run forever. (If any error message occurs which causes Emacs to beep, the keyboard macro will also be halted; this is a standard feature of Emacs. You can also generally press *C-g* to halt a running keyboard macro, although not all versions of Unix support this feature.)

The conditional and looping constructs are not actually tied to keyboard macros, but they are most often used in that context. For example, the keystrokes *10 Z < 23 RET Z >* push ten copies of 23 onto the stack. This can be typed "live" just as easily as in a macro definition.

See Section 17.2.2 [Conditionals in Macros], page 365, for some additional notes about conditional and looping commands.

17.2.4 Local Values in Macros

Keyboard macros sometimes want to operate under known conditions without affecting surrounding conditions. For example, a keyboard macro may wish to turn on Fraction mode, or set a particular precision, independent of the user's normal setting for those modes.

Macros also sometimes need to use local variables. Assignments to local variables inside the macro should not affect any variables outside the macro. The Z ` (`calc-kbd-push`) and $Z$ ' (`calc-kbd-pop`) commands give you both of these capabilities.

When you type Z ` (with a grave accent), the values of various mode settings are saved away. The ten "quick" variables q0 through q9 are also saved. When you type $Z$ ' (with an apostrophe), these values are restored. Pairs of $Z$ ` and Z ' commands may be nested.

If a keyboard macro halts due to an error in between a Z ` and a $Z$ ', the saved values will be restored correctly even though the macro never reaches the $Z$ ' command. Thus you can use $Z$ ` and Z ' without having to worry about what happens in exceptional conditions.

If you type Z ` "live" (not in a keyboard macro), Calc puts you into a "recursive edit." You can tell you are in a recursive edit because there will be extra square brackets in the mode line, as in '[(Calculator)]'. These brackets will go away when you type the matching Z ' command. The modes and quick variables will be saved and restored in just the same way as if actual keyboard macros were involved.

The modes saved by Z ` and Z ' are the current precision and binary word size, the angular mode (Deg, Rad, or HMS), the simplification mode, Algebraic mode, Symbolic mode, Infinite mode, Matrix or Scalar mode, Fraction mode, and the current complex mode (Polar or Rectangular). The ten "quick" variables' values (or lack thereof) are also saved.

Most mode-setting commands act as toggles, but with a numeric prefix they force the mode either on (positive prefix) or off (negative or zero prefix). Since you don't know what the environment might be when you invoke your macro, it's best to use prefix arguments for all mode-setting commands inside the macro.

In fact, C-u Z ` is like Z ` except that it sets the modes listed above to their default values. As usual, the matching Z ' will restore the modes to their settings from before the C-u Z `. Also, Z ` with a negative prefix argument resets the algebraic mode to its default (off) but leaves the other modes the same as they were outside the construct.

The contents of the stack and trail, values of non-quick variables, and other settings such as the language mode and the various display modes, are *not* affected by Z ` and Z '.

17.2.5 Queries in Keyboard Macros

The Z # (calc-kbd-query) command prompts for an algebraic entry which takes its input from the keyboard, even during macro execution. All the normal conventions of algebraic input, including the use of $ characters, are supported. The prompt message itself is taken from the top of the stack, and so must be entered (as a string) before the Z # command. (Recall, as a string it can be entered by pressing the " key and will appear as a vector when it is put on the stack. The prompt message is only put on the stack to provide a prompt for the Z # command; it will not play any role in any subsequent calculations.) This command allows your keyboard macros to accept numbers or formulas as interactive input.

As an example, 2 RET "Power: " RET Z # 3 RET ^ will prompt for input with "Power: " in the minibuffer, then return 2 to the provided power. (The response to the prompt that's given, 3 in this example, will not be part of the macro.)

See Section "Keyboard Macro Query" in *the Emacs Manual*, for a description of C-x q (kbd-macro-query), the standard Emacs way to accept keyboard input during a keyboard macro. In particular, you can use C-x q to enter a recursive edit, which allows the user to perform any Calculator operations interactively before pressing C-M-c to return control to the keyboard macro.

17.3 Invocation Macros

Calc provides one special keyboard macro, called up by C-x * z (calc-user-invocation), that is intended to allow you to define your own special way of starting Calc. To define this "invocation macro," create the macro in the usual way with C-x (and C-x), then type Z I (calc-user-define-invocation). There is only one invocation macro, so you don't need to type any additional letters after Z I. From now on, you can type C-x * z at any time to execute your invocation macro.

For example, suppose you find yourself often grabbing rectangles of numbers into Calc and multiplying their columns. You can do this by typing *C-x * r* to grab, and *V R : *** to multiply columns. To make this into an invocation macro, just type *C-x (C-x * r V R : * C-x)*, then *Z I*. Then, to multiply a rectangle of data, just mark the data in its buffer in the usual way and type *C-x * z*.

Invocation macros are treated like regular Emacs keyboard macros; all the special features described above for *Z K*-style macros do not apply. *C-x * z* is just like *C-x e*, except that it uses the macro that was last stored by *Z I*. (In fact, the macro does not even have to have anything to do with Calc!)

The *m m* command saves the last invocation macro defined by *Z I* along with all the other Calc mode settings. See Section 6.1 [General Mode Commands], page 137.

17.4 Programming with Formulas

Another way to create a new Calculator command uses algebraic formulas. The *Z F* (`calc-user-define-formula`) command stores the formula at the top of the stack as the definition for a key. This command prompts for five things: The key, the command name, the function name, the argument list, and the behavior of the command when given non-numeric arguments.

For example, suppose we type *' a+2b RET* to push the formula 'a + 2*b' onto the stack. We now type *Z F m* to define this formula on the *z m* key sequence. The next prompt is for a command name, beginning with 'calc-', which should be the long (*M-x*) form for the new command. If you simply press *RET*, a default name like `calc-User-m` will be constructed. In our example, suppose we enter *spam RET* to define the new command as `calc-spam`.

If you want to give the formula a long-style name only, you can press *SPC* or *RET* when asked which single key to use. For example *Z F RET spam RET* defines the new command as *M-x calc-spam*, with no keyboard equivalent.

The third prompt is for an algebraic function name. The default is to use the same name as the command name but without the 'calc-' prefix. (If this is of the form 'User-m', the hyphen is removed so it won't be taken for a minus sign in algebraic formulas.) This is the name you will use if you want to enter your new function in an algebraic formula. Suppose we enter *yow RET*. Then the new function can be invoked by pushing two numbers on the stack and typing *z m* or *x spam*, or by entering the algebraic formula 'yow(x,y)'.

The fourth prompt is for the function's argument list. This is used to associate values on the stack with the variables that appear in the formula. The default is a list of all variables which appear in the formula, sorted into alphabetical order. In our case, the default would be '(a b)'. This means that, when the user types *z m*, the Calculator will remove two numbers from the stack, substitute these numbers for 'a' and 'b' (respectively) in the formula, then simplify the formula and push the result on the stack. In other words, *10 RET 100 z m* would replace the 10 and 100 on the stack with the number 210, which is $a + 2b$ with $a = 10$ and $b = 100$. Likewise, the formula 'yow(10, 100)' will be evaluated by substituting $a = 10$ and $b = 100$ in the definition.

You can rearrange the order of the names before pressing *RET* to control which stack positions go to which variables in the formula. If you remove a variable from the argument list, that variable will be left in symbolic form by the command. Thus using an argument list of '(b)' for our function would cause *10 z m* to replace the 10 on the stack with the formula 'a + 20'. If we had used an argument list of '(b a)', the result with inputs 10 and 100 would have been 120.

You can also put a nameless function on the stack instead of just a formula, as in '<a, b : a + 2 b>'. See Section 9.8.1 [Specifying Operators], page 235. In this example, the command will be defined by the formula 'a + 2 b' using the argument list '(a b)'.

The final prompt is a y-or-n question concerning what to do if symbolic arguments are given to your function. If you answer **y**, then executing **z m** (using the original argument list '(a b)') with arguments 10 and x will leave the function in symbolic form, i.e., 'yow(10,x)'. On the other hand, if you answer **n**, then the formula will always be expanded, even for non-constant arguments: '10 + 2 x'. If you never plan to feed algebraic formulas to your new function, it doesn't matter how you answer this question.

If you answered **y** to this question you can still cause a function call to be expanded by typing **a "** (`calc-expand-formula`). Also, Calc will expand the function if necessary when you take a derivative or integral or solve an equation involving the function.

Once you have defined a formula on a key, you can retrieve this formula with the *Z G* (`calc-user-define-get-defn`) command. Press a key, and this command pushes the formula that was used to define that key onto the stack. Actually, it pushes a nameless function that specifies both the argument list and the defining formula. You will get an error message if the key is undefined, or if the key was not defined by a *Z F* command.

The *Z E* (`calc-user-define-edit`) command on a key that has been defined by a formula uses a variant of the `calc-edit` command to edit the defining formula. Press *C-c C-c* to finish editing and store the new formula back in the definition, or kill the buffer with *C-x k* to cancel the edit. (The argument list and other properties of the definition are unchanged; to adjust the argument list, you can use *Z G* to grab the function onto the stack, edit with `, and then re-execute the *Z F* command.)

As usual, the *Z P* command records your definition permanently. In this case it will permanently record all three of the relevant definitions: the key, the command, and the function.

You may find it useful to turn off the default simplifications with *m O* (`calc-no-simplify-mode`) when entering a formula to be used as a function definition. For example, the formula 'deriv(a^2,v)' which might be used to define a new function 'dsqr(a,v)' will be "simplified" to 0 immediately upon entry since `deriv` considers a to be constant with respect to v. Turning off default simplifications cures this problem: The definition will be stored in symbolic form without ever activating the `deriv` function. Press *m D* to turn the default simplifications back on afterwards.

17.5 Programming with Lisp

The Calculator can be programmed quite extensively in Lisp. All you do is write a normal Lisp function definition, but with `defmath` in place of `defun`. This has the same form as `defun`, but it automagically replaces calls to standard Lisp functions like + and `zerop` with calls to the corresponding functions in Calc's own library. Thus you can write natural-looking Lisp code which operates on all of the standard Calculator data types. You can then use *Z D* if you wish to bind your new command to a *z*-prefix key sequence. The *Z E* command will not edit a Lisp-based definition.

Emacs Lisp is described in the GNU Emacs Lisp Reference Manual. This section assumes a familiarity with Lisp programming concepts; if you do not know Lisp, you may find keyboard macros or rewrite rules to be an easier way to program the Calculator.

This section first discusses ways to write commands, functions, or small programs to be executed inside of Calc. Then it discusses how your own separate programs are able to call Calc from the outside. Finally, there is a list of internal Calc functions and data structures for the true Lisp enthusiast.

17.5.1 Defining New Functions

The `defmath` function (actually a Lisp macro) is like `defun` except that code in the body of the definition can make use of the full range of Calculator data types. The prefix 'calcFunc-' is added to the specified name to get the actual Lisp function name. As a simple example,

```
(defmath myfact (n)
  (if (> n 0)
      (* n (myfact (1- n)))
    1))
```

This actually expands to the code,

```
(defun calcFunc-myfact (n)
  (if (math-posp n)
      (math-mul n (calcFunc-myfact (math-add n -1)))
    1))
```

This function can be used in algebraic expressions, e.g., 'myfact(5)'.

The 'myfact' function as it is defined above has the bug that an expression 'myfact(a+b)' will be simplified to 1 because the formula 'a+b' is not considered to be `posp`. A robust factorial function would be written along the following lines:

```
(defmath myfact (n)
  (if (> n 0)
      (* n (myfact (1- n)))
    (if (= n 0)
        1
      nil)))    ; this could be simplified as: (and (= n 0) 1)
```

If a function returns `nil`, it is left unsimplified by the Calculator (except that its arguments will be simplified). Thus, 'myfact(a+1+2)' will be simplified to 'myfact(a+3)' but no further. Beware that every time the Calculator reexamines this formula it will attempt to resimplify it, so your function ought to detect the returning-`nil` case as efficiently as possible.

The following standard Lisp functions are treated by `defmath`: +, -, *, /, %, ^ or `expt`, =, <, >, <=, >=, /=, 1+, 1-, `logand`, `logior`, `logxor`, `logandc2`, `lognot`. Also, ~= is an abbreviation for `math-nearly-equal`, which is useful in implementing Taylor series.

For other functions *func*, if a function by the name 'calcFunc-*func*' exists it is used, otherwise if a function by the name 'math-*func*' exists it is used, otherwise if *func* itself is defined as a function it is used, otherwise 'calcFunc-*func*' is used on the assumption that this is a to-be-defined math function. Also, if the function name is quoted as in '('integerp a)' the function name is always used exactly as written (but not quoted).

Variable names have 'var-' prepended to them unless they appear in the function's argument list or in an enclosing `let`, `let*`, `for`, or `foreach` form, or their names already contain a '-' character. Thus a reference to 'foo' is the same as a reference to 'var-foo'.

A few other Lisp extensions are available in `defmath` definitions:

- The `elt` function accepts any number of index variables. Note that Calc vectors are stored as Lisp lists whose first element is the symbol `vec`; thus, '(elt v 2)' yields the second element of vector v, and '(elt m i j)' yields one element of a Calc matrix.

- The `setq` function has been extended to act like the Common Lisp `setf` function. (The name `setf` is recognized as a synonym of `setq`.) Specifically, the first argument of `setq` can be an `nth`, `elt`, `car`, or `cdr` form, in which case the effect is to store into the specified element of a list. Thus, '(setq (elt m i j) x)' stores x into one element of a matrix.

- A `for` looping construct is available. For example, '(for ((i 0 10)) body)' executes body once for each binding of i from zero to 10. This is like a `let` form in that i is temporarily bound to the loop count without disturbing its value outside the `for` construct. Nested loops, as in '(for ((i 0 10) (j 0 (1- i) 2)) body)', are also available. For each value of i from zero to 10, j counts from 0 to $i-1$ in steps of two. Note that `for` has the same general outline as `let*`, except that each element of the header is a list of three or four things, not just two.

- The `foreach` construct loops over elements of a list. For example, '(foreach ((x (cdr v))) body)' executes body with x bound to each element of Calc vector v in turn. The purpose of `cdr` here is to skip over the initial `vec` symbol in the vector.

- The `break` function breaks out of the innermost enclosing `while`, `for`, or `foreach` loop. If given a value, as in '(break x)', this value is returned by the loop. (Lisp loops otherwise always return `nil`.)

- The `return` function prematurely returns from the enclosing function. For example, '(return (+ x y))' returns $x+y$ as the value of a function. You can use `return` anywhere inside the body of the function.

Non-integer numbers (and extremely large integers) cannot be included directly into a `defmath` definition. This is because the Lisp reader will fail to parse them long before `defmath` ever gets control. Instead, use the notation, ':"3.1415"'. In fact, any algebraic formula can go between the quotes. For example,

```
(defmath sqexp (x)      ; sqexp(x) == sqrt(exp(x)) == exp(x*0.5)
  (and (numberp x)
       (exp :"x * 0.5")))
```

expands to

```
(defun calcFunc-sqexp (x)
  (and (math-numberp x)
       (calcFunc-exp (math-mul x '(float 5 -1)))))
```

Note the use of `numberp` as a guard to ensure that the argument is a number first, returning `nil` if not. The exponential function could itself have been included in the expression, if we had preferred: ':"exp(x * 0.5)"'. As another example, the multiplication-and-recursion step of `myfact` could have been written

```
:"n * myfact(n-1)"
```

A good place to put your `defmath` commands is your Calc init file (the file given by `calc-settings-file`, typically `~/.emacs.d/calc.el`), which will not be loaded until Calc starts. If a file named `.emacs` exists in your home directory, Emacs reads and executes the Lisp forms in this file as it starts up. While it may seem reasonable to put your favorite `defmath` commands there, this has the unfortunate side-effect that parts of the Calculator must be loaded in to process the `defmath` commands whether or not you will actually use the Calculator! If you want to put the `defmath` commands there (for example, if you redefine `calc-settings-file` to be `.emacs`), a better effect can be had by writing

```
(put 'calc-define 'thing '(progn
(defmath ... )
(defmath ... )
))
```

The `put` function adds a *property* to a symbol. Each Lisp symbol has a list of properties associated with it. Here we add a property with a name of `thing` and a '`(progn ...)`' form as its value. When Calc starts up, and at the start of every Calc command, the property list for the symbol `calc-define` is checked and the values of any properties found are evaluated as Lisp forms. The properties are removed as they are evaluated. The property names (like `thing`) are not used; you should choose something like the name of your project so as not to conflict with other properties.

The net effect is that you can put the above code in your `.emacs` file and it will not be executed until Calc is loaded. Or, you can put that same code in another file which you load by hand either before or after Calc itself is loaded.

The properties of `calc-define` are evaluated in the same order that they were added. They can assume that the Calc modules `calc.el`, `calc-ext.el`, and `calc-macs.el` have been fully loaded, and that the `*Calculator*` buffer will be the current buffer.

If your `calc-define` property only defines algebraic functions, you can be sure that it will have been evaluated before Calc tries to call your function, even if the file defining the property is loaded after Calc is loaded. But if the property defines commands or key sequences, it may not be evaluated soon enough. (Suppose it defines the new command `tweak-calc`; the user can load your file, then type *M-x tweak-calc* before Calc has had chance to do anything.) To protect against this situation, you can put

```
(run-hooks 'calc-check-defines)
```

at the end of your file. The `calc-check-defines` function is what looks for and evaluates properties on `calc-define`; `run-hooks` has the advantage that it is quietly ignored if `calc-check-defines` is not yet defined because Calc has not yet been loaded.

Examples of things that ought to be enclosed in a `calc-define` property are `defmath` calls, `define-key` calls that modify the Calc key map, and any calls that redefine things defined inside Calc. Ordinary `defun`s need not be enclosed with `calc-define`.

17.5.2 Defining New Simple Commands

If a `defmath` form contains an `interactive` clause, it defines a Calculator command. Actually such a `defmath` results in *two* function definitions: One, a '`calcFunc-`' function as was just described, with the `interactive` clause removed. Two, a '`calc-`' function with a suitable `interactive` clause and some sort of wrapper to make the command work in the Calc environment.

In the simple case, the `interactive` clause has the same form as for normal Emacs Lisp commands:

```
(defmath increase-precision (delta)
  "Increase precision by DELTA."    ; This is the "documentation string"
  (interactive "p")                 ; Register this as a M-x-able command
  (setq calc-internal-prec (+ calc-internal-prec delta)))
```

This expands to the pair of definitions,

```
(defun calc-increase-precision (delta)
  "Increase precision by DELTA."
  (interactive "p")
  (calc-wrapper
   (setq calc-internal-prec (math-add calc-internal-prec delta))))

(defun calcFunc-increase-precision (delta)
  "Increase precision by DELTA."
  (setq calc-internal-prec (math-add calc-internal-prec delta)))
```

where in this case the latter function would never really be used! Note that since the Calculator stores small integers as plain Lisp integers, the `math-add` function will work just as well as the native + even when the intent is to operate on native Lisp integers.

The 'calc-wrapper' call invokes a macro which surrounds the body of the function with code that looks roughly like this:

```
(let ((calc-command-flags nil))
  (unwind-protect
      (save-current-buffer
        (calc-select-buffer)
        body of function
        renumber stack
        clear Working message)
    realign cursor and window
    clear Inverse, Hyperbolic, and Keep Args flags
    update Emacs mode line))
```

The `calc-select-buffer` function selects the *Calculator* buffer if necessary, say, because the command was invoked from inside the *Calc Trail* window.

You can call, for example, `(calc-set-command-flag 'no-align)` to set the above-mentioned command flags. Calc routines recognize the following command flags:

`renum-stack`

> Stack line numbers '1:', '2:', and so on must be renumbered after this command completes. This is set by routines like `calc-push`.

`clear-message`

> Calc should call '(message "")' if this command completes normally (to clear a "Working..." message out of the echo area).

`no-align` Do not move the cursor back to the '.' top-of-stack marker.

`position-point`

> Use the variables `calc-position-point-line` and `calc-position-point-column` to position the cursor after this command finishes.

`keep-flags`

> Do not clear `calc-inverse-flag`, `calc-hyperbolic-flag`, and `calc-keep-args-flag` at the end of this command.

`do-edit`   Switch to buffer *Calc Edit* after this command.

`hold-trail`

Do not move trail pointer to end of trail when something is recorded there.

Calc reserves a special prefix key, shift-*Y*, for user-written extensions to Calc. There are no built-in commands that work with this prefix key; you must call **define-key** from Lisp (probably from inside a **calc-define** property) to add to it. Initially only *Y ?* is defined; it takes help messages from a list of strings (initially **nil**) in the variable **calc-Y-help-msgs**. All other undefined keys except for *Y* are reserved for use by future versions of Calc.

If you are writing a Calc enhancement which you expect to give to others, it is best to minimize the number of *Y*-key sequences you use. In fact, if you have more than one key sequence you should consider defining three-key sequences with a *Y*, then a key that stands for your package, then a third key for the particular command within your package.

Users may wish to install several Calc enhancements, and it is possible that several enhancements will choose to use the same key. In the example below, a variable **inc-prec-base-key** has been defined to contain the key that identifies the **inc-prec** package. Its value is initially "P", but a user can change this variable if necessary without having to modify the file.

Here is a complete file, **inc-prec.el**, which makes a *Y P I* command that increases the precision, and a *Y P D* command that decreases the precision.

```
;;; Increase and decrease Calc precision.  Dave Gillespie, 5/31/91.
;; (Include copyright or copyleft stuff here.)

(defvar inc-prec-base-key "P"
  "Base key for inc-prec.el commands.")

(put 'calc-define 'inc-prec '(progn

(define-key calc-mode-map (format "Y%sI" inc-prec-base-key)
            'increase-precision)
(define-key calc-mode-map (format "Y%sD" inc-prec-base-key)
            'decrease-precision)

(setq calc-Y-help-msgs
      (cons (format "%s + Inc-prec, Dec-prec" inc-prec-base-key)
            calc-Y-help-msgs))

(defmath increase-precision (delta)
  "Increase precision by DELTA."
  (interactive "p")
  (setq calc-internal-prec (+ calc-internal-prec delta)))

(defmath decrease-precision (delta)
  "Decrease precision by DELTA."
  (interactive "p")
  (setq calc-internal-prec (- calc-internal-prec delta)))

))  ; end of calc-define property

(run-hooks 'calc-check-defines)
```

17.5.3 Defining New Stack-Based Commands

To define a new computational command which takes and/or leaves arguments on the stack, a special form of `interactive` clause is used.

```
(interactive num tag)
```

where *num* is an integer, and *tag* is a string. The effect is to pop *num* values off the stack, resimplify them by calling `calc-normalize`, and hand them to your function according to the function's argument list. Your function may include `&optional` and `&rest` parameters, so long as calling the function with *num* parameters is valid.

Your function must return either a number or a formula in a form acceptable to Calc, or a list of such numbers or formulas. These value(s) are pushed onto the stack when the function completes. They are also recorded in the Calc Trail buffer on a line beginning with *tag*, a string of (normally) four characters or less. If you omit *tag* or use `nil` as a tag, the result is not recorded in the trail.

As an example, the definition

```
(defmath myfact (n)
  "Compute the factorial of the integer at the top of the stack."
  (interactive 1 "fact")
  (if (> n 0)
      (* n (myfact (1- n)))
    (and (= n 0) 1)))
```

is a version of the factorial function shown previously which can be used as a command as well as an algebraic function. It expands to

```
(defun calc-myfact ()
  "Compute the factorial of the integer at the top of the stack."
  (interactive)
  (calc-slow-wrapper
   (calc-enter-result 1 "fact"
     (cons 'calcFunc-myfact (calc-top-list-n 1)))))

(defun calcFunc-myfact (n)
  "Compute the factorial of the integer at the top of the stack."
  (if (math-posp n)
      (math-mul n (calcFunc-myfact (math-add n -1)))
    (and (math-zerop n) 1)))
```

The `calc-slow-wrapper` function is a version of `calc-wrapper` that automatically puts up a 'Working...' message before the computation begins. (This message can be turned off by the user with an *m w* (`calc-working`) command.)

The `calc-top-list-n` function returns a list of the specified number of values from the top of the stack. It resimplifies each value by calling `calc-normalize`. If its argument is zero it returns an empty list. It does not actually remove these values from the stack.

The `calc-enter-result` function takes an integer *num* and string *tag* as described above, plus a third argument which is either a Calculator data object or a list of such objects. These objects are resimplified and pushed onto the stack after popping the specified number of values from the stack. If *tag* is non-`nil`, the values being pushed are also recorded in the trail.

Note that if `calcFunc-myfact` returns `nil` this represents "leave the function in symbolic form." To return an actual empty list, in the sense that `calc-enter-result` will push zero elements back onto the stack, you should return the special value '`(nil)`', a list containing the single symbol `nil`.

The `interactive` declaration can actually contain a limited Emacs-style code string as well which comes just before *num* and *tag*. Currently the only Emacs code supported is '`"p"`', as in

```
(defmath foo (a b &optional c)
  (interactive "p" 2 "foo")
  body)
```

In this example, the command `calc-foo` will evaluate the expression '`foo(a,b)`' if executed with no argument, or '`foo(a,b,n)`' if executed with a numeric prefix argument of *n*.

The other code string allowed is '`"m"`' (unrelated to the usual '`"m"`' code as used with `defun`). It uses the numeric prefix argument as the number of objects to remove from the stack and pass to the function. In this case, the integer *num* serves as a default number of arguments to be used when no prefix is supplied.

17.5.4 Argument Qualifiers

Anywhere a parameter name can appear in the parameter list you can also use an *argument qualifier*. Thus the general form of a definition is:

```
(defmath name (param param...
                &optional param param...
                &rest param)
  body)
```

where each *param* is either a symbol or a list of the form

```
(qual param)
```

The following qualifiers are recognized:

'`complete`'
> The argument must not be an incomplete vector, interval, or complex number. (This is rarely needed since the Calculator itself will never call your function with an incomplete argument. But there is nothing stopping your own Lisp code from calling your function with an incomplete argument.)

'`integer`' The argument must be an integer. If it is an integer-valued float it will be accepted but converted to integer form. Non-integers and formulas are rejected.

'`natnum`' Like '`integer`', but the argument must be non-negative.

'`fixnum`' Like '`integer`', but the argument must fit into a native Lisp integer, which on most systems means less than $2\hat{}23$ in absolute value. The argument is converted into Lisp-integer form if necessary.

'`float`' The argument is converted to floating-point format if it is a number or vector. If it is a formula it is left alone. (The argument is never actually rejected by this qualifier.)

'*pred*' The argument must satisfy predicate *pred*, which is one of the standard Calculator predicates. See Section 17.5.7.4 [Predicates], page 391.

'not-*pred*'

> The argument must *not* satisfy predicate *pred*.

For example,

```
(defmath foo (a (constp (not-matrixp b)) &optional (float c)
              &rest (integer d))
  body)
```

expands to

```
(defun calcFunc-foo (a b &optional c &rest d)
  (and (math-matrixp b)
       (math-reject-arg b 'not-matrixp))
  (or (math-constp b)
      (math-reject-arg b 'constp))
  (and c (setq c (math-check-float c)))
  (setq d (mapcar 'math-check-integer d))
  body)
```

which performs the necessary checks and conversions before executing the body of the function.

17.5.5 Example Definitions

This section includes some Lisp programming examples on a larger scale. These programs make use of some of the Calculator's internal functions; see Section 17.5.7 [Internals], page 385.

17.5.5.1 Bit-Counting

Calc does not include a built-in function for counting the number of "one" bits in a binary integer. It's easy to invent one using b u to convert the integer to a set, and V # to count the elements of that set; let's write a function that counts the bits without having to create an intermediate set.

```
(defmath bcount ((natnum n))
  (interactive 1 "bcnt")
  (let ((count 0))
    (while (> n 0)
      (if (oddp n)
          (setq count (1+ count)))
      (setq n (lsh n -1)))
    count))
```

When this is expanded by **defmath**, it will become the following Emacs Lisp function:

```
(defun calcFunc-bcount (n)
  (setq n (math-check-natnum n))
  (let ((count 0))
    (while (math-posp n)
      (if (math-oddp n)
          (setq count (math-add count 1)))
      (setq n (calcFunc-lsh n -1)))
    count))
```

If the input numbers are large, this function involves a fair amount of arithmetic. A binary right shift is essentially a division by two; recall that Calc stores integers in decimal form so bit shifts must involve actual division.

To gain a bit more efficiency, we could divide the integer into n-bit chunks, each of which can be handled quickly because they fit into Lisp integers. It turns out that Calc's arithmetic routines are especially fast when dividing by an integer less than 1000, so we can set $n = 9$ bits and use repeated division by 512:

```
(defmath bcount ((natnum n))
  (interactive 1 "bcnt")
  (let ((count 0))
    (while (not (fixnump n))
      (let ((qr (idivmod n 512)))
        (setq count (+ count (bcount-fixnum (cdr qr)))
              n (car qr))))
    (+ count (bcount-fixnum n))))

(defun bcount-fixnum (n)
  (let ((count 0))
    (while (> n 0)
      (setq count (+ count (logand n 1))
            n (lsh n -1)))
    count))
```

Note that the second function uses **defun**, not **defmath**. Because this function deals only with native Lisp integers ("fixnums"), it can use the actual Emacs + and related functions rather than the slower but more general Calc equivalents which **defmath** uses.

The **idivmod** function does an integer division, returning both the quotient and the remainder at once. Again, note that while it might seem that '(logand n 511)' and '(lsh n -9)' are more efficient ways to split off the bottom nine bits of n, actually they are less efficient because each operation is really a division by 512 in disguise; **idivmod** allows us to do the same thing with a single division by 512.

17.5.5.2 The Sine Function

A somewhat limited sine function could be defined as follows, using the well-known Taylor series expansion for $\sin x$:

```
(defmath mysin ((float (anglep x)))
  (interactive 1 "mysn")
  (setq x (to-radians x))       ; Convert from current angular mode.
  (let ((sum x)                 ; Initial term of Taylor expansion of sin.
        newsum
        (nfact 1)               ; "nfact" equals "n" factorial at all times.
        (xnegsqr :"-(x^2)"))    ; "xnegsqr" equals -x^2.
    (for ((n 3 100 2))          ; Upper limit of 100 is a good precaution.
      (working "mysin" sum)     ; Display "Working" message, if enabled.
      (setq nfact (* nfact (1- n) n)
            x (* x xnegsqr)
            newsum (+ sum (/ x nfact)))
      (if (~= newsum sum)       ; If newsum is "nearly equal to" sum,
          (break))              ;   then we are done.
      (setq sum newsum))
    sum))
```

The actual **sin** function in Calc works by first reducing the problem to a sine or cosine of a nonnegative number less than $\pi/4$. This ensures that the Taylor series will converge quickly. Also, the calculation is carried out with two extra digits of precision to guard against cumulative round-off in 'sum'. Finally, complex arguments are allowed and handled by a separate algorithm.

```
(defmath mysin ((float (scalarp x)))
  (interactive 1 "mysn")
  (setq x (to-radians x))      ; Convert from current angular mode.
  (with-extra-prec 2           ; Evaluate with extra precision.
    (cond ((complexp x)
           (mysin-complex x))
          ((< x 0)
           (- (mysin-raw (- x)))    ; Always call mysin-raw with x >= 0.
          (t (mysin-raw x))))))

(defmath mysin-raw (x)
  (cond ((>= x 7)
         (mysin-raw (% x (two-pi))))       ; Now x < 7.
        ((> x (pi-over-2))
         (- (mysin-raw (- x (pi)))))       ; Now -pi/2 <= x <= pi/2.
        ((> x (pi-over-4))
         (mycos-raw (- x (pi-over-2))))    ; Now -pi/2 <= x <= pi/4.
        ((< x (- (pi-over-4)))
         (- (mycos-raw (+ x (pi-over-2))))) ; Now -pi/4 <= x <= pi/4,
        (t (mysin-series x))))             ; so the series will be efficient.
```

where `mysin-complex` is an appropriate function to handle complex numbers, `mysin-series` is the routine to compute the sine Taylor series as before, and `mycos-raw` is a function analogous to `mysin-raw` for cosines.

The strategy is to ensure that x is nonnegative before calling `mysin-raw`. This function then recursively reduces its argument to a suitable range, namely, plus-or-minus $\pi/4$. Note that each test, and particularly the first comparison against 7, is designed so that small roundoff errors cannot produce an infinite loop. (Suppose we compared with '`(two-pi)`' instead; if due to roundoff problems the modulo operator ever returned '`(two-pi)`' exactly, an infinite recursion could result!) We use modulo only for arguments that will clearly get reduced, knowing that the next rule will catch any reductions that this rule misses.

If a program is being written for general use, it is important to code it carefully as shown in this second example. For quick-and-dirty programs, when you know that your own use of the sine function will never encounter a large argument, a simpler program like the first one shown is fine.

17.5.6 Calling Calc from Your Lisp Programs

A later section (see Section 17.5.7 [Internals], page 385) gives a full description of Calc's internal Lisp functions. It's not hard to call Calc from inside your programs, but the number of these functions can be daunting. So Calc provides one special "programmer-friendly" function called `calc-eval` that can be made to do just about everything you need. It's not as fast as the low-level Calc functions, but it's much simpler to use!

It may seem that `calc-eval` itself has a daunting number of options, but they all stem from one simple operation.

In its simplest manifestation, '`(calc-eval "1+2")`' parses the string "1+2" as if it were a Calc algebraic entry and returns the result formatted as a string: "3".

Since `calc-eval` is on the list of recommended `autoload` functions, you don't need to make any special preparations to load Calc before calling `calc-eval` the first time. Calc will be loaded and initialized for you.

All the Calc modes that are currently in effect will be used when evaluating the expression and formatting the result.

17.5.6.1 Additional Arguments to `calc-eval`

If the input string parses to a list of expressions, Calc returns the results separated by ", ". You can specify a different separator by giving a second string argument to `calc-eval`: '(calc-eval "1+2,3+4" ";")' returns "3;7".

The "separator" can also be any of several Lisp symbols which request other behaviors from `calc-eval`. These are discussed one by one below.

You can give additional arguments to be substituted for '$', '$$', and so on in the main expression. For example, '(calc-eval "$/$$" nil "7" "1+1")' evaluates the expression "7/(1+1)" to yield the result "3.5" (assuming Fraction mode is not in effect). Note the `nil` used as a placeholder for the item-separator argument.

17.5.6.2 Error Handling

If `calc-eval` encounters an error, it returns a list containing the character position of the error, plus a suitable message as a string. Note that '1 / 0' is *not* an error by Calc's standards; it simply returns the string "1 / 0" which is the division left in symbolic form. But '(calc-eval "1/")' will return the list '(2 "Expected a number")'.

If you bind the variable `calc-eval-error` to `t` using a `let` form surrounding the call to `calc-eval`, errors instead call the Emacs **error** function which aborts to the Emacs command loop with a beep and an error message.

If you bind this variable to the symbol **string**, error messages are returned as strings instead of lists. The character position is ignored.

As a courtesy to other Lisp code which may be using Calc, be sure to bind `calc-eval-error` using `let` rather than changing it permanently with **setq**.

17.5.6.3 Numbers Only

Sometimes it is preferable to treat '1 / 0' as an error rather than returning a symbolic result. If you pass the symbol **num** as the second argument to `calc-eval`, results that are not constants are treated as errors. The error message reported is the first `calc-why` message if there is one, or otherwise "Number expected."

A result is "constant" if it is a number, vector, or other object that does not include variables or function calls. If it is a vector, the components must themselves be constants.

17.5.6.4 Default Modes

If the first argument to `calc-eval` is a list whose first element is a formula string, then `calc-eval` sets all the various Calc modes to their default values while the formula is evaluated and formatted. For example, the precision is set to 12 digits, digit grouping is turned off, and the Normal language mode is used.

This same principle applies to the other options discussed below. If the first argument would normally be x, then it can also be the list '(x)' to use the default mode settings.

If there are other elements in the list, they are taken as variable-name/value pairs which override the default mode settings. Look at the documentation at the front of the `calc.el` file to find the names of the Lisp variables for the various modes. The mode settings are restored to their original values when `calc-eval` is done.

For example, '(calc-eval '("$+$$" calc-internal-prec 8) 'num a b)' computes the sum of two numbers, requiring a numeric result, and using default mode settings except that the precision is 8 instead of the default of 12.

It's usually best to use this form of `calc-eval` unless your program actually considers the interaction with Calc's mode settings to be a feature. This will avoid all sorts of potential "gotchas"; consider what happens with '(calc-eval "sqrt(2)" 'num)' when the user has left Calc in Symbolic mode or No-Simplify mode.

As another example, '(equal (calc-eval '("$<$$") nil a b) "1")' checks if the number in string *a* is less than the one in string *b*. Without using a list, the integer 1 might come out in a variety of formats which would be hard to test for conveniently: "1", "8#1", "00001". (But see "Predicates" mode, below.)

17.5.6.5 Raw Numbers

Normally all input and output for `calc-eval` is done with strings. You can do arithmetic with, say, '(calc-eval "$+$$" nil a b)' in place of '(+ a b)', but this is very inefficient since the numbers must be converted to and from string format as they are passed from one `calc-eval` to the next.

If the separator is the symbol `raw`, the result will be returned as a raw Calc data structure rather than a string. You can read about how these objects look in the following sections, but usually you can treat them as "black box" objects with no important internal structure.

There is also a `rawnum` symbol, which is a combination of `raw` (returning a raw Calc object) and `num` (signaling an error if that object is not a constant).

You can pass a raw Calc object to `calc-eval` in place of a string, either as the formula itself or as one of the '$' arguments. Thus '(calc-eval "$+$$" 'raw a b)' is an addition function that operates on raw Calc objects. Of course in this case it would be easier to call the low-level `math-add` function in Calc, if you can remember its name.

In particular, note that a plain Lisp integer is acceptable to Calc as a raw object. (All Lisp integers are accepted on input, but integers of more than six decimal digits are converted to "big-integer" form for output. See Section 17.5.7.1 [Data Type Formats], page 385.)

When it comes time to display the object, just use '(calc-eval a)' to format it as a string.

It is an error if the input expression evaluates to a list of values. The separator symbol `list` is like `raw` except that it returns a list of one or more raw Calc objects.

Note that a Lisp string is not a valid Calc object, nor is a list containing a string. Thus you can still safely distinguish all the various kinds of error returns discussed above.

17.5.6.6 Predicates

If the separator symbol is `pred`, the result of the formula is treated as a true/false value; `calc-eval` returns `t` or `nil`, respectively. A value is considered "true" if it is a non-zero number, or false if it is zero or if it is not a number.

For example, '(calc-eval "$<$$" 'pred a b)' tests whether one value is less than another.

As usual, it is also possible for `calc-eval` to return one of the error indicators described above. Lisp will interpret such an indicator as "true" if you don't check for it explicitly. If you wish to have an error register as "false", use something like '`(eq (calc-eval ...) t)`'.

17.5.6.7 Variable Values

Variables in the formula passed to `calc-eval` are not normally replaced by their values. If you wish this, you can use the `evalv` function (see Section 10.2 [Algebraic Manipulation], page 251). For example, if 4 is stored in Calc variable `a` (i.e., in Lisp variable `var-a`), then '`(calc-eval "a+pi")`' will return the formula "`a + pi`", but '`(calc-eval "evalv(a+pi)")`' will return "`7.14159265359`".

To store in a Calc variable, just use `setq` to store in the corresponding Lisp variable. (This is obtained by prepending '`var-`' to the Calc variable name.) Calc routines will understand either string or raw form values stored in variables, although raw data objects are much more efficient. For example, to increment the Calc variable `a`:

```
(setq var-a (calc-eval "evalv(a+1)" 'raw))
```

17.5.6.8 Stack Access

If the separator symbol is `push`, the formula argument is evaluated (with possible '`$`' expansions, as usual). The result is pushed onto the Calc stack. The return value is `nil` (unless there is an error from evaluating the formula, in which case the return value depends on `calc-eval-error` in the usual way).

If the separator symbol is `pop`, the first argument to `calc-eval` must be an integer instead of a string. That many values are popped from the stack and thrown away. A negative argument deletes the entry at that stack level. The return value is the number of elements remaining in the stack after popping; '`(calc-eval 0 'pop)`' is a good way to measure the size of the stack.

If the separator symbol is `top`, the first argument to `calc-eval` must again be an integer. The value at that stack level is formatted as a string and returned. Thus '`(calc-eval 1 'top)`' returns the top-of-stack value. If the integer is out of range, `nil` is returned.

The separator symbol `rawtop` is just like `top` except that the stack entry is returned as a raw Calc object instead of as a string.

In all of these cases the first argument can be made a list in order to force the default mode settings, as described above. Thus '`(calc-eval '(2 calc-number-radix 16) 'top)`' returns the second-to-top stack entry, formatted as a string using the default instead of current display modes, except that the radix is hexadecimal instead of decimal.

It is, of course, polite to put the Calc stack back the way you found it when you are done, unless the user of your program is actually expecting it to affect the stack.

Note that you do not actually have to switch into the `*Calculator*` buffer in order to use `calc-eval`; it temporarily switches into the stack buffer if necessary.

17.5.6.9 Keyboard Macros

If the separator symbol is `macro`, the first argument must be a string of characters which Calc can execute as a sequence of keystrokes. This switches into the Calc buffer for the duration of the macro. For example, '`(calc-eval "vx5\rVR+" 'macro)`' pushes the vector

'[1,2,3,4,5]' on the stack and then replaces it with the sum of those numbers. Note that '\r' is the Lisp notation for the carriage-return, RET, character.

If your keyboard macro wishes to pop the stack, '\C-d' is safer than '\177' (the DEL character) because some installations may have switched the meanings of DEL and C-h. Calc always interprets C-d as a synonym for "pop-stack" regardless of key mapping.

If you provide a third argument to calc-eval, evaluation of the keyboard macro will leave a record in the Trail using that argument as a tag string. Normally the Trail is unaffected.

The return value in this case is always nil.

17.5.6.10 Lisp Evaluation

Finally, if the separator symbol is eval, then the Lisp eval function is called on the first argument, which must be a Lisp expression rather than a Calc formula. Remember to quote the expression so that it is not evaluated until inside calc-eval.

The difference from plain eval is that calc-eval switches to the Calc buffer before evaluating the expression. For example, '(calc-eval '(setq calc-internal-prec 17) 'eval)' will correctly affect the buffer-local Calc precision variable.

An alternative would be '(calc-eval '(calc-precision 17) 'eval)'. This is evaluating a call to the function that is normally invoked by the p key, giving it 17 as its "numeric prefix argument." Note that this function will leave a message in the echo area as a side effect. Also, all Calc functions switch to the Calc buffer automatically if not invoked from there, so the above call is also equivalent to '(calc-precision 17)' by itself. In all cases, Calc uses save-excursion to switch back to your original buffer when it is done.

As usual the first argument can be a list that begins with a Lisp expression to use default instead of current mode settings.

The result of calc-eval in this usage is just the result returned by the evaluated Lisp expression.

17.5.6.11 Example

Here is a sample Emacs command that uses calc-eval. Suppose you have a document with lots of references to temperatures on the Fahrenheit scale, say "98.6 F", and you wish to convert these references to Centigrade. The following command does this conversion. Place the Emacs cursor right after the letter "F" and invoke the command to change "98.6 F" to "37 C". Or, if the temperature is already in Centigrade form, the command changes it back to Fahrenheit.

```
(defun convert-temp ()
  (interactive)
  (save-excursion
    (re-search-backward "[^-.0-9]\\([-.0-9]+\\) *\\([FC]\\)")
    (let* ((top1 (match-beginning 1))
           (bot1 (match-end 1))
           (number (buffer-substring top1 bot1))
           (top2 (match-beginning 2))
           (bot2 (match-end 2))
           (type (buffer-substring top2 bot2)))
```

```
(if (equal type "F")
    (setq type "C"
            number (calc-eval "($ - 32)*5/9" nil number))
  (setq type "F"
          number (calc-eval "$*9/5 + 32" nil number)))
(goto-char top2)
(delete-region top2 bot2)
(insert-before-markers type)
(goto-char top1)
(delete-region top1 bot1)
(if (string-match "\\.$" number)    ; change "37." to "37"
    (setq number (substring number 0 -1)))
(insert number))))
```

Note the use of `insert-before-markers` when changing between "F" and "C", so that the character winds up before the cursor instead of after it.

17.5.7 Calculator Internals

This section describes the Lisp functions defined by the Calculator that may be of use to user-written Calculator programs (as described in the rest of this chapter). These functions are shown by their names as they conventionally appear in `defmath`. Their full Lisp names are generally gotten by prepending 'calcFunc-' or 'math-' to their apparent names. (Names that begin with 'calc-' are already in their full Lisp form.) You can use the actual full names instead if you prefer them, or if you are calling these functions from regular Lisp.

The functions described here are scattered throughout the various Calc component files. Note that `calc.el` includes `autoloads` for only a few component files; when Calc wants to call an advanced function it calls '(calc-extensions)' first; this function autoloads `calc-ext.el`, which in turn autoloads all the functions in the remaining component files.

Because `defmath` itself uses the extensions, user-written code generally always executes with the extensions already loaded, so normally you can use any Calc function and be confident that it will be autoloaded for you when necessary. If you are doing something special, check carefully to make sure each function you are using is from `calc.el` or its components, and call '(calc-extensions)' before using any function based in `calc-ext.el` if you can't prove this file will already be loaded.

17.5.7.1 Data Type Formats

Integers are stored in either of two ways, depending on their magnitude. Integers less than one million in absolute value are stored as standard Lisp integers. This is the only storage format for Calc data objects which is not a Lisp list.

Large integers are stored as lists of the form '(bigpos $d0$ $d1$ $d2$ ...)' for sufficiently large positive integers (where "sufficiently large" depends on the machine), or '(bigneg $d0$ $d1$ $d2$ ...)' for negative integers. Each d is a base-10^n "digit" (where again, n depends on the machine), a Lisp integer from 0 to 99...9. The least significant digit is $d0$; the last digit, dn, which is always nonzero, is the most significant digit. For example, the integer -12345678 might be stored as '(bigneg 678 345 12)'.

The distinction between small and large integers is entirely hidden from the user. In `defmath` definitions, the Lisp predicate `integerp` returns true for either kind of integer, and in general both big and small integers are accepted anywhere the word "integer" is used in this manual. If the distinction must be made, native Lisp integers are called *fixnums* and large integers are called *bignums*.

Fractions are stored as a list of the form, '(`frac n d`)' where *n* is an integer (big or small) numerator, *d* is an integer denominator greater than one, and *n* and *d* are relatively prime. Note that fractions where *d* is one are automatically converted to plain integers by all math routines; fractions where *d* is negative are normalized by negating the numerator and denominator.

Floating-point numbers are stored in the form, '(`float mant exp`)', where *mant* (the "mantissa") is an integer less than '10^p' in absolute value (*p* represents the current precision), and *exp* (the "exponent") is a fixnum. The value of the float is '`mant * 10^exp`'. For example, the number -3.14 is stored as '(`float -314 -2`) = $-314*10^{-2}$'. Other constraints are that the number 0.0 is always stored as '(`float 0 0`)', and, except for the 0.0 case, the rightmost base-10 digit of *mant* is always nonzero. (If the rightmost digit is zero, the number is rearranged by dividing *mant* by ten and incrementing *exp*.)

Rectangular complex numbers are stored in the form '(`cplx re im`)', where *re* and *im* are each real numbers, either integers, fractions, or floats. The value is '`re + imi`'. The *im* part is nonzero; complex numbers with zero imaginary components are converted to real numbers automatically.

Polar complex numbers are stored in the form '(`polar r theta`)', where *r* is a positive real value and *theta* is a real value or HMS form representing an angle. This angle is usually normalized to lie in the interval '(`-180 .. 180`)' degrees, or '(`-pi .. pi`)' radians, according to the current angular mode. If the angle is 0 the value is converted to a real number automatically. (If the angle is 180 degrees, the value is usually also converted to a negative real number.)

Hours-minutes-seconds forms are stored as '(`hms h m s`)', where *h* is an integer or an integer-valued float (i.e., a float with '`exp >= 0`'), *m* is an integer or integer-valued float in the range '[`0 .. 60`)', and *s* is any real number in the range '[`0 .. 60`)'.

Date forms are stored as '(`date n`)', where *n* is a real number that counts days since midnight on the morning of January 1, 1 AD. If *n* is an integer, this is a pure date form. If *n* is a fraction or float, this is a date/time form.

Modulo forms are stored as '(`mod n m`)', where *m* is a positive real number or HMS form, and *n* is a real number or HMS form in the range '[`0 .. m`)'.

Error forms are stored as '(`sdev x sigma`)', where *x* is the mean value and *sigma* is the standard deviation. Each component is either a number, an HMS form, or a symbolic object (a variable or function call). If *sigma* is zero, the value is converted to a plain real number. If *sigma* is negative or complex, it is automatically normalized to be a positive real.

Interval forms are stored as '(`intv mask lo hi`)', where *mask* is one of the integers 0, 1, 2, or 3, and *lo* and *hi* are real numbers, HMS forms, or symbolic objects. The *mask* is a binary integer where 1 represents the fact that the interval is closed on the high end, and 2 represents the fact that it is closed on the low end. (Thus 3 represents a fully closed interval.) The interval '(`intv 3 x x`)' is converted to the plain number *x*; intervals '(`intv mask x x`)' for any other *mask* represent empty intervals. If *hi* is less than *lo*, the interval is converted to a standard empty interval by replacing *hi* with *lo*.

Vectors are stored as '(vec v1 v2 ...)', where v1 is the first element of the vector, v2 is the second, and so on. An empty vector is stored as '(vec)'. A matrix is simply a vector where all v's are themselves vectors of equal lengths. Note that Calc vectors are unrelated to the Emacs Lisp "vector" type, which is generally unused by Calc data structures.

Variables are stored as '(var name sym)', where name is a Lisp symbol whose print name is used as the visible name of the variable, and sym is a Lisp symbol in which the variable's value is actually stored. Thus, '(var pi var-pi)' represents the special constant 'pi'. Almost always, the form is '(var v var-v)'. If the variable name was entered with # signs (which are converted to hyphens internally), the form is '(var u v)', where u is a symbol whose name contains # characters, and v is a symbol that contains – characters instead. The value of a variable is the Calc object stored in its sym symbol's value cell. If the symbol's value cell is void or if it contains nil, the variable has no value. Special constants have the form '(special-const value)' stored in their value cell, where value is a formula which is evaluated when the constant's value is requested. Variables which represent units are not stored in any special way; they are units only because their names appear in the units table. If the value cell contains a string, it is parsed to get the variable's value when the variable is used.

A Lisp list with any other symbol as the first element is a function call. The symbols +, -, *, /, %, ^, and | represent special binary operators; these lists are always of the form '(op lhs rhs)' where lhs is the sub-formula on the lefthand side and rhs is the sub-formula on the right. The symbol neg represents unary negation; this list is always of the form '(neg arg)'. Any other symbol func represents a function that would be displayed in function-call notation; the symbol func is in general always of the form 'calcFunc-name'. The function cell of the symbol func should contain a Lisp function for evaluating a call to func. This function is passed the remaining elements of the list (themselves already evaluated) as arguments; such functions should return nil or call reject-arg to signify that they should be left in symbolic form, or they should return a Calc object which represents their value, or a list of such objects if they wish to return multiple values. (The latter case is allowed only for functions which are the outer-level call in an expression whose value is about to be pushed on the stack; this feature is considered obsolete and is not used by any built-in Calc functions.)

17.5.7.2 Interactive Functions

The functions described here are used in implementing interactive Calc commands. Note that this list is not exhaustive! If there is an existing command that behaves similarly to the one you want to define, you may find helpful tricks by checking the source code for that command.

calc-set-command-flag *flag*   [Function]
> Set the command flag *flag*. This is generally a Lisp symbol, but may in fact be anything. The effect is to add *flag* to the list stored in the variable calc-command-flags, unless it is already there. See Section 17.5.2 [Defining Simple Commands], page 373.

calc-clear-command-flag *flag*   [Function]
> If *flag* appears among the list of currently-set command flags, remove it from that list.

`calc-record-undo` *rec*   [Function]

>   Add the "undo record" *rec* to the list of steps to take if the current operation should
>   need to be undone. Stack push and pop functions automatically call `calc-record-`
>   `undo`, so the kinds of undo records you might need to create take the form '(`set`
>   *sym value*)', which says that the Lisp variable *sym* was changed and had previously
>   contained *value*; '(`store` *var value*)' which says that the Calc variable *var* (a string
>   which is the name of the symbol that contains the variable's value) was stored and
>   its previous value was *value* (either a Calc data object, or `nil` if the variable was
>   previously void); or '(`eval` *undo redo args* ...)', which means that to undo requires
>   calling the function '(*undo args* ...)' and, if the undo is later redone, calling '(*redo*
>   *args* ...)'.

`calc-record-why` *msg args*   [Function]

>   Record the error or warning message *msg*, which is normally a string. This message
>   will be replayed if the user types `w` (`calc-why`); if the message string begins with a
>   '`*`', it is considered important enough to display even if the user doesn't type `w`. If
>   one or more *args* are present, the displayed message will be of the form, '*msg*: `arg1`,
>   `arg2`, ...', where the arguments are formatted on the assumption that they are ei-
>   ther strings or Calc objects of some sort. If *msg* is a symbol, it is the name of a Calc
>   predicate (such as `integerp` or `numvecp`) which the arguments did not satisfy; it is ex-
>   panded to a suitable string such as "Expected an integer." The `reject-arg` function
>   calls `calc-record-why` automatically; see Section 17.5.7.4 [Predicates], page 391.

`calc-is-inverse`   [Function]

>   This predicate returns true if the current command is inverse, i.e., if the Inverse (`I`
>   key) flag was set.

`calc-is-hyperbolic`   [Function]

>   This predicate is the analogous function for the `H` key.

17.5.7.3 Stack-Oriented Functions

The functions described here perform various operations on the Calc stack and trail. They
are to be used in interactive Calc commands.

`calc-push-list` *vals n*   [Function]

>   Push the Calc objects in list *vals* onto the stack at stack level *n*. If *n* is omitted it
>   defaults to 1, so that the elements are pushed at the top of the stack. If *n* is greater
>   than 1, the elements will be inserted into the stack so that the last element will end
>   up at level *n*, the next-to-last at level *n*+1, etc. The elements of *vals* are assumed to
>   be valid Calc objects, and are not evaluated, rounded, or renormalized in any way. If
>   *vals* is an empty list, nothing happens.
>
>   The stack elements are pushed without any sub-formula selections. You can give an
>   optional third argument to this function, which must be a list the same size as *vals*
>   of selections. Each selection must be `eq` to some sub-formula of the corresponding
>   formula in *vals*, or `nil` if that formula should have no selection.

`calc-top-list` *n m*   [Function]

>   Return a list of the *n* objects starting at level *m* of the stack. If *m* is omitted it defaults
>   to 1, so that the elements are taken from the top of the stack. If *n* is omitted, it also

defaults to 1, so that the top stack element (in the form of a one-element list) is returned. If m is greater than 1, the mth stack element will be at the end of the list, the m+1st element will be next-to-last, etc. If n or m are out of range, the command is aborted with a suitable error message. If n is zero, the function returns an empty list. The stack elements are not evaluated, rounded, or renormalized.

If any stack elements contain selections, and selections have not been disabled by the `j e` (`calc-enable-selections`) command, this function returns the selected portions rather than the entire stack elements. It can be given a third "selection-mode" argument which selects other behaviors. If it is the symbol `t`, then a selection in any of the requested stack elements produces an "invalid operation on selections" error. If it is the symbol `full`, the whole stack entry is always returned regardless of selections. If it is the symbol `sel`, the selected portion is always returned, or `nil` if there is no selection. (This mode ignores the `j e` command.) If the symbol is `entry`, the complete stack entry in list form is returned; the first element of this list will be the whole formula, and the third element will be the selection (or `nil`).

calc-pop-stack *n m*   [Function]

Remove the specified elements from the stack. The parameters n and m are defined the same as for `calc-top-list`. The return value of `calc-pop-stack` is uninteresting.

If there are any selected sub-formulas among the popped elements, and `j e` has not been used to disable selections, this produces an error without changing the stack. If you supply an optional third argument of `t`, the stack elements are popped even if they contain selections.

calc-record-list *vals tag*   [Function]

This function records one or more results in the trail. The *vals* are a list of strings or Calc objects. The *tag* is the four-character tag string to identify the values. If *tag* is omitted, a blank tag will be used.

calc-normalize *n*   [Function]

This function takes a Calc object and "normalizes" it. At the very least this involves re-rounding floating-point values according to the current precision and other similar jobs. Also, unless the user has selected No-Simplify mode (see Section 6.5 [Simplification Modes], page 142), this involves actually evaluating a formula object by executing the function calls it contains, and possibly also doing algebraic simplification, etc.

calc-top-list-n *n m*   [Function]

This function is identical to `calc-top-list`, except that it calls `calc-normalize` on the values that it takes from the stack. They are also passed through `check-complete`, so that incomplete objects will be rejected with an error message. All computational commands should use this in preference to `calc-top-list`; the only standard Calc commands that operate on the stack without normalizing are stack management commands like `calc-enter` and `calc-roll-up`. This function accepts the same optional selection-mode argument as `calc-top-list`.

calc-top-n *m*   [Function]

This function is a convenient form of `calc-top-list-n` in which only a single element of the stack is taken and returned, rather than a list of elements. This also accepts an optional selection-mode argument.

`calc-enter-result` *n tag vals*   [Function]

    This function is a convenient interface to most of the above functions. The *vals* argument should be either a single Calc object, or a list of Calc objects; the object or objects are normalized, and the top *n* stack entries are replaced by the normalized objects. If *tag* is non-`nil`, the normalized objects are also recorded in the trail. A typical stack-based computational command would take the form,

```
(calc-enter-result n tag (cons 'calcFunc-func
                                (calc-top-list-n n)))
```

    If any of the *n* stack elements replaced contain sub-formula selections, and selections have not been disabled by *j e*, this function takes one of two courses of action. If *n* is equal to the number of elements in *vals*, then each element of *vals* is spliced into the corresponding selection; this is what happens when you use the `TAB` key, or when you use a unary arithmetic operation like `sqrt`. If *vals* has only one element but *n* is greater than one, there must be only one selection among the top *n* stack elements; the element from *vals* is spliced into that selection. This is what happens when you use a binary arithmetic operation like `+`. Any other combination of *n* and *vals* is an error when selections are present.

`calc-unary-op` *tag func arg*   [Function]

    This function implements a unary operator that allows a numeric prefix argument to apply the operator over many stack entries. If the prefix argument *arg* is `nil`, this uses `calc-enter-result` as outlined above. Otherwise, it maps the function over several stack elements; see Section 3.7 [Prefix Arguments], page 111. For example,

```
(defun calc-zeta (arg)
  (interactive "P")
  (calc-unary-op "zeta" 'calcFunc-zeta arg))
```

`calc-binary-op` *tag func arg ident unary*   [Function]

    This function implements a binary operator, analogously to `calc-unary-op`. The optional *ident* and *unary* arguments specify the behavior when the prefix argument is zero or one, respectively. If the prefix is zero, the value *ident* is pushed onto the stack, if specified, otherwise an error message is displayed. If the prefix is one, the unary function *unary* is applied to the top stack element, or, if *unary* is not specified, nothing happens. When the argument is two or more, the binary function *func* is reduced across the top *arg* stack elements; when the argument is negative, the function is mapped between the next-to-top $-arg$ stack elements and the top element.

`calc-stack-size`   [Function]

    Return the number of elements on the stack as an integer. This count does not include elements that have been temporarily hidden by stack truncation; see Section 6.7.8 [Truncating the Stack], page 157.

`calc-cursor-stack-index` *n*   [Function]

    Move the point to the *n*th stack entry. If *n* is zero, this will be the '.' line. If *n* is from 1 to the current stack size, this will be the beginning of the first line of that stack entry's display. If line numbers are enabled, this will move to the first character of the line number, not the stack entry itself.

calc-substack-height *n*   [Function]
> Return the number of lines between the beginning of the *n*th stack entry and the bottom of the buffer. If *n* is zero, this will be one (assuming no stack truncation). If all stack entries are one line long (i.e., no matrices are displayed), the return value will be equal *n*+1 as long as *n* is in range. (Note that in Big mode, the return value includes the blank lines that separate stack entries.)

calc-refresh   [Function]
> Erase the *Calculator* buffer and reformat its contents from memory. This must be called after changing any parameter, such as the current display radix, which might change the appearance of existing stack entries. (During a keyboard macro invoked by the *X* key, refreshing is suppressed, but a flag is set so that the entire stack will be refreshed rather than just the top few elements when the macro finishes.)

17.5.7.4 Predicates

The functions described here are predicates, that is, they return a true/false value where **nil** means false and anything else means true. These predicates are expanded by **defmath**, for example, from **zerop** to **math-zerop**. In many cases they correspond to native Lisp functions by the same name, but are extended to cover the full range of Calc data types.

zerop *x*   [Function]
> Returns true if *x* is numerically zero, in any of the Calc data types. (Note that for some types, such as error forms and intervals, it never makes sense to return true.) In **defmath**, the expression '(= x 0)' will automatically be converted to '(math-zerop x)', and '(/= x 0)' will be converted to '(not (math-zerop x))'.

negp *x*   [Function]
> Returns true if *x* is negative. This accepts negative real numbers of various types, negative HMS and date forms, and intervals in which all included values are negative. In **defmath**, the expression '(< x 0)' will automatically be converted to '(math-negp x)', and '(>= x 0)' will be converted to '(not (math-negp x))'.

posp *x*   [Function]
> Returns true if *x* is positive (and non-zero). For complex numbers, none of these three predicates will return true.

looks-negp *x*   [Function]
> Returns true if *x* is "negative-looking." This returns true if *x* is a negative number, or a formula with a leading minus sign such as '-a/b'. In other words, this is an object which can be made simpler by calling (- x).

integerp *x*   [Function]
> Returns true if *x* is an integer of any size.

fixnump *x*   [Function]
> Returns true if *x* is a native Lisp integer.

natnump *x*   [Function]
> Returns true if *x* is a nonnegative integer of any size.

fixnatnump *x*   [Function]
  Returns true if *x* is a nonnegative Lisp integer.

num-integerp *x*   [Function]
  Returns true if *x* is numerically an integer, i.e., either a true integer or a float with
  no significant digits to the right of the decimal point.

messy-integerp *x*   [Function]
  Returns true if *x* is numerically, but not literally, an integer. A value is `num-integerp`
  if it is `integerp` or `messy-integerp` (but it is never both at once).

num-natnump *x*   [Function]
  Returns true if *x* is numerically a nonnegative integer.

evenp *x*   [Function]
  Returns true if *x* is an even integer.

looks-evenp *x*   [Function]
  Returns true if *x* is an even integer, or a formula with a leading multiplicative coefficient which is an even integer.

oddp *x*   [Function]
  Returns true if *x* is an odd integer.

ratp *x*   [Function]
  Returns true if *x* is a rational number, i.e., an integer or a fraction.

realp *x*   [Function]
  Returns true if *x* is a real number, i.e., an integer, fraction, or floating-point number.

anglep *x*   [Function]
  Returns true if *x* is a real number or HMS form.

floatp *x*   [Function]
  Returns true if *x* is a float, or a complex number, error form, interval, date form, or
  modulo form in which at least one component is a float.

complexp *x*   [Function]
  Returns true if *x* is a rectangular or polar complex number (but not a real number).

rect-complexp *x*   [Function]
  Returns true if *x* is a rectangular complex number.

polar-complexp *x*   [Function]
  Returns true if *x* is a polar complex number.

numberp *x*   [Function]
  Returns true if *x* is a real number or a complex number.

scalarp *x*   [Function]
  Returns true if *x* is a real or complex number or an HMS form.

vectorp *x*   [Function]

> Returns true if *x* is a vector (this simply checks if its argument is a list whose first element is the symbol **vec**).

numvecp *x*   [Function]

> Returns true if *x* is a number or vector.

matrixp *x*   [Function]

> Returns true if *x* is a matrix, i.e., a vector of one or more vectors, all of the same size.

square-matrixp *x*   [Function]

> Returns true if *x* is a square matrix.

objectp *x*   [Function]

> Returns true if *x* is any numeric Calc object, including real and complex numbers, HMS forms, date forms, error forms, intervals, and modulo forms. (Note that error forms and intervals may include formulas as their components; see **constp** below.)

objvecp *x*   [Function]

> Returns true if *x* is an object or a vector. This also accepts incomplete objects, but it rejects variables and formulas (except as mentioned above for **objectp**).

primp *x*   [Function]

> Returns true if *x* is a "primitive" or "atomic" Calc object, i.e., one whose components cannot be regarded as sub-formulas. This includes variables, and all **objectp** types except error forms and intervals.

constp *x*   [Function]

> Returns true if *x* is constant, i.e., a real or complex number, HMS form, date form, or error form, interval, or vector all of whose components are **constp**.

lessp *x* *y*   [Function]

> Returns true if *x* is numerically less than *y*. Returns false if *x* is greater than or equal to *y*, or if the order is undefined or cannot be determined. Generally speaking, this works by checking whether '*x* − *y*' is **negp**. In **defmath**, the expression '(< x y)' will automatically be converted to '(lessp x y)'; expressions involving >, <=, and >= are similarly converted in terms of **lessp**.

beforep *x* *y*   [Function]

> Returns true if *x* comes before *y* in a canonical ordering of Calc objects. If *x* and *y* are both real numbers, this will be the same as **lessp**. But whereas **lessp** considers other types of objects to be unordered, **beforep** puts any two objects into a definite, consistent order. The **beforep** function is used by the *V S* vector-sorting command, and also by Calc's algebraic simplifications to put the terms of a product into canonical order: This allows 'x y + y x' to be simplified easily to '2 x y'.

equal *x* *y*   [Function]

> This is the standard Lisp **equal** predicate; it returns true if *x* and *y* are structurally identical. This is the usual way to compare numbers for equality, but note that **equal** will treat 0 and 0.0 as different.

math-equal *x y*   [Function]

   Returns true if *x* and *y* are numerically equal, either because they are `equal`, or
   because their difference is `zerop`. In `defmath`, the expression '(= x y)' will automatically be converted to '(math-equal x y)'.

equal-int *x n*   [Function]

   Returns true if *x* and *n* are numerically equal, where *n* is a fixnum which is not a
   multiple of 10. This will automatically be used by `defmath` in place of the more
   general `math-equal` whenever possible.

nearly-equal *x y*   [Function]

   Returns true if *x* and *y*, as floating-point numbers, are equal except possibly in the
   last decimal place. For example, 314.159 and 314.166 are considered nearly equal if
   the current precision is 6 (since they differ by 7 units), but not if the current precision
   is 7 (since they differ by 70 units). Most functions which use series expansions use
   `with-extra-prec` to evaluate the series with 2 extra digits of precision, then use
   `nearly-equal` to decide when the series has converged; this guards against cumulative
   error in the series evaluation without doing extra work which would be lost when the
   result is rounded back down to the current precision. In `defmath`, this can be written
   '(~= x y)'. The *x* and *y* can be numbers of any kind, including complex.

nearly-zerop *x y*   [Function]

   Returns true if *x* is nearly zero, compared to *y*. This checks whether *x* plus *y* would
   by be `nearly-equal` to *y* itself, to within the current precision, in other words, if
   adding *x* to *y* would have a negligible effect on *y* due to roundoff error. X may be a
   real or complex number, but *y* must be real.

is-true *x*   [Function]

   Return true if the formula *x* represents a true value in Calc, not Lisp, terms. It tests
   if *x* is a non-zero number or a provably non-zero formula.

reject-arg *val pred*   [Function]

   Abort the current function evaluation due to unacceptable argument values. This
   calls '(calc-record-why *pred val*)', then signals a Lisp error which `normalize` will
   trap. The net effect is that the function call which led here will be left in symbolic
   form.

inexact-value   [Function]

   If Symbolic mode is enabled, this will signal an error that causes `normalize` to leave
   the formula in symbolic form, with the message "Inexact result." (This function has
   no effect when not in Symbolic mode.) Note that if your function calls '(sin 5)'
   in Symbolic mode, the `sin` function will call `inexact-value`, which will cause your
   function to be left unsimplified. You may instead wish to call '(normalize (list
   'calcFunc-sin 5))', which in Symbolic mode will return the formula 'sin(5)' to
   your function.

overflow   [Function]

   This signals an error that will be reported as a floating-point overflow.

underflow   [Function]

   This signals a floating-point underflow.

17.5.7.5 Computational Functions

The functions described here do the actual computational work of the Calculator. In addition to these, note that any function described in the main body of this manual may be called from Lisp; for example, if the documentation refers to the `calc-sqrt` [`sqrt`] command, this means `calc-sqrt` is an interactive stack-based square-root command and `sqrt` (which `defmath` expands to `calcFunc-sqrt`) is the actual Lisp function for taking square roots.

The functions `math-add`, `math-sub`, `math-mul`, `math-div`, `math-mod`, and `math-neg` are not included in this list, since `defmath` allows you to write native Lisp +, -, *, /, %, and unary -, respectively, instead.

`normalize` *val*   [Function]
> (Full form: `math-normalize`.) Reduce the value *val* to standard form. For example, if *val* is a fixnum, it will be converted to a bignum if it is too large, and if *val* is a bignum it will be normalized by clipping off trailing (i.e., most-significant) zero digits and converting to a fixnum if it is small. All the various data types are similarly converted to their standard forms. Variables are left alone, but function calls are actually evaluated in formulas. For example, normalizing '`(+ 2 (calcFunc-abs -4))`' will return 6.
>
> If a function call fails, because the function is void or has the wrong number of parameters, or because it returns `nil` or calls `reject-arg` or `inexact-result`, `normalize` returns the formula still in symbolic form.
>
> If the current simplification mode is "none" or "numeric arguments only," `normalize` will act appropriately. However, the more powerful simplification modes (like Algebraic Simplification) are not handled by `normalize`. They are handled by `calc-normalize`, which calls `normalize` and possibly some other routines, such as `simplify` or `simplify-units`. Programs generally will never call `calc-normalize` except when popping or pushing values on the stack.

`evaluate-expr` *expr*   [Function]
> Replace all variables in *expr* that have values with their values, then use `normalize` to simplify the result. This is what happens when you press the = key interactively.

`with-extra-prec` *n body*   [Macro]
> Evaluate the Lisp forms in *body* with precision increased by *n* digits. This is a macro which expands to
>
> ```
> (math-normalize
>   (let ((calc-internal-prec (+ calc-internal-prec n)))
>     body))
> ```
>
> The surrounding call to `math-normalize` causes a floating-point result to be rounded down to the original precision afterwards. This is important because some arithmetic operations assume a number's mantissa contains no more digits than the current precision allows.

`make-frac` *n d*   [Function]
> Build a fraction '*n*:*d*'. This is equivalent to calling '`(normalize (list 'frac n d))`', but more efficient.

`make-float` *mant exp*   [Function]

Build a floating-point value out of *mant* and *exp*, both of which are arbitrary integers. This function will return a properly normalized float value, or signal an overflow or underflow if *exp* is out of range.

`make-sdev` *x sigma*   [Function]

Build an error form out of *x* and the absolute value of *sigma*. If *sigma* is zero, the result is the number *x* directly. If *sigma* is negative or complex, its absolute value is used. If *x* or *sigma* is not a valid type of object for use in error forms, this calls `reject-arg`.

`make-intv` *mask lo hi*   [Function]

Build an interval form out of *mask* (which is assumed to be an integer from 0 to 3), and the limits *lo* and *hi*. If *lo* is greater than *hi*, an empty interval form is returned. This calls `reject-arg` if *lo* or *hi* is unsuitable.

`sort-intv` *mask lo hi*   [Function]

Build an interval form, similar to `make-intv`, except that if *lo* is less than *hi* they are simply exchanged, and the bits of *mask* are swapped accordingly.

`make-mod` *n m*   [Function]

Build a modulo form out of *n* and the modulus *m*. Since modulo forms do not allow formulas as their components, if *n* or *m* is not a real number or HMS form the result will be a formula which is a call to `makemod`, the algebraic version of this function.

`float` *x*   [Function]

Convert *x* to floating-point form. Integers and fractions are converted to numerically equivalent floats; components of complex numbers, vectors, HMS forms, date forms, error forms, intervals, and modulo forms are recursively floated. If the argument is a variable or formula, this calls `reject-arg`.

`compare` *x y*   [Function]

Compare the numbers *x* and *y*, and return -1 if '`(lessp x y)`', 1 if '`(lessp y x)`', 0 if '`(math-equal x y)`', or 2 if the order is undefined or cannot be determined.

`numdigs` *n*   [Function]

Return the number of digits of integer *n*, effectively '`ceil(log10(n))`', but much more efficient. Zero is considered to have zero digits.

`scale-int` *x n*   [Function]

Shift integer *x* left *n* decimal digits, or right $-n$ digits with truncation toward zero.

`scale-rounding` *x n*   [Function]

Like `scale-int`, except that a right shift rounds to the nearest integer rather than truncating.

`fixnum` *n*   [Function]

Return the integer *n* as a fixnum, i.e., a native Lisp integer. If *n* is outside the permissible range for Lisp integers (usually 24 binary bits) the result is undefined.

sqr *x*   [Function]

Compute the square of *x*; short for '(* *x* *x*)'.

quotient *x y*   [Function]

Divide integer *x* by integer *y*; return an integer quotient and discard the remainder. If *x* or *y* is negative, the direction of rounding is undefined.

idiv *x y*   [Function]

Perform an integer division; if *x* and *y* are both nonnegative integers, this uses the **quotient** function, otherwise it computes 'floor(*x*/*y*)'. Thus the result is well-defined but slower than for **quotient**.

imod *x y*   [Function]

Divide integer *x* by integer *y*; return the integer remainder and discard the quotient. Like **quotient**, this works only for integer arguments and is not well-defined for negative arguments. For a more well-defined result, use '(% *x* *y*)'.

idivmod *x y*   [Function]

Divide integer *x* by integer *y*; return a cons cell whose **car** is '(quotient *x* *y*)' and whose **cdr** is '(imod *x* *y*)'.

pow *x y*   [Function]

Compute *x* to the power *y*. In **defmath** code, this can also be written '(^ *x* *y*)' or '(expt *x* *y*)'.

abs-approx *x*   [Function]

Compute a fast approximation to the absolute value of *x*. For example, for a rectangular complex number the result is the sum of the absolute values of the components.

pi   [Function]

The function '(pi)' computes 'pi' to the current precision. Other related constant-generating functions are **two-pi**, **pi-over-2**, **pi-over-4**, **pi-over-180**, **sqrt-two-pi**, **e**, **sqrt-e**, **ln-2**, **ln-10**, **phi** and **gamma-const**. Each function returns a floating-point value in the current precision, and each uses caching so that all calls after the first are essentially free.

math-defcache *func initial form*   [Macro]

This macro, usually used as a top-level call like **defun** or **defvar**, defines a new cached constant analogous to **pi**, etc. It defines a function *func* which returns the requested value; if *initial* is non-**nil** it must be a '(float ...)' form which serves as an initial value for the cache. If *func* is called when the cache is empty or does not have enough digits to satisfy the current precision, the Lisp expression *form* is evaluated with the current precision increased by four, and the result minus its two least significant digits is stored in the cache. For example, calling '(pi)' with a precision of 30 computes 'pi' to 34 digits, rounds it down to 32 digits for future use, then rounds it again to 30 digits for use in the present request.

full-circle *symb*   [Function]

If the current angular mode is Degrees or HMS, this function returns the integer 360. In Radians mode, this function returns either the corresponding value in radians to the current precision, or the formula '2*pi', depending on the Symbolic mode. There are also similar function `half-circle` and `quarter-circle`.

power-of-2 *n*   [Function]
Compute two to the integer power *n*, as a (potentially very large) integer. Powers of two are cached, so only the first call for a particular *n* is expensive.

integer-log2 *n*   [Function]
Compute the base-2 logarithm of *n*, which must be an integer which is a power of two. If *n* is not a power of two, this function will return `nil`.

div-mod *a b m*   [Function]
Divide *a* by *b*, modulo *m*. This returns `nil` if there is no solution, or if any of the arguments are not integers.

pow-mod *a b m*   [Function]
Compute *a* to the power *b*, modulo *m*. If *a*, *b*, and *m* are integers, this uses an especially efficient algorithm. Otherwise, it simply computes '(% (^ a b) m)'.

isqrt *n*   [Function]
Compute the integer square root of *n*. This is the square root of *n* rounded down toward zero, i.e., 'floor(sqrt(n))'. If *n* is itself an integer, the computation is especially efficient.

to-hms *a ang*   [Function]
Convert the argument *a* into an HMS form. If *ang* is specified, it is the angular mode in which to interpret *a*, either `deg` or `rad`. Otherwise, the current angular mode is used. If *a* is already an HMS form it is returned as-is.

from-hms *a ang*   [Function]
Convert the HMS form *a* into a real number. If *ang* is specified, it is the angular mode in which to express the result, otherwise the current angular mode is used. If *a* is already a real number, it is returned as-is.

to-radians *a*   [Function]
Convert the number or HMS form *a* to radians from the current angular mode.

from-radians *a*   [Function]
Convert the number *a* from radians to the current angular mode. If *a* is a formula, this returns the formula 'deg(a)'.

to-radians-2 *a*   [Function]
Like `to-radians`, except that in Symbolic mode a degrees to radians conversion yields a formula like 'a*pi/180'.

from-radians-2 *a*   [Function]
Like `from-radians`, except that in Symbolic mode a radians to degrees conversion yields a formula like 'a*180/pi'.

random-digit   [Function]
Produce a random base-1000 digit in the range 0 to 999.

random-digits *n*   [Function]

Produce a random *n*-digit integer; this will be an integer in the interval '[0, 10^n)'.

random-float   [Function]

Produce a random float in the interval '[0, 1)'.

prime-test *n iters*   [Function]

Determine whether the integer *n* is prime. Return a list which has one of these forms: '(nil f)' means the number is non-prime because it was found to be divisible by *f*; '(nil)' means it was found to be non-prime by table look-up (so no factors are known); '(nil unknown)' means it is definitely non-prime but no factors are known because *n* was large enough that Fermat's probabilistic test had to be used; '(t)' means the number is definitely prime; and '(maybe i p)' means that Fermat's test, after *i* iterations, is *p* percent sure that the number is prime. The *iters* parameter is the number of Fermat iterations to use, in the case that this is necessary. If **prime-test** returns "maybe," you can call it again with the same *n* to get a greater certainty; **prime-test** remembers where it left off.

to-simple-fraction *f*   [Function]

If *f* is a floating-point number which can be represented exactly as a small rational number, return that number, else return *f*. For example, 0.75 would be converted to 3:4. This function is very fast.

to-fraction *f tol*   [Function]

Find a rational approximation to floating-point number *f* to within a specified tolerance *tol*; this corresponds to the algebraic function **frac**, and can be rather slow.

quarter-integer *n*   [Function]

If *n* is an integer or integer-valued float, this function returns zero. If *n* is a half-integer (i.e., an integer plus 1:2 or 0.5), it returns 2. If *n* is a quarter-integer, it returns 1 or 3. If *n* is anything else, this function returns **nil**.

17.5.7.6 Vector Functions

The functions described here perform various operations on vectors and matrices.

math-concat *x y*   [Function]

Do a vector concatenation; this operation is written '*x* | *y*' in a symbolic formula. See Section 9.2 [Building Vectors], page 223.

vec-length *v*   [Function]

Return the length of vector *v*. If *v* is not a vector, the result is zero. If *v* is a matrix, this returns the number of rows in the matrix.

mat-dimens *m*   [Function]

Determine the dimensions of vector or matrix *m*. If *m* is not a vector, the result is an empty list. If *m* is a plain vector but not a matrix, the result is a one-element list containing the length of the vector. If *m* is a matrix with *r* rows and *c* columns, the result is the list '(r c)'. Higher-order tensors produce lists of more than two dimensions. Note that the object '[[1, 2, 3], [4, 5]]' is a vector of vectors not all the same size, and is treated by this and other Calc routines as a plain vector of two elements.

dimension-error   [Function]

> Abort the current function with a message of "Dimension error." The Calculator will leave the function being evaluated in symbolic form; this is really just a special case of `reject-arg`.

build-vector *args*   [Function]

> Return a Calc vector with *args* as elements. For example, '(build-vector 1 2 3)' returns the Calc vector '[1, 2, 3]', stored internally as the list '(vec 1 2 3)'.

make-vec *obj dims*   [Function]

> Return a Calc vector or matrix all of whose elements are equal to *obj*. For example, '(make-vec 27 3 4)' returns a 3x4 matrix filled with 27's.

row-matrix *v*   [Function]

> If *v* is a plain vector, convert it into a row matrix, i.e., a matrix whose single row is *v*. If *v* is already a matrix, leave it alone.

col-matrix *v*   [Function]

> If *v* is a plain vector, convert it into a column matrix, i.e., a matrix with each element of *v* as a separate row. If *v* is already a matrix, leave it alone.

map-vec *f v*   [Function]

> Map the Lisp function *f* over the Calc vector *v*. For example, '(map-vec 'math-floor v)' returns a vector of the floored components of vector *v*.

map-vec-2 *f a b*   [Function]

> Map the Lisp function *f* over the two vectors *a* and *b*. If *a* and *b* are vectors of equal length, the result is a vector of the results of calling '(f ai bi)' for each pair of elements *ai* and *bi*. If either *a* or *b* is a scalar, it is matched with each value of the other vector. For example, '(map-vec-2 'math-add v 1)' returns the vector *v* with each element increased by one. Note that using ''+'' would not work here, since `defmath` does not expand function names everywhere, just where they are in the function position of a Lisp expression.

reduce-vec *f v*   [Function]

> Reduce the function *f* over the vector *v*. For example, if *v* is '[10, 20, 30, 40]', this calls '(f (f (f 10 20) 30) 40)'. If *v* is a matrix, this reduces over the rows of *v*.

reduce-cols *f m*   [Function]

> Reduce the function *f* over the columns of matrix *m*. For example, if *m* is '[[1, 2], [3, 4], [5, 6]]', the result is a vector of the two elements '(f (f 1 3) 5)' and '(f (f 2 4) 6)'.

mat-row *m n*   [Function]

> Return the *n*th row of matrix *m*. This is equivalent to '(elt m n)'. For a slower but safer version, use `mrow`. (See Section 9.3 [Extracting Elements], page 225.)

mat-col *m n*   [Function]

> Return the *n*th column of matrix *m*, in the form of a vector. The arguments are not checked for correctness.

mat-less-row *m n*   [Function]
>   Return a copy of matrix *m* with its *n*th row deleted. The number *n* must be in range
>   from 1 to the number of rows in *m*.

mat-less-col *m n*   [Function]
>   Return a copy of matrix *m* with its *n*th column deleted.

transpose *m*   [Function]
>   Return the transpose of matrix *m*.

flatten-vector *v*   [Function]
>   Flatten nested vector *v* into a vector of scalars. For example, if *v* is '[[1, 2, 3],
>   [4, 5]]' the result is '[1, 2, 3, 4, 5]'.

copy-matrix *m*   [Function]
>   If *m* is a matrix, return a copy of *m*. This maps `copy-sequence` over the rows of
>   *m*; in Lisp terms, each element of the result matrix will be `eq` to the corresponding
>   element of *m*, but none of the `cons` cells that make up the structure of the matrix
>   will be `eq`. If *m* is a plain vector, this is the same as `copy-sequence`.

swap-rows *m r1 r2*   [Function]
>   Exchange rows *r1* and *r2* of matrix *m* in-place. In other words, unlike most of the
>   other functions described here, this function changes *m* itself rather than building up
>   a new result matrix. The return value is *m*, i.e., '(eq (swap-rows m 1 2) m)' is true,
>   with the side effect of exchanging the first two rows of *m*.

17.5.7.7 Symbolic Functions

The functions described here operate on symbolic formulas in the Calculator.

calc-prepare-selection *num*   [Function]
>   Prepare a stack entry for selection operations. If *num* is omitted, the stack entry con-
>   taining the cursor is used; otherwise, it is the number of the stack entry to use. This
>   function stores useful information about the current stack entry into a set of vari-
>   ables. `calc-selection-cache-num` contains the number of the stack entry involved
>   (equal to *num* if you specified it); `calc-selection-cache-entry` contains the stack
>   entry as a list (such as `calc-top-list` would return with `entry` as the selection
>   mode); and `calc-selection-cache-comp` contains a special "tagged" composition
>   (see Section 17.5.7.8 [Formatting Lisp Functions], page 409) which allows Calc to
>   relate cursor positions in the buffer with their corresponding sub-formulas.
>
>   A slight complication arises in the selection mechanism because formulas may contain
>   small integers. For example, in the vector '[1, 2, 1]' the first and last elements
>   are `eq` to each other; selections are recorded as the actual Lisp object that appears
>   somewhere in the tree of the whole formula, but storing 1 would falsely select both 1's
>   in the vector. So `calc-prepare-selection` also checks the stack entry and replaces
>   any plain integers with "complex number" lists of the form '(cplx *n* 0)'. This list will
>   be displayed the same as a plain *n* and the change will be completely invisible to the
>   user, but it will guarantee that no two sub-formulas of the stack entry will be `eq` to
>   each other. Next time the stack entry is involved in a computation, `calc-normalize`
>   will replace these lists with plain numbers again, again invisibly to the user.

calc-encase-atoms *x*   [Function]

> This modifies the formula *x* to ensure that each part of the formula is a unique atom, using the '(cplx *n* 0)' trick described above. This function may use `setcar` to modify the formula in-place.

calc-find-selected-part   [Function]

> Find the smallest sub-formula of the current formula that contains the cursor. This assumes `calc-prepare-selection` has been called already. If the cursor is not actually on any part of the formula, this returns `nil`.

calc-change-current-selection *selection*   [Function]

> Change the currently prepared stack element's selection to *selection*, which should be `eq` to some sub-formula of the stack element, or `nil` to unselect the formula. The stack element's appearance in the Calc buffer is adjusted to reflect the new selection.

calc-find-nth-part *expr n*   [Function]

> Return the *n*th sub-formula of *expr*. This function is used by the selection commands, and (unless *j b* has been used) treats sums and products as flat many-element formulas. Thus if *expr* is '((a + b) - c) + d', calling `calc-find-nth-part` with *n* equal to four will return 'd'.

calc-find-parent-formula *expr part*   [Function]

> Return the sub-formula of *expr* which immediately contains *part*. If *expr* is 'a*b + (c+1)*d' and *part* is `eq` to the 'c+1' term of *expr*, then this function will return '(c+1)*d'. If *part* turns out not to be a sub-formula of *expr*, the function returns `nil`. If *part* is `eq` to *expr*, the function returns `t`. This function does not take associativity into account.

calc-find-assoc-parent-formula *expr part*   [Function]

> This is the same as `calc-find-parent-formula`, except that (unless *j b* has been used) it continues widening the selection to contain a complete level of the formula. Given 'a' from '((a + b) - c) + d', `calc-find-parent-formula` will return 'a + b' but `calc-find-assoc-parent-formula` will return the whole expression.

calc-grow-assoc-formula *expr part*   [Function]

> This expands sub-formula *part* of *expr* to encompass a complete level of the formula. If *part* and its immediate parent are not compatible associative operators, or if *j b* has been used, this simply returns *part*.

calc-find-sub-formula *expr part*   [Function]

> This finds the immediate sub-formula of *expr* which contains *part*. It returns an index *n* such that '(calc-find-nth-part *expr n*)' would return *part*. If *part* is not a sub-formula of *expr*, it returns `nil`. If *part* is `eq` to *expr*, it returns `t`. This function does not take associativity into account.

calc-replace-sub-formula *expr old new*   [Function]

> This function returns a copy of formula *expr*, with the sub-formula that is `eq` to *old* replaced by *new*.

simplify *expr*   [Function]

> Simplify the expression *expr* by applying Calc's algebraic simplifications. This always returns a copy of the expression; the structure *expr* points to remains unchanged in memory.
>
> More precisely, here is what `simplify` does: The expression is first normalized and evaluated by calling `normalize`. If any `AlgSimpRules` have been defined, they are then applied. Then the expression is traversed in a depth-first, bottom-up fashion; at each level, any simplifications that can be made are made until no further changes are possible. Once the entire formula has been traversed in this way, it is compared with the original formula (from before the call to `normalize`) and, if it has changed, the entire procedure is repeated (starting with `normalize`) until no further changes occur. Usually only two iterations are needed: one to simplify the formula, and another to verify that no further simplifications were possible.

simplify-extended *expr*   [Function]

> Simplify the expression *expr*, with additional rules enabled that help do a more thorough job, while not being entirely "safe" in all circumstances. (For example, this mode will simplify 'sqrt(x^2)' to 'x', which is only valid when x is positive.) This is implemented by temporarily binding the variable `math-living-dangerously` to t (using a `let` form) and calling `simplify`. Dangerous simplification rules are written to check this variable before taking any action.

simplify-units *expr*   [Function]

> Simplify the expression *expr*, treating variable names as units whenever possible. This works by binding the variable `math-simplifying-units` to t while calling `simplify`.

math-defsimplify *funcs body*   [Macro]

> Register a new simplification rule; this is normally called as a top-level form, like `defun` or `defmath`. If *funcs* is a symbol (like + or `calcFunc-sqrt`), this simplification rule is applied to the formulas which are calls to the specified function. Or, *funcs* can be a list of such symbols; the rule applies to all functions on the list. The *body* is written like the body of a function with a single argument called `expr`. The body will be executed with `expr` bound to a formula which is a call to one of the functions *funcs*. If the function body returns `nil`, or if it returns a result `equal` to the original `expr`, it is ignored and Calc goes on to try the next simplification rule that applies. If the function body returns something different, that new formula is substituted for *expr* in the original formula.
>
> At each point in the formula, rules are tried in the order of the original calls to `math-defsimplify`; the search stops after the first rule that makes a change. Thus later rules for that same function will not have a chance to trigger until the next iteration of the main `simplify` loop.
>
> Note that, since `defmath` is not being used here, *body* must be written in true Lisp code without the conveniences that `defmath` provides. If you prefer, you can have *body* simply call another function (defined with `defmath`) which does the real work.
>
> The arguments of a function call will already have been simplified before any rules for the call itself are invoked. Since a new argument list is consed up when this happens,

this means that the rule's body is allowed to rearrange the function's arguments destructively if that is convenient. Here is a typical example of a simplification rule:

```
(math-defsimplify calcFunc-arcsinh
  (or (and (math-looks-negp (nth 1 expr))
           (math-neg (list 'calcFunc-arcsinh
                           (math-neg (nth 1 expr)))))
      (and (eq (car-safe (nth 1 expr)) 'calcFunc-sinh)
           (or math-living-dangerously
               (math-known-realp (nth 1 (nth 1 expr))))
           (nth 1 (nth 1 expr)))))
```

This is really a pair of rules written with one `math-defsimplify` for convenience; the first replaces 'arcsinh(-x)' with '-arcsinh(x)', and the second, which is safe only for real 'x', replaces 'arcsinh(sinh(x))' with 'x'.

common-constant-factor *expr*   [Function]

Check *expr* to see if it is a sum of terms all multiplied by the same rational value. If so, return this value. If not, return `nil`. For example, if called on '6x + 9y + 12z', it would return 3, since 3 is a common factor of all the terms.

cancel-common-factor *expr factor*   [Function]

Assuming *expr* is a sum with *factor* as a common factor, divide each term of the sum by *factor*. This is done by destructively modifying parts of *expr*, on the assumption that it is being used by a simplification rule (where such things are allowed; see above). For example, consider this built-in rule for square roots:

```
(math-defsimplify calcFunc-sqrt
  (let ((fac (math-common-constant-factor (nth 1 expr))))
    (and fac (not (eq fac 1))
         (math-mul (math-normalize (list 'calcFunc-sqrt fac))
                   (math-normalize
                    (list 'calcFunc-sqrt
                          (math-cancel-common-factor
                           (nth 1 expr) fac)))))))
```

frac-gcd *a b*   [Function]

Compute a "rational GCD" of *a* and *b*, which must both be rational numbers. This is the fraction composed of the GCD of the numerators of *a* and *b*, over the GCD of the denominators. It is used by `common-constant-factor`. Note that the standard `gcd` function uses the LCM to combine the denominators.

map-tree *func expr many*   [Function]

Try applying Lisp function *func* to various sub-expressions of *expr*. Initially, call *func* with *expr* itself as an argument. If this returns an expression which is not `equal` to *expr*, apply *func* again until eventually it does return *expr* with no changes. Then, if *expr* is a function call, recursively apply *func* to each of the arguments. This keeps going until no changes occur anywhere in the expression; this final expression is returned by `map-tree`. Note that, unlike simplification rules, *func* functions may *not* make destructive changes to *expr*. If a third argument *many* is provided, it is an integer which says how many times *func* may be applied; the default, as described above, is infinitely many times.

compile-rewrites *rules*   [Function]

Compile the rewrite rule set specified by *rules*, which should be a formula that is either a vector or a variable name. If the latter, the compiled rules are saved so that later `compile-rules` calls for that same variable can return immediately. If there are problems with the rules, this function calls `error` with a suitable message.

apply-rewrites *expr crules heads*   [Function]

Apply the compiled rewrite rule set *crules* to the expression *expr*. This will make only one rewrite and only checks at the top level of the expression. The result `nil` if no rules matched, or if the only rules that matched did not actually change the expression. The *heads* argument is optional; if is given, it should be a list of all function names that (may) appear in *expr*. The rewrite compiler tags each rule with the rarest-looking function name in the rule; if you specify *heads*, `apply-rewrites` can use this information to narrow its search down to just a few rules in the rule set.

rewrite-heads *expr*   [Function]

Compute a *heads* list for *expr* suitable for use with `apply-rewrites`, as discussed above.

rewrite *expr rules many*   [Function]

This is an all-in-one rewrite function. It compiles the rule set specified by *rules*, then uses `map-tree` to apply the rules throughout *expr* up to *many* (default infinity) times.

match-patterns *pat vec not-flag*   [Function]

Given a Calc vector *vec* and an uncompiled pattern set or pattern set variable *pat*, this function returns a new vector of all elements of *vec* which do (or don't, if *not-flag* is non-`nil`) match any of the patterns in *pat*.

deriv *expr var value symb*   [Function]

Compute the derivative of *expr* with respect to variable *var* (which may actually be any sub-expression). If *value* is specified, the derivative is evaluated at the value of *var*; otherwise, the derivative is left in terms of *var*. If the expression contains functions for which no derivative formula is known, new derivative functions are invented by adding primes to the names; see Section 10.5 [Calculus], page 264. However, if *symb* is non-`nil`, the presence of nondifferentiable functions in *expr* instead cancels the whole differentiation, and `deriv` returns `nil` instead.

Derivatives of an *n*-argument function can be defined by adding a `math-derivative-n` property to the property list of the symbol for the function's derivative, which will be the function name followed by an apostrophe. The value of the property should be a Lisp function; it is called with the same arguments as the original function call that is being differentiated. It should return a formula for the derivative. For example, the derivative of `ln` is defined by

```
(put 'calcFunc-ln\' 'math-derivative-1
     (function (lambda (u) (math-div 1 u))))
```

The two-argument `log` function has two derivatives,

```
(put 'calcFunc-log\' 'math-derivative-2     ; d(log(x,b)) / dx
     (function (lambda (x b) ... )))
(put 'calcFunc-log\'2 'math-derivative-2    ; d(log(x,b)) / db
     (function (lambda (x b) ... )))
```

tderiv *expr var value symb*   [Function]

Compute the total derivative of *expr*. This is the same as `deriv`, except that variables other than *var* are not assumed to be constant with respect to *var*.

integ *expr var low high*   [Function]

Compute the integral of *expr* with respect to *var*. See Section 10.5 [Calculus], page 264, for further details.

math-defintegral *funcs body*   [Macro]

Define a rule for integrating a function or functions of one argument; this macro is very similar in format to `math-defsimplify`. The main difference is that here *body* is the body of a function with a single argument u which is bound to the argument to the function being integrated, not the function call itself. Also, the variable of integration is available as `math-integ-var`. If evaluation of the integral requires doing further integrals, the body should call '`(math-integral x)`' to find the integral of x with respect to `math-integ-var`; this function returns `nil` if the integral could not be done. Some examples:

```
(math-defintegral calcFunc-conj
  (let ((int (math-integral u)))
    (and int
         (list 'calcFunc-conj int))))

(math-defintegral calcFunc-cos
  (and (equal u math-integ-var)
       (math-from-radians-2 (list 'calcFunc-sin u))))
```

In the `cos` example, we define only the integral of '`cos(x) dx`', relying on the general integration-by-substitution facility to handle cosines of more complicated arguments. An integration rule should return `nil` if it can't do the integral; if several rules are defined for the same function, they are tried in order until one returns a non-`nil` result.

math-defintegral-2 *funcs body*   [Macro]

Define a rule for integrating a function or functions of two arguments. This is exactly analogous to `math-defintegral`, except that *body* is written as the body of a function with two arguments, u and v.

solve-for *lhs rhs var full*   [Function]

Attempt to solve the equation '`lhs = rhs`' by isolating the variable *var* on the lefthand side; return the resulting righthand side, or `nil` if the equation cannot be solved. The variable *var* must appear at least once in *lhs* or *rhs*. Note that the return value is a formula which does not contain *var*; this is different from the user-level `solve` and `finv` functions, which return a rearranged equation or a functional inverse, respectively. If *full* is non-`nil`, a full solution including dummy signs and dummy integers will be produced. User-defined inverses are provided as properties in a manner similar to derivatives:

```
(put 'calcFunc-ln 'math-inverse
     (function (lambda (x) (list 'calcFunc-exp x))))
```

This function can call '`(math-solve-get-sign x)`' to create a new arbitrary sign variable, returning x times that sign, and '`(math-solve-get-int x)`' to create a new arbitrary integer variable multiplied by *x*. These functions simply return *x* if the caller requested a non-"full" solution.

solve-eqn *expr var full*   [Function]
>   This version of `solve-for` takes an expression which will typically be an equation or inequality. (If it is not, it will be interpreted as the equation '*expr* = 0'.) It returns an equation or inequality, or `nil` if no solution could be found.

solve-system *exprs vars full*   [Function]
>   This function solves a system of equations. Generally, *exprs* and *vars* will be vectors of equal length. See Section 10.6.2 [Solving Systems of Equations], page 270, for other options.

expr-contains *expr var*   [Function]
>   Returns a non-`nil` value if *var* occurs as a subexpression of *expr*.
>
>   This function might seem at first to be identical to `calc-find-sub-formula`. The key difference is that `expr-contains` uses `equal` to test for matches, whereas `calc-find-sub-formula` uses `eq`. In the formula '`f(a, a)`', the two '`a`'s will be `equal` but not `eq` to each other.

expr-contains-count *expr var*   [Function]
>   Returns the number of occurrences of *var* as a subexpression of *expr*, or `nil` if there are no occurrences.

expr-depends *expr var*   [Function]
>   Returns true if *expr* refers to any variable the occurs in *var*. In other words, it checks if *expr* and *var* have any variables in common.

expr-contains-vars *expr*   [Function]
>   Return true if *expr* contains any variables, or `nil` if *expr* contains only constants and functions with constant arguments.

expr-subst *expr old new*   [Function]
>   Returns a copy of *expr*, with all occurrences of *old* replaced by *new*. This treats `lambda` forms specially with respect to the dummy argument variables, so that the effect is always to return *expr* evaluated at *old* = *new*.

multi-subst *expr old new*   [Function]
>   This is like `expr-subst`, except that *old* and *new* are lists of expressions to be substituted simultaneously. If one list is shorter than the other, trailing elements of the longer list are ignored.

expr-weight *expr*   [Function]
>   Returns the "weight" of *expr*, basically a count of the total number of objects and function calls that appear in *expr*. For "primitive" objects, this will be one.

expr-height *expr*   [Function]
>   Returns the "height" of *expr*, which is the deepest level to which function calls are nested. (Note that '`a + b`' counts as a function call.) For primitive objects, this returns zero.

`polynomial-p` *expr var*   [Function]

 Check if *expr* is a polynomial in variable (or sub-expression) *var*. If so, return the
 degree of the polynomial, that is, the highest power of *var* that appears in *expr*. For
 example, for '(x^2 + 3)^3 + 4' this would return 6. This function returns `nil` unless
 expr, when expanded out by `a x` (`calc-expand`), would consist of a sum of terms in
 which *var* appears only raised to nonnegative integer powers. Note that if *var* does
 not occur in *expr*, then *expr* is considered a polynomial of degree 0.

`is-polynomial` *expr var degree loose*   [Function]

 Check if *expr* is a polynomial in variable or sub-expression *var*, and, if so, return a
 list representation of the polynomial where the elements of the list are coefficients of
 successive powers of *var*: 'a + b x + c x^3' would produce the list '(a b 0 c)', and '(x
 + 1)^2' would produce the list '(1 2 1)'. The highest element of the list will be nonzero, with the special exception that if *expr* is the constant zero, the returned value
 will be '(0)'. Return `nil` if *expr* is not a polynomial in *var*. If *degree* is specified,
 this will not consider polynomials of degree higher than that value. This is a good
 precaution because otherwise an input of '(x+1)^1000' will cause a huge coefficient
 list to be built. If *loose* is non-`nil`, then a looser definition of a polynomial is used in
 which coefficients are no longer required not to depend on *var*, but are only required
 not to take the form of polynomials themselves. For example, 'sin(x) x^2 + cos(x)'
 is a loose polynomial with coefficients '((calcFunc-cos x) 0 (calcFunc-sin x))'.
 The result will never be `nil` in loose mode, since any expression can be interpreted
 as a "constant" loose polynomial.

`polynomial-base` *expr pred*   [Function]

 Check if *expr* is a polynomial in any variable that occurs in it; if so, return that
 variable. (If *expr* is a multivariate polynomial, this chooses one variable arbitrarily.)
 If *pred* is specified, it should be a Lisp function which is called as '(*pred subexpr*)',
 and which should return true if `mpb-top-expr` (a global name for the original *expr*)
 is a suitable polynomial in *subexpr*. The default predicate uses '(polynomial-p
 mpb-top-expr *subexpr*)'; you can use *pred* to specify additional conditions. Or, you
 could have *pred* build up a list of every suitable *subexpr* that is found.

`poly-simplify` *poly*   [Function]

 Simplify polynomial coefficient list *poly* by (destructively) clipping off trailing zeros.

`poly-mix` *a ac b bc*   [Function]

 Mix two polynomial lists *a* and *b* (in the form returned by `is-polynomial`) in a linear
 combination with coefficient expressions *ac* and *bc*. The result is a (not necessarily
 simplified) polynomial list representing 'ac a + bc b'.

`poly-mul` *a b*   [Function]

 Multiply two polynomial coefficient lists *a* and *b*. The result will be in simplified form
 if the inputs were simplified.

`build-polynomial-expr` *poly var*   [Function]

 Construct a Calc formula which represents the polynomial coefficient list *poly* applied
 to variable *var*. The `a c` (`calc-collect`) command uses `is-polynomial` to turn an
 expression into a coefficient list, then `build-polynomial-expr` to turn the list back
 into an expression in regular form.

check-unit-name *var*   [Function]

   Check if *var* is a variable which can be interpreted as a unit name. If so, return the
   units table entry for that unit. This will be a list whose first element is the unit
   name (not counting prefix characters) as a symbol and whose second element is the
   Calc expression which defines the unit. (Refer to the Calc sources for details on the
   remaining elements of this list.) If *var* is not a variable or is not a unit name, return
   `nil`.

units-in-expr-p *expr sub-exprs*   [Function]

   Return true if *expr* contains any variables which can be interpreted as units. If *sub-
   exprs* is `t`, the entire expression is searched. If *sub-exprs* is `nil`, this checks whether
   expr is directly a units expression.

single-units-in-expr-p *expr*   [Function]

   Check whether *expr* contains exactly one units variable. If so, return the units table
   entry for the variable. If *expr* does not contain any units, return `nil`. If *expr* contains
   two or more units, return the symbol `wrong`.

to-standard-units *expr which*   [Function]

   Convert units expression *expr* to base units. If *which* is `nil`, use Calc's native base
   units. Otherwise, *which* can specify a units system, which is a list of two-element lists,
   where the first element is a Calc base symbol name and the second is an expression
   to substitute for it.

remove-units *expr*   [Function]

   Return a copy of *expr* with all units variables replaced by ones. This expression is
   generally normalized before use.

extract-units *expr*   [Function]

   Return a copy of *expr* with everything but units variables replaced by ones.

17.5.7.8 I/O and Formatting Functions

The functions described here are responsible for parsing and formatting Calc numbers and
formulas.

calc-eval *str sep arg1 arg2 ...*   [Function]

   This is the simplest interface to the Calculator from another Lisp program. See
   Section 17.5.6 [Calling Calc from Your Programs], page 380.

read-number *str*   [Function]

   If string *str* contains a valid Calc number, either integer, fraction, float, or HMS form,
   this function parses and returns that number. Otherwise, it returns `nil`.

read-expr *str*   [Function]

   Read an algebraic expression from string *str*. If *str* does not have the form of a
   valid expression, return a list of the form '(`error` *pos* `msg`)' where *pos* is an integer
   index into *str* of the general location of the error, and *msg* is a string describing the
   problem.

read-exprs *str*   [Function]
> Read a list of expressions separated by commas, and return it as a Lisp list. If an error occurs in any expressions, an error list as shown above is returned instead.

calc-do-alg-entry *initial prompt no-norm*   [Function]
> Read an algebraic formula or formulas using the minibuffer. All conventions of regular algebraic entry are observed. The return value is a list of Calc formulas; there will be more than one if the user entered a list of values separated by commas. The result is **nil** if the user presses Return with a blank line. If *initial* is given, it is a string which the minibuffer will initially contain. If *prompt* is given, it is the prompt string to use; the default is "Algebraic:". If *no-norm* is **t**, the formulas will be returned exactly as parsed; otherwise, they will be passed through **calc-normalize** first.
>
> To support the use of *$* characters in the algebraic entry, use **let** to bind **calc-dollar-values** to a list of the values to be substituted for *$*, *$$*, and so on, and bind **calc-dollar-used** to 0. Upon return, **calc-dollar-used** will have been changed to the highest number of consecutive *$*s that actually appeared in the input.

format-number *a*   [Function]
> Convert the real or complex number or HMS form *a* to string form.

format-flat-expr *a prec*   [Function]
> Convert the arbitrary Calc number or formula *a* to string form, in the style used by the trail buffer and the **calc-edit** command. This is a simple format designed mostly to guarantee the string is of a form that can be re-parsed by **read-expr**. Most formatting modes, such as digit grouping, complex number format, and point character, are ignored to ensure the result will be re-readable. The *prec* parameter is normally 0; if you pass a large integer like 1000 instead, the expression will be surrounded by parentheses unless it is a plain number or variable name.

format-nice-expr *a width*   [Function]
> This is like **format-flat-expr** (with *prec* equal to 0), except that newlines will be inserted to keep lines down to the specified *width*, and vectors that look like matrices or rewrite rules are written in a pseudo-matrix format. The **calc-edit** command uses this when only one stack entry is being edited.

format-value *a width*   [Function]
> Convert the Calc number or formula *a* to string form, using the format seen in the stack buffer. Beware the string returned may not be re-readable by **read-expr**, for example, because of digit grouping. Multi-line objects like matrices produce strings that contain newline characters to separate the lines. The *w* parameter, if given, is the target window size for which to format the expressions. If *w* is omitted, the width of the Calculator window is used.

compose-expr *a prec*   [Function]
> Format the Calc number or formula *a* according to the current language mode, returning a "composition." To learn about the structure of compositions, see the comments in the Calc source code. You can specify the format of a given type of function call by putting a **math-compose-lang** property on the function's symbol, whose value is a Lisp function that takes *a* and *prec* as arguments and returns a composition. Here

lang is a language mode name, one of `normal`, `big`, `c`, `pascal`, `fortran`, `tex`, `eqn`, `math`, or `maple`. In Big mode, Calc actually tries `math-compose-big` first, then tries `math-compose-normal`. If this property does not exist, or if the function returns `nil`, the function is written in the normal function-call notation for that language.

`composition-to-string` *c w*   [Function]
> Convert a composition structure returned by `compose-expr` into a string. Multi-line compositions convert to strings containing newline characters. The target window size is given by *w*. The `format-value` function basically calls `compose-expr` followed by `composition-to-string`.

`comp-width` *c*   [Function]
> Compute the width in characters of composition *c*.

`comp-height` *c*   [Function]
> Compute the height in lines of composition *c*.

`comp-ascent` *c*   [Function]
> Compute the portion of the height of composition *c* which is on or above the baseline. For a one-line composition, this will be one.

`comp-descent` *c*   [Function]
> Compute the portion of the height of composition *c* which is below the baseline. For a one-line composition, this will be zero.

`comp-first-char` *c*   [Function]
> If composition *c* is a "flat" composition, return the first (leftmost) character of the composition as an integer. Otherwise, return `nil`.

`comp-last-char` *c*   [Function]
> If composition *c* is a "flat" composition, return the last (rightmost) character, otherwise return `nil`.

17.5.7.9 Hooks

Hooks are variables which contain Lisp functions (or lists of functions) which are called at various times. Calc defines a number of hooks that help you to customize it in various ways. Calc uses the Lisp function `run-hooks` to invoke the hooks shown below. Several other customization-related variables are also described here.

`calc-load-hook`   [Variable]
> This hook is called at the end of `calc.el`, after the file has been loaded, before any functions in it have been called, but after `calc-mode-map` and similar variables have been set up.

`calc-ext-load-hook`   [Variable]
> This hook is called at the end of `calc-ext.el`.

`calc-start-hook`   [Variable]
> This hook is called as the last step in a *M-x calc* command. At this point, the Calc buffer has been created and initialized if necessary, the Calc window and trail window have been created, and the "Welcome to Calc" message has been displayed.

`calc-mode-hook`   [Variable]
> This hook is called when the Calc buffer is being created. Usually this will only happen once per Emacs session. The hook is called after Emacs has switched to the new buffer, the mode-settings file has been read if necessary, and all other buffer-local variables have been set up. After this hook returns, Calc will perform a `calc-refresh` operation, set up the mode line display, then evaluate any deferred `calc-define` properties that have not been evaluated yet.

`calc-trail-mode-hook`   [Variable]
> This hook is called when the Calc Trail buffer is being created. It is called as the very last step of setting up the Trail buffer. Like `calc-mode-hook`, this will normally happen only once per Emacs session.

`calc-end-hook`   [Variable]
> This hook is called by `calc-quit`, generally because the user presses `q` or `C-x * c` while in Calc. The Calc buffer will be the current buffer. The hook is called as the very first step, before the Calc window is destroyed.

`calc-window-hook`   [Variable]
> If this hook is non-`nil`, it is called to create the Calc window. Upon return, this new Calc window should be the current window. (The Calc buffer will already be the current buffer when the hook is called.) If the hook is not defined, Calc will generally use `split-window`, `set-window-buffer`, and `select-window` to create the Calc window.

`calc-trail-window-hook`   [Variable]
> If this hook is non-`nil`, it is called to create the Calc Trail window. The variable `calc-trail-buffer` will contain the buffer which the window should use. Unlike `calc-window-hook`, this hook must *not* switch into the new window.

`calc-embedded-mode-hook`   [Variable]
> This hook is called the first time that Embedded mode is entered.

`calc-embedded-new-buffer-hook`   [Variable]
> This hook is called each time that Embedded mode is entered in a new buffer.

`calc-embedded-new-formula-hook`   [Variable]
> This hook is called each time that Embedded mode is enabled for a new formula.

`calc-edit-mode-hook`   [Variable]
> This hook is called by `calc-edit` (and the other "edit" commands) when the temporary editing buffer is being created. The buffer will have been selected and set up to be in `calc-edit-mode`, but will not yet have been filled with text. (In fact it may still have leftover text from a previous `calc-edit` command.)

`calc-mode-save-hook`   [Variable]
> This hook is called by the `calc-save-modes` command, after Calc's own mode features have been inserted into the Calc init file and just before the "End of mode settings" message is inserted.

calc-reset-hook   [Variable]

This hook is called after C-x * 0 (`calc-reset`) has reset all modes. The Calc buffer will be the current buffer.

calc-other-modes   [Variable]

This variable contains a list of strings. The strings are concatenated at the end of the modes portion of the Calc mode line (after standard modes such as "Deg", "Inv" and "Hyp"). Each string should be a short, single word followed by a space. The variable is `nil` by default.

calc-mode-map   [Variable]

This is the keymap that is used by Calc mode. The best time to adjust it is probably in a `calc-mode-hook`. If the Calc extensions package (`calc-ext.el`) has not yet been loaded, many of these keys will be bound to `calc-missing-key`, which is a command that loads the extensions package and "retypes" the key. If your `calc-mode-hook` rebinds one of these keys, it will probably be overridden when the extensions are loaded.

calc-digit-map   [Variable]

This is the keymap that is used during numeric entry. Numeric entry uses the minibuffer, but this map binds every non-numeric key to `calcDigit-nondigit` which generally calls `exit-minibuffer` and "retypes" the key.

calc-alg-ent-map   [Variable]

This is the keymap that is used during algebraic entry. This is mostly a copy of `minibuffer-local-map`.

calc-store-var-map   [Variable]

This is the keymap that is used during entry of variable names for commands like `calc-store` and `calc-recall`. This is mostly a copy of `minibuffer-local-completion-map`.

calc-edit-mode-map   [Variable]

This is the (sparse) keymap used by `calc-edit` and other temporary editing commands. It binds RET, LFD, and C-c C-c to `calc-edit-finish`.

calc-mode-var-list   [Variable]

This is a list of variables which are saved by `calc-save-modes`. Each entry is a list of two items, the variable (as a Lisp symbol) and its default value. When modes are being saved, each variable is compared with its default value (using `equal`) and any non-default variables are written out.

calc-local-var-list   [Variable]

This is a list of variables which should be buffer-local to the Calc buffer. Each entry is a variable name (as a Lisp symbol). These variables also have their default values manipulated by the `calc` and `calc-quit` commands; see Section 3.10 [Multiple Calculators], page 113. Since `calc-mode-hook` is called after this list has been used the first time, your hook should add a variable to the list and also call `make-local-variable` itself.

Appendix A GNU GENERAL PUBLIC LICENSE

Version 3, 29 June 2007

Copyright © 2007 Free Software Foundation, Inc. http://fsf.org/

Everyone is permitted to copy and distribute verbatim copies of this license document, but changing it is not allowed.

Preamble

The GNU General Public License is a free, copyleft license for software and other kinds of works.

The licenses for most software and other practical works are designed to take away your freedom to share and change the works. By contrast, the GNU General Public License is intended to guarantee your freedom to share and change all versions of a program—to make sure it remains free software for all its users. We, the Free Software Foundation, use the GNU General Public License for most of our software; it applies also to any other work released this way by its authors. You can apply it to your programs, too.

When we speak of free software, we are referring to freedom, not price. Our General Public Licenses are designed to make sure that you have the freedom to distribute copies of free software (and charge for them if you wish), that you receive source code or can get it if you want it, that you can change the software or use pieces of it in new free programs, and that you know you can do these things.

To protect your rights, we need to prevent others from denying you these rights or asking you to surrender the rights. Therefore, you have certain responsibilities if you distribute copies of the software, or if you modify it: responsibilities to respect the freedom of others.

For example, if you distribute copies of such a program, whether gratis or for a fee, you must pass on to the recipients the same freedoms that you received. You must make sure that they, too, receive or can get the source code. And you must show them these terms so they know their rights.

Developers that use the GNU GPL protect your rights with two steps: (1) assert copyright on the software, and (2) offer you this License giving you legal permission to copy, distribute and/or modify it.

For the developers' and authors' protection, the GPL clearly explains that there is no warranty for this free software. For both users' and authors' sake, the GPL requires that modified versions be marked as changed, so that their problems will not be attributed erroneously to authors of previous versions.

Some devices are designed to deny users access to install or run modified versions of the software inside them, although the manufacturer can do so. This is fundamentally incompatible with the aim of protecting users' freedom to change the software. The systematic pattern of such abuse occurs in the area of products for individuals to use, which is precisely where it is most unacceptable. Therefore, we have designed this version of the GPL to prohibit the practice for those products. If such problems arise substantially in other domains, we stand ready to extend this provision to those domains in future versions of the GPL, as needed to protect the freedom of users.

Finally, every program is threatened constantly by software patents. States should not allow patents to restrict development and use of software on general-purpose computers, but in those that do, we wish to avoid the special danger that patents applied to a free program could make it effectively proprietary. To prevent this, the GPL assures that patents cannot be used to render the program non-free.

The precise terms and conditions for copying, distribution and modification follow.

TERMS AND CONDITIONS

0. Definitions.

   "This License" refers to version 3 of the GNU General Public License.

   "Copyright" also means copyright-like laws that apply to other kinds of works, such as semiconductor masks.

   "The Program" refers to any copyrightable work licensed under this License. Each licensee is addressed as "you". "Licensees" and "recipients" may be individuals or organizations.

   To "modify" a work means to copy from or adapt all or part of the work in a fashion requiring copyright permission, other than the making of an exact copy. The resulting work is called a "modified version" of the earlier work or a work "based on" the earlier work.

   A "covered work" means either the unmodified Program or a work based on the Program.

   To "propagate" a work means to do anything with it that, without permission, would make you directly or secondarily liable for infringement under applicable copyright law, except executing it on a computer or modifying a private copy. Propagation includes copying, distribution (with or without modification), making available to the public, and in some countries other activities as well.

   To "convey" a work means any kind of propagation that enables other parties to make or receive copies. Mere interaction with a user through a computer network, with no transfer of a copy, is not conveying.

   An interactive user interface displays "Appropriate Legal Notices" to the extent that it includes a convenient and prominently visible feature that (1) displays an appropriate copyright notice, and (2) tells the user that there is no warranty for the work (except to the extent that warranties are provided), that licensees may convey the work under this License, and how to view a copy of this License. If the interface presents a list of user commands or options, such as a menu, a prominent item in the list meets this criterion.

1. Source Code.

   The "source code" for a work means the preferred form of the work for making modifications to it. "Object code" means any non-source form of a work.

   A "Standard Interface" means an interface that either is an official standard defined by a recognized standards body, or, in the case of interfaces specified for a particular programming language, one that is widely used among developers working in that language.

The "System Libraries" of an executable work include anything, other than the work as a whole, that (a) is included in the normal form of packaging a Major Component, but which is not part of that Major Component, and (b) serves only to enable use of the work with that Major Component, or to implement a Standard Interface for which an implementation is available to the public in source code form. A "Major Component", in this context, means a major essential component (kernel, window system, and so on) of the specific operating system (if any) on which the executable work runs, or a compiler used to produce the work, or an object code interpreter used to run it.

The "Corresponding Source" for a work in object code form means all the source code needed to generate, install, and (for an executable work) run the object code and to modify the work, including scripts to control those activities. However, it does not include the work's System Libraries, or general-purpose tools or generally available free programs which are used unmodified in performing those activities but which are not part of the work. For example, Corresponding Source includes interface definition files associated with source files for the work, and the source code for shared libraries and dynamically linked subprograms that the work is specifically designed to require, such as by intimate data communication or control flow between those subprograms and other parts of the work.

The Corresponding Source need not include anything that users can regenerate automatically from other parts of the Corresponding Source.

The Corresponding Source for a work in source code form is that same work.

2. Basic Permissions.

    All rights granted under this License are granted for the term of copyright on the Program, and are irrevocable provided the stated conditions are met. This License explicitly affirms your unlimited permission to run the unmodified Program. The output from running a covered work is covered by this License only if the output, given its content, constitutes a covered work. This License acknowledges your rights of fair use or other equivalent, as provided by copyright law.

    You may make, run and propagate covered works that you do not convey, without conditions so long as your license otherwise remains in force. You may convey covered works to others for the sole purpose of having them make modifications exclusively for you, or provide you with facilities for running those works, provided that you comply with the terms of this License in conveying all material for which you do not control copyright. Those thus making or running the covered works for you must do so exclusively on your behalf, under your direction and control, on terms that prohibit them from making any copies of your copyrighted material outside their relationship with you.

    Conveying under any other circumstances is permitted solely under the conditions stated below. Sublicensing is not allowed; section 10 makes it unnecessary.

3. Protecting Users' Legal Rights From Anti-Circumvention Law.

    No covered work shall be deemed part of an effective technological measure under any applicable law fulfilling obligations under article 11 of the WIPO copyright treaty adopted on 20 December 1996, or similar laws prohibiting or restricting circumvention of such measures.

When you convey a covered work, you waive any legal power to forbid circumvention of technological measures to the extent such circumvention is effected by exercising rights under this License with respect to the covered work, and you disclaim any intention to limit operation or modification of the work as a means of enforcing, against the work's users, your or third parties' legal rights to forbid circumvention of technological measures.

4. Conveying Verbatim Copies.

You may convey verbatim copies of the Program's source code as you receive it, in any medium, provided that you conspicuously and appropriately publish on each copy an appropriate copyright notice; keep intact all notices stating that this License and any non-permissive terms added in accord with section 7 apply to the code; keep intact all notices of the absence of any warranty; and give all recipients a copy of this License along with the Program.

You may charge any price or no price for each copy that you convey, and you may offer support or warranty protection for a fee.

5. Conveying Modified Source Versions.

You may convey a work based on the Program, or the modifications to produce it from the Program, in the form of source code under the terms of section 4, provided that you also meet all of these conditions:

a. The work must carry prominent notices stating that you modified it, and giving a relevant date.

b. The work must carry prominent notices stating that it is released under this License and any conditions added under section 7. This requirement modifies the requirement in section 4 to "keep intact all notices".

c. You must license the entire work, as a whole, under this License to anyone who comes into possession of a copy. This License will therefore apply, along with any applicable section 7 additional terms, to the whole of the work, and all its parts, regardless of how they are packaged. This License gives no permission to license the work in any other way, but it does not invalidate such permission if you have separately received it.

d. If the work has interactive user interfaces, each must display Appropriate Legal Notices; however, if the Program has interactive interfaces that do not display Appropriate Legal Notices, your work need not make them do so.

A compilation of a covered work with other separate and independent works, which are not by their nature extensions of the covered work, and which are not combined with it such as to form a larger program, in or on a volume of a storage or distribution medium, is called an "aggregate" if the compilation and its resulting copyright are not used to limit the access or legal rights of the compilation's users beyond what the individual works permit. Inclusion of a covered work in an aggregate does not cause this License to apply to the other parts of the aggregate.

6. Conveying Non-Source Forms.

You may convey a covered work in object code form under the terms of sections 4 and 5, provided that you also convey the machine-readable Corresponding Source under the terms of this License, in one of these ways:

a. Convey the object code in, or embodied in, a physical product (including a physical distribution medium), accompanied by the Corresponding Source fixed on a durable physical medium customarily used for software interchange.

b. Convey the object code in, or embodied in, a physical product (including a physical distribution medium), accompanied by a written offer, valid for at least three years and valid for as long as you offer spare parts or customer support for that product model, to give anyone who possesses the object code either (1) a copy of the Corresponding Source for all the software in the product that is covered by this License, on a durable physical medium customarily used for software interchange, for a price no more than your reasonable cost of physically performing this conveying of source, or (2) access to copy the Corresponding Source from a network server at no charge.

c. Convey individual copies of the object code with a copy of the written offer to provide the Corresponding Source. This alternative is allowed only occasionally and noncommercially, and only if you received the object code with such an offer, in accord with subsection 6b.

d. Convey the object code by offering access from a designated place (gratis or for a charge), and offer equivalent access to the Corresponding Source in the same way through the same place at no further charge. You need not require recipients to copy the Corresponding Source along with the object code. If the place to copy the object code is a network server, the Corresponding Source may be on a different server (operated by you or a third party) that supports equivalent copying facilities, provided you maintain clear directions next to the object code saying where to find the Corresponding Source. Regardless of what server hosts the Corresponding Source, you remain obligated to ensure that it is available for as long as needed to satisfy these requirements.

e. Convey the object code using peer-to-peer transmission, provided you inform other peers where the object code and Corresponding Source of the work are being offered to the general public at no charge under subsection 6d.

A separable portion of the object code, whose source code is excluded from the Corresponding Source as a System Library, need not be included in conveying the object code work.

A "User Product" is either (1) a "consumer product", which means any tangible personal property which is normally used for personal, family, or household purposes, or (2) anything designed or sold for incorporation into a dwelling. In determining whether a product is a consumer product, doubtful cases shall be resolved in favor of coverage. For a particular product received by a particular user, "normally used" refers to a typical or common use of that class of product, regardless of the status of the particular user or of the way in which the particular user actually uses, or expects or is expected to use, the product. A product is a consumer product regardless of whether the product has substantial commercial, industrial or non-consumer uses, unless such uses represent the only significant mode of use of the product.

"Installation Information" for a User Product means any methods, procedures, authorization keys, or other information required to install and execute modified versions of a covered work in that User Product from a modified version of its Corresponding Source.

The information must suffice to ensure that the continued functioning of the modified object code is in no case prevented or interfered with solely because modification has been made.

If you convey an object code work under this section in, or with, or specifically for use in, a User Product, and the conveying occurs as part of a transaction in which the right of possession and use of the User Product is transferred to the recipient in perpetuity or for a fixed term (regardless of how the transaction is characterized), the Corresponding Source conveyed under this section must be accompanied by the Installation Information. But this requirement does not apply if neither you nor any third party retains the ability to install modified object code on the User Product (for example, the work has been installed in ROM).

The requirement to provide Installation Information does not include a requirement to continue to provide support service, warranty, or updates for a work that has been modified or installed by the recipient, or for the User Product in which it has been modified or installed. Access to a network may be denied when the modification itself materially and adversely affects the operation of the network or violates the rules and protocols for communication across the network.

Corresponding Source conveyed, and Installation Information provided, in accord with this section must be in a format that is publicly documented (and with an implementation available to the public in source code form), and must require no special password or key for unpacking, reading or copying.

7. Additional Terms.

"Additional permissions" are terms that supplement the terms of this License by making exceptions from one or more of its conditions. Additional permissions that are applicable to the entire Program shall be treated as though they were included in this License, to the extent that they are valid under applicable law. If additional permissions apply only to part of the Program, that part may be used separately under those permissions, but the entire Program remains governed by this License without regard to the additional permissions.

When you convey a copy of a covered work, you may at your option remove any additional permissions from that copy, or from any part of it. (Additional permissions may be written to require their own removal in certain cases when you modify the work.) You may place additional permissions on material, added by you to a covered work, for which you have or can give appropriate copyright permission.

Notwithstanding any other provision of this License, for material you add to a covered work, you may (if authorized by the copyright holders of that material) supplement the terms of this License with terms:

  a. Disclaiming warranty or limiting liability differently from the terms of sections 15 and 16 of this License; or

  b. Requiring preservation of specified reasonable legal notices or author attributions in that material or in the Appropriate Legal Notices displayed by works containing it; or

  c. Prohibiting misrepresentation of the origin of that material, or requiring that modified versions of such material be marked in reasonable ways as different from the original version; or

    d. Limiting the use for publicity purposes of names of licensors or authors of the material; or

    e. Declining to grant rights under trademark law for use of some trade names, trademarks, or service marks; or

    f. Requiring indemnification of licensors and authors of that material by anyone who conveys the material (or modified versions of it) with contractual assumptions of liability to the recipient, for any liability that these contractual assumptions directly impose on those licensors and authors.

All other non-permissive additional terms are considered "further restrictions" within the meaning of section 10. If the Program as you received it, or any part of it, contains a notice stating that it is governed by this License along with a term that is a further restriction, you may remove that term. If a license document contains a further restriction but permits relicensing or conveying under this License, you may add to a covered work material governed by the terms of that license document, provided that the further restriction does not survive such relicensing or conveying.

If you add terms to a covered work in accord with this section, you must place, in the relevant source files, a statement of the additional terms that apply to those files, or a notice indicating where to find the applicable terms.

Additional terms, permissive or non-permissive, may be stated in the form of a separately written license, or stated as exceptions; the above requirements apply either way.

8. Termination.

You may not propagate or modify a covered work except as expressly provided under this License. Any attempt otherwise to propagate or modify it is void, and will automatically terminate your rights under this License (including any patent licenses granted under the third paragraph of section 11).

However, if you cease all violation of this License, then your license from a particular copyright holder is reinstated (a) provisionally, unless and until the copyright holder explicitly and finally terminates your license, and (b) permanently, if the copyright holder fails to notify you of the violation by some reasonable means prior to 60 days after the cessation.

Moreover, your license from a particular copyright holder is reinstated permanently if the copyright holder notifies you of the violation by some reasonable means, this is the first time you have received notice of violation of this License (for any work) from that copyright holder, and you cure the violation prior to 30 days after your receipt of the notice.

Termination of your rights under this section does not terminate the licenses of parties who have received copies or rights from you under this License. If your rights have been terminated and not permanently reinstated, you do not qualify to receive new licenses for the same material under section 10.

9. Acceptance Not Required for Having Copies.

You are not required to accept this License in order to receive or run a copy of the Program. Ancillary propagation of a covered work occurring solely as a consequence of using peer-to-peer transmission to receive a copy likewise does not require acceptance.

However, nothing other than this License grants you permission to propagate or modify any covered work. These actions infringe copyright if you do not accept this License. Therefore, by modifying or propagating a covered work, you indicate your acceptance of this License to do so.

10. Automatic Licensing of Downstream Recipients.

Each time you convey a covered work, the recipient automatically receives a license from the original licensors, to run, modify and propagate that work, subject to this License. You are not responsible for enforcing compliance by third parties with this License.

An "entity transaction" is a transaction transferring control of an organization, or substantially all assets of one, or subdividing an organization, or merging organizations. If propagation of a covered work results from an entity transaction, each party to that transaction who receives a copy of the work also receives whatever licenses to the work the party's predecessor in interest had or could give under the previous paragraph, plus a right to possession of the Corresponding Source of the work from the predecessor in interest, if the predecessor has it or can get it with reasonable efforts.

You may not impose any further restrictions on the exercise of the rights granted or affirmed under this License. For example, you may not impose a license fee, royalty, or other charge for exercise of rights granted under this License, and you may not initiate litigation (including a cross-claim or counterclaim in a lawsuit) alleging that any patent claim is infringed by making, using, selling, offering for sale, or importing the Program or any portion of it.

11. Patents.

A "contributor" is a copyright holder who authorizes use under this License of the Program or a work on which the Program is based. The work thus licensed is called the contributor's "contributor version".

A contributor's "essential patent claims" are all patent claims owned or controlled by the contributor, whether already acquired or hereafter acquired, that would be infringed by some manner, permitted by this License, of making, using, or selling its contributor version, but do not include claims that would be infringed only as a consequence of further modification of the contributor version. For purposes of this definition, "control" includes the right to grant patent sublicenses in a manner consistent with the requirements of this License.

Each contributor grants you a non-exclusive, worldwide, royalty-free patent license under the contributor's essential patent claims, to make, use, sell, offer for sale, import and otherwise run, modify and propagate the contents of its contributor version.

In the following three paragraphs, a "patent license" is any express agreement or commitment, however denominated, not to enforce a patent (such as an express permission to practice a patent or covenant not to sue for patent infringement). To "grant" such a patent license to a party means to make such an agreement or commitment not to enforce a patent against the party.

If you convey a covered work, knowingly relying on a patent license, and the Corresponding Source of the work is not available for anyone to copy, free of charge and under the terms of this License, through a publicly available network server or other readily accessible means, then you must either (1) cause the Corresponding Source to be so available, or (2) arrange to deprive yourself of the benefit of the patent license for this particular work, or (3) arrange, in a manner consistent with the requirements of this License, to extend the patent license to downstream recipients. "Knowingly relying" means you have actual knowledge that, but for the patent license, your conveying the covered work in a country, or your recipient's use of the covered work in a country, would infringe one or more identifiable patents in that country that you have reason to believe are valid.

If, pursuant to or in connection with a single transaction or arrangement, you convey, or propagate by procuring conveyance of, a covered work, and grant a patent license to some of the parties receiving the covered work authorizing them to use, propagate, modify or convey a specific copy of the covered work, then the patent license you grant is automatically extended to all recipients of the covered work and works based on it.

A patent license is "discriminatory" if it does not include within the scope of its coverage, prohibits the exercise of, or is conditioned on the non-exercise of one or more of the rights that are specifically granted under this License. You may not convey a covered work if you are a party to an arrangement with a third party that is in the business of distributing software, under which you make payment to the third party based on the extent of your activity of conveying the work, and under which the third party grants, to any of the parties who would receive the covered work from you, a discriminatory patent license (a) in connection with copies of the covered work conveyed by you (or copies made from those copies), or (b) primarily for and in connection with specific products or compilations that contain the covered work, unless you entered into that arrangement, or that patent license was granted, prior to 28 March 2007.

Nothing in this License shall be construed as excluding or limiting any implied license or other defenses to infringement that may otherwise be available to you under applicable patent law.

12. No Surrender of Others' Freedom.

If conditions are imposed on you (whether by court order, agreement or otherwise) that contradict the conditions of this License, they do not excuse you from the conditions of this License. If you cannot convey a covered work so as to satisfy simultaneously your obligations under this License and any other pertinent obligations, then as a consequence you may not convey it at all. For example, if you agree to terms that obligate you to collect a royalty for further conveying from those to whom you convey the Program, the only way you could satisfy both those terms and this License would be to refrain entirely from conveying the Program.

13. Use with the GNU Affero General Public License.

Notwithstanding any other provision of this License, you have permission to link or combine any covered work with a work licensed under version 3 of the GNU Affero General Public License into a single combined work, and to convey the resulting work. The terms of this License will continue to apply to the part which is the covered work, but the special requirements of the GNU Affero General Public License, section 13, concerning interaction through a network will apply to the combination as such.

14. Revised Versions of this License.

The Free Software Foundation may publish revised and/or new versions of the GNU General Public License from time to time. Such new versions will be similar in spirit to the present version, but may differ in detail to address new problems or concerns.

Each version is given a distinguishing version number. If the Program specifies that a certain numbered version of the GNU General Public License "or any later version" applies to it, you have the option of following the terms and conditions either of that numbered version or of any later version published by the Free Software Foundation. If the Program does not specify a version number of the GNU General Public License, you may choose any version ever published by the Free Software Foundation.

If the Program specifies that a proxy can decide which future versions of the GNU General Public License can be used, that proxy's public statement of acceptance of a version permanently authorizes you to choose that version for the Program.

Later license versions may give you additional or different permissions. However, no additional obligations are imposed on any author or copyright holder as a result of your choosing to follow a later version.

15. Disclaimer of Warranty.

    THERE IS NO WARRANTY FOR THE PROGRAM, TO THE EXTENT PERMITTED BY APPLICABLE LAW. EXCEPT WHEN OTHERWISE STATED IN WRITING THE COPYRIGHT HOLDERS AND/OR OTHER PARTIES PROVIDE THE PROGRAM "AS IS" WITHOUT WARRANTY OF ANY KIND, EITHER EXPRESSED OR IMPLIED, INCLUDING, BUT NOT LIMITED TO, THE IMPLIED WARRANTIES OF MERCHANTABILITY AND FITNESS FOR A PARTICULAR PURPOSE. THE ENTIRE RISK AS TO THE QUALITY AND PERFORMANCE OF THE PROGRAM IS WITH YOU. SHOULD THE PROGRAM PROVE DEFECTIVE, YOU ASSUME THE COST OF ALL NECESSARY SERVICING, REPAIR OR CORRECTION.

16. Limitation of Liability.

    IN NO EVENT UNLESS REQUIRED BY APPLICABLE LAW OR AGREED TO IN WRITING WILL ANY COPYRIGHT HOLDER, OR ANY OTHER PARTY WHO MODIFIES AND/OR CONVEYS THE PROGRAM AS PERMITTED ABOVE, BE LIABLE TO YOU FOR DAMAGES, INCLUDING ANY GENERAL, SPECIAL, INCIDENTAL OR CONSEQUENTIAL DAMAGES ARISING OUT OF THE USE OR INABILITY TO USE THE PROGRAM (INCLUDING BUT NOT LIMITED TO LOSS OF DATA OR DATA BEING RENDERED INACCURATE OR LOSSES SUSTAINED BY YOU OR THIRD PARTIES OR A FAILURE OF THE PROGRAM TO OPERATE WITH ANY OTHER PROGRAMS), EVEN IF SUCH HOLDER OR OTHER PARTY HAS BEEN ADVISED OF THE POSSIBILITY OF SUCH DAMAGES.

17. Interpretation of Sections 15 and 16.

    If the disclaimer of warranty and limitation of liability provided above cannot be given local legal effect according to their terms, reviewing courts shall apply local law that most closely approximates an absolute waiver of all civil liability in connection with the Program, unless a warranty or assumption of liability accompanies a copy of the Program in return for a fee.

END OF TERMS AND CONDITIONS

How to Apply These Terms to Your New Programs

If you develop a new program, and you want it to be of the greatest possible use to the public, the best way to achieve this is to make it free software which everyone can redistribute and change under these terms.

To do so, attach the following notices to the program. It is safest to attach them to the start of each source file to most effectively state the exclusion of warranty; and each file should have at least the "copyright" line and a pointer to where the full notice is found.

```
one line to give the program's name and a brief idea of what it does.
Copyright (C) year name of author

This program is free software: you can redistribute it and/or modify
it under the terms of the GNU General Public License as published by
the Free Software Foundation, either version 3 of the License, or (at
your option) any later version.

This program is distributed in the hope that it will be useful, but
WITHOUT ANY WARRANTY; without even the implied warranty of
MERCHANTABILITY or FITNESS FOR A PARTICULAR PURPOSE.  See the GNU
General Public License for more details.

You should have received a copy of the GNU General Public License
along with this program.  If not, see http://www.gnu.org/licenses/.
```

Also add information on how to contact you by electronic and paper mail.

If the program does terminal interaction, make it output a short notice like this when it starts in an interactive mode:

```
program Copyright (C) year name of author
This program comes with ABSOLUTELY NO WARRANTY; for details type 'show w'.
This is free software, and you are welcome to redistribute it
under certain conditions; type 'show c' for details.
```

The hypothetical commands 'show w' and 'show c' should show the appropriate parts of the General Public License. Of course, your program's commands might be different; for a GUI interface, you would use an "about box".

You should also get your employer (if you work as a programmer) or school, if any, to sign a "copyright disclaimer" for the program, if necessary. For more information on this, and how to apply and follow the GNU GPL, see http://www.gnu.org/licenses/.

The GNU General Public License does not permit incorporating your program into proprietary programs. If your program is a subroutine library, you may consider it more useful to permit linking proprietary applications with the library. If this is what you want to do, use the GNU Lesser General Public License instead of this License. But first, please read http://www.gnu.org/philosophy/why-not-lgpl.html.

Appendix B GNU Free Documentation License

Version 1.3, 3 November 2008

Copyright © 2000, 2001, 2002, 2007, 2008 Free Software Foundation, Inc.
`http://fsf.org/`

0. PREAMBLE

The purpose of this License is to make a manual, textbook, or other functional and useful document *free* in the sense of freedom: to assure everyone the effective freedom to copy and redistribute it, with or without modifying it, either commercially or non-commercially. Secondarily, this License preserves for the author and publisher a way to get credit for their work, while not being considered responsible for modifications made by others.

This License is a kind of "copyleft", which means that derivative works of the document must themselves be free in the same sense. It complements the GNU General Public License, which is a copyleft license designed for free software.

We have designed this License in order to use it for manuals for free software, because free software needs free documentation: a free program should come with manuals providing the same freedoms that the software does. But this License is not limited to software manuals; it can be used for any textual work, regardless of subject matter or whether it is published as a printed book. We recommend this License principally for works whose purpose is instruction or reference.

1. APPLICABILITY AND DEFINITIONS

This License applies to any manual or other work, in any medium, that contains a notice placed by the copyright holder saying it can be distributed under the terms of this License. Such a notice grants a world-wide, royalty-free license, unlimited in duration, to use that work under the conditions stated herein. The "Document", below, refers to any such manual or work. Any member of the public is a licensee, and is addressed as "you". You accept the license if you copy, modify or distribute the work in a way requiring permission under copyright law.

A "Modified Version" of the Document means any work containing the Document or a portion of it, either copied verbatim, or with modifications and/or translated into another language.

A "Secondary Section" is a named appendix or a front-matter section of the Document that deals exclusively with the relationship of the publishers or authors of the Document to the Document's overall subject (or to related matters) and contains nothing that could fall directly within that overall subject. (Thus, if the Document is in part a textbook of mathematics, a Secondary Section may not explain any mathematics.) The relationship could be a matter of historical connection with the subject or with related matters, or of legal, commercial, philosophical, ethical or political position regarding them.

The "Invariant Sections" are certain Secondary Sections whose titles are designated, as being those of Invariant Sections, in the notice that says that the Document is released under this License. If a section does not fit the above definition of Secondary then it is not allowed to be designated as Invariant. The Document may contain zero Invariant Sections. If the Document does not identify any Invariant Sections then there are none.

The "Cover Texts" are certain short passages of text that are listed, as Front-Cover Texts or Back-Cover Texts, in the notice that says that the Document is released under this License. A Front-Cover Text may be at most 5 words, and a Back-Cover Text may be at most 25 words.

A "Transparent" copy of the Document means a machine-readable copy, represented in a format whose specification is available to the general public, that is suitable for revising the document straightforwardly with generic text editors or (for images composed of pixels) generic paint programs or (for drawings) some widely available drawing editor, and that is suitable for input to text formatters or for automatic translation to a variety of formats suitable for input to text formatters. A copy made in an otherwise Transparent file format whose markup, or absence of markup, has been arranged to thwart or discourage subsequent modification by readers is not Transparent. An image format is not Transparent if used for any substantial amount of text. A copy that is not "Transparent" is called "Opaque".

Examples of suitable formats for Transparent copies include plain ASCII without markup, Texinfo input format, LaTeX input format, SGML or XML using a publicly available DTD, and standard-conforming simple HTML, PostScript or PDF designed for human modification. Examples of transparent image formats include PNG, XCF and JPG. Opaque formats include proprietary formats that can be read and edited only by proprietary word processors, SGML or XML for which the DTD and/or processing tools are not generally available, and the machine-generated HTML, PostScript or PDF produced by some word processors for output purposes only.

The "Title Page" means, for a printed book, the title page itself, plus such following pages as are needed to hold, legibly, the material this License requires to appear in the title page. For works in formats which do not have any title page as such, "Title Page" means the text near the most prominent appearance of the work's title, preceding the beginning of the body of the text.

The "publisher" means any person or entity that distributes copies of the Document to the public.

A section "Entitled XYZ" means a named subunit of the Document whose title either is precisely XYZ or contains XYZ in parentheses following text that translates XYZ in another language. (Here XYZ stands for a specific section name mentioned below, such as "Acknowledgements", "Dedications", "Endorsements", or "History".) To "Preserve the Title" of such a section when you modify the Document means that it remains a section "Entitled XYZ" according to this definition.

The Document may include Warranty Disclaimers next to the notice which states that this License applies to the Document. These Warranty Disclaimers are considered to be included by reference in this License, but only as regards disclaiming warranties: any other implication that these Warranty Disclaimers may have is void and has no effect on the meaning of this License.

2. VERBATIM COPYING

You may copy and distribute the Document in any medium, either commercially or noncommercially, provided that this License, the copyright notices, and the license notice saying this License applies to the Document are reproduced in all copies, and that you add no other conditions whatsoever to those of this License. You may not use technical measures to obstruct or control the reading or further copying of the copies you make or distribute. However, you may accept compensation in exchange for copies. If you distribute a large enough number of copies you must also follow the conditions in section 3.

You may also lend copies, under the same conditions stated above, and you may publicly display copies.

3. COPYING IN QUANTITY

If you publish printed copies (or copies in media that commonly have printed covers) of the Document, numbering more than 100, and the Document's license notice requires Cover Texts, you must enclose the copies in covers that carry, clearly and legibly, all these Cover Texts: Front-Cover Texts on the front cover, and Back-Cover Texts on the back cover. Both covers must also clearly and legibly identify you as the publisher of these copies. The front cover must present the full title with all words of the title equally prominent and visible. You may add other material on the covers in addition. Copying with changes limited to the covers, as long as they preserve the title of the Document and satisfy these conditions, can be treated as verbatim copying in other respects.

If the required texts for either cover are too voluminous to fit legibly, you should put the first ones listed (as many as fit reasonably) on the actual cover, and continue the rest onto adjacent pages.

If you publish or distribute Opaque copies of the Document numbering more than 100, you must either include a machine-readable Transparent copy along with each Opaque copy, or state in or with each Opaque copy a computer-network location from which the general network-using public has access to download using public-standard network protocols a complete Transparent copy of the Document, free of added material. If you use the latter option, you must take reasonably prudent steps, when you begin distribution of Opaque copies in quantity, to ensure that this Transparent copy will remain thus accessible at the stated location until at least one year after the last time you distribute an Opaque copy (directly or through your agents or retailers) of that edition to the public.

It is requested, but not required, that you contact the authors of the Document well before redistributing any large number of copies, to give them a chance to provide you with an updated version of the Document.

4. MODIFICATIONS

You may copy and distribute a Modified Version of the Document under the conditions of sections 2 and 3 above, provided that you release the Modified Version under precisely this License, with the Modified Version filling the role of the Document, thus licensing distribution and modification of the Modified Version to whoever possesses a copy of it. In addition, you must do these things in the Modified Version:

A. Use in the Title Page (and on the covers, if any) a title distinct from that of the Document, and from those of previous versions (which should, if there were any, be listed in the History section of the Document). You may use the same title as a previous version if the original publisher of that version gives permission.

B. List on the Title Page, as authors, one or more persons or entities responsible for authorship of the modifications in the Modified Version, together with at least five of the principal authors of the Document (all of its principal authors, if it has fewer than five), unless they release you from this requirement.

C. State on the Title page the name of the publisher of the Modified Version, as the publisher.

D. Preserve all the copyright notices of the Document.

E. Add an appropriate copyright notice for your modifications adjacent to the other copyright notices.

F. Include, immediately after the copyright notices, a license notice giving the public permission to use the Modified Version under the terms of this License, in the form shown in the Addendum below.

G. Preserve in that license notice the full lists of Invariant Sections and required Cover Texts given in the Document's license notice.

H. Include an unaltered copy of this License.

 I. Preserve the section Entitled "History", Preserve its Title, and add to it an item stating at least the title, year, new authors, and publisher of the Modified Version as given on the Title Page. If there is no section Entitled "History" in the Document, create one stating the title, year, authors, and publisher of the Document as given on its Title Page, then add an item describing the Modified Version as stated in the previous sentence.

J. Preserve the network location, if any, given in the Document for public access to a Transparent copy of the Document, and likewise the network locations given in the Document for previous versions it was based on. These may be placed in the "History" section. You may omit a network location for a work that was published at least four years before the Document itself, or if the original publisher of the version it refers to gives permission.

K. For any section Entitled "Acknowledgements" or "Dedications", Preserve the Title of the section, and preserve in the section all the substance and tone of each of the contributor acknowledgements and/or dedications given therein.

L. Preserve all the Invariant Sections of the Document, unaltered in their text and in their titles. Section numbers or the equivalent are not considered part of the section titles.

M. Delete any section Entitled "Endorsements". Such a section may not be included in the Modified Version.

N. Do not retitle any existing section to be Entitled "Endorsements" or to conflict in title with any Invariant Section.

O. Preserve any Warranty Disclaimers.

If the Modified Version includes new front-matter sections or appendices that qualify as Secondary Sections and contain no material copied from the Document, you may at your option designate some or all of these sections as invariant. To do this, add their titles to the list of Invariant Sections in the Modified Version's license notice. These titles must be distinct from any other section titles.

You may add a section Entitled "Endorsements", provided it contains nothing but endorsements of your Modified Version by various parties—for example, statements of peer review or that the text has been approved by an organization as the authoritative definition of a standard.

You may add a passage of up to five words as a Front-Cover Text, and a passage of up to 25 words as a Back-Cover Text, to the end of the list of Cover Texts in the Modified Version. Only one passage of Front-Cover Text and one of Back-Cover Text may be added by (or through arrangements made by) any one entity. If the Document already includes a cover text for the same cover, previously added by you or by arrangement made by the same entity you are acting on behalf of, you may not add another; but you may replace the old one, on explicit permission from the previous publisher that added the old one.

The author(s) and publisher(s) of the Document do not by this License give permission to use their names for publicity for or to assert or imply endorsement of any Modified Version.

5. COMBINING DOCUMENTS

You may combine the Document with other documents released under this License, under the terms defined in section 4 above for modified versions, provided that you include in the combination all of the Invariant Sections of all of the original documents, unmodified, and list them all as Invariant Sections of your combined work in its license notice, and that you preserve all their Warranty Disclaimers.

The combined work need only contain one copy of this License, and multiple identical Invariant Sections may be replaced with a single copy. If there are multiple Invariant Sections with the same name but different contents, make the title of each such section unique by adding at the end of it, in parentheses, the name of the original author or publisher of that section if known, or else a unique number. Make the same adjustment to the section titles in the list of Invariant Sections in the license notice of the combined work.

In the combination, you must combine any sections Entitled "History" in the various original documents, forming one section Entitled "History"; likewise combine any sections Entitled "Acknowledgements", and any sections Entitled "Dedications". You must delete all sections Entitled "Endorsements."

6. COLLECTIONS OF DOCUMENTS

You may make a collection consisting of the Document and other documents released under this License, and replace the individual copies of this License in the various documents with a single copy that is included in the collection, provided that you follow the rules of this License for verbatim copying of each of the documents in all other respects.

You may extract a single document from such a collection, and distribute it individually under this License, provided you insert a copy of this License into the extracted document, and follow this License in all other respects regarding verbatim copying of that document.

7. AGGREGATION WITH INDEPENDENT WORKS

A compilation of the Document or its derivatives with other separate and independent documents or works, in or on a volume of a storage or distribution medium, is called an "aggregate" if the copyright resulting from the compilation is not used to limit the legal rights of the compilation's users beyond what the individual works permit. When the Document is included in an aggregate, this License does not apply to the other works in the aggregate which are not themselves derivative works of the Document.

If the Cover Text requirement of section 3 is applicable to these copies of the Document, then if the Document is less than one half of the entire aggregate, the Document's Cover Texts may be placed on covers that bracket the Document within the aggregate, or the electronic equivalent of covers if the Document is in electronic form. Otherwise they must appear on printed covers that bracket the whole aggregate.

8. TRANSLATION

Translation is considered a kind of modification, so you may distribute translations of the Document under the terms of section 4. Replacing Invariant Sections with translations requires special permission from their copyright holders, but you may include translations of some or all Invariant Sections in addition to the original versions of these Invariant Sections. You may include a translation of this License, and all the license notices in the Document, and any Warranty Disclaimers, provided that you also include the original English version of this License and the original versions of those notices and disclaimers. In case of a disagreement between the translation and the original version of this License or a notice or disclaimer, the original version will prevail.

If a section in the Document is Entitled "Acknowledgements", "Dedications", or "History", the requirement (section 4) to Preserve its Title (section 1) will typically require changing the actual title.

9. TERMINATION

You may not copy, modify, sublicense, or distribute the Document except as expressly provided under this License. Any attempt otherwise to copy, modify, sublicense, or distribute it is void, and will automatically terminate your rights under this License.

However, if you cease all violation of this License, then your license from a particular copyright holder is reinstated (a) provisionally, unless and until the copyright holder explicitly and finally terminates your license, and (b) permanently, if the copyright holder fails to notify you of the violation by some reasonable means prior to 60 days after the cessation.

Moreover, your license from a particular copyright holder is reinstated permanently if the copyright holder notifies you of the violation by some reasonable means, this is the first time you have received notice of violation of this License (for any work) from that copyright holder, and you cure the violation prior to 30 days after your receipt of the notice.

Termination of your rights under this section does not terminate the licenses of parties who have received copies or rights from you under this License. If your rights have been terminated and not permanently reinstated, receipt of a copy of some or all of the same material does not give you any rights to use it.

10. FUTURE REVISIONS OF THIS LICENSE

The Free Software Foundation may publish new, revised versions of the GNU Free Documentation License from time to time. Such new versions will be similar in spirit to the present version, but may differ in detail to address new problems or concerns. See http://www.gnu.org/copyleft/.

Each version of the License is given a distinguishing version number. If the Document specifies that a particular numbered version of this License "or any later version" applies to it, you have the option of following the terms and conditions either of that specified version or of any later version that has been published (not as a draft) by the Free Software Foundation. If the Document does not specify a version number of this License, you may choose any version ever published (not as a draft) by the Free Software Foundation. If the Document specifies that a proxy can decide which future versions of this License can be used, that proxy's public statement of acceptance of a version permanently authorizes you to choose that version for the Document.

11. RELICENSING

"Massive Multiauthor Collaboration Site" (or "MMC Site") means any World Wide Web server that publishes copyrightable works and also provides prominent facilities for anybody to edit those works. A public wiki that anybody can edit is an example of such a server. A "Massive Multiauthor Collaboration" (or "MMC") contained in the site means any set of copyrightable works thus published on the MMC site.

"CC-BY-SA" means the Creative Commons Attribution-Share Alike 3.0 license published by Creative Commons Corporation, a not-for-profit corporation with a principal place of business in San Francisco, California, as well as future copyleft versions of that license published by that same organization.

"Incorporate" means to publish or republish a Document, in whole or in part, as part of another Document.

An MMC is "eligible for relicensing" if it is licensed under this License, and if all works that were first published under this License somewhere other than this MMC, and subsequently incorporated in whole or in part into the MMC, (1) had no cover texts or invariant sections, and (2) were thus incorporated prior to November 1, 2008.

The operator of an MMC Site may republish an MMC contained in the site under CC-BY-SA on the same site at any time before August 1, 2009, provided the MMC is eligible for relicensing.

ADDENDUM: How to use this License for your documents

To use this License in a document you have written, include a copy of the License in the document and put the following copyright and license notices just after the title page:

```
Copyright (C)  year  your name.
Permission is granted to copy, distribute and/or modify this document
under the terms of the GNU Free Documentation License, Version 1.3
or any later version published by the Free Software Foundation;
with no Invariant Sections, no Front-Cover Texts, and no Back-Cover
Texts.  A copy of the license is included in the section entitled ``GNU
Free Documentation License''.
```

If you have Invariant Sections, Front-Cover Texts and Back-Cover Texts, replace the "with...Texts." line with this:

```
with the Invariant Sections being list their titles, with
the Front-Cover Texts being list, and with the Back-Cover Texts
being list.
```

If you have Invariant Sections without Cover Texts, or some other combination of the three, merge those two alternatives to suit the situation.

If your document contains nontrivial examples of program code, we recommend releasing these examples in parallel under your choice of free software license, such as the GNU General Public License, to permit their use in free software.

Appendix C Customizing Calc

The usual prefix for Calc is the key sequence `C-x *`. If you wish to use a different prefix, you can put

```
(global-set-key "NEWPREFIX" 'calc-dispatch)
```

in your .emacs file. (See Section "Customizing Key Bindings" in *The GNU Emacs Manual*, for more information on binding keys.) A convenient way to start Calc is with `C-x * *`; to make it equally convenient for users who use a different prefix, the prefix can be followed by `=`, `&`, `#`, `\`, `/`, `+` or `-` as well as `*` to start Calc, and so in many cases the last character of the prefix can simply be typed twice.

Calc is controlled by many variables, most of which can be reset from within Calc. Some variables are less involved with actual calculation and can be set outside of Calc using Emacs's customization facilities. These variables are listed below. Typing *M-x customize-variable RET variable-name RET* will bring up a buffer in which the variable's value can be redefined. Typing *M-x customize-group RET calc RET* will bring up a buffer which contains all of Calc's customizable variables. (These variables can also be reset by putting the appropriate lines in your .emacs file; See Section "Init File" in *The GNU Emacs Manual*.)

Some of the customizable variables are regular expressions. A regular expression is basically a pattern that Calc can search for. See Section "Regular Expression Search" in *The GNU Emacs Manual* to see how regular expressions work.

`calc-settings-file`   [Variable]

> The variable `calc-settings-file` holds the file name in which commands like `m m` and `Z P` store "permanent" definitions. If `calc-settings-file` is not your user init file (typically `~/.emacs`) and if the variable `calc-loaded-settings-file` is `nil`, then Calc will automatically load your settings file (if it exists) the first time Calc is invoked.
>
> The default value for this variable is `"~/.emacs.d/calc.el"` unless the file `~/.calc.el` exists, in which case the default value will be `"~/.calc.el"`.

`calc-gnuplot-name`   [Variable]

> See Chapter 13 [Graphics], page 329.
>
> The variable `calc-gnuplot-name` should be the name of the GNUPLOT program (a string). If you have GNUPLOT installed on your system but Calc is unable to find it, you may need to set this variable. You may also need to set some Lisp variables to show Calc how to run GNUPLOT on your system, see Section 13.5 [Graphical Devices], page 335, . The default value of `calc-gnuplot-name` is `"gnuplot"`.

`calc-gnuplot-plot-command`   [Variable]
`calc-gnuplot-print-command`   [Variable]

> See Section 13.5 [Graphical Devices], page 335.
>
> The variables `calc-gnuplot-plot-command` and `calc-gnuplot-print-command` represent system commands to display and print the output of GNUPLOT, respectively. These may be `nil` if no command is necessary, or strings which can include '`%s`' to signify the name of the file to be displayed or printed. Or, these variables may contain Lisp expressions which are evaluated to display or print the output.

The default value of `calc-gnuplot-plot-command` is `nil`, and the default value of `calc-gnuplot-print-command` is `"lp %s"`.

`calc-language-alist`   [Variable]

See Section 16.1 [Basic Embedded Mode], page 351.

The variable `calc-language-alist` controls the languages that Calc will associate with major modes. When Calc embedded mode is enabled, it will try to use the current major mode to determine what language should be used. (This can be overridden using Calc's mode changing commands, See Section 16.4 [Mode Settings in Embedded Mode], page 358.) The variable `calc-language-alist` consists of a list of pairs of the form (*MAJOR-MODE . LANGUAGE*); for example, (`latex-mode . latex`) is one such pair. If Calc embedded is activated in a buffer whose major mode is *MAJOR-MODE*, it will set itself to use the language *LANGUAGE*.

The default value of `calc-language-alist` is

```
((latex-mode . latex)
 (tex-mode    . tex)
 (plain-tex-mode . tex)
 (context-mode . tex)
 (nroff-mode . eqn)
 (pascal-mode . pascal)
 (c-mode . c)
 (c++-mode . c)
 (fortran-mode . fortran)
 (f90-mode . fortran))
```

`calc-embedded-announce-formula`   [Variable]
`calc-embedded-announce-formula-alist`   [Variable]

See Section 16.5 [Customizing Embedded Mode], page 360.

The variable `calc-embedded-announce-formula` helps determine what formulas `C-x * a` will activate in a buffer. It is a regular expression, and when activating embedded formulas with `C-x * a`, it will tell Calc that what follows is a formula to be activated. (Calc also uses other patterns to find formulas, such as '`=>`' and '`:=`'.)

The default pattern is `"%Embed\n\\(% .*\n\\)*"`, which checks for '`%Embed`' followed by any number of lines beginning with '`%`' and a space.

The variable `calc-embedded-announce-formula-alist` is used to set `calc-embedded-announce-formula` to different regular expressions depending on the major mode of the editing buffer. It consists of a list of pairs of the form (*MAJOR-MODE . REGEXP*), and its default value is

```
((c++-mode      . "//Embed\n\\(// .*\n\\)*")
 (c-mode        . "/\\*Embed\\*/\n\\(/\\* .*\\*/\n\\)*")
 (f90-mode      . "!Embed\n\\(! .*\n\\)*")
 (fortran-mode . "C Embed\n\\(C .*\n\\)*")
 (html-helper-mode . "<!-- Embed -->\n\\(<!-- .* -->\n\\)*")
 (html-mode    . "<!-- Embed -->\n\\(<!-- .* -->\n\\)*")
 (nroff-mode   . "\\\\\"Embed\n\\(\\\\\" .*\n\\)*")
 (pascal-mode  . "{Embed}\n\\({.*}\n\\)*")
```

```
(sgml-mode    . "<!-- Embed -->\n\\(<!-- .* -->\n\\)*")
(xml-mode     . "<!-- Embed -->\n\\(<!-- .* -->\n\\)*")
(texinfo-mode . "@c Embed\n\\(@c .*\n\\)*"))
```

Any major modes added to `calc-embedded-announce-formula-alist` should also be added to `calc-embedded-open-close-plain-alist` and `calc-embedded-open-close-mode-alist`.

`calc-embedded-open-formula`   [Variable]
`calc-embedded-close-formula`   [Variable]
`calc-embedded-open-close-formula-alist`   [Variable]

> See Section 16.5 [Customizing Embedded Mode], page 360.
>
> The variables `calc-embedded-open-formula` and `calc-embedded-close-formula` control the region that Calc will activate as a formula when Embedded mode is entered with `C-x * e`. They are regular expressions; Calc normally scans backward and forward in the buffer for the nearest text matching these regular expressions to be the "formula delimiters".
>
> The simplest delimiters are blank lines. Other delimiters that Embedded mode understands by default are:
>
> 1. The TEX and LATEX math delimiters '$ $', '$$ $$', '\[\]', and '\(\)';
> 2. Lines beginning with '\begin' and '\end' (except matrix delimiters);
> 3. Lines beginning with '@' (Texinfo delimiters).
> 4. Lines beginning with '.EQ' and '.EN' (*eqn* delimiters);
> 5. Lines containing a single '%' or '.\"' symbol and nothing else.
>
> The variable `calc-embedded-open-close-formula-alist` is used to set `calc-embedded-open-formula` and `calc-embedded-close-formula` to different regular expressions depending on the major mode of the editing buffer. It consists of a list of lists of the form (*MAJOR-MODE OPEN-FORMULA-REGEXP CLOSE-FORMULA-REGEXP*), and its default value is `nil`.

`calc-embedded-word-regexp`   [Variable]
`calc-embedded-word-regexp-alist`   [Variable]

> See Section 16.5 [Customizing Embedded Mode], page 360.
>
> The variable `calc-embedded-word-regexp` determines the expression that Calc will activate when Embedded mode is entered with `C-x * w`. It is a regular expressions.
>
> The default value of `calc-embedded-word-regexp` is `"[-+]?[0-9]+\\(\\.[0-9]+\\)?\\([eE][-+]?[0-9]+\\)?"`.
>
> The variable `calc-embedded-word-regexp-alist` is used to set `calc-embedded-word-regexp` to a different regular expression depending on the major mode of the editing buffer. It consists of a list of lists of the form (*MAJOR-MODE WORD-REGEXP*), and its default value is `nil`.

`calc-embedded-open-plain`   [Variable]
`calc-embedded-close-plain`   [Variable]
`calc-embedded-open-close-plain-alist`   [Variable]

> See Section 16.5 [Customizing Embedded Mode], page 360.
>
> The variables `calc-embedded-open-plain` and `calc-embedded-open-plain` are

used to delimit "plain" formulas. Note that these are actual strings, not regular expressions, because Calc must be able to write these string into a buffer as well as to recognize them.

The default string for `calc-embedded-open-plain` is `"%% "`, note the trailing space. The default string for `calc-embedded-close-plain` is `" %%\n"`, without the trailing newline here, the first line of a Big mode formula that followed might be shifted over with respect to the other lines.

The variable `calc-embedded-open-close-plain-alist` is used to set `calc-embedded-open-plain` and `calc-embedded-close-plain` to different strings depending on the major mode of the editing buffer. It consists of a list of lists of the form (*MAJOR-MODE OPEN-PLAIN-STRING CLOSE-PLAIN-STRING*), and its default value is

```
((c++-mode      "// %% "    " %%\n")
 (c-mode        "/* %% "    " %% */\n")
 (f90-mode      "! %% "      " %%\n")
 (fortran-mode "C %% "      " %%\n")
 (html-helper-mode "<!-- %% " " %% -->\n")
 (html-mode "<!-- %% " " %% -->\n")
 (nroff-mode    "\\\" %% "    " %%\n")
 (pascal-mode   "{%% "       " %%}\n")
 (sgml-mode      "<!-- %% " " %% -->\n")
 (xml-mode       "<!-- %% " " %% -->\n")
 (texinfo-mode "@c %% "     " %%\n"))
```

Any major modes added to `calc-embedded-open-close-plain-alist` should also be added to `calc-embedded-announce-formula-alist` and `calc-embedded-open-close-mode-alist`.

`calc-embedded-open-new-formula`   [Variable]
`calc-embedded-close-new-formula`   [Variable]
`calc-embedded-open-close-new-formula-alist`   [Variable]

See Section 16.5 [Customizing Embedded Mode], page 360.

The variables `calc-embedded-open-new-formula` and `calc-embedded-close-new-formula` are strings which are inserted before and after a new formula when you type `C-x * f`.

The default value of `calc-embedded-open-new-formula` is `"\n\n"`. If this string begins with a newline character and the `C-x * f` is typed at the beginning of a line, `C-x * f` will skip this first newline to avoid introducing unnecessary blank lines in the file. The default value of `calc-embedded-close-new-formula` is also `"\n\n"`. The final newline is omitted by `C-x * f` if typed at the end of a line. (It follows that if `C-x * f` is typed on a blank line, both a leading opening newline and a trailing closing newline are omitted.)

The variable `calc-embedded-open-close-new-formula-alist` is used to set `calc-embedded-open-new-formula` and `calc-embedded-close-new-formula` to different strings depending on the major mode of the editing buffer. It consists of a list of lists of the form (*MAJOR-MODE OPEN-NEW-FORMULA-STRING CLOSE-NEW-FORMULA-STRING*), and its default value is `nil`.

`calc-embedded-open-mode`   [Variable]
`calc-embedded-close-mode`   [Variable]
`calc-embedded-open-close-mode-alist`   [Variable]

>   See Section 16.5 [Customizing Embedded Mode], page 360.
>
>   The variables `calc-embedded-open-mode` and `calc-embedded-close-mode` are strings which Calc will place before and after any mode annotations that it inserts. Calc never scans for these strings; Calc always looks for the annotation itself, so it is not necessary to add them to user-written annotations.
>
>   The default value of `calc-embedded-open-mode` is `"% "` and the default value of `calc-embedded-close-mode` is `"\n"`. If you change the value of `calc-embedded-close-mode`, it is a good idea still to end with a newline so that mode annotations will appear on lines by themselves.
>
>   The variable `calc-embedded-open-close-mode-alist` is used to set `calc-embedded-open-mode` and `calc-embedded-close-mode` to different strings expressions depending on the major mode of the editing buffer. It consists of a list of lists of the form (*MAJOR-MODE OPEN-MODE-STRING CLOSE-MODE-STRING*), and its default value is

```
((c++-mode      "// "    "\n")
 (c-mode        "/* "    " */\n")
 (f90-mode      "! "     "\n")
 (fortran-mode "C "      "\n")
 (html-helper-mode "<!-- " " -->\n")
 (html-mode     "<!-- " " -->\n")
 (nroff-mode    "\\\"" "\n")
 (pascal-mode   "{ "     " }\n")
 (sgml-mode     "<!-- " " -->\n")
 (xml-mode      "<!-- " " -->\n")
 (texinfo-mode "@c "     "\n"))
```

>   Any major modes added to `calc-embedded-open-close-mode-alist` should also be added to `calc-embedded-announce-formula-alist` and `calc-embedded-open-close-plain-alist`.

`calc-lu-power-reference`   [Variable]
`calc-lu-field-reference`   [Variable]

>   See Section 11.5 [Logarithmic Units], page 319.
>
>   The variables `calc-lu-power-reference` and `calc-lu-field-reference` are unit expressions (written as strings) which Calc will use as reference quantities for logarithmic units.
>
>   The default value of `calc-lu-power-reference` is `"mW"` and the default value of `calc-lu-field-reference` is `"20 uPa"`.

`calc-note-threshold`   [Variable]

>   See Section 11.6 [Musical Notes], page 320.
>
>   The variable `calc-note-threshold` is a number (written as a string) which determines how close (in cents) a frequency needs to be to a note to be recognized as that note.
>
>   The default value of `calc-note-threshold` is 1.

`calc-highlight-selections-with-faces`   [Variable]
`calc-selected-face`   [Variable]
`calc-nonselected-face`   [Variable]

See Section 10.1.3 [Displaying Selections], page 246.

The variable `calc-highlight-selections-with-faces` determines how selected sub-formulas are distinguished. If `calc-highlight-selections-with-faces` is nil, then a selected sub-formula is distinguished either by changing every character not part of the sub-formula with a dot or by changing every character in the sub-formula with a '#' sign. If `calc-highlight-selections-with-faces` is t, then a selected sub-formula is distinguished either by displaying the non-selected portion of the formula with `calc-nonselected-face` or by displaying the selected sub-formula with `calc-nonselected-face`.

`calc-multiplication-has-precedence`   [Variable]

The variable `calc-multiplication-has-precedence` determines whether multiplication has precedence over division in algebraic formulas in normal language modes. If `calc-multiplication-has-precedence` is non-nil, then multiplication has precedence (and, for certain obscure reasons, is right associative), and so for example 'a/b*c' will be interpreted as 'a/(b*c)'. If `calc-multiplication-has-precedence` is nil, then multiplication has the same precedence as division (and, like division, is left associative), and so for example 'a/b*c' will be interpreted as '(a/b)*c'. The default value of `calc-multiplication-has-precedence` is t.

`calc-context-sensitive-enter`   [Variable]

The commands `calc-enter` and `calc-pop` will typically duplicate the top of the stack. If `calc-context-sensitive-enter` is non-nil, then the `calc-enter` will copy the element at the cursor to the top of the stack and `calc-pop` will delete the element at the cursor. The default value of `calc-context-sensitive-enter` is nil.

`calc-undo-length`   [Variable]

The variable `calc-undo-length` determines the number of undo steps that Calc will keep track of when `calc-quit` is called. If `calc-undo-length` is a non-negative integer, then this is the number of undo steps that will be preserved; if `calc-undo-length` has any other value, then all undo steps will be preserved. The default value of `calc-undo-length` is 100.

`calc-gregorian-switch`   [Variable]

See Section 4.9 [Date Forms], page 122.

The variable `calc-gregorian-switch` is either a list of integers (*YEAR MONTH DAY*) or nil. If it is nil, then Calc's date forms always represent Gregorian dates. Otherwise, `calc-gregorian-switch` represents the date that the calendar switches from Julian dates to Gregorian dates; (*YEAR MONTH DAY*) will be the first Gregorian date. The customization buffer will offer several standard dates to choose from, or the user can enter their own date.

The default value of `calc-gregorian-switch` is nil.

Appendix D Reporting Bugs

If you find a bug in Calc, send e-mail to Jay Belanger,

> `jay.p.belanger@gmail.com`

There is an automatic command *M-x report-calc-bug* which helps you to report bugs. This command prompts you for a brief subject line, then leaves you in a mail editing buffer. Type *C-c C-c* to send your mail. Make sure your subject line indicates that you are reporting a Calc bug; this command sends mail to the maintainer's regular mailbox.

If you have suggestions for additional features for Calc, please send them. Some have dared to suggest that Calc is already top-heavy with features; this obviously cannot be the case, so if you have ideas, send them right in.

At the front of the source file, `calc.el`, is a list of ideas for future work. If any enthusiastic souls wish to take it upon themselves to work on these, please send a message (using *M-x report-calc-bug*) so any efforts can be coordinated.

The latest version of Calc is available from Savannah, in the Emacs repository. See `http://savannah.gnu.org/projects/emacs`.

Appendix E Calc Summary

This section includes a complete list of Calc keystroke commands. Each line lists the stack entries used by the command (top-of-stack last), the keystrokes themselves, the prompts asked by the command, and the result of the command (also with top-of-stack last). The result is expressed using the equivalent algebraic function. Commands which put no results on the stack show the full *M-x* command name in that position. Numbers preceding the result or command name refer to notes at the end.

Algebraic functions and *M-x* commands that don't have corresponding keystrokes are not listed in this summary. See [Command Index], page 471. See [Function Index], page 477.

C-x * a		33	calc-embedded-activate
C-x * b			calc-big-or-small
C-x * c			calc
C-x * d			calc-embedded-duplicate
C-x * e		34	calc-embedded
C-x * f*formula*			calc-embedded-new-formula
C-x * g		35	calc-grab-region
C-x * i			calc-info
C-x * j			calc-embedded-select
C-x * k			calc-keypad
C-x * l			calc-load-everything
C-x * m			read-kbd-macro
C-x * n		4	calc-embedded-next
C-x * o			calc-other-window
C-x * p		4	calc-embedded-previous
C-x * q*formula*			quick-calc
C-x * r		36	calc-grab-rectangle
C-x * s			calc-info-summary
C-x * t			calc-tutorial
C-x * u			calc-embedded-update-formula
C-x * w			calc-embedded-word
C-x * x			calc-quit
C-x * y		1, 28, 49	calc-copy-to-buffer
C-x * z			calc-user-invocation
C-x * :		36	calc-grab-sum-down
C-x * _		36	calc-grab-sum-across
C-x * '*editing*		30	calc-embedded-edit
C-x * 0(*zero*)			calc-reset

0-9	*number*		*number*
.	*number*		*0.number*
_	*number*		*-number*
e	*number*		*1e number*
#	*number*		*current-radix#number*
P	(*in number*)		*+/-*
M	(*in number*)		*mod*
@ ' "	(*in number*)		*HMS form*
h m s	(*in number*)		*HMS form*

'	*formula*	37, 46	*formula*
$	*formula*	37, 46	*$formula*
"	*string*	37, 46	*string*

a b	+	2	**add**(*a, b*) *a+b*

Stack	Key		Num	Function
a b	-		2	sub(a, b) a−b
a b	*		2	mul(a, b) a b, a*b
a b	/		2	div(a, b) a/b
a b	^		2	pow(a, b) a^b
a b	I ^		2	nroot(a, b) a^(1/b)
a b	%		2	mod(a, b) a%b
a b	\		2	idiv(a, b) a\b
a b	:		2	fdiv(a, b)
a b	|		2	vconcat(a, b) a|b
a b	I |			vconcat(b, a) b|a
a b	H |		2	append(a, b)
a b	I H |			append(b, a)
a	&		1	inv(a) 1/a
a	!		1	fact(a) a!
a	=		1	evalv(a)
a	M-%			percent(a) a%
... a	RET		1	... a a
... a	SPC		1	... a a
... a b	TAB		3	... b a
. a b c	M-TAB		3	... b c a
... a b	LFD		1	... a b a
... a	DEL		1	...
... a b	M-DEL		1	... b
	M-RET		4	calc-last-args
a	'	editing	1, 30	calc-edit
... a	C-d		1	...
	C-k		27	calc-kill
	C-w		27	calc-kill-region
	C-y			calc-yank
	C-_		4	calc-undo
	M-k		27	calc-copy-as-kill
	M-w		27	calc-copy-region-as-kill
	[			[...
[.. a b	]			[a, b]
	(			(...
(.. a b	)			(a, b)
	,			*vector or rect complex*
	;			*matrix or polar complex*
	..			*interval*
	~			calc-num-prefix
	<		4	calc-scroll-left
	>		4	calc-scroll-right
	{		4	calc-scroll-down
	}		4	calc-scroll-up
	?			calc-help
a	n		1	neg(a) −a
	o		4	calc-realign
	p	*precision*	31	calc-precision
	q			calc-quit
	w			calc-why
	x	*command*		M-x calc-*command*
a	y		1, 28, 49	calc-copy-to-buffer
a	A		1	abs(a)
a b	B		2	log(a, b)

a b	I	B		2	alog(a, b) b^a
a		C		1	cos(a)
a	I	C		1	arccos(a)
a	H	C		1	cosh(a)
a	I H	C		1	arccosh(a)
		D		4	calc-redo
a		E		1	exp(a)
a	H	E		1	exp10(a) 10.^a
a		F		1, 11	floor(a, d)
a	I	F		1, 11	ceil(a, d)
a	H	F		1, 11	ffloor(a, d)
a	I H	F		1, 11	fceil(a, d)
a		G		1	arg(a)
		H	*command*	32	*Hyperbolic*
		I	*command*	32	*Inverse*
a		J		1	conj(a)
		K	*command*	32	*Keep-args*
a		L		1	ln(a)
a	H	L		1	log10(a)
		M			calc-more-recursion-depth
	I	M			calc-less-recursion-depth
a		N		5	evalvn(a)
		O	*command*	32	*Option*
		P			*pi*
	I	P			*gamma*
	H	P			*e*
	I H	P			*phi*
a		Q		1	sqrt(a)
a	I	Q		1	sqr(a) a^2
a		R		1, 11	round(a, d)
a	I	R		1, 11	trunc(a, d)
a	H	R		1, 11	fround(a, d)
a	I H	R		1, 11	ftrunc(a, d)
a		S		1	sin(a)
a	I	S		1	arcsin(a)
a	H	S		1	sinh(a)
a	I H	S		1	arcsinh(a)
a		T		1	tan(a)
a	I	T		1	arctan(a)
a	H	T		1	tanh(a)
a	I H	T		1	arctanh(a)
		U		4	calc-undo
		X		4	calc-call-last-kbd-macro
a b		a =		2	eq(a, b) a=b
a b		a #		2	neq(a, b) a!=b
a b		a <		2	lt(a, b) a<b
a b		a >		2	gt(a, b) a>b
a b		a [		2	leq(a, b) a<=b
a b		a]		2	geq(a, b) a>=b
a b		a {		2	in(a, b)
a b		a &		2, 45	land(a, b) a&&b
a b		a |		2, 45	lor(a, b) a||b
a		a !		1, 45	lnot(a) !a
a b c		a :		45	if(a, b, c) a?b:c
a		a .		1	rmeq(a)
a		a "		7, 8	calc-expand-formula

a	a +	i, l, h	6, 38	$\text{sum}(a, i, l, h)$
a	a -	i, l, h	6, 38	$\text{asum}(a, i, l, h)$
a	a *	i, l, h	6, 38	$\text{prod}(a, i, l, h)$
$a\,b$	a _		2	$\text{subscr}(a, b)$ a_b
$a\,b$	a \		2	$\text{pdiv}(a, b)$
$a\,b$	a %		2	$\text{prem}(a, b)$
$a\,b$	a /		2	$\text{pdivrem}(a, b)$ $[q, r]$
$a\,b$	H a /		2	$\text{pdivide}(a, b)$ $q\text{+}r/b$
a	a a		1	$\text{apart}(a)$
a	a b	old, new	38	$\text{subst}(a, old, new)$
a	a c	v	38	$\text{collect}(a, v)$
a	a d	v	4, 38	$\text{deriv}(a, v)$
a	H a d	v	4, 38	$\text{tderiv}(a, v)$
a	a e			$\text{esimplify}(a)$
a	a f		1	$\text{factor}(a)$
a	H a f		1	$\text{factors}(a)$
$a\,b$	a g		2	$\text{pgcd}(a, b)$
a	a i	v	38	$\text{integ}(a, v)$
a	a m	$pats$	38	$\text{match}(a, pats)$
a	I a m	$pats$	38	$\text{matchnot}(a, pats)$
$data\,x$	a p		28	$\text{polint}(data, x)$
$data\,x$	H a p		28	$\text{ratint}(data, x)$
a	a n		1	$\text{nrat}(a)$
a	a r	$rules$	4, 8, 38	$\text{rewrite}(a, rules, n)$
a	a s			$\text{simplify}(a)$
a	a t	v, n	31, 39	$\text{taylor}(a, v, n)$
a	a v		7, 8	calc-alg-evaluate
a	a x		4, 8	$\text{expand}(a)$
$data$	a F	$model, vars$	48	$\text{fit}(m, iv, pv, data)$
$data$	I a F	$model, vars$	48	$\text{xfit}(m, iv, pv, data)$
$data$	H a F	$model, vars$	48	$\text{efit}(m, iv, pv, data)$
a	a I	v, l, h	38	$\text{ninteg}(a, v, l, h)$
$a\,b$	a M	op	22	$\text{mapeq}(op, a, b)$
$a\,b$	I a M	op	22	$\text{mapeqr}(op, a, b)$
$a\,b$	H a M	op	22	$\text{mapeqp}(op, a, b)$
$a\,g$	a N	v	38	$\text{minimize}(a, v, g)$
$a\,g$	H a N	v	38	$\text{wminimize}(a, v, g)$
a	a P	v	38	$\text{roots}(a, v)$
$a\,g$	a R	v	38	$\text{root}(a, v, g)$
$a\,g$	H a R	v	38	$\text{wroot}(a, v, g)$
a	a S	v	38	$\text{solve}(a, v)$
a	I a S	v	38	$\text{finv}(a, v)$
a	H a S	v	38	$\text{fsolve}(a, v)$
a	I H a S	v	38	$\text{ffinv}(a, v)$
a	a T	i, l, h	6, 38	$\text{table}(a, i, l, h)$
$a\,g$	a X	v	38	$\text{maximize}(a, v, g)$
$a\,g$	H a X	v	38	$\text{wmaximize}(a, v, g)$
$a\,b$	b a		9	$\text{and}(a, b, w)$
a	b c		9	$\text{clip}(a, w)$
$a\,b$	b d		9	$\text{diff}(a, b, w)$
a	b l		10	$\text{lsh}(a, n, w)$
$a\,n$	H b l		9	$\text{lsh}(a, n, w)$
a	b n		9	$\text{not}(a, w)$
$a\,b$	b o		9	$\text{or}(a, b, w)$
v	b p		1	$\text{vpack}(v)$

Args	Pre	Key	Extra	#	Command
a		b r		10	`rsh`(a, n, w)
$a\ n$	H	b r		9	`rsh`(a, n, w)
a		b t		10	`rot`(a, n, w)
$a\ n$	H	b t		9	`rot`(a, n, w)
a		b u		1	`vunpack`(a)
		b w	w	9, 50	`calc-word-size`
$a\ b$		b x		9	`xor`(a, b, w)
$c\ s\ l\ p$		b D			`ddb`(c, s, l, p)
$r\ n\ p$		b F			`fv`(r, n, p)
$r\ n\ p$	I	b F			`fvb`(r, n, p)
$r\ n\ p$	H	b F			`fvl`(r, n, p)
v		b I		19	`irr`(v)
v	I	b I		19	`irrb`(v)
a		b L		10	`ash`(a, n, w)
$a\ n$	H	b L		9	`ash`(a, n, w)
$r\ n\ a$		b M			`pmt`(r, n, a)
$r\ n\ a$	I	b M			`pmtb`(r, n, a)
$r\ n\ a$	H	b M			`pmtl`(r, n, a)
$r\ v$		b N		19	`npv`(r, v)
$r\ v$	I	b N		19	`npvb`(r, v)
$r\ n\ p$		b P			`pv`(r, n, p)
$r\ n\ p$	I	b P			`pvb`(r, n, p)
$r\ n\ p$	H	b P			`pvl`(r, n, p)
a		b R		10	`rash`(a, n, w)
$a\ n$	H	b R		9	`rash`(a, n, w)
$c\ s\ l$		b S			`sln`(c, s, l)
$n\ p\ a$		b T			`rate`(n, p, a)
$n\ p\ a$	I	b T			`rateb`(n, p, a)
$n\ p\ a$	H	b T			`ratel`(n, p, a)
$c\ s\ l\ p$		b Y			`syd`(c, s, l, p)
$r\ p\ a$		b #			`nper`(r, p, a)
$r\ p\ a$	I	b #			`nperb`(r, p, a)
$r\ p\ a$	H	b #			`nperl`(r, p, a)
$a\ b$		b %			`relch`(a, b)
a		c c		5	`pclean`(a, p)
a		c 0-9			`pclean`(a, p)
a	H	c c		5	`clean`(a, p)
a	H	c 0-9			`clean`(a, p)
a		c d		1	`deg`(a)
a		c f		1	`pfloat`(a)
a	H	c f		1	`float`(a)
a		c h		1	`hms`(a)
a		c p			`polar`(a)
a	I	c p			`rect`(a)
a		c r		1	`rad`(a)
a		c F		5	`pfrac`(a, p)
a	H	c F		5	`frac`(a, p)
a		c %			`percent`$(a\text{*}100)$
		d .	*char*	50	`calc-point-char`
		d ,	*char*	50	`calc-group-char`
		d <		13, 50	`calc-left-justify`
		d =		13, 50	`calc-center-justify`
		d >		13, 50	`calc-right-justify`
		d {	*label*	50	`calc-left-label`

	d }	*label*	50	`calc-right-label`
	d [		4	`calc-truncate-up`
	d]		4	`calc-truncate-down`
	d "		12, 50	`calc-display-strings`
	d SPC			`calc-refresh`
	d RET		1	`calc-refresh-top`
	d 0		50	`calc-decimal-radix`
	d 2		50	`calc-binary-radix`
	d 6		50	`calc-hex-radix`
	d 8		50	`calc-octal-radix`
	d b		12, 13, 50	`calc-line-breaking`
	d c		50	`calc-complex-notation`
	d d	*format*	50	`calc-date-notation`
	d e		5, 50	`calc-eng-notation`
	d f	*num*	31, 50	`calc-fix-notation`
	d g		12, 13, 50	`calc-group-digits`
	d h	*format*	50	`calc-hms-notation`
	d i		50	`calc-i-notation`
	d j		50	`calc-j-notation`
	d l		12, 50	`calc-line-numbering`
	d n		5, 50	`calc-normal-notation`
	d o	*format*	50	`calc-over-notation`
	d p		12, 50	`calc-show-plain`
	d r	*radix*	31, 50	`calc-radix`
	d s		5, 50	`calc-sci-notation`
	d t		27	`calc-truncate-stack`
	d w		12, 13	`calc-auto-why`
	d z		12, 50	`calc-leading-zeros`
	d B		50	`calc-big-language`
	d C		50	`calc-c-language`
	d E		50	`calc-eqn-language`
	d F		50	`calc-fortran-language`
	d M		50	`calc-mathematica-language`
	d N		50	`calc-normal-language`
	d O		50	`calc-flat-language`
	d P		50	`calc-pascal-language`
	d T		50	`calc-tex-language`
	d L		50	`calc-latex-language`
	d U		50	`calc-unformatted-language`
	d W		50	`calc-maple-language`
a	f [		4	$\mathrm{decr}(a, n)$
a	f]		4	$\mathrm{incr}(a, n)$
a b	f b		2	$\mathrm{beta}(a, b)$
a	f e		1	$\mathrm{erf}(a)$
a I	f e		1	$\mathrm{erfc}(a)$
a	f g		1	$\mathrm{gamma}(a)$
a b	f h		2	$\mathrm{hypot}(a, b)$
a	f i		1	$\mathrm{im}(a)$
n a	f j		2	$\mathrm{besJ}(n, a)$
a b	f n		2	$\min(a, b)$
a	f r		1	$\mathrm{re}(a)$
a	f s		1	$\mathrm{sign}(a)$
a b	f x		2	$\max(a, b)$
n a	f y		2	$\mathrm{besY}(n, a)$

a	f A		1	abssqr(a)
$x\ a\ b$	f B			betaI(x, a, b)
$x\ a\ b$	H f B			betaB(x, a, b)
a	f E		1	expm1(a)
$a\ x$	f G		2	gammaP(a, x)
$a\ x$	I f G		2	gammaQ(a, x)
$a\ x$	H f G		2	gammag(a, x)
$a\ x$	I H f G		2	gammaG(a, x)
$a\ b$	f I		2	ilog(a, b)
$a\ b$	I f I		2	alog(a, b) b^a
a	f L		1	lnp1(a)
a	f M		1	mant(a)
a	f Q		1	isqrt(a)
a	I f Q		1	sqr(a) a^2
$a\ n$	f S		2	scf(a, n)
$y\ x$	f T			arctan2(y, x)
a	f X		1	xpon(a)
$x\ y$	g a		28, 40	calc-graph-add
	g b		12	calc-graph-border
	g c			calc-graph-clear
	g d		41	calc-graph-delete
$x\ y$	g f		28, 40	calc-graph-fast
	g g		12	calc-graph-grid
	g h	*title*		calc-graph-header
	g j		4	calc-graph-juggle
	g k		12	calc-graph-key
	g l		12	calc-graph-log-x
	g n	*name*		calc-graph-name
	g p		42	calc-graph-plot
	g q			calc-graph-quit
	g r	*range*		calc-graph-range-x
	g s		12, 13	calc-graph-line-style
	g t	*title*		calc-graph-title-x
	g v			calc-graph-view-commands
	g x	*display*		calc-graph-display
	g z		12	calc-graph-zero-x
$x\ y\ z$	g A		28, 40	calc-graph-add-3d
	g C	*command*		calc-graph-command
	g D	*device*	43, 44	calc-graph-device
$x\ y\ z$	g F		28, 40	calc-graph-fast-3d
	g H		12	calc-graph-hide
	g K			calc-graph-kill
	g L		12	calc-graph-log-y
	g N	*number*	43, 51	calc-graph-num-points
	g O	*filename*	43, 44	calc-graph-output
	g P		42	calc-graph-print
	g R	*range*		calc-graph-range-y
	g S		12, 13	calc-graph-point-style
	g T	*title*		calc-graph-title-y
	g V			calc-graph-view-trail
	g X	*format*		calc-graph-geometry
	g Z		12	calc-graph-zero-y
	g C-l		12	calc-graph-log-z
	g C-r	*range*		calc-graph-range-z
	g C-t	*title*		calc-graph-title-z

	h b			calc-describe-bindings
	h c	*key*		calc-describe-key-briefly
	h f	*function*		calc-describe-function
	h h			calc-full-help
	h i			calc-info
	h k	*key*		calc-describe-key
	h n			calc-view-news
	h s			calc-info-summary
	h t			calc-tutorial
	h v	*var*		calc-describe-variable
	j 1-9			calc-select-part
	j RET		27	calc-copy-selection
	j DEL		27	calc-del-selection
	j '	*formula*	27	calc-enter-selection
	j `	*editing*	27, 30	calc-edit-selection
	j "		7, 27	calc-sel-expand-formula
	j +	*formula*	27	calc-sel-add-both-sides
	j -	*formula*	27	calc-sel-sub-both-sides
	j *	*formula*	27	calc-sel-mul-both-sides
	j /	*formula*	27	calc-sel-div-both-sides
	j &		27	calc-sel-invert
	j a		27	calc-select-additional
	j b		12	calc-break-selections
	j c			calc-clear-selections
	j d		12, 50	calc-show-selections
	j e		12	calc-enable-selections
	j l		4, 27	calc-select-less
	j m		4, 27	calc-select-more
	j n		4	calc-select-next
	j o		4, 27	calc-select-once
	j p		4	calc-select-previous
	j r	*rules*	4, 8, 27	calc-rewrite-selection
	j s		4, 27	calc-select-here
	j u		27	calc-unselect
	j v		7, 27	calc-sel-evaluate
	j C		27	calc-sel-commute
	j D		4, 27	calc-sel-distribute
	j E		27	calc-sel-jump-equals
	j I		27	calc-sel-isolate
H	j I		27	calc-sel-isolate (*full*)
	j L		4, 27	calc-commute-left
	j M		27	calc-sel-merge
	j N		27	calc-sel-negate
	j O		4, 27	calc-select-once-maybe
	j R		4, 27	calc-commute-right
	j S		4, 27	calc-select-here-maybe
	j U		27	calc-sel-unpack
	k a			calc-random-again
n	k b		1	bern(n)
n x	H k b		2	bern(n, x)
n m	k c		2	choose(n, m)
n m	H k c		2	perm(n, m)
n	k d		1	dfact(n) $n!!$
n	k e		1	euler(n)
n x	H k e		2	euler(n, x)

Args		Keys	Page	Function
n		k f	4	prfac(n)
$n\ m$		k g	2	gcd(n, m)
$m\ n$		k h	14	shuffle(n, m)
$n\ m$		k l	2	lcm(n, m)
n		k m	1	moebius(n)
n		k n	4	nextprime(n)
n	I	k n	4	prevprime(n)
n		k p	4, 28	calc-prime-test
m		k r	14	random(m)
$n\ m$		k s	2	stir1(n, m)
$n\ m$	H	k s	2	stir2(n, m)
n		k t	1	totient(n)
$n\ p\ x$		k B		utpb(x, n, p)
$n\ p\ x$	I	k B		ltpb(x, n, p)
$v\ x$		k C		utpc(x, v)
$v\ x$	I	k C		ltpc(x, v)
$n\ m$		k E		egcd(n, m)
$v1\ v2\ x$		k F		utpf($x, v1, v2$)
$v1\ v2\ x$	I	k F		ltpf($x, v1, v2$)
$m\ s\ x$		k N		utpn(x, m, s)
$m\ s\ x$	I	k N		ltpn(x, m, s)
$m\ x$		k P		utpp(x, m)
$m\ x$	I	k P		ltpp(x, m)
$v\ x$		k T		utpt(x, v)
$v\ x$	I	k T		ltpt(x, v)
$a\ b$		l +		lupadd(a, b)
$a\ b$	H	l +		lufadd(a, b)
$a\ b$		l -		lupsub(a, b)
$a\ b$	H	l -		lufsub(a, b)
$a\ b$		l *		lupmul(a, b)
$a\ b$	H	l *		lufmul(a, b)
$a\ b$		l /		lupdiv(a, b)
$a\ b$	H	l /		lufdiv(a, b)
a		l d		dbpower(a)
$a\ b$	O	l d		dbpower(a, b)
a	H	l d		dbfield(a)
$a\ b$	O H	l d		dbfield(a, b)
a		l n		nppower(a)
$a\ b$	O	l n		nppower(a, b)
a	H	l n		npfield(a)
$a\ b$	O H	l n		npfield(a, b)
a		l q		lupquant(a)
$a\ b$	O	l q		lupquant(a, b)
a	H	l q		lufquant(a)
$a\ b$	O H	l q		lufquant(a, b)
a		l s		spn(a)
a		l m		midi(a)
a		l f		freq(a)
		m a	12, 13	calc-algebraic-mode
		m d		calc-degrees-mode
		m e		calc-embedded-preserve-modes
		m f	12	calc-frac-mode
		m g	52	calc-get-modes
		m h		calc-hms-mode
		m i	12, 13	calc-infinite-mode
		m m		calc-save-modes

	m p		12	calc-polar-mode
	m r			calc-radians-mode
	m s		12	calc-symbolic-mode
	m t		12	calc-total-algebraic-mode
	m v		12, 13	calc-matrix-mode
	m w		13	calc-working
	m x			calc-always-load-extensions
	m A		12	calc-alg-simplify-mode
	m B		12	calc-bin-simplify-mode
	m C		12	calc-auto-recompute
	m D			calc-default-simplify-mode
	m E		12	calc-ext-simplify-mode
	m F	*filename*	13	calc-settings-file-name
	m N		12	calc-num-simplify-mode
	m O		12	calc-no-simplify-mode
	m R		12, 13	calc-mode-record-mode
	m S		12	calc-shift-prefix
	m U		12	calc-units-simplify-mode
	r s	*register*	27	calc-copy-to-register
	r i	*register*		calc-insert-register
	s c	*var1, var2*	29	calc-copy-variable
	s d	*var, decl*		calc-declare-variable
	s e	*var, editing*	29, 30	calc-edit-variable
	s i	*buffer*		calc-insert-variables
	s k	*const, var*	29	calc-copy-special-constant
a b	s l	*var*	29	*a* (letting var=b)
a ...	s m	*op, var*	22, 29	calc-store-map
	s n	*var*	29, 47	calc-store-neg (v/-1)
	s p	*var*	29	calc-permanent-variable
	s r	*var*	29	*v* (recalled value)
	r 0-9			calc-recall-quick
a	s s	*var*	28, 29	calc-store
a	s 0-9			calc-store-quick
a	s t	*var*	29	calc-store-into
a	t 0-9			calc-store-into-quick
	s u	*var*	29	calc-unstore
a	s x	*var*	29	calc-store-exchange
	s A	*editing*	30	calc-edit-AlgSimpRules
	s D	*editing*	30	calc-edit-Decls
	s E	*editing*	30	calc-edit-EvalRules
	s F	*editing*	30	calc-edit-FitRules
	s G	*editing*	30	calc-edit-GenCount
	s H	*editing*	30	calc-edit-Holidays
	s I	*editing*	30	calc-edit-IntegLimit
	s L	*editing*	30	calc-edit-LineStyles
	s P	*editing*	30	calc-edit-PointStyles
	s R	*editing*	30	calc-edit-PlotRejects
	s T	*editing*	30	calc-edit-TimeZone
	s U	*editing*	30	calc-edit-Units
	s X	*editing*	30	calc-edit-ExtSimpRules
a	s +	*var*	29, 47	calc-store-plus (v+a)
a	s -	*var*	29, 47	calc-store-minus (v-a)
a	s *	*var*	29, 47	calc-store-times (v*a)
a	s /	*var*	29, 47	calc-store-div (v/a)
a	s ^	*var*	29, 47	calc-store-power (v^a)

a	s |	*var*	29, 47	calc-store-concat $(v\|a)$
	s &	*var*	29, 47	calc-store-inv $(v\text{\textasciicircum}\text{-}1)$
	s [	*var*	29, 47	calc-store-decr $(v\text{-}1)$
	s]	*var*	29, 47	calc-store-incr $(v\text{-}(\text{-}1))$
$a\ b$	s :		2	assign(a, b) a := b
a	s =		1	evalto(a, b) a =>
	t [		4	calc-trail-first
	t]		4	calc-trail-last
	t <		4	calc-trail-scroll-left
	t >		4	calc-trail-scroll-right
	t .		12	calc-full-trail-vectors
	t b		4	calc-trail-backward
	t d		12, 50	calc-trail-display
	t f		4	calc-trail-forward
	t h			calc-trail-here
	t i			calc-trail-in
	t k		4	calc-trail-kill
	t m	*string*		calc-trail-marker
	t n		4	calc-trail-next
	t o			calc-trail-out
	t p		4	calc-trail-previous
	t r	*string*		calc-trail-isearch-backward
	t s	*string*		calc-trail-isearch-forward
	t y		4	calc-trail-yank
d	t C	*oz, nz*		tzconv(d, oz, nz)
$d\ oz\ nz$	t C	*$*		tzconv(d, oz, nz)
d	t D		15	date(d)
d	t I		4	incmonth(d, n)
d	t J		16	julian(d, z)
d	t M		17	newmonth(d, n)
	t N		16	now(z)
d	t P	*1*	31	year(d)
d	t P	*2*	31	month(d)
d	t P	*3*	31	day(d)
d	t P	*4*	31	hour(d)
d	t P	*5*	31	minute(d)
d	t P	*6*	31	second(d)
d	t P	*7*	31	weekday(d)
d	t P	*8*	31	yearday(d)
d	t P	*9*	31	time(d)
d	t U		16	unixtime(d, z)
d	t W		17	newweek(d, w)
d	t Y		17	newyear(d, n)
$a\ b$	t +		2	badd(a, b)
$a\ b$	t -		2	bsub(a, b)
	u a		12	calc-autorange-units
a	u b			calc-base-units
a	u c	*units*	18	calc-convert-units
defn	u d	*unit, descr*		calc-define-unit
	u e			calc-explain-units
	u g	*unit*		calc-get-unit-definition
	u n	*units*	18	calc-convert-exact-units
	u p			calc-permanent-units
a	u r			calc-remove-units
a	u s			usimplify(a)

a	u t	*units*	18	calc-convert-temperature
	u u	*unit*		calc-undefine-unit
	u v			calc-enter-units-table
a	u x			calc-extract-units
a	u 0-9			calc-quick-units
$v1\ v2$	u C		20	$vcov(v1, v2)$
$v1\ v2$	I u C		20	$vpcov(v1, v2)$
$v1\ v2$	H u C		20	$vcorr(v1, v2)$
v	u G		19	$vgmean(v)$
$a\ b$	H u G		2	$agmean(a, b)$
v	u M		19	$vmean(v)$
v	I u M		19	$vmeane(v)$
v	H u M		19	$vmedian(v)$
v	I H u M		19	$vhmean(v)$
v	u N		19	$vmin(v)$
v	u R			$rms(v)$
v	u S		19	$vsdev(v)$
v	I u S		19	$vpsdev(v)$
v	H u S		19	$vvar(v)$
v	I H u S		19	$vpvar(v)$
	u V			calc-view-units-table
v	u X		19	$vmax(v)$
v	u +		19	$vsum(v)$
v	u *		19	$vprod(v)$
v	u #		19	$vcount(v)$
	V (		50	calc-vector-parens
	V {		50	calc-vector-braces
	V [		50	calc-vector-brackets
	V]	*ROCP*	50	calc-matrix-brackets
	V ,		50	calc-vector-commas
	V <		50	calc-matrix-left-justify
	V =		50	calc-matrix-center-justify
	V >		50	calc-matrix-right-justify
	V /		12, 50	calc-break-vectors
	V .		12, 50	calc-full-vectors
$s\ t$	V ^		2	$vint(s, t)$
$s\ t$	V -		2	$vdiff(s, t)$
s	V ~		1	$vcompl(s)$
s	V #		1	$vcard(s)$
s	V :		1	$vspan(s)$
s	V +		1	$rdup(s)$
m	V &		1	$inv(m)$ $1/m$
v	v a	n		$arrange(v, n)$
a	v b	n		$cvec(a, n)$
v	v c	$n > 0$	21, 31	$mcol(v, n)$
v	v c	$n < 0$	31	$mrcol(v, -n)$
m	v c	0	31	$getdiag(m)$
v	v d		25	$diag(v, n)$
$v\ m$	v e		2	$vexp(v, m)$
$v\ m\ f$	H v e		2	$vexp(v, m, f)$
$v\ a$	v f		26	$find(v, a, n)$
v	v h		1	$head(v)$
v	I v h		1	$tail(v)$
v	H v h		1	$rhead(v)$

args	keys	extra	page	command
v	I H v h		1	rtail(v)
	v i	n	31	idn($1, n$)
	v i	0	31	idn(1)
$h\ t$	v k		2	cons(h, t)
$h\ t$	H v k		2	rcons(h, t)
v	v l		1	vlen(v)
v	H v l		1	mdims(v)
$v\ m$	v m		2	vmask(v, m)
v	v n		1	rnorm(v)
$a\ b\ c$	v p		24	calc-pack
v	v r	$n > 0$	21, 31	mrow(v, n)
v	v r	$n < 0$	31	mrrow($v, \text{-}n$)
m	v r	0	31	getdiag(m)
$v\ i\ j$	v s			subvec(v, i, j)
$v\ i\ j$	I v s			rsubvec(v, i, j)
m	v t		1	trn(m)
v	v u		24	calc-unpack
v	v v		1	rev(v)
	v x	n	31	index(n)
$n\ s\ i$	C-u v x			index(n, s, i)
v	V A	op	22	apply(op, v)
$v1\ v2$	V C		2	cross($v1, v2$)
m	V D		1	det(m)
s	V E		1	venum(s)
s	V F		1	vfloor(s)
v	V G			grade(v)
v	I V G			rgrade(v)
v	V H	n	31	histogram(v, n)
$v\ w$	H V H	n	31	histogram(v, w, n)
$v1\ v2$	V I	$mop\ aop$	22	inner($mop, aop, v1, v2$)
m	V J		1	ctrn(m)
$m1\ m2$	V K			kron($m1, m2$)
m	V L		1	lud(m)
v	V M	op	22, 23	map(op, v)
v	V N		1	cnorm(v)
$v1\ v2$	V O	op	22	outer($op, v1, v2$)
v	V R	op	22, 23	reduce(op, v)
v	I V R	op	22, 23	rreduce(op, v)
$a\ n$	H V R	op	22	nest(op, a, n)
a	I H V R	op	22	fixp(op, a)
v	V S			sort(v)
v	I V S			rsort(v)
m	V T		1	tr(m)
v	V U	op	22	accum(op, v)
v	I V U	op	22	raccum(op, v)
$a\ n$	H V U	op	22	anest(op, a, n)
a	I H V U	op	22	afixp(op, a)
$s\ t$	V V		2	vunion(s, t)
$s\ t$	V X		2	vxor(s, t)
	Y			*user commands*
	z			*user commands*
c	Z [		45	calc-kbd-if
c	Z			45	calc-kbd-else-if
	Z :			calc-kbd-else
	Z]			calc-kbd-end-if

	Z {		4	`calc-kbd-loop`
c	Z /		45	`calc-kbd-break`
	Z }			`calc-kbd-end-loop`
n	Z <			`calc-kbd-repeat`
	Z >			`calc-kbd-end-repeat`
n m	Z (			`calc-kbd-for`
s	Z)			`calc-kbd-end-for`
	Z C-g			*cancel if/loop command*
	Z '			`calc-kbd-push`
	Z '			`calc-kbd-pop`
	Z #			`calc-kbd-query`
comp	Z C	*func, args*	50	`calc-user-define-composition`
	Z D	*key, command*		`calc-user-define`
	Z E	*key, editing*	30	`calc-user-define-edit`
defn	Z F	*k, c, f, a, n*	28	`calc-user-define-formula`
	Z G	*key*		`calc-get-user-defn`
	Z I			`calc-user-define-invocation`
	Z K	*key, command*		`calc-user-define-kbd-macro`
	Z P	*key*		`calc-user-define-permanent`
	Z S		30	`calc-edit-user-syntax`
	Z T		12	`calc-timing`
	Z U	*key*		`calc-user-undefine`

NOTES

1. Positive prefix arguments apply to n stack entries. Negative prefix arguments apply to the $-n$th stack entry. A prefix of zero applies to the entire stack. (For `LFD` and `M-DEL`, the meaning of the sign is reversed.)

2. Positive prefix arguments apply to n stack entries. Negative prefix arguments apply to the top stack entry and the next $-n$ stack entries.

3. Positive prefix arguments rotate top n stack entries by one. Negative prefix arguments rotate the entire stack by $-n$. A prefix of zero reverses the entire stack.

4. Prefix argument specifies a repeat count or distance.

5. Positive prefix arguments specify a precision p. Negative prefix arguments reduce the current precision by $-p$.

6. A prefix argument is interpreted as an additional step-size parameter. A plain `C-u` prefix means to prompt for the step size.

7. A prefix argument specifies simplification level and depth. 1=Basic simplifications, 2=Algebraic simplifications, 3=Extended simplifications

8. A negative prefix operates only on the top level of the input formula.

9. Positive prefix arguments specify a word size of w bits, unsigned. Negative prefix arguments specify a word size of w bits, signed.

10. Prefix arguments specify the shift amount n. The w argument cannot be specified in the keyboard version of this command.

11. From the keyboard, d is omitted and defaults to zero.

12. Mode is toggled; a positive prefix always sets the mode, and a negative prefix always clears the mode.

13. Some prefix argument values provide special variations of the mode.

14. A prefix argument, if any, is used for m instead of taking m from the stack. M may take any of these values:

    Integer   Random integer in the interval $[0..m)$.

    Float   Random floating-point number in the interval $[0..m)$.

    0.0   Gaussian with mean 1 and standard deviation 0.

    Error form   Gaussian with specified mean and standard deviation.

    Interval   Random integer or floating-point number in that interval.

    Vector   Random element from the vector.

15. A prefix argument from 1 to 6 specifies number of date components to remove from the stack. See Section 7.5.1 [Date Conversions], page 192.

16. A prefix argument specifies a time zone; *C-u* says to take the time zone number or name from the top of the stack. See Section 7.5.4 [Time Zones], page 197.

17. A prefix argument specifies a day number (0–6, 0–31, or 0–366).

18. If the input has no units, you will be prompted for both the old and the new units.

19. With a prefix argument, collect that many stack entries to form the input data set. Each entry may be a single value or a vector of values.

20. With a prefix argument of 1, take a single $n \times 2$ matrix from the stack instead of two separate data vectors.

21. The row or column number n may be given as a numeric prefix argument instead. A plain *C-u* prefix says to take n from the top of the stack. If n is a vector or interval, a subvector/submatrix of the input is created.

22. The *op* prompt can be answered with the key sequence for the desired function, or with *x* or *z* followed by a function name, or with *$* to take a formula from the top of the stack, or with *'* and a typed formula. In the last two cases, the formula may be a nameless function like '<#1+#2>' or '<x, y : x+y>'; or it may include *$*, *$$*, etc., where *$* will correspond to the last argument of the created function; or otherwise you will be prompted for an argument list. The number of vectors popped from the stack by *V M* depends on the number of arguments of the function.

23. One of the mapping direction keys _ (horizontal, i.e., map by rows or reduce across), : (vertical, i.e., map by columns or reduce down), or = (map or reduce by rows) may be used before entering *op*; these modify the function name by adding the letter *r* for "rows," *c* for "columns," *a* for "across," or *d* for "down."

24. The prefix argument specifies a packing mode. A nonnegative mode is the number of items (for *v p*) or the number of levels (for *v u*). A negative mode is as described below. With no prefix argument, the mode is taken from the top of the stack and may be an integer or a vector of integers.

    -1   (*2*) Rectangular complex number.

    -2   (*2*) Polar complex number.

    -3   (*3*) HMS form.

-4   (2) Error form.

-5   (2) Modulo form.

-6   (2) Closed interval.

-7   (2) Closed .. open interval.

-8   (2) Open .. closed interval.

-9   (2) Open interval.

-10   (2) Fraction.

-11   (2) Float with integer mantissa.

-12   (2) Float with mantissa in [1..10).

-13   (1) Date form (using date numbers).

-14   (3) Date form (using year, month, day).

-15   (6) Date form (using year, month, day, hour, minute, second).

25. A prefix argument specifies the size n of the matrix. With no prefix argument, n is omitted and the size is inferred from the input vector.

26. The prefix argument specifies the starting position n (default 1).

27. Cursor position within stack buffer affects this command.

28. Arguments are not actually removed from the stack by this command.

29. Variable name may be a single digit or a full name.

30. Editing occurs in a separate buffer. Press `C-c C-c` (or `LFD`, or in some cases `RET`) to finish the edit, or kill the buffer with `C-x k` to cancel the edit. The `LFD` key prevents evaluation of the result of the edit.

31. The number prompted for can also be provided as a prefix argument.

32. Press this key a second time to cancel the prefix.

33. With a negative prefix, deactivate all formulas. With a positive prefix, deactivate and then reactivate from scratch.

34. Default is to scan for nearest formula delimiter symbols. With a prefix of zero, formula is delimited by mark and point. With a non-zero prefix, formula is delimited by scanning forward or backward by that many lines.

35. Parse the region between point and mark as a vector. A nonzero prefix parses n lines before or after point as a vector. A zero prefix parses the current line as a vector. A `C-u` prefix parses the region between point and mark as a single formula.

36. Parse the rectangle defined by point and mark as a matrix. A positive prefix n divides the rectangle into columns of width n. A zero or `C-u` prefix parses each line as one formula. A negative prefix suppresses special treatment of bracketed portions of a line.

37. A numeric prefix causes the current language mode to be ignored.

38. Responding to a prompt with a blank line answers that and all later prompts by popping additional stack entries.

39. Answer for v may also be of the form $v = v_0$ or $v - v_0$.

40. With a positive prefix argument, stack contains many y's and one common x. With a zero prefix, stack contains a vector of ys and a common x. With a negative prefix, stack contains many $[x, y]$ vectors. (For 3D plots, substitute z for y and x, y for x.)

41. With any prefix argument, all curves in the graph are deleted.

42. With a positive prefix, refines an existing plot with more data points. With a negative prefix, forces recomputation of the plot data.

43. With any prefix argument, set the default value instead of the value for this graph.

44. With a negative prefix argument, set the value for the printer.

45. Condition is considered "true" if it is a nonzero real or complex number, or a formula whose value is known to be nonzero; it is "false" otherwise.

46. Several formulas separated by commas are pushed as multiple stack entries. Trailing),], }, >, and " delimiters may be omitted. The notation $$$ refers to the value in stack level three, and causes the formula to replace the top three stack levels. The notation $3 refers to stack level three without causing that value to be removed from the stack. Use LFD in place of RET to prevent evaluation; use M-= in place of RET to evaluate variables.

47. The variable is replaced by the formula shown on the right. The Inverse flag reverses the order of the operands, e.g., I s - x assigns $x := a - x$.

48. Press ? repeatedly to see how to choose a model. Answer the variables prompt with iv or $iv; pv$ to specify independent and parameter variables. A positive prefix argument takes $n + 1$ vectors from the stack; a zero prefix takes a matrix and a vector from the stack.

49. With a plain C-u prefix, replace the current region of the destination buffer with the yanked text instead of inserting.

50. All stack entries are reformatted; the H prefix inhibits this. The I prefix sets the mode temporarily, redraws the top stack entry, then restores the original setting of the mode.

51. A negative prefix sets the default 3D resolution instead of the default 2D resolution.

52. This grabs a vector of the form [*prec, wsize, ssize, radix, flfmt, ang, frac, symb, polar, matrix, simp, inf*]. A prefix argument from 1 to 12 grabs the nth mode value only.

(Space is provided below for you to keep your own written notes.)

Index of Key Sequences

C

D

E

I

W

X

Y

Z

Index of Calculator Commands

Since all Calculator commands begin with the prefix 'calc-', the x key has been provided as a variant of *M-x* which automatically types 'calc-' for you. Thus, *x last-args* is short for *M-x calc-last-args*.

Index of Algebraic Functions

This is a list of built-in functions and operators usable in algebraic expressions. Their full Lisp names are derived by adding the prefix 'calcFunc-', as in calcFunc-sqrt. All functions except those noted with "*" have corresponding Calc keystrokes and can also be found in the Calc Summary.

Concept Index

Index of Variables

The variables in this list that do not contain dashes are accessible as Calc variables. Add a 'var-' prefix to get the name of the corresponding Lisp variable.

The remaining variables are Lisp variables suitable for `setq`ing in your Calc init file or `.emacs` file.

Index of Lisp Math Functions

The following functions are meant to be used with `defmath`, not `defun` definitions. For names that do not start with 'calc-', the corresponding full Lisp name is derived by adding a prefix of 'math-'.

www.ingramcontent.com/pod-product-compliance
Lightning Source LLC
LaVergne TN
LVHW060132070326
832902LV00018B/2763